INTRODUCING COMPARATIVE POLITICS

INTRODUCING COMPARATIVE POLITICS

Concepts and Cases in Context

Carol Ann Drogus

Stephen Orvis

Hamilton College

CQ PRESS

A Division of SAGE
Washington, D.C.

CQ Press
2300 N Street, NW, Suite 800
Washington, DC 20037

Phone: 202-729-1900; toll-free, 1-866-4CQ-PRESS (1-866-427-7737)

Web: www.cqpress.com

Cover design: Jeffrey Everett–El Jefe Design
Interior design: Matthew Simmons
Composition: Judy Myers
Map composition: International Mapping Associates

Photo Credits:
AP Images: Cover (all), 6, 8, 27, 56, 63, 65, 72, 73, 76, 78, 95, 99, 103, 109, 116, 124, 131, 137, 144, 166, 174, 187, 190, 220, 221, 227, 233, 255, 267, 279, 287, 303, 318, 348, 357, 369, 374, 378, 389, 392, 399, 402, 406, 418, 425, 427, 446, 448, 460, 463, 465, 521
Corbis: 3, 67
Getty Images: 147, 451, 475, 478, 498, 511, 523
The Granger Collection: 45, 61, 87
Landov: 59, 69
Reuters: 20, 111, 178, 199, 207, 215, 243, 284, 291, 326, 332, 473, 501, 514
Wikipedia Commons: 422

♾ The paper used in this publication exceeds the requirements of the American National Standard for Information Sciences—Permanence of Paper for Printed Library Materials, ANSI Z39.48-1992.

Printed and bound in the United States of America

12   11   10   09   08   1   2   3   4   5

Library of Congress Cataloging-in-Publication Data

Drogus, Carol Ann.
  Introducing comparative politics : concepts and cases in context / Carol Ann Drogus, Stephen Orvis.
    p. cm.
  Includes bibliographical references (p.   ) and index.
  ISBN 978-0-87289-343-6 (alk. paper)
  1. Comparative government. 2. Comparative government—Case studies. I. Orvis, Stephen Walter
II. Title.
  JF51.D76 2008
  320.3—dc22

                                                                            2008037001

*To Nick and Will, in the hope that their generation
will better understand the world,
in order to improve it.*

Brief Contents

INTRODUCING COMPARATIVE POLITICS
Concepts and Cases in Context

Contents

INTRODUCING COMPARATIVE POLITICS
Concepts and Cases in Context

Timelines, Figures, Tables, Maps, Boxes

Maps

Boxes

PREFACE

The teaching of introductory comparative politics has long been divided, and to some extent confounded, by the question of "country" or "concept": Should the course be taught, as it traditionally has been, as a series of country studies highlighting the key similarities and differences among political institutions around the world, or should it be focused on the important concepts in the discipline? Throughout twenty years of teaching Introduction to Comparative Politics, we have been frustrated by this "either/or" proposition, as well as by the textbooks that have been built upon it. The country approach is far too descriptive, and it is not at all easy to tease major concepts out of country case studies in any sustained way. This makes it difficult for students to get to the intellectual "meat" of our discipline. A purely conceptual approach, on the other hand, leaves students with little concrete knowledge, even when they're given examples here and there. We want our students to know the difference between a president and a prime minister. We've found that it is impossible for them to assess theories in an empirical vacuum. Students need the context that studying actual country cases provides.

We traded syllabi back and forth over the years, trying to combine the two approaches. Our goal was to introduce a set of related concepts and then immediately examine in some detail how they matter in the real world in a comparative context. To do this, we started using two textbooks, one conceptual and the other country-based, in an iterative fashion. But the parts never fit together well, even if written by the same team. In particular, we found that the conceptual books didn't lend themselves well to connecting key theoretical concepts to case study material. We also found that the case studies in most country-based books were either too detailed, leaving the student overwhelmed by unnecessary information, or too simplistic, leaving the student without adequate knowledge with which to understand the utility of the theoretical concepts.

This textbook tries to resolve this country-or-concept dilemma, using what we've come to think of as a "hybrid" approach. The book is organized conceptually, but each chapter introduces concepts and then immediately uses them to examine a series of topical, interesting, and relevant case studies. For instance, chapter 5 on the state and markets lays out the key concepts in political economy and major economic theories and inserts case studies, where they best fit, of the U.S. laissez faire model, the German social market economy, the Japanese developmental state, Brazil's history of import substitution industrialization and recent move toward global integration, and Nigeria's underdevelopment and oil dependence.

We use ten countries throughout the book as "touchstones" (approximately five cases in each chapter), returning to these countries to illustrate the debates we address. The ten countries—Brazil, China, Germany, India, Iran, Japan, Nigeria, Russia, the United Kingdom, and the United States—span the globe, illustrate a wide array of current and past regimes, and avoid a Eurocentrism still too common in the field of comparative politics. Since we know, however, that not all aspects of comparative politics can best be represented by these ten countries alone, we also include what we call "mini-cases" throughout the book. These briefer cases are interspersed throughout the chapters where they make the most sense and cover some of the most important topics of current research. In this way we are able to introduce students to such topics as Tanzania's one-party regime, civic nationalism in France, genocide and ethnic violence in Rwanda, succession in Egypt and Zimbabwe, and economic development in the Middle East region.

By the end of the book, students not only will have been introduced to a wide array of important concepts and theoretical debates, but also will have learned a lot about the most interesting aspects of each of the ten countries. We do not and cannot systematically examine all elements of all ten as a standard country-by-country book would. Instead, after a brief overview of each country in chapter 2 to give students a basic context, we identify the most conceptually interesting elements of each country. For instance, for Japan, we cover the developmental state, the role of that state's bureaucracy and level of corruption, its electoral system, and the country's recent efforts to deal with globalization and resuscitate economic growth; whereas for Germany, we cover the rise and structure of the Nazi regime, Germany's cultural nationalism and citizenship debates, the social market economy, the role of the country's powerful judiciary, its electoral system, and its effort to reform the social market economy and welfare state in the face of globalization and EU integration. The case studies are organized and written in a way that allows students to understand the context of the interesting debates and concepts without having to read an entire "country chapter" on each. And the cases are not overly long, which leaves faculty members the option of lecturing to fill in any additional detail that they may feel important or to provide comparisons with cases not covered in a chapter.

Rather than using any one theoretical or methodological approach, in chapter 1 we introduce students to the broad debates in the field to show throughout the book how comparativists have used various theories and methodologies to understand political phenomena. We do not generally offer definitive conclusions about which approach is best for understanding a particular issue, preferring instead to show students the strengths and weaknesses of each. Occasionally, we make clear that one approach has become the "conventional wisdom" in the field or that we believe it is the most accurate way to analyze a particular phenomenon, but we do this in the context of a broader debate. Our primary focus on ten countries gives the book an implicit bias toward comparative case studies over large-N quantitative methodology, but we introduce students to the core ideas and benefits of the latter and refer to large-N studies throughout the book as useful. We believe our approach will allow faculty to generate debates among students over key approaches and methodologies. By focusing on the key conceptual debates and illustrating them in the real world, the book enables instructors to move their introductory students beyond the memorization of basic information and toward an ability to assess and debate the real issues in our discipline.

The book also moves firmly away from the traditional Cold War division of the world into first-, second-, and third-world countries. While many textbooks claim to do this, we have found that they typically suffer from a "Cold War hangover," with the old division lurking just beneath the surface. We consciously set out to show how many theoretical concepts in the discipline are useful in a wide array of settings, that is, that political phenomena are not fundamentally different in one part of the world than they are in another. For instance, we illustrate the parliamentary system not only with Britain, but also with India; we use both Germany and Brazil to analyze the role of the judiciary and judicial review in a democracy; and we examine women's struggle for equality in Russia and Iran. Throughout, we try to show how long-standing concepts and debates in the discipline illuminate current "hot topics," including women's status in Iran, Russia's growing authoritarianism, and China's economic expansion.

ORGANIZATION OF THE BOOK

This book is divided into three main parts. It moves from examining the theories and concepts that inform and drive research as a way to frame our investigation, on to a survey of political institutions and institutional change, and lastly, to an examination of several current policy debates. Part I introduces the major theoretical approaches to the discipline and focuses on the modern state and its relationship to citizens and civil society, regimes, identity groups, and the market economy. It provides an introduction to the discipline and its key concepts in the modern world, applying them to case studies throughout. Chapter 1 provides a broad overview of key conceptual debates, and it divides the field into three broad questions to help students organize these debates: Who rules? What explains political behavior? and Where and why? These help orient students by grouping the many debates in the field into broad categories tied to clear and compelling questions. "Who rules?" addresses the dispersion of political power, focusing mainly on the debate between pluralist and elite theorists. While that debate is typically subsumed under the study of American politics, we think it helps illuminate important areas of comparative politics as well. "What explains political behavior?" gets at the heart of the discipline's major disputes, which we divide among rational-actor theories, theories of political culture and ideology, and structural theories. "Where and why?" introduces students to the importance of and approaches to comparison.

The rest of Part I focuses on the modern state and its relationship to other key areas of modern politics. Chapter 2 defines and provides an overview of the modern state and uses a brief history of the modern state in our ten case studies to give students an overview of each. Chapter 3 examines modern states in relation to citizens, civil society, and political regimes, arguing that the latter are based first and foremost on political ideologies having to do with the relationship between state and citizen. Chapter 4 looks at the debate over political identity and the state's relationship to nations, ethnic and religious groups, and racial groups. Chapter 5 examines the abstract and historical relationship between the state and the market economy, including key concepts in political economy, economic theories, and globalization. Each of these chapters uses case studies to illustrate and assess the concepts and debates it introduces.

Part II examines political institutions in both democratic and authoritarian regimes as well as regime transitions. It is the "nuts-and-bolts" section of the book, providing what traditionally has been a core feature of the course. While this part of the book is essential, we have endeavored to keep it as succinct as possible to allow room to develop the thematic and theoretical elements of Part I as well as the contemporary policy debates of Part III. Chapters 6 and 7 examine political institutions in democratic regimes. Chapter 6 focuses on governing institutions: executive/legislative systems, the judiciary, the bureaucracy, and federalism. The theme throughout is the question of accountability in democracies. Chapter 7 looks at institutions of participation and representation: electoral systems, parties and party systems, and interest groups and social movements. It focuses primarily on how to achieve different kinds of representation and the potential trade-off between active participation and effective governance. Chapter 8 looks at institutions in authoritarian regimes, drawing on the previous two chapters to show how similar institutions function quite differently in nondemocratic regimes. Chapter 9, on regime transition, not only focuses on democratic transitions, but also sets them in the longer-term debate over regime change, looking first at military coups and social revolutions.

Part III examines some key current policy issues that have been foreshadowed earlier in the book. The conceptual and empirical knowledge that the students have gained in Parts I and II are used to address important current issues. Chapter 10 looks at different states' efforts to respond effectively to globalization, revisiting in a more current context the debates developed in chapter 5. It looks at the debate over convergence versus the varieties of capitalism approach in understanding the response to globalization in wealthy countries, as well as developing countries' efforts to respond to globalization in order to further develop, including the East Asian model and China's rise. The theme of chapter 11 is market failure, examining social policy, health policy, and environmental policy in turn. It draws on chapters 5 and 10, as well as material from Part II, to look at different approaches to current hot topics such as universal health care and climate change. Chapter 12 returns to themes first developed in a theoretical and historical framework in chapter 4 on identity politics. Its theme is how states respond to demands for inclusion in full citizenship by groups typically not included in the past and the clashes of fundamental values those demands raise in the areas of religion, gender, and sexual orientation.

KEY FEATURES

This text includes a number of pedagogical features that reappear throughout the chapters. Each of them is designed to help students marry the conceptual and country-specific material in the most effective way possible. We think students can manage the concepts without losing sight of the important facts they've learned about the countries if they're given the right tools. The three questions set out in chapter 1 are introduced at the start of each chapter in the form of specific chapter-opener questions relevant to the content of the chapter. They are intended to provide students with key material to consider as they read the chapter, study the cases, and then debate in class. The chapters do sometimes provide conclusive answers to some of the opener questions, but more often than not they show the students different ways they can be answered or approached. Each chapter also opens with a map showing the countries used as case studies and mini-cases. This feature helps readers locate chapters in which specific countries are discussed, facilitating the development of country-specific knowledge.

A "Country and Concept" table is included for chapters 2 through 12 that showcases empirical material. These provide key data of relevance to each chapter's case study countries, as well as offer succinct information on the theme of the chapter for all ten, even those not included as case studies in a particular chapter. The text refers to the tables at various points, but students and faculty can use these for much more, comparing the countries across the variables and asking questions about what might explain the observable variation.

As described earlier, each chapter after chapter 1 includes mini-cases as well as case studies of our ten countries. Mini-cases are one-shot interesting examples of particular themes. They illustrate alternatives to the models our case studies provide, or in some cases they introduce students to "classic" case studies not included in our ten. For instance, we include mini-cases on Sierra Leone and Liberia when discussing failed states, the Philippines when discussing the Third Wave of democratic transitions, and South Korea when presenting the "East Asian Miracle."

Most chapters have a "Where and Why" feature that provides a brief overview of a major theoretical debate in comparative politics relevant to the chapter but not directly addressed in the main text. Chapter 5 on political economy, for instance, outlines the debate over why structural adjustment programs have been more successful in some countries than in others, and chapter 11 includes one on why different kinds of welfare states have developed in different countries.

Most chapters also include one or more "In Context" features that present basic data that allow students to set a case study or idea into a comparative (and sometimes provocative) context. Students can use these to asses how representative some of our case studies are or to see the distribution of an institution, type of event, or set of factors around the world. For example, the "In Context" in chapter 4 focuses on identity politics in Latin America and shows racial and ethnic demography across the entire region. This is set next to the case study of race relations in Brazil.

In addition to these themed features, readers will find many original tables, figures, and maps throughout the book that illustrate key relationships or variables around the world. Students will find end-of-chapter lists of key concepts with page references to help study and review, as well as a list of works cited and a list of important references for further research. At the back of the book, we've also included a bibliography of major works for each of the ten core countries we discuss. We hope the design of the book strikes a balance as well: colorful and well illustrated to help engage student attention, but without adding significantly to cost.

ANCILLARIES

Because we know from experience that making the leap into a new textbook is no small chore, we also offer a full suite of high-quality instructor and student ancillary materials (prepared by Amy Forster Rothbart, University of Wisconsin–Madison). Specifically tailored to *Introducing Comparative Politics: Concepts and Cases in Context,* all of these materials are available online.

Adopters can register to access the instructor resources at www.cqpress.com/college. Click on "Ancillaries for Download," and you will find:

- A comprehensive test bank with more than 600 multiple-choice, fill-in-the-blank, and short- and long-essay questions. The test bank is available in Word and WordPerfect formats as well as fully loaded in Respondus, a flexible and easy-to-use test-generation software that allows instructors to build, customize, and even integrate exams into course management systems.
- A set of 180 PowerPoint lecture slides tailored around the core concepts of the book.
- A set of graphics from the text, including all of the maps, tables, and figures, in PowerPoint and .pdf formats for classroom presentations.

Students also have access to a customized companion Web site at http:// IntroducingCP.cqpress.com. Organized by chapter, the Web site offers opportunities to self-test and study that include clear and concise chapter summaries for each chapter, multiple-choice quizzes, interactive flashcards, and an interactive crossword puzzle based on the key concepts of the book.

ACKNOWLEDGMENTS

We have developed numerous debts in the process of writing this book. Perhaps the longest standing is to our students over twenty years of teaching Introduction to Comparative Politics at Hamilton College. Figuring out how to teach the course in a way that is interesting, relevant, and clear to them led us to develop the approach taken in this book. We kept them in mind as we wrote the book: Will it be clear to them? Will it interest them? Will it help them see the important concepts and how they matter in the real world?

We owe a substantial thank you to the office of the Dean of Faculty at Hamilton College as well. It has provided support for research assistants for this project over three years, primarily from the Steven Sands Fund for Faculty Innovation. The office also provided sabbatical support for Steve Orvis on Hamilton's program at Pembroke College, Oxford University, where the first elements of this project were written. Additional thanks go to the fellows and staff at Pembroke College for providing a hospitable venue for a sabbatical leave for research and writing. Deep thanks go as well to four especially talented Hamilton College undergraduates who worked for us as research assistants, pulling together vital data and information for many of the book's case studies. They are Luke Forster, Derek King, Joshua Meah, and Natalie Tarallo. They were invaluable help for two faculty taking on a project of this magnitude. Thanks go also to Andrew Rogan and Dawn Woodward for assistance in preparing the bibliographies in the book. We are very grateful to Amy Forster Rothbart for ably crafting all of the ancillary materials for this book.

The staff at CQ Press has been pleasant, professional, and efficient throughout this process. Our association began with a chance meeting between one of us and a sales representative from CQ Press, in which complaints were made about the quality of textbooks in the field and the sales rep asked the inevitable: "So how would you write one?" A quick response was met with the sales rep's enthusiastic statement: "We're looking for a book just like that! Can my acquisitions editor call you to talk about it?" We said sure, but, to be honest, didn't expect to hear from anyone. A week later the phone rang; Charisse Kiino, now chief acquisitions editor for CQ Press's College Publishing Group, was on the line to talk through the ideas further. This led to a long process through which Charisse expertly led us, starting with developing a proposal and draft chapter and responding to the first round of reviews. Charisse patiently walked us through the process with constant good cheer and support. Our development editor, Elise Frasier, has been invaluable, putting forth tremendous ideas for pedagogical elements of the book that we would have never thought of on our own, doing much of the research to develop these elements (with the help of her interns Serena Golden and Joe Farrell, whom we thank as well), and being herself an insightful reader and critic of the text. She has been supportive and flexible enough to help us get through this process efficiently but on a schedule we could handle. We deeply appreciate all she's done. Finally, our project editor, Lorna Notsch, has been fabulous in the final stages of the project, improving the prose in innumerable places, pointing out inconsistencies, and working with us in an open, honest, and professional way that has made a tedious process as easy as it could be. We deeply appreciate the work of everyone at CQ Press who have made the process of writing this book as painless as we could imagine it being.

We wish also to thank the numerous reviewers who read chapters of the book at various stages. Their comments led us to revise a number of elements, drop others, and further develop still others. They have collectively made it a much better book that we hope will serve students well. They are:

William Avilés, University of Nebraska–Kearney
Michael Bernhard, Penn State University
Gitika Commuri, University of California–Santa Barbara
William Crowther, University of North Carolina–Greensboro
Clement M. Henry, University of Texas–Austin
Eric H. Hines, University of Montana
Christian B. Jensen, University of Iowa
Eric Langenbacher, Georgetown University
Ricardo Laremont, SUNY Binghamton
Carol S. Leff, University of Illinois–Urbana Champaign
Mona Lyne, University of Missouri–Kansas City
Scott Morgenstern, University of Pittsburgh
Anthony Spanakos, Montclair State University
Sarah Tenney, University of Mississippi
Erica Townsend-Bell, University of Iowa
Kellee Tsai, Johns Hopkins University
Thomas Turner, Virginia Commonwealth University
Eleanor E. Zeff, Drake University
Darren Zook, University of California–Berkeley

Last, but far from least, we have to extend thanks to our children, Nick and Will. They didn't contribute ideas or critique the book, but they showed real enthusiasm for understanding things like who the prime minister of Britain is and why there is a Monster Raving Loony Party, and they endured and even participated in occasional dinner table debates on things like the relative merits of parliamentary systems and different concepts of citizenship. Most of all, they gave of themselves in the form of great patience. This project became more of an obsession, at least at key points, than our work usually is. It took us away from them more than we like and made our family life rather hectic, especially in the final year of writing. They bore it well, going on with their lives in their typically independent way. We deeply appreciate that, and hope we can make it up to them now that the writing is done.

INTRODUCING COMPARATIVE POLITICS

PART I

A FRAMEWORK FOR UNDERSTANDING COMPARATIVE POLITICS

COUNTRY CASES IN PART 1

Chapter	Brazil	China	Germany	India	Iran	Japan	Nigeria	Russia	UK	US
1. Introduction										
2. The Modern State	●	●	●	●	●	●	●	●	●	●
3. States and Citizens	●		●	●			●	●	●	
4. State and Identity	●		●				●			●
5. The State and the Market	●		●	●	●	●	●	●		●

Country	Area sq. mi.	Capital	Population	Age Structure*
Brazil	3,286,470	Brasilia	184,225,000	0–14 years: 25.3% 15–64 years: 68.4% 65 years and older: 6.3%
China	3,705,805	Beijing	1,334,210,000 including Hong Kong, Macao, Taiwan	0–14 years: 20.4% 15–64 years: 71.7% 65 years and older: 7.9%
Germany	137,854	Berlin	82,503,000 (2005 E)	0–14 years: 13.9% 15–64 years: 66.3% 65 years and older: 19.8%
India	1,222,559	New Delhi	1,124,000,000 (2005 E)	0–14 years: 31.8% 15–64 years: 63.1% 65 years and older: 5.1%
Iran	636,293	Tehran	68,492,000 (2005 E)	0–14 years: 23.2% 15–64 years: 71.4% 65 years and older: 5.4%
Japan	145,850	Tokyo	127,988,000	0–14 years: 13.8% 15–64 years: 65.2% 65 years and older: 21%
Nigeria	356,667	Abuja	130,445,000	0–14 years: 42.2% 15–64 years: 54.7% 65 years and older: 3.1%
Russia	6,592,800	Moscow	144,738,000	0–14 years: 14.6% 15–64 years: 71.1% 65 years and older: 14.4%
United Kingdom	94,249	London	60,021,000 (2005 E)	0–14 years: 17.2% 15–64 years: 67% 65 years and older: 15.8%
United States	3,732,396	Washington, D.C.	297,810,000	0–14 years: 20.2% 15–64 years: 67.2% 65 years and older: 12.6%

*CIA Factbook

An ethnic Albanian man shouts during a protest in Pristina, Kosovo, in October 2003.

Principal Languages	Monetary Unit	Major Natural Resources*
Portuguese	Real	Bauxite, gold, hydropower, iron ore, manganese, nickel, petroleum, phosphates, platinum, timber, tin, uranium
Standard Chinese or Mandarin (Putonghua, based on the Beijing dialect), Yue (Cantonese), Wu (Shanghainese), Minbei (Fuzhou), Minnan (Hokkien-Taiwanese), Xiang, Gan, Hakka dialects	Yuan	Aluminum, antimony, coal, iron ore, lead, magnetite, manganese, mercury, molybdenum, natural gas, petroleum, tin, tungsten, uranium, vanadium, zinc, hydropower potential
German	Euro	Arable land, coal, construction materials, copper, iron ore, lignite, natural gas, nickel, potash, salt, timber, uranium
Hindi, English (in addition to other languages that are official at the state levels)	Rupee	Arable land, bauxite, coal (world's fourth-largest reserves), chromite, diamonds, iron ore, limestone, manganese, mica, natural gas, petroleum, titanium ore
Persian (Farsi)	Rial	Coal, chromium, copper, iron ore, lead, manganese, natural gas, petroleum, sulfur, zinc
Japanese	Yen	Negligible mineral resources, fish
English, Hausa, Igbo, and Yoruba	Naira	Arable land, coal, iron ore, lead, limestone, natural gas, niobium, petroleum, tin, zinc
Russian, in addition to languages recognized by the constituent republics	Ruble	Broad natural resource base, including major deposits of coal, natural gas, oil, timber, and many strategic minerals
English (Gaelic is spoken in portions of Scotland and Northern Ireland, while Welsh is spoken in northern and central Wales)	Pound Sterling	Arable land, chalk, clay, coal, gold, gypsum, iron ore, lead, limestone, natural gas, petroleum, potash, salt, sand, silica, slate, tin, zinc
English. At the time of the 2000 census approximately 82.1% spoke only English; 10.7% Spanish; 7.2% other	Dollar	Bauxite, coal, copper, gold, iron, lead, mercury, molybdenum, natural gas, nickel, petroleum, phosphates, potash, silver, timber, tungsten, uranium, zinc

*CIA Factbook

Sources: Political Handbook of the World, 2008 (Washington, D.C.: CQ Press, 2008) and CIA *The World Factbook,* https://www.cia.gov/library/publications/the-world-factbook

Who Rules?

- How much power do different people or groups have in different political systems?

- Is power widely shared or concentrated among a few individuals?

What Explains Political Behavior?

- Do self-interest, beliefs, or underlying structural forces best explain how people act in the political realm?

- What kind of evidence can help us determine why political actors do what they do?

Where and Why?

- What can be learned through comparing political behavior and outcomes across countries?

INDIA

IRAN

USA

NIGERIA

JAPAN

GERMANY

UK

CHINA

RUSSIA

BRAZIL

1

INTRODUCTION

Understanding political developments and disputes around the world has never seemed more important to Americans than in the aftermath of the September 11, 2001, attacks on the World Trade Center and the Pentagon. The plot was conceived in Afghanistan and carried out primarily by individuals originally from Saudi Arabia, and in its wake, the United States invaded Afghanistan in search of terrorists, and stayed to engage in a difficult process of democratization. The United States then invaded Iraq ostensibly to rid it of weapons of mass destruction, but again ended up trying to build a democracy. U.S. policy tried to help a new Iraqi leadership navigate extremely difficult and, to Americans, unfamiliar political differences among Shiite Arabs, Sunni Arabs, and Kurds.

To many Americans, the world seemed suddenly more complicated and less comprehensible than it had in the post–Cold War era, a period perceived as one of unprecedented peace and stability when foreign politics were of relatively little importance. Indeed, Francis Fukuyama, an official in the George H. W. Bush administration, called the end of the Cold War "the end of history" (1992). The end of Communist rule in the Soviet Union and Eastern Europe seemed to foreshadow a period in which liberal democracies and market economies would spread, erasing the differences that made countries and their politics so incomprehensible to one another; understanding political differences appeared at once easier and less important.

In reality, the post–Cold War era from 1989 to 2001 was not nearly as peaceful and change not nearly as homogenizing and uniform as Fukuyama and others believed. Instead, this was a period of dramatic political change around the world: Communist rule collapsed, several countries literally split, the number of ethnic and religious civil wars rose significantly, and two full-scale genocides took place. Yet the number of countries that could claim to have democratic governments also increased substantially, even as East Asia, led by China, achieved unprecedented

Sunni Arab Deputy Prime Minister Salam Zikam Ali al-Zubaie, Shiite Prime Minister Nouri al-Maliki, and Kurd Deputy Prime Minister Barham Saleh (left to right), sit in front of other parliamentarians at the inauguration of the national unity government in 2006, three years after the U.S. invasion of Iraq. The government has officially ruled since that time, but still has difficulty forming a coherent national army or agreeing on how to share the country's oil wealth among the three major groups. Building democracy is often a very difficult process.

economic growth that removed more people from poverty more quickly than ever before in history. So while 9/11 and its aftermath may have refocused Americans' attention on the differences among nations and the perplexities of understanding them, those differences are not new.

Diversity of political, economic, and social life among nations persists in every period of history. The field of comparative politics primarily focuses on the fundamental and longstanding questions this diversity raises: Why do governments form? Why does a group of people come to see itself as a nation? Why do those nations sometimes fall apart? How can governments convince people they have a right to rule? Do some forms of government last longer than others? Do some forms of government serve their people's interests better than others? How do democracies form, and how do they fall apart? Can democracy work anywhere or only in particular countries and at particular times? Are certain political institutions more democratic than others? Can government policy reduce poverty and improve economic well-being? This book introduces you to the many and often conflicting answers that political scientists have come up with after examining these and other questions comparatively, and helps you start to assess which answers are most convincing and why.

THE BIG ISSUES

Current "hot button" political issues around the world are just the latest manifestations of a set of enduring questions that students of comparative politics have been studying for the last half century. Many could be listed. For the moment, though, let's focus on just five to illustrate the major interests of comparative politics: political development, regime type and change, participation and representation, policy-making processes, and political economy. The logical starting point is the question of **political development**.

You may be accustomed to seeing the word "development" applied to economics, where it relates to the growth of modern industrial economies, but development has important political dimensions as well. Historically, the biggest political development question is how and why modern **nations**—groups with a shared identity that also share or seek to share a territory and government—and **states**—ongoing administrative apparatuses that control territory and monopolize the use of force to govern—arose. Why did the entity now known as France, and a group of people that thinks of itself as French, come into existence? Is this process similar for all countries? If not, how and why does it vary?

Political scientists began thinking about these issues in a European historical context, but since World War II most questions about political development have emerged out of the experience of former European colonies in Latin America, Africa, and Asia. As these colonies gained independence, the relationship between the two types of development—economic and political—came into focus. Most observers assumed former colonies would go through a process of economic development dubbed **modernization**—the transformation from poor agrarian to wealthy industrial societies. Political scientists initially assumed that as this transformation occurred political systems that were more or less democratic also would emerge in these "new nations."

In truth, neither the economic nor the political aspects of this process evolved as planned. Some countries, such as South Korea, have achieved rapid economic transformation and have established electoral democracies. Many others, however, have not. In some cases democracy has emerged in very poor countries, whereas in others nondemocratic governments have presided over great economic change. In many a sense of being a "nation" has not even fully emerged, and some have completely collapsed into civil war and fragmentation. Yet even though the assumptions of modernization have not systematically answered the question of how economic and political development are related, scholars continue to produce more complex studies of the process of political development, because it remains crucial, as the cases of Afghanistan and Iraq demonstrate so vividly today.

Closely related to the issue of political development is the question of regime type and regime change. Americans often use "regime" to refer to some sort of "bad" government: we (democracies) have governments (for example, "the Blair government") or administrations ("the Bush administration"), whereas they (nondemocracies) have regimes. Political scientists, however, define a **regime** as a set of fundamental rules and institutions that govern political activity. Germany has existed as a state and a nation since at least the 1860s, but it has had several different regimes. Otto von Bismarck and Kaiser Wilhelm ruled over the first regime of a united Germany until the destruction of this modernizing authoritarian regime in World War I. Out of that emerged a second regime, the democratic Weimar Republic. Its instability led to the rise of the fascist Nazi regime under Adolf Hitler. The Cold War split the country into two states, each with its own regime—a democratic one in West Germany and a Communist one in East Germany. The reunification of Germany in 1990 brought both countries under the democratic regime as the Communist regime crumbled entirely. Germany has continuously existed for well over a century as one state (and, for a time, two), but it has had five different regimes.

Political scientists try to classify regimes into categories, or **regime types**, for greater ease of comparison. A broad initial division is into democratic and authoritarian regimes. Many definitions of democracy exist, but for purposes of systematic comparison, most political scientists adhere to what is often called the "minimal definition" of **democracy** as a regime in which citizens have basic rights of open association and expression and the ability to change the government through some sort of electoral process. This is not to say that democratic regimes are all the same: besides being "more" or "less" democratic, they are also organized in different ways, for example, as presidential or parliamentary systems (see chapter 6). Conversely, an **authoritarian regime** is simply a regime lacking democratic characteristics, and, like democratic regimes, numerous kinds exist. The most important of these in the twentieth century were **fascist**, such as Nazi Germany; **communist**, including the Soviet Union; **modernizing authoritarian**, like that of the shah of Iran or the military government of Brazil from 1964–1985; and **theocratic**, such as the Islamic Republic of Iran since 1979.

Britain's Prince Philip passes the Instruments of Independence to Kenyan nationalist leader Jomo Kenyatta at Kenya's independence ceremony on December 12, 1963. Kenyatta presided over a relatively successful economy but also created a one-party dictatorship that lasted until 1992. Even after opposition parties were allowed and democratic elections began, Kenyatta's party continued to rule for another ten years, finally relinquishing power after losing an election in 2002.

Once the various regimes are identified, we can ask questions about how they differ and how they are similar. On the surface, the answer seems obvious: democracies have elections and authoritarian regimes have dictators. In fact, the differences and similarities are much more complex. Some formally democratic regimes have significant informal limits on citizen input and participation, whereas some authoritarian regimes allow dissent and even power-sharing within certain bounds. We define and explore regimes in detail, as well as various subtypes of each, in chapter 3.

As our earlier German example suggests, we also need to ask questions about **regime change**, the process through which one regime is transformed into another. Recent dramatic political changes often direct political scientists' focus in studying this topic. For much of the last century, most political science research focused on **revolution**, a sudden and violent socioeconomic and political transformation that constitutes the most dramatic form of regime change. This type of study was spurred by the overthrow of Russia's autocratic regime in 1917 and intensified with the triumph of Chinese Communists over a nominal democracy in 1949. In the 1950s and 1960s, researchers looking primarily at Latin America also developed theories about the causes of **democratic breakdowns** brought about by military coups d'etat.

The spread of democracy since the late 1970s has shifted attention to the form of regime change most common today: **democratic transition**. Scholars studying democratic transitions ask questions about when and why authoritarian regimes give way to democracies, what kind of democracies are likely to emerge in particular circumstances, and how truly democratic new democracies are and how likely they are to last.

Closely related to the issues of regime type and democratization are **participation** and **representation**. Since Aristotle, if not before, political scientists and political philosophers have sought to understand why and how people participate in the political process, as well as how that participation differs across cultures and regimes. In some countries citizens participate as part of self-conscious identity groups, such as ethnic, religious, or racial groups (see chapter 4). In others identity groups have little relevance to politics. When and why do these differences emerge? What are the effects of strong "identity politics" on the stability of democracy? In relatively poor, agrarian societies, participation is often individual in nature, with citizens seeking out individuals above them in the political system who can help them secure what they need. In more industrial societies citizens may band together in what is called civil society to pursue common interests in the political process. **Civil society** is the sphere of organized, nonviolent activity by groups smaller and less inclusive than the state or government, but larger than the family or individual firm. Its most familiar elements are **interest groups** such as the Sierra Club or a chamber of commerce.

Political participation also occurs in **political parties**, of course. Different regimes have quite distinct kinds of parties and party systems that encourage different kinds and degrees of citizen participation, but whatever the type, parties are meant to represent citizens' concerns in the formal political process. No surprise then that political scientists want to know what electoral system most accurately represents the interests of citizens in the political process. How can citizens ensure that their representatives actually represent them? Can representation exist in authoritarian regimes? How do different societies conceptualize political representation in different cultural contexts? Each of these questions is an enduring element of comparative politics, and is discussed in chapters 7 and 8.

Two final major issues in comparative politics are **policymaking** and political economy. All governments, whatever the regime, ultimately make policies that govern society. How do different regimes decide on which policies to pursue? What role do different political institutions have in the policy-making process? Who is most influential in the process and why? Do the policies that finally gain approval reflect the will of the people? Which decisions should be made at the level of the national government, and which should be delegated to more local governments such as states or provinces? Different regimes provide different answers to these questions.

Political economy is the study of the interaction between political and economic phenomena. In the modern world, virtually all governments are concerned with and (at least in theory) held responsible for the economic well-being of their societies. Political economists try to determine what kinds of economic policies are most likely to prove beneficial in particular cultural, social, and political contexts. Do some types of regimes produce better economic outcomes than others? Many observers have argued, for instance, that modernizing authoritarian regimes are better able to achieve rapid economic growth in poor countries than are democratic regimes, but in recent years scholars of comparative politics have found substantial evidence that the relationship is far less black and white. Some authoritarian regimes, such as China's, have been quite capable of achieving growth, whereas others, including Nigeria, have not. Similarly, some kinds of democratic regimes seem capable of achieving beneficial economic outcomes even as others do not. A detailed comparative study of regimes and economic success can help unravel an answer to this all-important question.

These big issues do not encompass all of comparative politics, but they do raise the most prominent questions that **comparativists**, political scientists who study comparative politics, have been grappling with for the past half century. Today these questions are alive and well in the countries making headlines, from Iraq and Afghanistan to China and Sudan. Comparativists try to look beyond the momentary hot topics to systematically examine the enduring questions, seeking ever-clearer understanding of how politics works in the world and how it might be made better. Doing this requires some thought about how to study a very complex subject.

COMPARATIVE POLITICS: WHAT IS IT? WHY STUDY IT? HOW TO STUDY IT?

Politics can be defined as the process by which human communities make collective decisions. These communities can be of any size, from small villages or neighborhoods to nations and international organizations. In addition, the process of collective decision making always involves elements of **power**, the ability of one person or group to get another person or group to do something it otherwise would not do.

Comparative politics is one of the major subfields of **political science**, the systematic study of politics and power. In comparative politics, the primary focus is on power and decision making within national boundaries. This includes the politics of entire countries as well as more local-level politics. Politics among national governments and beyond national boundaries is generally the purview of the field of **international relations**, and while comparativists certainly take into account the domestic effects of international events, they do not try to explain the international events themselves. Perhaps it is self-evident, but comparativists also compare; we systematically examine political phenomena in more than one place and during more than one period, and try to develop a generalized understanding of and explanation for political activity that seems to work in many different situations.

Why study comparative politics? For one thing, comparativists are interested in understanding political events and developments in various countries. Why did the Taliban come to power in Afghanistan? Why did the Conservative Party rule Britain continuously from 1979 to 1997, and why was the Labour Party able to defeat it and rule continuously since? Also, as the Taliban example shows, understanding political events in other countries can be very important to foreign policy. If Americans and the U.S. government had understood better and paid more attention to events in Afghanistan in the 1990s, perhaps the country would not be faced with the crisis it has since 2001, or at least officials might have been better able to respond to it.

Systematic comparison of different political systems and events around the world also can generate important lessons from one place that can be applied in another. Americans often see their system of government, with a directly elected president, as a very successful and stable model of democracy. Certainly it has been used successfully elsewhere as well, but not everywhere. Much evidence suggests that in a situation of intense political conflict, such as an ethnically divided country that has had a recent civil war, a system with a single and powerful popularly elected president might not be such a great idea. A candidate from only one side can win this coveted post, and the sides that lose might choose to restart the war rather than live with the results of the election. A democratic system that gives all major groups some share of political power at the national level might work better in such a situation. That is not obvious when examining the United States alone. A systematic comparison of a number of different countries, however, reveals this possibility.

A third reason for examining politics comparatively is to develop broad theories about how politics works. A **theory** is an abstract argument that provides a systematic explanation of some phenomenon. The theory of evolution, for instance, makes an argument about how species change over time in response to their environment. The social sciences, including political science, use two different kinds of theory. An **empirical theory** is an argument that explains what actually occurs. Empirical theorists first notice and *describe* a pattern, and then attempt to *explain* what causes it. The theory of evolution is an empirical theory in that evolutionary biologists do not argue that evolution is inherently good or bad, they simply describe evolutionary patterns and explain their causes. A good theory should then allow theorists to *predict* what will happen. For example, a comparison of democratic systems in post–civil war conflicts would lead us to predict that presidential systems are more likely to lead to renewed conflict.

A **normative theory** is an argument that explains what *ought* to occur. For instance, socialists support a normative theory that the government and economy *ought* to be structured in a way that produces a relatively equal distribution of wealth. While comparativists certainly hold various normative theories, most of the discipline focuses on empirical theory. We attempt to explain the political world around us, and we do this by looking across multiple cases to come up with generalizations about politics.

Comparison is important because an empirical theory cannot be proved or disproved on the basis of a single case, although that single case may suggest a theory. For instance, the U.S. case suggests a theory about presidentialism as an inherently stable form of government. Once an empirical theory has been developed, however, it must be tested multiple times to see if it explains behavior across many cases. If it does not, the theory must be modified or abandoned in light of the evidence.

Unfortunately, political scientists do not have perfect scientific conditions in which to do research. We do not have a controlled laboratory, because the real world of politics cannot begin to be controlled. Physicists can use a laboratory to control all elements of an experiment, and they can repeat that same experiment to achieve identical results because molecules do not notice what the scientists are doing, think about the situation, and change their behavior. In political science, political actors think about the changes going on around them and modify their behavior accordingly. The research completed by political scientists, disseminated via publications and teaching, can influence the real world of politics. By producing the results of our research, we sometimes cause those we are studying to change their behavior, making the original ideas no longer applicable.

Comparativists use several **research methods** to try to overcome at least some of these difficulties, and we use scientific terminology, as explained in the following box. A **single case study** examines a particular political phenomenon in just one country or community and can generate ideas for theories or test theories developed from different cases. A single case, of course, can never be definitive proof of anything beyond that case itself, but it can be suggestive of further research and be of interest to people researching that particular country. Scholars use **multiple case studies** to examine the same phenomenon in several cases and try to mimic laboratory conditions by carefully selecting cases that are similar in many ways but differ in the area being studied. For instance, we can examine several countries that have had civil wars along roughly similar ethnic lines and subsequently adopted different kinds of democratic systems to see which kind of democratic system seems most stable in the aftermath of such wars. Alternatively, we could look at a number of examples of presidential systems in different countries to see which social, cultural, or economic conditions make presidential systems more or less stable.

With about two hundred countries in the world, however, no one can systematically examine every single case, or even multiple cases, in depth on any subject. For large-scale studies, political scientists rely on a third method, **quantitative**

statistical techniques. When evidence can be reduced to sets of numbers, statistical methods can be used to systematically compare a huge number of cases. Recent research on the causes of civil war, for instance, looked at all identifiable civil wars over several decades, literally hundreds of cases. The results indicated that ethnic divisions, which often seem to be the cause of civil war, are not as important as had been assumed. Although they may play a role, civil war is much more likely in cases in which groups are fighting over control of a valuable resource such as oil; where no such resource exists, ethnic divisions are far less likely to result in war (Collier and Hoeffler 2001).

Each of these methods has its advantages and disadvantages. A single case study allows a political scientist to look at a phenomenon in great depth and come to a more thorough understanding of a particular case (usually a country). Multiple case studies retain some, but not all, of this depth and gain the advantage of systematic comparison. Quantitative techniques can show broad patterns, but only for questions for which the evidence can be presented numerically, and they provide little depth on any particular case. Case studies are best at generating new ideas and insights that can lead to new theories. Quantitative techniques are best at showing the tendency of two or more phenomena to vary together, such as civil war and the presence of valuable resources. Understanding how the phenomena are connected, and what causes what, often requires case studies that can provide greater depth to see the direct connections involved.

No matter how much political scientists attempt to mimic science, though, the subject matter will not allow the kind of scientific conclusions that exist in chemistry or biology. The real world of politics is too complex and self-consciously changing for any type of universal theories to be supported in the long run by completely convincing evidence. As the world changes, ideas and theories have to adapt to explain it. That does not mean that old theories are not useful; they very often are. It does mean that no theory will ever become a universal and unchanging law, like the law of gravity. The political world simply isn't that certain.

Comparative politics will also never become a true science because of political scientists' own human passions about and positions in the various debates we study. A biologist might become determined to gain fame or fortune by proving a particular theory, even if laboratory tests don't support it, as the example of Woo Suk Hwang in South Korea who fabricated stem cell research, attests. Biologists, however, do not usually become ethically or morally committed to finding particular research results or engage in particular kinds of research because of their moral beliefs.

Political scientists, in contrast, very often do, and should. Normative theories affect our science because our science is in part the study of people. Our ethical and moral positions often influence the very questions we ask. Those who ask questions about the level of "cheating" in the welfare system, for instance, are typically critics of the system who tend to think the government is wasting money on welfare payments to people who could get by without them. Those who ask questions about the effects of budget cuts on the poor, on the other hand, probably believe

Scientific Method in Comparative Politics

While political science can never be a pure science because of rather imperfect laboratory conditions (the real world, over which we have very little control), political scientists nonetheless think in scientific terms. Most use key scientific concepts, including the following:

- **hypothesis:** a claim that certain things cause other things to happen or change
- **variable:** a measurable phenomenon that changes across time or space
- **dependent variable:** the phenomenon a scientist is trying to explain
- **independent variable:** the thing that explains the dependent variable
- **control:** holding variables constant so the effects of one independent variable on the dependent variable can be examined

The questions in political science are complex enough that an explanation usually requires the inclusion of several independent variables simultaneously to come close to a complete explanation of a dependent variable. In quantitative studies, each variable is explicitly measured, and complex statistical techniques can allow simultaneous examination of how all the independent variables correlate with the dependent variable. This in turn suggests the extent to which each explains variation in the dependent variable. For instance, one recent study of civil war by Paul Collier and Anke Hoeffler includes, among other things, measurements of poverty, ethnic fragmentation, and dependence on natural resources to explain where civil wars start and how long they last. This demonstrates that the presence of natural resources is more closely correlated with civil war than is ethnic fragmentation.

Using the scientific method in political science is quite complex because we do not control our laboratory and the political world is opaque. Often, the first challenges are defining the variables clearly and measuring them accurately. We conceive of the variables by developing hypotheses. But what constitutes, for instance, a "civil war"? How much violence must occur and for how long before a particular country is considered to be having a civil war? In 2007 critics of the U.S. presence in Iraq argued that Iraq was experiencing a civil war, while defenders of the United States denied this, so should Iraq in 2007 be counted as having a civil war or not?

A second challenge is including all the potentially relevant variables. In a laboratory, scientists control many of the variables they work with, holding them constant so they can examine the effects of one independent variable on the dependent variable. Political scientists can rarely do this directly, as we cannot hold variables constant, so we measure the simultaneous effects of them all through quantitative studies. Single or comparative case studies attempt to control variables via careful selection of the cases. For instance, a comparative case study examining the same questions Collier and Hoeffler studied might select as cases only poor countries, hypothesizing that natural resources only cause civil wars in poor countries. In the context of poverty, is ethnic fragmentation or natural resources more important in causing civil war? If, on the other hand, we think poverty itself affects the outcome, we might select several cases from poor countries and several others from rich countries to see if the presence of natural resources has a different effect in the different contexts. None of this provides the perfect control that a laboratory can achieve, but rather attempts to mimic those conditions as closely as possible to arrive at scientifically defensible conclusions.

the government should be involved in alleviating poverty. These ethical positions do not mean that the evidence can or should be ignored. Recent research on the effects of the 1996 welfare reform initiative in the United States, for example, suggested that it neither reduced the income of the poor as much as critics initially feared nor helped the poor get jobs and rise out of poverty as much as its proponents predicted (Jacobson 2001). Good political scientists can approach such a subject with a set of ethical concerns but recognize the results of careful empirical research nonetheless. Their normative position may not change, but they might modify their support for particular solutions to the problems in light of new evidence.

Normative theories can be important and legitimate purposes for a research project. This book includes extensive discussion of different kinds of democratic political institutions. We systematically compare them in part to try to understand their effects in particular contexts. One of the key trade-offs, we argue, is between greater levels of representation and participation on the one hand and efficient policymaking on the other. We demonstrate this by looking at abstract logic and the actual functioning of different institutions in particular countries. This is only interesting, however, if we care about the trade-off. We have to hold a normative position on which of the two—representation and participation or efficient policymaking—is more important and why. Only then can we use the lessons learned from our empirical examination to make recommendations about which institutions a country ought to adopt.

Where does this leave the field of comparative politics? Is there a way to study it systematically that can actually provide convincing answers? The answer to the latter is "only partially." The answer to the former is that it leaves us aware of our own biases but still attempting to use various methods to generate the most systematic evidence possible to come to logical conclusions. We approach the subject with our ethical concerns, our own ideas about what a "good society" should be and what role a government should have in it. We try to do research on interesting questions as scientifically and systematically as possible to develop the best evidence we can so that government policy can be based on solid ground. Because we care passionately about the issues, we ought to study them as rigorously as possible. Comparative politics is all about trying to find as solid answers as we can to crucial political questions.

THREE KEY QUESTIONS IN COMPARATIVE POLITICS

Comparative politics is a huge field that encompasses all political activity except international relations. The questions that can be asked and the debates that can be held are virtually limitless. Spanning this huge range, however, are three major questions. The first two are fundamental to the field of political science, of which comparative politics is a part. The third is comparativists' particular contribution to the broader field of political science.

Probably the most common question political scientists ask is: What explains political behavior? The heart of the discipline is trying to understand why people do what they do in the world of politics. We can ask why voters vote the way they do. Why do interest groups champion particular causes so passionately? Why does the U.S. Supreme Court make the decisions it does? Why did the United States invade Iraq? All of these ask why individuals, groups, institutions, or countries take particular political actions. Comparativists ask all but the last of these—we usually leave the question of why one country invades another to international relations. Political scientists have developed many theories to explain various kinds of political actions. Below, we discuss them in three broad approaches that focus on individual motivation, culture and ideology, and underlying structures.

The second large question animating political science is: Who rules? Who has power in a particular country, political institution, or political situation, and why? Formal power is often clear in modern states: particular officials have prescribed functions and rules that give them certain powers. For example, the U.S. Congress passes legislation, which the president has the power to sign or veto and which the Supreme Court can rule as constitutional or not. But does the legislation Congress passes reflect the will of the citizens? Are citizens really ruling through their elected representatives, as the U.S. Constitution implies, or are powerful lobbyists calling the shots or can members of Congress do what they want once in office? The Constitution and laws can't fully answer this broader question of who really has a voice, is able to participate, and therefore has power.

Virtually all questions in political science derive from these two fundamental questions, and virtually all empirical theories are part of the debate these two questions raise. Comparativists add a third particular focus by asking: Where and why? Where and why do particular types of political behavior occur? If we can explain why Americans on the left side of the political spectrum vote for Democrats, does the same explanation work for Germans and Brazilians with left-leaning views? If special interests have the real power over economic policy in the U.S. presidential system, is this the case in Britain's parliamentary democracy as well? Why have military coups d'etat happened rather frequently in Latin America and Africa but very rarely in Europe and North America? Comparativists start with the same basic theories other political scientists do to try to explain political behavior and understand who really has power, but we add a comparative dimension to try to develop explanations that work in different times and places. In addition to helping develop more scientific theories, comparing different cases and contexts can help us know what lessons we can take from one situation and apply to another.

These three questions—what explains political behavior, who rules, and where and why—guide this book. Each chapter touches on each of them in one way or another. As is true for most political scientists, explaining political behavior occupies much of our attention. Throughout, though, we raise the question of who really has power in particular situations and why. Each chapter also includes a separate box asking a where and why question, one that has been the subject of significant attention in the field. In addition, each chapter opens with key questions specific to the subject matter in that chapter, but these derive from these three broader questions. As we examine specific material, we introduce new questions and concepts, but all originate in these three questions and the broad theoretical approaches to answering them that we outline below.

What Explains Political Behavior?

The core activity in all political science is explaining political behavior: Why do people, groups, and governments act as they do in the political arena? It's easy enough to observe and describe behavior, but what explains it? In daily discussions we tend to attribute the best of motives to those with whom we agree—they are "acting in the best interests" of the community or nation. We tend to see those with whom we disagree, on the other hand, as acting selfishly or even with evil intent. You can see this tendency in the way Americans use the phrase "special interest." Groups whose causes or ideological leanings we agree with we perceive as benevolent and general; those we disagree with are "special interests." Logically, however, any **political actor**, that is, any person or group engaged in political behavior, can be motivated by a variety of factors. Political scientists have developed three broad answers to the question of what explains political behavior: individual motivation, culture and ideology, and underlying structures. Each answer includes within it several theoretical approaches.

Individual Motivation. It is a common assumption that most people involved in politics are in it for their own good. Even when political actors claim to be working for the greater good or for some specific principle, many people suspect they are really just using those ideas to hide their self-interested motives. The assumption of self-interest is also a major element in political science theories about political behavior. **Rational choice theory** assumes that individuals are rational and bring a set of self-defined interests into the political arena. This does not mean that all people are greedy, but rather that they rationally pursue their self-defined preferences, whatever those may be. The theory borrows heavily from the field of modern economics, which makes the same assumptions in analyzing behavior in the market. Scholars use this model to explain political behavior and its results by making assumptions about political actors' self-interests, modeling the political context in which they pursue those interests, and demonstrating how political outcomes can be explained as the result of the self-interested interactions of those actors in that context. For instance, allocating money for building new roads is a result of an agreement among members of a congressional committee. All of the members have certain interests, based mainly on the districts they represent and their desire for reelection. They pursue those interests rationally, and the final bill is a negotiated solution reflecting the committee members' relative power and interests within the context of the committee and Congress more broadly.

Rational choice theories start their analysis at the level of the individual, but often seek to explain group behavior. They model group behavior from their assumptions about the interests of individual members of the groups. Group behavior is essentially considered a result of the collective actions of rational individual actors in the group in a particular context. Racial or ethnic minority groups, women's groups, or environmental and religious groups can all be analyzed in this way. Rational choice theorists would argue, for instance, that environmentalists are just as rational and self-interested as polluters, they just have different preferences. Environmentalists gain benefits from breathing clean air and walking through unpolluted forests; their pursuit of those goals is no less self-interested than is the oil industry's opposition to environmental regulations. Even if the environmentalists do not consciously perceive their concern for the environment as self-interested, rational choice theorists would argue that it is, or else the environmentalists would not pursue that concern in the political arena. While self-interest may be easier to see when analyzing political battles over material goods and money, it exists throughout the political arena.

This example, however, raises one of the major criticisms of rational choice theories. Critics contend that rational choice theorists have some difficulty explaining outcomes because it is often difficult to know in advance exactly which individuals or groups might be involved in a particular political dispute, exactly how they will define their interests, and exactly what their relative power will be in the dispute. When a new political issue arises, individuals or groups have to figure out if they have an interest in it and, if so, what that interest is, and this process is not easily discerned. For instance, how can a rational theorist explain the electoral choice of a Catholic voter who is also a member of a labor union when faced with a Democratic candidate who favors raising the minimum wage and other workers' benefits but also favors legalized abortion, and a Republican candidate with the opposite views? Will he vote as a Catholic or as a union member? How can his vote be predicted by looking at his self-interests?

Many comparativists also ask whether rational choice theories can explain the different political behavior seen around the world. For most of the twentieth century, for example, the most important French labor unions were closely affiliated with the Communist Party and pursued many objectives tied to that set of beliefs, beyond the basic "shop floor" issues of wages and working conditions. In the United States, by contrast, no major unions were tied to Communist or socialist parties, and unions focused much more closely on improving wages and working conditions, with less concern for broader social changes. In Britain labor unions were not Communist, but ultimately they created the Labour Party to represent their interests in government. Rational choice theorists might be able to explain political outcomes involving these unions after correctly understanding the preferences of each, but they have a hard time explaining why unions in different countries seem to develop strikingly different self-interests. Did something in the working conditions of the three countries produce different definitions of "self-interest," or do different workers define their interests differently based on factors other than rational calculation?

Psychological theories also focus on individual motivation. These explain political behavior on the basis of individuals' psychological experiences or dispositions; this stands in opposition to rational choice theory's assumption of rational behavior. Instead, psychological theories look for nonrational explanations for political behavior. Comparativists who study individual leaders often use this approach, trying to explain leaders' choices and actions by understanding personal backgrounds and psychological states. Psychological theories are also sometimes used to explain group identity and behavior, such as strong attachments to racial or ethnic groups, and the willingness to join a group engaging in political actions outside the norms and values of a particular society at a particular time, including revolutions, political violence, or genocide. In these cases rational choice explanations seem quite unhelpful. Critics of this approach question whether the inherent focus on the individual that is fundamental to psychological theories makes them relevant to explaining group behavior. If not, their utility in political science is limited. Explanations beyond the level of individual motivation, however, might help explain these situations.

Culture and Ideology. Culture and ideology are probably second only to self-interest in popular ideas about political behavior. If people think someone is acting out of something other than self-interest, they usually assume that something to be a value or belief. Environmentalists care about the environment; regardless of their own personal interests, they think everyone ought to have clean air to breathe and forests to walk through. People who are against abortion believe that life begins at conception and therefore abortion is murder; self-interest has nothing to do with it. Political scientists have developed various formal theories that relate to this commonsense notion that values and beliefs matter. These approaches focus on either political culture or political ideology.

A **political culture** is a set of widely held attitudes, values, beliefs, and symbols about politics. These provide people with ways to understand the political arena, with justification for a particular set of political institutions and practices, and with a definition of appropriate political behavior. Political cultures emerge from various historical processes and can change over time, although they usually change rather slowly, as they are often deeply embedded in a society. They tend to endure, in part, because of **political socialization**, the process through which people, especially young people, learn about politics and are taught a society's common political values and beliefs. Yet while a society may have a common political culture in the form of certain shared values, beliefs, and symbols about politics, it also may have various **subcultures** within it that hold different beliefs and values in certain areas. Indeed, no political culture is truly monolithic; political minorities with distinct beliefs, values, and symbols exist everywhere.

Theories of political culture argue that the extent to which a society shares a common political culture and the values and beliefs in that culture are crucial explanations of political behavior. Two broad schools of thought within political culture theory exist: modernist and postmodernist. **Modernists** believe that clear attitudes, values, and beliefs can be identified within any particular political culture. The best known example of this approach was presented in the 1963 book *The Civic Culture*. Based on a broad survey of citizens of five countries in North America and Europe, the authors developed a **typology**, or list of different types, of political cultures. They saw each country as dominated primarily by one particular type of political culture and argued that the more stable and democratic countries, such as the United States and Great Britain, had a **civic culture**. This meant that their citizens held democratic values and beliefs that supported their democracies; these attitudes led them to participate actively in politics but also to defer enough to the leadership to let it govern effectively. Mexico, on the other hand, was described as an authoritarian culture in which citizens viewed themselves primarily as subjects with no right to control the government. The

Women vote in Jordan in November 2007. Comparativists seek to explain why people vote as they do, not just in one country but around the world. Are they motivated by ideological beliefs, long-standing values, self-interest? Are different kinds of voters influenced by similar factors in different countries?

authors argued that these attitudes helped produce an authoritarian one-party state, a state that went on to govern Mexico until 2000 (Almond and Verba 1963).

Critics of this approach question the assumption that any country has a clearly defined political culture that is relatively fixed and unchanging and contest the argument that cultural values cause political outcomes rather than the other way around. They note, for instance, that subcultures exist in all societies; racial or religious minorities, for instance, may not fully share the political attitudes and values of the majority. Therefore, the assumption that one political culture is key to understanding a country masks some of the most important political conflicts within countries. Furthermore, political attitudes themselves may be symptoms rather than causes of political activity or a governmental system. For example, Mexican citizens in the 1960s may not have viewed themselves as active participants in government for a very rational reason: they had lived for forty years under one party that had effectively suppressed all meaningful opposition and participation. They really did not have any effective voice in government or chance for effective participation, so the political institutions created the political attitudes, rather than vice versa.

Some political scientists also accuse the approach of ethnocentrism, in that it argues that Anglo-American values are superior to others for establishing stable democracies. Still other critics suggest that political culture is more malleable than *The Civic Culture*'s approach assumed. The attitudes that surveys identified in the 1960s were just that, attitudes of the 1960s. Over time, as societies change and new political ideas arise, attitudes and values change to match, sometimes with breathtaking speed (Almond and Verba 1989).

A somewhat more recent modernist approach examines this kind of change in political culture. Ronald Inglehart (1971) coined the term **postmaterialist** in the 1970s to describe what he saw as a new predominant element in political culture in wealthy democracies. He argued that with the post–World War II economic expansion, most citizens in wealthy societies were no longer as concerned about economic (materialist) issues by the 1960s and 1970s and were more concerned with "quality of life" issues; they had become "postmaterialist." Economic growth allowed most citizens to attain a level of material comfort that led to a change in attitudes and values. Individuals became more concerned with things like human rights, civil rights, women's rights, environmentalism, and moral values.

This shift in political culture led to a sea change in the issues that politicians came to care about and the outcome of elections. It explained, for instance, why a number of self-identified Catholic voters in the United States shifted from voting

Democratic in the middle of the twentieth century to voting Republican by the end. In the 1950s they voted their mostly working-class economic interests, supporting the party that created what many saw as "pro-worker" policies. Later, as they moved into greater security as part of an expanding middle class, they came to care more about postmaterial moral values, such as their religious opposition to abortion, and shifted their party allegiance accordingly. As the bulk of American voters went through this shift in political culture, political battles focused less on economic issues and more on debates over the moral and cultural values that many analysts see dividing the country today.

Inglehart's approach, and others like it, shows how political culture can change over time and how it could be seen as the result of other changes in society, such as economic prosperity, as well as the cause of political action and outcomes. They nonetheless continued to argue that it was useful to think about societies as having identifiable political cultures that explain much political behavior. **Postmodernist** approaches to political culture, however, criticize the assumption that one clear set of values can be identified that has a clear meaning to all involved and defines the politics of a society at a particular time. Postmodernists, influenced primarily by postmodern French philosophers such as Michel Foucault, see cultures not as sets of fixed and clearly defined values, but rather as sets of symbols subject to interpretation. Postmodernists focus primarily on **political discourse**, the ways in which a people speaks and writes about politics, when examining political culture. They argue that a culture has a set of symbols that, through a particular historical process, has come to be highly valued, but that is not to say that these symbols are not subject to varying interpretations. They are not fixed values that all agree on but are instead symbols that political actors can use by interpreting them through political discourse.

One possible example is the symbol of "family values." Politicians in the United States seldom say they are opposed to family values. In the 1980s Republicans under President Ronald Reagan used this concept in their campaign discourse very effectively to paint themselves as supporters of the core concerns of middle-class families; Democrats and their policies came to be seen at times as threatening to the ideal of the nuclear family. In the 1990s under President Bill Clinton, Democrats were able to gain back some political advantage by reinterpreting family values to mean what they argued was support for "real" American families: single mothers trying to raise kids on their own or two-income families in which the parents were worried about the quality of after-school programs and the cost of a college education. Democrats created a new discourse about family values that allowed them to connect that powerful symbol to the kinds of government programs they supported. Family values, the postmodernists would argue, are not a fixed set of values that all agree on but rather a symbol through which political leaders build support by developing a particular discourse at a particular time. Such symbols are always subject to reinterpretation in this way.

Critics of the postmodern approach argue that it can really explain nothing: if everything is subject to interpretation, then how can anything be explained or predicted, other than that "things will change" somehow as new interpretations arise? Postmodernists respond that the discourses themselves matter by setting symbolic boundaries within which political actors must engage to mobilize political support. The ability of political leaders to interpret these symbols to develop support for themselves and their policies is a central element to understanding political activity in any country.

A recent example of this approach is discussed in a book by political scientist Michael Schatzberg (2001) that examines African politics. He argues that each society has a "moral matrix of legitimate governance" that places boundaries on what is "politically thinkable." In Africa that moral matrix involves symbols of the family and the political leader as "father-chief." This symbol, however, is not fixed. The father is seen as the head and leader of the family and as such he is due respect, but he also is responsible for the well-being of his children. In addition, he is expected to eventually turn over his position to someone in the next generation.

Political discourse in Africa, then, is often about what a leader owes his "children"—the citizens—and how well he is providing for them, but it is also about when the leader will relinquish power to the next generation. While the image of the father may appear quite undemocratic, it can also be interpreted in ways that are much more democratic, ways that involve concern for the well-being of citizens and the transfer of power from one generation to the next. The moral matrix sets boundaries on what is acceptable, but leaves room for many political battles within these boundaries. Political culture, in this view, affects political behavior by limiting it to certain boundaries and providing the discourse through which political actors debate one another and mobilize political support.

Advocates of political culture, whether modernist or postmodernist, argue that explaining political behavior requires understanding the effects of political culture at the broadest level. A related but distinct way to examine the effect of value and beliefs is the study of **political ideology**, a systematic set of beliefs about how a political system ought to be structured. Political ideologies typically are quite powerful, overarching worldviews that incorporate both normative and empirical theories and explicitly state an understanding of how the political world does operate and how it ought to operate. Political ideology is distinct from political culture in that it is much more consciously elaborated. In chapter 3 we examine the predominant political ideologies of the last century: liberalism, communism, fascism, modernizing authoritarianism, and theocratic ideology.

Advocates of a particular political ideology attempt to mobilize support for their position by proclaiming a vision of a just and good society, a goal toward which political actors should strive. The most articulate proponents of a particular political ideology can expound on its points, define its key terms, and argue for why it is right. Communists, for instance, envision a communist society in which all people are equal and virtually all serious conflicts disappear, meaning government itself can disappear. They appeal to people's sense of injustice with the existing order in a capitalist society, and encourage people to work with them through various means to achieve a better society in the future.

A political ideology may be related to a particular political culture, but political ideologies are conscious and well-developed sets of beliefs, rather than vague sets of values or attitudes that typically constitute a political culture. Some scholars take political ideology at face value, at least implicitly accepting the idea that political leaders, and perhaps followers as well, should be taken at their word. These scholars believe that political actors have thought about politics and adopted a particular set of beliefs that they use as a basis for their own political actions and for judging the actions of others. Comparativists Evelyne Huber and John Stephens (2001), for instance, argue that the strength of social democratic ideology in several northern European governments partly explains why those states created and have maintained exceptionally generous welfare policies.

Critics of this approach point to what they see as the underlying motives of ideology and the real explanation for political behavior. The Italian Marxist Antonio Gramsci (1971) argued that ideology is part of **hegemony**, or the ruling class's political dominance. For Gramsci ideology is a means by which the ruling class convinces the population that its rule is natural, justified, or both (see the "Who Rules?" element in this chapter for a discussion of the ruling class). Advocates of rational choice models might argue that a particular leader or group adopts a particular ideology because it is in its own self-interest: business owners support an ideology of "free markets" because it maximizes opportunities to make profits. Similarly, advocates of a political culture approach see cultural values as lying behind ideology. In the United States, for instance, vague but deep-seated American values of individualism and individual freedom may explain why Americans are far less willing to support socialist ideologies than are Europeans. The debate between proponents of political ideology as an explanation of political behavior and their critics is about whether the political actors' ideological statements should be accepted at face value as explanations of their behavior, or if scholars should dig deeper to look for underlying causes of why those actors support that ideology.

Underlying Structures. The third broad approach to explaining political behavior is **structuralism**. Structuralists argue that broader structures in a society at the very least influence and limit, and perhaps even determine, political behavior. These structures can be socioeconomic or political. An early and particularly influential structuralist argument was **Marxism**, which states that economic structures largely determine political behavior. Karl Marx contended that the production process of any society creates distinct **social classes**—groups of people with the same relationship to the means of production. He argued that in modern capitalist society the key classes are the **bourgeoisie** who owns and controls capital, and the **proletariat** who owns no capital and must sell its labor to survive. According to Marx, this economic structure explains political behavior: the bourgeoisie uses its economic advantage to control the state in its interest, while the proletariat will eventually recognize and act on its own, opposing interests.

A more recent structuralist theory is institutionalism. Institutionalists argue that political institutions are crucial to understanding political behavior. A **politi-**

cal institution is most commonly defined as a set of rules, norms, or standard operating procedures that is widely recognized and accepted by a society and structures and constrains individuals' political actions. In short, institutions are the "rules of the game" within which political actors must operate. These rules are quite formal and widely recognized in some cases, such as the U.S. Constitution.

Other institutions can be informal or even outside government, but nonetheless are very important in influencing political behavior. In the United States, George Washington established a long-standing informal institution, the two-term limit on the presidency. After he stepped down at the end of his second term, no other president, no matter how popular, attempted to run for a third term until Franklin Roosevelt did so in 1940, as the country was coming out of the Great Depression and about to enter World War II. In that context, voters supported this decision and reelected him, but after his death the country quickly and easily passed a constitutional amendment that created a formal rule limiting a president to two consecutive terms. Informal institutions can be quite enduring, as the two-term presidency tradition shows. It held for more than 150 years simply because the vast majority of political leaders and citizens believed it should; in that context, no politician dared go against it.

Broadly speaking, two schools of thought exist among institutionalists. **Rational-choice institutionalists** follow the assumptions of rational choice theory outlined above. They argue that institutions are the products of the interaction and bargaining of rational actors. Barry Weingast, for instance, claims that for democracies to succeed, major political forces must come to a rational compromise on key political institutions in order to create a system that gives all important political players incentives to remain involved in it. Institutions that create such incentives will be self-enforcing, therefore creating a stable democratic political system. Weingast (1997) applies this argument to several countries, including the United States; he argues that political stability in early U.S. history was due to the Constitution's provision of federalism, a particular separation of powers, and the equal representation of each of the states in the Senate. This gave both North and South an effective veto power over major legislation, which enforced compromise and, thereby, stability. The Civil War broke out, in part, because by the 1850s the creation of more nonslave states threatened the South's veto power.

Historical institutionalists believe institutions play an even bigger role in explaining political behavior. They argue that institutions not only limit self-interested political behavior, but actually shape individuals' political preferences and what they see as their self-interests. Because societies value long-standing political institutions, members typically instill belief in those institutions in each succeeding generation. As children go through the process of political socialization they come to accept and value existing institutions and define their own interests partly in terms of preserving those institutions. Historical institutionalists also argue that institutions often determine what a government is capable of accomplishing, thereby explaining what people try to achieve politically, and what they succeed at and fail to accomplish. Stephan Haggard and Robert Kaufman (1995), for example, argue that two key institutions, a strong executive and coherent party system, are crucial to explaining which countries in Latin America and East Asia were able to respond positively to economic crises in the 1980s and 1990s and produce not only better economies but stable democracies as well. Regardless of people's self-interests or cultural values, historical institutionalists argue that the institutions themselves profoundly shape what policies are possible and what political outcomes are likely.

Critics of institutionalism argue that institutions are rarely the actual explanation of political behavior. Skeptics who follow rational choice theory argue that institutions are simply based on rational actions and compromises among elites who will continue to be "constrained" by these only as long as doing so serves their own interests. Scholars who focus on political culture or ideology, on the other hand, suggest that institutions are derived from those sources. Institutions reflect either a society's underlying values and beliefs or a more self-conscious ideology. In either case, the real explanation for political behavior and the shape of the institutions is the underlying values, beliefs, or ideology.

Political scientists look to three different sources as explanations of political behavior: rational self-interest, values and beliefs, and political institutions. Quite often, different scholars use each of these approaches to analyze the same political event. For instance, Chile made one of the smoother and, by most accounts, most successful transitions to democracy in the 1990s. A rational choice theorist might argue that this smooth transition resulted from the strategic interaction of the major political actors, regardless of what they personally believed about democracy. They came to a compromise with the former military regime and with each other around a set of electoral procedures that, given the political context, they thought was better for them than the available nondemocratic alternatives, so they accepted acting within the democratic "game." A political culture theorist would point to values in Chilean society that favored democracy, perhaps deriving in part from much of the population's European origins, as well as the country's past history with democracy. A historical institutionalist, on the other hand, while also looking at Chile's past history with democracy, would argue that its prior stable democratic institutions were easy to resurrect because of their past success; these institutions represented a legacy that many other Latin American countries did not have. So, the question becomes: Which of these theories is most convincing and why, and what evidence can we find to support one or another theory? This is the primary work of much of political science, the kind of question we will return to frequently in this book. The theories we use are summarized in Table 1.1.

Who Rules?

The second great question in comparative politics is: Who rules? What individual, group, or groups control power, and how much do they really control? At first glance, the answer may seem obvious. In a democracy, legislators are elected for a set term to make the laws. They rule, after the voters choose them, until the next election. Because of elections, it is the voters who really rule in the long term. In a dictatorship, on the other hand, one individual, one ruling party, or one small group such as a military junta rule. This ruling entity has all the power and keeps it as long as it pleases, or at least as long as it is able.

Comparativists, however, question this surface view. Even in democracies, it can be argued that the voters don't really hold the power and that a small group at the top really controls things. Conversely, many argue that dictatorships may not really be the monoliths they appear to be in that those officially in charge may have to unofficially share power with others in society in one way or another. Political scientists, in trying to dig beneath the surface of the question, have developed many theories grouped into two broad categories, pluralist theories and elite theories.

Pluralist Theories: Each Group Has Its Voice. **Pluralist theories** contend that society is divided into various political groups and power is dispersed among these groups so that no group has complete or permanent power. This is most obvious in democracies in which different parties capture power via elections. When pluralists look at political groups, however, they look at far more than just parties. They argue that politically organized groups exist in all societies, sometimes formally and legally, but at other times informally or illegally. These groups compete for access to and influence over power. Policy is almost always the result of a compromise among groups to some extent, and no single group is able to dominate continuously. Furthermore, over time and on different issues, the power and influence of groups vary, so a group that is particularly successful at gaining power or influencing government on one particular issue will not be as successful on another. No group will ever win all battles.

This process is less obvious in countries that do not have electoral democracies, but many pluralists argue their ideas are valid in these cases as well. Even in the Soviet Union under Communist rule, some analysts saw elements of pluralism. They believe that for most of the Soviet period, at least after the death of Stalin in 1953, the ruling Communist Party had numerous internal factions that were essentially informal and unofficial political groups. These were based on a person's position in the party and government bureaucracy or on economic position, regional loyalty, or personal loyalty to a key leader. For instance, people in the secret police, the KGB, or the military would be one group, quietly lobbying the official rulers to expand the influence and power of their organization. Leaders of particular industries, such as the oil industry, could be seen as a group seeking the ruling party's support for greater resources and prestige for their area of the economy. Leaders of a region or city could also act as a group, seeking greater government spending in their area. In all these cases, the pluralist politics was hidden behind a façade of iron-clad party rule in which the politburo, the Communist Party's central decision-making elite, made all decisions and all others obeyed. Pluralist analysts of the Soviet Union argue, however, that behind closed doors a great deal of lobbying, coalition-building, and power-seeking was occurring, not unlike the more public version that happens in democracies.

Dictatorships in postcolonial countries can also be analyzed via pluralism. On the surface, a military government in Africa looks like one individual or small group holding all power for as long as able or desired. Pluralists argue, however, that many of these governments have very limited central control. They rule through **patron-client relationships** in which the top leaders, the patrons, mobilize political support by providing resources to their followers, the clients. The internal politics of this type of rule revolve around the competition of the leaders for access to resources they can pass on to their clients. Their top clients are themselves patrons of clients further down the chain. Mid-level clients might decide to shift their loyalty from one patron to another if they don't receive adequate resources, meaning those on the top must continuously work to maintain their support. In many cases, patrons use resources to mobilize support from others in their own ethnic group, so the main informal groups competing for power are ethnically defined (see chapter 4). Various factions compete for power and access to resources, again behind a façade of unitary and centralized power.

Elite Theory: Concentrated Power.

While pluralists see competing groups, even in countries that appear to be ruled by dictators, proponents of **elite theory** argue that all societies are ruled by an elite that has effective control over virtually all power. The longest tradition within elite theory is Marxism, first mentioned above. Marx argued that in any society political power reflects control of the economy. In feudal Europe, for instance, the feudal lord, by virtue of his ownership of land, had power over the peasants dependent on the lord for access to land and their survival. The peasants were forced to live on the land of the lord under whom they were born, work that land for their own survival and produce a surplus for the lord, and carry out the lord's will in virtually all things. The lord, by virtue of his economic position, had tremendous political power over them. Similarly, in modern capitalist society, Marx contended that the bourgeoisie and proletariat are the two great social classes. By virtue of their ownership of capital, Marx said, the bourgeoisie are the **ruling class**, as the feudal lords were centuries ago. The general population,

Konstantin Chernenko, the last leader of the Soviet Union before economic and political reforms began, waves to other members of the politburo, the Soviet Union's top leadership council. Communist systems seem to be ruled by a small elite, but some pluralist theorists argue that even such dictatorial regimes include an element of pluralism. The men on the podium often represent different factions in the ruling party–state, vying for resources and power behind closed doors.

or proletariat, is forced to work in the bourgeoisie's factories or sell its labor to survive, and generally serve the desires of the bourgeoisie. Thus, in *The Communist Manifesto* Marx famously called the modern state "the executive committee of the whole bourgeoisie."

In postcolonial societies, Marxist analysts often argue that at least part of the ruling class is outside the country it rules. With the end of colonialism, a new situation of **neocolonialism** arose. The leaders of the newly independent countries of Africa and Asia benefited politically and economically by helping Western businesses maintain access to their countries' wealth. The new governments came to serve the interests of Western corporations as much or more than they served their own people. Marxist theorists debate among themselves how much power and autonomy the local elite within the country had vis-à-vis Western influences, but all agree that internal groups had at most very limited power in relation to the new elite supported by the West.

The Marxist tradition is only one type of elite theory. C. Wright Mills, in *The Power Elite* (1956), argued that the United States was ruled by a set of interlocking elites sitting at the top of economic, political, and military hierarchies. Mills shared with the Marxist tradition an emphasis on a small

TABLE 1.1 What Explains Political Behavior?

TYPE	INDIVIDUAL MOTIVATION Understanding what internal factors explain political actions	
Theory or Framework	Rational choice	Psychological theory
Assumptions	Political actors bring a set of self-defined interests, adequate knowledge and ability to pursue those interests, and rationality to the political arena.	Nonrational influences explain political behavior.
Unit of Analysis	Individual actors.	Group and individual identity and behavior.
Methods	Observe outcome of political process; identify actors involved, relative power, and interests; demonstrate how outcome was result of actors' self-interested interaction.	Explain actors' choices and actions by understanding their personal background and psychological state.
Critiques	Some difficulty predicting future behavior; hard to explain variation across cases.	Difficult to verify connections between internal state and actions, partcularly for groups.

CULTURE AND IDEOLOGY		UNDERLYING STRUCTURES	
Understanding the effect of values or beliefs		Understanding how broad structures or forces shape or determine behavior	
Political culture	**Political ideology**	**Marxism**	**Institutionalism**
A set of widely held attitudes, values, beliefs, and symbols about politics shapes what actors do.	Systematic set of beliefs about how the political system ought to be structured motivates political action.	Economic structures determine political behavior. Production process creates distinct social classes—groups of people with same relationship to means of production.	Political institutions are rules, norms, or standard operating procedures widely recognized and accepted that structure and constrain individuals' political actions—the "rules of the game."
Individual actors and groups, political institutions, discourses, and practices.	Individual actors and groups.	Groups: social classes in particular.	Interaction of both formal and informal institutions with groups and individuals.
Modernist approach identifies clear attitudes, values, and beliefs within any particular political culture—for example, civic culture or postmaterialist culture. Postmaterialist approach holds that cultures do not have fixed and clearly defined values, but rather a set of symbols subject to interpretation; focuses primarily on political discourse.	Analyze written and verbal statements of political actors and correlate with behavior.	Historical analysis of economic systems.	Rational choice institutionalists follow rational choice theory; institutions are products of the interaction and bargaining of rational actors. Historical institutionalists examine the historical evolution of institutions to demonstrate how these institutions limit self-interested political behavior and shape individuals' political preferences.
Political culture is not a monolithic, unchanging entity within a given country; cultural values not necessarily the cause of political outcomes, but perhaps the other way around. If everything is subject to interpretation, then how can anything be explained or predicted?	Focus on ideology obscures what may be underlying motives, the real explanation for political behavior.	Ignores noneconomic motives and groups other than social classes.	Difficult to determine if institutions limit behavior, rather than self-interest or culture.

group controlling all real power, but did not see the economy as the sole source of this power. He believed that the three spheres, while interlocking, are distinct and that all serve as key elements in the ruling elite. A more recent example of this view is Charles Lindblom (1977), who refers to the "privileged position of business" in a capitalist society in that government is dependent on business for taxes and the bulk of the population is dependent on business for employment, so business is in a unique position to influence those in power and therefore government policy. Lindblom argues that two spheres of power exist in modern democracies. One of these spheres is subject to democratic control, the other (the owners of business) is not. Modern democracies, including the United States, are not fully governed by "the people" in any real sense of the word according to these theorists, but rather by elites who serve the interests of the owners and managers of capital.

More recently, feminist scholars have also developed elite theories of rule based on the concept of **patriarchy**, or rule by men. They argue that throughout history men have controlled virtually all power. Even though women have gained the right to vote in most countries, men remain the key rulers virtually everywhere. Today this may be caused more by social mores and political discourse than actual law, but men remain in power nonetheless, and the political realm, especially its military aspects, continues to be linked to masculinity. A leader needs to be able to command a military, "take charge," "act boldly and aggressively," all things most societies associate with masculinity. Men also continue to enjoy greater income and wealth than women and can translate that into political power. According to feminist theorists, men thus constitute an elite that continues to enjoy a near monopoly on political power in many societies.

Similarly, some analysts argue that a racial elite exists in some societies in which one race has been able to maintain a hold on power. Historically, this was done via laws that prevented other races from participating in the political process, such as under apartheid in South Africa or the Jim Crow laws of the southern United States. But, as with feminists, analysts of race often argue that one race can maintain dominance through a disproportionate share of wealth or through the preservation of a political discourse in which its attributes are considered to be those most desirable for leadership. Such theorists contend that in the United States cultural attributes associated with being white, such as personal manner-isms, musical preferences, and accent and dialect of English, are all assumed to be not only "normal" but implicitly superior and expected of those in leadership positions. This gives an inherent advantage to white aspirants for political posi-tions, even when no overt discrimination against others exists.

As shown here, pluralists and elite theorists disagree over where power lies in society. Pluralists tend to see power as dispersed among many groups, and while this theory arose in the context of explaining democracy, it has been ap-plied in various forms to nondemocratic societies as well. These societies may be less pluralistic than democracies, but they can still be analyzed as including various groups that either share or at least have influence on power and govern-ment policy.

TABLE 1.2 Who Rules?

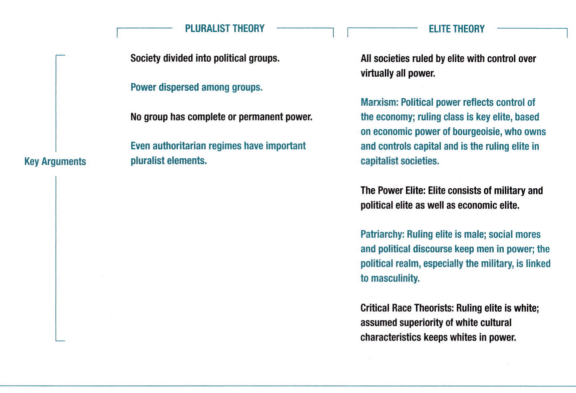

	PLURALIST THEORY	ELITE THEORY
Key Arguments	Society divided into political groups. Power dispersed among groups. No group has complete or permanent power. Even authoritarian regimes have important pluralist elements.	All societies ruled by elite with control over virtually all power. Marxism: Political power reflects control of the economy; ruling class is key elite, based on economic power of bourgeoisie, who owns and controls capital and is the ruling elite in capitalist societies. The Power Elite: Elite consists of military and political elite as well as economic elite. Patriarchy: Ruling elite is male; social mores and political discourse keep men in power; the political realm, especially the military, is linked to masculinity. Critical Race Theorists: Ruling elite is white; assumed superiority of white cultural characteristics keeps whites in power.

Elite theorists, in contrast, see all societies as controlled by one or more small group of elites. The most common type of elite theory is based on social class, following from Marx and other nineteenth-century theorists, but other elite groups, such as those based on gender and race, might exist as well. Determining which of these theories best answers the question of who rules requires answering: Who is in power? Who has influence on government decision making? Who benefits from the decisions made? If the answer to all of these seems to be one or a select few individuals, then the evidence points to elite theory as more accurate. If various groups seem to have access to power, influence on decision making, or both, then pluralism would seem more accurate. Table 1.2 summarizes these theories, which we investigate throughout this book, and the following Where and Why? takes a closer look at how comparativists explore these questions.

PLAN OF THE BOOK

This book takes a thematic approach to exploring the world of comparative politics. Each chapter examines a set of issues by presenting the major theoretical

WHERE AND WHY

"What explains political behavior?" and "Who rules?" are central questions to all of political science. The particular focus of comparative politics is to ask these questions across countries in an attempt to develop a common understanding of political phenomena in all places and times. Then there is the third major question that orients this book: Where and why? Where do particular political phenomena occur, and why do they occur where they do and how they do? As noted earlier, comparativists often use single case studies to develop hypotheses that can then be examined comparatively. Comparison requires looking at carefully chosen cases, and comparativists often try to pick countries that are similar in certain ways but different in others to understand the effects of those differences, like lab scientists control certain variables in order to understand the specific effects of others in which they are interested.

For instance, Sweden is famous for its extensive and expensive welfare state, while the U.S. government spends much less money and attention on providing for people's needs directly via "welfare." Why are these two wealthy democracies so different? Can their differences be explained on the basis of competing rational choices—by business interests overpowering the interests of workers and poor people in the United States, while a large and well-organized labor movement in Sweden overcame a small, weaker business class to produce a more extensive welfare state? Or is it because the Swedish Socialist Party, which has been dominant over most of the last century, has simply been successful at convincing the bulk of the population that its social democratic ideology produces a better society, while Americans' cultural belief in "making it on one's own" leads them to reject any form of socialism? Or is it because a strong nongovernmental institution, the LO (Landsorganisationen I Sverige), arose in Sweden, uniting virtually all labor unions under one organization that the government came to recognize as

a central part of the policy-making process, whereas in the United States the country's more decentralized political institutions resulted in decentralized labor institutions that were not as capable of gaining the government's ear on welfare policy? Comparative politics attempts to resolve this kind of puzzle by examining the various theories of political behavior in light of the evidence found.

We engage in similar efforts to understand who rules comparatively. A case study of the United States, for instance, might argue (as many have) that a corporate elite holds great power in American democracy, perhaps so great that it raises questions of how democratic the system actually is. A Marxist might argue that this is due to the unusually centralized and unequal control of wealth in the United States. A political culture theorist would point instead to American culture's belief in individualism, which leads few to question the leaders of major businesses who are often depicted as "self-made" individuals many citizens admire. An institutionalist, on the other hand, would argue that American political institutions allow great corporate influence via expensive campaigns and the fact that members of Congress have little incentive to vote in support of their party and so are more open to pressure from individual lobbyists. A comparativist might take this case study and examine several European countries, examining the level of corporate influence, the level of wealth concentration, cultural values, and the ability of lobbyists to influence legislators. Such a study might reveal comparative patterns that suggest, for instance, that corporate influence is highest in countries where wealth is most concentrated, regardless of the type of political system or cultural values. We examine this kind of question throughout the book, highlighting in each chapter some of the best-known examples of comparativists asking where and why questions about the subject matter of that chapter.

ideas and debates in that area of comparative politics and then examining how those ideas and issues play out in the real world in a set of countries. The rest of Part I looks at a set of key relationships crucial to an understanding of modern politics. These relationships all involve the **modern state** (defined fully in chapter 2)—to understand the modern political world, we must first come to an understanding of how the modern state arose. Our examination then looks at the relationship of the state to citizens (chapter 3), group identity (chapter 4), and the market economy (chapter 5). Part II examines the basic institutions of modern politics in both democratic and authoritarian regimes, and also explores the process of transition from one regime to another. Part III turns to an examination of a set of important issues in contemporary politics around the world.

Throughout the book, we draw on a set of ten countries to illustrate the ideas, debates, institutions, and issues we're examining. Each chapter focuses on a comparison of several of these countries, chosen to illustrate the key ideas and debates in the chapter. The ten countries include a majority of the most populous countries in the world and are a representative sample of different kinds of modern political history. They include four wealthy democracies (the United States, Britain, Germany, and Japan), two post-Communist countries (Russia and China), the largest and one of the most enduring democracies in the world (India), the world's only theocracy (Iran), and two examples of countries that have struggled to establish democratic systems after lengthy military dictatorships (Brazil and Nigeria). Collectively, our countries come from every continent and major region of the world. Our task is to see what we can learn from a comparative examination of politics in this diverse array of settings.

Key Concepts

authoritarian regime (p. 8)
bourgeoisie (p. 23)
civic culture (p. 19)
civil society (p. 9)
communist regime (p. 8)
comparative politics (p. 10)
comparativists (p. 10)
democracy (p. 8)
democratic breakdowns (p. 9)
democratic transition (p. 9)
elite theory (p. 27)
empirical theory (p. 11)
fascist regime (p. 8)
hegemony (p. 23)
historical institutionalists (p. 24)
interest groups (p. 9)
international relations (p. 11)
Marxism (p. 23)
modernists (p. 19)
modernization (p. 7)
modernizing authoritarian
   regime (p. 8)
modern state (p. 33)

multiple case studies (p. 12)
nations (p. 7)
neocolonialism (p. 28)
normative theory (p. 12)
participation (p. 9)
patriarchy (p. 30)
patron-client relationships
   (p. 27)
pluralist theories (p. 26)
policymaking (p. 9)
political actor (p. 17)
political culture (p. 19)
political development (p. 6)
political discourse (p. 21)
political economy (p. 10)
political ideology (p. 22)
political institution (p. 23)
political parties (p. 9)
political science (p. 10)
political socialization (p. 19)
politics (p. 10)
postmaterialist (p. 20)
postmodernist (p. 21)

power (p. 10)
proletariat (p. 23)
psychological theories (p. 18)
quantitative statistical techniques
   (p. 12)
rational-choice institutionalists
   (p. 24)
rational choice theory (p. 17)
regime (p. 7)
regime change (p. 8)
regime types (p. 8)
representation (p. 9)
research methods (p. 12)
revolution (p. 9)
ruling class (p. 27)
single case study (p. 12)
social classes (p. 23)
states (p. 7)
structuralism (p. 23)
subcultures (p. 19)
theocratic regime (p. 8)
theory (p. 11)
typology (p. 19)

Works Cited

Almond, Gabriel A., and Sidney Verba. 1963. *The Civic Culture: Political Attitudes and Democracy in Five Nations.* Princeton: Princeton University Press.

———. 1989. *The Civic Culture Revisited.* Thousand Oaks, Calif.: Sage.

Collier, Paul, and Anke Hoeffler. 2001. *Greed and Grievance in Civil War.* Washington, D.C.: World Bank.

Fukuyama, Francis. 1992. *The End of History and the Last Man.* New York: Free Press.

Gramsci, Antonio. 1971. *Selections from the Prison Notebooks.* Ed. and trans. Quintin Hoare and Geoffrey Nowell Smith. New York: International Publishers.

Haggard, Stephan, and Robert Kaufman. 1995. *The Political Economy of Democratic Transitions.* Princeton: Princeton University Press.

Huber, Evelyne, and John Stephens. 2001. *Development and Crisis of the Welfare State.* Chicago: University of Chicago Press.

Inglehart, Ronald. 1971. "The Silent Revolution in Post-Industrial Societies." *American Political Science Review* 65: 991–1017.

Jacobson, Linda. 2001. "Experts Debate Welfare Reform's Impact on Children." *Education Week* 21 (September 19): 1–8.

Lindblom, Charles E. 1977. *Politics and Markets: The World's Political Economic Systems.* New York: Basic Books.

Mills, C. Wright. 1956. *The Power Elite.* New York: Oxford University Press.

Schatzberg, Michael G. 2001. *Political Legitimacy in Middle Africa: Father, Family, Food.* Bloomington: Indiana University Press.

Weingast, Barry R. 1997. "The Political Foundations of Democracy and the Rule of Law." *American Political Science Review* 91, no. 2 (June): 245–263.

Resources for Further Study

Blank, Rebecca. 2001. "Declining Caseloads/Increased Work: What Can We Conclude about the Effects of Welfare Reform?" *Economic Policy Review* 7, no. 2 (September).

Dahl, Robert. 1961. *Who Governs?* New Haven: Yale University Press.

Katznelson, I., and H. V. Milner, ed. 2002. *Political Science: State of the Discipline.* New York: Norton.

King, Gary, Robert Keohane, and Sidney Verba. 1994. *Designing Social Inquiry.* Princeton: Princeton University Press.

Landman, Todd. 2003. *Issues and Methods in Comparative Politics,* 2nd ed. New York: Routledge.

Pierson, Paul, and Theda Skocpol. 2002. "Historical Institutionalism in Contemporary Political Science." In *Political Science: State of the Discipline,* ed. I. Katznelson and H. V. Milner, 693–721. New York: Norton.

Tucker, Robert C. 1978. *The Marx-Engels Reader.* New York: Norton.

Weingast, Barry R. 2002. "Rational-choice Institutionalism." In *Political Science: State of the Discipline,* ed. I. Katznelson and H. V. Milner, 660–692. New York: Norton.

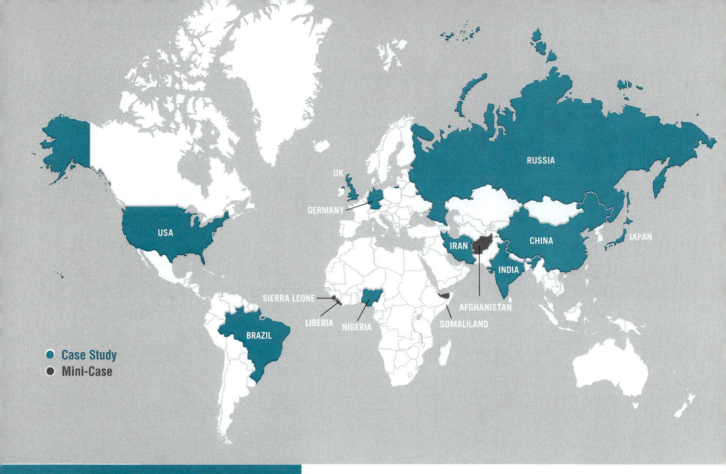

Who Rules?

- What common characteristics do all modern states have, and how do they give their rulers power?

What Explains Political Behavior?

- Why did modern states arise and become universal?

- Do the common characteristics of modern states limit power in any way?

Where and Why?

- Why are some states stronger than others? Why do some states fail completely?

2

THE MODERN STATE

Political development—the origin and development of the modern state—is the main starting point for the study of comparative politics. What is meant by "the modern state"? The answer is not obvious, because although "state" is often used interchangeably with both "country" and "nation," political scientists use the term in a more specific way. "Country" is essentially a specific, geographic location; "nation" more broadly includes connotations of tradition, language, or culture. The "state" is more than a location, but it does not share the full connotations of "nation." We say more about the relationship between state and nation ("country" is not a conceptual term in political science) in this chapter, but for now we will point out that it is perfectly possible to have stateless nations (Israel prior to 1949 or the Kurds today) and states comprised of more than one nation (former Yugoslavia, contemporary Iraq).

For political analysis, we need to find a more exact definition of state. One approach is to ask how and when we "see" or "contact" the state. Purpose-built capitals like Abuja, Brasilia, and Washington, D.C., make it visible because they "house" a range of state functions, including administration, courts, the legislature, and the executive, in close proximity. On some level, these buildings and the people working in them are the "state." Similarly, if you have attended public school, gotten a driver's license, received a traffic ticket, or paid income taxes, you've come into contact with the state, which provides public goods and enforces laws and uses public money in the form of taxes to do so. These observations lead to a very basic definition of the state as a set of ongoing institutions that develops and administers laws and generates and implements public policies in a specific territory. The *ongoing* nature of a state's institutions sets it apart from yet another similar term, "government." Americans use "government" and "state" interchangeably, but "governments," which Americans call "administrations," are transient in that they occupy and utilize the ongoing apparatus of the state.

The complex relationship among these terms—state, nation, and government—highlights the way the concept of the state can help address that perennial question of political scientists: "Who rules?" Understanding the state itself does not answer that question, because the state is a set of institutions and people performing a range of public and political functions. Any number of groups or individuals, such as dictators, elites, democratically elected politicians, or the "government of the day," can rule through the same institutions. Identifying and understanding the key features of the state, however, help in analyzing who is utilizing them and for what ends—in short, who rules and how.

In addition, looking at how much institutional apparatus a particular country has developed and how effectively that apparatus can be deployed (Are people really paying taxes? Are neighborhoods run by drug lords or the police?) can also help identify the effective limits of official rule in a particular country. Where such structures are poorly developed, it may be concluded that no one rules on a national level, although powerful local groups may effectively rule in place of the nominal state. Comparativists also always seek to answer the "where and why" questions: Where did the modern state emerge, and why did it do so at different times in different places? Why did strong state structures develop sooner in some countries and later or not at all in others?

The brief definition and discussion above clearly leaves some open questions. As Christopher Pierson says, "We think that we know the state when we see it, but it proves extremely difficult to bring it under some brief but generally acceptable definition" (1996, 5). Like Pierson, though, we believe that political scientists generally agree on a fuller set of shared characteristics that are common among *modern* states. These characteristics help set the state apart from other concepts like nation, government, and regime, as well as from earlier forms of political organization.

CHARACTERISTICS OF THE MODERN STATE

The first characteristic of the modern state is so obvious that you might overlook it. A state must have **territory**, an area with clearly defined borders to which it lays claim. In fact, borders are one of the places the state is "seen" most clearly, not only by the signs that welcome visitors, but also by the customs inspectors and immigration officers who patrol and represent it. Territories vary enormously, from Russia, the largest geographical state at 6,520,800 square miles, to the seventeen recognized states with territories of less than 200 square miles. The differences between vast Russia and tiny Tuvalu are significant, but territories and borders allow both to claim the status of state, and both are recognized as such.

A glance at any map of the world's states suggests there's little room for change; one look shows no unclaimed territories or great expanses not enclosed by state borders. Many states also have inhabited their present borders for so long that we may think of them as being relatively fixed. In truth, the number of states and their borders continue to change rather frequently. As recently as 2008, Kosovo's independence caused mapmakers to redraw the map of Europe, and it was only the most recent addition to the numerous border changes and state creations that have characterized Eastern Europe since 1989. This particular shake-up is a recent manifestation of the state turmoil found in that region throughout the twentieth century. Border changes and the creation of new states are often attempts to make "states" coincide more closely with "nations," and what this means is that we cannot conclude that we are now "done" and that today's states will be the same as tomorrow's. On the contrary, the lesson of history seems to be that states will continue to change their shapes and borders.

The example of Kosovo reminds us of another important aspect of territoriality: states exist in an international system of other states (see Table 2.1 on level of state recognition). It is not enough for a state to claim a defined territory; other states must also recognize that overall claim, even if they dispute a particular border. Political scientists call internationally recognized states **sovereign**. Essentially, a sovereign state is legally recognized by the family of states as the sole legitimate governing authority within its territory and as the legal equal of other states, even if this is not actually the case. This legal recognition is the minimal standard for **external sovereignty**, or sovereignty relative to outside powers. Legal external sovereignty, which entails being given the same vote in world affairs as all other states, is vital for sovereignty.

In a world of competitive and conflicting states, to achieve real, effective external sovereignty, that is, to truly be free of external interference in governing, a state must be able to defend its territory and must not be overly dependent on the resources or decisions of another power. Invasion, colonialism, and "puppet states" are the most obvious cases of lack of true external sovereignty. Examples include the Japanese-backed and controlled state headed by the Chinese emperor Puyi in Manchukuo (Manchuria) from 1932 to 1945, the Vichy government in collaborationist occupied France during World War II, and many colonial states. In all such cases, although some kind of local government apparatus may operate on a day-to-day basis, it is not a sovereign state, because its most crucial decisions are subject to an external authority.

IN CONTEXT New States and the United Nations

Since 1959 the vast majority of new member states in the United Nations were admitted after declaring independence. In the 1960s and 1970s, most newly admitted states were former colonies. In the 1990s, most of those admitted were the result of the break-up of the Soviet Union and other Eastern-bloc countries. New members continue to be added to the list in the new millennium.

1945–1949	81 member states admitted
1960–1969	42 member states admitted
1970–1979	25 member states admitted
1980–1989	6 member states admitted
1990–1999	31 member states admitted
2000–2007	5 member states admitted

MINI-CASE Somaliland

Somaliland is a most interesting recent case of disputed sovereignty. It is a state that has achieved almost unquestioned internal sovereignty, a stable constitutional democracy, and a growing economy, but no other state recognizes it so it has no international legal sovereignty. This unusual outcome is a result of the collapse of the larger state of Somalia and the international efforts to resolve that country's civil war. Somaliland, the northernmost region of Somalia, originally was a separate colony from the rest of what is now Somalia. It fell under British control, while the rest of the country was an Italian colony. In 1960 the former British colony gained independence for a few days but then quickly agreed to become part of the larger state of Somalia, which had also just gained independence.

The civil war that has engulfed Somalia really began in Somaliland in the late 1980s. When dictator Siad Barre fell in the capital, Mogadishu, in 1991, the rebel movement in Somaliland, the Somali National Movement (SNM), declared the region independent within a few months. This was not especially surprising, given that all of Somalia is deeply divided into rival clans. Somaliland is no exception. The Isaaq clan represents about two-thirds of that region's population and dominates the SNM leadership, but members reached out to other clans in the newly independent country to coalesce their control. An initial agreement among clan elders put the SNM in power in 1991, but disputes with other clans and within the SNM led to further fighting. A conference of the elders of all the major clans in 1993 produced a new government that was a ci-

vilian administration no longer controlled exclusively by the SNM. This administration created a parliament modeled after traditional Somali institutions, with representation based on clan membership. In 2001 a referendum approved a new constitution that was fully democratic, with a bicameral legislature: one house is filled by directly elected representatives and the other by clan elders. By 2005 successful democratic elections had been held for president, parliament, and local governments.

The Somaliland economy has grown substantially, based mainly on exports of livestock to the Middle East and money sent home by Somalis living and working around the world. The government has established much better social services and greater security than exist in the rest of war-wracked Somalia. Yet because it has no official recognition from other governments, Somaliland receives no official aid from other countries, has no embassies in its capital, and sends no ambassadors abroad. Unofficially, some Western aid has reached Somaliland via private charities, and the leadership has met with representatives of Western countries, including the United States, but the country remains largely on its own. Most of the world fears that officially recognizing Somaliland will encourage other regions of Somalia to attempt to break away as well, so the wait is on for resolution of the larger civil war in Somalia, after which many expect full recognition of Somaliland for what it is: an unusually successful African state that has established its effective sovereignty without the support of legal recognition.

Modern states also strive for **internal sovereignty**, that is, to be the sole authority within a territory capable of making and enforcing laws and policies. They must defend their internal sovereignty against domestic groups that challenge it, just as they defend it externally against possible invasion. These challenges typically take the form of a declaration of independence from some part of the state's territory, and perhaps a declaration of civil war. Rarely is a state willing to accept such an act of defiance. Most states, from the United States in 1861 at the start of the Civil War to the former Soviet Republic of Georgia when

TABLE 2.1 The Shifting Borders of Modern States: Not Recognized, Limited Recognition, and Majority Recognition States

Not Recognized		
State	**Disputed Since**	**Status**
Nagorno-Karabakh	1991	Claimed by Azerbaijan
Somaliland	1991	Claimed by Somalia
Transnistria	1990	Claimed by Moldova

Limited Recognition		
State	**Disputed Since**	**Status**
Abkhazia	2008	Recognized only by Russian Federation
Kosovo	2008	Recognized by 40 countries
South Ossetia	2008	Recognized only by Russian Federation
Palestine	1988	Recognized as a proposed state by 96 UN member states
Turkish Republic of Northern Cyprus (TRNC)	1983	Recognized only by Turkey
Sahrawi Arab Democratic Republic (SADR)	1976	Recognized by 45 countries as legitimate government of Western Sahara
Republic of China (Taiwan) (ROC)	1949	Recognized by 23 countries

Majority Recognition		
State	**Disputed Since**	**Status**
Czech Republic	1993	Not recognized by Liechtenstein
Liechtenstein	1993	Not recognized by Czech Republic or Slovakia
Slovakia	1993	Not recognized by Liechtenstein
Cyprus	1974	Recognized by all countries except Turkey
People's Republic of China (PRC)	1949	Not recognized by the Republic of China (Taiwan); the PRC does not accept diplomatic relations with the 22 other UN member states that recognize the ROC.
Israel	1948	Not recognized by Iran or SADR, no diplomatic relations with 34 countries
North Korea	1948	Not recognized by South Korea
South Korea	1948	Not recognized by North Korea

faced with the breakaway region of South Ossetia in the 1990s, use all means in their power to preserve their sovereignty over their recognized territories. Even a relatively insignificant challenge will draw the full attention of a state. In Waco, Texas, in 1993, a small religious sect called the Branch Davidians broke various U.S. laws and declared its compound beyond the reach of U.S. authority. Though a small and isolated group that most of the country thought was simply "crazy," its direct rejection of U.S. sovereignty ultimately led to intervention by President Bill Clinton's administration; Attorney General Janet Reno was personally involved in the standoff on a daily basis. Even a superpower will react with full force to the smallest threat to its claim to sovereignty.

States try to enforce their sovereignty by claiming, in the words of famous German sociologist Max Weber, a "monopoly on the legitimate use of physical force" (1970). Put simply, the state claims to be the only entity within its territory with the right to hold a gun to your head and tell you what to do. Some governments claim a virtually unlimited right to use force when and as they choose. At least in theory, and usually in practice, liberal democracies include strict guidelines under which force can be used. For example, law enforcement can be called in when a citizen runs a red light or fails to pay taxes, but not when a citizen criticizes government policy. All states, though, insist on the right to use force to ensure their internal as well as external sovereignty. As one political philosopher reportedly said in response to complaints from students about the government calling in police during a demonstration, "The difference between fascism and democracy is not whether the police are called, but when."

Sovereignty does not mean, however, that a state is all powerful. Real internal and external sovereignty varies greatly and depends on many factors. The size and wealth of the United States mean its sovereignty results in much greater power than does the sovereignty of Vanuatu, though both are recognized as legitimate sovereigns over a clear territory. Wealthier states can defend their territories from attack better than poorer and weaker ones, and they can also more effectively ensure that their citizens comply with their laws. This ability to enforce sovereignty fully comes not only from wealth, however, but also from legitimacy and bureaucracy, the final two key characteristics of states.

Remember that Weber argued that a state claims a "monopoly on the legitimate use of physical force." **Legitimacy** is the recognized right to rule. This right has at least two sides: the claims that states and others make about why they have a right to rule, and the empirical fact of whether their populations accept or at least tolerate this claimed right. All modern states argue at length for a particular normative basis for their legitimacy, and this claim is the basis of the various kinds of regimes in the world today (a subject explored more fully in chapter 3). Weber described three types of legitimate authority: traditional, charismatic, and rational-legal. **Traditional legitimacy** is the right to rule based on a society's long-standing patterns and practices. The European "divine right of kings" and the blessing of ancestors over the king in many precolonial African societies are examples of this. **Charismatic legitimacy** is the right to rule based on personal virtue, heroism, sanctity, or other extraordinary characteristics. Wildly popular leaders of revolutions, such as Mao Zedong in his early years in power, have charismatic legitimacy; people recognize their authority to rule because they trust and believe these individuals to be exceptional. **Rational-legal legitimacy** is the right of leaders selected according to an accepted set of laws to command. Leaders who come to power via electoral processes and rule according to a set of laws such as a constitution are the chief examples of this. Weber argued that the third of these distinguishes modern rule from its predecessors, but recognized that in practice most legitimate authority is based on a combination of the three. For example, modern democratically elected leaders may achieve office and rule on the basis of rational-legal processes, but a traditional status or personal charisma may have gained them the electoral victory and may enhance their legitimacy in office.

Legitimacy enhances a state's sovereignty. Modern states often control an overwhelming amount of coercive power, but its use is expensive and difficult. States cannot maintain effective internal sovereignty in a large, modern society solely through the constant use or even threat of force. Legitimacy, whatever its basis, enhances sovereignty at much lower cost. If most citizens obey the government because they believe it has a right to rule, little force will be necessary to maintain order. For this reason, governments proclaim their legitimacy and spend a great deal of effort trying to convince their citizens of it, especially if it is brought into serious question.

Modern **bureaucracy** is the final important characteristic of the state. We defined the state at the outset as a set of institutions that develops and administers laws. In contemporary societies, the state plays many complicated roles. It must collect revenue from some source or another and use these resources to shore up its monopoly on the use of force and its legitimacy. Typically, as discussed further in chapter 5, modern states spend revenues not only on coercive force, but also on ways to strengthen the economy and provide for the well-being of at least some of their citizens in order to enhance legitimacy. Collecting taxes, paving roads, building schools, and providing retirement pensions all require a bureaucracy. Weber saw bureaucracy as a central part of modern, rational-legal legitimacy, since in theory individuals obtain official positions in a modern bureaucracy via a rational-legal process of appointment and are restricted to certain tasks by a set of laws. Like legitimacy, effective bureaucracy enhances sovereignty. A bureaucracy that efficiently carries out laws, collects taxes, and expends revenues as directed by the central authorities gives the state greater power than it would have otherwise. As we discuss further below, weak legitimacy and bureaucracy are two key causes of state weakness in the contemporary world.

From this overview we can expand our notion of the modern state as a set of ongoing institutions that develops and administers laws and generates and implements public policies in a specific territory. We can see that this definition implies internal sovereignty and adds that a state must also maintain its external sovereignty. We can also add that the distinctive features of modern states include performing these activities not only on the basis of a monopoly on the use of force, but also through the cultivation of legitimacy, and particularly rational-legal legitimacy. Finally, we can add that bureaucracy is an important and effective way of carrying out these administrative tasks and potentially enhancing legitimacy.

Where modern states overlap with nations, national identity can be a powerful source of legitimacy as well. This is not always the case, however, and most modern states must find other ways to cultivate the allegiance of their inhabitants. They usually do so by attempting to gain legitimacy based on some claim of representation or service to the people, or citizens. The relationship between states and citizens is central to modern politics, and chapter 3 addresses it at length.

We explore the contentious relationship among states, nations, and other identity groups more fully in chapter 4.

HISTORICAL ORIGINS OF MODERN STATES

Now that we have clarified what a state is, we need to understand the diverse historical origins of modern states, which greatly influence their strength and relationships to their citizens and nation. A world of modern states controlling virtually every square inch of territory and every person on the globe may seem natural today, but it is a fairly recent development. The modern state arose first in Europe between the fifteenth and eighteenth centuries. The concept spread via conquest, colonialism, and then independence for former colonies, becoming truly universal only with the independence of most African states in the 1960s.

Prior to approximately 1500, Europe consisted of **feudal states**, which were distinct from modern states in several ways. Most importantly, they neither claimed nor had undisputed sovereignty. Feudal rule involved multiple and overlapping sovereignties. At the heart of it was the **fief**, a relationship between lord and vassal in which the lord gave a vassal the right to rule a piece of land, its products, and people in exchange for political and military loyalty. This relationship, however, was subject to frequent change. Once a vassal had control of a fief, he could shift his loyalty from one lord to another if he was dissatisfied. The system often involved several layers of these relationships, from the highest and most powerful king in a region to the local lord. The loyalty of the peasants—the bulk of the population who were simply subjects and had virtually no rights—followed that of their lord. At any given time, each individual was subject to the sovereignty of not only his immediate lord, but also at least one higher lord and often more, and that loyalty could and did change. In addition, the Catholic Church claimed a separate and universal religious sovereignty over all, and gave religious legitimacy to the kings and lords who recognized church authority.

By the fifteenth century, feudalism was giving way to **absolutism**, rule by a single monarch who claimed complete, exclusive sovereignty over a territory and its people. Absolutist rulers were the winners of battles for power among feudal lords who used superior economic and military resources to permanently vanquish their rivals. Most continued to recognize officially the religious authority of the Catholic Church, but in practice they increasingly proclaimed their undisputed rule within their territories. Scholars debate the extent to which the absolutist state was a truly modern state, but it certainly introduced a number of its key elements. Perry Anderson (1974), one of the most influential scholars on the subject, argued that the absolutist state included at least rudimentary forms of a standing army and diplomatic service, both of which are crucial for external sovereignty; centralized bureaucracy; systematic taxation; and policies to encourage economic development. It took centuries for these to develop fully modern form, however. Legitimacy remained based largely on tradition and heredity, and most people, though now under a single sovereign, remained distant subjects with few legal rights. Because many kingdoms lacked a common language, state officials, both military and civilian, often were not identified as members of the same cultural group as the common people and were seen as, in effect, foreigners appointed by the king. Perhaps of greatest importance, the state was not conceived as a set of ongoing institutions separate from the king; rather, as Louis XIV of France famously declared, "l'etat, c'est moi" (I am the state).

The **Peace of Westphalia** in 1648 codified the idea of states as legal equals that recognized each other's external and internal sovereignty within specified territories, and that were prepared to defend that sovereignty and their interests via diplomacy if possible or war if necessary. The subsequent survival-of-the-fittest process gradually whittled the number of European states from approximately five hundred in 1500 to about fifty today. Besides reducing numbers, this competition to actualize and preserve external sovereignty helped further the development of the fully modern state. A state that developed a more effective system of taxation, a more efficient bureaucracy, and a stronger military won. Along the way, political leaders realized that a sense of personal loyalty (legitimacy) on the part of their subjects was of great benefit, particularly because these subjects were increasingly required to pay taxes and serve in the military. States therefore began the process of creating nations, expanding public education, and shifting from the use of Latin or French in official circles to the local vernacular so that rulers and ruled could communicate directly, thus adding a new dimension to the rulers' legitimacy. This was a long process, but it ultimately helped create modern nations, most of which emerged by the mid-nineteenth century.

Thomas Hobbes, an important early modern British political philosopher, believed a strong state to which subjects gave their undivided loyalty was essential to prevent the brutality that would inevitably result from anarchy.

The truly modern state emerged as the state came to be seen as separate from an individual ruler. This developed in conjunction with some concept of limits on a ruler's power. The state as a set of institutions retained its claim to absolute sovereignty, but the powers of individual officials, ultimately including the supreme ruler, were increasingly limited. A political philosophy that came to be known as liberalism, which we discuss in greater depth in chapter 3, provided the theoretical justification and argument for limiting the power of officials to ensure the rights of individuals. The common people were ultimately transformed from subjects to citizens of the state. Bellwether events in this history included the Glorious Revolution in Great Britain in which Parliament forced King James II's resignation, the French Revolution of 1789, and a series of revolutions that established new democratic republics in 1848.

Europe exported the modern state to the rest of the world through colonial conquest, and began to do so as early as the sixteenth century in the Americas. Modern states in the Americas, Africa, and Asia, however, were not established by colonial rule, because colonial states by definition lacked sovereignty. Colonial rule in the Americas began with military invasion and the destruction of Native American states and empires. In North America, disease and war decimated local populations, and this paved the way for extensive European settlement. In South America, larger indigenous populations survived to be subjugated, and one of the products of this was substantial mixed race, or mestizo, populations. In many areas, including Brazil and the southern part of the United States, African slaves were brought in to supplement Native populations and meet labor demands. These demographic patterns ultimately produced today's varied racial patterns across the Americas.

The earliest colonies, such as those in the Americas, were ruled by European absolutist states that were not fully modern themselves. This is not to say that these ruling states did not try to develop some modern methods to administer their distant domains. European kings appointed officials to represent them and rule over newly acquired territories, and effective administration ultimately required the appointment of numerous such officials. Yet over time, settlers identified their interests as distinct from and often in opposition to those of the colonizers and their officials, and colonists began to question the legitimacy of rule by distant sovereigns. The first rebellion against colonial rule ultimately produced the United States. Its Founders were heavily influenced by European liberalism, and as such, they rejected the notion of an absolute ruler. They instead wrote a constitution that established a sovereign but limited state that carved out a rational-legal basis for its monopoly on the legitimate use of force. This was a major event in the development of both the modern state and liberal democracy.

The second major rebellion came at the hands of black slaves, whose rebellion in 1793 led to the first abolition of slavery in the world and, in 1804, to Haitian independence. By the 1820s and 1830s, most of the populations of Central and South America had rebelled as well. As in the United States, the leaders of these rebellions were mostly wealthy, landholding elites. This landed elite often relied on state force to keep peasant and slave labor working on its behalf, so while some early efforts at democracy emerged after independence, most Central and South American states ultimately went through many decades of strongman rule.

Early modern states in the Americas emerged from colonialism, which is a very different context for the birth of a modern state than that of early European states. European states went through several centuries of developing a sense of national identity, which emerged strongly in most areas by the nineteenth century. In the Americas, the racial divisions produced by colonization, European settlement, and slavery meant that none of the newly independent states had a widely shared sense of national identity. Where slavery continued to exist, as in the United States, citizenship was restricted to the "free" and therefore primarily white (and exclusively male) population. Where significant Native American populations had survived, as in Peru and Guatemala, they continued to be politically excluded and economically marginalized by the primarily white, landholding elite who controlled the new states. This historical context would make the ability of the new states to establish strong national identities difficult and would produce ongoing racial and ethnic problems explored further in chapter 4.

After most of the first wave of colonies achieved independence, growing economic and military rivalry among Britain, France, and Germany beginning in the

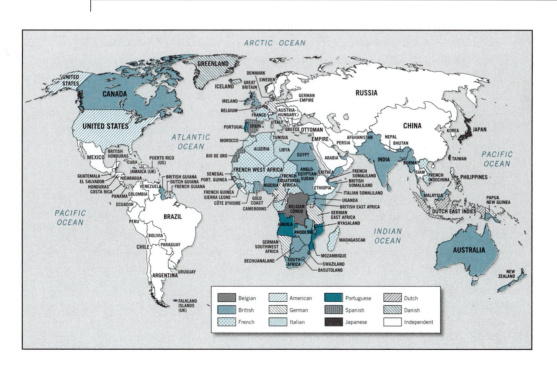

MAP 2.1
Imperialism in the Modern World, circa 1900

mid-nineteenth century spurred a new round of colonization, first in Asia and then in Africa. This time far fewer European settlers were involved. The vast majority of the populations of these new colonies remained indigenous, ruled over by a rather thin layer of European officials. Colonizers effectively destroyed the political power of precolonial indigenous states and empires, but did not exterminate the population en masse. (Long-standing exposure to Europe via trade also meant that the indigenous people in these regions had some immunity to the European diseases that killed countless millions in the Americas.)

Challenges to this new wave of colonialism, on both the home front and abroad, were quick and numerous. The independence of the first-wave colonies and the end of slavery in the industrialized world raised questions about European subjugation of African and Asian peoples. Colonization in this context had to be justified as bringing "advanced" European civilization and Christianity to the "backward" peoples. Education, provided primarily by Christian missionaries, was seen as a key part of this "civilizing" mission. It had a more practical aspect as well: with limited European settlement, colonial rulers needed indigenous individuals to serve in the bureaucracies of the colonial states. These chosen few were educated in colonial languages and customs and became elites among those colonized, although European officials remained at the top of the colonial hierarchy with nearly unlimited power. In time, the indigenous elites began to see themselves as equal to the ruling Europeans and chafed at the limits to their political position and economic advancement under colonial rule. They became the key leaders of the movements for independence that emerged in the early twentieth century in Asia and by mid-century in Africa. This new elite demanded and, following World War II, finally received independence. At that point, modern states covered virtually every square inch of the globe.

The postcolonial countries, however, faced huge obstacles and challenges to consolidating their modern states. Although they enjoyed legal external sovereignty and had inherited at least minimal infrastructure from colonial bureaucracies, legitimacy and internal sovereignty remained problematic for most. The nationalist movements that brought the colonies independence created genuine enthusiasm for new nations, but the colonizers had tried to inhibit a strong sense of national unity to prevent possible united action against them. What this meant was that they often had established borders with little regard for precolonial political boundaries. Some precolonial states—Siam (Thailand), Rwanda, Burundi—survived with their borders more or less intact; most did not. This meant that numerous political entities and many distinct religious and linguistic groups were brought together under one colonial state.

The new indigenous elite emerged as literate in the colonial language and sometimes, for a variety of reasons, came disproportionately from one area of a colony, which caused resentment in other areas. In all cases, the new elites communicated among themselves and with the rest of the world in the colonial language, which almost always became the language of higher education and government. Additionally, while precolonial states had been subjugated, they had not been forgotten, and colonial rulers frequently had allowed them to continue to exist at the local level, subject to colonial control. What this meant was that after the colonizers left, political loyalty was often divided between the new nation and its central government on the one hand, and local rulers, often remnants of precolonial states, on the other. Finally, huge disparities in wealth, education, and access to power between the elite and the majority of the population reduced popular support, and this made the new democracies extremely fragile.

In summary, modern states arose around the world at different times and in very different contexts. Although they shared some common difficulties, such as the need to cultivate a more cohesive national identity as a basis for legitimacy, European and non-European states experienced rather different timelines for developing both their modern states and national identities. A colony often inherited rather a minimal bureaucracy and infrastructure that were not necessarily geared toward developing the country's resources, and if this bureaucracy and infrastructure were controlled by local elites, they were often perceived to be of questionable legitimacy and utility by the rest of the population.

The result of colonial history for many countries was late development of a modern state and deeply divided loyalty that proved problematic for legitimacy, cohesion, and internal sovereignty. Many succumbed to some form of authoritarian rule not long after independence, though democratic movements have emerged more recently. These new states were modern in terms of their most basic characteristics, but most were very weak versions. The differences between strong and weak states, and the causes of state weakness and collapse, are the last subject we need to address to complete our conceptual overview of the modern state.

WEAK AND FAILED STATES

No state indisputably enjoys complete external or internal sovereignty, absolute legitimacy and a monopoly on the use of force, and a completely effective and efficient bureaucracy. Some states, however, are clearly much closer to this ideal than others. States typically use their sovereignty, territory, legitimacy, and bureaucracy to provide what political scientist Robert Rotberg (2004) calls "political goods" to their population, such as security, the rule of law, and a functioning legal system, and infrastructure, such as roads, public education, and health care. A **weak state** is one that cannot provide adequate political goods to its population. Obviously, knowing exactly what "adequate" means in this definition is not easy, and an absolutely clear-cut distinction cannot be made between "strong" and "weak" states. Rather, all states exist on a continuum of relative strength, with no state perfectly strong in all conceivable categories. States that seem persistently unable to provide adequate security and other essential political goods, however, are demonstrably weaker than those that can and do. The table in the following Where and Why? ranks our case studies based on the "Failed States Index," a recent effort to quantify state strength. As the Country and Concept table shows,

WHERE AND WHY Failed States

In response to growing international concern about the failure of states, the Fund for Peace developed a "Failed States Index" to highlight countries of imminent concern. In 2007 the third annual index ranked 177 countries on twelve factors in three categories considered essential to state strength: four social indicators (demographic pressures, refugees or internally displaced persons creating humanitarian emergencies, vengeance-seeking group grievance or group paranoia, and chronic, sustained human flight); two economic indicators (uneven economic growth along group lines and sharp/severe economic decline); and six political indicators (criminalization/delegitimization of the state, deterioration of public services, suspension of rule of law/human rights abuses, the operation of a security apparatus as a "state within a state," factionalized elites, and intervention of external political actors). Thirty-two countries were placed on the 2007 "alert" list based on these factors. Each factor was scored 1–10, with 10 as the worst ranking, so absolute failure in all areas would score 120. Sudan ranked first in 2007, with a score of 113.7.

Which states end up on the alert list and why? Some geographic patterns are clear: no European, North American, or South American country is on the alert list. Eighteen of the thirty-two failed states are in Africa. In contrast, the fifteen strongest states include eleven European countries (of which five are in Scandinavia), Australia and New Zealand, Canada, and Japan. All but three (Ethiopia, Nepal, and Yemen) on the alert list were previously colonies. Twenty-five of the twenty-nine former colonies gained independence during World War II or later, the exceptions being Afghanistan, Haiti, Iraq, and Liberia. And twenty-eight of the thirty-two alert countries are among the fifty-three lowest-income countries (countries with per capita incomes of less than $905) according to the World Bank. Three of the remaining four are in the next highest income group. The only higher-income country in the group is Lebanon, a country whose integrity and internal and external sovereignty have been repeatedly violated due to the ongoing conflict among its Middle Eastern neighbors. Lastly, many of the countries on the alert list are "enclave economies" whose one or two key, very valuable resources (often oil, diamonds, or other minerals) can produce tensions between areas of the country that have the resources and those that do not, and can be easily exploited by venal leaders. Many of these countries have been beset by the rise of warlords, civil conflict, or both, including the Democratic Republic of the Congo, Nigeria, Liberia, and Sierra Leone.

While this information alone is not enough to reach any firm conclusions, some hypotheses might explain state failure. Based on these patterns, one could hypothesize that state failure might be geographically or culturally rooted, but there are also other equally suggestive patterns. Colonialism and its aftermath may have contributed to ineffectual institutions or produced incentives to develop weak, ineffective governments. Ethnic pluralism, one legacy of colonialism in many of these countries, may be a significant obstacle to consolidating a strong state. Poverty and enclave economies may themselves inhibit state development, or may interact with other factors like ethnic divisions to produce internal conflict and otherwise jeopardize the creation of strong states.

Comparativists don't agree on which of these factors is most important yet, but we do look at such evidence of state weakness and try to generate testable hypotheses for state failure. Which of these hypotheses seems most persuasive? What kind of evidence would help confirm it or disprove it? What other hypotheses might explain state failure? Comparativists will continue to study this question in an effort to help states develop stronger institutions, because the human consequences of state weakness—civil conflict, refugees, human rights violations—and the consequences for the international system of states are severe.

Failed States, 2007

Rank and State	Total Score
1. Sudan	113.7
2. Iraq	111.4
3. Somalia	111.1
4. Zimbabwe	110.1
5. Chad	108.8
6. Côte d'Ivoire	107.3
7. Democratic Republic of Congo	105.5
8. Afghanistan	102.3
9. Guinea	101.3
10. Central African Republic	101
11. Haiti	100.9
12. Pakistan	100.1
13. North Korea	97.7
14. Burma/Myanmar	97
15. Uganda	96.4
16. Bangladesh	95.9
17. Nigeria	95.6
18. Ethiopia	95.3
19. Burundi	95.2
20. Timor-Leste	94.9
21. Nepal	93.6
22. Uzbekistan	93.5
23. Sierra Leone	93.4
24. Yemen	93.2
25. Sri Lanka	93.1
26. Republic of the Congo	93
27. Liberia	92.9
28. Lebanon	92.4
29. Malawi	92.2
30. Solomon Islands	92
31. Kenya	91.3
32. Niger	91.2

Source: From Fund for Peace, "Failed States Index 2007," www.fundforpeace.org/web/index.php?option=com_content&task=view&id=229&Itemid=366

stronger states tend to consume a larger share of economic resources; they are simply economically bigger than weak states. They also are less corrupt, indicating the presence of stronger bureaucracies.

Prior to the twentieth century, states that were weak internationally sooner or later faced a hostile invasion; they were the losers in the history of state formation in Europe. The new international system incorporated after World War II fundamentally changed this dynamic. Starting with the League of Nations in 1919 and expanding under the United Nations after 1945, the international system collectively came to an agreement that the hostile takeover of other states was unacceptable. While there have been exceptions, usually based on an inability or unwillingness of great powers to intervene, outright invasion and permanent conquest have become rare. This means weak states are more likely to survive, at least for longer than they would have a century or two ago, so we need to understand what a weak state is and what effect weakness has on domestic politics.

Virtually all elements of state strength are interconnected. State weakness is both caused by and causes declines in effective sovereignty, bureaucracy, legitimacy, and even control over territory. If a state lacks the resources to provide basic infrastructure and security, its legitimacy most likely will decline. Lack of resources also may mean civil servants are paid very little, which may lead to corruption and an even further decline in the quality of state services. Corruption in some bureaucracies, such as the military and border patrol, can cause a loss of security and territorial integrity. If the state cannot provide basic services such as education, citizens will likely find alternative routes to success that may well involve illegal activity such as smuggling; if they are successful, these efforts undermine the state's sovereignty that much further. If the state does not provide the rule of law impartially, citizens will turn to private means to settle their disputes, undermining the state's monopoly on the legitimate use of violence, and so on. Weak states can be caught in a vicious cycle that is difficult to break.

A state that is so weak that it loses effective sovereignty over part of its territory is known as a **failed state**. Failed states make headlines: Sierra Leone, the Democratic Republic of the Congo, Liberia, Sudan, Angola, Afghanistan. The "Failed States Index" ranks all states on twelve indicators of strength. Several of these, including a security apparatus that operates as a "state within the state," external intervention in state affairs, and criminalization or delegitimization of the state, address characteristics like external and internal sovereignty and legitimacy directly. Others, such as violation of human rights or uneven economic development, can be considered indirect measures of effective administration, legitimacy, or both.

In extreme cases, the state collapses totally, as Somalia did in 1991. Since then the territory has been divided among competing warlords in the south and Somililand in the north, which has declared itself a separate country, though with no international recognition. The total collapse of the Somali state has resulted in a decade and a half of near-total anarchy for much of the population, as well as the famous "Black Hawk Down" episode in 1993, in which sixteen U.S. soldiers were killed and dragged through the streets of the capital. In 2006 the United States feared that an Islamic group that gained control of the capital was linked to Islamic terrorists elsewhere. State failure and collapse, as the cases of Somalia and Afghanistan suggest, can have effects far beyond the borders of the failed state itself.

MINI-CASE Afghanistan

In 2001 Afghanistan became probably the world's most famous failed state because it served as a refuge for and supporter of al-Qaida leader Osama bin Laden. But its failure as a state long predates the September 11, 2001, attacks on the World Trade Center and the Pentagon. Indeed, its failure figured prominently in the late Cold War era, when the Soviet Union invaded it in 1979 and the United States subsequently supported the country's Islamist *mujahedeen* resistance fighters. Afghanistan serves as a case study of the debilitating interaction between a weak state and self-interested international forces.

The coronation of Ahmad Shah as king in 1747 is generally accepted as the start of a united Afghanistan, though it was far from a modern state. Numerous ethnic groups, all Islamic but practicing different branches of the faith, were united, with the Pashtun, Ahmad Shah's group, as the largest. The kingdom relied on local rulers for its support, and political loyalty remained focused primarily at the local level as ethnic and religious elders wielded most of the real power. The kingdom fell apart in a succession of battles in 1818, and for the rest of the nineteenth century Afghanistan faced intermittent civil war, as well as increasing British and Russian encroachment. By the end of that century, much of the country was virtually a British colony. The British helped establish Amir Abdur Rahman Khan as ruler and began a negotiated evacuation in 1880. Abdur Rahman ruled for the last two decades of the century and began an ambitious modernization plan that favored Western culture and also established the start of a modern state, creating a united army that gained control of virtually all of modern-day Afghanistan. Although Afghanistan's monarchy ruled until 1973, the state remained rather weak. There was no real national Afghan identity, and most ethnic groups, including the Pashtun, extended into neighboring countries, which meant that people's ethnic loyalty across national borders was often greater than their loyalty to the Afghan state.

Afghanistan also remained susceptible to external powers. The Soviet Union had long been actively involved in the country, but the government that overthrew the king in 1973 began to move away from the Soviet sphere and toward the West. In response, the Soviets invaded in 1979, installing the local Communist Party to power. The Communist government launched a series of land, local government, and educational reforms that struck at the heart of local elder control of society. The response was widespread resistance, which soon took on an Islamic ideology. The *mujahedeen* resistance fighters battled the Soviet army in guerilla warfare throughout the 1980s. While never able to defeat the Soviets, they nonetheless kept the Communist regime from effectively ruling. Divided along both religious and ethnic lines, the *mujahedeen* still received significant U.S. support. They also became a heroic force in the eyes of many Muslims worldwide: young religious fighters from across the Muslim world streamed into Afghanistan to join the fight, including a Saudi by the name of Osama bin Laden.

The reform policies of Mikhail Gorbachev in the Soviet Union led to a Soviet withdrawal and the creation of a *mujahedeen* government in 1989, but it collapsed into civil war among the various ethnic militia almost immediately. A decade of warfare had left the economy in ruins, encouraging the rise of poppy growing as the only viable alternative for many farmers. As a consequence, Afghanistan became the world's top source of heroin by the 1980s. Warlords arose via control of weaponry and poppy production, and the state collapsed nearly completely.

In the midst of this a new, radical Islamist group emerged among the Pashtun, the Taliban. Supported by external Muslim financing, much of it from individuals in Saudi Arabia (including bin Laden) and Pakistan, the Taliban defeated the divided *mujahedeen* and in 1996 took control of most of the country. The group seemed to care little about the state, instead focusing its policies almost solely on religious concerns of moral purity, religious observance, and gender relations (mostly involving the seclusion of women). Infamously, the group also provided a refuge for bin Laden and his followers.

In retaliation for the September 11 attacks, the United States invaded Afghanistan in late 2001, supporting the northern, non-Pashtun opposition to the Taliban. The United States and the UN helped create a new democratic government, which seven years later continues to rely heavily on U.S. and NATO military support. The country has democratic institutions but remains quite weak, without full control over its territory. The elected president, Hamid Karzai, continues to rely in part on former warlords, who retain considerable local control. Some of their power comes from their continued control of Afghanistan's lucrative poppy production. (The rest of the economy has begun to rebound, but poppies remain the largest source of wealth.)

The Taliban launched a major offensive to regain territory in 2006. Though the forces were pushed back, they still have the ability to pursue low-scale guerilla war in some Pashtun areas, and security remains far from certain in much of the country. The United States, the UN, and NATO have spent seven years trying to help put a strong and stable state in place, and the process still remains uncertain and far from concluded. International interventions from several sources helped produce the country's total collapse but similar international forces are having a much harder time rebuilding Afghanistan.

States become weak and fail for a variety of reasons. Overall level of wealth certainly plays a role. States need resources to provide security and other political goods. Resources come from some form of taxation, but to have taxation a state must have some viable economic activity. States in the poorest regions of the world simply lack resources, regardless of the intentions or administrative competence of their rulers. In eighteenth-century Europe, these weakest states would have simply been annexed by a larger and stronger neighbor, but the contemporary international system by and large does not allow that to happen.

The result can be what Robert Jackson (1990) calls **quasi-states**: states that have legal sovereignty and international recognition but lack almost all the domestic attributes of a functioning state. Jackson argues that many postcolonial states, especially those in Africa, the poorest region in the world, are quasi-states. At independence, nationalist leaders formed governments and sent their delegates to the United Nations to receive official recognition, usually with a great deal of initial support at home. Their extremely poor economies left them with few resources to provide the most basic political goods, however, so their governments turned to international aid donors to provide revenue. In the worst cases, this revenue came to constitute the majority of a government's funding. The government subsequently survived not on the basis of internal legitimacy but instead on the basis of support from external sources. This left rulers with no incentive to provide basic goods to their people, and as people became increasingly disenchanted, these states lost most of their domestic legitimacy. As the economic and political downward spiral continued, armed rebellion arose in some states, creating not just weak but failed states. One can see how the logic of quasi-states could lead to a spiraling of conditions—economic weakness, external dependency, disrespect for human rights—that leads to a state's designation on the "Failed States Index" alert list.

Weak or failed states also can be caused by venal leadership, even when other circumstances are favorable. If a dictator arises and has the resources to stay in power even without much legitimacy, a state is likely to become weaker and weaker. International aid is one way such dictators maintain power. During the Cold War, the rivalry between the United States and the Soviet Union led both to back dictators who would support their respective side in global politics. Both sides provided generous aid to dictators who ruled with little interest in providing services to their people. Mobutu Sese Seko of Zaire (now the Democratic Republic of the Congo), in power from 1965 to 1997, was an example of such a U.S. "client"; Mengistu Haile Mariam of Ethiopia, in power from 1974 to 1991, was an example of a Soviet one. These states both failed a few years after the end of the Cold War because the elimination of the U.S.-Soviet global rivalry meant that neither side was interested in continuing its support. Rebels pushed Mobutu out of power in Zaire and changed the country's name, but lost control of much of the territory. The world's bloodiest civil war since World War II ensued, with peace only partially established by 2006. In Ethiopia, Mengistu's fall not only changed the government, but also resulted in one region seceding entirely, becoming the separate country of Eritrea.

In addition, leaders can create weak or failed states despite the presence of relatively plentiful resources. Countries with tremendous mineral wealth, such as oil or diamonds, often suffer this fate. A government that can gain enough revenue from mineral extraction alone does not need to worry about the strength of the rest of the economy or the well-being of the rest of the population. If the asset exists in one particular economic enclave, the government simply has to control that area and export the resources to gain revenue to survive, at least for a while. Rebel groups often recognize that if they can overpower the government they could seize the wealth. Given the government's lack of legitimacy in most of the country, these rebels find it relatively easy to gain local support, and a full-scale civil war follows. This may be based on real, popular grievances on the part of an ignored and oppressed populace, but it also can be based on the greed of a rebel group that simply wants to gain control of the mineral wealth for itself. The sad twin stories of Sierra Leone and Liberia illustrate this well.

MINI-CASE Sierra Leone and Liberia: Collapsed States

Liberia and Sierra Leone, neighboring states in West Africa, tragically illustrate the worst effects of weak states controlling significant mineral wealth. Ironically, both countries began as beacons of hope for liberated slaves. Britain founded Sierra Leone to provide a refuge for liberated slaves captured from slaving vessels, and the United States founded Liberia as a home for former American slaves. Descendants of these slaves became the ruling elite in both countries. Liberia became the first independent postcolonial African state in 1847 with a constitution modeled after the U.S. Constitution but with voting rights restricted to owners of private property. This meant that virtually no indigenous Africans could vote; only the Americo-Liberian elite (as they were called) had political rights. Similarly, Sierra Leone had a colonial elite composed almost exclusively of the "Krio," descendants of freed slaves, until its independence in 1961.

Both countries were heavily dependent on key natural resources from the beginning. The bulk of government revenue in Sierra Leone came from diamond mining; in Liberia it was derived from iron mining and rubber plantations owned by the Firestone Tire Company of the United States. Each country was also the recipient of a great deal of aid from its respective former colonial power; during the Cold War Liberia was Africa's single biggest recipient of U.S. foreign aid.

These resources, however, did not produce strong states. In Sierra Leone, six years of democracy gave way to one-party rule in 1968 under Siaka Stevens, who remained in power until 1985, when he resigned to transfer power to his handpicked successor. Members of the one-party regime used the revenues from diamond mining to support the leaders' own ethnic groups and enrich themselves, while the overall economy, government services, and regime legitimacy declined. Similarly, in Liberia the Americo-Liberian ruling party won every election from 1847 to 1980, the longest continuously ruling political party in world history, and used government resources to enrich the key ruling families while the bulk of the indigenous population was ignored and the economy worsened. The legitimacy of both governments declined further as corruption and favoritism toward their supporters destroyed each state's ability to provide the most basic services expected of modern states.

The dramatic downward spiral began with a military coup in Liberia in 1980, in which the top Americo-Liberian leaders were executed. The new government was led by a twenty-eight-year-old sergeant, Samuel Doe, who shifted power from the Americo-Liberian elite to his own Krahn ethnic group. Doe continued to receive generous U.S. support in spite of holding what all saw as completely fraudulent elections. After enduring a decade of Doe's increasingly brutal and corrupt rule, an exiled former member of his government, Charles Taylor, launched a guerilla war in rural areas inhabited by ethnic groups whom Doe ignored and repressed. Given the government's near total lack of legitimacy, the uprising spread rapidly. Taylor became the first and worst warlord in West Africa, arming young men who had grievances against the government and allowing them to take whatever spoils of victory they would. His march to the capital was stopped only by the intervention of forces from other countries, mainly Nigeria. He financed his war by selling timber and other resources that he took from areas of Liberia he controlled on the international market.

In 1991, after he was stopped from taking the Liberian capital, Taylor adjusted his sights and helped finance a guerilla uprising in neighboring Sierra Leone. Once the guerilla forces gained control of Sierra Leone's lucrative diamond mines, Taylor smuggled the diamonds onto the international market to finance the rebellions in both countries. The Sierra Leonean rebellion led to a coup that replaced the one-party state with a military government. The state was so weak, however, that it ultimately was forced to turn to a private South African company to bring in mercenary forces to regain control of the diamond mines in exchange for the company receiving a share of the mines' profits. At the same time, the government significantly expanded the official armed forces, arming young men in several parts of the country to defend their areas against rebels. Many of these armed but poorly trained and paid young soldiers ultimately came to be known as "sobels," soldiers in the government army by day and rebels by night, looting and maiming the civilian population in both roles. After another coup, the military government privately cooperated with the rebels to exploit the diamond wealth.

A peace deal was finally brokered in Liberia in 1997, and elections for a new government were held. Charles Taylor, the warlord, was democratically elected president. Many Liberians reasoned that unless they gave him power he would continue the war, so better to elect him and hope the war would end. Once in power officially, Taylor continued to exploit the country's exportable resources and Sierra Leone's diamonds for his own benefit. He also continued to finance the Sierra Leonean rebels, who briefly gained control of the entire country in 1998–1999. A regional military force led by Nigeria forced the rebels out of Sierra Leone's capital and set the conditions for a peace process in which the rebels finally gave up their efforts. At about the same time, an anti-Taylor rebel movement invaded Liberia. Taylor continued to smuggle diamonds out of Sierra Leone and timber out of Liberia to finance his government and line his own pockets until international sanctions against West African diamonds finally reduced his cash flow and ultimately forced him out of power in 2003.

Both countries are now at peace, with new, if fragile, elected governments. Liberia elected the first woman president in African history, Ellen Johnson-Sirleaf, in January 2006. Charles Taylor and several Sierra Leonean rebel leaders are on trial in international tribunals for violations of international human rights laws. Left from the wars is a legacy of more than two hundred thousand killed and millions maimed and displaced.

Ellen Johnson-Sirleaf became Liberia's president and Africa's first woman head of state in January 2006. Her inauguration raised the country's hopes that Johnson-Sirleaf would deliver what she promised: a "fundamental break" with its conflict-ridden past.

Rebel armies used large numbers of child soldiers: thousands of young boys in both countries grew up in the 1990s with guns in their hands and looting as a way of life, rather than being schooled and trained for future careers. In addition, both countries remain among the world's poorest: in 2007 Sierra Leone, despite its diamond wealth, was in last place on the UN's Human Development Index, a measure of overall well-being. While the future looks much brighter than the past, both countries still have relatively weak states that must be reconstructed to regain some sense of legitimacy and reestablish the basic functions states are supposed to provide: security, infrastructure, social services, and general well-being.

In the post–Cold War era, the international system and major powers have come to see weak and failed states as a significant problem. Weak states produce corruption and illegal activity. They have porous borders through which all manner of illegal arms, biological or nuclear weapons, and illegal drugs might pass. They undermine economic growth and political stability, and democracy is difficult or impossible to foster when a state is unable or unwilling to provide at least the basic political goods citizens expect. People may reason that if the state cannot provide basic security or infrastructure to citizens, what is the point of voting officials into office? And failed or collapsed states cause even bigger problems than poor voter turnout, including refugee crises, outbreaks of contagious diseases, and opportunities for infiltration by terrorist groups. Afghanistan prior to the September 11 attacks is only the best-known example of this worst-case scenario. One of the most important reasons for studying comparative politics is to understand how and why political institutions work effectively to produce strong states that can maintain security, gain real legitimacy, and avoid the humanitarian costs and dangers of state weakness and failure.

CASE STUDIES OF STATE FORMATION

We have chosen ten countries to illustrate the trends, theories, and debates in comparative politics. We introduce all ten below by describing the historical development of each state. Nations, citizenship, and political regimes are all examined more fully in the following chapters, but we touch on these issues as well to provide a general political history here.

These countries represent a diverse set of political and economic situations. Some have been under the same type of government—democratic or authoritarian—for many years; others have seen frequent changes in their governmental systems. Some have been and are democratic; others have struggled to establish democracy. Some are quite wealthy and have achieved high rates of education and health for their populations; others are among the poorest countries on the planet. Together, they provide a full array of the realities of politics in the contemporary world. (The following Country and Concept table presents some basic information about the formation of our ten case study states.)

COUNTRY AND CONCEPT The Modern State

Country	Approximate Year Modern State Established	FAILED STATE INDEX, 2007		Gov't Revenue as % of GDP	Corruption Perception Index (0-highly corrupt, 10-highly clean)
		Rank among 177 Countries	Score (12-lowest risk of state failure, 144-highest risk of state failure)		
Brazil	1889	117	66.9	20.12%	3.5
China	1949	62	81.2	4.83%	3.5
Germany	1871	154	38.4	26.94%	7.8
India	1947	110	70.8	9.81%	3.5
Iran	1925	57	82.8	9.25%	2.5
Japan	1867	164	28.5	17.6%	7.5
Nigeria	1960	17	95.6	—	2.2
Russia	1917	62	81.2	—	2.3
United Kingdom	1707	157	34.1	33.1%	8.4
United States	1787	160	33.6	19.3%	7.2

Sources: Failed state data is from the Fund For Peace, 2007. Data on government revenue as percentage of GDP are from the UN's "Central Government Tax Revenue as Percentage of GDP, 1990 and 1997," http://unpan1.un.org/intradoc/groups/public/documents/un/un-000028.pdf. All data for government revenues are from 1997 except for Brazil (1994), China (1996), Germany (1996), Japan (2003), India (1996), and the United Kingdom (1995). Data on corruption are from Transparency International, 2007.

To illustrate the process of state formation, we present them now in the order in which the modern state arose in each country, rather than by region. Most people tend to think of political development as emanating outward from Europe, eventually reaching the former colonies in Asia and Africa. While the modern state certainly arose first in Europe, the order of the case studies below illustrates clearly that some leaders in other areas of the world adopted the form relatively early on; some of our non-Western cases created modern states before some of our European cases.

CASE STUDY United Kingdom

The full union of England and Scotland under the Act of Union of 1707 officially established the United Kingdom of Great Britain and Northern Ireland (also called the UK, Great Britain, or simply Britain), but the origins of the state lay much earlier. Most of England was under Roman rule until the fourth century. Roman withdrawal led to the creation of numerous small, feudal kingdoms, but by the time the Normans invaded from northern France in 1066, much of the southern part of the island had been united under one kingdom. The Norman invasion created a new kingdom that initially included part of what is now northern France. The indigenous Anglo-Saxons saw the Norman invaders, who came to constitute the bulk of the nobility of the new kingdom, as foreign oppressors. Over several centuries, however, the cultural and linguistic division between conqueror and conquered slowly disappeared, and a new language, English, emerged.

This state expanded over the centuries. The ascension of King Henry VII of the Welsh Tudor family to the throne of England in 1485 began the process of the unification of England and Wales (the western edge of the island) that was completed with the Act of Union of 1542. Similarly, Scotland and England were first united under a single crown when James VI of Scotland also became King James I of England. That union finally brought the entire island under a single state, created a single British parliament, and eliminated the separate Scottish and Welsh parliaments. While a distinct Welsh language survived among a small portion of the population, the Scottish tongue died out completely. Both areas came to be primarily English speaking, linguistically uniting the kingdom, though some cultural distinctions remain to this day.

While a parliament existed as early as 1236, the king remained the primary holder of power until the nineteenth century (see chapter 3 for details on the emergence of liberal democracy in Britain). The greatest turmoil along the way took the form of religious wars between Protestants and Catholics. After King Henry VIII broke with the Catholic Church and established the

One of the earliest modern states, Britain has become an increasingly globalized society. Its membership in the EU is symbolic of how it has opened its borders to the world economy. London's main airport, Heathrow, is one of the busiest in the world, and London itself has become one of the most multinational cities in the world.

Church of England (known as the Anglican Church in the UK and the Episcopal Church in the United States) in 1534, religious conflicts dominated politics for well over a century. Protestant monarchs, starting with Henry VIII, persecuted Catholics, and when Catholic monarch Mary Tudor (Mary Queen of Scots) regained the throne, she persecuted Protestants. This culminated in a civil war in the 1640s that brought to power a nonroyal dictatorship under Protestant Oliver Cromwell. The monarchy was restored after about twenty years, only to be removed again, this time peacefully, by Parliament in the so-called Glorious Revolution of 1688. After this, the doctrine of liberalism gained greater prominence, and slowly the two faiths learned to live under the same government.

Starting in the mid-eighteenth century, Britain became one of the first countries to begin the process of industrialization. By the nineteenth century, rapid economic transformation helped Britain become the most powerful country in the world, enhancing and securing its external sovereignty. British industry and trade dominated the newly independent countries of Latin America and much of Asia. In the 1860s, Britain led the second round of European colonization so that by

1900 it could be said "the sun never set on the British Empire." Domestically, industrialization transformed the state and politics. By the early nineteenth century, Parliament had gained nearly full power from the monarch, who remains today as a figurehead only. Industrialization and urbanization led to successful demands to expand voting rights beyond property owners (see chapter 3), which in turn gave politicians the incentive by the 1880s to create the first mass political parties to appeal directly to the general population.

The British Empire declined with World War II. While Britain helped win the war, it became a distant second power vis-à-vis its ally and former colony, the United States. World War II helped inspire a growing nationalist movement across Asia and Africa that resulted in nearly all British (and other) colonies gaining their independence by the 1960s. Domestically, the sacrifices made to defeat fascism produced a consensus in favor of a more egalitarian society, such that shortly after the war the major pieces of the British welfare state were established, which provided income support to those in need and government-funded health care for all. Today, Britain's welfare state is less extensive than many in Europe, but is far more extensive than similar programs in the United States.

Starting in the 1960s, the British state slowly yielded some sovereignty to the European Economic Community, which became the European Union (EU) in 1993. The EU requires member states to yield sovereign power over various issues to the larger body and abide by a wide array of EU standards and regulations. In 1999 many members adopted a common currency, the euro, thereby giving up major areas of economic policy to the new European Central Bank. But even as it has participated in various EU programs and policies, Britain has never completely embraced the EU, and it chose not to adopt the euro. Indeed, as late as 2005, one facetious British "political party" (the Monster Raving Looney Party) joked that rather than joining the euro, Britain should invite the rest of Europe to join the pound!

Yet while it has chosen to maintain greater sovereignty than most EU members, Britain has nonetheless yielded its sovereignty in significant areas to the larger body. The EU perhaps represents a new phase in the development of states, one in which states for the first time voluntarily cede elements of sovereignty to a larger body. While it lost its empire, Britain remains a strong, modern state with a functioning democracy and important role in Europe and the world.

CASE STUDY The United States

At first glance, the origin of the United States in a conference that brought together thirteen separate colonies appears most unusual. Few states were so completely created by design rather than slow historical evolution. Prior to 1776, Britain's thirteen North American colonies were separate colonial entities with significant cultural and political differences. These "united states" declared independence in 1776, but did not put a national government in place until 1781, and an effective one did not take shape until 1787. A real sense of national unity did not emerge until after the Civil War, fought from 1861 until 1865. Yet while the origin of the U.S. state was unusual, its early trials and tribulations, and questions about its very existence, are similar to those of many other postcolonial states.

North America's colonial history was not unlike that of South America, despite primarily British rather than Spanish and Portuguese conquest. The earliest settlers came looking for wealth; others followed looking for freedom to practice their religion, which is not to be confused with believing in or practicing freedom of religion. From early on, the economy of the southern colonies was based on large-scale plantation agriculture, which required extensive labor. Because British conquest had decimated the Native American population through disease and displacement, this group was not available as a labor force. Labor instead came at first in the form of indentured servants from Britain, but was soon augmented by African slaves with no rights and no possibility of gaining freedom. While

The signing of the Declaration of Independence in 1776 was a unique event at the time: a state actually being created by conscious design rather than emerging from political battles among rival monarchs. It would take much more work to draft a working form of government, and a civil war to create a real sense of national unity. Many colonies would follow the example of the United States in later centuries, demanding independence and writing their own constitutions.

most northern colonies allowed slavery, their economies did not depend on it, initially because small family farms predominated in these areas and subsequently because industrialization took hold about the time of the revolution. Neither required slave labor, although the wage laborers in early factories and mills were extremely poor and ill-treated.

Acting as representatives of poor and rich alike, the white, wealthy authors of the Declaration of Independence adopted the enlightened views then prevalent among European intellectuals. They envisioned a nation in which "all men are created equal and endowed by their Creator with certain inalienable rights." The five-year war that followed achieved independence for the American colonies, but the first effort at creating a functioning state, the Articles of Confederation, fell into disarray within a few years, in part because of a lack of effective sovereignty. The Articles severely curtailed the national government's power, preserving for the separate thirteen states the right to approve all taxes and trade policy. The mess caused by this national weakness led to the Second Continental Congress, during which what we now know as the U.S. Constitution was written. The document laid out a plan for a stronger central government with powers to establish a coherent national economy and uniform foreign policy. States did retain significant areas of sovereignty, such as responsibility over policing, infrastructure, and education; indeed, all powers not specifically vested in the national government were reserved for the states.

This created the first modern form of **federalism**, a system in which a state's power is divided among more than one level of government. The Constitution also made clear that the political elite at the time had a very limited concept of "all men are created equal." The Framers certainly meant "men," since women had no political rights, but they also did not mean "all." To secure the support of the southern states, slavery was preserved, and while slaves had no rights, each was to be counted as two-thirds of a person for purposes of establishing representation in the House of Representatives. This would give the slave-holding states more representation in Congress than their number of voters justified.

The new state consisted of three branches—executive, legislative, and judicial—each with distinct powers meant to limit the overall power of the central government. In 1803 the Supreme Court's famous *Marbury vs. Madison* decision gave the Court the sole right to interpret all matters of constitutional principle, including the power to reverse congressional or presidential acts when necessary to preserve what the Court saw as proper constitutional processes and powers. So, nearly thirty years after the Declaration of Independence, the basic institutions of the modern state were established. This state, however, remained very weak compared to the contemporary U.S. federal government. Its overall size was quite small, governing a relatively poor and primarily agricultural society.

That changed. Westward expansion by white settlers pushed Native populations ever further west, industrialization produced a stronger economy, and the population of the new state continued to grow. Each of these contributed to the establishment of the first mass political parties by the 1830s. The "Jacksonian Revolution" gave all free white men the right to vote, which was a great expansion of political rights, and created the first more or less modern parties: the Democrats in the 1830s and the Republicans in the 1850s. Immigration and industrialization increased the size and power of the northern states relative to the southern ones, while a growing abolitionist movement questioned the continuing legitimacy of slavery, a position on which the new Republican Party took the strongest stand.

When the country elected Abraham Lincoln as its first Republican president in 1860, southern states began seceding from the Union almost immediately. This soon led to the Civil War, a four-year, failed effort by the South to preserve a slaveholding society. In the middle of the war, following his abolitionist principles and appealing to support from European powers opposed to slavery, Lincoln signed the Emancipation Proclamation, freeing the slaves. Lacking effective sovereignty over the South, however, the state could not enforce emancipation until the Northern armies definitively defeated the Southern forces and the South surrendered and reentered the Union. The long-simmering issue of slavery, though not the last chapter in the saga of American race relations, was finally brought to an end.

Shortly after the war, the Thirteenth, Fourteenth, and Fifteenth Amendments to the Constitution were passed, ending slavery and in theory giving black citizens the same rights as whites. African Americans faced continuing discrimination in various ways, however, and most severely in the former slaveholding states. During the ten-year period now known as Reconstruction, Union troops and Union-supported government officials enforced these new amendments in the South, and blacks in the former slave states began to participate in the political process. As soon as the troops left and the officials were ousted from office, however, the white majority passed laws at the state level to reverse this trend. Blacks would not truly achieve full legal citizenship, including the right to vote, for another hundred years. These rights would come with the passage of the Civil Rights and Voting Rights Acts in 1964 and 1965, in response to Martin Luther King Jr.'s growing civil rights movement. White women actually received political rights earlier, with a constitutional amendment in 1920.

The United States became a global power with the second industrial revolution of the late nineteenth century. Cities grew dramatically, immigrants poured into urban areas to provide labor for rapidly expanding factories, and the country was transformed from a primarily agricultural society into one that was predominantly urban and industrial. This brought demands for changes in the state. The United States had been well known for corruption: political leaders at all levels regularly appointed their supporters to government jobs, often regardless of their qualifications. After a long period of such "machine politics," reformists lobbied for and successfully established a civil service under which most jobs in the government bureaucracy would be permanent and based on some concept of merit, rather than on the whims of the next elected politician. The same reform movement ultimately produced the Federal Reserve Board, which gave control over currency to appointed officials, as well as a 1913 constitutional amendment that created the national income tax, which became the state's primary source of revenue. This helped create the state's modern bureaucracy, which expanded significantly as the government took on additional roles in the twentieth century, especially after World War II.

That expansion of the state began with the New Deal in the 1930s. After being on the winning side of World War I and fully establishing itself as a superpower, the United States was the first country to feel the effects of the depression that swept the globe after 1929. Newly elected president Franklin Roosevelt envisioned an expanded government that helped to provide jobs and old-age pensions to people in need as part of the effort to bring the country back to economic stability. The New Deal, followed by policies aimed at improving health care (Medicare and Medicaid) and reducing poverty (Aid to Families with Dependent Children, or AFDC, and food stamps) in the Great Society program of the 1960s, increased the size and reach of the U.S. state, though it remained quite a bit smaller than most of its European counterparts (see chapter 5).

These new roles also strengthened the central government vis-à-vis the states. While the formal rules in the Constitution did not change, the central government's ability to fund popular programs run by the states gave it much greater power than it had possessed a century earlier. Some of this has been reversed in the past twenty-five years, but much of it remains in place, and the state remains far more important to American lives than it was a century ago.

CASE STUDY Japan

Japan is one of the few places in the world that successfully avoided European colonization. It went on to become the first "non-Western" country to join the ranks of the world's wealthy and most powerful states, creating a new model of capitalism in the process: the developmental state. Japan also was unusual centuries earlier, when it reduced the monarchy to a largely symbolic role much earlier than did the countries of Europe. As early as the twelfth century, military leaders called shoguns wrested effective power from the emperor, who remained the symbolic source of legitimacy, as he is today. Japan then suffered a period of "warring states" until two victors of these wars, Oda Nobunaga and Toyotomi Hideyoshi, began to reestablish a central authority.

Completion of that task fell to another victor, Tokugawa Ieyasu, who claimed the title of shogun in 1603. He consolidated a central state that came to be called the Tokugawa Bakufu, or shogunate, similar to those found under European feudalism. The ruling Tokugawa family did not hold all power, but rather shared it with 260 landlords called *daimyo*. These *daimyo,* however, were not as powerful as most European feudal lords because the central government regularly used its superior military power to extract funds and labor from them, which limited their wealth. The third important class in medieval society, the warriors or samurai, were a "landless aristocracy."

Under the Tokugawa Shogunate (1603–1867), Japan virtually isolated itself from outside influence, until U.S. warships under the command of Commodore Matthew Perry sailed into the harbor at Edo (present-day

Japan was the first non-Western state to create a fully modern economy. By first isolating itself from Western control and then borrowing Western technology as rapidly as possible, Japan's unusually strong state helped create the world's second largest economy.

Tokyo) in 1853. Perry refused to leave until Japanese officials agreed to undertake trade talks. The officials eventually agreed to a series of unfavorable treaties with the United States, France, and Britain, the closest the country would come to succumbing to Western control until the end of World War II. These agreements produced immediate protests, led by the samurai, against what was seen as undue Western influence. The protests broadened, and by the early 1860s, a samurai alliance had formed in opposition to the shogunate. After a series of battles, the shogunate ceded power in October 1867, establishing what came to be known as the Meiji Restoration, so called because the new government claimed to be restoring the Emperor

Meiji to his full powers. In truth, the new government was controlled by the samurai, who eliminated the feudal classes of both the shogun and *daimyo*.

The Meiji government went on to create the first truly modern state in Japan. Though unhappy with the earlier treaties with Western powers, the new government launched a series of modernizations, borrowing openly and heavily from the West, especially Western technology. Successful economic growth and industrialization gave Japan the power to renegotiate its treaties with the Western powers by the end of the nineteenth century, this time on more favorable terms. The new state ultimately included a modern army and navy, the beginnings of compulsory education, and the establishment of a single school to train all government civil servants. Significantly, the new military had nearly complete autonomy as no form of civilian control existed over it.

Japan's opening to the outside world also allowed Western ideas of liberal democracy (still only partially implemented in the West at the time) to enter the country, and a movement for democracy developed in the 1870s. Though unsuccessful, it did lead the Meiji government to write a constitution in 1889 that established the first Japanese parliament, the *Diet,* and the first political parties. (The *Diet* had very limited powers; the emperor, controlled by the samurai rulers, could overrule anything ordered by it.) The new constitution also established the first, albeit limited, civil and political rights.

After the death of Emperor Meiji, a period of greater political liberalization emerged under his successor, Emperor Taisho. While the institution of democratic reforms was still limited, this period did include the adoption in 1925 of the first universal male suffrage. Economic recession led the military to reverse this liberalization by 1927, however, with Gen. Tanaka Giichi becoming prime minister. Military leaders and right-wing parties blamed democracy for the country's economic woes, leading the military to enter politics directly. This ushered in a period of growing Japanese imperialism. The military effectively intimidated all civilian political leaders and pushed the government toward a more aggressive foreign policy. This new approach led to

Japan's invasion of China starting in 1931, its alliance with fascist Germany and Italy, and its attack on Pearl Harbor in 1941, which contributed to the entry of the United States into World War II.

This war would end for Japan with the dropping of atomic bombs on Hiroshima and Nagasaki by the United States in August 1945. The Japanese surrender led to the country's full occupation by the United States in the name of the victorious Allies. Under Gen. Douglas MacArthur, the United States completely demilitarized Japanese society and then established a new democratic constitution, written by the occupying Americans, in 1947. The document's provisions prohibited Japan from creating a military or ever engaging in war, although Japan ultimately did create a "self-defense" force that has since become the second most funded military in the world. In addition, the new constitution created a complex electoral system that favored rural over urban areas and helped the Liberal Democratic Party (LDP) maintain electoral control for more than forty years. This single party won every election from 1955 to 1993, and most subsequent ones, something which is discussed at greater length in later chapters.

The LDP governments created what came to be known as the "developmental state," a democracy that actively used the government to guide rapid economic growth. The bureaucracy became very powerful under LDP rule, working much more closely with Japanese businesses than was the case with governments in most Western countries. The result was a period of extremely rapid economic growth from the 1950s to 1973 that ultimately made Japan the second largest economy in the world (see chapter 5 for more details on this).

Since 1990, however, Japan's unusually powerful bureaucracy has been rocked by a seeming inability to restart economic growth and a series of corruption scandals. Nonetheless, sixty years after its defeat in World War II, the country remains the second largest economy in the world, a functioning democracy with an exceptionally important bureaucracy, and the highest ranking (that is, the strongest) state on the "Failed States Index."

CASE STUDY Germany

Germany, Europe's largest country, lies at the heart of the continent. This central position has made it important throughout European history; indeed, with no clear natural boundaries between German-speaking and neighboring areas, German speakers spread across central Europe in the Middle Ages. Yet it is a relative latecomer to the ranks of modern statehood, although some German nationalists trace their earliest state to the Holy Roman Empire, founded by Charlemagne in 800 A.D., which ruled over most German speakers for many centuries. This was a loose, medieval empire, however, not a modern state. For centuries Germans were split into hundreds of small principalities, duchies, and the like, and political loyalty and identity were primarily local. To add to this, the formation of Protestantism by German monk Martin Luther beginning in 1521 created religious divisions that only exacerbated long-standing political divisions among the German people.

The first stirrings of a united Germany occurred in response to Napoleon's destruction of the Holy Roman Empire in 1813: a loose confederation of German states emerged when the French emperor was defeated. Prussia, centered on the city of Berlin, quickly became the economically and militarily dominant member of the confederation, which was still not a unified state. The democratic revolutions that swept much of Europe in 1848 only slightly affected the German states, all of which remained monarchies. Democratic reformers did organize an election for a constitutional assembly, with delegates from several German states. After a year of deliberation, however, no constitution emerged, as each monarch successfully resisted any element of democratic reform.

A unified Germany finally did emerge under Otto von Bismarck, the chancellor (equivalent of a prime minister) of Prussia. Bismarck came to power in 1862 and set about expanding and uniting Germany under Prussian control. Between 1864 and 1870, he initiated wars with Denmark, Austria-Hungary, and France to conquer lands populated by German speakers that were under "foreign" control. In 1871 a new, united Germany was proclaimed, with the Prussian king named

East Berliners stand atop the Berlin Wall in 1989, shortly before it was brought down to reunite the divided German state. Reunification in 1990 meant the elimination of the separate and largely illegitimate East German state, absorbed by the much stronger and more legitimate West German state. This was only the most recent change in the boundaries of the German state. Because it lies at the heart of Europe, World Wars I and II and the Cold War had profound influences on what territory the German state controlled.

as the German kaiser and Bismarck as the chancellor. This new Germany had a legislature and elections, but virtually all power was in the hands of Kaiser Wilhelm I and Bismarck.

The new German state became actively involved in the economy, pursuing rapid industrialization in an attempt to catch up with the economic might of Britain, at that time Europe's most powerful state. The primary opposition to Bismarck came out of this industrialization in the form of the Social Democratic Party (SDP), founded in 1875, which demanded greater workers' rights and democracy. Bismarck successfully resisted the party's efforts, both by brutal repression when necessary and by creating Europe's first social welfare programs, including health insurance and old-age pensions.

By 1900 Germany had become an industrial powerhouse with aspirations of becoming an empire. The country colonized what is now Namibia in southern Africa as well as parts of Cameroon and Togo in West Africa. Such territorial gains would contribute toward Germany's entry into World War I in 1914. Its involvement and subsequent loss in "the Great War" ended the country's first united government. As Allied forces moved on Berlin in 1918, the kaiser fled and the leaders of the SDP proclaimed a democratic republic. Communist groups did attempt a revolution on the heels of the one that had just succeeded in Russia, and uprisings in several cities were put down with some difficulty. Ultimately, though, a new, democratic constitution was put in place once stability was restored in 1919.

The Weimar Republic survived only fourteen years. Defeat in the war and subsequent reparations to the victorious Allies left the nation devastated. Throughout the 1920s, voters became increasingly disenchanted with "mainstream" politicians who seemed unable to resolve the country's growing economic crisis. Popular support shifted toward the extreme political groups: the Communists and the Nazis. National Socialist Adolf Hitler became chancellor in 1932 and effectively eliminated democracy a year later (see chapter 3). He went on to create a rigid authoritarian state and launched Germany into World War II in 1939, proclaiming the state the rightful ruler not only of all German-speaking people, but of all Europe.

Hitler's eventual defeat in 1945 led to Germany's division. At the end of the war, the victorious Allies (the United States, UK, France, and the Soviet Union) each oversaw a separate German occupational zone. While the United States, Britain, and France came to unite their zones under one government, the Soviet Union ultimately refused to allow its sector to rejoin the rest. This zone would become the German Democratic Republic (GDR), better known as East Germany, a Communist state closely controlled by the Soviet Union. The other three united sectors formed the Federal Republic of Germany (FRG), governed by the Basic Law (the equivalent of a constitution) that took effect in 1949. West Germany, as it came to be known, reemerged as an industrial powerhouse in central Europe. It joined France in creating what would become the European Union and also created what came to be known as the "social market economy," a distinct form of capitalism (see chapter 5).

Germany and the city of Berlin were to remain divided for nearly thirty years. It was not until the fall of communism brought an end to the Cold War in 1989 that the country and city were reunited. Nothing signified this more dramatically than the destruction of the Berlin Wall, which had split the German capital since 1961. By 1990 Germany had been reunified under the constitution of the former West Germany. This process was economically and politically difficult, requiring the integration of the much poorer East German population into the unified nation.

Once the worst of its growing pains were behind it, a reunited German state led the way in transforming what had been the European Community into the European Union, even giving up significant economic sovereignty to the larger body. This transformation culminated with the creation of the euro and European Central Bank in 1999.

Since the mid-nineteenth century, the German state consciously and effectively created an industrial powerhouse in the heart of Europe. Democracy emerged much more slowly but was secure and universal throughout Germany after 1990. Today the modern state is widely considered to be one of the world's strongest, wealthiest, and most stable. And like Germany, Brazil, the subject of the next case study, also faced difficulties in achieving democracy, even though, like Germany, it was the largest and wealthiest state in its region.

CASE STUDY Brazil

Like most countries, Brazil's modern state was the product of European colonial rule. Prior to Portuguese colonization in 1500, its population was relatively small compared to that of many other areas of the Americas. The Portuguese effectively subjugated what indigenous population there was, and colonial Brazil became a major producer of sugarcane and other agricultural products, farmed largely with slave labor. Indeed, Brazil had more slaves than any other colony in the Americas. The economic heart of the colonial economy was the northeastern sugar-producing region, even though Rio de Janeiro in the south became the capital. A Portuguese, landowning elite emerged as the socially and economically dominant force in the colonial society.

In contrast to the Spanish colonies in South America, Brazil gained independence from Portugal as a single country. This was partly due to its unusual route to independence. In most of South America in the early nineteenth century, the landowning elite helped lead rebellions against continued Spanish rule, which Spain initially resisted, but lacked the power to stop. In contrast, the Portuguese government actually moved to the colony, and the royal family later declared itself independent of the mother country.

The royal family originally fled to Brazil in 1808 to evade Napoleon's conquest of Portugal, taking sanctuary in Rio de Janeiro, the capital of its American colony. In 1821 King João VI returned to Portugal after regaining his throne, leaving his son, Prince Dom Pedro, in Rio as prince regent to rule on his behalf. A year later, Dom Pedro declared Brazil independent and himself emperor, with no real opposition from Portugal. In 1840 his son, Dom Pedro II, became emperor and ruled until 1889. Dom Pedro II reigned over a political system that allowed the landowning elite to form parties and have representation in a legislature, but everything was subject to his ultimate approval. The economy remained based in northeastern agriculture using slave labor.

By the late nineteenth century, profits from coffee production in the south were rivaling those of the decaying sugar industry in the northeast. Brazil was at that point the last remaining slaveholding society in the world, and while coffee growers needed labor, many came to believe that importing wage labor would be easier and more accepted than maintaining slavery. In addition, growing international and domestic pressure was being applied to end the institution. Both factors ultimately led the emperor to abolish slavery in 1888, and the same liberal ideas that led some Brazilian elites to oppose that institution also led them to oppose the empire and favor democracy instead. Just a year after the abolition of slavery, civilian and military reformers convinced key military leaders to overthrow the emperor in a bloodless coup that sent him into exile in Portugal and established a republic.

The leaders of the new republic created Brazil's modern state, drafting a constitution that created a democratic system of government but gave voting

Downtown São Paulo, one of the largest cities in the world, shows the results of the Brazilian state's conscious effort to rapidly industrialize the economy starting in the 1960s. The modern state emerged as the center of economic life shifted from the rural northeast to the urban southeast. São Paulo was the seat of the movement for Brazilian democracy in the 1970s as well. Present here are all of the benefits and costs, including a rapidly expanding urban population and growing inequality, that state-led industrialization has produced.

rights to literate men only, which restricted the voting population to 3.5 percent of the citizenry. This was due in part to the fact that slavery had been abolished only a year earlier, and virtually all the former slaves were illiterate, so the literacy restriction effectively eliminated their ability to vote. What they were able to do was migrate in massive numbers to São Paulo and Rio, where the expanding coffee industry and industrialization had shifted economic and political power.

Economic influence was shifting to southern urban areas, but political control remained vested in the rural landowning elite. Known as *coroneis,* or "colonels," these individuals used their socioeconomic dominance to control the votes in their regions in a type of machine politics. Meanwhile, in the growing urban areas, **clientelism**, the exchange of material resources for political support, developed as the key means of mobilizing political support. As more urban dwellers became literate and gained the right to vote, elite politicians would gain their support by providing direct benefits to them, such as jobs or government services to their neighborhoods. Clientelism and *coronelismo* (rule by *coroneis*) became ways to shore up political power in Brazil's first, partial democracy. Corruption and clientelistic use of bureaucratic jobs as perks for supporters simultaneously bloated and undermined Brazil's young bureaucracy, an indication of a rather weak modern state.

One politician to rise out of this system was Getúlio Vargas. After losing a disputed presidential election in 1930, Vargas used his support in the military to launch a coup that brought him to power, ending Brazil's first republic. Vargas was a quintessential populist politician who used nationalist rhetoric and clientelism to gain the first truly mass following in Brazil's political history. He and other populists in South America appealed directly to the growing population of urban poor via populist and nationalist rhetoric, and the provision of goods and services overcame the power of the rural *coroneis.* He used this support to establish the *Estado Novo* (New State), a quasi-fascist regime that he ruled from 1937 to 1945. During this period, he created trade unions ostensibly to represent the growing number of urban workers, although these essentially were puppet groups controlled by the government. He had the

government create its own steel and oil industries and expanded health and welfare systems to gain popular support, all while ruling an authoritarian state. However, when the end of World War II brought U.S. and domestic pressure against his state, which too closely resembled those of the discredited fascists of Europe, Vargas was forced to allow a return to democratic rule.

The New Republic was plagued by such economic problems as very high inflation and by political instability, including Vargas's suicide (he had been elected back into power in 1950) and another president's sudden resignation only a year into his term. (The quixotic Jânio Quadros resigned a year after being elected, leaving the mercurial leftist vice president, João Goulart, as the new president.) No president seemed able to create a formula for economic success. By the early 1960s, the elite and military saw growing militancy on the part of workers as a threat, and many in the military believed this to be the first movement toward a communist revolution.

In a preemptive strike against such a revolution, the military overthrew the elected government, with U.S. and considerable upper- and middle-class support, in 1964. The military ruled until 1985, leading what we will term a "modernizing authoritarian" regime (see chapter 3) that produced very rapid economic growth and industrialization, but also great inequality. The Brazilian military government was less brutal than many South American military governments of the time, but nonetheless exiled, imprisoned, and executed opponents. It allowed a two-party parliament to exist in which one party officially supported the government and the other opposed it, but the body had very limited power, and given the level of electoral tampering, the legislature was too weak to challenge the military.

By the late 1970s, growing inequality and a slowdown in economic growth led workers in the expanding industrial cities to organize illegal unions. Despite government efforts to stop them, these unions and followers of liberation theology in the Catholic Church led a growing movement for democracy that ultimately forced the military to slowly shift power back to elected officials (see chapter 9). Democratic governments have ruled since the first president was directly elected in 1989.

Brazil's democracy now seems to be fully established, with a complex party system and quite intense partisan competition in a primarily industrialized economy that is one of the world's largest. This modern state does continue to be plagued by high levels of corruption and clientelism that at times undermine the rule of law and bureaucratic effectiveness, but it is nonetheless a sovereign state, with effective control of its territory and people, and it presides over the largest economy in the Southern Hemisphere.

CASE STUDY Russia

Our third "European" case, Russia, is actually only partly in Europe. Since its founding, Russian leaders have struggled with how much to identify with Europe and how much with Asia, as the country's landmass, the largest single state in the world, stretches from eastern Europe to the borders of China and Japan. Many Russians consider the first Russian state, a medieval kingdom, to have been founded in Kiev, now the capital of Ukraine, in 882. Kievan Russia lasted until the twelfth century and first had the name of "Rus." Overrun by Mongol invaders from central Asia in 1236, much of what is now Russia subsequently came under Mongol control.

A new kingdom emerged in Moscow in the fourteenth century, and a monarchy was created that would last until 1917. Ivan IV Vasilyevich (who would come to be known as Ivan the Terrible) took the title "tsar" in 1547 and greatly increased the monarchy's power and reach by initiating military campaigns to take over vast swaths of territory to the east and west. By 1660 Russia was the largest country in the world, its rulers having taken control of the previously independent Ukraine and territory stretching far into Asia. The country became a great, multiethnic empire in which more than one hundred separate languages were spoken.

Over all of this reigned the tsar, who was an absolutist ruler with even greater power than most monarchs in Europe. For example, Russian tsars succeeded in preventing any private land ownership until Empress Catherine II Alekseyevna (known widely as Catherine the Great) came to allow it in 1765. Prior to that, the tsar effectively owned all of Russia, keeping all political and economic power in royal hands. Over the centuries, an expanding bureaucracy did emerge to administer the

Members of the pro-Kremlin youth movement Nashi rally in support of Vladimir Putin in front of the Kremlin and St. Basils Cathedral. The new Russian state emerged from the collapse of the Soviet Union in 1991. After a decade as a very weak state, it became significantly stronger under Putin, often to the detriment of democracy. Putin consciously identified himself with the symbols of the Soviet and pre-Communist Russian state, both to project an image of strength and to gain greater legitimacy.

tsar's lands, but the Russian monarchy essentially had the attributes of an early modern absolutist state in terms of effective sovereignty and control over territory, though not necessarily in terms of legitimacy.

The tsar faced pressure to reform the government throughout the nineteenth century. Tsar Alexander II gave in to the most major reform in 1862 by permitting the emancipation of serfs. For centuries before this, the bulk of the Russian population had lived under the control of the landed nobility and held virtually no rights. Local noble landowners were in effect the local government. Serfs, essentially owned by the landlords and barred from leaving their place of birth, paid taxes and were forced into the tsar's army when needed, but had no other direct relationship with the monarch. Alexander's freeing of the serfs from landlord control was a belated but essential step in the transition to capitalism. Emancipated serfs gained collective control over their land, reducing the power of the landlord, and rapid industrialization in the late nineteenth century gave freed serfs a reason to move to urban areas, which exploded in size.

Radical movements grew in these newly expanded cities, including groups demanding democracy and a growing Marxist movement. Tsar Alexander III responded to this by expanding his secret police force and writing new laws to make any opposition to tsarist rule a crime, but after police brutally put down a demonstration in 1905, widespread opposition arose that bordered on anarchy. This finally forced the tsar to agree to the creation of an elected legislature, the *Duma.* He dissolved the body after only three months, however, changing the electoral laws, and spearheading the election of a new, more compliant legislature. Russia's first, very brief experiment with democracy was over.

Not long after, Russia was drawn into what would become World War I, which proved economically disastrous for the country. Still primarily an agricultural society, it was far poorer than Germany, France, or Britain. Fighting against Germany required massive popular sacrifices. As the war proceeded, soldiers were sent to the front ill equipped and hungry, and as conditions worsened, mass desertions began to occur.

By the end of the war, the Bolsheviks, a Communist group under Vladimir Ilyich Lenin, had gained popularity. The makings of another electoral democracy emerged in February 1917, only to be overtaken by a communist revolution that October. The Communists assassinated the tsar and his family, after which many of the non-Russian areas of the empire declared themselves independent. It took the Communist movement three years to fully recapture what had been the tsarist empire. A new government called the Union of Soviet Socialist Republics, or the Soviet Union (see chapter 3 for more details), was formed, a brutal but nonetheless modern state. The Communists created a dictatorial regime that appeared to create a federal state in which local regions (the soviet republics) had significant power; in truth, all were controlled tightly from Moscow by the Communist Party.

Communist rule modernized Russia in a way the tsars had not. At tremendous human cost (estimates range as high as ten million dead), Lenin's successor, Josef Stalin, rapidly industrialized the country, taking resources and laborers from the countryside as needed. The state took complete control of all economic activity. The secret police dealt with anyone who opposed the state's methods, which contributed to the formation of one of the most oppressive police states in history. Yet Stalin also created a superpower, which became the only serious rival to the United States after World War II. After his death, Soviet leaders reduced the degree of terror held over the population but still kept centralized control over an increasingly bureaucratic form of communism. And while it had been successful at initial industrialization, the Soviet Union could not keep pace with the West's economic growth. Recognizing the need for change, a new leadership under Mikhail Gorbachev began a process of reform in 1985 that eventually resulted in the collapse of the Soviet state.

When elements of the Soviet military, led by men opposed to Gorbachev's reforms, attempted a coup in August 1991, Boris Yeltsin, the leader of the Russian part of the Soviet federation and himself a Communist reformer, successfully stood up to the tanks and proclaimed the end of Soviet rule. The military, faced with masses of people in the streets and with the eyes of the world on it, was forced to back down. By December Gorbachev had agreed to the dissolution of the Soviet state. The old tsarist empire split into fifteen separate states, with Russia the largest by far.

Today Russia remains a very multiethnic state, with a federal system of government that gives some power, at least in theory, to the various regions, which are defined loosely along ethnic lines. After the dissolution of the Soviet regime, Russia proclaimed itself a democracy and Yeltsin became president. A growing power battle between Yeltsin and the parliament (elected under Gorbachev's last major reform in 1990) led to a standoff in 1993 during which members of the parliament barricaded themselves in the building. Yeltsin eventually had the military force them out, and his victory allowed him to write a new constitution as he wanted and hold elections by the end of the year. He went on to be elected president twice, resigning in 2000 to allow his heir apparent, Vladimir Putin, to assume command.

The collapse of Communist rule allowed an electoral democracy to emerge in the 1990s. It was, however, characterized by very fragile and rapidly changing political parties, and for a while, it appeared that the former Communist Party might actually be elected back into power as the new government. Yeltsin refused to participate in party politics, claiming to be "above it all." While his proclamation made good headlines, in practice, this made it very difficult for the president and parliament to work together effectively.

The state became demonstrably weaker in the early to mid-1990s. Because the state had limited ability to protect the population, powerful mafias arose in Moscow, further reducing internal sovereignty. Yeltsin encouraged a rapid but often corrupt shift to a capitalist economy, which allowed some former Communist leaders, among others, to become "oligarchs" in the new Russia by gaining control of huge private companies. Under Putin's leadership, control increasingly was returned to the executive office. Examples of this included Putin getting a majority elected to parliament from several different parties, all of which supported him. He also strengthened the state, reduced crime, and restored order. After a period of fairly extreme weakness in the 1990s, the state has become stronger in most areas. It gained strength under Putin, but lost much of its democratic character, and most political scientists now term it as a semi-authoritarian, rather than a democratic, state (see chapter 9).

CASE STUDY Iran

Iran is the modern descendant of the great ancient empire of Persia, and it is a state that has been heavily influenced by a series of invasions. The most important of these, by Arabs in the seventh-century, brought Islam to the region. The territory of Iran as it is known today, however, was not united under one state until the Safavid invasion of 1501.

The Safavids were Turkic-speaking invaders from the north who established the first great Iranian empire of the modern era, which lasted as a united entity until 1722. Yet the power of the Safavids, while seemingly absolute, was actually quite limited. Like many other early modern or feudal states, the shah, as the supreme ruler was known, had to rely on local scribes who could speak and write Persian to administer his state and on militaries loyal to local chieftains to maintain order. This dependency limited the Safavids' power over the population so that their internal sovereignty was far from complete. The lasting legacy of their empire, though, was Shiite Islam. Iran had up to that point been pri-

marily Sunni, the majority sect of Islam (see chapter 3). The Safavid were Shiite, and by the middle of the seventeenth century they had converted 90 percent of the country to their version of Islam.

Yet another invasion, led by Afghans from the east, overthrew the Safavids in 1722. This provoked intermittent civil war until 1794, when another Turkic group, the Qajars, was victorious in establishing a new empire. The Qajar Empire was similar to that of the Safavids in terms of daily operation, but it differed in one crucial aspect: the Qajars were Sunni. This meant that the local Shiite clergy retained legitimacy as the true interpreters of the faith, and therefore most judicial questions, which gave them much greater power than they had under the Shiite Safavids. The Qajar monarchs ruled until 1921, but in the nineteenth century their real power was drastically reduced by Russian and British imperialism. Like China, Iran was never formally colonized, but the government came to be extremely dependent upon and compliant with the Russians and British, granting them

Iranian president Mohammad Khatami, left, and Iran's parliament speaker, Mehdi Karrubi, attend a meeting of lawmakers and cabinet members in Tehran. Iran's Islamic rulers govern a state modernized by the regime they overthrew, which had been led by the shah of Iran. The current rulers attempt to combine the institutions of a more or less modern state with a form of government based on their Islamic beliefs.

very favorable economic terms for key resources such as oil and depending on them for military support when needed. This meant that Iran's sovereignty was compromised in many ways.

By the start of the twentieth century, popular discontent with this foreign influence led to street demonstrations from citizens demanding a new constitution. In 1906 the shah agreed to a constitution that included a bill of rights and allowed for the creation of an elected legislature with greater power than the shah himself. The new democratic state allowed open discussion, but became polarized between social reformers and conservatives who wanted to preserve traditional Shiite values. Perhaps more important, the central state still had limited sovereignty over the provinces, which continued to control the bulk of revenue collection and the military. By the end of World War I, Russian (by that point Soviet) and British interests were once again gaining control over the weak and divided Iranian state.

In the midst of this, Col. Reza Khan led a coup d'etat that overthrew the weakened Qajar dynasty and established what came to be known as the Pahlavi dynasty, ruled first by Reza Shah and then by his son, Mohammed Reza Pahlavi. The Pahlavis created the first truly modern state in Iran. During their rule from 1925 to 1979, they increased the size of the central army tenfold, dramatically expanded the bureaucracy, and gained full control over the provinces. The Pahlavis established a modernizing authoritarian state, modernizing both the state and the economy, increasing agricultural and industrial production, and building tremendous infrastructure, with the government itself directly involved in most of these efforts. Indeed, the Pahlavi family became the country's largest landowners and industrialists. They also centralized power in their hands: the elected legislature continued to exist with an elected prime minister at its helm, but its power was greatly reduced.

When the second Pahlavi took control in 1941, he allowed greater press freedom and political competition than had existed during his father's time. The Pahlavis remained very supportive of foreign ownership in Iran, however, and when a left-leaning prime minister, Mohammad Mosaddeq, was elected in 1951 on a platform of taking government control of the foreign-owned oil industry, his economic policies were anathema to them and to their foreign backers. In 1953 the shah, with active British and U.S. support, overthrew Mosaddeq and established a fully authoritarian state that had no place in it for elected officials.

From the start, the 1953 coup was unpopular, seen by many as directed by foreigners. Soon after, the shah launched a series of social and economic reforms to modernize, as he saw it, Iranian society even further. He called this period the White Revolution, and his modernizations included land reform and the elimination of many areas of Islamic law. In the 1970s, he created a ruling party so that he could gain further political control over a restive population, as an economic crisis in the latter part of that decade created growing opposition to his policies. Merchants and professionals began to speak out against the government, joined by long-time critics such as the Communist Party and Mossaddeq's party, the National Front. These groups coalesced behind the leadership of the exiled Shiite spiritual leader Ayatollah Ruhollah Khomeini. Protests spread through streets and mosques, and local Islamic militias took over entire neighborhoods. These events led to a general strike in 1978 and gave birth to an antigovernment rally of more than two million people in December of that year.

Faced with such opposition, the shah went into what was supposed to be temporary exile in January 1979, but he never returned. A month later, Khomeini came back from exile and led the creation of the Islamic Republic of Iran, the first theocratic government in the modern era. Shortly thereafter, students stormed the U.S. embassy in Tehran with Khomeini's support and took U.S. diplomatic personnel hostage. The crisis lasted 444 days and resulted in the breaking of virtually all relations between Iran and its powerful former ally. Also in 1980, Iraq began an eight-year war with Iran that was mostly fought in Iran.

The Islamic Republic during this period went through phases of greater openness to political debate and greater repression (see chapter 8), but still endured as a powerful state, both domestically and regionally. Its bid to become a nuclear power, or at least to acquire much greater nuclear capabilities, has recently made it the center of major global debate. The Pahlavis established the first modern state and attempted to reduce the influence of Islam. The Ayatollah Khomeini, his followers and successor, have re-Islamized the country, but within the confines of a modern and relatively powerful state.

CASE STUDY India

As the world's largest democracy, India is one of the few postcolonial countries to maintain democratic rule for nearly all of its history. Arguably, it is also the world's most diverse country, with more than 250 different languages, five major religions, and a complex caste system that has crucial political implications. Its independence movement, led by the charismatic Mahatma Gandhi, was the first successful anticolonial effort of the post–World War II era and inspired many other anticolonial leaders to pursue independence.

The territory that is now India, Pakistan, and Bangladesh was once divided among many kingdoms, most of which were Hindu. Muslim invaders created the Moghul Empire in 1526, which dominated most of northern and central India and ruled over a mostly Hindu population, while the south remained under the control of local Hindu kings. Like other premodern states, both the Hindu kings and Muslim emperors had only loose sovereignty over daily life: at the local level, members of the elite caste, the Brahmin, governed.

Beginning in 1612, the British East India Company established trading centers on India's coast. The company then used its power to eliminate Indian textile and other early industrial production to ensure the export of cheap cotton and other raw materials to feed its

factories back in Britain. By the middle of the 1700s, the company had established an informal empire over most of the country, breaking Moghul rule and acting

India's parliament, the Lok Sabha, shows the colonial influence on state creation around the world. The Indian state was founded out of the nationalist movement that ovethrew British rule but then adopted the British parliamentary system of government. While it is weakened by corruption, has suffered from widespread religious and ethnic tensions, and remains extremely poor despite recent economic gains, India's democratic state has endured for more than six decades, a rare feat in the postcolonial world.

as a government. Much of the earliest British colonial rule in Asia and Africa came about in this manner: companies became governments.

Like the overseers of other colonies, the company ultimately had trouble ruling effectively. The Sepoy Rebellion in the Indian army in 1857 ended company rule, and the British government took direct control of its largest formal colony. The new colonial government ruled through the five hundred or so *maharajas,* or local Hindu rulers, and the *zamindars,* local landowners. Both groups were given more power than they had possessed in the precolonial era, with the British even providing military support when necessary. In exchange for their loyalty, these elites were given wide latitude to rule at the local level as they saw fit.

As colonizers often did, the British required educated local people to fill the administrative offices of their colonial state. Creating an all-Indian civil service, the start of a modern bureaucracy, and military helped create greater unity among the subcontinent's disparate regions, and newly educated Indians filled the offices of these new institutions. Unfortunately for the British, the first stirrings of nationalism would arise from this educated elite.

The Indian National Congress, which eventually became the Congress Party that has ruled India for most of its independent history, was founded by urban elites in 1885. Although its top leadership was primarily Hindu, the congress operated along democratic and secular principles and claimed to represent all Indians in a society with numerous religious and ethnic divisions. The National Congress initially demanded only greater Indian participation in government, but in 1915 Gandhi transformed this single demand into a mass nationalist movement. As the nationalist struggle continued through the 1920s and 1930s under Gandhi's leadership, Hindu nationalists pressed the Congress Party to adopt a more overtly Hindu orientation. On the other end of the spectrum, India's Muslim leaders increasingly felt unrepresented in the organization, and by the end of the 1930s, some Muslim leaders were beginning to demand a separate Muslim state.

The push for independence succeeded after World War II. The British agreed to grant India independence if the Congress Party supported Britain during the war. Muslim leaders, however, demanded and received from the British a separate Muslim state, Pakistan. The simultaneous creation of the two separate states (against Gandhi's fierce opposition) resulted in the mass migration of millions of citizens, as Hindus moved from what was to be Pakistan into what would become India, and Muslims went the other direction. At least a million people perished in violence associated with the massive migration.

India thus gained independence under the rule of the Congress Party, with Jawaharlal Nehru, a close associate of Gandhi, as prime minister. The new state was a federal system, much like that of the United States. Besides economic development, Nehru's other great challenge was the demand for greater recognition by India's diverse ethnic and religious groups. Throughout the 1950s, leaders of local language groups demanded, and some received, states of their own.

After Nehru's death, his daughter, Indira Gandhi (no relation to Mahatma), gained leadership of the Congress Party and the country. She made a mass appeal directly to the populace, asking for its support with the slogan *Garibi Hatao!* (End Poverty Now!), and won the crucial 1971 election that broke the power of many local Brahmin elites on whom her father had relied. Gandhi went on to create an increasingly centralized state: in 1975 she declared a "state of emergency" that gave her the power to disband local governments and replace them with those loyal to her. This was the only period since India's independence that democracy was threatened, and her actions were met with increasing opposition.

Indira was assassinated by a Sikh, yet another of India's religious groups, who was part of a growing movement for an independent Sikh state. While this movement was never successful, it was the first significant example of violent religious-political division since the partition of India and Pakistan. Since then, political battles have increased between Muslims and Hindu nationalists, both of whom reject the official secularism of the national government. Out of this has emerged a renewed Hindu nationalist party that gained control of the legislature in 1996.

Since the mid-1990s, India's rapidly developing economy has carved out a major niche in the global economy, especially in areas related to computer services and programming. It remains, however, a country with widespread malnutrition and has the largest population of poor people in the world. While presiding over an expanding economy, the current government, again under Congress Party rule but with the country's first non-Hindu prime minister (a Sikh), faces continuing religious tensions, especially vis-à-vis the large and rather impoverished Muslim minority, many of whom seem to believe India's democracy is not for them. Through all of this, however, India's democracy has survived, although its state remains relatively weak, a weakness manifested in continuing corruption, religious tensions, and poverty.

India's democracy has survived, although its state remains relatively weak, a weakness manifested in continuing corruption, religious tensions, and poverty. In recent years, however, it has presided over a rapidly growing economy, and many observers see elements of a potential economic superpower. It increasingly rivals its largest neighbor, China, as an up-and-coming economic power, yet China remains well ahead of India economically and has maintained a very strong state through a dramatic process of economic transformation. What it lacks is India's democracy, at least so far.

CASE STUDY China

China is the world's most populous country, had the world's fastest growing economy in the 1990s, and is widely recognized as the world's "oldest civilization." Although its modern state arose only in 1949 under Communist rule, the Chinese empire was first united in 221 B.C. While several different dynasties came to power over the centuries, the empire existed, more or less unified, until 1911, making it the longest continuous political entity in human history. The various dynasties ruled over a remarkable society that produced great technological and philosophical advances at an early period. The empire survived for so long in part because of its geographic isolation and protection from invaders, its urbanization compared to other societies (including those in Europe) at the time, and the presence of a unifying system of beliefs in Confucianism.

The empire's demise began in the mid-nineteenth century. While trade with the outside world had long existed, the expanding European imperial powers and the United States began demanding greater access to China in the 1840s. The Opium Wars between China and Britain were most immediately about Britain's right to sell opium in China but were ultimately about greater European and American access to and control over China. While China was never formally colonized, its losses in the Opium Wars from 1840 to 1864 resulted in a series of very unequal treaties with Western powers that gave the latter access to Chinese markets and trade as well as effective sovereignty over key areas of the country, including Hong Kong, which Britain would eventually return to China in 1997.

A period of extensive Western influence over the state began, with European powers implementing Western laws in areas they controlled and allowing Christian missionaries to enter the country for the first time. In reaction to increasing foreign control and economic decline, a series of revolts known as the Taiping Rebellion broke out in the 1850s. Led by a millenarian reformer who identified himself with Jesus Christ, the rebellion united as many as one thousand local peasant protest movements against foreign domination and the unresponsiveness of the old empire. The rebellion

China has surpassed the United States as the country with the largest number of Internet users, only one result of the Chinese state's policies of rapid economic expansion that have lifted millions out of poverty since 1979. As has always been true in China, however, economic changes bring questions of political stability. While the Chinese state is modern in many ways and presides over a quite modern economy, it has resisted almost all forms of democracy. The Internet connects growing numbers of people to the rest of the world, but the state blocks Web sites that portray it in a poor light.

gained control of a significant share of the country, with a capital based in the city of Nanjing, but was ultimately defeated with the help of European forces that wanted to preserve the favorable treatment they received from the emperor. After 1864 the dynastic government regained control, though with a continuing quasi-colonial European presence.

The restoration of the empire brought relative stability, but only until the end of the century. What many saw as continued excessive foreign domination and economic stagnation produced growing discontent. Sun Yat-sen, an American-educated doctor and revolutionary leader, started a nationalist movement that proclaimed its opposition to the empire and foreign imperialism. The first stirrings of this movement came in 1905, and by 1911 military uprisings in Shanghai and elsewhere signaled the empire's imminent collapse. On January 1, 1912, the emperor resigned and the Republic of China was established.

While the nationalist movement, which came to be known as the Guomindang (GMD), proclaimed democracy, its members were forced to compromise with the military and allow military leader Yuan Shikai to be appointed president. Shikai quickly created a dictatorship that betrayed the GMD by banning the party and giving in to key Japanese demands. His premature death from kidney failure in 1916 ushered in more than a decade of chaos and war in which warlords gained control of various parts of the country as the Chinese state crumbled.

The GMD fought to gain back power. In the 1920s, it slowly regained control with the help of an alliance with a new political force, the Chinese Communist Party (CCP). Chiang Kai-shek, Sun's successor after Sun died in 1925, ordered the killing of CCP members in 1927, effectively breaking with the party after it helped him regain power. By 1928 the GMD under Chiang had gained power over the entire country and established a nationalist dictatorship. Its sovereignty was seriously compromised by reliance on warlords in some areas and the continuous threat of civil war with the CCP and Japanese invasion. The GMD promised reforms such as land redistribution but implemented little, and the government's legitimacy declined as the GMD became increasingly corrupt and unpopular. While the nationalists had regained control, they ruled a very weak state.

The CCP under its new leader, Mao Zedong, moved to the countryside after the GMD broke the alliance. Starting in the southeast, Mao put together a revolutionary movement based in the peasantry, the poor majority of the country, and that movement began an intermittent civil war between the CCP and GMD government. As the government was more concerned about the internal threat from the CCP than the external threat from the Japanese, it made overtures to partially appease Japan and reduce the possibility of attack. The CCP, in contrast, took a strongly nationalist, anti-Japanese stance that gained much support in the country. In 1934–1935 Mao led the famous Long March, a six-thousand-mile trek by party supporters from the southeast part of the country to the northwest, where supporters would be more secure from government attack. The CCP then took effective control of the northwestern section of the country and began creating the prototype of its future Communist government.

The Japanese invasion of 1937 left the country divided, with the CCP controlling the northwest, the GMD ruling part of the southwest, and Japan occupying the rest. Japan's invasion and World War II benefited the CCP, which had a better relationship with the peasantry and created a peasant army to resist the Japanese. By the end of World War II, a full-scale civil war had ensued between supporters of the CCP and the GMD. The CCP won the internal conflict in 1949, despite U.S. military support for the GMD. The GMD fled to the island of Taiwan and formed a government there. For many years, it claimed to be the true government of China, and the UN recognized it as such until 1972.

Communist rule brought massive changes to China. It led to the creation of the first truly unified modern Chinese state, but at horrific cost. The new government led many dramatic reform efforts in the early 1950s, including massive land reform programs and campaigns against corruption, opium use, and other common socially harmful practices. It also took control of the economy, creating a Soviet-style command economy that attempted to industrialize the world's largest agrarian society. The result was the Great Leap Forward, an effort at rapid rural industrialization that led to a famine that killed at least twenty million people. Political purges sent many others to "re-education camps," prison, or execution. The Cultural Revolution from 1966 to 1976 was a period in which Mao mobilized his followers against what he saw as entrenched bureaucrats in his own party and state; his efforts created widespread political uncertainty, repression, and economic and social dislocation.

The Cultural Revolution ended with Mao's death in 1976. After a three-year period of jockeying for power among his potential successors, including his wife, a victor emerged. Deng Xiaopeng, one of Mao's earliest comrades who had been removed from power during the Cultural Revolution, established his supremacy over the party and state in 1979. Deng initiated a series of slow but ultimately sweeping economic reforms that focused on allowing greater market forces in the economy and reducing the direct role of the state. These reforms continue today, a nearly thirty-year process of introducing market reforms that is still not complete. The result has been the fastest economic growth in the world that has moved millions of Chinese out of poverty, created a huge exodus from rural areas to cities, and allowed much greater inequality than existed under Mao.

Politically, Deng and his successors have resisted most efforts toward greater freedoms and democracy. Many observers see a fundamental contradiction between allowing economic freedoms but denying political ones and argue that ultimately the CCP will have to allow much greater political freedoms if its economic success is to continue. The most dramatic popular protest for such political liberalization occurred in Tiananmen Square in 1989. The demonstrations, initially led by students, began as a demand for greater openness and less corruption within the ruling party, but ultimately expanded to include demands for more fundamental democratic change. Deng successfully resisted these demands by sending in the army to crush the demonstration, earning the government the opprobrium of much of the world as a result.

More recently, small-scale political changes have occurred. The level of political debate in the country is significantly more open than it was under Mao, and elections to some local offices have been allowed on an experimental basis, though all are still ultimately controlled by the CCP. Deng engineered his own succession in 1993 when Jiang Zemin became head of the party, and he in turn was succeeded by Hu Jintao in 2003. Overall, China remains a Communist government in name and in political practice, and the CCP rules a stable authoritarian state that so far has resisted democracy. The party has presided over perhaps the most remarkable economic advance in human history, making China the fourth largest economy in the world and a potential economic and political superpower.

CASE STUDY Nigeria

Nigeria, like most African states, is a product of colonialism. It is by far the largest African country (approximately one-seventh of all Africans are Nigerians) and a major oil producer, making it an important country to understand both in Africa and around the world. Approximately 250 languages are spoken within its borders; colonialism amalgamated a huge number of separate societies into one "nation." Ethnic competition led to a three-year civil war in the 1960s, and today the country is deeply divided along religious lines between Muslims, primarily in the north, and Christians in the south. This has produced extensive violence since the early 1990s, though no civil war. Similarly, grievances among people living near the oil wells in the southeast, who have benefited very little from the region's oil production, have produced significant violence that has at

Nigerian women occupy an oil terminal, demanding that the oil company provide more jobs. The postcolonial state has seen numerous political changes, but one thing has remained constant since the late 1960s: the overwhelming importance of oil. While it provides the state with massive revenues, it also has allowed equally massive corruption that has weakened the state and siphoned benefits from oil production away from the common people. A democracy has emerged over the last decade, but the corruption and lack of local benefits from oil revenues remain a problem.

times disrupted oil production and caused global oil prices to rise.

Prior to colonial conquest in the late nineteenth century, the territory that is now Nigeria was home to numerous and varied societies. The northern half was primarily Muslim and was ruled by Islamic emirs based in twelve separate city-states. The southern half consisted of many societies, the two biggest of which were the Yoruba and Igbo. The Yoruba lived in a series of kingdoms, sometimes politically united and sometimes not, though they shared a common language and religion. The Igbo in the southwest also shared a common language and culture, but were governed only at the most local level by councils of elders; the group had no kings or chiefs.

The opening of trade with the West starting around 1500 and the subsequent rise of extensive slave raiding profoundly altered these societies, especially in the south. Slave raiding devastated the southern region by taking huge numbers of able-bodied young people, primarily men, and causing numerous wars among kingdoms. After the end of slavery in the nineteenth century, however, southerners responded with alacrity to market opportunities by producing palm oil, peanuts, and cocoa for export.

The British conquest of what became Nigeria began around 1870. European powers, increasingly competing with each other economically and politically, collectively decided to carve up the African continent in their own interests. In 1885 they agreed not to go to war over African territory, but instead to allow whoever gained military control over a territory to keep it: the "scramble for Africa" ensued. The British united Nigeria as one colony in 1914. In northern Nigeria, they created Indirect Rule, the form of rule they would use throughout their African empire. Under Indirect Rule, the British, in theory, left precolonial kingdoms intact to be ruled through their leaders. In northern Nigeria, this meant ruling through the emirs, who in general accepted British oversight as long as they were left to run their internal affairs mostly as they pleased. In the south, kings and chiefs fulfilled this role where they existed, but in areas such as Igboland, there were no chiefs. The British, therefore, invented them, appointing elders to be chiefs.

In all cases, including that of the emirs in the north, British rule gave local rulers more power than they had before. They could call on British military power to enforce their will if necessary. In return, the British required local leaders to implement unpopular policies such as forced labor and the collection of colonial taxes. This put the local leaders in a bind because to maintain local support, they could not implement the policies the British required of them. Some leaders chose to support the British and lost most of their local legitimacy; others tried to resist the British and were ultimately replaced. While Indirect Rule was supposed to preserve "traditional" rulers, they in truth were replaced whenever they refused to cooperate with colonial authority.

As in India, the colonial state required educated Natives to help staff essential services. Christian missionaries provided virtually all of the education for many decades. In the south, particularly among the Igbo, Christianity and Western education expanded rapidly; southerners filled most of the positions in the colonial state. The northern emirs, on the other hand, convinced colonial authorities to keep Christian missionaries out in order to preserve Islam, on which their legitimacy was based. This meant that northerners received far less Western education. The north, already poorer than most of the south, fell behind in educational attainment and subsequent job opportunities. As the colonial state expanded, especially after World War II, more and more southerners moved north to take up positions as clerks for the government, actions that would prove explosive after independence.

Again like India, the educated elite became the leadership of the nationalist movement after World War II. Given the history of divisions in the country, it is no surprise that this movement was split from the start. Northern leaders actually resisted independence for many years, fearing their region would lose out to the more educated southerners who had most of the government jobs. Southerners were split between the Yoruba in the southwest and Igbo in the southeast. The British finally were able to negotiate a new government

for an independent Nigeria that would be federal, with three regions corresponding to the three major ethnic groups. Parties formed mainly along regional and ethnic lines, and the government that took power at independence in 1960 was a coalition of one northern and the main southwestern parties.

As in virtually all African countries, the new government was quite fragile. After fifty years of oppressive, authoritarian colonial rule, the British began introducing the institutions of British-style democracy just a few years before independence. Nigerians had no prior experience with electoral democracy, and little reason to believe it would be a superior system for them. The northern leadership of the new government quickly asserted itself as the dominant partner, weakening the power of the Yoruba leaders from the west. Just two years after independence, this produced violence in the west that the central government used as an excuse to undermine the leading Yoruba party. In 1965 the northern party won the second national election, but the victory was seen as fraudulent. Tensions were also growing in the north, where locals who resented Igbo power and wealth attacked Igbo civil servants and businessmen.

In response to the fraudulent elections and anti-Igbo violence, the army, also led primarily by Igbo, overthrew the elected government in January 1966 in the country's first military coup. The new government ended federalism entirely, creating a unified central government. Northerners saw this as an Igbo power grab. A countercoup six months later brought a new, northern-dominated government to power. This new government reestablished federalism, creating twelve states from the three regions in an attempt to reduce regional and ethnic rivalry. The Igbo military leadership refused to accept this new government, and by January 1967 the Igbo declared their region of the country the independent state of Biafra. Not coincidentally, large-scale oil production had just begun, and the oil wells were in the area claimed as Biafra. Full state collapse ensued, with a three-year civil war that cost the lives of a million people, mostly due to starvation. The central government defeated the separatists in Biafra and reestablished a single state in 1970. After the war, the government pursued a policy of reconciliation that encouraged Igbo (other than the top leadership of the rebel forces) to reintegrate into Nigerian society. This policy was relatively successful, and ethnic tensions eased somewhat.

The quadrupling of oil prices in 1973 gave the government a massive windfall. Nigeria was poised to become much wealthier; many saw it as the emerging leader of Africa and a growing power on the world stage. Ultimately, however, high oil revenues produced more corruption than anything else. Weak state institutions meant little control over the oil money, which major political leaders pocketed or used as patronage for their supporters. The military continued to rule until 1979, repeatedly promising a return to democracy but not delivering. It finally did, producing a new constitution very similar to that of the United States, but with the additon of elaborate rules on how political parties could form, an effort to prevent ethnically based parties from rising again.

A fraudulent election in 1983 under the four-year-old democracy was soon reversed by the military, again under northern leadership. This began a sixteen-year period of military rule under four different leaders. While all pledged to reduce corruption, in reality, each actively participated in it. Oil revenue, even when world prices were relatively low, overwhelmed all other economic activity. The government invested virtually nothing in developing agriculture or industry, using oil money for governmental largesse and personal corruption. Then when oil prices dropped, the government went deeply into debt and required external aid from donors who demanded reforms to reduce corruption. The government claimed to pursue these policies in order to get the aid, but little changed (see chapter 5). A weak state grew ever weaker and more corrupt. The military maintained control, even as the institutions of government became increasingly ineffective and government popularity plummeted.

When a movement for a return to democracy arose throughout Africa in the early 1990s, the Nigerian military government appeared to capitulate by calling for elections in 1993. Yet after the party that the military opposed won, the government annulled the elections and arrested the winning presidential candidate. The military leader did step down but was soon replaced with the most brutal and corrupt leader in Nigeria's history, Gen. Sani Abacha. Abacha ruled from 1993 until his death in 1998, engaging in massive corruption while in power. His death produced a new military government that promised elections and actually carried them out. In 1999 Nigeria had its first truly free and fair election in twenty years. A former military ruler and respected elder statesman, Gen. Olusegun Obasanjo, won the election. He is a Yoruba from the south but had much support from northern military leaders. Obasanjo launched a much publicized drive against corruption, the results of which have been modest. After being reelected in 2003, his handpicked successor, Umaru Yar'Adua, won an election most observers saw as fraudulent in 2007.

Obasanjo also faced growing religious tension in the northern states, many of which have adopted Islamic law as state law; non-Muslims have responded to this with alarm, and violence has occasionally broken out between Muslim and Christian groups (see chapter 4). In the oil-rich areas of the former Biafra, ethnic militias have demanded greater benefits for their people. Despite its natural resources, the area's residents are among the poorest in the country. In the 1990s, when a nonviolent movement arose among the Ogoni people of the oil-producing region, Abacha had its leader, poet Ken Saro-Wiwa, executed. More recently, violent ethnic movements have arisen in the same area; members have blown up pipelines and kidnapped oil workers. The central government has responded with military force. The violence disrupted oil production and helped drive up world prices in 2005 and 2006. The Nigerian state has managed to survive, mostly under military rule, but continues to be extremely weak. The new democratic government is a great improvement over previous regimes but has had limited success so far in solving the deeply entrenched problems the country faces. Ironically, the state's weakness results in part from its oil wealth, which has been a huge incentive for corruption and has weakened the state further.

CONCLUSION

The modern state is a political form that has been singularly successful. Arising nearly five hundred years ago, it has spread to every corner of the globe. In fact, the modern world demands that we all live in states. Strong states can provide the political goods that help improve citizens' lives, though nothing guarantees that they will. In the short term, state strength can also be used to oppress the citizenry. Many political scientists argue that long-term strength, however, must come from legitimacy and the effective provision of political goods.

We asked at the outset why modern states arose. What common characteristics do they have, and how do those characteristics make these states powerful? European history seems to point to the successful combination of military and economic advantage that feudal kings might have used to gain unrivaled control of a territory. Maintaining that control, however, required the establishment of permanent institutions in the form of an army and a bureaucracy and of a source of continuous revenue through direct taxation. This is why Marxists often argue that the modern state is dependent on the success of capitalism and always works to enhance capitalist production to gain revenue. Other analysts, though, argue that sustaining the state takes more than just economic and military might; eventually, it requires some degree of acceptance on the part of the subjects. Legitimacy is crucial to state strength in the long run. One source of this legitimacy is a sense of belonging to a nation that the state represents, a subject we return to in greater depth in chapter 4.

Not all states are equally successful. Why are some weaker than others, and why do some fail completely? The answers are obviously very complex, but the story usually starts with colonialism. The external creation of a state, as opposed to its emergence from political rivals within a particular territory, often meant that it did not have effective internal sovereignty, even after a nationalist movement led it to legal independence. In centuries past, such weak states would have been absorbed by stronger

TIMELINE The Modern State

Modern State Established / State collapse	Historic Events / Empire or colony established
	2000
	1999 Euro established as common European currency
	1997 China regains control of Hong Kong
	1993 European Union established
Russia 1991 Collapse of Soviet Union	1990 Reunification of East and West Germany
	1989 Germany: Fall of Berlin Wall
	1979 Iran: Islamic revolution
Nigeria 1960	
China 1949	
India 1947	1945 Germany: Split of East and West Germany
Iran 1925	
Russia/Soviet Union 1917	1914 Nigeria: United in one British colony
China 1912 Empire collapses	
	1900
Brazil 1889	1885 Berlin Conference: Scramble for Africa begins
Germany 1871	1861–1865 United States: Civil War
Japan 1867	1858 India: Start of formal British colonial rule
	1840–1864 China Opium Wars
Nigeria 1835–1890 Oyo Empire collapses and Yoruba wars	1822 Brazil Independence
	1800 1800s Slave rebellions in the Americas
United States 1787	1789 French Revolution
	1722 Iran: Qajar Empire established
United Kingdom 1707	**1700**
	1648 Peace of Westphalia
	1600 1603 Japan: Tokugawa shogunate established
	1550 Nigeria: Oyo Empire established
	1526 India: Moghul Empire established
	1500 1500s Colonial rule begins in the Americas
	Before 1500 European feudal states

ones, but the current international system makes that virtually unheard of today. These days weak states can survive as recognized entities, often with significant external financial support, even though they may have little real sovereignty and provide little benefit to their populations. The weakest are prone to collapse, as violent opponents can challenge any monopoly on the use of force with relative ease. This scenario has produced many of the most brutal wars of recent years, including those in Somalia, Liberia, Afghanistan, and the Democratic Republic of the Congo.

The successful modern states, though, raise another question we asked at the outset: Does anything limit the power of the modern state? In one sense, modern political institutions do, because they limit the power possessed by any individual ruler. A king can no longer do just exactly as he pleases; the modern state has become an entity separate from the monarch, something more than his personal property. But the power of the modern state is nonetheless a potential threat to liberty, as it can very easily be abused. One result of this potential threat is the biggest political debate of the modern era: What justifies a state's right to rule over its citizens? Can and should the state's power be limited, and if, so how? These are the central questions we take up in the next chapter.

Key Concepts

absolutism (p. 44)

bureaucracy (p. 43)

charismatic legitimacy (p. 42)

clientelism (p. 68)

external sovereignty (p. 39)

failed state (p. 52)

federalism (p. 61)

feudal states (p. 44)

fief (p. 44)

internal sovereignty (p. 40)

legitimacy (p. 42)

Peace of Westphalia (p. 45)

quasi-states (p. 54)

rational-legal legitimacy (p. 42)

sovereign (p. 39)

territory (p. 38)

traditional legitimacy (p. 42)

weak state (p. 49)

Works Cited

Anderson, Perry. 1974. *Lineages of the Absolutist State.* London: New Left Books.

Fund for Peace. www.fundforpeace.org.

Jackson, Robert H. 1990. *Quasi-States: Sovereignty, International Relations, and the Third World.* New York: Cambridge University Press.

Pierson, Christopher. 1996. *The Modern State.* New York: Routledge.

Rotberg, Robert I., ed. 2004. *When States Fail: Causes and Consequences.* Princeton: Princeton University Press.

Weber, Max. 1970. *Politics as Vocation.* In *From Max Weber,* ed. H. H. Gaert and C. W Mills. London: Routledge and Kegan Paul.

Resources for Further Study

International Crisis Group. www.crisisgroup.org.

Jessop, Bob. 1990. *State Theory: Putting Capitalist States in Their Place.* Cambridge, UK: Polity Press.

Levi, Margaret. 2002. "The State of the Study of the State." In *Political Science: State of the Discipline,* ed. I. Katznelson and H. V. Milner, 33–55. New York: Norton.

Poggi, Gianfranco. 1990. *The State: Its Nature, Development, and Prospects.* Cambridge, UK: Polity Press.

Tilly, Charles, ed. 1975. *The Formation of National States in Western Europe.* Princeton: Princeton University Press.

Who Rules?

- How do different ideologies balance the rights and duties of citizens with the ability of the state to compel obedience?

- On what grounds do different ideologies give citizens an opportunity to participate in politics? Who rules where citizens do not seem to have such an opportunity? Can this be justified?

What Explains Political Behavior?

- To what extent does ideology explain how different regimes are organized and justify themselves? What else helps explain how different kinds of regimes actually function?

Where and Why?

- Do our case studies suggest patterns for where different regime types emerge and why?

3

STATES AND CITIZENS

The proper relationship between a state and its people, individually and collectively, is one of the most interesting and debated questions in political science. All successful modern states are able to compel their citizens to obey and to regulate many areas of citizens' individual and collective lives. No modern state can do this, however, without answering questions about the legitimate boundaries of such compulsion and regulation. Each state must decide how far and under what circumstances it can compel individuals and groups to obey, how extensively it can intervene in people's lives, and how and whether some areas of individual and collective life should not be subject to the state's monopoly on violence and ability to force compliance. In practice, decisions about these issues vary greatly, for there are states that claim carefully restricted and circumscribed authority; those that claim virtually unlimited authority to act against their citizens, both individually and collectively; and those that fill virtually every variation between these extremes. Each state, no matter where it falls on this continuum, however, tries to justify the level and extent of compulsion and control it exercises.

In this chapter, we examine various models of the relationship between a state and its people, and how states seek to legitimize these models. Each model is embodied in a regime, which we defined in chapter 1 as a set of fundamental rules and institutions governing political activity. Regimes are more enduring than governments, but less enduring than states. Democratic regimes, for example, may persist through many individual governments. The United States elected its forty-fourth presidential government in 2008, yet its democratic regime has remained intact. Similarly, a modern state may persist though its regime changes from democratic to authoritarian or the other way around. The state—the existence of a bureaucracy, state territory, and so on—is continuous, but its fundamental rules can change.

Each regime is based at least partially on a political ideology that is usually explicitly stated and often quite elaborately developed. Political ideologies, at their core, are about answering the question we posed at the outset: What is the appropriate relationship between the state and its people? Thus, we will focus on some familiar political ideologies and how they have been used to underpin regimes in various countries. As we discuss each ideology, we stress the way it conceives of the appropriate relationship between a state and the people over whom it claims sovereignty. We also examine the ways in which regimes diverge from their ideological justifications. Before we begin discussing any of this, however, it is helpful to understand a little bit more about the historical development of the "people" over whom modern states claim sovereignty, for the basic ideas about how the people stand in relation to the state have changed greatly over time and evolved in tandem with the modern state described in chapter 2.

At the most basic level, a **citizen** is a member of a political community or state. Notice that a citizen is more than an inhabitant within a state's borders. An inhabitant may be a member of a physical community, but a citizen inhabits a political community that places him or her in a relationship with the state. Think of the difference between a resident alien and a citizen: only the latter is a member of the political community or state. In the modern world, everyone needs to be from somewhere. It is almost inconceivable (although it does happen) to be a "man without a country." By this minimal definition, everyone is considered a citizen of some state.

The word "citizen" is also much more complex than this simple definition may lead us to believe, however. Up until about two or three hundred years ago, most Europeans would not have called themselves citizens. They were certainly members of political communities or states, but they would have thought of themselves as "subjects" of their monarchs, not citizens. Most people had little say in their relationship with the state; their side of that relationship consisted primarily of duty and obedience. The very nature of the absolutist state meant that few mechanisms existed to protect them and enable them to claim things as their "right." If the king wanted your land or decided to throw you in jail as a possible conspirator, no court could or would overrule him.

This began to change with the transition to the modern state. As the state was separated from the person of the monarch and its apparatus was modernized, states gained both the ability and the need to make their people more than just subjects. The concept of sovereignty, like the state itself, was divorced from the person of the sovereign, and many European states began to toy with the idea that sovereignty could lie with the people as a whole (or some portion, such as male landowners) rather than with a sovereign monarch. This was an important step in the development of the concept of modern citizenship: citizens, unlike subjects, were inhabitants of states that claimed that sovereignty resided with the people. Thus, after the French Revolution overthrew the absolutist *ancien régime*, people addressed one another as "citizen."

Citizens are legal subjects of a state, but because modern states represent and act on behalf of the people, they are also, in principle, more than just subjects. Over time, as the modern state developed, people began to associate a complex set of rights with the concept of citizenship. In the mid-twentieth century, the philosopher T. H. Marshall (1963) usefully characterized the rights of citizenship into three areas: civil, political, and social. **Civil rights** are designed to guarantee individual freedom and equal, just, and fair treatment by the state. Examples include the right to trial by jury, habeas corpus, and freedom of expression, association, and worship. **Political rights** are those associated with active political participation: the right to vote, run for office, or otherwise participate in political activity. **Social rights** are those related to basic well-being and socioeconomic equality. Examples of these rights include the provision of public education, pensions, or national health care. Marshall believed that modern citizenship included basic legal (civil)

The French overthrew their monarch in a series of violent actions, including this march on Versailles in October 1789. The French Revolution abruptly ended their status as "subjects," leading them to celebrate their new status by greeting one another as "citizen."

status in society and protection by the state as well as the right to actively participate in the political process by which a society chooses its leaders and makes policy. He further argued that full citizenship required enough socioeconomic equality to make the civil and political equality of citizenship meaningful.

Like citizenship, civil society in Europe developed in conjunction with the modern state. We defined civil society in chapter 1 as the sphere of organized, nonviolent activity between the state and the family or firm. Absolutist states would not have conceived of such a realm of society separate from the state itself, for what would this have meant? If a king could dispose of lands and goods, grant monopolies on tax collection, and head the church or at least determine which religion his realm would follow, what could "society" mean apart from that? The rise of religious pluralism and of modern, capitalist economies alongside the modern state meant that there were now areas of social life outside the immediate control of the state, and the gradual evolution of civil and political rights made it possible for individuals to organize themselves into new civil societies for all kinds of purposes, including political action.

Citizens with rights and the emergence of a civil society where they could organize themselves to act politically proved to be mutually reinforcing. As Sidney Tarrow argues in his 1998 book, *Power in Movement*, the ability to share ideas in public spaces such as coffeehouses meant that citizens with minimal rights could organize themselves in groups to demand even more rights. A nascent civil society and some basic civil rights meant that people could organize to demand expanded suffrage, more political rights, and, eventually, labor and other social rights.

This history should not be romanticized or thought of as a linear movement toward "progress" to the goal of modern, democratic citizenship. Even within the countries that most closely fit this cursory description, it was more often a case of one step forward and two steps back, and change was never inevitable or always even good. The same changes that gave us the modern state, however, also gave us the modern concept of the citizen and the modern concept of an independent civil society in which citizens could organize collectively for all sorts of purposes, from religious worship to entrepreneurship to political action.

Today ideas of citizenship and civil society are connected via the concept of "popular sovereignty" to claims to legitimacy by regimes, and the two are closely related. Although it is a distinctly European and liberal democratic notion, the idea of popular sovereignty has deeply influenced all subsequent political ideologies. Since sovereignty was conceptually separated from the person of the monarch, all modern states claim, at least in theory, to be working on behalf of the people, even if they have very different ideas of what this means in practice. Even dictators claim to be working on behalf of the citizenry. They may claim that they must deny certain rights in the short term to benefit society as a whole in the long term (or, in the case of theocracy, that God has willed certain exceptions to citizens' rights), but they still lay some claim to working toward the well-being of the citizens. This is part of the ideological justification of virtually all modern regimes.

Like the concept of the modern state, the concepts of citizenship, civil society, and popular sovereignty spread globally via colonialism and the international dominance of Europe and the United States. They have become, for better or for worse, modern standards to which states must respond. Marshall's norms of citizenship, for example, are recognized in the Universal Declaration of Human Rights of the United Nations, which explicitly recognizes various civil rights, the right to participate in political life, and various social rights such as education. States don't always act in accordance with this declaration and it is not binding, but its very existence suggests that ideologies and states that depart from this model may feel compelled to provide an explanation defending their choices. It may seem that these are very European standards against which to measure global behavior, but just as the modern European state became a standard other states needed to respond to in order to be competitive within the international system, modern citizenship and the toleration of civil society have become hallmarks of legitimacy to which regimes and ideologies that question those standards must respond.

In reality, regimes vary enormously in their relationships to both citizen rights and civil society. Virtually no country fully provides all three types of rights described by Marshall, and authoritarian regimes deny that some rights, such as political participation, are even important. Similarly, the manifestation of civil society varies from flourishing, lively groups of independently organized citizens to highly controlled or actively repressed. In short, modern citizens and civil society are much like the modern state: modern in the sense of being an ideal, but not in the sense of being universally implemented in contemporary societies. This means that we can compare regimes and ideologies on the basis of their attitudes toward their individual and collective citizenry. Which rights do they privilege, and which do they ignore? How much room do they allow for collective organization, and under what conditions? How do they attempt to restrict, channel, or repress collective organization, and how do they seek to justify these decisions?

Thus, while everyone is a citizen by the minimal definition, understanding the history and connotations of the term alerts us to look for the combination of citizen rights that different regimes actually provide. All states claim to provide some rights, but the exact details of the relationship between a state and its citizens—the rights and duties of each—vary significantly from one kind of regime to another, across different countries, and at different times. By looking at a regime's political ideology, we can learn how it attempts to justify and legitimize its particular relationship with its citizens.

REGIMES, IDEOLOGIES, AND CITIZENS

Not all political ideologies have been embodied in regimes, but every regime has some sort of ideology that attempts to justify its existence in the eyes of its citizens and the world. Regimes are much more than just the legal and institutional embodiments of their ideologies, however. All regimes have formal rules and institutions that reflect, at least to some extent, their ideological claims to legitimacy, but they also may have informal rules and institutions that conflict with those ideological claims. As we noted in chapter 2, weak states are characterized by relatively weak formal institutions. In such states, knowledge of informal rules and institutions may be more important to understanding how a regime actually functions and how power is mobilized than is knowledge of the formal institutions embodied in a constitution. The major regime types we delineate below include examples of those in which the official ideology and related formal institutions represent the most important elements of a regime. Other examples we have chosen exemplify situations in which informal institutions are more important to how a state actually functions, even though some sort of ideological claim to legitimacy exists and justifies the formal institutions of a regime.

What this all means is that we do not intend to say that a regime that claims to rule on the basis of a particular ideological blueprint actually does so. Informal institutions may be more important than official ones; rulers may not actually believe the ideology they proclaim; or the realities of being in power, of trying to govern a complex society, may necessitate ideological modifications. Ideologies are important nonetheless. The major political ideologies have defined the terms of the most important political debates of the past century. (For a description of the major ideologies, see the following text box.) Most regimes have come to power in the name of one or another of the ideologies outlined below, and many have made serious efforts to rule along the lines prescribed by them.

Major Political Ideologies and Regimes

Liberal Democracy

- Individuals are free and autonomous with natural rights.
- Social contract theory: legitimate governments form when free and independent individuals join in a contract to permit representatives to govern over them.
- Government must preserve the core liberties—life, liberty, and property—possessed by all free individuals.
- Representative democracy: direct citizen control, with leaders who can be removed.
- Legislature essential.
- Separation of powers, federalism, and social citizenship supplement, but are not essential, to legitimate government.

Communism

- Based on Marxism.
- Historical materialism: material (economic) forces are the prime movers of history and politics.
- Ruling class oppresses other classes, based on mode of production: bourgeoisie rules in capitalist society.
- Liberal democracy is political and ideological shell that allows capitalism to function and serves the interests of the bourgeoisie.
- Social revolution is transition from one mode of production to another at time of economic and political crisis.
- Proletariat will lead socialist revolution.
- Socialist society after revolution will be ruled as dictatorship of the proletariat over other classes; will eventually create classless communist society in which class oppression ends.
- Lenin: vanguard party can lead socialist revolution in interests of present and future proletariat.
- Vanguard party rules socialist society using democratic centralism; justified in oppressing classes that oppose it.

Fascism

- Rejects materialism and rationality; "spiritual attitude."
- Organic conception of society: society akin to living organism, rather than a set of disparate groups and individuals.
- The state as head of the corporate body: all-embracing, and outside of it no human or spiritual values can exist.
- "Accepts the individual only in so far as his interests coincide with those of the State."
- The state creates the nation, a "higher personality"; intensely nationalistic.

- Supreme leader rules the state.
- Corporatism: state recognizes one entity to lead each group in society (for example, official trade union).

Modernizing Authoritarianism

- Not based on a single, consciously elaborated ideology but rather on an appeal to a common set of precepts.
- Claim to legitimacy: government will modernize or "develop" the country.
- Modernization theory: postcolonial societies must go through same process to develop as the West did.
- Modern elite: relatively few highly educated people should have power.
- Technocratic legitimacy: claim to rule based on knowledge.
- Development requires national unity.
- Three institutional forms: one-party regimes, military regimes, and personalist regimes.
- Neopatrimonial regimes: common subtype:
  - Combine trappings of modern, bureaucratic states with underlying informal institutions.
  - Constitutions, laws, courts, and bureaucracies exist, but really work on basis of personal favors and patronage.
  - Patron-client relations central: rulers maintain power by distributing patronage; this is more important than formal powers.
  - Politics is competition among patrons for access to state's resources.
  - Can be military, one-party, or personalist.

Theocracy

- Rule by divine inspiration or divine right.
- God is sovereign, not people.
- Islamist version:
  - Islamism: Islamic law, as revealed by God to the Prophet Mohammed, can and should provide basis for government in Muslim communities.
  - *Ijtihad:* belief that Muslims should read and interpret the original Islamic texts for themselves, not simply follow traditional religious leaders and beliefs.
  - *Sharia:* Muslim law should be law of society for all Muslims.

Even where leaders do not seem to believe in a proclaimed ideology, some sort of ideology remains important for their claim to legitimacy. All of the major political ideologies address the key question of the proper relationship between the state and its citizens. While liberal democracy is certainly not universally accepted, it has become powerful enough that all regimes, implicitly or explicitly, must respond to its claims. Authoritarian regimes always at least partially justify themselves by criticizing liberal democracy and showing why their ideology and regime are superior at ruling in the interests of the people. Since liberal democracy is central to the ideological debates of the past two centuries, we will turn to it first.

Liberal Democracy

"Democracy" means different things to different people. For average citizens, it may well be very difficult to define clearly, but they know it when they see it. As we noted in chapter 1, we will follow the main convention in comparative politics and use a minimal definition of the term, typically referred to as "liberal democracy." The two parts of the phrase are stated together so frequently that in many people's minds they have become one, but the distinction between the two is important to understanding both the development of liberal democracy and current debates over its expansion around the world, which we discuss in subsequent chapters.

Classical liberalism, the predecessor of liberal democracy, arose in the sixteenth and seventeenth centuries amidst the religious wars in England and the later revolution in France. The key liberal thinkers of the period created a model of political philosophy known as **social contract theory**. Although there are many variations, all social contract theories begin from the premise that legitimate governments are formed when free and independent individuals join in a contract to permit representatives to govern over them in their common interests. The originators of this idea, Thomas Hobbes and John Locke in England and the Baron de Montesquieu and Jean-Jacques Rousseau in France, started from a new and innovative assumption: all citizens should be considered free and equal. They posited an original "state of nature" in which all men (and they meant men—women weren't included until much later) lived freely and equally with no one ruling over them. They argued that the only government that could be justified was one that men living in such a state of nature would freely choose.

These philosophers did have somewhat different visions of what this state of nature looked like and therefore different reasons for why men would choose to create a government to rule over them, but beginning with Locke, they ultimately came to the same basic conclusion about what such a freely chosen government would look like. Locke argued that in the state of nature government would only arise if it helped preserve the core liberties of all free men: life, liberty, and property (a phrase Thomas Jefferson later adopted and modified into "life, liberty and the pursuit of happiness" in the Declaration of Independence). This became the central doctrine of liberalism: a regime is only justified if it preserves and protects the core liberties of autonomous, free, and equal individuals. A state can only infringe on these liberties in very particular circumstances, such as when an action is essential for the well-being of all or when a particular citizen has denied others their rights. Preservation of rights is essential and severely limits what governments can do.

Civil Rights and Representative Democracy.

Civil Rights and Representative Democracy. This focus by classical liberals on the preservation of rights justifies limited government to enhance what are seen as individual freedoms, but it says nothing about how a government will come to power or make decisions. It was argued that men in a state of nature would desire a government over which they had some direct control, with leaders they could remove from office if they wished as protection against a state overstepping its bounds and trying to destroy basic liberties. The idea of representative democracy was thus born and justified. By voting, citizens would choose the government. Those chosen would be in office for a limited period, with some mechanism for removal if necessary.

With elected representatives, some type of legislature would be essential and central to government. This would be a body in which elected officials would debate and decide the important issues of the day. While kings and courts had long existed in Europe as the executive and judicial branches, liberals argued that the most important branch ought to be the legislative, the body of elected representatives of free and equal citizens. Montesquieu added the idea of separating the main powers of government into distinct institutions to divide and thereby further limit power. This doctrine, adopted in the United States but not in the United Kingdom, is not essential to liberal democracy, but is rather an extension of the liberal ideal of limited government.

Who Could Vote and Why.

Who Could Vote and Why. Most classical liberals, for all of their forward thinking about equality and limited government, still conceived of the citizens to which these concepts applied as male property owners. An important nineteenth-century exception was the English philosopher John Stuart Mill, who made one of the earliest philosophical arguments in favor of women's political rights in his 1870 book *The Subjection of Women*, which he most likely cowrote with his wife. Most liberals, however, argued that while everyone had some basic civil rights, only men who owned property were adequately mature, rational, and independent of the whims of others to be given the right to vote and participate in governing. Restricting full citizenship to this group also meant all citizens could be considered equal. Different men held different amounts of property and had different abilities, of course, so they certainly were not truly equal in reality, but compared to the rest of society they were roughly similar.

It was not long before groups not initially granted full citizenship, such as men without property, women, and racial minorities, began asking why they weren't considered as free and equal as anybody else. This question produced the largest political struggles of the nineteenth and twentieth centuries in Europe and the United States, struggles to fully democratize liberalism. As citizenship slowly expanded to include more and more groups, real inequality among citizens increasingly began to conflict with the proposition that "all men (and later, all people) are created equal." Reformers started to demand that citizens gain what Marshall called social citizenship: decent living standards so that they could be respected in their communities and fully participate in the rights of citizenship as moral equals.

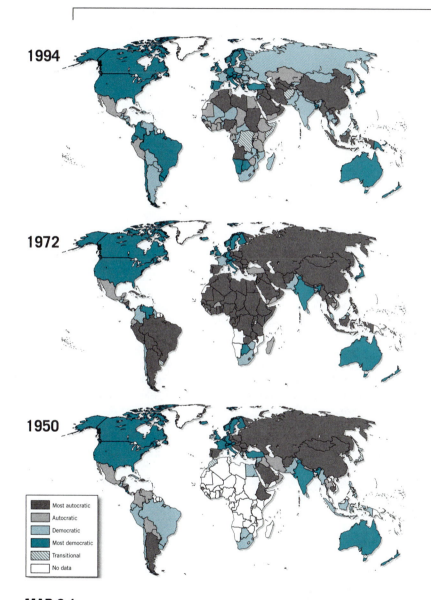

MAP 3.1
Spread of Democracy around the World by Era

Source: John O'Loughlin et al., "The Diffusion of Democracy, 1946–1994," *Annals of the Association of American Geographers* 88, no. 4: 556. Reproduced with the permission of Blackwell Publishing.

The Birth of Modern Liberal Democracy. Social democratic parties emerged in Europe in part because of the argument that all individuals had the right to be treated with respect by the state and the right to take part in the creation of the regime. These parties had originated in Marxist movements, but by the early twentieth century, members had come to accept the basic precepts of liberal democracy: individual rights should be protected and political change should come via elections. Proponents argued, however, that the state had to intervene in the economy to provide effective citizenship to all of the population, not just to those with more resources. Social democratic ideology, while not creating a separate regime, became an important variant in the internal debates of liberal democracy. (See What is Democracy? box below.)

Modern liberal democratic regimes arose from this history. Leaders in these regimes justify their actions by claiming to preserve and protect core civil and

What Is Democracy?

"Democracy" is one of those words that many people find hard to define, but they know it when they see it. It literally means rule by the demos, or the people, but that doesn't tell us very much. In this book, we use the definition used by most comparativists, often called the minimal definition. This is essentially what political scientist Robert Dahl called "polyarchy," a system of government that provides eight key guarantees: freedom of association, freedom of expression, the right to vote, broad citizen eligibility for public office, the right of political leaders to compete for support, alternative sources of information, free and fair elections, and institutions that make government policies depend on votes and other forms of citizen preferences. A system of this nature is generally referred to as **liberal democracy**.

Liberal democracy is certainly not the only form of democracy that democratic theorists have imagined or advocated. Perhaps the best known alternative is **social democracy**, which combines liberal democracy with much greater provision of social rights of citizenship and typically greater public control of the economy. Advocates argue that citizen control over the political sphere implies that this control should be extended to the economic sphere as well. They favor public ownership or at least extensive regulation of key sectors of the economy to enhance equal citizenship and the well-being of all. They believe in maintaining a market economy, but one regulated in the interests of the greater good of the citizens as a whole. Advocates also believe that Marshall's third category, social rights, is very important to achieving full democracy, so social programs must be generously funded in an attempt to achieve greater economic equality among citizens.

Participatory democracy is also a long-standing expansion of liberal democracy. Proponents argue that real democracy must include far more than the minimal list of institutional guarantees associated with Dahl's polyarchy. Real democracy requires direct citizen participation in the decisions that affect their lives, and so advocates support decentralizing decisions to local communities to the greatest extent possible to involve citizens directly in decision making. Many also support the democratization of the workplace, advocating for worker participation in the key decisions of the companies for which they work. Like social democrats, supporters of participatory democracy believe real democracy requires citizen control over economic as well as political activity, but they want to see it directly in the hands of citizens and workers at the local level.

With the spread of democracy around the world in the last thirty years (see chapter 9), an additional kind of democracy has emerged. Many countries, especially in Africa, have instituted elections that have allowed multiple candidates and parties to compete for power in what had been authoritarian regimes; however, these states have not fully implemented the institutional guarantees listed above for liberal democracy. They hold elections and allow opposition to exist and win some legislative seats, but the ruling parties limit various rights to ensure their ultimate survival in office. Analysts refer to this type of regime as **electoral democracy**: opposition and elections are present, but not the fully protected rights of liberal democracy. Those who use the term do not advocate for it as a good form of government; rather, they use it to distinguish what they see as partial democracies from fully institutionalized liberal democracies.

political liberties: freedom from government intervention in private lives except under clearly defined and limited circumstances, freedom of religious practice, freedom of expression, freedom of association, and the rights to vote and hold office. The citizens in a liberal democracy use these freedoms to create civil society, though civil society's strength, organization, and daily relationship with the state vary from country to country (we discuss this in detail in chapter 7). All liberal democracies are characterized by some system of elections by which voters, now defined almost universally as all adult citizens, choose key members of the government, who serve limited terms and may be removed. Some liberal democracies include other safeguards, such as separation of powers. Some include the provision of extensive government services to attempt to achieve something closer to equal social citizenship. These are variations on the core principles.

CASE STUDY United Kingdom: "Cradle of Democracy"

Many of the most important developments in the history of liberal democracy occurred in the United Kingdom, or England before it became the UK. The core ideas of limiting a sovereign's power and creating what was called a parliament (from the French word *parler,* meaning to talk) arose long before they were codified in the philosophy of Locke and others. The earliest document of importance to this principle was the Magna Carta, signed by King John in 1215. Feudal lords forced the king to sign the document, which restricted his ability to abuse various laws. It included the first implementation of the idea of trial by peers, guaranteed the freedom of the (Catholic) church from monarchical intervention, created an assembly of twenty-five barons chosen by all the barons to ensure enforcement of the document, and guaranteed nobles the right to be called together to discuss any significant new taxes. Ultimately, all of these rights and guarantees were strictly to preserve the dominance of the nobility.

For four centuries, the Magna Carta restricted the powers of the monarchy, but the sovereigns' powers remained strong. King Henry VIII's break with the Catholic Church would ultimately lead the English into a civil war in the 1640s that resulted in the beheading of King Charles I. Carried out in the name of gaining control over the monarchy, the war ended in a dictatorship under Oliver Cromwell that was subsequently overthrown prior to restoration of the monarchy; Locke developed

his ideas largely in reaction to the deep religious divisions and violence of the civil war. The Glorious Revolution of 1688 saw Parliament's bloodless removal of King James II from the throne and the installation of a new monarch. The following year the legislative body passed a Bill of Rights that substantially expanded the rights of citizenship, and from that point forward,

Since the establishment of the Magna Carta, the monarch's relationship to the British parliament has evolved to become one that is largely ceremonial, but debate remains a key function, as the derivation of "parliament" suggests. In 2005 both houses of Parliament went into a highly unusual all-night session to debate the Blair government's controversial antiterrorism law.

Parliament gained increasing power vis-à-vis the monarchy. This became especially true after the American Revolution, when King George III became increasingly incapacitated and the power of the prime minister—an individual appointed by the king but who worked closely with Parliament—grew significantly.

The growing power of the elected Parliament was significant, but political citizenship was still restricted primarily to men with substantial property holdings, which was less than 5 percent of the population. The nineteenth century saw significant changes to this system, starting with the Reform Act of 1832, which expanded the vote to the growing middle class. Still, the electorate remained all male and grew only to about 7 percent of the population. Political citizenship later was expanded to most adult males through the Representation of the People Act of 1867 and the Franchise Act of 1884. A movement for women's suffrage emerged by the mid-nineteenth century, but it wasn't until 1918 that all men and women thirty years of age and older were given the right to vote, with the age dropping to twenty-one in 1928. None of this expansion of political citizenship occurred easily. Large-scale pressure from civil society, first from the growing middle class in the early nineteenth century, then from the growing working class in the industrializing cities in the latter part of the century, and finally from women, was necessary to achieve each reform.

The British model of liberal democracy is unusual, in part because of its history. At no point did the equivalent of the American or French Revolution occur that caused a definitive break from monarchy and establishment of democracy. The development of the liberal democratic regime in Britain was much more gradual. It is often portrayed as nonviolent as well, which is true only if you ignore the widespread and prolonged violence that occurred from the Norman Conquest in 1066 through the Glorious Revolution. Britain did see the worst of its political violence in the premodern era; after the Glorious Revolution in 1688, the expansion of the power of Parliament and voting rights was gradual and mostly peaceful, though always politically contentious.

The result of this history is a liberal democracy based on the concept of **parliamentary sovereignty**: Parliament is supreme in all matters. Members can write any law they choose via majority vote. Britain lacks a written constitution like that of the United States, and while basic liberal rights have long been established in law, Parliament can easily change that. Rights are preserved only by a collective consensus that Parliament should not reverse them. This is a great example of a powerful but *informal* political institution, a set of implicit rules and norms that are not violated even though in theory they could be. Political culture theorists would explain this institution by pointing to British cultural values; institutionalists might suggest that the institution, established primarily in the Bill of Rights of 1689, has served citizens' interests well and therefore is preserved. In any case, the system has continued to operate without fundamental change for more than three centuries.

This is not to say that Britain's liberal democracy has not faced all of the challenges of other liberal democracies over the past half century. Like most of Europe, Britain created a fairly extensive welfare state after World War II in an effort toward greater social citizenship. Although less extensive than many others found in Europe, Britain's welfare state is significantly more extensive than its counterpart in the United States, even after significant reductions were made to it in the 1980s during the government of Prime Minister Margaret Thatcher. These reductions were in line with the economic policies dominant at the time and coincided with a decline in the strength and power of labor unions, which earlier in the century had been perhaps the most important single element in British civil society. In addition, Britain has seen significant immigration from its former colonies since the end of its colonial empire in Africa and Asia. This immigration has created a more racially diverse society and caused growing racial and religious tensions that raise questions about the ability of a liberal democracy to politically integrate people of diverse backgrounds and cultures in one society, a subject we explore further in the next chapter.

Communism

The first and most influential ideological alternative to liberal democracy was communism, which became the basis for regimes in Russia, China, and a number of other countries. Communism arose from the philosophy of Karl Marx, whose primary works were written between the 1840s and 1880s. Marx, a German forced into exile first to France and ultimately to England, created a philosophy based on what he called **historical materialism**, the assumption that material (economic) forces are the prime movers of history and politics. He believed that understanding politics requires first understanding the economic structure of a society and the economic interests that arise from it. As the material forces in the society—technology, raw materials, and the way they are combined to make goods—change, so too will the political system and political ideologies. Feudalism produced all-powerful lords and kings, with religious sanction from the church as the chief ideological justification, to keep the peasants in their place producing a surplus for the lords. According to Marx, when the production process changes, the political, social, and ideological systems must also change to allow the productive forces to work to their fullest. Thus the shift to capitalism produced liberalism, in which political power was no longer vested in the landed aristocracy but was instead given to all men of property. This allowed the rising bourgeoisie to gain political power. Capitalism requires labor that can move from place to place, what is known as **free wage labor** (see chapter 5 for more on capitalism), so serfdom ultimately was abolished, and many peasants were forced off their land to work for a daily wage in cities.

Liberal democracy, according to Marx, is the political and ideological shell that allows capitalism to work and serve the interests of the bourgeoisie, capitalism's ruling class. As was true for the UK and many countries when Marx was developing his ideas, only men of property had full political rights. Even where those rights expanded to others, as in the United States by the 1830s, Marx argued this was only a charade. He called liberal rights "equal rights for unequal people," arguing that where workers did have the vote and rights of expression it was virtually meaningless because those with wealth were the only ones with any real power. Civil society, he argued, was a realm dominated by capitalists as well, a sphere created to give capitalists independence from the state and a means by which they could control the state.

Marx saw the transition from one **mode of production** to another, such as from feudalism to capitalism, as a process of **social revolution**. He argued that all such modes ultimately produce contradictions they cannot overcome, leading to revolution. Capitalism, he believed, would be characterized by an ever greater division between the bourgeoisie and the proletariat (wage laborers). As more and more wealth and power accrued in the hands of capitalists, the proletariat would become so poor that individuals would not be able to consume all of capitalism's products, creating an economic crisis that would usher in a new era of social revolution. Just as the liberal revolutions had been led by the bourgeoisie and had established liberal democracy, the next revolutions would be communist revolutions led by the proletariat—what he called the "specter haunting Europe" in his *The Communist Manifesto* of 1848. This was inevitable, and it was the job of the communist movement to recognize when and where social revolutions were emerging and bring them to fruition to create a new and better society and political system.

The communist society that Marx believed would emerge from these revolutions would abolish class distinctions and collectively own the means of production. All people (or at least men—Marx was no more feminist than most other nineteenth-century philosophers) would be paid the same amount for the same work, and everyone would have to work. This he saw as the first stage of communism, which he also called socialism. He referred to the government of this system as the **dictatorship of the proletariat**, an absolute rule by workers as a class over all other classes. This dictatorship was not of one man, but of the entire class, that would control and ultimately eliminate all other classes. Civil society distinct from this workers' state would no longer be needed. This was justified in Marx's view because all governments, including all liberal democracies, have been class dictatorships: liberal democracies are simply dictatorships of the bourgeoisie. As this socialist society developed everyone eventually would become equal in the sense of all being part of the proletariat. At that point, the second, higher stage of communism would develop in which no state would be necessary because no class divisions existed, and all dictatorships would end.

Marx did not write in detail about what this communist society and its government would look like, in part because he did not believe in prescription and speculation about the future. Philosophically, he believed that communism was both inevitable and the final stage of human historical evolution. Just as political systems and ideologies are the product of economic forces, Marx believed human nature was as well. With class division and exploitation eliminated, he believed that human nature itself would change from being self-interested and greedy under capitalism to being what he viewed as more fully human under communism. This would facilitate the creation of his ultimate and, he believed, inevitable goal of a communist utopia.

CASE STUDY Russia

Marx was an active revolutionary for most of his life, but he did not live to see a communist revolution succeed. Based on his analysis of capitalism, he believed the revolution would start in the wealthiest and most advanced capitalist societies, such as the UK, Germany, or France. Russia at the turn of the twentieth century was nothing like these powers. It was what would later be called a third-world country, still primarily rural, with growing multinational investment controlled by foreigners and an unstable and oppressive political system. The liberal, bourgeois revolution, let alone the socialist one, had yet to happen there. In fact, late in his life Marx wrote to Russian revolutionaries, counseling patience and telling them to wait for the revolutions in the wealthier parts of Europe before pursuing their own socialist dreams.

Vladimir Lenin never met Marx; he did, however, read and admire his writings, and by the late nineteenth century, shortly after Marx's death, Lenin had become a committed communist revolutionary. As Russia writhed in the throes of World War I, a disastrous and unpopular war in Russia, Lenin would lead his **Bolshevik** forces to victory in the October Revolution of 1917 and create the first self-proclaimed Communist regime. Lenin knew that according to Marx, Russia was not ripe for revolution, so to legitimize his regime, Lenin modified Marx's political theories. He argued that where capitalism had not developed sufficiently to produce the economic crisis and socialist revolution, a committed band of revolutionaries, a **vanguard party**, could still lead a revolution. This party would take power and wield it on behalf of the proletariat until such time as the country was fully industrialized and therefore fully proletarian. Socialism, the first stage of communism, would last longer than Marx had envisioned, but the revolution could occur sooner. Lenin also believed that once the revolution succeeded in Russia, the proletariat of the wealthier European countries would see the possibility of a proletarian regime and rise up to create their own; he fully expected the communist revolution to spread quickly across Europe to create a set of socialist regimes that would build communism together.

Once in power, and seeing that the revolution was not going to spread rapidly across Europe, Lenin had to figure out how the Soviet Union would survive as the lone socialist state. The regime he created was led by his Communist Party, which claimed to act on behalf of the present and future proletariat. The dictatorship of the proletariat would, for the time being, be the dictatorship of a single party, which was justified in ruthlessly suppressing those who opposed it if they represented other class interests, especially the nobility and bourgeoisie of pre-revolutionary Russia. The party thus became the sole representative of the people, with the regime it created based on Lenin's idea of **democratic centralism** as the key organizing principle. This was an organization of state power in which lower organs of the party and state would vote on issues and individuals to represent them at higher levels, ultimately reaching the top level, which would make final, binding decisions. Once these decisions were made, all lower levels were

Marx thought Russia was not ready for communism, but Vladimir Lenin, above, led a revolution there. He modified Marxist doctrine to adapt it to Russian circumstances and suggested that a vanguard party of committed revolutionaries could lead a precapitalist, agrarian nation into communism.

expected to follow orders without question. In practice, those at the top controlled virtually all power, allowing only ideas and people they already had approved to rise through the hierarchy.

The regime consisted of a set of **soviets**, or legislative bodies, that made decisions at all levels. After gaining full control of the pre-revolutionary Russian empire and some additional territories, the new regime and state was named the Union of Soviet Socialist Republics (USSR). Officially, the soviet was the decision-making body at each level of the regime, from the village to the province to the national state, but in reality each was tightly controlled by the Communist Party, which was the only legal party to which any politically active person or official had to belong. At the top of the entire system was the **politburo**, the party's chief decision-making organ. This small, mostly male group collectively and secretly selected each new general secretary of the party. The country's most powerful rulers, most general secretaries served in that position until their death.

Lenin came to recognize by 1921 that while central state control of the government had merit, similar control of the economy was hurting production, especially in agriculture, the largest sector of the economy.

In response, he created the New Economic Policy, under which state control of the economy was partially loosened, but he died at a relatively young age only three years later, before seeing this policy and others come to fruition. Most never would. After a five-year succession struggle, Josef Stalin eventually came to power in 1929, and he radically changed Soviet socialism. Stalin launched a plan to rapidly institute state control of the economy, taking ownership of virtually all land and extracting huge surpluses from agriculture to build industry. The result was the beginning of a rapid industrialization that transformed the Soviet Union from a poor agricultural country to an industrial powerhouse and superpower by World War II. Those who opposed Stalin or his policies were quickly suppressed: estimates of deaths under his rapid industrialization and political reign range from two to ten million. He held complete control and created a **totalitarian regime** that controlled virtually all aspects of society and eliminated all vestiges of civil society.

After Stalin's death in 1953, his successors, Nikita Khrushchev (1956–1964) and Leonid Brezhnev (1964–1982) restored broader party control of the state, reduced aspects of the reign of terror and created what became an oppressive but predictable communist system. Political scientists of the time debated extensively over how centralized or pluralist this regime was, and while it certainly was not pluralist in the democratic sense of the term, many observers argued that factions jockeyed for power and influence behind the scenes. It was clearly less totalitarian than it had been under Stalin.

With Brezhnev's death, a new generation of leadership emerged in the person of Mikhail Gorbachev (1985–1991). Stalin's policies had rapidly industrialized the economy, but the inefficiencies of central state control had grown over time, and the wealth and productivity of the Soviet Union declined compared to that of Western countries. To try to increase economic productivity and allow a modicum of open political debate, Gorbachev launched new economic and political policies, called **perestroika** and **glasnost**, respectively. The implementation of these policies would initiate a cycle of events over which Gorbachev would eventually lose control. When the military attempted a coup d'etat in August

1991 to try to restore some of the old order and failed, the Soviet Union itself began to crumble. In December 1991 it officially came to an end, and fifteen separate states, including Russia, emerged once the dust settled. This began the difficult process of transition to democracy in Russia that we explore further in chapter 9.

For nearly a century, Russia's Communist regime, based on the principles of Marx as modified by Lenin, claimed to be working on behalf of the proletariat. Regime members argued, however, that only highly trained and educated communists could use Marxist analysis to fully see to the proletariat's interests. This claim to legitimacy justified repression of all public dissent; any opposition was automatically liable to be called out as a class-based attempt to reverse the inevitable and morally justifiable movement toward true communism. The regime thus defined citizenship as restricted to those who accepted the party's wisdom and rule; those who opposed it were traitors to the class that rightfully should rule.

Civil society under Communist Party rule was completely eliminated and the state, led by the party, controlled virtually all aspects of individuals' lives, including where they worked, the clubs and organizations they could belong to, and the prices they paid at the cash register. The initial revolution had been extremely popular, seen by many as freeing the country from the yoke of tsarist rule and promising a movement into the "modern" and wealthy world. Centralized control, at least from Stalin on, destroyed this legitimacy. The regime nonetheless worked hard to justify itself in terms of its official ideology, educating its citizens from a young age to believe in and work within the Communist system.

The Russian Communist Party set the basic model of communist rule that was copied, with some modifications, in China and elsewhere after World War II. Only China, Cuba, Vietnam, and North Korea still maintain a claim to communism, and only Cuba and North Korea still maintain the centralized economic system that was at the heart of the effort. China and Vietnam, as we will see later in the book, have essentially allowed capitalism to emerge and, while still claiming to be communist, are in fact modernizing authoritarian regimes.

Fascism

Fascism was the other major European alternative to liberal democracy in the early to mid-twentieth century. It was also a very self-consciously anticommunist ideology and set of regimes. Fascist ideology espouses a conception of society akin to a living organism, rather than a set of disparate groups and individuals. The state is central to and dominant within this organic society; it regulates and assures the smooth functioning of the organism, much as the brain does for the body. Italian fascist leader Benito Mussolini, in *Fascism: Doctrine and Institutions* (1968, reprint) argued that "the State is all-embracing; outside of it no human or spiritual values can exist … [T]he Fascist State … interprets, develops, and potentiates the whole life of a people." He goes on to say that the state creates the nation, which is itself a "higher personality." Fascists are thus intensely nationalistic, but conceive of the nation as created by and loyal to the state first and foremost. Unlike liberals, who emphasize individual freedom, fascists perceive that the individual is and should be subsumed within the nation and the state; Mussolini said the fascist "accepts the individual only in so far as his interests coincide with those of the State, which stands for the conscience and the universal will of man as a historic entity." Thus the interests of the state are justifiably dominant over both individual citizens and civil society. This state, in turn, is led by one man who becomes the supreme leader and head of the state, which itself is both the head and the spirit of the nation.

Fascists also reject Marxists' emphasis on materialism and economic life. Instead, Mussolini calls fascism "[a] spiritual attitude," describing a fascist life as "serious, austere, religious." Fascists reject much of the rationality that is the basis of all types of Western philosophy, appealing instead to spiritual principles and traditions of a nation as a living organism. Fascist doctrine sees life as a struggle and proclaims a life of action. It views each nation as a unique and historical force that must work to maximize its power and position in the world, and it accepts war as a part of this struggle for the glorification of the state, the nation, and the leader.

Fascists generally glorify the nation, but do not explicitly proclaim one nation as inherently superior to all others. They also do not define the nation as being of one racial or cultural group, though they do appeal to national cultural traditions. Since the nation is created by the state, however, it follows that those loyal to the state can become part of that nation, at least in theory, regardless of their background. Germany's National Socialists (Nazis) modified the tenets of fascism by adding explicit racism. Following their leader Adolf Hitler, they married fascism and racism, claiming that not only was the state the embodiment of the nation, but the German nation, defined in racial terms as "Aryan," was superior to all others and deserved to rule over them.

Fascists shared the modern conception of citizenship in the sense of a direct relationship between citizens and a state. Like communists, however, they defined citizens not as everyone legally in the state's territory but much more narrowly. First and foremost, only those loyal to the state and nation could be citizens. Second, for Nazis only those of Aryan racial bloodlines could be citizens. Even these citizens, however, did not have rights in the liberal sense of the word. Since they had no existence outside the state, the concept of individual rights pre-existing or separate from the state was nonsensical. Citizens were left with only duties, which they fulfilled as part of achieving a more complete life. Fascists, like communists, thus justified the complete elimination of civil society, but in contrast to the communists, Mussolini openly admitted the fascist state was and should be totalitarian.

CASE STUDY Nazi Germany

Germany's economy was in dire straits in the 1920s, due in part to its defeat in World War I and the subsequent peace treaty that forced it to pay massive war reparations. The global Great Depression that started in 1929 simply made things worse. Blaming the mainstream parties in power for their increasingly difficult lives, German voters began shifting their allegiance to the "radical" parties: the communists and National Socialists, or Nazis. By the 1932 election, the Nazis had won 37 percent of the vote, the largest percentage of any party. What this means is that Adolf Hitler did not grab power via a violent revolution or military coup: he was elected. He had become leader of the Nazi Party in 1920, and his party had competed with others in the very unstable democracy of the Weimar Republic, the regime in Germany from the end of World War I to Hitler's rise to absolute power in 1933.

Following the norms of Weimar's parliamentary democracy (see chapter 6 for an explanation of parliamentary democracy), Hitler became chancellor (the German equivalent of a prime minister) and as such Germany's key leader of the government. Because his party did not have a majority of seats in the Reichstag, the German legislature, he had to invite members of other parties to join his government to form a coalition. Members of the Nationalist Party, the chief mainstream conservative party, sympathized with enough of Hitler's goals to support their party becoming his partner in government. The party's leaders believed that, despite Hitler's antidemocratic rhetoric and writings, they could use their influence in the government to keep him in check. They were wrong.

The Nazis, while willing to operate within electoral channels temporarily, had no respect for democracy in the long run. Shortly after Hitler became chancellor in early 1933, the Reichstag burned to the ground. Hitler arrested a Communist activist and launched an anti-Communist campaign, claiming that a communist revolution threatened the nation. In reality, it is almost certain that the Nazis themselves burned the Reichstag to initiate their grab of total power. Hitler used the "emergency" to temporarily ban personal liberties, allowing him to arrest Communist members of the Reichstag as well as other opponents. Within months, he had convinced his coalition partners to pass the Enabling Act. ("Convinced" being a nice way of saying coerced, given that the act was passed while the Nazi Party militia surrounded and entered the Reichstag, intimidating many legislators who had seen what had happened to their Communist colleagues.) This piece of legislation effectively eliminated the Reichstag's legislative powers, and a dictatorship was born. Hitler and his party used this new law to immediately ban all opposition political parties and all trade unions. Their offices and assets were seized, and any leaders who resisted were imprisoned and many killed.

The Nazi Party set out to create the totalitarian state that fascist doctrine calls for. The party completely eliminated autonomous civil society and replaced it with organizations under its control. Fascist belief in society as an organic whole leads to the argument that society should not have competing organizations potentially working against each other; instead, just one organization should represent the interests of each

Fascists believed the state was preeminent over society, so just one state-sanctioned organization should represent and speak for each group, whether workers, business, or youth. Here, Nazi leader Adolf Hitler leaves a rally of the Hitler Youth and the Nazi-led German League of Girls in Nuremberg in September 1938.

component of society. This idea is known as **corporatism**. Therefore all German trade unions were replaced with the German Labor Front, and independent youth organizations were eliminated in favor of the National Socialist Youth.

Pluralists argue, however, that even this totalitarian state had factions within it. Some members of the National Socialist Party took the socialist part seriously, favoring government control of the economy to build a stronger nation. Hitler, however, sided with business in the interest of rapid economic growth. Early in June 1934, he had "radical elements" in the Nazi Party's paramilitary force, the SA, murdered during the "Night of the Long Knives." The regime then sided unequivocally with business, though it interfered in the economy to control prices and wages when it deemed this necessary for the national interest. Large industries worked relatively closely with the Nazis. They initially favored

Hitler's elimination of trade unions, and later benefited from heavy government investment in infrastructure and military production in the build-up to World War II. Within the regime itself, factions continued to exist, with fierce internal battles for power in various ministries. While the regime was as close as any has ever been to being fully totalitarian, factionalism nonetheless continued to exist behind the scenes and within limits.

Nazi fascism was combined with racism, aimed primarily at Jews. The regime slowly and systematically implemented anti-Semitic policies, first encouraging boycotts of Jewish businesses and firing Jewish civil servants in 1933 then officially classifying people as Jewish and registering Germany's entire population by race in 1935. Jewish businesses were looted and burned during *Kristallnacht* ("night of broken glass") in November 1937, and shortly after Jewish citizenship was eliminated and Jews were encouraged to migrate from Germany to "purify" the state. The Holocaust did not begin in earnest until the start of World War II, when Jews could no longer flee, at least not in large numbers, but by the end of the war approximately six million Jews had died at the hands of the Nazis and their allies across Europe. In addition to Jews and political opponents, the systematic killing included the sick and disabled who could not contribute to the national good, homosexuals because they were considered "morally depraved," members of various faiths in part because religious faith was seen as denying the supremacy of fascism and Hitler's control, and gypsies (Romanis) because they were seen as impure and flawed.

The horror of Nazi rule, and fascist rule in general (most notably in Italy and Spain), delegitimized the ideology the world over. No regime proclaims itself as fascist today. While small fascist political movements and parties exist, none that claims the name has any significant political influence. Many observers, however, argue that fascism, or at least fascist tendencies, continue to threaten democracy in many countries. Parties that espouse a virulent nationalism, often defined on a cultural or religious basis and opposed to immigrants as threats to the "soul of the nation," are frequently termed **neofascist**. These groups vehemently deny the label, however. The best-known example of neofascism is France's National Front, led by Jean-Marie Le Pen.

Le Pen argues that the greatest danger facing France is the immigration of Muslims, mainly from North Africa. He claims Muslim immigration is destroying the French nation, and he calls for policies that would reward white French women for having more babies and severely restrict or even eliminate immigration. Shockwaves rippled through France and much of Europe in 2002 when Le Pen came in second in that year's presidential election. Although he ultimately lost in the second round of voting, winning less than 20 percent of the vote, many people are still deeply concerned by the development and worry about what it may mean for the future.

Modernizing Authoritarianism

While no regime currently uses fascism as an acceptable claim to legitimacy, the argument that the needs of the state and nation must take precedence over liberalism's individual rights remains common. Many postcolonial regimes can be termed modernizing authoritarian: their common claim to legitimacy is that they will modernize or "develop" their countries. These regimes are not all based on a single and consciously elaborated ideology like the other types of regimes in this chapter, but each nonetheless explicitly or implicitly appeals to a common set of precepts. Some have an elaborate ideological justification for their legitimacy; others do not. Many of these states are relatively weak so their informal institutions may reveal more about how they actually rule than the formal institutions based on their claim to legitimacy. What they all share, however, is a set of core assumptions that is the basis of their official claim to legitimacy.

The first of these assumptions is that *development requires the leadership of a "modern elite."* In societies with relatively few highly educated people, the assumption is that the reins of power should be in the hands of those who understand the modern world and how to advance within it. It is an appeal to a **technocratic legitimacy**, a claim to rule based on knowledge that was part of **modernization theory**, a theory of development that argued that in order to develop postcolonial societies needed to go through the same process of modernization that the West underwent. Modernization theorists argued that the modern elite—a "[n]ew type of enterprising men" in the words of Walt Rostow (1960), one of the pioneers of the theory and one of the originators of U.S. president John Kennedy's foreign aid program—would lead the development process. Modernization theorists assumed, as we noted in chapter 1, that democracy would develop along with economic development.

The leaders of the modernizing authoritarian regimes that emerged, however, recognized the contradiction between arguing that development requires the leadership of an educated elite and assuming that democracy would evolve: the latter does not necessarily produce the former. Postcolonial elites, in particular, believed that in a country in which a large percentage of the population was illiterate, democracy would not necessarily put the "right" people in power. In their eyes, this justified and legitimized truncating democracy and limiting citizens' rights in favor of some form of authoritarian rule led by elites who claimed to have special leadership abilities based on their education.

The second common assumption of modernizing authoritarian regimes is that *they can produce the benefits of "development."* The word means many things to many people, but in political discourse throughout the postcolonial world since the 1950s, it has meant moving in the direction of creating societies like those found in the West, at least economically, to bring very poor populations closer to the standard of living found in wealthier countries. Rostow saw this economic goal as entering "the age of high mass consumption." For the poorest countries this meant transforming poor, overwhelmingly agricultural societies into urbanized, industrialized societies with dramatically higher productivity and wealth. For middle-income countries, such as Brazil, development meant continuing the industrialization that had already started, "deepening" it from relatively low technology to higher technology and higher productivity industries, as well as continuing the overall shift of economic activity and people from countryside to city. All of this required the application of modern science and technology, which the educated and technocratic elite claimed to understand and be able to employ on behalf of the entire country. The goal, and the main justification for authoritarian rule, was development.

Development also required *national unity,* the third assumption underpinning these regimes. Postcolonial elites argued that achieving the Herculean task of "catching up" to the West necessitated unusual measures. Their countries did not have time to fight internally by engaging in political battles for control of the government or lengthy debates about what policies to pursue. Instead, the modern elite should take control to move the country forward. Debate and democracy had to wait until the "big push" for development was completed, or at least well underway. Some groups in civil society, such as labor unions demanding higher wages or better working conditions, might oppose policies that the elite believed were beneficial. Modernizing elites found such resistance unacceptable because it was not in the interest of development; everyone had to be united to move forward rapidly. They typically tied this appeal to unity to nationalism, citing the unity needed to build a more powerful nation in which people could take pride.

Modernizing authoritarianism has taken three distinct institutional forms: one-party regimes, military regimes, and personalist regimes. While they all share the key assumptions of the general model, each has different origins and somewhat different institutions (or lack thereof). **One-party regimes**, once common in Africa and Asia, were based on a single party gaining power after independence and systematically eliminating all opposition in the name of development and national unity. These regimes eliminated all effective opposition, but some did achieve notable economic progress, such as Mexico and, to a lesser extent, Kenya and Côte d'Ivoire. **Military regimes** took power via **coups d'etat**, military takeovers of government, and they justified elimination of the previous government, whether democratic or not, in terms of modernizing authoritarianism. Often citing prolonged economic stagnation or growing social unrest as their impetus, military leaders argued that they would "clean up the mess" of the prior government and get the country at least started down the road to development before returning to civilian and democratic rule. Some military regimes were more serious in this intent and more economically successful; others seem to have used the assumptions of modernizing authoritarianism to justify their own hold on power, with little development taking place, as the case of Nigeria illustrates. **Personalist regimes** usually arose either via one party or via military coup, but a central leader came to dominate, typically eliminating not only all opposition, but also weakening the state's institutions in order to centralize power. Mobutu Sese Seko of Zaire (now the Democratic Republic of the Congo) and Ferdinand Marcos of the Philippines were classic examples of this type. Such individuals justify their rule using the assumptions of modernizing authoritarianism, and occasionally the state sees some economic successes, but personalist regimes typically centralize power for the benefit of the leader, achieving very little in the way of real development.

MINI-CASE Tanzania's One-Party Regime

From the 1960s until the 1980s, the African state of Tanzania was an interesting example of a modernizing authoritarian one-party regime. Julius Nyerere, the president of Tanzania from 1962 to 1985, has been called Africa's "philosopher-king," in part because he was far more self-conscious and explicit in justifying the regime he helped create than most heads of state. He argued that political parties in Western democracies are based primarily on social class divisions, and that since Africa has few and minor class divisions, there was no need for opposing parties. He suggested that in Africa "when a village of a hundred people have sat and talked together until they agreed where a well should be dug they have practised [sic] democracy" (1966). This led to his justification of a one-party state. His party, the Tanzanian African National Union (TANU), overwhelmingly won the country's first election on the eve of independence, and it didn't take much to change the constitution to legally eliminate the opposition.

In addition to his vision of "African democracy," Nyerere also envisioned creating an "African socialism," dubbed *ujamaa* in Swahili. He argued that this would return the country to its precolonial origins, but with distinctly modern additions. In line with this, the government took ownership of most major sectors of the economy, but the centerpiece of the effort was the creation of *ujamaa* villages. Nyerere argued that prior to

colonial influence Africans had lived and worked communally, and they ought to return to that lifestyle, living together in villages or working communal farms rather than spread out on their individual farms. This would also facilitate the provision of more modern social services such as schools, health clinics, and clean water. While Nyerere justified *ujamaa* as a return to precolonial "tradition," it was in fact an example of a modernizing authoritarian regime in action. Nyerere's vision of precolonial Africa was historically inaccurate, and the rural majority had no interest in farming communally or moving into villages. The government first tried to cajole people to form the new villages and then tried incentives. When neither worked, Nyerere turned to force; the state moved millions into new villages and tried to force communal labor. The results were disastrous for agricultural production and the country's economy, though the government was able to improve health care and education, achieving the amazing feat of nearly universal literacy in one of the world's poorest countries.

Even with all of this, TANU ruled for thirty years. Nyerere's commitment to village democracy ultimately proved limited; public debate became more and more circumscribed over time. His twin goals of African democracy and African socialism were contradictory. He claimed both came from African traditions, but when the populace did not accept his vision of socialism, he used the modern state to try to force it on them. When they tried to dissent, the ruling party reduced open debate. Throughout TANU's rule, the party did hold parliamentary elections once every five years, allowing two party-approved candidates to compete for each seat. The candidates could not, however, question the ruling party's overall policies. They could and did compete over the question of who would best represent the area, so the elections were fair, if not free.

Nyerere ultimately created a modernizing authoritarian state, restricting dissent and political opposition in the interests of achieving a specific vision of "devel-opment." By 1985 he realized his vision had produced a bankrupt country and that the key economic policies would have to change. He resigned the presidency, only the third postcolonial African president to ever do so, rather than implement a reversal of his vision. In the 1990s and following the trend across the continent (see chapter 9), Nyerere argued in favor of opening the country to multiparty democracy, saying the time for one-party rule was over. The country did allow full legal opposition, starting with the election of 1995, but TANU (renamed CCM, Chama Cha Mapinduzi, or Party of the Revolution) continues to rule against only token opposition.

Modernizing authoritarian regimes arose primarily in postcolonial states, many of which still tend to be relatively weak states with weak formal institutions. Informal institutions are therefore often quite important in understanding how these regimes function. Power in these weak state regimes becomes quite personalized, and the rule of law is inconsistent at best. These traits can characterize any of the forms of modernizing authoritarian regimes noted above, though are most likely in personalist regimes. Military and one-party regimes also vary widely in their level of formal institutionalization. They too can have very weak institutions in which the personal authority of key leaders matters more than the formal organization of power under the party or military as an institution.

Comparativists studying Africa have dubbed these regimes in the weakest states *neopatrimonial*. German sociologist Max Weber (1978) defined "patrimonial" rule as rule in which personal ties and favors, not bureaucratic institutions, determine power. **Neopatrimonial regimes** combine the trappings of modern, bureaucratic states with underlying informal institutions that work behind the scenes to determine real power. Constitutions, laws, courts, and bureaucracies all exist, but they really work mainly on the basis of personal favors and patronage. Patron-client relations are central in these regimes; gaining state employment, power, and resources requires knowing the right people. Rulers maintain their power by distributing patronage, which is actually more important than the powers they have via their formal positions in the state. Politics becomes a competition among key patrons for access to the state's resources to distribute to their supporters. Neopatrimonial regimes in Africa and elsewhere can be military, one-party, or personalist. Indeed, many scholars argue that new democracies in Africa, including our case study of Nigeria, retain many elements of neopatrimonial rule: they may now have the formal institutions of electoral democracy, but power remains based primarily on personal access to the state (now via elections) and distribution of its resources as patronage.

The modernizing authoritarian regime type is different from the other regime types in that both its forms and the extent to which a particular government consciously elaborates the ideology can vary significantly. These regimes do share a common set of assumptions, at least some of which they use to legitimize their rule. They all make a central claim that democracy, citizens' rights, and civil society must be curtailed to provide development because development requires national unity and democracy would threaten that unity. While their formal institutions are derived from the precepts of modernizing authoritarianism, in many cases informal institutions are at least as important. Our case studies present two military modernizing authoritarian regimes: Brazil, in which formal institutions were relatively strong and the regime really did develop the country significantly, and Nigeria, a neopatrimonial military regime that made similar claims to legitimacy based on development but achieved very little.

Semi-Authoritarian Rule: A New Regime Type?

The regime types reviewed in this chapter are the major ones that have characterized the last century of political history, but a growing number of scholars now recognize a new addition to this list: **semi-authoritarian regimes**. These have developed out of attempts at transitions to democracy that have taken place in many former Communist and postcolonial states. Comparativist Marina Ottaway coined the term "semi-authoritarianism" to characterize regimes that "allow little real competition for power … [but] leave enough political space for political parties and organizations of civil society to form, for an independent press to function to some extent, and for some political debate to take place" (2003, 3). A closely related concept is Andreas Schedler's notion of **electoral authoritarianism**: "[e]lectoral authoritarian regimes play the game of multiparty elections…. Yet they violate the liberal-democratic principles of freedom and fairness so profoundly and systematically as to render elections instruments of authoritarian rule rather than 'instruments of democracy'" (2006, 3).

Unlike modernizing authoritarian regimes, semi-authoritarian regimes proclaim themselves democratic and point to elements of liberal democracy within their states to justify this claim. In truth, manipulation of the electoral process, limits on basic freedoms, and powerful informal institutions such as patronage limit real competition and ensure the ruling party or leader continued power. Many scholars initially saw these regimes as simply part of a prolonged transition to democracy, but Ottaway and others now argue that they are stable regimes, with internal formal and informal rules of their own. Most are so recent, however, that it is difficult to conclude definitively that they constitute a distinct, long-term regime type. We examine them in greater detail in chapter 9 when we address the broader issues of transitions to democracy, including examining our case study of Russia, one of the most recent additions to the list of semi-authoritarian regimes.

CASE STUDY Brazil: The Bureaucratic Authoritarian State, 1964–1985

Brazil emerged from World War II as a semi-industrialized economy. It had its own version of a quasi-fascist regime, the *Estado Novo* (New State), under Getúlio Vargas in the 1930s and through the war. (This regime eventually did become a member of Allied powers in the war rather than a supporter of the Axis powers.) Like other fascist regimes, it established a system of corporatism that allowed but controlled the creation of, for instance, trade unions. It was also relatively successful at industrializing: the country had shifted from an agricultural economy dependent on coffee and cattle at the beginning of the century to a mostly industrial economy by the end of World War II.

When fascism became disgraced after the war, Brazil returned to being a democracy, but a very unstable one. Elections were held from 1946 to 1960 and significant economic growth occurred, but the population became increasingly divided economically and politically. The democratic regime loosened the limitation the *Estado Novo* had placed on civil society, and debates raged between the right and the left over the direction of the state's development model and the sharing of its benefits.

After the abrupt resignation of President Jânio Quadros, who had been elected in 1960, Vice President João Goulart stepped up to the presidency. Seen by laborers, peasants, and other members of the working poor as sympathetic to their cause, Goulart and his new position of influence emboldened these groups to organize in increasing numbers of street protests to show their displeasure over not receiving what they saw as their fair share of the fruits of development. These in turn led to rising concern from business owners, landowners, and other conservatives, who organized their own demonstrations. It was not long before the Brazilian military, with quiet support from the United States, decided that the ensuing instability threatened the country's development. Military officials stepped in and overthrew Goulart in a coup d'etat in 1964.

The Brazilian military came to power at the height of the Cold War, just five years after Fidel Castro led a communist revolution in Cuba. This meant that anti-

Brazil's military regime was less violent than its infamous neighbors in Chile and Argentina of the same period, but violence was certainly used to repress dissent, and student and worker protests were often targets. In 1968 cavalrymen charged students gathered to protest the killing of a student by police in Rio de Janeiro.

communism was an important addition to the common justifications of modernizing authoritarian regimes. Brazilian officials created what Argentine political scientist Guillermo O'Donnell (1979) called a **bureaucratic-authoritarian state**, a specific version of the modernizing authoritarian regime type. O'Donnell argued that the military came to power to further the economic development model because the continued profitability of Brazil's growing industries was being threatened by workers' demands for a greater share of the rewards. The military regime suppressed independent unions and returned the country to the corporatist model of the *Estado Novo*. It then proceeded to expand industrialization by a very conscious policy of significant government investment in new industries, particularly in heavy industry such as auto manufacturing and airplanes, and industries related to the military. The regime very consciously claimed legitimacy on the basis of technocratic expertise and anticommunism and brought many talented economists into the government to develop the new economic plan. The result came to be known as the "Brazilian Miracle," a period of particularly rapid economic growth at its zenith from 1967 to 1973. Despite this growth, however, much of the population remained mired in poverty.

The Brazilian military government certainly repressed its opponents as necessary to implement its economic model, though it was less repressive than many Latin American military governments of the time. It allowed elections for a national congress but controlled the body by allowing only two legal parties: one that supported the government and one that was a legal opposition. The opposition, however, was limited in what it was allowed to say, the congress itself had quite limited powers, and the military was quite willing to resort to electoral tampering to maintain government party control. Ultimate decision making remained with the top military leaders.

By the late 1970s, the world oil shocks had contributed to an economic slowdown across the country. Independent unions once again formed, in open violation of the law. Strikes became more common and had greater impact given the rapid industrialization of the past two decades: there were now more industrial workers, and their industries were more important to the economy. Trade unions and political activists in the Catholic Church became more active in civil society, playing a key role in starting a movement for democracy that eventually brought Brazil's modernizing authoritarian regime to an end in 1989, the year in which the first direct election of a civilian president since 1960 was held.

CASE STUDY Nigeria: Neopatrimonial Military Rule, 1966–1979 and 1983–1999

The Brazilian modernizing authoritarian regime took its ideology and its economic model quite seriously and had formal institutions strong enough to effect significant economic development. Nigeria, on the other hand, suffered through several military regimes whose claims to legitimacy followed the modernizing authoritarian model but did not always take their own claims seriously in practice. Each of these regimes was neopatrimonial, using the state to distribute resources to top leaders and their clients rather than investing in economic development, despite the presence of significant oil reserves. Indeed, oil wealth allowed for greater patronage and corruption. These informal institutions of rule affected Nigeria's efforts at democracy as well, as seen in chapter 9.

Nigeria's first electoral democracy survived six tumultuous years after independence. The country was deeply divided along regional and therefore ethnic and religious lines from the outset. The democratic constitution, negotiated with the departing British colonizers, recognized this division by creating three separate regions with significant autonomy from the central government. Corruption among those in power and mutual suspicion among the political leaders of each region produced an increasingly chaotic and, at election time, violent democracy. The northern region controlled the most power in the central government because it was the most populous, which created resentment in the other regions. By 1965 this numerical superiority and fraudulent elections produced a central government overwhelmingly controlled by northern officials, as well as widespread violence, especially in the western region.

The first of six successful military coups took place in January 1966. A group of mid-level military officers, ethnically Igbo and from the eastern region, attempted to take power, an effort that was only partially successful. The crisis, however, allowed the military's top commander, Gen. Johnson Aguiyi-Ironsi, also an Igbo, to

Sani Abacha presided over a dark period (1993–1998) during which his personal interests trumped his stated ideological goals of modernization and development. His unexpected death released Nigeria from military rule and permitted a transition to democracy. This 1998 photo was taken just before rumors about his ill-health began circulating through the capital of Abuja.

convince the democratic government to give him full power, pronouncing the alternative to be civil war. Each of the military governments in Nigeria, starting with that of Ironsi, took power claiming that its primary aims were to restore order, end violence and corruption to restart development, and return the country to a more stable and peaceful democratic rule. The previous civilian government was portrayed as corrupt and incompetent, and the military was touted as a national institution that would serve only as a "corrective" regime to solve the worst of the crisis and return the country to democracy. This too was all in the name of restoring the possibility of development, particularly in the context of Nigeria's oil wealth, which increased immensely in 1973 when the world price of oil quadrupled.

General Ironsi saw himself as a nationalist and used the language of modernizing authoritarianism to justify his takeover, which was popular in the southern half of the country. To overcome the regional tensions that had plagued the country since independence, Ironsi eliminated the regional governments entirely and centralized power in the capital. While this probably was a sincere effort at national unity, political and military leaders in the north saw it as an attempt by the Igbo in the east to grab all the power. Northern military leaders responded with a counter-coup that overthrew Ironsi after his being in power only six months.

The military leadership in the east rejected the new government led by Gen. Yakubu Gowon. This resulted in a three-year civil war (see chapter 2). Gowon eventually was successful in defeating the rebels and reuniting the country, proclaiming a policy of forgiveness for those from the east and reintegration of all citizens into one nation to achieve unity once again. He also promised to restore democratic civilian rule by 1976, after the reconciliation process was complete. His economic policy focused on using government oil revenues to invest in industry to begin the industrialization process, though corruption and inefficiency plagued the effort. Rapidly growing oil revenues led to parallel growth in corruption in Gowon's regime and a desire to cling to power to continue gaining the corrupt benefits of high oil prices. Not long after Gowon announced in 1974 that the country was "not ready" for a return to civilian rule, a new military government overthrew him and proclaimed, once again, that it was dedicated to reducing corruption and restoring democracy. This regime did make some progress on reducing corruption, though not a lot, but it carried out its pledge to allow democracy, with elections taking place for a new government in 1979.

Nigeria's new democracy, the Second Republic, was short-lived, lasting only four years. At that point, the military once again intervened. When Gen. Muhammadu Buhari took power in 1983, he proclaimed his regime in favor of national unity, the elimination of corruption, and the restoration of economic growth ("development"). He launched a major and, at times, brutal campaign against corruption, and shifted economic policy toward more market-oriented policies with less government involvement, as was demanded by international aid agencies in the 1980s (see chapter 5).

Buhari was overthrown in 1985 by another northerner, Gen. Ibrahim Babangida, who would rule until 1993. Babangida accelerated the shift to a more market-oriented economic policy and promised yet again to restore democracy. After much delay and continuing corruption in the northern-dominated military government, elections were finally held in 1993, but Babangida annulled them, unhappy with who had won. He instead created a short-lived transitional government that was overthrown by Gen. Sani Abacha. Abacha led Nigeria into its darkest period, with the most brutal suppression of dissent and greatest corruption in its history. His regime quickly became a personalist one, and while still proclaiming the goals of modernizing authoritarianism, in practice he ruled in his personal interests, with no coherent development policy in place. His death in 1998 finally allowed a transition to democracy through the Third Republic, which remains in power.

Prior to Abacha, Nigeria's military governments, while certainly corrupt and authoritarian, ruled less harshly than many military regimes. At times, they seemed to take the mandate of modernizing authoritarianism seriously, attempting to unify the country and pursue some sort of development policy. They all banned political parties and other associations, but all prior to Abacha allowed a relatively free press to continue to criticize their actions, and some allowed elements of civil society to operate with some autonomy. All relied on the continuing work of the country's civil servants, the government's bureaucrats, which meant that the bureaucratic institutions of the state continued to function, though weakened by growing corruption, under both military and civilian regimes. This was especially true under Abacha, when corruption weakened state institutions quite profoundly. The military leadership sat atop and ruled over a civilian state. All proclaimed to be working for national unity and development; all argued that after a brief and necessary authoritarian period, in which the country would be put back on the "right track" toward development, democracy would be restored. All, however, ruled over a neopatrimonial system that slowly but systematically undermined the formal institutions of the state, making the military's claims of aiding the nation's development appear ever more hollow.

Theocracy

Theocracy is rule by religious authorities. Thirty years ago, it's very unlikely that you would have found it included in a textbook on comparative politics, except perhaps as historical background. If it were mentioned at all, it would have been in connection with the "divine right of kings" of medieval and early modern Europe, under which the monarchy was thought to represent God on Earth, sanctioned as such by the universal Catholic Church. Today the prime example of theocracy is not Christian but Muslim. Like other kinds of regimes, the Muslim theocracy in Iran is based on a well-elaborated political ideology, but in practice it does not or cannot always adhere perfectly to that ideology. Iran currently is the world's only existing theocracy, but political movements aimed at achieving similar regimes elsewhere exist throughout the Muslim world. We focus on Islamic theocracy as an ideology and regime type not because it is the only conceivable kind of theocracy but because it is the only contemporary example of a theocratic regime and theocratic political ideology that is an important challenger to liberal democracy today.

The political ideology that has inspired such fear in much of the West and such admiration in much of the Muslim world is typically known as "Islamic fundamentalism," a name that implies a set of ideas that is often quite different from what its adherents actually believe. The word "fundamentalist" implies "traditional" to many people, but nothing could be further from the truth in this case. "Traditional" Islamic beliefs, as developed over the centuries, certainly posit that religious law ought to be the basis for government, but in practice these precepts are compromised significantly by local cultural traditions and rulers. In many countries in the twenty-first century, traditional religious authorities compromise with modernity and the increasing secularization of the state by, among other things, ignoring the secular and political world as much as possible, withdrawing from politics nearly completely, and allowing effectively secular, modernizing authoritarian regimes to emerge.

Given this reality, most scholars use the term **Islamism** instead of Islamic fundamentalism in their discourse. While it contains many variations, Islamism is generally defined as a belief that Islamic law, as revealed by God to the Prophet Mohammed, can and should provide the basis for government in Muslim communities, with little equivocation or compromise. It arose in the nineteenth and twentieth centuries with the goal of "purifying" Muslim society of the creeping influences of the West and secularism that traditional Muslim religious leaders had often been willing to accept, or at least ignore. In line with this, most Islamists explicitly reject the Muslim concept of *taqlid,* the acceptance of all past legal and moral edicts of the traditional clergy, and instead embrace *ijtihad,* the belief that Muslims should read and interpret the original Islamic texts for themselves. They base their ideology on their interpretation of the Quran and Sunnah, the two holiest books of Islam, and focus primarily on the original Muslim society and state created by Mohammed as their model. Islamists do vary in the degree to which they are willing to compromise with aspects of the contemporary world, but most adhere to a fairly strict belief in Muslim law, ***sharia***, as written in the Quran and Sunnah. Past compromises by traditional clergy are therefore unacceptable.

Islamists believe that sovereignty rests with God, so they ultimately reject democracy and its idea of popular sovereignty. Some, however, such as the early Palestinian leader Taqi al-Din al-Nabhani (1905–1978), reserve a place for *shura,* which means "consultation with the people." He believed the Muslim state should be led by a caliph, a supreme religious and political leader, but that the caliph should be acceptable to the population as a whole and be advised by an elected council. Some religious authorities have since used this concept to argue in favor of allowing an ideologically limited civil society, one that stays within the bounds of Islamic practices, ideas, and law.

Then there are those such as the members of the Algerian Islamic Front (FIS), who believe in participating in democracy. In December 1991 the party won the first round of Algeria's first democratic elections, only to see the second round cancelled and the military take effective control of the government and subsequently ban the party. Some FIS followers believed that in a true Islamic state, democracy would be eliminated, but they were willing to participate in democratic politics until they were able to create such a state. Other Islamists, such as Sayyid Qutb, a key early leader of the Egyptian Muslim Brotherhood, reject the notion of short- or long-term democracy altogether. More recently, however, the Muslim Brotherhood has taken a path similar to that of the FIS, unofficially participating in Egypt's rather restricted elections and winning a significant number of legislative seats in the 2006 election.

French political scientist Oliver Roy (2004) and other scholars of Islam argue that Islamist movements face a contradiction between their abstract goals and actual practice if they gain power. Islam certainly has a long tradition of providing legal structure for many areas of life, but by no means all. If Islamists gain power, as they have in Iran, they must confront the complexities and political pressures of governing modern states. This always requires them to compromise their theologically driven blueprint to govern effectively. The alternative, Roy argues, is a regime like Afghanistan's Taliban government. The Taliban is what Roy calls a **neofundamentalist** group, which he distinguishes from Islamists. It had no particular plan on how to govern and, in fact, cared little about governing. Followers virtually ignored the state, and many state functions nearly ceased operations while the group ruled in Afghanistan; for example, foreign policy was essentially run by and through the Pakistani government. The Taliban instead focused only on implementing an extremely rigid vision of *sharia* at the local level that was directed toward how people lived their daily lives. Rule was implemented based purely on theological principles, but this could not really be called governing in the modern sense of the word.

As the electoral participation of some groups demonstrates, while all Islamists place great significance on *jihad*, not all advocate violence. ***Jihad*** comes from an Arabic word for "struggle" and, although it is not one of the "five pillars" of the faith, it is an important concept in Islam. The Quran identifies three kinds of *jihad*. The first and most important is the individual's internal struggle to renounce evil and live faithfully by following proper religious practices. The second is the struggle of the individual to right evils and injustice within the **umma**, the Muslim community as a whole. The third and least important is protection, armed and violent if necessary, of the *umma*. The most radical Islamists and neofundamentalists, which Roy terms *jihadists*, argue that the *umma* is under attack externally from the West and internally via secularization and Westernization. For groups like al-Qaida, this justifies violent opposition to these types of forces, both outside and within the *umma*. Furthermore, following *ijtihad*, these individuals reject the traditional teaching that violent *jihad* should only be carried out on the orders of high religious authorities; they argue instead that individuals, and religiously untrained leaders like Osama bin Laden, can discern for themselves when and where violent *jihad* is not only a justifiable option but a moral necessity.

Iran's Muslim regime may be a fairly recent development, but theocracy is perhaps the oldest form of government in existence. Its sole contemporary version, however, is Islamic. Like all theocrats, Islamists believe in a government established according to their understanding of God's teaching, giving sovereignty not to "we the people" but rather to God. Followers vary widely in the methods they use to achieve Islamist regimes and in the details of what that regime would look like. Some include quasi-democratic elements such as consultation with some sort of legislative body, and some are willing to try to gain power via electoral democracy, give limited rights to citizens, and allow some civil society. All, however, would give great power to religious authorities to interpret and implement God's sovereignty on earth. Islamist philosophers and ideologues have created many variants of Islamist regimes in the abstract, but only one has gained power and ruled for a sustained period: Iran's revolutionary Islamic government.

CASE STUDY The Islamic Republic of Iran, 1979–

Islam in Iran is unusual in that the vast majority of the country's population and major religious authorities are Shiites, not Sunnis. In the seventh century, Islam split over the succession to the Prophet Mohammed. Those who became Shiite believe the Prophet's son-in-law, Imam Ali, was rightful heir to the leadership of the *umma* and that descendants of Imam Ali remain the only rightful religious authorities; major Shiite religious authorities are chosen from among his heirs. Sunnis, who constitute approximately 85 percent of the world's Muslims, believe that any religiously educated person of appropriate stature and training can become a major leader of the *umma,* and they reject the claim that a particular bloodline should rule. Iran and Iraq are the only Muslim countries with Shiite majorities; Iran is nearly all Shiite. The Islamic Republic in Iran nonetheless exemplifies the ideology and contradictions of Islamist theocracy more broadly.

Prior to 1979, Iran had a modernizing authoritarian regime under the leadership of the Pahlavi dynasty: father and then son ruled the country from 1925 to 1979. In the 1960s and 1970s, Shah Reza Pahlavi attempted to "modernize" the country via close relations with the West, Westernization of Iranian culture, and industrialization. The dynasty, however, preserved whatever benefits came out of this modernization for itself and its close supporters, and domestic opposition mounted. One of the country's major religious leaders, Ayatollah Ruhollah Khomeini, emerged as a major spokesman and leader of this opposition. At first jailed for his ac-

tions and later forced to live in exile in neighboring Iraq, Khomeini was the symbol and by far the most popular leader of the revolution that swept the shah from power in 1978–1979. His Islamist ideals became the basis for the new government.

Khomeini's most original contribution to Islamist doctrine was the concept of the supreme leader. He argued that one leader with enough religious authority and popular support should be the ultimate guide of the Islamic state, with the power to veto any law he deemed as contrary to *sharia.* Khomeini also believed, however, in consultation, or *shura,* and so was quite willing to allow the existence of an elected parliament, the *Majlis,* as long as its laws were subject to the approval of the supreme leader or other major clergy he might deputize to fulfill that function.

An Assembly of Experts wrote the new Iranian constitution, which was ratified by referendum in December 1979. The assembly had been elected, though virtually all politicians opposed to Khomeini boycotted the elections on the grounds that the election was rigged. The new constitution established Iran as an Islamic Republic that specifically followed Shiite doctrine and declared God as sovereign. The position of supreme leader was created, with Khomeini filling that role, and a Guardian Council of twelve clergy was formed. Six members of this council were appointed by the leader and six by the parliament, and its task would be to examine and approve or veto every law the parliament passed. A directly elected president would

Ayatollah Ruhollah Khomenei launched Iran's Islamic Revolution from Qom, one of the holiest cities in Shiite Islam and home to a theological center and many of the grand ayatollahs Khomenei brought into the postrevolutionary regime. Here, a cleric stands before a wall painting in Qom depicting Khomenei.

administer the government on a daily basis. Khomeini, in his earlier Islamist writings, had envisioned local *sharia* courts as the only judicial system necessary, but upon taking power quickly realized the benefit of preserving the shah's relatively modern and hierarchical judicial system. This system, however, would henceforth use *sharia* as its sole source of law, and would be headed at all major levels by clergy. Government ministers, those in charge of the various departments of the government, would be appointed by the president but also be monitored by clergy in each ministry.

The regime was clearly theocratic from its origin; supreme religious authorities could ultimately make

or unmake any governmental decision. Some democratic elements were allowed, however, in the regular elections for the president and parliament, which have been held on schedule since the incorporation of the new constitution into Iranian life, a subject discussed in greater detail in chapter 8. The Guardian Council, however, can disapprove any candidate for office if he is deemed not adequately committed to the goals of the Islamic revolution, and the degree of openness of the elections has varied greatly over time depending on political circumstance. In the first parliamentary election in 1980, a large number of parties competed and entered parliament, and the somewhat "moderate" Abolhassan Bani Sadr won the presidency. He claimed commitment to the revolution, but also believed in being practical in modifying Islam to meet the necessities of running a modern state. By 1983 Khomeini had forced him and other moderates out of office and into exile and had banned all but the Islamic Republican Party (IRP), the party officially supported by most major clergy. By 1986 even the IRP was banned; Khomeini argued that political parties were divisive and in the future all candidates for parliamentary elections would run as independents.

As real political options narrowed and the power of the *Majlis* vis-à-vis the Guardian Council declined, elections became much more lackluster, with less interest and lower voter turnout. A decade later, in the late 1990s, elections again became more exciting and popular affairs after the clergy once again allowed a moderate reformer, Mohammad Khatami, to run for president. Following his election, however, the clergy proceeded to frustrate virtually every reform effort he undertook, and they made sure that a candidate more loyal to them, current president Mahmoud Ahmadinejad, won the election held in 2005. Yet by the time of Khomeini's death in late 1989, the most important religious leaders had withdrawn from active politics, and the clergy who were engaged politically were only mid-level religious authorities. The contradiction between running a modern state and Islamist purity had been won by the former: politics had beat out religion in the world's premier theocracy.

Given the structure of the Iranian constitution, one might imagine that the supreme leader, Guardian Council, and other major institutions controlled exclusively by religious authorities would have total power and eliminate any real internal political factions or battles. This has certainly not been the case to date. Shiite Islam has a long tradition of internal debate about religious and secular affairs. After Khomeini banned all political parties, he specifically said clergy could form alternative factions to discuss important issues and compete in the *Majlis* elections, as long as all factions remained true to the ideals of the revolution. Various informal factions have emerged over the years, with the clergy of the Guardian Council and the supreme leader working against and ultimately, if necessary, banning candidates from factions that take "reform" of the system too far.

Despite such factional battles for power, citizen ability to voice opinions and engage in political activity has been quite limited. When allowed, a very active press has emerged, as it did right after the revolution and again in the late 1990s. Whenever this press begins to question the goals of the revolution beyond certain limits, however, religious authorities close it down and a period of repression sets in. Still, compared to the civil societies of much of the Middle East or that of the shah's regime, civil society and political debate have been relatively open in the Islamic Republic. Intellectual critics and university students have repeatedly spoken out, and repeatedly been repressed when they have spoken out too strongly. In 1999 some student leaders began to question a continued commitment to Islam as the key identity of the state, arguing for democracy and Iranian nationalism instead. Their arrest and the closure of a reformist newspaper resulted in demonstrations across Iran's universities in mid-1999, a brutal police response, and violent student riots. Religious authorities successfully repressed the students, but not without losing further legitimacy in the eyes of many. The Iranian theocracy certainly limits civil society severely, especially when the key religious authorities feel threatened with a potential loss of power, but the country has nonetheless seen growing pressure for change, and a more active civil society than is present in many Middle Eastern countries.

Because of this, some call Iran's theocracy a combination of theocracy and democracy. It is clearly theocratic in the sense that Islam remains the supreme source of official legitimacy and the test against which all policies are measured. Khomeini's revolutionary ideology, however, recognized a place for some voicing of opinion and advice about which direction the revolution ought to take. Following Islamist principles, Khomeini allowed and at times even encouraged a degree of *ijtihad*. Ultimately, of course, he maintained the final word. His death allowed stronger reformist movements and politicians to emerge in the 1990s, ensconced in the democratic elements of the regime: the presidency and *Majlis.* Conservative clergy have used the religious institutions the revolution created to frustrate reform and preserve what they see as the pure path of the Islamist regime, but mounting pressures for change clearly exist. As socioeconomic changes continue and Iranians increasingly use the Internet and other means of communication to access the outside world, theocracy still survives, but the democratic elements it has allowed to operate in partial form continue to question it and threaten more fundamental change.

CONCLUSION

All political ideologies involve the question of the proper relationship between individual citizens and the state. Most citizens of established democracies probably consider liberal democracy's insistence on limited state power and citizens' rights, especially the right to participate in politics through voting, as the presumptive norm. Liberal democracy, however, is an outlier in this regard. Communism, fascism, modernizing authoritarianism, and theocracy all tilt the balance in varying degrees in favor of the state. Each finds some grounds for arguing that government should not rest in the hands of citizens or elected representatives

COUNTRY AND CONCEPT Modern Regimes

Country	Current Regime	Year Established	Number of Regimes in 20th Century	Freedom House Score
Brazil	Liberal democracy	1989	5	Free
China	"Communist" modernizing authoritarian	People's Republic, est. 1949	3	Not free
Germany	Liberal democracy	Federal Republic of Germany, est. 1945; reunited w German Democratic Republic in 1991	4	Free
India	Liberal democracy	Independence, 1947	2	Free
Iran	Theocracy	Islamic Republic, proclaimed 1979	4	Not free
Japan	Liberal democracy	1947	2	Free
Nigeria	Democracy (though with neopatrimonial elements)	1999	8	Partly free
Russia	Semi-authoritarian	Constitution promulgated, 1993	3	Not free
United Kingdom	Liberal democracy	Glorious Revolution, 1688	1	Free
United States	Liberal democracy	1789	1	Free

alone. Whether it's the working class, the fascist state itself, or a technocratic or religious elite, most ideologies offer some sort of rationale for giving a select group more say and limiting the participation of others. Many people around the world have found persuasive the arguments that development, equality, nationalism, or a more properly moral and religious nation require the political guidance of various elites. Today these arguments hold less appeal globally and democracy seems to be expanding, but we should not rule out the power of ideologies that insist that some kind of specialized rule and limitations on individual freedoms and participation are necessary in the face of great challenges.

Ideology offers what regimes hope is a compelling justification for their actions, but regimes do not always abide strictly by their ideologies. Democracies vary in their institutional structures, for instance, and even the most established ones have only relatively recently granted full citizenship rights, including the right to participate, to all adult citizens regardless of gender or race. Similarly, communist regimes modified Marx's ideal of rule by the proletariat in favor of Lenin's concept of rule by the vanguard party. Many modernizing authoritarian regimes have failed to meet their own goals of technocratic government and instead have lapsed into neopatrimonial or other forms of corrupt rule. Sometimes these lapses are based on culture and history and depend on a patriarchal culture that shaped emerging ideas of democracy in the seventeenth century or a postcolonial culture possessed of strong traditions of patrimonialism and patron-client linkages. In other instances, practical circumstances make leaders choose paths that diverge from their stated ideology, as when Lenin espoused the New Economic Policy. Similarly, after Mao Zedong's death, reformers in the Chinese Communist Party were able to push for gradual economic liberalization, seeing this as a necessary remedy to the country's frequent agricultural crises and low level of industrialization. The government remains officially communist, but the regime now diverges in many ways from that ideology.

Comparativists ask why certain ideologies and regime types seem to cluster in certain regions. Most long-established democracies are in Europe and North America, whereas modernizing authoritarian regimes have tended to dominate postcolonial Africa and parts of Asia. Latin America has seen regular regional shifts between predominantly democratic and authoritarian regimes. Some analysts find an explanation in culture, arguing, for instance, that democratic ideas first emerged in the UK and Europe and so found a more ready home there, or that Islam provides a more ready cultural base for theocracy. If we look closely, we must conclude that other factors are certainly at work as well. After all, fascism as well as democracy had its primary home in Europe, India is one of the world's longest standing democracies, and Christianity generated theocracies of a sort in an earlier period in Europe.

Moreover, regimes change all over the world: authoritarian and communist regimes have undergone democratization, and Germany, as well as many Latin American cases, reminds us that democracies can collapse into nondemocratic regimes. Our cases above suggest other factors that may be at work. For example, the existence and emergence of an independent and relatively powerful civil society seems to be important to establishing and maintaining democracy. Postcolonial status seems particularly connected with social and economic problems that favor modernizing authoritarianism. Particular challenges, such as lagging economic development and economic and security crises, may also favor nondemocratic ideologies and regimes that proclaim a particular ability to solve these problems. You may wish to generate some hypotheses of your own on this question, which we return to in chapters 8 and 9.

Key Concepts

Bolshevik (p. 99)
bureaucratic-authoritarian state
   (p. 109)
citizen (p. 86)
civil rights (p. 87)
corporatism (p. 103)
coups d'etat (p. 105)
democratic centralism (p. 99)
dictatorship of the proletariat
   (p. 98)
electoral authoritarianism
   (p. 108)
electoral democracy (p. 94)
free wage labor (p. 97)
glasnost (p. 100)

historical materialism (p. 97)
Islamism (p. 113)
jihad (p. 114)
liberal democracy (p. 94)
military regimes (p. 105)
mode of production (p. 97)
modernization theory (p. 104)
neofascist (p. 103)
neofundamentalist (p. 114)
neopatrimonial regimes (p. 107)
one-party regimes (p. 105)
parliamentary sovereignty (p. 96)
participatory democracy (p. 94)
perestroika (p. 100)
personalist regimes (p. 106)

politburo (p. 99)
political rights (p. 87)
semi-authoritarian regimes
   (p. 108)
sharia (p. 113)
social contract theory (p. 91)
social democracy (p. 94)
social revolution (p. 97)
social rights (p. 87)
soviets (p. 99)
technocratic legitimacy (p. 104)
theocracy (p. 112)
totalitarian regime (p. 100)
umma (p. 114)
vanguard party (p. 99)

Works Cited

Marshall, T. H. 1963. *Class, Citizenship, and Social Development.* Chicago: University of Chicago Press.

Mussolini, Benito. 1968. *Fascism: Doctrine and Institutions.* Reprint. New York: Howard Fertig.

O'Donnell, Guillermo A. 1979. *Modernization and Bureaucratic-Authoritarianism: Studies in South American Politics.* Text ed. Berkeley: Institute of International Studies, University of California.

Ottaway, Marina. 2003. *Democracy Challenged: The Rise of Semi-Authoritarianism.* Washington, D.C.: Carnegie Endowment for International Peace.

Rostow, W. W. 1960. *The Stages of Economic Growth: A Non-Communist Manifesto.* Cambridge: Cambridge University Press.

Roy, Oliver. 2004. *Globalized Islam: The Search for a New Ummah.* New York: Columbia University Press.

Schedler, Andreas, ed. 2006. *Electoral Authoritarianism: The Dynamics of Unfree Competition.* Boulder, Colo.: Lynne Rienner Publishers.

Tarrow, Sidney G. 1998. *Power in Movement: Social Movements and Contentious Politics.* New York: Cambridge University Press.

Weber, Max. 1978. *Economy and Society: An Outline of Interpretive Sociology.* Berkeley: University of California Press.

Resources for Further Study

Dahl, Robert. 1971. *Polyarchy: Participation and Opposition.* New Haven, Conn.: Yale University Press.

Esposito, John L. 1997. *Political Islam: Revolution, Radicalism, or Reform?* Boulder, Colo.: Lynne Rienner Publishers.

Held, David. 1996. *Models of Democracy.* Stanford: Stanford University Press.

Husain, Mir Z. Z. 2003. *Global Islamic Politics.* 2nd ed. New York: Longman.

Mill. John Stuart. S. 1870. *The Subjection of Women.* New York: D. Appleton and Company.

Nyerere, Julius. 1966. *Freedom and Unity: Uhuru Na Umoja: A Selection from Writings and Speeches, 1952–65.* London: Oxford University Press.

Sargent, Lyman Tower. 1987. *Contemporary Political Ideologies: A Comparative Analysis.* 7th ed. Homewood, Ill.: Dorsey Press.

Tucker, Robert C., ed. 1978. *The Marx-Engels Reader.* New York: Norton.

Who Rules?

- What means are used by identity groups within a state to ensure or augment their access to power?

- How do differences among identity groups—ethnic, religious, racial—affect the type of representation or access to power they pursue?

What Explains Political Behavior?

- How and why do identity groups form and become politically important?

Where and Why?

- Why does ethnic, religious, or racial diversity lead to violent conflict in some places but not in others?

- What lessons can be learned that might help prevent identity-based conflict in the future?

4

STATE AND IDENTITY

The great political battle of the second half of the twentieth century was between liberalism and communism, but by the end of the century it appeared that a dark-horse contender, nationalism, was the winner. Nationalist, ethnic, and religious movements seemed to be the main beneficiaries of the fall of communism as well as the greatest challenges to democracy. Since the end of the Cold War, an internationalist Islamist movement has gained strength in many countries, a number of countries in the former Soviet sphere have been wracked by ethnically based political battles, and full-scale genocide has occurred in Bosnia and Rwanda. From the battles to create new governments in Iraq and Afghanistan, to the increasingly tense relations between China and Japan, to genocidal violence in Rwanda and secessionist struggles in Chechnya, "identity politics" have come to the fore.

Studying the political impact of identity is a long-standing core feature of comparative politics. Comparativists want to know what explains the current global surge of conflictual political behavior based on nationalist, ethnic, and religious identity. We debate whether these conflicts are continuations of ancient differences or products of our modern world and what can be done to contain them. We also ask how race, ethnicity, and religion influence groups' access to power and how groups seek to share power during periods of normal politics. Finally, we question why ethnic, religious, or racial fragmentation leads to explosive politics in some places but not in others. This chapter examines the most politically important categories of identity in the modern world—nation, ethnicity, race, and religion. We look at the conceptual debate over the origins of identity groups, the similarities and differences across the different categories of identity, the political impact of these similarities and differences, and how these similarities and differences can be the basis of bloody political battles. The Country and Concept table at the end of this chapter portrays the linguistic, ethnic, racial, and religious diversity in our case study countries as well as the major conflicts that have arisen from that diversity.

As we noted in chapter 2, states and nations are intimately connected. Internationally, the state is seen as the representative and voice of the nation. Domestically, political leaders can gain great legitimacy and power by proclaiming their nationalism and castigating their opponents as "traitors" to the nation. But identities such as ethnicity or race also can serve as foundations of political mobilization and power within nation-states. We noted in chapter 3 that groups based on some sense of common identity are only one of many kinds of political groups, but these in particular have an intense hold on people's loyalties. Few people would risk their lives defending the Sierra Club or the local chamber of commerce, but everyone is expected to do so for their nation, and many would do so for their ethnic or religious group (or groups) as well. The potential for this kind of ultimate political commitment means states must and do care deeply about identity politics, because mobilization around identity can threaten national unity and even the continued existence of a state. All states seek to develop and gain legitimacy from some sense of identity, but the "wrong" identity can be the gravest threat a state can face.

Ethnic identity is a primary source of violent conflict in the world today. Triggered by drought and struggles over scarce resources, conflict in Sudan's Darfur region has raged along ethnic lines since 2003, creating a severe humanitarian crisis.

Many people view loyalty to their nation, ethnic group, or religion as natural, or even divinely ordained, but the intensity and political impact of this loyalty can vary widely across different countries and over time within any particular country. While some type of group membership may be "natural" to humans, a particularly intense political loyalty to the "nation," "tribe," or "faith" seems not to be, given how greatly it varies. The **political saliency**, that is, the political impact and importance of identity groups is created, not innate. Explaining this process is our first major task.

THE DEBATE OVER IDENTITY

Given the enduring importance of identity to politics, it's not surprising that social scientists have developed several different approaches to understanding how identities are formed and why they become politically salient. The debate over identity politics illustrates some of the theoretical divisions we outlined in chapter 1. Theorists disagree over whether identity politics should be explained by focusing on the elite or society as a whole, and on rational self-interest or political culture.

The oldest approach to addressing this debate is now commonly called **primordialism**. Primordialism provides the central assumptions of many people's understanding of group origins and difference and is implicit in the arguments of many nationalist, ethnic, and racial leaders. The purest primordialists believe exactly what we mentioned above: that identity groups are in some sense "natural" or God given, that they have existed since "time immemorial," and that they can be defined unambiguously by such clear criteria as kinship, language, culture, or phenotype (physical characteristics, including skin color, facial features, and hair). Based on these assumptions, many primordialists see conflict among groups as understandable, and perhaps even inevitable, given their innate differences. Few social scientists see the world in such black and white terms, and so there are few pure primordialists today, but the approach still holds important influence.

Primordialism largely holds sway as a political culture argument: cultural values and beliefs are deeply ingrained in people and are therefore the basis of more or less immutable group identities. Religious tenets understood in this way served as the basis of a very influential 1997 work by Samuel Huntington entitled *The Clash of Civilizations*. Huntington argued that the world can be divided into seven or eight major "civilizations" based largely on religious identity and that the major wars of the future will occur along the boundaries of these civilizations. Given that the belief systems of many of these civilizations are fundamentally different from those of Western society, the latter must recognize and address them as possible threats.

The first major challenge to such a line of thought came from scholars propounding a theory now known as **instrumentalism** whose proponents reject the idea that politically important identity groups originate only from the deeply held, enduring characteristics emphasized by primordialists. Instrumentalism is instead an elite theory of identity politics: rational and self-interested elites manipulate symbols and feelings of identity to mobilize a political following. Paul Brass, the first to put this view into words, argues that ethnic groups "are created and transformed by particular elites ... [and t]his process invariably involves competition and conflict for political power, economic benefits, and social status between competing elite, class and leadership groups" (1991, 25). Without elite leadership and context, "primordial" identities have little political relevance, the "cultural givens" won't matter much, and people who possess common cultural traits may not even see themselves as part of a cohesive group deserving of their political loyalty.

In addition to primordialism and instrumentalism, the most recent and currently dominant approach to understanding identity is **constructivism**. Like primordialism, it is partly based on political culture, but instead of accepting the primordialists' view of cultural identities as unchanging it utilizes the more recent ideas of political culture outlined in chapter 1, which emphasize the shifting interpretation of symbols and stories. This approach also accepts much of the instrumentalists' focus on the malleability of identity, but suggests the process is more complex because elites cannot manipulate identities in any way they please. In this sense, constructivists take a more pluralistic approach to understanding identity groups and group conflict. They argue that a complex process usually referred to as **social construction** creates identities. Societies collectively "construct" identities as a wide array of actors continually discusses the question of who "we" are.

This discourse is crucial to defining identities, or "imagined communities." Identity communities are "imagined" in the sense that they exist because people believe they do: people come to see themselves as parts of particular communities based on particular traits. These communities are not frozen in time, though they probably change relatively slowly. Furthermore, individuals see themselves as members of a number of different groups at the same time. Elites can attempt to mobilize people using the discourse and symbols of any one of several such communities in a particular time and place, but they cannot create a community no one else has imagined, and the ongoing social discourse provides the cultural material for and limits on elite manipulation.

This creation of social and cultural boundaries, even where no legal ones exist, is central to the social construction of identity. As a group defines who "we" are, it also creates boundaries that define who "they" are. To take the most obvious example, the concepts and identities of "man" and "woman" could not exist without each other. If humans were a species of only one gender, neither word would exist. The same is true, constructivists argue, for all types of identity, though usually there are more than just two categories. Afrikaner identity in South Africa, for instance, emerged in the nineteenth century among the descendants of Dutch and French settlers in juxtaposition to both the indigenous black African population and the invasion of British colonists. The social construction of this particular identity inherently included and excluded, and who was included and excluded had crucial consequences in regard to who ruled. Someone perceived as not part of a nation is unlikely to have significant social standing or political influence. Within a nation, if a powerful racial or ethnic group sees itself as superior, other groups may have difficulty asserting significant political power.

Constructivists argue that identities and boundaries are created by the interpretation and reinterpretation of symbols and stories, so they are at least partially postmodernist theorists of political culture. Through families, the media, and the public education system in all countries, individuals develop a sense of identity as they learn the importance and meaning of key symbols and stories. The state always plays an important role in this process. As a government develops and implements educational curricula, it requires that children be taught the "national history," which can include only certain events interpreted in certain ways if the "facts" are to continue supporting a specific national identity. Schools may also teach more localized ethnic or racial histories, although these are often more the purview of the family. The end result of this partly planned and always amorphous process is adherence to certain beliefs, values, symbols, and stories that come to constitute an identity: a flag, a monarch, the struggle for independence, the fight for racial equality, monuments to fallen heroes.

Like most contemporary social scientists, in this text we adopt a primarily constructivist approach, as it seems to combine the best of past theories. It is clear that identities are not fixed, and, as we'll see below, their political saliency varies greatly. Elites certainly play an important role in the process of creating and politically mobilizing identity groups, but identities develop over too long a period and are too intensely felt to be subject to complete manipulation. Culture matters, not as a static entity, but rather as a set of symbols and stories available for interpretation. Elites, working in their own rational self-interest, can interpret the symbols and stories of identity categories to connect them to particular political contexts, to raise passions of various sorts, and often to challenge the status quo. Therefore, state leaders typically work to reinforce a sense of national identity tied to support for the state and to find ways to accommodate other identities without threatening the strength and political legitimacy of the state itself. Conversely, their opponents

What about Gender?

Gender is an important identity category that we do not investigate in depth in this chapter. We chose not to focus as much on it because, in contrast to all the other categories, gender has never been the basis of a widespread movement for political autonomy, and it has never threatened the very existence of a state. It has, however, been the basis of very important movements for greater representation and equality. The women's movement has arguably been the most successful political and social movement of the last generation, especially in wealthy and middle-income nations, which we examine in detail in chapter 12.

The "third wave" of feminism has demanded greater access to education, which has improved women's economic standing, though in most countries their income still lags behind men's in spite of equal or greater educational achievement. Education and birth control have freed many women from traditional gender roles, allowing them to enter the political and economic spheres far more than at any time in the past. In the last twenty years, the women's movement in the Global South has expanded tremendously as well, as women battle for greater access to birth control, education, employment opportunities, and an end to female genital mutilation in parts of Africa and the Middle East. While perhaps not as successful at changing government policy as in the wealthier areas of the world, the women's movement in poorer countries is nonetheless well on its way to similar results.

Gender does share some clear similarities with the other identity categories, but in other ways it is fundamentally different. The demands of women's movements have been broadly similar to those of most racial movements: recognition and representation. And as in the case of race, once basic legal recognition and equality are achieved, women's movements have gone on to demand greater inclusion and integration in politics, the economy, and civil society. Yet because gender always cuts across communities—men and women exist in all communities—it does not serve as the basis of an exclusive communal identity. With a few minor exceptions, no all-women's community has demanded autonomy or its own state.

Gender also has a unique relationship to the other identity categories. While some notions of nationalism can be tied to race (Hitler) or religion (some versions of Islamism), most are not. Gender, on the other hand, is intrinsic in all other categories. As Nira Yuval-Davis and Flora Anthias (1989) have argued, gender symbols and women in general are used to define national, ethnic, religious, and racial boundaries. By having babies, women literally reproduce the community. As the primary child care providers in almost all societies, they also pass on key cultural elements to the next generation. Lastly, they serve as symbolic markers of community identity and boundaries. A recent example of this is the issue of wearing the Islamic veil, both in Europe and in several Middle Eastern countries (see chapter 12). What women do, how they behave, and where and how they are seen can all be issues of identity. Women's movements, whatever their origins and goals, threaten other communal identities that rely in part on particular gender roles and symbols to define themselves.

seek to interpret prevailing symbols and stories in different ways to undermine the political influence of those in power at the moment or perhaps even to bring into question the very existence of the state itself. We examine these processes by looking at each of the major categories of modern identity in turn: nation, ethnicity and religion, and race.

NATIONS AND NATIONALISM

The nation remains a fundamental building block of the global political system. Each state claims to be the sole legitimate representative of a nation, and each nation claims the right to its own state. Despite this, clearly defining the word "nation" is no easy task. Writing a century ago, French theorist Ernest Renan (1882), after trying to figure out which particular cultural characteristics produced nations in Europe, finally concluded that no single cultural feature was crucial. Instead:

> [a] nation is a soul, a spiritual principle. Two things, which are really only one, go to make up this soul or spiritual principle. One of these things lies in the past, the other in the present. The one is the possession in common of a rich heritage of memories; and the other is actual agreement, the desire to live together, and the will to continue to make the most of the joint inheritance.

The resemblance of Renan's deduction to contemporary notions of social construction is striking. A nation is an "imagined community," imagined through shared memories. All of those memories beyond the immediate experience of the individuals themselves are shared only because a group has learned to share them, in part through state-sponsored education.

Like the distinction between a state and a nation, the distinction between a nation and an ethnic group is also not always clear. The Irish are members of a nation, but when they immigrate to the United States they become, sooner or later, part of an "ethnic group." The Zulu in South Africa are an ethnic group, but the Palestinians, who are less culturally distinct from their neighbors (or at least from other Arabs) than the Zulu are from neighboring African groups, are generally regarded as a nation. As Renan concluded long ago, no particular set of cultural markers fully distinguishes a nation from an ethnic group. The only clear definition ties back to the state. A nation is a group that proclaims itself a nation and has or seeks control of a state. Ethnic groups do not think of themselves as nations and often do not desire to control their own state as much as they want autonomy within a larger state. This desire to be a nation and thus to control a national state is **nationalism**.

Perhaps not surprisingly, most nationalist leaders are primordialists: each claims his or her nation has existed since the mists of time as a mighty and proud people. As we saw in chapter 2, however, most scholars see nationalism as a fundamentally modern concept tied to the rise of the modern state and economy. The first European nations, such as France and England, were largely the products of pre-existing states. Once nationalism emerged as an idea, though, political and intellectual leaders started propagating a sense of national identity long before they controlled their own states, as the development of Germany demonstrates. In former colonies, nationalism emerged as a movement for independence from colonial oppressors. And once the creation of the state is accomplished, the process of developing a national identity continues. As Italian nationalist Massimo d'Azeglio declared shortly after the unification of Italy in the 1860s: "We have made Italy. Now we must make Italians."

Nationalism also has a complicated relationship with liberal democracy. At least until the mid-twentieth century, many nationalists saw themselves as carving democratic nations out of the remnants of feudal or colonial empires. Before "we, the people" can declare ourselves sovereign, "we" must have a sense of "us" as a "people": who is and is not included in "us" defines who has the rights of democratic citizenship. If "we" use particular cultural or physical characteristics to define "us," then we exclude as well as include people in our "nation." For this reason, most observers see **civic nationalism** as most supportive of democracy. This sense of national unity and purpose is based on a set of commonly held political beliefs. Those who share the beliefs are part of the nation. In contrast, **cultural nationalism** is national unity based on a common cultural characteristic, and those people who don't share that particular cultural characteristic cannot be included in the nation. How, then, can they be full citizens with democratic rights?

France and Germany provide a classic comparison of different kinds of nationalism. They illustrate that even what are perceived to be strong and deeply rooted nations were, in fact, constructed, and relatively recently at that. They also demonstrate the intermingling and competition of civic and cultural nationalism that exists in most countries, and therefore the complicated relationship of nationalism to democracy. As Rogers Brubaker (1992, 1) puts it, "For two centuries … France and Germany have been constructing, elaborating, and furnishing to other states distinctive, even antagonistic, models of nationhood and national self-understanding." He goes on to express how these two models illustrate the variation in the relationship between the state and the nation that we outlined above:

> In the French tradition, the nation has been conceived in relation to the institutions and territorial frame of the state. Revolutionary and Republican definitions of nationhood … reinforced what was already in the ancient regime an essentially political understanding of nationhood.…
> [T]he German understanding has been *Volk*-centered and differentialist. Since national feeling developed before the nation-state, the German idea of the nation was not originally political.… This prepolitical German nation, this nation in search of a state, was conceived not as the bearer of universal political values, but as an organic cultural, linguistic, or racial community.… On this understanding, nationhood is an ethnocultural, not a political fact.

These generalizations have regularly been contested within each country, however. French nationalism at first glance seems predominantly civic, but it has strong cultural elements, and German nationalism is clearly cultural, but that notion has been continually challenged, especially since Adolf Hitler's time in power. As the following mini-case on France and case study on Germany show, neither country's nationalism is monolithic and unchanging.

MINI-CASE Civic Nationalism in France

France, the "Great Nation," might seem an example of a primordial, culturally based nation *par excellence*. Its current borders encompass a number of distinctive cultures, however. Although most people think of the French language as intimately connected to French cultural and national identity, the territory of France includes speakers not only of *langue d'oil* (the precursor of modern French spoken in the central region), but also of *langue d'oc* in the south, Breton in the northeast, and other distinctive regional languages. It took Cardinal Richelieu's creation of the Académie Française in 1634 and a concerted effort to forge a unified, purified modern French language. Even so, perhaps only 50 percent of the population spoke modern French in 1789.

As the example of the Académie suggests, France's absolutist state was instrumental in forging a unified concept of a French nation. The French state under the monarchy was an absolutist state with many modern characteristics that expanded outward from Paris, incorporating neighboring regions into a single political unit. The concept of nationalism did not fully enter French political discourse until the Revolution of 1789, long after the state was fully established and quite extensive. This allowed a political and territorial nationalism to emerge, but while based on civic values of liberty, equality, and fraternity, French revolutionary nationalism was nonetheless culturally **assimilationist** from the start. Regional linguistic and cultural divisions were seen not as the democratic right of separate peoples but rather as unacceptable divisions in the unity of revolutionary and democratic France. Regional variation needed to be eliminated to achieve unity and equality, just as the absolutist monarchy had tried to do.

This nationalist ideal fully developed under the Third Republic after 1870, when the country's first universal and public education system was created, consciously designed to instill a common version of the French language and a common set of democratic political values in the population. By the end of the century, France's citizenship laws officially defined "the nation" as including virtually all people born within it. Legally, this took the form of *jus soli* laws, citizenship based on "soil," or residence in the state's territory, that conferred citizenship to second-generation immigrants.

This primarily civic nationalism did not go without challenge, however. Throughout the nineteenth century, France's political right called for a restoration of the monarchy and the official position of the Catholic Church. By late in the century, leaders in this movement had created a strongly cultural and primordial nationalism that focused on an often quasi-racial definition of the "pure" France that excluded immigrants, Protestants, and Jews, among others. This tradition was enunciated and carried forward by the Ligue des Patriotes founded in 1882, the Nazi puppet regime of Vichy France during World War II, and the opponents of Algerian independence in the 1960s.

The contemporary heir to the movement is the National Front (FN) led by Jean-Marie Le Pen. The FN openly calls for restrictions on immigration and immigrant rights, particularly in regard to France's large Muslim population. It advocates a shift from *jus soli* to *jus sanguinis,* citizenship based on blood rather than residence, a demand that reflects a primordial understanding of the nation. The FN also calls for a policy of encouraging white French to have more babies to maintain their percentage of the population. The National Front's efforts to redefine French nationality and citizenship in the direction of *jus sanguinis* have never succeeded, but the party's appeal has been substantial. As described in chapter 3, LePen's first-round win in the 2002 presidential election shocked the nation and the world. His vote share fell from a high of nearly 18 percent in 2002's second round to about 10 percent in 2007's presidential election. Nonetheless, the FN's persistence shows the continued appeal of cultural nationalism despite the strength of France's legal and historical commitment to civic nationalism.

CASE STUDY Nationalism in Germany

German nationalism long predates the modern German state. German speakers migrated widely across central and eastern Europe during the Middle Ages and lived side by side with Slavs and other ethnic groups while retaining their German language and culture. Modern German nationalism emerged in response to Napoleon's invasion of the region in the early nineteenth century and was influenced by the Romantic movement popular across Europe at the time. Advocates of this movement envisioned the nation as an organic whole with a "distinct personality." Intellectual leaders of German nationalism defined "Germany" in linguistic and cultural terms that juxtaposed German identity with those of the neighboring Slavs in the east and French in the west. The largest German state, Prussia, included large populations of minorities, however, especially Poles. In acknowledgment of this, Prussian reformers tried to develop a state-based sense of nationalism after the defeat of Napoleon in 1815, which ran counter to the linguistically based German nationalism advocated throughout the rest of the region. German nationalism, Brubaker argues, has been characterized by a "duality" between a state-based and a cultural nationalism ever since.

As outlined in chapter 2, Otto von Bismarck finally united much of what is now Germany in 1871. Like his contemporaries in France's Third Republic, he tried to use education to create greater cultural homogeneity in the new state, and he wrote citizenship laws that were partly based on *jus soli*, literally, citizenship dependent on "soil," or residence within the national territory. His new Reich, however, still included large populations of linguistic minorities and excluded huge numbers of German speakers in Austria and eastern Europe, and continuing emigration of Germans to eastern Europe and immigration of non-Germans into the Reich led nationalists such as the Pan-German League to successfully demand a revision to the citizenship laws in 1913.

Until 2000 Germany's "jus sanguinis" definition of citizenship meant that millions of Turkish workers and their German-born children were not citizens. These Turkish parents pose with their daughter, one of the first children born under a recent law that grants automatic citizenship to anyone born in Germany.

The new laws fully legalized the long-standing German nationalist conceptualization of the nation by basing citizenship quite strictly on *jus sanguinis*, or "blood" ties. This amendment legally codified a cultural and primordial understanding of what it meant to be "German."

Nazi ideology developed out of German cultural nationalism but distorted it by marrying it to explicit racism. The nation was thought of not only in cultural, but also racial, terms. The master Aryan race was superior to all others, and Hitler's regime stripped non-Aryans of all citizenship rights, expelling or exterminating many, especially Jews. With the end of the war and the establishment of West Germany, German nationalism remained primarily cultural. The Soviet Union expelled millions of ethnic Germans from Eastern Europe shortly after the war, and by 1950 they constituted one-sixth of West Germany's population. Germany once again was a nation divided across more than one state. Citizenship continued to reflect the concept of the cultural nation: all ethnic Germans were welcome into West Germany and automatically granted the rights of citizenship. This open-arms policy was in stark contrast to the treatment of the growing number of non-German immigrants, who rarely gained citizenship no matter how many generations they resided within Germany's national borders.

The debate over who is and should be "German" continues today, especially in the context of growing immigration. The large numbers of Turks who immigrated to Germany in recent decades were initially welcomed to fulfill essential jobs. Following German national self-conception, these immigrants were known as *gastarbeiter,* or "guest workers"; they were to stay as long as employed and then return home. Today more than two million Turks live in Germany, and many have raised children there. Until recently, however, very few could gain German citizenship because of Germany's *jus sanguinis* law. In 2000 the government finally allowed German-born children of immigrants who had been in the country at least eight years to apply for citizenship, provided they could pass a German language test. Approximately half a million former Turkish citizens now have German citizenship, though three quarters of Turkish residents remain noncitizens despite the fact that many have lived in Germany for decades.

The German case shows the complexity of what may seem to be a very stable national identity. Neither civic nor cultural nationalism has become the unquestioned and universal conception, at least not for very long. Political battles between contending visions of the national identity are fought in the realm of citizenship laws, meaning they have a direct bearing on who gains democratic rights and who does not. Nationality is not the only identity that has an important influence on and an ambiguous relationship with democracy, however, ethnicity and religion do as well.

ETHNICITY AND RELIGION

Ethnicity and Ethnic Conflict

Now that we have defined and illustrated what a nation is, defining an ethnic group becomes a little easier. An **ethnic group** is a group of people who see themselves as united by one or more cultural attributes or a sense of common history but do not see themselves as a nation seeking their own state. Like a nation and all other identity categories, people's perceptions, not actual attributes or some "objective" interpretation of history, are crucial because just like nations, ethnic groups are imagined. They may be based on very real cultural attributes such as a common language, but even these are subject to perception and change. In the former Yugoslavia, Serbs, Croats, and Bosnians all spoke closely related versions of what was known as Serbo-Croatian. As ethnic conflict and then war emerged in the

What's in a Name? Tribe, Ethnicity, and Nation

When Westerners think of Africans and Native Americans, they think of "tribes," but no one refers to the Basques in Spain or Scots in Britain as a tribe. Instead they are ethnic groups, linguistic groups, or "nations." A nation, it is argued, is a group of people who have or want their own state. By that definition, Basques and Scots only partially qualify: some of them want their own state, but many simply want greater autonomy within Spain or Britain. In this sense, they are very similar to a good portion of the Zulu in South Africa, who want much the same thing. So why are the Zulu a tribe while the Scots and Basques are not?

The word "tribe" usually conjures up the image of a small, primitive group tied together by a common culture, language, kinship, and system of government based on a chief. People tend to understand tribes in very primordialist and negative terms, that is, they are "traditional" groups that have survived into the modern world and therefore cause political problems. As our case study of Nigeria shows, nothing could be further from the truth. Modern African ethnic groups arose in their current form from varying precolonial identities or states during the colonial era. The Kalenjin of Kenya consist of eight separate groups speaking closely related languages that were brought together as an ethnic identity only in the 1950s, primarily via a radio program. To say "tribe," with its image of a small and primitive group, masks this history and variation.

The real reason tribe is associated with Africans and Native Americans is rooted in eighteenth- and nineteenth-century racist assumptions about these people. At least since Julius Caesar, tribe has implicitly meant a backward and inferior group of people. Caesar used "tribus" to refer to the "barbarian," blue-eyed blonds he conquered in northern Europe. European slavers and colonists used it to classify people they saw as backward and inferior, and the term stuck. (For an interesting discussion of the use of tribe in Africa, see www.africaaction.org/bp/ethall.htm.) Contemporary scholars of Africa prefer the term ethnic group for people in Africa, Europe, or anywhere else who have an identity derived from some cultural characteristic but who are not a nation in the Western sense of that term. Many Native Americans, on the other hand, prefer the term "nation," even though most of them do not seek complete sovereignty from the larger states in which they reside.

early 1990s, each group began claiming it spoke a distinct language—"Serbian," "Croatian," or "Bosnian"—and nationalists in all three groups began to emphasize the minor linguistic differences among them.

People think of African "tribes" as modern remnants of ancient, unchanging groups, but the Nigerian case below shows how even there ethnicity is socially constructed and quite modern. If ethnic groups do not desire to have their own state, what do they want? Their political interests generally revolve around what Charles Taylor (1994) calls the **politics of recognition**. All identity groups, including nations, want to be recognized, and each ethnic group usually desires this recognition within the confines of a nation-state that it shares with other ethnic groups. Recognition may include things like official state support of cultural events, instruction in the local language, a specific language being one of the official languages in which government business is conducted, or explicit inclusion in the national history curriculum. Where an ethnic group resides primarily in one area of the country, it also may demand some type of regional **autonomy**, such as a federal system of government in which members can control their own state or province. The issue became so contentious in India in the 1960s that the national government created a commission to examine it. This commission recommended the creation of a number of new states based on linguistic boundaries. For practical reasons, not all of India's hundreds of language areas could receive their own states, but the largest ones did.

In contrast to national identity, ethnicity is not always political. In the United States today, white ethnic identity has very little political content. Irish Americans may be proud of their heritage and identify culturally with Ireland, but few feel any common political interests based on that. This can change, of course: a century ago many Irish Americans felt their identity was tied very strongly to their political interests. A crucial question then is when and why ethnicity becomes politically salient. As instrumentalists point out, leadership can be a key cause. Because of the potential intensity of ethnic attachments, they are a tempting resource for ambitious politicians. A leader who can tie ethnic identity to political demands that people come to see as important can gain tremendous support.

Constructivists point out, however, that leaders cannot create such an appeal at will. The context is almost always important. If a group believes those in power have discriminated against it economically, socially, or politically, members may see their political interests and ethnic identity as one and the same. Their history, which they may well pass from parent to child, is one of discrimination at the hands of the powerful "other." Similarly, if they feel **relative deprivation**, a belief that they are not getting their share relative to others in the society or relative to their own expectations, they may come to see that deprivation in ethnic terms. On the other hand, sometimes relative wealth can lead to ethnic mobilization. If an ethnic group is based in a particular region, as many are, and that region has a particularly valuable resource such as oil, members of that group may feel that they should receive all or most of the benefits from what they see as "their" resource. The national government, on the other hand, will see the resource as belonging to the nation as a whole, to be controlled by the central government. This is a central issue in the ethnic and religious divisions in Iraq because the country's oil reserves are located in both Kurd and Shiite areas, but not in Sunni areas. Sunni leaders, not surprisingly, want oil revenue fully controlled by the central government in Baghdad, not by regional governments.

Political or economic uncertainty can also lead to ethnic mobilization. With the fall of communism in Eastern Europe and the former Soviet Union, many people felt great fear about the future. The old institutions had collapsed, and the new ones were untested. In this situation, it is relatively easy for a political leader to mobilize support with an ethnic or nationalist appeal by using history to suggest that other groups will take advantage of the uncertain situation and try to dominate everyone else. A classic case is Serbian leader Slobodan Milosevic, who proclaimed sympathy with the Serb minority in Kosovo in a famous speech in 1987, taking upon himself the mantle of Serb nationalism. Croatian and Bosnian Muslim leaders, fearful of Serb domination, soon responded in kind. The eventual result was war and genocide in which the three ethnic-religious groups who had lived together rather peacefully under Communist rule developed increasingly strident cultural nationalisms and ultimately dismembered the country.

Government leaders who want to remain in power and preserve peace must respond to such politically mobilized ethnic groups. Indeed, in a country with significant ethnic diversity or ethnic conflict, the government will often seek to preempt ethnic mobilization. One means of doing this that is common in authoritarian governments is simply to ban all public appeals to ethnicity, religion, or other "sectarian" identities. From the 1960s to 1980s, the party in Tanzania's one-party state had internal elections that were actually competitive, but candidates were strictly forbidden to make any ethnic, regional, or religious appeals when campaigning. Many a military leader has banned not only political parties, but all sorts of ethnic groups and clubs as well.

Less draconian measures are frequently taken in an attempt to grant ethnic groups some of the recognition and autonomy they seek while preserving a coherent central government. Federalism is one means of doing this. By creating regional states or provinces based on ethnicity or linguistics, central governments can try to shift the focus of ethnic politics from the center to the regional governments. A group still may not hold many official positions or much influence in the central government, but members may hold all of the offices in a specific province, whether the government is democratic or authoritarian.

Another means of granting some recognition and autonomy to ethnic groups is known as **consociationalism** (Lijphart 1977). A consociational system recognizes the existence of specific ethnic groups and grants each some share of power in the central government; for this reason it is often prescribed as a constitutional remedy for multi-ethnic countries recovering from conflict, such as Iraq. Switzerland and Belgium also are considered examples of this system. Power-sharing can be done formally, as in Lebanon where the distribution exists along religious lines: by agreement of all parties, the president is always a Christian, the prime minister a Sunni Muslim, and the Speaker of the Parliament a Shiite Muslim. It can also be done more informally. The electoral system, for instance, can be designed to encourage the formation of ethnically based parties, if this is a fundamental political cleavage in the society. The parties, once elected, can then work out power-sharing arrangements in some type of government of national unity.

Religion as Group Identity

We can apply most of what we have learned about ethnic groups to religious groups as well. A religious group identifies itself by a particular set of cultural characteristics centered on religious membership or beliefs. When membership alone is the criterion, the group is identified simply by nominal affiliation with the religion, regardless of actual practice or belief. The three major groups in the former Yugoslavia were defined primarily in this manner: Serbs are Orthodox, Croats are Catholic, and Bosnians are Muslim. As noted above, once tension and conflict began to emerge, leaders in each of the groups started to emphasize cultural distinctions. Ironically, because Communists had ruled the country since World War II, religious belief and practice were very low among all three groups prior to the outbreak of conflict: religious affiliation was a marker of identity based on birth, not a matter of personal faith. As the conflict spread, religious observance actually increased within all three groups. Once people start shooting at you because of your religion, the latter starts to loom larger in your consciousness.

One might assume that religious group membership can be more inclusive and flexible than ethnicity. Virtually all religions allow conversion to the faith, so while one may not be able to become Chechen, except perhaps through marriage, one can convert to Islam. In practice this may be more difficult, especially where religious identity has become a form of cultural marker and religion has become the basis of political mobilization. Such mobilization is at least implicitly targeted against other groups. It is unlikely that members of these other groups will desire conversion at this point, or be accepted if they did. Conversion is much more likely when the political salience of religious identity is relatively low.

The demands of religiously mobilized groups are comparable to those of ethnic groups: recognition and autonomy. For religious groups, recognition certainly involves the right to practice one's faith openly, but it might also include demands for the state to officially recognize the religion in the form of state-sponsored religious holidays or recognition of and perhaps funding for religious schools. Autonomy could take the form of a demand for federalism if the religious group lives in a particular region. Within its own state or province, the group can then practice its religion and use the state or provincial government to support it. Demands for autonomy can also take the form of granting religious leaders and organizations legal control over marriage, death, and other personal matters.

Multi-ethnic and multi-religious states need not be conflictual, though they often are. The wrong context combined with ambitious leaders can produce deep-seated, potentially violent political battles. Authoritarian states often try to avoid such conflict by simply banning any expression of ethnicity or religion, but in the long run this is unlikely to work. Some degree of recognition, autonomy, or both is usually essential if a mobilized group is to find its place peacefully inside a larger state. Nigeria provides an interesting case study of the possibility and problems of this type of approach.

CASE STUDY The Strange History of Ethnicity and Religion in Nigeria

Nigeria is demonstrative of the social construction of ethnic identity under colonialism, the role of relative deprivation and battles over resources in politicizing ethnic difference, and the limited ability of federalism and constitutional engineering to contain ethnic and religious conflict. It is also a case in which people hold multiple identities—regional, ethnic, and religious—the political salience of which has changed over time for each.

As outlined briefly in chapter 2, Nigeria is the quintessential colonial creation. People of many different languages and faiths were brought together within its boundaries, where approximately four hundred languages are now spoken. Three groups emerged as numerically predominant: the Hausa in the north, the Yoruba in the west, and the Igbo in the east. We say "emerged" because that is exactly what happened. While many Nigerians perceive their ethnic identity in primordial terms, those identities were in fact socially constructed primarily in the twentieth century. The Hausa are a Muslim people sharing a common language who were governed in twelve separate city-states by Muslim emirs in the eighteenth and nineteenth centuries. Today they constitute approximately 30 percent of Nigeria's population. The Yoruba shared a common language and a common indigenous religion that later became the basis for Haitian *voodoo* and Brazilian *candomblé*. Like the Hausa, for most of their precolonial history the Yoruba were not politically united and were instead divided into a series of kingdoms that sometimes lived in peace but which suffered through a time of prolonged warfare in the late precolonial period. Under colonial rule, most Yoruba converted to Christianity, though a large minority today is Muslim. Yoruba constitute about 20 percent of Nigeria's current population. The Igbo, on the other hand, had no conception of themselves as a people prior to colonial rule. They lived in small, mostly independent villages ruled by councils of elders—a classic **acephalous**, or stateless, society. The word "Igbo" first appears in documents in the 1930s. Under colonial rule, members of this group converted to Christianity more quickly and completely than did the Yoruba. By independence, they constituted 18 percent of Nigeria's population.

Despite these different origins, all three emerged as ethnic groups by the end of colonial rule. Each came to perceive its collective interests as tribal, defined by region and language. Indirect rule (described in chapter 2) played a part in this, as colonial chiefs became leaders over what the British, and the Nigerians, increasingly came to see as tribes. Missionaries and anthropologists were crucial in the recognition of the Igbo and other stateless societies as distinct groups. As they wrote down "tribal histories" that told primordialist stories of ancient and noble traditions and political unity and transcribed a common "Igbo" language, they codified that language and the Igbo culture.

For the Hausa and Yoruba, internal political disagreements faded in the face of their common interests vis-à-vis the colonizer and, increasingly, each other. As members of these groups moved to the growing colonial cities to work, they encountered members of other groups and gained employment and other benefits from members of their own group who had moved to the urban areas before them. These migrants began to compete for jobs, with members of each group supporting their own, and patron-client networks like those discussed in chapter 3 emerged. Separate networks developed within the groups, which established the importance of ethnicity to one's material well-be-

Conflict over ethnicity and oil led to an unsuccessful secession attempt by the Igbo and then civil war in 1968. Oil and ethnicity are still a volatile mix in southeastern Nigeria.

ing. Those individuals who became Christian were the first to be educated in colonial schools and in the English language, which gave them an advantage in the job market. The Igbo in particular benefited from this; the Hausa, being Muslim and therefore receiving little Christian education, lost out. Military employment, however, required less education than most sectors of the economy, and the Hausa and other northerners found greater success in this arena. Southerners, and especially the Igbo, dominated in education, civil service, and private business, even in other regions of the country.

The approach of independence in 1960 provided a context for solidifying ethnic and regional identity, and separate nationalist movements emerged in each of the three regions, each led by one of the three major ethnic groups. Budding national leaders mobilized followings on ethnic and regional bases, as instrumentalists would predict. Obafemi Awolowo rallied the Yoruba by creating a cultural organization, the Egbe Omo Oduduwa, that is, "the descendants of Oduduwa" (the mythical founder of the Yoruba people). Northern leaders used memories of the independent Muslim Sokoto caliphate of the nineteenth century to mobilize support for the Northern People's Congress. There was no comparable Igbo cultural organization, but the National Council of Nigeria and Cameroons, which originated as a broader nationalist party, became a de facto Igbo party led by Nnamdi Azikiwe by the late 1950s. When leaders of the three groups and the British negotiated a federal system of government on the eve of independence, some autonomy was given to each of the three regions. This meant that a coalition of two of the three would be required to form a national government. The northerners, led by the Hausa, shared the country's first independent government with the Igbo; by dint of numbers, the northerners were the dominant partner. The Yoruba in the west were left in opposition.

The newly independent government was fragile from the start. The three major parties, one representing each ethnic group, consolidated their power over the minorities in their own regions. The minorities, members of Nigeria's roughly two hundred much smaller ethnic groups, resented the political power of the larger groups and began demanding their own regions. By the 1990s, this pressure would result in the Nigerian government creating thirty-six states out of the original three regions. Growing tensions between the central government and the regions, as well as friction among the three major parties, led to a chaotic and violent second election in 1964. The military stepped in with the nation's first coup d'etat in 1966, led mainly by Igbo officers. The new government eliminated federalism, arguing it had caused much of the division and conflict of the prior years. Whatever the military's actual reason for taking power, the Yoruba and Hausa saw the coup and the elimination of federalism as an Igbo effort to grab power. In response, widespread rioting broke out in northern cities. Hausa attacked Igbo working as civil servants and in business, and tens of thousands were killed.

This violence combined with a battle over a new resource, oil, and ultimately escalated to full-scale civil war. A second military coup six months after the first brought a northern military government to power that restored federalism, this time creating twelve states. This gave some smaller ethnic groups their own states by dividing each of the three existing states into several. It was also an attempt to keep control of oil revenues out of Igbo hands, as oil production in the eastern region was rapidly on the rise. After the second coup and further violence against Igbo in the north, the Igbo military leader of the eastern region declared the independence of a new country, Biafra, in 1967. The effort to create a new

nation foundered when non-Igbo minorities in the region did not support this effort at nationalism. The result was a three year civil war (1967–1970), ultimately unsuccessful, in which more than a million people perished.

Northerners have pretty much ruled Nigeria ever since. Under the first two democratic republics (1960–1966 and 1979–1983), their numerical strength gave them electoral victory in voting that was sharply divided along ethnic lines. (In the current Third Republic, inaugurated in 1999, leading northern politicians decided to support a southerner, former Yoruba military ruler Olusegun Obasanjo, who ruled with greater support from the north than from his own region.) Because of their predominance in the military, northerners also controlled most of the military governments that ruled between the democratic regimes. With each return to democracy, a new constitution was drafted to try to contain ethnoregional conflict through the use of federalism and strict rules on how political parties could form. The 1979 constitution required that all political parties have representatives in all areas of the country; to win the presidency, a candidate had to win not just the most votes but also at least 25 percent of the vote in two thirds of the (at that point) nineteen states. Similar provisions in the 1999 constitution seem to have coincided with less ethnically tense politics at the national level.

The reduction in ethnic tension, however, is due in part to a shift of political saliency from ethnic to religious identity. With the rise of the global Islamist movement in the later part of the twentieth century, identity politics began to subtly shift in Nigeria. A marginal Muslim sect led by a self-proclaimed prophet emerged in the north and criticized both the government and mainstream Islam. Sect followers, mostly the urban poor and unemployed, engaged in extensive rioting in 1980, Nigeria's first religiously based conflict of any significance. The riots led to growing Muslim-Christian tensions as non-Muslims came to fear that a Muslim government might try to "Islamize" the new capital of Abuja. Religious tension continued to simmer throughout the 1990s, and the country's north-south regional division came to be seen as primarily religious rather than ethnic.

The 1999 constitution gave state governments the right to set their own legal systems. Newly elected governors in several northern states used this provision to rally a religious following by proclaiming Islamic *sharia* as state law. One reason for the popularity of this move was the weakness of the Nigerian state itself. The new government seemed incapable of controlling crime, reviving the economy, or controlling growing ethnic militias in parts of the south. Given this uncertain context, both ethnic and religious identity appealed to many people as possible sources of security. Yet although in theory *sharia* can apply to only Muslims, and a secular legal system would remain for non-Muslims, Christians were nonetheless mobilized to oppose what they saw as the Islamization of their states. Increasing competition over land between ethnic groups, some Christian and others Muslim, also helped fuel this conflict. So while proclaiming *sharia* was an attempt by Muslim leaders to clearly demonstrate that they were in control, local Christian opposition was an effort to assert religious rights, maintain some power in government, and protect land rights.

In the southeastern part of the country, local ethnic movements emerged in the mid 1990s around the issue of benefits from oil. Members of these movements, which contained both peaceful and violent elements, argued that all the oil revenue went to the central government and they were left with environmental devastation and poverty, in spite of living in the oil-rich region. The best known of these movements originated among the Ogoni, who were led by internationally known poet Ken Saro-Wiwa until his assassination in 1995. He and his movement successfully linked Ogoni ethnic demands with environmental and oil revenue concerns in a locally powerful movement that the military government ultimately tried to quell by executing Saro-Wiwa and several other leaders of the movement. To date, oil revenues remain under the control of the central government and the situation on the ground remains tense. Violent clashes, mostly involving young men from the Ijaw ethnic group, erupted in 1999 on the day after the newly elected government was sworn in, and in 2002 a group of Ijaw youth took over a ChevronTexaco oil facility to demand better treatment for Ijaw workers. In 2003 several oil producers suspended operations in Nigeria entirely until the country's military regained control of the situation. Among the Yoruba, a separatist movement, the O'odua People's Congress, emerged before the 1999 election in response to the military government, and continues to attract young urban Yoruba to its sometimes violent activities. Though not focused on oil, the group does advocate Yoruba nationalism and strong federalism.

A number of lessons can be taken from the history of Nigerian ethnicity and religion. First, although they are socially constructed and usually quite modern, once ethnic and religious divisions are politicized they become difficult to contain. Both military and civilian governments struggled with these forces, and at times their efforts at control exacerbated the problems rather than provided solutions. Even seemingly logical solutions such as creating more state governments and requiring that political parties have some degree of support across the country were of limited success because in the context of economic inequality, relative deprivation, political insecurity, and conflict over oil, political leaders have been able to raise ethnic and religious support quite easily.

Second, the political saliency and focus of different identities can shift in a relatively short span of time. In the 1960s, national political divisions were primarily a three-way split among the major ethnic groups and regions. Thirty years later, the major political division was along a two-way, north-south, Muslim-Christian divide. Ethnicity had not disappeared; it had simply become more localized. In areas of religious conflict over the use of *sharia* as state law, ethnic and religious divisions often overlapped at the local level. In the southeastern oil region, local ethnicity continued to be very powerful, and Yoruba and "Biafran" separatist movements still exist today, ready to gain more followers when the time is right and their numbers swell. All of this has posed severe challenges for Nigeria's efforts at democracy. Ethnic conflict has been a primary force undermining the two prior attempts at democracy, and religious and ethnic tensions threaten to undermine the current democracy.

MINI-CASE Rwanda: Genocide and Ethnic Violence

When does politicized ethnicity or religion become violent? Can we understand why and when it happens? The factors that explain ethnic and religious political mobilization also help explain the next step, violence. Key leaders can incite ethnic violence in the context of relative deprivation, battles over control of resources, and political and economic uncertainty. The tiny central African country of Rwanda is an example. In three months in 1994, Rwandan Hutus murdered approximately eight hundred thousand other Rwandans, the vast majority being Tutsi, the other ethnic group in the country. Yet no situation shows the inaccuracy of the concept of primordial "tribal conflict" better than Rwanda, a precolonial kingdom that survived colonialism with its borders more or less intact. Hutu and Tutsi speak the same language, live in the same communities and neighborhoods, have the same customs, follow the same religions, and lived for centuries in the same kingdom. Cultural differences between them don't exist.

What do exist are all the other elements of political mobilization of ethnicity listed above. Tutsis dominated the precolonial kingdom, and Belgian colonial rule reinforced this by increasing Tutsi power and control. At independence in 1960, a "Hutu revolution" overthrew the Tutsi monarchy and established a Hutu-led government that would rule until the genocide in 1994. The revolution produced hundreds of thousands of Tutsi refugees, who fled to neighboring countries. An entire generation grew up in neighboring Uganda but was never granted citizenship or full rights there, and these individuals longed to return home. Some launched a successful invasion of the country in 1990. By 1993 a ceasefire had been established, and democratic elections were planned with the goal being a new govern-

ment of both Hutu and Tutsi. Elements on both sides, however, feared the results. Hutu leaders enjoyed the privileges of power and wanted to maintain them, and some Tutsi rebel leaders seemed unwilling to allow the majority (overwhelmingly Hutu) to rule.

A group of Hutu extremists in the government, some of whom have since been convicted of genocide by UN tribunals, began propagating an anti-Tutsi ideology, primarily via radio. These individuals continuously told their followers that the Tutsi were trying to regain complete power, take away Hutu land and power, and kill many Hutu. In a very densely populated country dependent on agriculture, the threat to land ownership was particularly explosive. The Hutu extremists also created private militia of unemployed and desperate young Hutu men, and when the Hutu president's plane was shot down on April 6, 1994, the extremists and their armed militia swung into action. First their military supporters staged a coup, then barriers went up all over the capital and the militia began systematically executing "moderate" Hutu who might oppose the genocide (lists of the first to be killed had been prepared in advance), as well as any Tutsi they found. The extremist hate-radio directed much of the effort, telling the militia where Tutsi were hiding and urging them to "chop down the trees." (The stereotype of a Tutsi person is tall and thin, hence the image of cutting down trees.)

Members of the militia demanded that other Hutu join them in identifying and killing Tutsi; those who refused would themselves be killed as moderates who could not be trusted. The rest of the world watched in horror but did little to stop the killing. Finally, a Tutsi-led rebellion swept into the capital, took over the country, and stopped the genocide, but not until more than three-quarters of the entire Tutsi population had been killed. While such crimes are impossible to fully explain, a context of fear and a battle over resources (land) and power, enflamed by irresponsible, hate-mongering leaders, helps us understand how such an event could happen. It is the logical conclusion of any ideology demanding national, racial, or ethnic purity.

RACE

While the distinction between ethnic group and nation is relatively clear, the difference between ethnic group and race is much more ambiguous. In a particular context it may seem quite obvious, but at a more abstract level, a consistent distinction is difficult to apply systematically. Most ethnic identities focus on cultural rather than physical characteristics, though many do see specific physical characteristics as markers of particular groups as well. Most racial groups are distinguished by physical characteristics, though they and others may also perceive cultural distinctions. We define a **race** as a people who sees itself as a group based primarily on one or more perceived common physical characteristics and common history. The distinction between this and ethnicity is still not crystal clear, but this is probably the best we can do.

An interesting example of the interconnectedness of the terms comes from ethnic and racial categorizations in much of Latin America. In many Latin American countries with substantial indigenous populations, such as Guatemala, indigenous people who keep their traditional language, dress, and customs regard themselves as an ethnic group. The dominant groups in society, however, may regard these people in both ethnic and racial terms. This is made clear when a separate term (such as "ladino" in Guatemala) is reserved for persons of indigenous descent who adopt Spanish and no longer maintain indigenous customs. In this case, race and ethnicity are clearly intertwined and depend very much on whose opinion is being asked.

For the concept of race, just as for that of nation and ethnicity, we emphasize perception. Genetically, members of racial groups, such as white and black Americans, have as much in common with each other as they do with members of their own groups: genetic variation is no greater across the two groups than it is within each. Races are constructed by focusing on particular differences, such as skin color, and ignoring the far more numerous similarities. Discussing sex, Sigmund Freud referred to this process as "the narcissism of minor differences," the process by which humans amplify the importance of very minor biological variations, such as x versus y chromosomes or skin color.

Like all socially constructed categories of identity, racial identity varies across time and space, as the case studies of the United States and Brazil below demonstrate. While racial groups may seem absolutely fixed and "natural" to most people in a particular time and place, they are just as subject to change as national and ethnic identities. This is also true in the context of political mobilization and political saliency. Like ethnicity, a racial identity need not be political in the sense of being a basis for common political goals. The extent to which it is depends on the ability of particular leaders to articulate a common agenda by using the symbols of racial identity and discrimination in a way that is compelling to people in a particular context. A dominant or majority group, such as white Americans, typically will not see itself as pursuing a common political agenda, though members of other races may think otherwise. Groups in a minority or subordinate position are more likely to view their political interests as tied to their racial identity. Like national and ethnic movements, this is most likely when they sense some deprivation or discrimination tied to their race, and a leadership group is able to articulate this successfully.

Politicized racial groups usually desire recognition and representation. Autonomy is a less common goal because racial groups usually do not share a distinct geographical home. Recognition usually means official governmental recognition of the race as a socially important group through such means as inclusion on a census form, the teaching of the group's historical role in the larger national history, and the celebration of its leaders and contribution to the nation's culture. In addition, racial groups desire representation, in the sense of full formal and informal participation, in their government and society. Thus, racial demands typically do not involve such mechanisms as federalism, but instead focus on inclusion in public and private employment, political office, and the educational system. Frequently, as in the United States, members of minority races may argue that past discrimination justifies some type of preferential system that works to relatively rapidly achieve representation equal to their share of the population. Mechanisms to do this might include numerical targets or goals for hiring, increased funding for training and education for particular races, or adjustments to the electoral system that make the election of racial minorities more likely. As the cases of the Unites States and Brazil show, racial politics can be just as intense as ethnic or national politics, so state leaders often see it as in their interests to respond, or at least appear to respond, to racial demands.

MINI-CASE Bolivia: Regional Conflict

Bolivia has always been deeply divided along racial, economic, and geographic lines. When the Spaniards first arrived, they subjugated and enslaved the Native population, descendants of the Incas, although geographic isolation in the country's western *Altiplano,* a high plateau between two Andean ranges, limited the impact of European diseases, so the indigenous population remained significant. Even after independence, this large indigenous population continued to be subjugated and disenfranchised, and the economic benefits of the precious metals they mined from the *Altiplano* flowed to economic elites, doing little to develop or enrich the people of the region. Today about 55 percent of Bolivians are indigenous, speaking thirty-seven different languages, with Aymara and Quechua being the most prevalent. They continue to live primarily on the *Altiplano,* where the descendants of those enslaved to work in the mines labor as subsistence farmers or coca growers. Most live below the poverty line. In contrast, Bolivia's eastern lowlands are tropical forest or grassland, home to the wealthiest part of the population. (Most of this region is now inhabited by white Bolivians, descendants of European immigrants.) These days the region's wealth is based on oil, natural gas, and agribusiness, but during much of the country's history it was an economic backwater compared to the mining region.

Bolivia's government structure even reflects the long-standing social divide between indigenous groups on the *Altiplano* and white, European-descended Bolivians in the eastern lowlands. It is one of a very few countries to have two capital cities: La Paz on the *Altiplano* houses the executive and legislative branches; Sucre, 250 miles away in the lowlands, is home to the judiciary. At independence in 1825, Sucre was the national capital. A civil war in 1899 pitted the Liberal Party based in La Paz against the Conservatives with a stronghold in Sucre; when the Liberals won they created the current divided capital arrangement. The civil war was not, as we might expect, over the ethnic differences between the regions, but rather over resources. Although the capital was in Sucre, railways connecting La Paz to the Pacific meant that region became the wealthier of the two by exporting silver and tin. The exports did not benefit the indigenous people, but European elites became wealthy and wanted to control politics as well as the national economy.

For the last several decades, the east has been the wealthier region, and the white population has been politically dominant through both democratic and military regimes. That political dominance was upset in 2006, when Evo Morales was elected the nation's first indigenous president. A Socialist with close ties to peasant groups and coca growers on the *Altiplano,* Morales proposed a number of radical measures, including nationalizing the nation's energy resources to redistribute wealth to the impoverished *Altiplano.* He also called for a constitutional assembly to draft a new document that would recognize many indigenous rights and guarantee indigenous representation in the legislature. Perhaps not surprisingly, conflict between Morales and his supporters and political and economic elites in the eastern lowlands quickly escalated. The easterners demanded that the constitutional assembly once again make Sucre the sole capital of Bolivia. When the assembly rejected this, four eastern lowland states refused to recognize the new charter and issued their own declarations of autonomy. Both the constitution and the declarations of autonomy went before voters in 2007, but the results are still being debated.

There are certainly elements of long-standing ethnic tension in the current conflict, but this struggle also illustrates the way in which ethnic conflicts interact with and are stimulated by other factors. In 2007, as in 1899, a significant part of the conflict was based on economic disparities between the two regions. In 1899 the tensions were found among the white elite, but as economic power shifted eastward, the economic conflict has been superimposed along the same lines as the country's ethnic and racial divide. Interestingly, the easterners have demanded autonomy, not national independence, despite the clear regional division. Perhaps this is because they have not historically perceived themselves as an ethnic group (being composed primarily of descendants of white Europeans from Spain but also many other countries), and so they lack the wherewithal to develop a national consciousness. They do, however, perceive a common benefit in regional autonomy from a government they currently see as controlled by an indigenous agenda.

CASE STUDY Racial Politics in the United States

While most Americans today see racial categories as self-evident and more or less fixed, nothing could be further from the truth in U.S. history. The three oldest racial categories in the United States are white, black/ African American, and Native American. The white-Native conflict reduced Native populations nearly to extinction. The black population, on the other hand, grew substantially, and the white-black division would become the racial division that had the greatest impact on American political history and national identity. For most of the country's colonial and independent history, this racial division was legally defined to distinguish clearly between black slave and white citizen and eventually took the form of the "one drop" rule, which classified anyone with virtually any black heritage as black and therefore slave. This ensured that the offspring of slave women and white masters remained slaves and thus property. In the immediate aftermath of slavery, legal racial definitions remained important in underpinning the segregationist laws of the Jim Crow era. The famous *Plessy v. Ferguson* case of 1896 would codify such postslavery racial definitions by classifying a person as "black" if the individual had one-eighth black ancestry (that is, one of eight great grandparents was classified as black). Like the one drop rule before it, this definition served to keep the black population clearly identified as such and the black-white boundary as distinct as possible.

The black-white division, though, has not been the only racial question in U.S. history. The clear categorization of all European immigrants as white that is so accepted today was by no means automatic. Writing in 1897 in *The Conservation of Races,* and reflecting the racial understanding of his time, the great black intellectual W. E. B. du Bois lists the following races

> the Slavs of eastern Europe, the Teutons of middle Europe, the English of Great Britain and America, the Romance nations of Southern and Western Europe, the Negroes of Africa and America, the Semitic people of Western Asia and Northern Africa, the Hindoos of Central Asia and the Mongolians of Eastern Asia.

The predominantly Anglo population of the United States in the late nineteenth century shared du Bois's categorization, which meant that immigrants from southern and eastern Europe were not viewed as racial equals. This changed only with the passage of significant time and the slow assimilation across generations of Irish, Italians, Poles, Jews, and others, into the white majority. A recent study of this era and this process is *How the Irish Became White* (Ignatiev 1995).

The ultimate success of these groups in claiming a place of equality within the white majority had significant effects. First, most discriminatory practices against them ended over time; by the end of the twentieth century no discernable differences in socioeconomic standing existed between members of these groups and the larger white population. Second, this assimilation process helped preserve a clear white majority in the country as a whole. Given the huge number

Racial thinking in the United States has long been dominated by the categories "white" and "black," but Hispanics are now the country's single largest "minority" group. Many non-Hispanics may think of this group as a third "racial" category, but language, not race, is its key characteristic, as this bilingual sign outside a Texas polling place in 2004 suggests.

of immigrants, had they ultimately been classified into the distinct races listed by du Bois, today the country would have a number of racial minorities, but no clear racial majority. Third, white "ethnics," as they are sometimes called, see themselves as white and American first, and "ethnic" only secondarily, if at all. Their ethnic origin may be a source of pride and may influence their culture in various ways, but it has virtually no impact on their political allegiance or activity.

This is certainly not true, on the other hand, for African Americans and other blacks, whose racial identity has always profoundly affected their political activity. Du Bois (1897) wrote that the "American Negro" (the term he used at the time) suffered from a "double consciousness [in which o]ne ever feels this two-ness—an American a Negro; two souls, two thoughts, two unreconciled strivings; two warring ideals in one dark body, whose dogged strength alone kept it from being torn asunder." The very history of racial terminology reflects the struggle descendants of African slaves have had to assert a positive racial identity. A century ago, "Negro" replaced "Colored" as the preferred term, an assertion of identity against prior derogatory terms. In the late

1960s, "black" came to replace "Negro" via the "black power" movement, which was an attempt to unite around the most obvious sign of racial character, skin color, and proclaim "black is beautiful." In the 1980s, Jesse Jackson helped popularize "African-American," arguing that his people should have the same status as any other "hyphenated" immigrant group.

Throughout this terminological evolution, African Americans have been united and politically mobilized most successfully by their common experience in the face of discrimination. Until at least the early 1960s, local laws of various sorts throughout the United States kept most blacks restricted to impoverished ghettoes or isolated rural areas with limited access to social, economic, or political opportunities. They were, at best, second-class citizens. This situation produced two major branches of thinking about their identity, both of which have always involved important political positions and demands. From Frederick Douglass to Martin Luther King Jr. and Jesse Jackson, one strand has focused primarily on proclaiming and demanding racial equality within the existing U.S. political and social system. King's core demands were the rights enshrined in the Declaration of Independence and the U.S. Constitution: a system that actually operates on the precept that "all men are created equal." The legal elements of this effort were achieved with the Civil Rights Act of 1964 and the Voting Rights Act of 1965, finally and permanently granting African Americans the complete rights of citizenship.

These laws did not fully eliminate the effects of past discrimination, however. In the last four decades, the efforts of leaders within the African American community have focused on programs to achieve full social and economic integration that will ensure equal representation of African Americans in the political system, the economy, and civil society. These efforts have included demands for: 1) "affirmative action," that is, programs in education, employment, and business that accommodate specific hiring policies directed toward minorities; 2) equal funding for educational opportunities; 3) greater funding for programs to improve conditions for the poor, who are disproportionately black and Hispanic; 4) changes in the electoral system to enhance the possibility that African Americans will be elected into public office; and 5) encouragement of African American voting and other forms of participation in the electoral process.

Running parallel to this first line of defining black identity is the second strand, usually referred to as "black nationalism," though only some of its adherents qualify as nationalists in our terms. In the words of William Van Deburg (1997, 3), proponents of this movement "seek to strengthen in-group values while holding those promoted by the larger society at arm's length. Withdrawing from the body politic as much as practicable, they strive to win and maintain sociocultural autonomy." One of the earliest manifestations of this was promoted by Caribbean-born activist Marcus Garvey, who popularized the "back to Africa" movement in the early twentieth century. Based on the belief that blacks would never be accepted as full citizens in the United States, he proposed a large-scale immigration to a new, or renewed, homeland in Africa. This was the ultimate demand for autonomy rather than representation.

A much more recent, and slightly less extreme, version of this same strand of thinking was the "black power" movement of the 1960s. Black power leaders went beyond proclaiming blacks' rightful place in U.S. society by emphasizing that fundamental change in the U.S. socioeconomic system was needed before racial equality could be achieved. Their actions aimed first at creating a more positive self-image among the black community rather than demanding immediate changes in white behavior or attitudes. Groups like the Black Panthers worked to improve the lives of poor blacks in urban areas, provided self-defense and protection (from the police as well as from criminals), and educated blacks in the glories of their African past, all with little support from or interest in white society at large. Advocates of this approach argued that not until black power was achieved in this way could blacks ultimately force racist whites to move toward racial equality.

Blacks and whites, of course, are not the only racial groups in the United States. The people now called "Asian Americans" and "Hispanics" have been present since at least the mid-nineteenth century, and Mexicans lived in the Southwest long before it became part of the United States. The terms "Asian American," "Hispanic," and "Latino," however, are of very recent origin. Immigrants from China, Japan, and other Asian countries, as well as residents of Mexican descent, identified themselves primarily by nationality until the mid-twentieth century. Chinese immigrants, for instance, thought of themselves as Chinese, and later Chinese American, but not as Asian American. A relatively small population and often poor, they had little influence on national politics. Like other immigrants, they were treated as second-class citizens in many ways, even in areas where their populations were fairly large.

Intellectual and political activists in these minority communities were influenced by the black power movement in the 1960s and began to conceive of themselves and their political demands in new ways. Rather than focusing on their separate countries of origin, leaders began to shift the focus of their identity to their common experiences in the United States. They argued that Chinese, Japanese, Filipino, and other immigrants faced common linguistic and racial hurtles and experiences in the United States, and so they coined the term "Asian American" to unite them under one identity. This new movement began with a student strike in San Francisco in 1968, as Japanese, Chinese, and Filipino students came together from separate ethnically defined organizations to form a new "Asian-American Political Alliance." Similarly, leaders of Mexican, Puerto Rican, Dominican, and other South and Central American groups began to use the more overarching "Hispanic" to assert their common identity tied to their common language and experience of discrimination.

Hispanics are the fastest growing census group in the United States: this population increased by nearly 60 percent between the 1990 and 2000 censuses to officially become the largest "minority" group in the country. While most Americans probably think of Hispanic or Latino as a racial category, each is legally a linguistic category, that is, Hispanics and Latinos identify themselves as speakers of Spanish or descendants of Spanish speakers. Officially, these individuals can be of any race. The U.S. census, however, still has not come to reflect accurately the self-perception of Hispanic Americans: in the 2000 census, 48 percent of Hispanics identified themselves racially as white. Another 42 percent identified themselves as "some other race," which indicates an unwillingness to accept any of the official U.S. racial categories. After 2000 the Census Bureau tried unsuccessfully to eliminate the category of "some other race" in an attempt to force Hispanics to choose among the existing racial categories, but political pressure by the Hispanic community successfully resisted this effort. Clearly, the construction of the category "Hispanic/Latino"—socially, politically, and legally—is still very fluid.

As this discussion shows, racial inequality in the United States remains considerable despite the political mobilization of racial groups in recent decades. Table 4.1 shows recent data for education and income for the largest racial groups. As this data make clear, while Asian Americans have achieved, and indeed surpassed, the levels of education and income achieved by whites, African Americans and Hispanics continue to suffer much lower levels of both. And Asian Americans do not graduate from high school in as high a percentage as do whites, indicating something of a divided Asian American population, with many earning

TABLE 4.1 Racial Disparity in the United States

	White (not Hispanic)	African American	Asian	Hispanic (all racial categories)
Percentage with college degree	27	14	44	10
Median household income, 2006 ($US)	52,375	32,372	63,642	38,747

Sources: Income, earnings, and poverty data from the 2006 American Community Survey, U.S. Census Bureau, August 2007; U.S. Census Bureau, "Educational Attainment: 2000," www.census.gov/prod/2003pubs/c2kbr-24.pdf.

college degrees but quite a few others not even finishing high school. African Americans and Hispanics each constituted about 12 percent of the U.S. population in 2000, and forty-three African Americans, just short of 10 percent of the total, served in the House of Representatives in 2005, while one served in the Senate that same year. Twenty-three Hispanics were elected to the House in 2004, and, for the first time ever, two were elected to the Senate, but overall, Hispanics remain underrepresented in both houses. African Americans have come close to parity in the House, but still lag far behind in representation in the Senate, to which only five African Americans have ever been elected—two in the 1860s and three since World War II.

CASE STUDY Race in Brazil

A comparison of the United States and Brazil demonstrates in stark terms the variation and importance of racial identity and racial politics in different contexts. Like the United States, Brazil was a major slaveholding society. Indeed, Brazilian slavery was much more extensive and lasted longer than slavery in the United States: abolition did not occur until 1888, making the country the last in the Americas to outlaw slavery. At the time of abolition, approximately half of Brazil's population was at least partially of African slave descent.

Despite very different conceptions of racial identity and politics, racial discrimination and inequality in Brazil are rather similar to what is found in the United States. The different conceptions of race, however, have made it much more difficult for a clear black racial consciousness to emerge in Brazil and effectively demand black recognition and representation. Only in the last thirty years has a sustained Afro-Brazilian political movement emerged and achieved some success in altering the country's racial policies.

The black/white dichotomy that characterizes U.S. racial history makes little sense to most Brazilians. Brazil contains literally dozens of informal racial categories and distinctions. Intermarriage between light-skinned and dark-skinned people has been and remains fairly common. More important, Brazil's social construction of race is nearly opposite of that of the United States. Throughout the twentieth century, Brazil proclaimed itself a racial democracy because no legal racial segregation had existed there since the end of slavery. Simultaneous and contradictory to these claims, however, has been an explicit desire to "whiten" the population in a variety of ways.

Brazilians say, "Money whitens," but as this photo of Brazilian socialites taken in 2005 shows, the elite is still white. A 2008 Brazilian government study found that it may take another fifty years to bridge the income gap between blacks and whites.

For many years, Brazilian intellectuals and leaders claimed that Brazilian slavery had been more humane than slavery in the United States, although few historians accept this view today. While no more humane, it was certainly different. Slaves in Brazil, working in tropical conditions to complete the plantation work demanded of them, tended to die younger than North American slaves. The system survived for centuries not by the biological reproduction of slaves but instead by the large-scale importation of new slaves to replace the old. This meant that defining the children of slaves as slaves was not as economically important as it was in the United States. Combined with the fact that for a long time Portuguese immigrants to Brazil were overwhelmingly male, the result was the early beginnings of a "**mulatto**," or mixed race, group. The ease of importing slaves also meant Brazilian slaveholders were less

IN CONTEXT Race and Ethnicity in Latin America

Nearly 50 percent of Brazilians are of African descent, whereas only 1 percent are indigenous. In most Latin American countries, though, identity politics focus on indigenous ethnicity. Survey data on race and ethnicity in Latin America are difficult to interpret, but the following data give some idea of issues of race, ethnicity, and access to power and resources in the region.

- 29% (about 150 million people) of the population of Latin America and the Caribbean is of African descent; more than half of these live in Brazil.

- 8% (about 40 million people) of the region's population is indigenous and lives in every country except Uruguay.

- 400 indigenous languages are spoken in the region.

- Indigenous people comprise 30% to 50% of the populations of Bolivia, Ecuador, Guatemala, and Peru.

- Nearly 25% of all Latin American indigenous people live in Mexico, but they comprise only 10% of Mexico's population.

- Indigenous people are disproportionately poor; for example, while approximately 66% of all Guatemalans are poor, 90% of indigenous Guatemalans are.

Source: Mayra Buvinic and Jacqueline Mazza, with Ruthanne Deutsch, ed. *Social Inclusion and Economic Development in Latin America.* Washington, D.C.: Inter-American Development Bank, 2004.

"whitening." This included encouraging and even subsidizing the immigration of European workers and completely banning black immigration. By 1920 half of the industrial workforce was composed of immigrants, and virtually all of them were from southern and eastern Europe. As in the United States, this large-scale immigration of people who came to be defined as "white" kept the black and mulatto proportion of the population lower than it would have been otherwise.

Whitening in Brazil also included active encouragement of racial intermarriage to "improve" black genetics with white genes, and those few blacks or mulattos who were able to crawl up the class ladder were also "whitened" in the process. Racial discrimination was milder for those with higher levels of education and wealth, which would come to be the source of the common Brazilian phrase "money whitens." Brazil's white population, facing a country in which at least half of the population was of slave descent, actively encouraged the creation of intermediate racial categories as buffers between them and poor, uneducated blacks. Even the census was employed for this purpose. Over the years, the Brazilian government used it to actively encourage people to identify with some intermediate category instead of "black," or to deny the existence of race entirely by simply not asking any racial questions at all. The policy worked: the 1890 census recorded 44 percent of the population as "white"; the 1950 census put the figure at 62 percent, with a similar increase in "mulatto" identification and a reduction in "black" identification.

opposed than their North American counterparts to slaves buying their freedom. This combination of factors resulted in a significant free population of mulattos and some blacks by the time of abolition. Since the country was a monarchy until 1889, no one could vote, so the existence of this group also created no immediate political threat to the white elites. And so Brazil achieved abolition peacefully and nearly simultaneously created a republic. With the growing industrialization of southern cities, many former slaves moved south, especially to Rio de Janeiro.

The central government in Rio never imposed legal segregation of the sort found in the United States during the Jim Crow era, but it did pursue the policy of

Brazilian historian and intellectual Gilberto Freyre is credited with coining the term "racial democracy" in the 1930s. At the same time, populist president Getúlio

Vargas embraced Afro-Brazilian cultural practices such as samba, *carnaval* (Brazilian mardi gras), and *condomblé* (a Brazilian descendent of Nigerian Yoruba religion). This meant that African heritage was celebrated as part of the racial democracy and national culture, even as discrimination and efforts to whiten the population continued. Political discrimination, when a democracy existed, was secured by a law requiring voters to be literate, disenfranchising the majority of the black population without imposing legal racial restrictions.

In this context, political activists had a difficult time creating and politically mobilizing an Afro-Brazilian identity. The policy of whitening allowed what was called the "mulatto escape hatch." If education, intermarriage, and a better income could whiten people and improve their social status, why actively try to identify yourself as "black"? For this reason, most poor blacks viewed their difficulties in terms of class, not race. Black activists complained of the difficulty of organizing: people preferred to view themselves as poor, a condition they could escape by winning the lottery or getting money some other way, than as black, a condition they could never change.

Black political movements eventually did emerge, the first significant one of which developed in the 1930s in the form of a black political party. Outlawed with all other parties when Vargas ended democracy in 1937, black organizations, except for a few that focused on culture, remained largely dormant even after the return to democracy in 1945. In contrast to the United States during the same period, no significant black movement emerged in the 1950s and 1960s.

The military government in power from 1964 until 1985 continued the policy of denying the importance of race, so when Brazilian social scientists in the 1960s produced the first studies demonstrating the extent of racial inequality, the military banned all studies of racial discrimination in 1969 and exiled several of the scholars involved. In response, the *Movimento Negro Unificado* (Unified Black Movement) became an active part of the struggle for democracy, but the group's long-term gains remained limited. Beginning in the 1980s, newly elected state governors, especially in the major urban areas like Rio de Janeiro, did start to place some blacks in leadership positions and officially begin to recognize Afro-Brazilians as a group by, for instance, incorporating Afro-Brazilian cultural events in schools. At the national level, however, the major political parties, even those on the left of the political spectrum, continued to focus on class issues and to downplay the importance of race, and very few self-identified blacks were elected to the National Congress.

By the 1990s, Brazil was still a racially unequal society. In 1999, blacks—defined as all those who did not identify as white on the census—were 45 percent of the national population but 64 percent of those living in poverty. Illiteracy among black adults was 20 percent, as opposed to 8 percent among adult whites. In 2003 only 9 of 513 members of the National Congress self-identified as black. One of these, Benedita da Silva, has spent many years trying to create an Afro-Brazilian caucus in the National Congress, an effort that has been successful only in the past few years, and then with only a handful of members. Most Brazilian politicians, whatever their background or skin color, still see little political gain from identifying as Afro-Brazilian. Through 2003, only three Afro-Brazilians had ever been appointed cabinet ministers: Benedita da Silva, soccer great Pelé, and pop musician Gilberto Gil.

The most dramatic change in Brazil's racial policies occurred quite recently with the government's official endorsement of a quota-based affirmative action program in 2001. Fernando Henrique Cardoso, president from 1995 to 2003, had been one of the pioneers of the study of racial discrimination who was forced into exile under the military government during the 1960s. Upon assuming the presidency, he actively encouraged a rethinking of Brazil's racial policy. This came together with large-scale preparation for the United Nations's 2001 World Conference on Racism to produce the country's biggest debate on race in decades. Those who opposed changing existing policies argued that it is impossible to determine at this point who is truly "black" and therefore deserving of affirmative action; proponents argued that all those who identify as "not white" face discrimination. As this debate shows, even with this policy shift and associated programs, the question of "who is black" is not resolved.

The U.S. and Brazilian cases show the importance of understanding even racial identity as a social construct that can vary over time and across countries. The very idea of what constitutes a race depends on distinct historical legacies in the two countries. While they share histories of slavery and racial discrimination, each is dramatically different from the other, resulting in different political movements in recent decades. Brazilians have long argued that the country is a racial democracy and have consciously distanced themselves from the legalized segregation of the United States and South Africa under apartheid, but Brazil's discrimination was simply different, not less. Indeed, the lack of stark racial divisions and legalized discrimination is a major explanation for the much more limited black political mobilization in Brazil. In both the United States and Brazil, however, those in subordinate racial positions have and will continue to attempt to mobilize a political following on the basis of race to demand greater recognition and representation.

COUNTRY AND CONCEPT Ethnicity, Race, and Religion

Country	Major Language Group	Largest Ethnic/Racial Group, % of Population
Brazil	1 major (Portuguese)	White, 53.7%
China	1 major (Mandarin), ~6–12 sublanguages (though categorization is controversial)	Han, Chinese 91.9%
Germany	1 major (German), 7 minor	German, 91.5%
India	1 major linguistic group (Hindi, 40%), with hundreds of other major and minor language groups and dialects	Hindi, 40%
Iran	4 major (Persian, Pashto, Kurdish, and Balochi); more than 80 other varieties	Persian, 51%
Japan	1 major (Japanese)	Japanese, 98.5%
Nigeria	6 major (English, Hausa, Yoruba, Igbo, Fulani, Ibibio); more than 250 total.	Hausa and Fulani, 29%
Russia	1 major linguistic group (Russian), with more than one hundred other major and minor languages.	Russian, 79.8%
United Kingdom	1 (English) with more than 5 others, including Welsh, Gaelic)	White British, 85%
United States	1 (English), but with 11% of the population speaking Spanish	White alone, 73.9%

Sources: Data are from most recent country census results, the CIA *World Factbook,* and the United Nations. Ethnic fragmentation data from James, "Ethnic and Cultural Diversity by Country," *Journal of Economic Growth* 8 (2003): 195–222.

CONCLUSION

Each person belongs to various identity groups: male or female, a member of a racial group as defined by our society, and a member of a nation. Individuals may have an ethnic or religious group identity as well. No one can escape membership in at least some larger identity groups, but whether these groups seem politically important, and whether people act politically based on group membership, depends on a variety of factors. First, the group in question must have a pre-existing sense of itself: it must be an "imagined community" with both historic ties and a forward-looking agenda. Second, it must have some felt grievance. This could be a sense of suffering historical discrimination or relative deprivation, a desire to claim a share of some newly important (and enriching) natural resource, or a reaction to a recent change in law, such as passage of a bill requiring all public schools to teach in a dominant national language. Finally, groups seem to need political leadership, elites who can build on and strengthen the identity and link it to the

Largest Religion, % of Population	Index of Ethnic Fractionalization	Major Modern, Identity-Based Conflicts
Roman Catholic (nominal) 73.6%, Protestant 15.4%, Spiritualist 1.3%	0.549	None
Officially atheist, so percentages unknown. Current estimates are Taoist, Buddhist, Christian 3–4%, Muslim 1–2% but likely percentages much higher.	0.154	None
Protestant 34%, Roman Catholic 34%, Muslim 3.7%	0.095	Nazi repression of Jews/Holocaust, 1933–1945
Hindu 80.5%, Muslim 13.4%	0.811	• India/Pakistan partition, 1947–1948 • Kashmir dispute, 1947– • Hindu-Muslim conflicts/riots, 1950– (intermittent) • Sikh independence movement, 1960s–1984
Shiite Muslim 89%, Sunni Muslim 9%	0.669	Islamic Revolution, 1978–1979
Shinto and Buddhist 84%, other 16%	0.012	None
Muslim (mostly Sunni) 50%, Christian 40% (Protestant 26% majority Christian religion), indigenous beliefs 10%	0.805	• Biafran civil war, 1967–1970 • Ogoni and related movements, 1993– • Muslim-Christian battles over *sharia*, 1999– (intermittent)
Russian Orthodox 15–20%, Muslim 10–15%, other Christian 2%	0.33	• War of Transniestira, 1990–1992 • Chechen Wars, 1994–1996, 1999–
Church of England, 22.2%, all Christian 71.6%	0.324	None
Protestant 51.3%, Roman Catholic 23.9%, Mormon 1.7%, Jewish 1.7%, other Christian 1.6%, Buddhist 0.7%, Muslim 0.6%	0.491	• Civil war over slavery, 1861–1865 • Urban race riots, 1965–1968

* 0 = perfectly homogeneous and 1= highly fragmented

grievance and to appropriate action. This is easier to accomplish if there is already a strongly felt imagined community. Elites can work with and strengthen a weakly felt sense of identity, as the example of the creation of countries like Germany or Italy out of many smaller regional groups suggests, but the groups must have some shared and accepted basis for this to work, and the elites must have resources to make it work as well.

It is also useful to remember that the political importance of even strongly felt, primordial identities can be rather fleeting. Nigeria and Sudan are both examples of this: in Nigeria, political conflict has shifted from a primarily ethnic to a primarily religious basis; in Sudan, the change has been in the opposite direction. Such changes may have to do with the nature of a conflict and how it overlaps pre-existing identities. As noted in the Nigerian case study, resource conflicts there over oil evoke a strong reaction from regionally based ethnic groups, while *sharia* law, which might once have been considered an ethnic issue due to Islam's connection with Hausa ethnicity, is now perceived as a religious issue, perhaps in part because of the growing numbers of Muslims of other ethnicities as well as increasing numbers of Christians in the northern Hausa areas. The case of Nigeria also suggests the influence of globalization on local identity groups: local groups may pick up the dominant global discourses and be influenced by them as they begin to mobilize. Today the resurgence of global Islamism provides a context that enhances the tendency of local groups to see their struggle in religious terms; for most of the twentieth century, in contrast, the dominant global discourse was about nationhood, encouraging local groups that saw themselves as culturally different to cast their struggles as struggles for a national state.

As these examples suggest, how a group defines itself influences what it may claim in order to gain or enhance its power: anything from specific legal protections like antidiscrimination laws or the right to school their children in a local language to regional autonomy, power-sharing arrangements, or national statehood. In addition, the strength of their grievances and the national response to demands may determine whether a regionally based ethnic group seeks autonomy or "national" sovereignty. Similarly, actions taken in pursuit of redress of grievances may range from lobbying, voting, and constitutional reform to armed violence, secessionist movements, or even genocide.

Because identity politics often threaten the very existence of states, governments have to care about the issues involved. The leaders of governments typically want to mobilize a national identity tied to the state, while simultaneously demobilizing all other identities. Sometimes, however, the very effort to create a unifying national identity spawns challenges from ethnic, religious, or other groups. As these groups are politically mobilized, state leaders must try to find a way either to eliminate that mobilization (the typical authoritarian option) or contain it within the institutional boundaries of the existing political system through federalism or other mechanisms of power-sharing (as democracies typically try to do). Containment, however, frequently is not easy. Political leaders often try to achieve this while yielding little in the way of real power or resources, which only causes opponents to demand more. Once mobilized, identity politics can thus be quite explosive.

Key Concepts

acephalous society (p. 137)

assimilationist (p. 130)

autonomy (p. 133)

civic nationalism (p. 129)

consociationalism (p. 135)

constructivism (p. 125)

cultural nationalism (p. 129)

ethnic group (p. 132)

instrumentalism (p. 125)

jus sanguinis (p. 130)

jus soli (p. 130)

mulatto (p. 147)

nationalism (p. 128)

political saliency (p. 124)

politics of recognition (p. 133)

primordialism (p. 125)

race (p. 141)

relative deprivation (p. 134)

social construction (p. 126)

Works Cited

Brass, Paul R. 1991. *Ethnicity and Nationalism: Theory and Comparison.* Newbury Park, Calif.: Sage Publications.

Brubaker, Rogers. 1992. *Citizenship and Nationhood in France and Germany.* Cambridge: Harvard University Press.

Du Bois, W.E.B. 1897. *The Conservation of Races.* www.teachingamericanhistory.org/library/index.asp?document=1119.

Huntington, Samuel P. 1997. *The Clash of Civilizations and the Remaking of World Order.* New York: Touchstone.

Ignatiev, Noel. 1995. *How the Irish Became White.* New York: Routledge.

Lijphart, Arend. 1977. *Democracy in Plural Societies: A Comparative Exploration.* New Haven: Yale University Press. Renan, Ernest. 1882. *What Is a Nation?* www.nationalismproject.org/what/renan.htm.

Taylor, Charles. 1994. "The Politics of Recognition" in *Multiculturalism: Examining the Politics of Recognition,* ed. Amy Gutmann. Princeton: Princeton University Press.

Van Deburg, William L., ed. 1997. *Modern Black Nationalism: From Marcus Garvey to Louis Farrakhan.* New York: New York University Press.

Youvall-Davis, Nira, and Flora Anthias, ed. 1989. *Women-Nation-State.* London: Macmillon.

Resources for Further Study

Ghai, Yash P. 2000. *Autonomy and Ethnicity: Negotiating Competing Claims in Multi-Ethnic States.* Cambridge: Cambridge University Press.

Hobsbawm, Eric J. 1990. *Nations and Nationalism since 1780: Programme, Myth, Reality.* Cambridge: Cambridge University Press.

Horowitz, D. 1985. *Ethnic Groups in Conflict.* Berkeley: University of California Press.

Hutchinson, John, and Anthony D. Smith, ed. 2000. *Nationalism: Critical Concepts in Political Science.* New York: Routledge.

Juergensmeyer, Mark. 1993. *The New Cold War? Religious Nationalism Confronts the Secular State.* Berkeley: University of California Press.

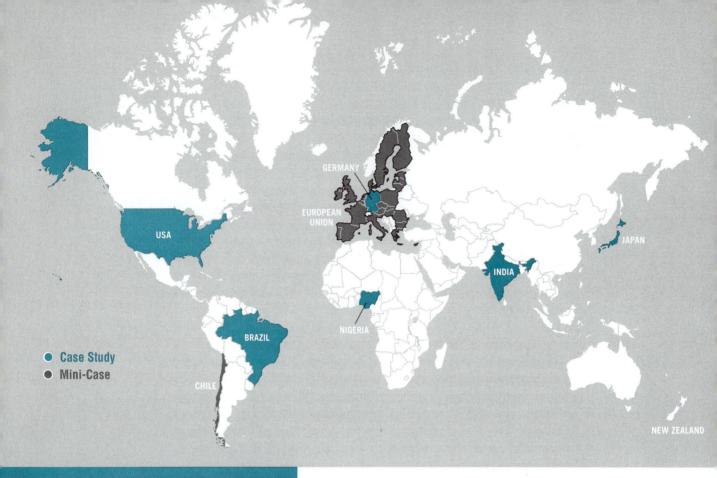

● Case Study
● Mini-Case

Who Rules?

- In what ways do economic policies reflect the relative power of different interest groups in a country?

- How important are international organizations in determining the economic policies of countries?

What Explains Political Behavior?

- Keynesianism and monetarism have been widely favored economic policies at different times in the twentieth century. What might explain the widespread changing of preferences in economic policy?

Where and Why?

- What factors might explain why states that industrialized later are more likely to intervene in the market with tariffs, state ownership, and social programs than are those, such as the United States, that industrialized earlier?

THE STATE AND THE MARKET

"It's the economy, stupid!" This was the motto of Bill Clinton's 1992 presidential campaign, posted on the wall at his campaign headquarters. The message worked. Clinton won the election, based heavily on voters' perceptions of the economy. They blamed President George H. W. Bush for the recession that had plagued much of his presidency. Like Bush, political leaders in democracies across the globe rise and fall on the basis of citizens' perceptions of the economy and their own economic well-being. Citizens have come to expect the state to guide the economy to improve their lives, not hurt their bottom lines.

In the "command economies" in Communist countries such as the Soviet Union and China during the Cold War, the government tried to control virtually all economic activities, and while some were successful at initial industrialization, as the decades passed they fell further and further behind the economic productivity of wealthy market economies in the West. Market economies have become nearly universal since the end of the Cold War, with the state involved in the process to varying degrees. In these economies, the state does not control the economy, but a government can and usually does try to encourage economic growth and influence how the benefits of that growth are distributed. Therefore the relationship between the state and the market, and the debates surrounding that relationship, are crucial to understanding modern politics virtually everywhere. As noted in chapter 1, the subfield of comparative politics that focuses on this set of issues is political economy. This chapter provides an analysis of the fundamental relationship between the modern state and market economy, contemporary debates over economic policy, and the questions raised by globalization, the latest major economic phenomenon.

THE MARKET, CAPITALISM, AND THE STATE

A **market economy** is an economic system in which individuals and firms exchange goods and services in a largely unfettered manner. This includes not only the exchange of finished products but also inputs into the production process, including labor. To most people, this seems like a natural state of affairs, but until fairly recently it was the exception, not the norm. In feudal Europe, for instance, most people were legally bound to a particular lord and manor; they could not exchange their labor for a wage anywhere they pleased. In many preindustrial societies, people subsisted on the fruits of their own labor and engaged in very limited trade. The creation of the modern market economy required that feudal bonds restricting labor be broken so that most people became dependent on market exchanges for their survival, and that productivity increase enough to allow the regular production of a surplus that could be traded. This combination in modern industrial and postindustrial societies has left virtually the entire population dependent on the ability to earn a wage or a share of profit via market exchanges.

Capitalism is not simply the same thing as a market economy, though the terms are typically used interchangeably (and we do the same in this chapter). Rather, capitalism is the combination of a market economy with private property rights. In theory, it is possible to imagine a market economy that does not include individual property rights. Firms could be owned collectively in some way but free to produce what they could for a profit in an unfettered market. Yugoslavia under the Communist rule of Jozef Tito attempted a modified version of such a system in the 1960s and 1970s, though never fully implemented it. Today virtually all countries have some form of a capitalist economy, but the degree to which the market is unfettered and the precise nature of private property rights vary widely. There is no absolute law in economics about how "free" market exchanges or private property must be for a capitalist economy to function. The debates over the extent to which the state should intervene to limit and shape market exchanges and property rights are at the core of many of the most important political issues around the globe. The end of the Cold War may have effectively eliminated the communist command economy as a viable political economy model, but it by no means ended the debate on what is and ought to be the relationship between the market and the state.

Because people tend to see the market economy as somehow natural, they also see it as existing independently of government. Nothing could be further from the truth. Command economies were ultimately of limited efficiency, but they proved that a state can exist for a long time without a market economy. A market economy, on the other hand, cannot exist without the state. In a situation of anarchy—the absence of a state—the market would be severely limited; without state provision of security, property and contract rights, and money, exchange would be limited to bartering and would require extensive provision of private security forces. Mafias are examples of this kind of capitalism, which arise where states are weak or absent: they provide their own security and enforce their own contracts. While this can certainly create some productive economic activity, the costs of private provision of security limit economic growth and create a society in which few would like to live.

The rise of the modern state occurred together with the state's separation from direct control of economic activity. Under European feudalism, political and economic power were fused in the person of a feudal lord. Political scientist Robert Bates (2001) uses rational choice theory to provide a succinct analysis of how the modern state arose and came to encourage capitalist economic growth. As agricultural productivity increased in early modern Europe, towns and economic activity outside of the sphere of agriculture grew rapidly as well. Feudal lords had financed their military conquests by raiding wealth from wherever they could get it. They took surplus production from peasants and other forms of wealth from conquered rivals to finance their increasing military and political power. When they turned to newly emerging towns as sources of wealth, however, they found them harder to conquer, in part because towns were easier to defend than castles in the countryside. More important, much of a town's wealth was mobile. Conquest, or even the threat of conquest, could provoke rapid movement of this wealth out of the town, which defeated one of the main purposes of the conquest in the first place.

And so the self-interests of kings and business owners led to a historic compromise: a king would provide the town military protection, instead of trying to conquer it outright by force, in exchange for a share of profits. Modern sovereignty and taxation were born. Political and economic power became distinct spheres; the state came to restrict its role in the economy, leaving most productive activity in private hands. The state, nonetheless, still had a crucial role to play; it and business came to be mutually dependent but separate spheres.

This compromise made security one of the state's essential functions in a market economy, but it was by no means the only one. The various roles the state has come to play can be divided into three categories: essential roles, beneficial roles, and politically generated roles. The essential roles are providing security, establishing and enforcing property and contract rights, and creating and controlling currency. Most essential roles, and many of the beneficial ones as well, involve a state's provision of **public goods**, those goods or services that cannot or will not be provided via the market because their costs are too high or their benefits too diffuse. National security is perhaps the best example of a public good. Individual provision of security is extremely expensive, and if any one company could pay for it, the benefits would accrue to everyone in the country anyway and so it wouldn't generate revenue sufficient to cover the costs. The state must provide this service if the market economy is to thrive.

The state's essential functions in a market economy also include protection of property and contract rights. Capitalism requires investing now with the expectation of future gains. Some uncertainty is always involved, but if there is no means of ensuring that the future gains will accrue to the person making the initial investment, no one will be interested in investing. Property rights not only protect the control individuals and firms have over property legally purchased in the market but also protect their future property—the profits of their current productive activity. Similarly, those profits require that market exchanges are honest: if a ton of cotton is promised for delivery at a set price, it must actually be delivered at that price. The state, through its legal system, must guarantee both property rights and contracts for this reason. The details of these rights can vary significantly from one country to another, but some legal guarantee that current and future property and exchanges will be protected is essential to achieving the productivity associated with modern market economies.

The modern state must also provide a currency to facilitate economic exchanges. States did not always print or control currency. Prior to the Civil War, for instance, private banks printed most currency in the United States (hence the term "banknote"). When the state took over this process and created a uniform currency, exchanges across the entire country were eased. This process continued in Europe with the adoption of the euro as the single currency of thirteen European Union countries since 2004, and this has greatly expanded the exchange process across much of the continent.

Several other roles the state commonly plays in the modern market economy are not absolutely essential, but most analysts consider them beneficial to the overall economy. These roles include providing infrastructure, education, and health care and preventing or regulating monopolies. Most infrastructure is a public good. Roads are a classic example. While private roads have existed, and still do in some countries, governments build the bulk of all inter- and intrastate systems. The costs of building private roads, the use of which is restricted to those who build them, are clearly prohibitive. Public provision of a road network lowers the cost of transporting goods and people, which improves the efficiency and profitability of many sectors of a state's economy.

Similarly, most economists and business leaders see an educated populace as beneficial to economic efficiency. Research has shown educated workers to be more productive than those who are not educated. This is especially true for basic education. Workers who can read, write, and do basic arithmetic are far more productive than those who cannot. Once again, companies could provide this education themselves, but because of the years education takes to complete, the fact that learning is done most efficiently and effectively during childhood, and the reality that workers are free to switch jobs and take their company-provided training and education with them, it is a nearly universal function of the state.

In most countries, the provision of basic health care is seen as very similar to the provision of basic education. Obviously, a healthy workforce is more productive than an unhealthy one. Like education, the most productive investments in health are in the early stages of life; the economic benefits of high-quality prenatal and early childhood health care are far greater than the benefits of health care for the elderly. Most countries, therefore, consider it worthwhile for the state to provide at least some basic health care, and in most wealthy countries this share may be significant. At the very least the government aggressively intervenes in the health care market to ensure that such care is provided to all.

The fourth beneficial economic function of the modern state is the prevention or regulation of monopolies. A **monopoly** is the control of the entire supply of a valued good or service by one economic actor. In a market economy, competition among alternative suppliers is a key incentive for efficiency. Monopolies eliminate this incentive. As many Marxist theorists have pointed out, while the state in a capitalist economy must work to ensure the successful functioning of capitalism as a whole, at times this may require the state to work against the interests of a particular capitalist. If one company has a monopoly, the state typically intervenes to preserve or restore competition to benefit the system as a whole.

Natural monopolies do exist in certain situations, however. These are sectors of the economy in which competition would raise costs and reduce efficiency. Where a natural monopoly exists, the state may choose to regulate or take control of it, rather than eliminate it. Natural monopolies can change over time as technology and market conditions change. A good example is telephone service. A generation ago, every phone had to be hardwired into a land line and all calls had to travel over wires; this meant that competition would have required more than one company running wires down the same street. This was obviously prohibitively expensive and inefficient, so virtually all telephone service was either provided by a government-regulated monopoly such as "Ma Bell" (as AT&T was nicknamed) in the United States or directly by a government-owned telephone company such

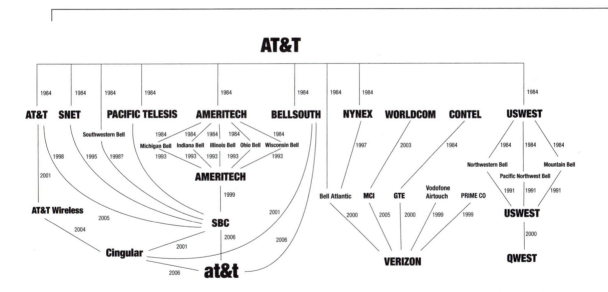

A 1984 lawsuit forced the breakup of AT&T's regulated monopoly on phone service. Cell phones have further eroded the natural monopoly in telephone service, but this chart shows the tendency toward reconcentration of services in a few large firms.

as British Telephone. With the advent of satellite and wireless technology, this natural monopoly evaporated; around the world, governments have privatized or deregulated phone services, and consumers now have a choice of services.

All of these beneficial functions of the state are subject to extensive debate today. How much infrastructure should be built? Is a new bridge or interstate really needed in a particular place, and how much will it cost and who will it benefit? While virtually all agree that basic education is beneficial and ought to be provided by the state (the United Nations has officially endorsed education as a right for all), that belief still leaves a great deal open to dispute: How much secondary and higher education should the state provide? Should the government pay for all or most of a person's higher education, as is true in most of Europe, or should the individual receiving the benefits of the education pay a substantial share, as in the United States? Health care is even more controversial. Should the government provide most basic care as in Canada or the UK, or should such care be left primarily to the private insurance and health industry as in the United States? What are the costs and benefits of each approach? While most agree a healthy workforce enhances a market economy, how to achieve such a healthy population is the subject of nearly constant debate. These issues are analyzed in greater depth in chapter 11.

COUNTRY AND CONCEPT The State and the Market

Country	GDP Growth[1]			Unemployment[2]	
	1980–1989	1990–1999	2000–2005	1990–1999	2000–2005
Brazil	2.7	2.9	2.2	7.5	9.3
China	9.8	10	9.4	—	4
Germany	2.2	1.5	0.7	8.9	8.5
India	5.7	5.6	6.5	—	5
Iran	-0.3	4.6	5.5	—	12
Japan	4	1.4	1.3	2.5	4.5
Nigeria	1.6	2.4	5.9	—	—
Russia	—	-4.9	6.9	1.15	8
United Kingdom	2.4	2.1	2.7	10.2	5.6
United States	3	3.4	2.8	6.8	5

[1] GDP growth data from the Organisation for Economic Cooperation and Development (OECD). All data are percentages except Inequality.

[2] Data for the unemployment rate, average annual (% of labor force). Reliable unemployment data for Nigeria are not available because of the difficulties of measuring it in an economy characterized by a large informal sector. Data are from UNDP's Human Development Report and KILM.

A third category of state functions in a market economy are politically generated. Most business leaders do not see these functions as either essential or even beneficial to capitalist growth, but states have taken on these roles because a large section of the populace has politically demanded them. Karl Polanyi argued in his 1944 book, *The Great Transformation,* that the rise of the modern industrial economy produced political demands to limit what many people saw as the negative effects of the market. This led to what is now termed the modern welfare state. Through the democratic process in European countries and the United States, in particular, citizens demanded protection from the market, and governments began to provide it, at least partially. Primary examples of these politically generated state functions are improved working conditions and the implementation of policies to redistribute income and protect the environment.

Because such state interventions as these are politically demanded rather than considered essential, they remain very contentious political issues and policies vary greatly by state. In wealthy industrial economies, modern working conditions, including a minimum wage, an eight-hour workday, and workers' health and safety standards, are largely the product of labor union demands. Yet as the case studies at the end of this chapter show, policies in wealthy countries vary significantly, particularly in areas such as the length of the work week, job security, length of maternity leave, and amount of vacation time.

Inflation			Inequality	Population Living below
1980–1989	1990–1999	2000–2005	(GINI Index)[3]	National Poverty Line[4]
284	264.3	10.1	57	21.5
5.3	7.7	3.1	46.9	4.6
—	2.0	0.9	28.3	8.3
8.7	8.8	3.9	36.8	28.6
16.5	27.5	19.3	—	—
1.7	0.1	-1.8	24.9	11.8
16.7	34.8	17.4	43.7	34.1
—	312	20.5	39.9	30.9
7.6	3.7	2.4	36	12.4
4.2	1.8	2.2	40.8	17

[3] The GINI Index measures overall income inequality, varying from 0 to 100. Higher numbers indicate greater inequality. Data are from UNDP, Human Development Report 2007/2008 GINI Index, http://hdrstats.undp.org/indicators/147.html.

[4] This is the relative poverty rate. Data are from UNDP, Human Development Report, http://hdrstats.undp.org/indicators/25.html and also http://hdr.undp.org/en/media/hdr06-complete.pdf.

As the preceeding Country and Concept table shows, the variation in outcomes related to poverty and distribution of wealth is much more dramatic if we compare the wealthy countries with those that have begun industrializing more recently, such as Brazil or China. In these countries, labor unions, if they exist at all, are recent creations that have not had the opportunity to successfully champion the same sort of reforms to working conditions that are now taken for granted in countries that industrialized much earlier. Minimum wages may be low or nonexistent, workdays may be as long as twelve hours, and paid vacations are rare. This disparity between wealthier and poorer countries is at the core of the controversies surrounding globalization, a subject we explore below.

Similar controversy and variation exist in income redistribution policies. Typically referred to as welfare in the United States (though Social Security is also an income redistribution policy), these policies exist to help mitigate the effects of unequal income distribution generated by the market. Markets generally provide great economic efficiency and growth under the right conditions, but they provide no rules on how wealth is distributed. As social and economic inequality expanded in the late nineteenth and early twentieth centuries, reformers began to demand that the state take action to help those who were gaining little or nothing in the market. For reasons we explore in the case studies at the end of this chapter, the extent to which the early industrializing countries in Europe and the United States ultimately pursued income redistribution and poverty amelioration varies considerably. As with proper and regulated working conditions, income redistribution policies barely exist at all in the poorest countries; the poorest people are left to survive in the market as best they can.

Environmental policies are the most recent addition to the list of state interventions in the market. Economists think of most environmental damage as an **externality**, a cost or benefit of the production process that is not fully included in the price of the final market transaction when the product is sold. For example, if a factory pollutes the air as it makes its product, that air pollution has costs to the long-term health of local residents and to everyone through global climate change. The factory owner, however, does not have to pay any of these costs as it makes and sells its products, and the price its customers pay doesn't accommodate these costs. Many economists argue, therefore, that the state should intervene either to limit the extent of such pollution or to make the producers and consumers of the product bear its costs. While this is the common economic justification for environmental protection, governments have adopted protective policies mainly because of pressure from environmental groups demanding improvements. The political strength of these movements has varied from country to country, so state intervention in this area has varied greatly as well, and the differential impact of environmental policies in different countries has become a major issue in the debate over globalization, which we explore in chapter 12.

Overall, the symbiotic relationship between the modern state and the market economy provides a means to analyze state interventions into modern economic life. The state must carry out certain roles if capitalism is to survive and thrive. Political leaders know that much of their popularity rests on the ability to generate goods and services, jobs, and taxes. In the modern economy, states pursue various policies and market interventions beyond just the bare essentials for the survival of capitalism. Some of these are widely recognized as beneficial to contemporary economies, though the details of how and how much to pursue them remain controversial. Other policies, however, are generated primarily by political demands emanating from society, especially in democracies. These policies remain the most controversial and vary the most from state to state, as we will see in the case studies at the end of the chapter and in chapters 10 and 11.

KEY ECONOMIC DEBATES

Understanding political economy and the relationship between the state and the market requires not only the application of political science but also some basic economics. Major economic theories lie behind the debates over how governments should intervene in the market. The central debate that first must be understood is between **Keynesian** and **monetarist** theories of when, why, and how the state ought to attempt to guide the economy. John Maynard Keynes, the most prominent economist of the mid-twentieth century, developed a theory that revolutionized economics after watching his native Britain and the rest of the world enter the Great Depression in the 1930s. Prior to Keynes, Western governments had engaged in rather minimal intervention in the economy, and officials believed that the market was best left alone. True, during economic downturns, unemployment rose and people suffered, but in the longer term, unemployment lowered wages until labor was cheap enough that businesses started to invest and employ people again, which created a new cycle of economic growth. In the meantime, policymakers believed government should do little but provide essential services and wait.

Keynes, after whom Keynesian economic theory is named, argued that the state could, and should, do more. In an economic downturn like the Great Depression, the main problem was lack of demand for goods and services, and he believed **fiscal policy**, government budgetary policy, could revive this demand and stimulate the economy. He suggested that the government could and should engage in **deficit spending**, that is, it should spend more than it collected in revenue to stimulate demand. To do this, the government would borrow money. By creating new programs and hiring people, the government would put that money into people's hands; they in turn would start to buy other goods and services, and the economy would start to rebound. When the economic downturn was over, the government could pay off the debt it had taken on while deficit spending, and this would help slow demand in the economy if needed, as too much demand too quickly can cause inflation. Keynes believed that in this way the state could manage capitalism by smoothing out the cycle of economic expansion and contraction—boom and bust—that seemed inherent in unchecked capitalism. If this was done properly, it might even be possible to achieve continuous full employment.

Keynesianism (and the onset of World War II) offered governments a way to help their economies out of the depression, and most Western governments adopted it either explicitly or implicitly. The power of the economic theory alone, however, was not the only reason Keynesian policies became so popular. Deficit spending, if it could be justified, was very popular with elected politicians because it allowed governments to create new programs of various sorts to benefit their constituents without having to raise taxes to pay for them: the appeal for politicians facing reelection is obvious. In Europe Keynesianism also helped social democratic parties economically justify a significant expansion of social spending and welfare policies after World War II. This political logic led to frequent distortion of pure Keynesian policies—deficit spending continued in many countries even in times of economic upturn, which contradicted Keynes's original idea that when the economy improved a government would pay off its debt.

By the 1970s, Keynesian policies came under sustained questioning, first in the discipline of economics and then in the political arena. Due in part to the quadrupling of oil prices in 1973, most Western countries by that time faced a new economic situation: **stagflation**, simultaneous high inflation and high unemployment. Keynes's prescription of more government borrowing was seen as potentially disastrous in this situation because such action was likely to produce more inflation. In this context, an alternative economic theory, monetarism, gained popularity. The core ideas of the theory were developed by American economist Milton Friedman in the 1950s, but they were largely ignored for over a decade.

Friedman and other monetarists argued that fiscal policy does not stimulate economic growth. Rather, government borrowing and deficit spending simply "crowd out" private sector borrowing, and this hurts the ability of businesses to invest, which potentially lowers long-term growth. So the key to economic growth, Friedman argued, is **monetary policy**, the amount of money a government prints and puts into circulation and the basic interest rates the government sets. Inflation, monetarists argue, is caused chiefly by excessive government printing of money, and low growth is due in part to government borrowing. Defeating stagflation and restoring growth would therefore require reducing the amount of money in circulation, raising interest rates, and reducing deficit spending. Monetarists also argue that every economy has a natural rate of unemployment, below which government policy is counterproductive, and that a government and a society must accept this, whatever the level is. U.S. president Ronald Reagan and UK prime minister Margaret Thatcher each put monetarist policies in place in the early 1980s. The economic boom that followed the institution of these policies was seen as a vindication of monetarism, and it remains the "conventional wisdom" in economic theory today.

Just because it is widely accepted in economics, however, does not mean all governments pursue it in its purest form at all times. As noted earlier, deficit spending is supported by a powerful political logic, especially in democracies. When the European Union agreed to adopt the euro as a common currency, the governments involved collectively forced themselves to restrict their deficit spending to a common percentage of their respective economies. Beginning in 1999, each government that wanted to "join" the euro had to limit its deficit to the agreed-upon level, which in general has worked so far, but has proven a challenge in times of economic stagnation. So while monetarism is the preferred policy among most economists, elements of Keynesianism remain important in actual policy.

Keynes also had an influential role in international economics, so his ideas ultimately influenced economic policy in the postcolonial world. He was instrumental in the creation of the International Monetary Fund (IMF) and the World Bank, and it was these two key institutions that helped stabilize the postwar economy and rebuild Europe. By the early 1960s, both also came to play an important role in the economic development of the newly independent countries of Africa and Asia, as well as Latin America. As the postwar world emerged, economists and policymakers in Latin America, joined by a growing list of independent postcolonial states such as India and Pakistan, began to rethink their economic policies. A new field, "development economics," emerged, the basic premise of which was that the policies that help create stability and growth in already wealthy industrial countries are not appropriate for countries just starting the industrialization process.

One basic assumption of this postwar global economic order was that free trade should be as widespread as possible. The economic argument in favor of this is known as **comparative advantage**, which puts forth that economic efficiency and well-being will be maximized if each country uses its resources to produce whatever it produces relatively well compared to other countries and then trades what it has produced with other countries for goods it does not produce. What this meant in practical terms was that the poor and agrarian countries of Asia, Africa, and Latin America would, for the foreseeable future, produce primarily agricultural products and raw materials. Their industries, where they existed, were quite new and as such were not likely to compete successfully against the well-established industrial conglomerates of the wealthy countries.

Latin American economists in particular argued that this scenario was not acceptable. Their research suggested that the **terms of trade**, the prices of their countries' exports versus their imports, would continuously move to favor industrial over agricultural products. Subsequently, their countries would have to produce more and more agricultural products to trade for the industrial products they needed, and they would fall further and further behind the industrialized powers. The nationalist leaders of the newly established countries of Africa and Asia also found reliance on agriculture and raw materials unacceptable: they wanted to "develop" their economies via industrialization.

Development economics, then, came to be about how a state could intervene in the economy to stimulate rapid industrialization and growth. It was argued that allowing the global market to run its course through the avenues of free trade would not lead to development, or at least not for a very long time. This position meshed with the general Keynesian theory that the state could manage capitalism to enhance growth; in the "developing countries" this management would simply have to take somewhat different forms. The central policy that developed out of these ideas was **import-substitution industrialization (ISI)**, which stated that restricting trade protected new industries and allowed them to grow to eventually be able to compete on the international market. By preventing the importation of or placing tariffs on manufactured products, postcolonial governments could encourage domestic and international investment in new industries in their countries. Most postcolonial countries pursued these policies, with the support of Western governments and the World Bank, from the 1950s to the 1970s. Where investment in an industry was not available, many governments even took on the role of business owner, creating wholly or partly owned government industries that supplied the domestic market with key goods.

At first, ISI was relatively successful in creating many new industries throughout middle-income and poorer countries. Countries such as Brazil, Mexico, and Turkey saw very rapid economic growth throughout the 1950s and 1960s. By the 1970s, though, momentum was waning. Protecting industry from competition to get it started perhaps was a good idea initially, but in the long run it resulted in inefficient industries that could not compete on the international market. These industries and their employees put political pressure on postcolonial governments to preserve the protections. When oil prices quadrupled in 1973, those postcolonial countries that did not produce their own oil had to pay a lot more for oil and other key imports, but because their industries could not compete globally the countries could not export enough to pay for the imports. The governments were forced to take out international loans to cover the difference, but in the meantime they changed relatively few policies. When another oil price increase occurred in 1979, many governments that had pursued ISI had to borrow even more money from international lenders. Some were on the brink of bankruptcy: Mexico's declaration in 1982 that it was unable to meet its international obligations by paying back its debt began a global "debt crisis" that ushered in a new period of economic policy in postcolonial countries.

The growing problems with ISI were emerging at the same time that economists and policymakers in the West were shifting from Keynesian to monetarist ideas and becoming increasingly skeptical of governments' ability to manage the

By the 1980s, ISI was becoming discredited, and neoliberals were advocating that developing countries should instead emulate the East Asian Miracle by promoting export-led growth. This 2006 photo shows the rapidly growing port of Ensenada, Mexico, where Asian exports that California's clogged ports cannot accommodate are offloaded for transport to the United States.

market. The World Bank abruptly shifted its development agenda and prescriptions in 1980 and embraced a monetarist-inspired development model now called **neoliberalism**. This shift was partly induced by the great economic success of a handful of East Asian countries that collectively came to be known as the "East Asian Miracle." In contrast to most of the postcolonial world, these rapidly growing countries, most notably South Korea, Taiwan, Singapore, and the city of Hong Kong, either had never adopted ISI or had abandoned it early on in favor of focusing on exporting in sectors in which they were competitive. Their success, especially in light of the problems ISI policies had begun to face, would come to suggest to many policymakers, including those at the World Bank, that a new approach to development was needed.

The neoliberal model that emerged by 1980 shared monetarists' skepticism of the ability of the state to lead economic growth via interventions in the market. Neoliberal economists argued that developing countries were no different from wealthy ones, and as such they should follow the same basic monetarist policies. These economists went on to compile a package of policies that came to be known as **structural adjustment programs (SAPs)**. Included in this bundle of programs were directives to end government protection of industries and other restrictions on free trade, **privatize** (sell off) government-owned industry, and reduce fiscal deficits. SAPs required a drastically reduced government that would participate far less in the economy; this would allow comparative advantage and the market to signal how resources should be invested, which would maximize efficiency and economic growth.

The IMF and World Bank would impose this model on much of the postcolonial world. The debt crisis that began in 1982 meant that many postcolonial governments had to ask the IMF for emergency assistance to get them out of what was essentially bankruptcy. Working in tandem, the IMF and World Bank demanded that the governments receiving assistance in the 1980s and 1990s move their policies in the direction of the neoliberal model. This was a slow process in many countries, as the necessary steps were politically unpopular because they initially resulted in high inflation and increased unemployment and meant drastic cuts in government services, including education and health care. The promise was that by enduring these transition pains now, the policies would maximize efficiency and encourage new investment and growth in the long term.

The success of the neoliberal model has been mixed at best. Supporters point to some striking successes, such as Chile and several countries in Southeast Asia. While the military government in Chile chose to adopt neoliberal policies of its own volition, Malaysia and Thailand, to name two, only partly followed the model. In many other countries, especially in Latin America and Africa, the new policies not only didn't produce growth but actually produced significant economic decline. Supporters of the policies argue that this was because those countries resisted the IMF and World Bank when possible and only partly implemented the SAPs. Critics counter that the policies themselves were flawed, producing little growth and greater unemployment and poverty and reducing educational opportunity and health care for those most in need.

WHERE AND WHY The Successes and Failures of SAPs

The neoliberal SAPs implemented in most postcolonial countries in the 1980s and 1990s had a distinctly mixed success rate. Chile, Ghana, and Uganda stand out as relative successes; many others are far less so. What explains these differences? The large theoretical and policy debate that arose over this very question pitted those who saw simply failure of implementation against those who saw fundamental flaws in the model and those who believed the model was applicable only in certain circumstances.

Most SAPs were implemented at the behest of the IMF and World Bank. To secure essential debt relief, poor countries had to accept the policy requirements the two institutions imposed. States would agree to make certain policy changes over a period of about three years, and the IMF/World Bank would subsequently monitor how the states followed through on their promises. Often political leaders would only partially fulfill their obligations, and everything went back to the drawing board. This resulted in very slow and partial implementation of the full set of neoliberal policies as countries went through several rounds of negotiation and implementation with the IMF/World Bank.

One body of critics, including the IMF and World Bank, concluded from this process that the model's limited success was due to failure of political will. Success happened when top political leaders took "ownership" of the ideas, understood their importance, and committed themselves to accomplishing them. In the absence of this, no amount of external arm-twisting would do the job, and partial implementation often made little economic sense.

Other critics contend that the model contained fundamental conceptual flaws, one of which was a failure to understand political dynamics. Lack of implementation, they argue, came not just from lack of understanding and commitment, but also from the rational action of self-interested political leaders in a particular context. This was particularly true in Africa, where neopatrimonial politics meant that leaders' survival depended on their ability to provide supporters with patronage, something the reforms clearly jeopardized.

Institutionalists point to a different flaw in the model. They contend that markets only work well when embedded in strong institutions such as clear property rights and contracts. The ultimate goal of the neoliberal

Overall, economic policy remains in flux. During the economic boom of the 1990s, quite a few governments were able to stick with more or less monetarist policies, and postcolonial governments embraced SAPs as necessary. As economic growth slowed after the turn of the century, it became more difficult to adhere to these policies and they again became subject to renewed questioning. Deficit spending increased, even in the United States, which arguably had the most monetarist policies of all. The World Bank began to question aspects of the neoliberal model is to improve efficiency to encourage greater domestic and international investment and thereby future growth, but weak states that fail to adequately provide key institutions will never gain greater investment because investors cannot be certain their investments and future profits will be secure. The initial neoliberal model ignored this essential area entirely, and so was successful only where the institutions were already relatively strong.

Another group of critics look at the global economy and argue that the neoliberal model suffered from a fallacy of composition. This is a term in logic that says that just because something is true in one particular case does not mean it will be true when applied to all cases. In relation to SAPs, it suggests that market-friendly policies designed to attract investment will succeed in some cases, probably the earliest ones and those with other attractions to investors, but when the same policies are extended to all countries, there will not be enough investment capital available to respond. Furthermore, the earliest success cases will be likely to attract even more investment, leaving the latter cases empty-handed. Even if later or less-attractive states pursue the "right" policies, they still may not see the investments necessary to spark economic growth.

Still another school of critics argues that the neoliberal model undermines the real fundamentals of long-term development: infrastructure and human capital. These individuals contend that states that are successful at instigating economic development do so by providing key political goods that investors will need, that is, infrastructure, especially efficient transportation and communications systems, and human capital, meaning an educated and healthy workforce. SAPs demanded fiscal austerity, typically meaning cuts to both. For countries with relatively little of either, these policies proved detrimental to economic growth.

The debate on SAPs has never been fully resolved. Clearly, more than one of these positions can be right simultaneously. The debate did help create a shift in the conventional wisdom about development by the new millennium however. While most economists and policymakers still argue in favor of the basics of market-friendly policies like SAPs, they also recognize the importance of strong institutions, infrastructure, and human capital to developmental success. The World Bank, in particular, now has active policies pursuing each of these goals.

development model as well, in particular acknowledging that quality education and health care are crucial to long-term development everywhere and must be funded accordingly. The bank's policies began to shift once again in favor of funding these sectors of the government, even though it continued to advocate open trade and a thriving and unfettered market in general as the best ways to create economic growth. In addition, by the turn of the century many observers saw states facing a new set of economic concerns vis-à-vis the forces of globalization.

The Role of the State in the Market

Essential Functions of the State

- Providing national and personal security—failure to do so produces anarchy or the creation of a mafia.
- Protecting property and contract rights—essential for investments to produce profits over time.
- Providing a currency—facilitates widespread exchange.

Beneficial Functions of the State

- Providing public goods—goods or services not provided via the market because their costs are too high or their benefits too diffuse. These include:
  - Building infrastructure—for example, highways, ports.

- Providing education and health care—improves labor productivity and nearly impossible for market to provide fully.
- Preventing or regulating monopolies—enhances competition or limits negative effects of natural monopolies.

Politically Generated Functions of the State

- Improving working conditions—for example, health and safety standards, eight-hour day, minimum wage.
- Redistributing income—for example, retirement benefits, unemployment compensation, welfare.
- Protecting the environment—corrects market failures due to externalities.

GLOBALIZATION: A NEW WORLD ORDER OR DÉJÀ VU ALL OVER AGAIN?

Globalization has become perhaps the most frequently used, and abused, term in political economy today. It first gained prominence in the 1990s, and since then hundreds of books and countless pages have been written about it. It has cultural as well as economic and political implications, but we will focus on only the latter two in order to understand its effects on the relationship between the state and the market. **Globalization** probably has as many different meanings as there are books written on it. For our purposes we can define it as a rapid increase in the flow of economic activity, technology, and communication around the globe. The key debate is whether this represents a brave new world in which the fundamental relationship between the state and the market has changed forever or simply the latest phase in that relationship—something new and interesting but not fundamentally different.

As is often the case when a new concept emerges, its earliest adherents saw it as a portent of fundamental change. Japanese scholar Kenichi Ohmae, writing in 1995, argued that globalization would result in the "end of the nation-state." He focused on economic aspects of globalization, but others have broadened this general argument, claiming that the rapid flow of money, goods and services, ideas, and cultural symbols around the globe would eventually make the nation-state irrelevant as it destroyed the ability of states to manage their economies. Regional, if not global, management would have to fill the role currently played by the state. The flow of ideas and culture would severely weaken national identity, as the

Internet in particular allowed people to form identities not linked to territories and their immediate local communities. All of these changes would ultimately require political responses in the form of strengthened international organizations for global governance, as well as global citizens' organizations because global problems would require global political solutions.

Ten years later, the scholarly consensus seems to be moving toward a more modest assessment of the effects of globalization. Certainly all of the trends described above exist, and most agree that they are likely to weaken the nation-state, but few now believe they are likely to destroy it. The state seems to be alive and well in the "global" era. Since the initial separation of the economic and political spheres, capital's greatest weapon has been its mobility: business can usually threaten to move if it does not receive adequate treatment from a state. The state, in sharp contrast, is tied to a territory. The increased speed and lowered cost of global transportation and communication, as well as neoliberal economic policies that have lowered barriers to cross-border economic activity, have significantly increased capital mobility so that businesses can credibly threaten to leave a country much more easily now than they could a generation ago. This has increased capital's power in relation to states. In trying to manage their economies, policymakers must be actively concerned about preserving the investments they have and attracting new ones. And with business able to move relatively easily, states increasingly must compete to attract it.

This competition is based largely on the policies discussed earlier in this chapter: states must provide security, property rights and contracts, and infrastructure and resist political pressure to enact policies that cost business money to benefit those hurt or marginalized by the market. For example, businesses usually prefer not to have to negotiate with labor unions or abide by many environmental regulations, and states that eliminate both are more likely to attract investment. Businesses decide to invest for a wide variety of reasons, some of which the state cannot control, but as a general rule the more favorable a state's policies are toward business the more likely it is to attract investment, jobs, and economic growth.

Similar changes in global finance—the flow of money around the world— also have weakened the state. Many countries now allow their currencies to be traded freely. More are moving toward full convertibility, allowing people to trade a currency for other currencies as often as they like, at whatever exchange rate they can get, all the time. India and Russia, for instance, both announced plans for full convertibility in 2006. China plans to make the yuan convertible by 2010. Electronic communications have made such currency transactions nearly instantaneous. For a government trying to pursue sound monetary policies through control of its money supply and interest rates, this new world of global currency flow can be extremely difficult. The collapse of many Southeast Asian economies in 1997 was caused at least in part by currency speculators, or traders who purchase a currency not to buy goods in the country but to simply try to buy it low and sell it high at a later date. When the speculators, led by international financier

George Soros, found the Southeast Asian economies were weaker than they had previously believed, they began to sell the currencies rapidly. This led to a classic market panic in which virtually all international traders sold their currency, which produced the biggest loss of wealth in the world since the Great Depression and caused immense economic loss and political instability in the region. States, especially in small and poor countries, must base monetary policy not only on domestic concerns but also on how "global markets" might react.

The rapid flow of all sorts of economic transactions across state borders seems to have shifted the relative power of capital and the state. States are arguably less able to manage capitalism than they were a generation ago, although the effects are not as great in wealthy and large countries as they have been in small and poor countries. States do still have an important role to play, however. Political scientist Geoffrey Garrett (1998) conducted a sophisticated quantitative study that showed that European countries can maintain policies favoring labor unions and related groups if they provide long-term stability and predictability for business. In poor countries, however, this seems unlikely to work. The kinds of investments now made in Europe mostly involve hiring highly trained labor, which business is willing to pay more for to ensure long-term stability. Europe also has the advantage of a huge and wealthy market, the EU, in which to sell products. Nigeria, by contrast, has none of these advantages. Investments there are in natural resources and perhaps "light manufacturing" involving large numbers of cheap, unskilled, and easily replaceable labor. The Nigerian government is in a significantly weaker bargaining position vis-à-vis likely international investors than is, for example, the German government.

In this era of globalization, the fundamental relationship between states and business has not been transformed into something entirely new, but there has been a shift in the relative power of each partner in that relationship. Any state interested in the economic well-being of its populace must negotiate the rapidly expanding global markets as well as possible, bargaining for the best "deal" for its people. Even for the best-intentioned government knowing how to do this effectively is not easy, as some of the case studies below illustrate.

The expanded global market and capital mobility also raise questions about the level at which political responses to economic problems can and should occur. More and more analysts argue that new global problems require collective, global political solutions. An obvious example is the ultimate global environmental problem: climate change. If pollution is an externality that states can and should intervene in the market to overcome, then climate change is a global externality that only global agreement can possibly remedy. Future generations, one way or another, will pay the costs of this externality that businesses and their consumers are not paying today, but no single state, even the largest and wealthiest, can solve the problem alone. Similarly, the competition among poor states with abundant labor to attract investment by keeping labor costs low and working conditions poor cannot be overcome by the individual governments acting alone. Those governments that change their policies will simply lose out to the competition.

A uniform global policy on wages and working conditions, though extremely difficult to achieve, would reduce this competition to the advantage of workers, at least in theory.

Many groups in civil society are not waiting for states to achieve these policies on their own and are actively organizing across borders to put pressure on governments or international bodies such as the UN, the IMF, and the World Bank to enact measures to address global problems. To the extent that they are successful, individual states may again be weakened because as citizens focus their political organization and pressure at the international level, they make individual states less relevant. Many core economic problems, including most discussed in this chapter, remain at the national level, however, particularly in large and wealthy countries. So while the state is weakened vis-à-vis capital, it is far from dead. The case studies below show this interplay between state and market and the continuing importance of states in the process.

STATES AND MARKETS AROUND THE WORLD

As with any area of comparative politics, economic policies in the real world do not follow perfectly the various abstract economic models. Many factors beyond the ideas, models, and theories of economists influence what policies governments pursue. These include broad political ideologies; the relative strength of particular groups, especially business and labor; and international influences. To illustrate real-world variation in the relationship of the market to the state, we look at five of our case study countries: three wealthy, industrialized democracies and two developing countries. The Country and Concept table earlier in the chapter provides an overview of key economic data for all five and offers some of the overall story of each country. The market-oriented model in the United States has produced relatively good growth and moderate unemployment and inflation, but relatively high inequality and poverty compared to that found in the other wealthy countries. Germany's social market economy struggles with low growth and high unemployment, though the country has controlled inflation very well and has far less poverty and inequality than the United States. Japan's developmental state achieved high growth prior to 1990 but has been in crisis since then, with growing unemployment and deflation and modest poverty and inequality. Brazil has achieved only modest economic growth since 1980 and struggles with growing unemployment, but has recently defeated its perpetual enemy, astronomically high inflation; it is also one of the most unequal economies in the world and, as a developing country, still has a much higher poverty rate than the wealthier cases. Nigeria, by far the poorest of the five, is dependent on one crucial export, oil, for its growth and suffers from rather high inflation and inequality and very high poverty.

CASE STUDY The United States: The Free Market Model

The United States has long been the greatest exemplar of the free market, or *laissez faire,* model of economic development and capitalism. Compared to the governments of most wealthy countries, including those of Germany and Japan, the U.S. government has intervened relatively little in the market, both in terms of guiding economic growth and providing social services. For most of its history, the United States took pretty much a "hands off" approach to the economy: it wasn't until the Great Depression and the New Deal of the 1930s that the government began to attempt to guide the economy to increase growth and employment and to redistribute income to ameliorate poverty. From the New Deal through the 1960s, the government more or less followed Keynesian policies, but by the 1980s it had shifted toward monetarism, moving back toward its historic reluctance to be involved in the economy. At least rhetorically, the United States has emerged as the chief champion of free trade and globalization in recent years, though the government has not always followed that position consistently when U.S. interests are in danger of being compromised.

The modern U.S. economy emerged with rapid industrialization in the late nineteenth and early twentieth centuries that transformed the country from a primarily agricultural and rural society into a rapidly growing urban and industrial economy. The government's nearly complete absence of involvement in the economy had to change in response to this transformation. Its initial policies, however, were aimed primarily at ensuring that the market would be as free as possible. The first major regulatory effort was directed toward the elimination or regulation of monopoly control of key sectors of the economy, starting with the railways and then expanding with the landmark Sherman Antitrust Act of 1890 that resulted in the breakup of the Standard Oil monopoly in 1910.

This might seem "antibusiness," but it does not mean the government was "pro-labor." The last two decades of the nineteenth century saw the rise not only of the large conglomerates that came to control entire sectors of the economy but also of national labor unions. The government opposed the increasingly frequent strikes organized by these unions, the most famous of which occurred in Chicago and became known as the Haymarket Riots of May 1886. This began as a strike to demand an eight-hour workday, but within days it included 350,000 people nationwide. On May 4, it ended with a rally during which a bomb killed a police officer and the police killed dozens of unarmed demonstrators. This event helped get May 1 declared "Labor Day" in most countries of the world in honor of workers' struggles for labor rights. (The United States is one of a very few countries to celebrate Labor Day on a different date.)

By the early twentieth century, the U.S. government recognized that it must broaden its role in the economy, and in 1913 it created both the Federal Reserve (the "Fed") as the nation's first central bank and the income and corporate tax system. The Fed was modeled after the British and German central banks, given a monopoly on printing legal currency, and charged with regulating the nation's money supply. Unlike central banks in many countries, however, the Fed is an autonomous agency that elected leaders cannot con-

Each president since Ronald Reagan has espoused expanding free trade, but critics argue that it leads to loss of jobs, especially factory jobs that can be done more cheaply abroad. Job loss and foreclosures are evident in Michigan, a former industrial stronghold and now a state that leads the nation in unemployment.

trol directly, which is meant to ensure its independence from immediate political demands. With growing industrialization, the government also recognized that taxes on trade, the primary source of government revenue in the nineteenth century, would no longer suffice. Since industry had come to generate the bulk of the nation's wealth, the federal government began permanently taxing businesses to provide a stronger revenue stream. Yet while the government began to play a larger role in the economy in this era, it remained focused on ensuring the smooth functioning of a free market by eliminating monopolies, opposing unions, providing a stable monetary system, and gaining government revenue from taxation of private economic activity.

This remained the model of economic policy until the Great Depression and the New Deal. The Great Depression, which produced 25 percent unemployment at its peak in 1933, shook the foundations of the nation's belief in the beneficial effects of the market. During this time of rapidly rising union membership and radical political demands, Franklin Roosevelt won the presidency in 1932 with a promise to fundamentally alter the nation's economic policy. The New Deal was the fruition of this promise, an ambitious program that began with unprecedented government spending on public works projects that employed large numbers of workers in improving the nation's infrastructure. By 1935 these programs would amount to nearly 7 percent of the country's gross domestic product (GDP). The initiative also included the first legislation creating a federally mandated eight-hour workday, collective bargaining rights for workers, a minimum wage, protection against unfair labor practices, federal subsidies for farmers, and federal income support for poor single mothers. With government acquiescence, union membership doubled between 1925 and 1941, reaching its peak in the 1960s.

Government social services also were expanded, with the most important component of this extension being the creation of the Social Security system. This

IN CONTEXT Central Banks

A central bank or some other monetary authority is a crucial institution of economic policy. Many started in part to create a unified national currency. In most wealthy countries today, central banks are usually independent institutions, supposedly free of political influence, that establish currency stability and monetary policy. The U.S. Federal Reserve System was a relative latecomer among monetary authorities:

- Bank of England, 1694
- Banque de France, 1800
- Reichsbank, 1876 (succeeded by Bundesbank in West Germany, 1957)
- Bank of Japan, 1882
- U.S. Federal Reserve System, 1913
- Bank of Canada, 1934
- European Central Bank (EU), 1998

began as a program to provide pensions to retired workers but was soon expanded to include pensions for their survivors and assistance for the disabled. Social Security has arguably done more to reduce poverty in the United States than any other government program before or since.

The New Deal era remains one of unprecedented growth in government involvement in the economy, employment creation, and worker protection. Put into practice, it also began a period of more or less Keynesian economic policy in which the government actively worked to improve economic growth and expand employment by, among other things, building infrastructure. The Employment Act of 1946 "declared it the policy of the federal government to maximize employment, production, and purchasing power." After World War II, the United States was by far the world's largest economy and experienced exceptionally rapid growth as the world recovered from the war. The middle class expanded at an unprecedented rate as the economy boomed, infrastructure continued to be expanded, and returning veterans took advantage of the GI Bill to pursue higher education opportunities.

In the 1960s, Lyndon Johnson's administration initiated the "Great Society" as the completion of the goals of the New Deal. The pillars of this effort were the creation of Medicare, which is medical insurance for Social Security recipients; Aid to Families with Dependent Children (AFDC), a much-expanded welfare program for poor mothers; and Medicaid, health care for AFDC and other welfare recipients. These programs, along with the earlier Social Security system, helped reduce poverty from 25 percent of the population in 1955 to 11 percent by 1973. Slower economic growth and waning political support subsequently led the government to reduce the real value of these various anti-poverty programs, however, which contributed to a rise in poverty rates to around 14 percent by the 1990s.

Sustained economic growth and Keynesian policies continued through the mid-1960s. By the late 1960s, continued deficit spending caused by involvement in the Vietnam War and by costs of Great Society programs helped produce rising inflation. The quadrupling of world oil prices in 1973 further slowed economic growth and spurred inflation, producing "stagflation" by the late 1970s that the government seemed incapable of reversing. Ronald Reagan won the presidency in 1980 on a platform that emphasized the need to reduce the size and scope of government by embracing monetarism's prescriptions for reduced government spending, accepting of a "natural rate of unemployment," and freeing the market to restart growth. President Jimmy Carter had begun some deregulation of industry in the late 1970s, but Reagan expanded this effort substantially, starting with the airline and trucking industries. Via his successful effort to defeat the air traffic controllers' strike in 1981, Reagan also reduced the power and reach of unions, whose membership had been declining throughout the 1970s. (This trend has continued, with union membership now reduced to about what it was a century ago, although the unionized workforce grew slightly in 2007 for the

first time since the 1970s, reaching 12.1 percent.) Reagan cut spending on social programs and cut taxes to spur economic growth. At the same time the Federal Reserve embraced monetarist policies, raising interest rates and reining in the money supply to reduce inflation. This combination produced the most severe economic downturn since the Great Depression between 1981 and 1983, but sustained economic growth reemerged for the rest of the decade. Reagan reversed the Keynesian effort of the New Deal–Great Society period, marking the most dramatic shift in economic policy since the 1930s.

He embraced monetarism, but Reagan's tax cuts and high military spending resulted in record budget deficits. President Bill Clinton and Congress finally eliminated these budget deficits in the 1990s. In combination with continued monetarist policies at the Fed, the elimination of these deficits helped spur renewed economic growth. Though Clinton was a Democrat like Johnson and Roosevelt, his economic policies continued the trend begun under Reagan, a Republican. Monetarism continued to be the accepted economic theory, and Clinton joined a Republican Congress to fundamentally alter AFDC, replacing it with TANF (Temporary Assistance for Needy Families), which limited most welfare payments to a maximum of five years and required virtually all recipients to work while receiving benefits. President George W. Bush continued these basic monetarist policies after taking office in 2000, although following September 11, 2001, he increased military spending and cut taxes, which returned the nation to the budget deficits characteristic of the 1970s and 1980s.

Except for a brief recession in 1989–1991 and slower growth since 2000, monetarist policies produced substantial economic expansion over the past twenty years, until early 2008, when slower growth, a mortgage crisis, and rising energy costs raised fears of a looming recession or even stagflation. These policies also have produced greater inequality and poverty. The GINI Index, an overall measure of inequality, was at about 37 in the late 1940s. It dropped (meaning greater equality) to 35 by the late 1960s, and by 1994 it had risen to 42, where it has remained since. As the earlier Country and Concept table showed, this is a much higher level than is found in other wealthy countries. In the late 1960s, the wealthiest fifth of the population had 40.6 percent of all income; by 2001 that figure had risen to 49.6. The poorest fifth's share of income, on the other hand, dropped from 5.6 to 3.5 percent over the same period.

Every president since Reagan has actively embraced the idea of expanding free trade and globalization, arguing that it maximizes efficiency and will produce the greatest possible wealth for the United States and the rest of the world. The United States has been a key champion of opening all borders to trade and investment, and U.S. companies have moved thousands of factories and hundreds of thousands of factory jobs out of the country. President Clinton got the North American Free Trade Agreement (NAFTA) ap-

proved, which has dramatically opened cross-border economic activity among the United States, Mexico, and Canada. Unions, environmentalists, and others have opposed much of this development, arguing that it is costing the United States jobs and exporting production to countries where workers and the environment are not protected. But official U.S. support of free trade is not universal. Agriculture is the prime example of an economic sector over which the government has maintained protective policies: both the United States and many European countries continue to protect their farming sectors from low-cost competition from poorer countries in Latin America and Africa. These issues caused the failure in 2008 of multiyear discussions of the World Trade Organization (WTO), in which the United States is the single largest player.

The U.S. model of free market growth is an exception, not the norm: most other governments choose to intervene more substantially in market processes. It took a half century of union effort, but the U.S. government eventually did agree to mitigate some of the worst effects of the market on workers by regulating their working conditions and protecting them against the advancement of age and possible disability. The mid-twentieth century saw a period of expanded government involvement starting with the New Deal, a set of policies that has been partially reversed since the 1980s. Some New Deal–Great Society policies, notably Social Security and Medicaid, have proved more popular and durable, despite monetarist demands for reduced government spending. The United States seems to have permanently embraced a somewhat expanded government role, though it remains far less invasive than almost any European country. Its championing of free trade and globalization have made the country a symbol of the new era, to supporters and critics alike, and its ability to prosper amidst globalization will have a major impact on how widespread the free market model of capitalism will become. For now, though, many countries maintain economic systems that include far more extensive state intervention, of which Germany is an exemplar.

CASE STUDY **Germany:** The Social Market Economy

Over the course of the twentieth century, Germany created a much-admired model of regulated capitalism known as the **social market economy**. This model combined a highly productive market economy that became the world's leading industrial exporter with an extensive and generous welfare state and unusually active involvement of both business and labor associations in setting and implementing economic policy. Productivity, wages, and job security were relatively high and inequality relatively low. Germany also led the way in creating the EU and then the euro, yielding its control over monetary policy to the new European Central Bank in 1999, which was modeled after Germany's own Bundesbank. Globalization has raised significant questions about the viability of the social market economy, as Germany has faced continuing high unemployment and difficulty in financing its generous social welfare benefits and maintaining the strict limits on deficit spending that the euro requires and Germany itself has long championed.

The modern German economy first developed under Otto von Bismarck in the 1860s and 1870s: Germany was a late industrializer compared to Britain or France. Bismarck set out to build German national strength via economic growth, and so he pursued a set of policies that protected industry and produced rapid industrialization and urbanization. This came at the expense of workers, who faced horrific working conditions, social dislocation in the expanding cities, and low wages. Under these conditions, an active communist movement arose in Germany, and some of the followers of this movement created the Social Democratic Party (SDP) in 1875 to work for socialism via nonviolent means. High tariffs protected German industry so it could grow but also resulted in high prices for food and other basic commodities, which further fueled worker unhappiness and the socialist movement.

Bismarck was very concerned about what he saw as a socialist threat, and so, starting in 1879, he introduced a series of laws that created an extensive (for its time) social policy network for workers while simultaneously outlawing socialist parties and labor unions.

Germany has been a leader in European Union monetary policy, including the creation of the euro and the European Central Bank. Here, the German finance minister unveils the German national euro coin.

The new policies included the world's first national health insurance system, accident insurance that was administered and financed by cooperative associations of employers, and old age and widows' pensions subsidized by the federal government, all developed a half century before similar policies in the United States. Working conditions, on the other hand, did not change. Basically, the program was a conscious effort to continue industrialization via cheap labor while protecting workers from the worst situations they might face.

These social policies slowly expanded after Bismarck left power in 1890. The government also relaxed restrictions on labor unions, which grew as well. After Germany's loss in World War I and the establishment of the Weimar Republic, social welfare policies expanded still further. The SDP was a prominent force in the Weimar governments of the early 1920s, and its socialist tendencies showed: the government broadened the insurance and pension systems in response to hyperinflation following the war. The influence of labor unions increased rapidly with their increased numbers, and by the mid-1920s, employers had agreed to establish an eight-hour workday, a forty-eight-hour work week, a system of collective bargaining with unions over wages and other benefits, and binding arbitration to settle disputes. Social expenditures leapt from 19 percent of government spending in 1919 to 40 percent by 1930, and wage rates rose as employers and unions agreed to mandatory collective bargaining (Crew 1998). In response to rapid inflation, many companies began paying what was termed a "social wage," a wage that was adjusted to account for the costs of supporting a family.

Hitler interrupted this process with his totalitarian state but after his defeat, the new government of West Germany took up pretty much where things had left off and extended the social welfare system again. The Christian Democratic Union (CDU) under Konrad Adenauer governed West Germany from its first election in 1949 until 1966. Though a "conservative" party, the CDU officially coined the term the "social market economy" and fully developed the model. Christian Democrats generally saw protection of workers as part of their Christian ideology. Granted, the SDP often wanted social spending to expand even more rapidly, but all the major parties agreed with the basic premises of the system. Not surprisingly, after the SDP became the governing party in 1969, social spending expanded more rapidly than in the past, but the shifts in economic and social policies from one government to the next were not large.

The social market economy has created a form of capitalism in which close relationships and interpenetration between the private and public sectors have helped create and implement economic and social policies. The national government passes broad regulatory standards for various sectors of the economy, industries, and professions, but allows state governments (*Lander*) to work with businesses to formulate any detailed implementation plans. The *Lander* work closely with industrial organizations to implement policies locally, which industries accept rather willingly because they've had a role in the formulation of these policies.

Unions also have a role to play, as the government channels some social programs through unions and religious organizations, which allows them to identify and provide money to local beneficiaries. More significantly, unions and employers' associations negotiate binding wage agreements that all employers in a given sector must follow, and unions are represented on the supervisory boards of all German firms of more than two thousand employees. This system, known as **co-determination**, was created in 1976 and gives German workers power through their unions to influence policy. One effect of this has been that the unions have come to understand what they must do to help achieve the high levels of productivity and product quality for which German firms have become famous. Each business of more than five employees also must have a workers' council. These councils must approve rules regarding working conditions, and many run vocational training programs that have helped make German workers among the most highly skilled in the world. Codetermination creates an element of democracy within the management of business enterprises, though ultimately businesses are still privately owned and must answer to their stockholders as in any other capitalist economy.

This economic model made Germany one of the most successful economies in the world from the end of World War II until the late 1980s. No economy is perfect, but Germany enjoyed relatively rapid growth and became one of the world's wealthiest economies with very low unemployment and inflation and exceptionally generous social welfare benefits. It also became one of the world's leading exporters of high-quality manufactured goods, but all of this began to change with the end of the Cold War and the acceleration of globalization, as can be seen in the Country and Concept table. German reunification required the economic absorption of the much poorer East Germany into the social market economy. Privatization of the former government-owned industries in East Germany created massive unemployment. West Germans had to fund huge social programs, infrastructure construction and improvement, and job training programs as they worked to integrate the eastern economy into the western (the bill for this was estimated to be about 4 percent of the entire German economy throughout the 1990s) (European World Year Book 2007). The biggest single problem became and remains unemployment, which hovered around 1 percent for decades in West Germany. By 1998 it had hit nearly 12 percent in reunified Germany and has been between 10 and 12 percent ever since. In the former East Germany, it is more than 18 percent. Economic growth has also slowed as a result of reunification and other factors, averaging only 1.2 percent per capita from 1990 to 2003.

In addition to pioneering the social market economy, Germany has been a key leader in the European Union. The creation of the euro in 1999 required that EU members who adopted it allow the new European Central Bank to control monetary policy (see the following Mini-Case on the European Union). The German central bank, the Bundesbank, restricted German monetary policy to keep inflation low, and the new European bank is charged with doing the same. To be part of the EU, countries must keep their fiscal deficit within strict limits, which restricts the ability of individual governments to spend on social or other programs unless they can raise the taxes to pay for them. Germany's social policies call for generous benefits to the growing numbers of unemployed, but membership in the euro requires it to maintain strict limits on government spending.

MINI-CASE The European Union, Economic Sovereignty, and Globalization

The creation of the European Union (EU), and especially the creation of the European Monetary Union (EMU) and the euro, has raised fundamental questions about globalization and state sovereignty over economic policy. The EU originated in the European Coal and Steel Community of 1952, becoming the more broadly defined European Economic Community (EEC) in 1958. It was at that point that a group of six states, led by West Germany and France, came together with their primary goal to open their economies to each other and ease trade and investment among them. The EEC, as it was known until 1987, did succeed in substantially reducing barriers to trade among member countries, and in effect created an enlarged, multistate market for goods. Member states, however, did not really yield substantial sovereignty because each retained the right to veto any decision of importance; each member state also retained the right to choose what it would agree to and what it would not. By 1981, this group had expanded to ten members, further expanding to fifteen by 1995, and twenty-seven by 2007, with the addition of twelve mostly eastern European countries.

The most ambitious of the original architects of the European Community (EC) envisioned it eventually becoming a "United States of Europe," a single state created as member states voluntarily yielded their sovereignty to the larger body over time. While this has never happened, many members have given substantial sovereignty over their economic policy to what is now called the European Union, which is governed by three key bodies. The first of these, the Council of Ministers, includes the foreign ministers of all member states and has ultimate decision-making authority. Next is the European Commission, the EU's administrative arm; members are appointed, and initiate most new policies. Lastly, the elected European Parliament must approve these polices and send them on to the Council of Ministers for final approval.

Member states were first required to yield real sovereign decision-making power to the larger body under the Single European Act of 1987. The act limited a single state's veto power in the Council of Ministers, and instead expanded a system of qualified majority voting, in which 55–72 percent (depending on the issue) of the total votes are needed to make policy decisions (each country's share of the total vote is based on its size). Under this system, no single state, not even the biggest, Germany, can veto decisions; several states must vote together to block a decision, which means that individual states have given up their sovereign right over key economic decisions. The Single European Act also eliminated most remaining trade barriers within the EC, creating a truly common market by the early 1990s.

The next and biggest step in the process of states yielding sovereignty was the Maastricht Treaty of 1992, which renamed the EC the EU and created the EMU. The plan of this treaty, which each member state could choose to accept or not, was to create a common currency—the euro—controlled by a new European Central Bank. The thirteen states that have so far agreed to participate essentially gave up their ability to control their monetary policy and agreed to strict limits on their fiscal policy. Given the centrality of monetary and fiscal policy to both Keynesian and monetarist economic management, these states have given up perhaps the most important tool they have to control their own economies. To "join" the euro, states had to bring their inflation and interest rates close to the European average, restrict their budget deficits to 3 percent of GDP and their public debt to 60 percent of GDP, and keep the exchange rate of their currency within a particular limit. The eleven states who initially met these criteria adopted the euro in 1999 as an electronic currency for business purposes (Greece joined in 2001 and Slovenia in 2007), and adopted it as their daily currency, in paper and coin form, in 2004. The European Central Bank controls the money supply and therefore key monetary policy for these thirteen states.

Maintaining the strict fiscal limitations has been difficult, especially during economic downturns. Indeed, even Germany and France, the main supporters of the euro, did not stick within the limits in 2003–2004, which led to EU procedures against them. Recognizing the importance of these two large countries, however, the EU ultimately revised the enforcement guidelines to make them less harsh so that the two could stay within the euro and avoid a financial crisis. In effect, the EMU relaxed its strict adherence to monetarist policies in favor of Keynesian policies to stimulate growth during an economic slowdown. Britain and Denmark have explic-

itly rejected participation in the euro, both unwilling to yield monetary sovereignty to the EU, but most other EU members hope to join the euro in the future.

The EU leadership attempted a final expansion of EU sovereignty in 2004 with a proposed European constitution. Despite, or perhaps because of, the successful expansion of EU power before that, the proposed constitution was unpopular in many countries. In 2005, French and Dutch voters rejected it in respective referendums, effectively killing the proposal. Critics were concerned about giving up greater sovereignty to the EU, especially since many viewed the document as having a "democratic deficit." Despite the existence of the directly elected European Parliament, EU critics argue that the EU is too large to be an effective democracy and that real power continues to lie with the appointed Council of Ministers and European Commission, rather than the elected parliament. The constitution would have expanded qualified majority voting, further reducing the veto power of member states and therefore sovereignty.

Opponents of the EU constitution also reacted against the fiscal and monetary policies imposed to join the euro, seeing them as requiring every country to follow the neoliberal economic orthodoxy popular with the IMF and World Bank and undermining European social welfare policies. They saw this as an expansion of the negative effects of globalization, in that their individual states would lose more and more power to the EU bureaucracy, which they saw as committed to expanding the unfettered market competition globalization entails. This has produced a sudden halt to the expanding sovereignty of the EU, though the euro continues to function effectively. Ironically, while the key governments were willing to yield more economic sovereignty to the EU, their citizens were not.

The expenses of reunification and the institution of the euro as a common currency have produced the most significant political discord and electoral shifts in Germany since the end of the Nazi era. In response,

Germany voted out the CDU, led by Helmut Kohl, who had championed German reunification whatever the cost, in 1998. The new SDP government under Gerhard Schröder introduced Agenda 2010, however, which was legislation that significantly lowered the protections and benefits the social market economy had provided Germans, and in 2005, German voters once again expressed their displeasure. Narrowly but definitively voting Schröder and the SDP out, voters returned the CDU to power under Germany's first woman chancellor, Angela Merkel, but the election was so close she had to rule in a grand coalition with the SDP. She faces the same difficult task as her predecessors: how to adjust Germany's social market economy in the face of the growing pressures of globalization and the demands of EU membership.

Germany stands as an economic model quite distinct from that of the United States's free market system; while certainly capitalist, the social market economy includes much more extensive state intervention. In its heyday, government, business, and labor organizations worked closely together to guide the economy on a path of growth and near full employment, with social services far more generous than those available in the United States. Globalization, the EU, and reunification have called the model into question as the country struggles to adapt to a new era. Japan, our next case study, represents a third model of successful capitalism, but one that has also struggled in the new globalized era.

CASE STUDY Japan: The Developmental State and Its Crisis

Japan was the first non-Western society to industrialize successfully and create a fully modern and wealthy economy. This process began under its first modern state, the Meiji regime, which led the country from 1868 until World War II, but the country became fully developed only after World War II, when a distinct model of market-state relations emerged: the developmental state. Interventionist like the German model, the Japanese model arose not from the fear or demands of organized labor and a socialist democratic party, but instead from the concerted effort of key governments to achieve rapid economic growth and industrialization. The primary purpose of intervention under the model has been to guide key sectors of the economy to achieve maximum growth, and the developmental state made Japan the second largest economy in the world by the 1980s. Many Americans at the time came to view it as a primary threat to U.S. economic hegemony. As the Country and Concept table shows, however, persistent economic stagnation since 1990 and only limited reform in the face of the vicissitudes of globalization have brought the developmental state model into question, both in Japan and around the world.

The Meiji Restoration of 1867 brought to power a fundamentally new state led by the militaristic samurai, who were determined to modernize the country after the humiliation of the country's forced opening to Western trade. The Meiji government focused on creating a strong and prosperous state, defined by its central slogan: "rich nation, strong army." The government actively intervened in economic activity, directly investing not only in infrastructure but also in key industries. Once the government started an industry, it often sold it to private investors at bargain bin prices and actively encouraged industrial mergers to create larger and more competitive firms. This produced a very concentrated business class, at the heart of which were the *zaibatsu,* three family-dominated industrial conglomerates that controlled key areas of the economy and had close relations with the government. In contrast to standard practice in capitalist economies, especially that of the United States, the government helped create business cartels to control specific sectors of the economy and trade associations to coordinate development efforts among firms in the same industry.

World War I was a major boon to the Japanese economy, as wartime demand from the United States greatly increased Japanese exports. This allowed Japan to pursue an early ISI policy under which it created even heavier industry than it had before, producing a period of very rapid economic growth, urbanization, and industrialization. After the war, this economic expansion made Japan an attractive place for those with foreign capital to invest, and by the 1930s, Japanese businesses were asking the government for even more support to create cartels to compete against foreign companies. Meanwhile, the increasingly powerful military was concerned that private capital, both domestic and foreign, was getting too powerful and would pursue its own private interests rather than broader national ones, so it initiated a system of government licensing of a wide array of economic investments and activities. The government used these licenses to encourage domestic ownership in key sectors, discourage foreign ownership, and encourage all firms to invest in areas it deemed of national interest. A firm that was Japanese-owned and willing to invest in an area the military-dominated government considered of national importance would receive a license to begin operations much more easily than other firms. This system not only fueled Japan's military machine, it also further concentrated ownership of capital.

After World War II the United States not only dethroned the emperor but also the *zaibatsu.* The United States saw the concentrated business conglomerates as part of the fascist Japanese past and antithetical to healthy competition in a market economy, and so it set out to establish a more decentralized and therefore more "democratic" business class by writing anti-

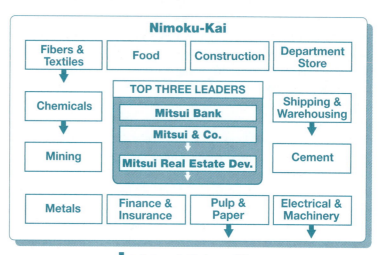

indicates subsidiaries or affiliates

Japan's *keiretsu,* like the Mitsui example shown here, are complex, interlocking, and sometimes vertically integrated industrial conglomerates. They are not technically monopolies, but their highly integrated structures make it difficult for firms outside the *keiretsu* to compete.

monopoly legislation to disband the *zaibatsu.* The Japanese civil service, including the bureaucracies that had helped create the prewar economy, were not substantially changed, however, which meant that what emerged from U.S. occupation was not exactly what had been intended. A shortage of capital for investment forced the United States to allow banks to own stocks in industrial companies and the latter to own stocks in each others' companies. The capital shortage also led Japan's ministry of finance to allow twelve key banks to "overlend" money to companies, meaning that the banks were allowed to lend more money than they had and more than other banks were allowed to lend.

The result of all this, fully developed by the 1960s, was the creation of *keiretsu,* which are still in existence today. These complex networks of firms are owned separately but work together closely. Some are direct descendants of the *ziabatsu.* At the center of most *keiretsu* is a major bank, which lends money on favorable terms to its *keiretsu* members and typically sends representatives to work in the firms to which it has lent money to ensure that its loans are being used wisely.

Firms in a *keiretsu* own stock in each others' companies and therefore give each other orders for products. "Vertical" *keiretsu* like Toyota and Nissan involve a major manufacturer tied to hundreds of favored suppliers of inputs. While ownership of capital is not as concentrated as it was under the Meiji regime, the system nonetheless encourages long-term relationships among firms and limits the ability of firms outside the *keiretsu,* including foreign firms, to do business.

What Chalmers Johnson (1982) termed the **developmental state** emerged along with the rise of the *keiretsu*. A developmental state does not seek just to establish the rules of the game for capitalism and encourage overall economic growth, but also to consciously create national strength in particular economic areas: it takes an active and conscious role in the development of specific sectors of the economy. The Japanese government did this via two key bureaucratic agencies, the Ministry of Finance (MOF) and the Ministry of International Trade and Industry (MITI). Until liberalization in the 1970s, the MOF had extensive influence over the banking sector via its control of interest rates and the role of banks in the *keiretsu*. The major banks were allowed to overlend to their *keiretsu* members to facilitate industrial investment. The banks could not cover all of these loans, so when a debtor failed to pay, the MOF guaranteed the loan, making the banks, and in turn the industrial companies, dependent on MOF goodwill. The MOF also controlled substantial funds via the postal saving system, a state-run system that provided a safe, convenient way for people to deposit their money in savings accounts through the post office. Most Japanese households invested their personal savings in postal savings accounts, and then the MOF used these funds to subsidize key industries it favored.

MITI influenced industrial policies more specifically through extensive licensing of technology and "administrative guidance," the ability of the bureaucracy to informally and successfully suggest that an industry or firm pursue a particular endeavor. MITI was able to use such an informal system to guide industrial growth because of the licensing, financial, and other powers it held over business, and because of the close relation-

ship that developed between key industries, bureaucracies, and the ruling party. Leaders in all three would move from one to the other over the course of their careers: former bureaucrats frequently became members of parliament, for instance.

T. J. Pempel (2000) argues that Japan's development state was fundamentally a "conservative regime" in the sense that it favored business and governing elites over labor. Labor unions have always been opponents of the ruling party, but have never been very powerful. This is due in part to what has been termed "lifetime employment" at major Japanese firms. In reality, the system is not lifetime, but rather a member of the core, "permanent" workforce has (or at least had) a near guarantee of employment with the same firm. This was made possible in part by the existence of a large, part-time, and flexible workforce of mostly women that firms could hire and fire as market conditions warranted. The permanent male workforce received nearly guaranteed employment and was assured health and retirement benefits via the firm, therefore many chose to remain loyal.

The developmental state created the "Japanese miracle"; the economy in 1975 was more than six times the size of what it had been in 1950. Japan became the world's second largest economy and "Japan, Inc." was the chief economic rival to the United States in the 1970s and 1980s. As Table 5.1 shows, Japan has also maintained a relatively low level of inequality and only moderate levels of poverty. This has not, however, been due to an extensive social welfare system. Japan's spending on social welfare is typically second lowest among wealthy countries, not far above that of the United States, and well below most European welfare states like Germany. Rather, Japan has maintained relative equality via the lifetime employment system and the extensive benefits large companies provide workers. Workers at large firms typically get a substantial lump sum payment upon retirement, and some also receive pensions after that. A governmental social security system exists but is very modest, even compared to the U.S. system. The retirement payment and the fact that many companies pay a substantial share of annual wages via occasional large bonuses have

TABLE 5.1 Profile of Japan's Economy, 1970–2005

	1970	1980	1990	2000	2005
GDP Growth (annual %)	10.7	2.8	5.2	2.9	1.9
Social Expenditures (total, as % of GDP)	..	10.3	11.2	16.1	..
Gross National Savings (as % of nominal GDP)	..	..	33.2	27.5	26.8
Share of Income or Consumption, Ratio of Richest 20% to Poorest 20%	..	..	4.3	3.4	3.4

Sources: Data from World Bank Indicators, OECD, UNDP Human Development Reports.

helped make Japan's savings rate one of the highest in the world. This savings helped fuel rapid investment and growth in earlier years, but some economists believe it is now hurting Japan's ability to move out of the recession it has been in since 1993.

Table 5.1 also illustrates the sharp difference between the last twenty years in Japan and earlier decades. Economic growth is only a third of what it was in the 1980s, unemployment has increased substantially, and prices are actually falling, a sign of serious economic stagnation or recession. The economic miracle ended in 1990. On the first business day of the year, rapidly escalating real estate and stock prices plummeted, and the bubble burst. There had been indications: productivity growth had been slowing since the 1970s, as had the government's ability to influence the direction of economic activity. Acquiescing to international pressure, the government had begun to slowly reduce its power to control flows of money and financing in the late 1970s. In the 1980s, the system of guaranteeing bank loans led Japanese corporations to take on excessive debt, which they invested in real estate and other unproductive areas. Because of deregulation, the MOF could do little to stop them, and it didn't really try. Simultaneously, the more efficient Japanese companies such as Toyota and Nissan fully entered the age of globalization, investing elsewhere in the world so that instead of exporting cars from Japan, they began building them in the United States and Europe, reducing Japan's key source of growth, exports.

All of this meant that when the bubble burst, the government had great difficulty responding effectively. It tried both Keynesian and monetarist policies, engaging in deficit spending and lowering official interest rates all the way to zero, but nothing seemed to revive economic growth. A key problem was massive bad bank debt from all the poorly invested loans. Government spending went to paying off the bad loans and keeping the banks that had made them in business. Corporations cut their permanent workforces and shifted to more part-time workers, reducing worker benefits and real wages.

In April 2001, Junichiro Koizumi was swept into power on his promises to reform the system, but he faced entrenched business and bureaucratic interests opposed to his efforts. His reforms were intended to reduce regulation and government control over the economy, thereby dismantling much of the developmental state, but was only partially successful. For example, only a minority of government-owned companies were sold. Koizumi has lowered deficit spending to reduce the size of the government but, following Keynesian economic logic, this hurt growth by reducing the demand for goods. In 2005, facing opposition from within his own party to privatizing the postal service, including its massive savings system, Koizumi called an early election and won. In a subsequent special session of the legislature, the postal service was privatized, a long process that began in 2007 that ultimately will take from the bureaucracy the giant savings system that it used to subsidize favored industries—a key mechanism of the developmental state. In 2005–2006, modest economic growth returned to the country, though huge bank and government debt remains a significant problem as Japan struggles to transform or at least adjust the developmental state to meet the demands of globalization.

Postwar Japan created a new model of political economy, the developmental state, that proved spectacularly successful at transforming the country into a global power and one of the wealthiest countries in the world. The mechanisms through which the state achieved this, however, proved to have negative effects when faced with the pressure of globalization in the form of more open financial systems, global investment by its own companies, and speculative investment in real estate and stock markets. Japan continues to struggle to adopt its model to the new era. Our next case study, Brazil, is a case of a much poorer, developing economy that met with significant success a generation ago but also struggled considerably in the 1980s and 1990s.

CASE STUDY Brazil: Modernizing Authoritarianism, ISI, and Debt Crisis

Brazil, Latin America's giant, is a classic example of the evolution of development economics theory outlined earlier in this chapter. The military government, a modernizing authoritarian regime, used ISI to industrialize quite successfully, until the underlying problems of the model and global oil shocks in the 1970s produced a debt crisis and forced it to shift to more neoliberal policies. Over the course of the past century, Brazil's development policies have transformed it from a primarily agricultural economy into one that is quite industrialized, though it has only achieved the status of "middle-income" country by world standards and still has tremendous inequality and poverty.

Industrialization began in the 1930s. Up to that point, the country was primarily agricultural, relying on coffee and sugar exports as its main sources of income. But with the Great Depression, Brazil's coffee economy was in crisis, and the government under Getúlio Vargas began its first ISI policies, manipulating the value of the national currency to discourage imports of manufactured goods. This process accelerated during World War II, when growth of the industrial sector was more than 5 percent per year. Under the neofascist

Estado Novo (1937–1945), the first state-owned companies were created, and the state invested heavily in the infrastructure needed by industry. The Estado Novo also controlled labor unions, keeping workers' wages low to attract investment. The democratic regime from 1945 to 1964 continued and intensified the ISI strategy. The first industries to receive favorable treatment and protection were consumer goods, including textiles and automobiles, but by the 1960s, ISI was extended to encourage domestic production of inputs to the industrialization process. The state was able to successfully expand into such heavy industry as chemicals and machinery.

The economic crisis that precipitated the military coup in 1964 produced a modernizing authoritarian regime officially dedicated to rapid economic development. The new military government viewed development as central to its official National Security Doctrine and pursued a policy of intensified ISI, rapidly expanding the state's involvement in the economy by creating more state-owned companies in heavy industry and by building more infrastructure. It was particularly interested in developing its own technological capacities and invested heavily in such areas as the aerospace industry. Like the *Estado Novo,* the military government also used the corporatist labor structure to severely restrict labor unions and workers' wages to encourage private investment.

The results from 1967 to 1973 formed what would become known as the "Brazilian Miracle," during which the economy grew at a rate of 9 to 10 percent per year, one of the fastest in the world. This completed the country's transition from an agricultural to an industrial economy but also produced much greater inequality. The southeastern states and cities, especially São Paulo and Rio de Janeiro, received the bulk of the investment and grew rapidly. The rural populace, with little to support them in agriculture, migrated to these two cities in huge numbers: at one point São Paulo was growing by more than half a million people a year. This left the northern part of the country and the interior depopulated and even poorer. Within the booming cities, however, inequality was also increasing. The wealthy and middle classes benefited tremendously from industrialization, as did the highest paid workers in the growing industries, but most laborers saw little improvement in their lives. Many of the new migrants from the countryside could find only menial work and moved into impoverished shantytowns called *favelas.* The government did begin creating social programs such as retirement pensions for workers—the beginnings of a welfare policy—but these programs primarily benefited government employees and workers in major industries.

The government responded to the oil price increases of the 1970s by trying to deepen ISI, creating many more state corporations and trying to produce more sophisticated technology. Not enough of these protected industries, however, could compete internationally to earn revenue via exports, and the government ultimately had to borrow heavily to purchase oil and other essential imports. By the early 1980s, continuing inability to export products and a sudden jump in international interest rates produced a debt crisis: Brazil became the world's biggest debtor. This resulted in several negotiated agreements over the next decade with the United States and the major banks to which

In 1969, even as the Brazilian Miracle was taking off, *favelas* continued to grow amidst the fashionable neighborhoods of Rio de Janeiro. Many Brazilians still live in *favelas,* as Brazil's bumpy path to industrialization and "middle-income" status has left it with high levels of poverty, unemployment, and inequality.

Brazil owed money. These agreements reduced some of the debt in exchange for promises of policy changes in line with the neoliberal model of development advocated by the IMF. With the transition to democracy underway in the 1980s, however, change to the state's role in the economy was relatively slow. High inflation remained a major concern as well. Some efforts at privatization and reducing the size of the government were made, but with limited success, in part because potential buyers found the large firms unlikely to be profitable. The privatization that did occur was often very unpopular, particularly if purchasers were foreign corporations, which raised nationalist sympathies.

The new democratic government that came to power at the end of the 1980s tried various economic reform plans to reduce inflation and restore economic growth. The only one to succeed was a plan crafted by Minister of Finance Fernando Henrique Cardoso in 1993, which created a new currency and promised reduced government spending. Political opposition to Cardoso's plan was initially significant, but once it succeeded at dramatically reducing inflation, it became very popular. Cardoso went on to win the presidency in 1994 and was reelected in 1999. Also in the late 1990s, Cardoso successfully accelerated privatization of state-owned companies and reduced the expensive pension plans for government workers. Economic growth returned but still was only 2.9 percent during the 1990s. Unemployment, meanwhile, went from around 2 percent in the mid-1970s to more than 12 percent by 2003. Neoliberal policies had reduced state deficits and inefficiency by reducing employment in the public sector and had restored some growth, but that growth was not enough to reach full employment through the private sector.

In the Brazilian economic development story, the state has played an active role in shaping the market to pursue development. It has built much of the country's infrastructure and created some welfare programs for certain segments of the population. Today Brazil is a major exporter of not only coffee but also of automobile parts and small airplanes, and the rising cost of oil may position it to become a major exporter of ethanol and ethanol technology, pioneered under the military to cut oil imports. ISI policies initiated this industrial upturn but also helped create an economic crisis by the end of the 1970s. International pressure forced a slow transition to neoliberal policies by the early 1990s. These policies have reduced debt and inflation and restored growth, but so far have not significantly reduced inequality, poverty, and unemployment. A new, leftist government was elected in 2004 to try to cope with the forces of globalization, a subject to which we return in chapter 10. While Brazil struggled with neoliberal policies, its neighbor Chile, discussed in the following Mini-Case, represents a case of striking success, in sharp contrast to our final case study of Nigeria.

MINI-CASE Chile: Early Neoliberal Reformer

Prior to the 1970s, Chile's economic history was similar to that of its Southern Cone peers. It depended heavily on mineral exports developed by foreign investors—first nitrates and then copper—and suffered the vicissitudes associated with primary product exports. It experimented with ISI, but it was still by no means an industrial economy. In 1970 Chile narrowly elected Salvador Allende, who came to power at the head of a left-wing coalition dedicated to following a "peaceful road to socialism." Allende's government nationalized industries including American-owned firms, imposed price controls, increased wages, and began a land reform, but opposition from the middle and upper classes of Chile as well as the United States was swift. Economic chaos ensued. By 1973, strikes, runaway inflation, and shortages had brought the economy to the brink of disaster. On September 11 the military intervened in a coup d'etat that left at least two thousand people dead—the first casualties of a long and brutal military dictatorship under General Augusto Pinochet.

The military turned economic policy over to a group of civilian technocrats who were quickly dubbed the "Chicago Boys." Trained at the University of Chicago, they were devotees of Milton Friedman's monetarist economic policies and sought to modernize the Chilean economy by opening it up fully to the world market and reducing state intervention. They intended to fully reverse Allende's policies, selling Chile's nearly 500 state-owned firms, eliminating subsidies, and forcing Chilean firms to compete with foreign firms. These policies successfully reduced Chile's runaway inflation and promoted growth throughout the 1970s, but ironically many of the Chilean business owners who had supported the coup lost out in the competition with foreign firms.

Like other poorer countries, Chile's economy shrank tremendously in the aftermath of Mexico's debt crisis in 1982, and nearly one-third of the workforce was unemployed by mid-1983. General Pinochet brought in new economic advisers who implemented even more radical free market reforms. GDP growth reached a strong average annual rate of 4.1 percent throughout the 1980s, compared with 2.8 percent in Brazil, 1.1 percent in Mexico, and -0.3 percent in Argentina. Unemployment also fell, but wages remained low and poverty high, while many poor Chileans did not have access to social services like health care that the government had privatized.

In 1988 Pinochet decided to risk a plebiscite on continued military rule. Perhaps he believed that people grateful for the returning economic growth would support him, but a unified opposition including the Socialists and the dominant centrist party, the Christian Democrats, mounted a dramatically successful campaign to vote "no" on continued military rule. After some tense moments, Pinochet accepted the result, paving the way for the election of the Christian Democrat Patricio Aylwin, who assumed office in 1990. Aylwin and his successors, Christian Democrat Eduardo Frei Ruiz-Tagle and Socialists Ricardo Lagos and Michele Bachelet (Chile's first female president, elected in 2006) all committed themselves to maintaining the basic structure of the free market economy, while espousing various types of social programs to deal with the poverty and inequality left over from the military era. Chile continued its commitment to trade liberalization, joining the Latin American MERCOSUR free trade zone as an associate member in 1996, and concluding free trade agreements with Canada (1996), the United States (2005), China (2005) and Japan (2005).

Chile's free market economy produced average annual GDP growth of nearly 8 percent throughout much of the 1990s, making it the fastest growing economy in Latin America. Beginning in 1998, the country experienced an economic slowdown and rising unemployment, but a rise in the price of copper, which still accounts for 40 percent of exports, and consistent macroeconomic policies led to renewed growth in 2003, reaching an estimated 5.8 percent in 2007. Unemployment has fallen as well, but remains around 8 percent. Chile appears to have successfully created strong financial institutions and the macroeconomic context for strong export-led growth into the future. High growth rates, lower birth rates, and government poverty-reduction programs also lowered Chile's poverty rate dramatically since Patricio Aylwin's election in 1990, especially in comparison with the rest of Latin America, but 18.2 percent of the population remained in poverty in 2005, and its GINI coefficient was 54.9 in 2003. The challenge now is to use future growth to continue to reduce poverty and income inequality, as Chile attempts to move further on the path toward solidifying its status as a middle-income country.

CASE STUDY Nigeria: Oil, Corruption, and Dependence

Like almost all African countries, when Nigeria gained independence in 1960 it was a poor, agricultural country with little industry of any kind. As much as 98 percent of the population worked in agriculture, producing 65 percent of the country's GDP and 70 percent of its exports. And like the governments of other African states, its new government initially attempted to industrialize via ISI. By the mid-1970s, however, oil production and revenue had overwhelmed all other aspects of the economy and made the government dangerously dependent on the global oil market for political and economic survival. The huge influx of oil revenue and the active involvement of the government in the economy helped create a situation ripe for corruption, and Nigeria ultimately became one of the most corrupt societies and governments in the world. Corruption, dependence, and mismanagement combined to leave average Nigerians gaining virtually nothing from the country's massive oil wealth. Very little development has occurred under either democratic or military governments, and the country's elite have come to use oil wealth to enrich themselves and maintain their political position among their political and economic clients.

The origins of Nigeria's economic problems, and the troubled relationship between the state and the market, lay in colonial rule. Like colonial rulers throughout sub-Saharan Africa, colonial rulers in Nigeria allowed only particular economic opportunities to Africans. In Nigeria peasant farmers were encouraged to produce food and export crops, and these crops became the backbone of an export economy based on cocoa, cotton, peanuts, and palm oil. Nigerians were not allowed any significant opportunity in industry, and foreign businesses controlled what little industry there was. Africans' sole route to economic advancement under colonial rule was education and employment in the colonial government, and in contrast to the situation in most capitalist economies, government employment became a key source of wealth. At independence, the educated elite was primarily employed in government, with virtually no involvement or expertise in private industry. This elite thus looked to an expansion of the government's role in the economy as central to development, and members saw this course of action to be in their own interests as well. As we noted earlier, development economists at the time agreed with this approach, arguing that in the absence of an indigenous capitalist class, the state could beneficially intervene to initiate the development process.

The earliest manifestation of this model of state intervention in the interests of development came in the agricultural sector with the creation of **marketing boards**. These were government entities with monopoly control over the domestic and international marketing of key crops. Of particular importance were the marketing boards for export crops such as cocoa and cotton. These boards used their monopoly to buy export crops from Nigerian farmers at low prices and sell them internationally at much higher prices. The difference between the money spent and the money earned became a key source of government revenue, as it was essentially an unofficial but quite substantial tax on farmers. British colonial rulers created this system, and the newly elected independent government continued it. When world prices for key crops were relatively high,

Colonial and independent Nigerian states used marketing boards to reap profits from exports like cocoa, but failed to reinvest these profits in productive development. Today oil has replaced cocoa as the country's primary revenue generator, but most Nigerians have benefited little from this wealth.

the system functioned, but when those prices dropped in the late 1960s, farmers faced even lower prices, and protests and riots broke out in key agricultural areas.

Despite farmers' opposition to this unofficial tax, if the government used the revenue gained from agricultural exports to make productive investments in industry, modernization theorists would argue that its actions were justified. However, this money was not distributed or invested in the most effective or efficient way possible: Nigeria's federal system of government, which included four rather autonomous regional governments in the 1960s, worked against either of these. The bulk of the revenue from the marketing boards went to the regional governments, each government used the revenue to build infrastructure and encourage industrialization, and in the process one often duplicated the efforts of another. The marketing board revenues also became an early source of corruption, further undermining efficient investment.

Given the lack of private Nigerian involvement in industry, the government, supported by aid donors and advisers, saw joint government investment with foreign companies as crucial to industrialization. In 1963 private Nigerian investment constituted only 10 percent of large-scale manufacturing, foreign investment controlled 68 percent, and the various governments controlled the remaining 22 percent. By the 1970s, the government had passed laws on "Nigerianization" that required investments in key sectors of the economy to include a particular percentage of Nigerian participation, either by the government or individual investors. Using these laws and revenue from oil reserves, the government rapidly expanded its investment in large-scale industry during the 1970s. Most of the private Nigerian investors were themselves government officials or political leaders, so participation in the government and politics remained the key source of wealth.

Until the early 1970s, Nigeria's economic story of taxation of agricultural exports and state-led investment in industry was typical of Africa as a whole. Nigeria, however, possessed large oil reserves. In 1961 money from oil exports constituted less than 8 percent of government revenue; by 1974 that number hit 80 percent. Oil production obviously increased steadily

after independence, and in the early 1970s it became subject to Nigerianization along with the rest of the economy. Throughout the decade, Nigerian governments invested virtually nothing in agriculture, which declined from being the most important sector of the economy to one that continued to employ many people but produced very little.

The biggest change would come with the quadrupling of world oil prices in 1973. Oil exports went from about 3 percent of the country's total exports at independence to 95 percent in the 1980s and 1990s. This gave the Nigerian government a windfall from which it has yet to recover. The military governments of the 1970s used the oil wealth to invest in large-scale infrastructure projects, borrowing money against future oil revenues to do so. The democratic government elected in 1979 did much the same thing, expanding infrastructure and government employment to purchase political support. When the oil market collapsed in the mid-1980s, the government was unable to pay back its loans and faced bankruptcy. Once again, it became a fairly typical African state, going to the IMF after 1983 to negotiate an SAP. The politically painful reductions in the government's size and activity insisted on by the IMF were more than even the military governments could bear, however, and the process of instituting neoliberal policies was long and remains incomplete. Certainly, the government has reduced its involvement in industry (other than oil) and cut its size, but it has still only partially liberalized.

The central role of the state in the economy prior to 1983 and the huge oil revenues created a situation ripe for corruption, and Nigeria became one of the world's most corrupt societies. Its worst ruler, Sani Abacha, is rumored to have stolen approximately $2 billion in government oil revenue in just five years in power in the 1990s. Transparency International ranked Nigeria at 147 out of 179 countries in terms of corruption in 2007. As in other parts of the postcolonial world, state intervention in the economy in the 1960s and 1970s gave government officials and politicians many opportunities to grease palms and stuff their own pockets. Every law that required government approval for some economic activity created a point at which an official could ask for a bribe. In Africa, the fact that government employment was the chief source of wealth contributed to this process. Ambitious young leaders went into government and politics not just to gain political power and to lead, but also to make money. Furthermore, political power and legitimacy were based heavily on patron-client ties. In the newly independent African states like Nigeria, legitimacy was officially based on democratic elections, but these democracies were new additions to the political scene. Average Nigerians had no reason to trust these new institutions, and so they "voted" what and who they knew.

Some analysts argue that Nigerian and other African political cultures encourage corruption. Leaders were long expected to provide for their followers. The colonial government was seen as a source of wealth and resources: it had no other legitimacy in the eyes of the people. A cultural norm arose, then, in which people expected government officials and politicians to provide something for them. Since democratic legitimacy was weak, and military governments had little legitimacy, patron-client links and the provision of resources became nearly the sole means of maintaining political support. Nigerian leaders took bribes and stole from government coffers both to feather their own nests and to provide resources to their supporters, who would then grant them political support. As we argued in chapter 2, weak state institutions are both the cause and the effect of corruption. The illegitimacy of the colonial government and the brand-new democracy after independence meant governmental institutions were weak, so people did not value them and were not interested in fighting to preserve them. Corruption, then, became quite easy to engage in for those who were interested. Oil revenue allowed that corruption to develop on a massive scale. Political leaders, whether civilian or military, used this wealth to amass personal fortunes and buy political support to stay in power as long as possible. Structural adjustment, which in theory should reduce the size of government and corruption, has made little difference. Oil revenue so overwhelms all other areas of the economy that corruption in that one sector alone provides all the money any

IN CONTEXT Nigeria as an Oil Exporter

The Country and Concept table allows you to compare Nigeria with two other oil exporters, Iran and the Russian Federation, but it is also instructive to compare Nigeria with its partners in the Organization of Petroleum Exporting Countries (OPEC). All the data below are for 2006.

- Nigeria has the second largest population in OPEC, after Indonesia.

- Nigeria has 134.41 million people, compared to an OPEC average of 47.6 million.

- Nigeria produced 2,234,000 barrels of oil per day, compared to an OPEC average of 2,672,000 barrels/day.

- It exported $52.52 billion of oil, but this amounted to only $391 of oil exports per capita. The OPEC average was $1136 per capita.

- Nigeria's per capita GDP of $858 made it the poorest OPEC country, in comparison with an average of $3128/person and Qatar's high of $61,977/person.

- Nigeria has only half the average proven crude oil reserves: 36.22 billion barrels compared to 76.87 billion barrels. Saudi Arabia has the highest OPEC reserves (264.25 billion barrels), and Indonesia the lowest (4.37 billion barrels).

- A recent IMF Report found that Nigeria and other sub-Saharan African oil exporters face much greater developmental challenges than exporters from other regions, including shorter oil horizons, lower reserves per capita, high oil dependence, and greater infrastructural and human development gaps.

individual could want or need, and plenty left over to pass on to clients. The long struggle for democracy in the 1990s, which we discuss further in chapter 9, somewhat increased the legitimacy of the system in the eyes of Nigerians and the world, but there is still a long way to go.

Nigeria is a case study of development gone wrong. The largest country in Africa and blessed (or cursed) with abundant oil reserves, it remains one of the world's poorest countries. The development models pursued—both ISI and, more recently, SAPs—were justified in terms of reigning theories of economic de-velopment in their respective eras, but neither led to significant development in Nigeria. Weak institutions, political demands, and massive oil wealth produced monumental levels of corruption that undermined vir-tually all development efforts. Neoliberal policies are designed to encourage such investment, but have achieved little success in the context of African states. Economic blueprints, in the absence of a strong and coherent set of state institutions and a favorable global economic context, do not produce the expected re-sults, though are frequently used to justify the politi-cally motivated actions of various leaders.

CONCLUSION

With the extension of the market economy to nearly every corner of the globe, a universal set of issues exists involving the relationship between the market and the state. The state must perform certain functions for the market to function efficiently and in turn produce revenue for the state. The market is likely to gen-erate greater wealth if the state is able to go beyond these essential functions by establishing policies to encourage investment and growth. Political pressure can lead to yet other policies, as organized groups in society demand particular state intervention in the market in their favor. Clear and consistent economic theories of how and why the state should intervene serve as intellectual guides for state actions; however, no government's policies follow the blueprints perfectly, as our cases studies have shown.

Indeed, the case studies demonstrate a wide array of approaches to and levels of state involvement in the market. Explaining this variation has long been a pre-occupation of comparativists. Marxist analysts, whose theories of the dominance of the bourgeoisie are challenged by the existence of extensive welfare states such as Germany's, argue that the elite create policies beneficial to workers to preserve capitalism in the long term, sacrificing the short-term interests of particular busi-nesses to preserve the system as a whole. Probably the most widespread explana-tion, however, is a pluralist one: countries in which there exists a strong workers' movement and in which unions have developed have created the policies these groups favor. This immediately raises the question of why some countries de-veloped stronger unions than others. Analysts comparing the United States with countries in Europe, in particular, have asked why unions are weaker and why no strong socialist party has emerged in the United States. One common explana-tion is the "frontier thesis" that cites the option of moving west as an escape valve that allowed workers to flee rather than organize and fight. Another is a racial thesis that proposes that racial divisions within the American union movement kept it from gaining more strength. Many historians have argued that U.S. business leaders, especially in the South, actively encouraged those racial divisions to keep unions weak.

Weak unions are just one example of weak institutions, which institutionalists argue are the key to explaining the different economic paths of different countries. They argue that more than just group strength is involved in creating stronger welfare states in some countries than in others. The strength of institutions is also crucial, especially the strength of parties, unions, and business associations. Proponents of this line of thought contend that a strong party that supports welfare policies, regardless of how or how much the working class is organized, produces stronger welfare policies. Similarly, unified labor unions and business associations can effectively limit the actions of their individual members, which gives the organizations strong bargaining power vis-à-vis the state and each other. Strong business associations can discipline their members to accept policies that the bulk of the association supports but which some individual businesses may not. In contrast, relatively weak unions and business associations in the United States resulted in local unions striking even when national associations opposed them and in local businesses demanding lower wages even when national associations might have agreed to higher ones. The ability of stronger institutions in Germany to discipline their members produced a less confrontational environment that allowed stronger welfare policies to gain support. Strong bureaucratic and party institutions similarly help explain the rise of the developmental state in Japan, where unions have always been exceptionally weak. Bureaucrats experienced in heavily guiding business in prewar Japan developed a similar system after the U.S. occupation with the support of party leaders who were themselves close allies of business interests. A state emerged that was dedicated to expanding key businesses in the interests of both the businesses themselves and national economic development.

In poorer countries, groups in civil society seem distinctly less able to influence economic policies. When labor unions in Brazil were demanding a significantly greater share of the wealth from industrialization in the 1950s and 1960s, the military carried out a coup that ushered in a period of rapid growth and investment but repression of labor and wages. In Nigeria policies that in theory were designed to use the state to enhance national development instead favored the elite who controlled key government machinery, thus providing few benefits for the majority of the population. In both countries, and throughout the "Global South," the ideas of development economists in the north have been very influential. Since the debt crisis of the early 1980s, structural adjustment policies imposed by the World Bank and IMF have forced both countries to pursue policies that have had little domestic support.

Without question, globalization has challenged all past models of political economy. Whether they were successful or not in earlier decades, they now face rapidly moving capital that seems to limit their options. Europe has used the EU to try to survive and prosper in this new era, but this has required individual nations to adhere to a common set of policies, especially if they wish to be part of the euro zone. Weaker nations seem to have even less room to maneuver in an era in which international forces are increasingly powerful vis-à-vis domestic ones. The pluralist and institutionalist approaches that help explain past economic policies and outcomes may be less helpful in understanding how states can and do deal with globalization. We return to this subject in chapters 10 and 11, in the final part of the book in which we examine a series of crucial contemporary issues facing the nations of the world and the field of comparative politics.

Key Concepts

capitalism (p. 156)
codetermination (p. 179)
comparative advantage (p. 165)
deficit spending (p. 163)
developmental state (p. 184)
externality (p. 162)
fiscal policy (p. 163)
globalization (p. 170)
import-substitution industrialization (ISI) (p. 166)

Keynesian theory (p. 163)
market economy (p. 156)
marketing boards (p. 190)
monetarist theory (p. 163)
monetary policy (p. 164)
monopoly (p. 159)
natural monopolies (p. 159)
neoliberalism (p. 167)
privatize (p. 167)
public goods (p. 157)

social market economy (p. 178)
stagflation (p. 164)
structural adjustment
   programs (SAPs) (p. 167)
terms of trade (p. 165)

Works Cited

Bates, Robert H. 2001. *Prosperity and Violence: The Political Economy of Development.* New York: W. W. Norton.

Crew, David F. 1998. *Germans on Welfare: From Weimer to Hitler.* New York: Oxford University Press.

The European World Year Book. 2007. London: Europa Publications.

Garrett, Geoffrey. 1998. *Partisan Politics in the Global Economy.* Cambridge: Cambridge University Press.

Johnson, Chalmers A. 1982. *MITI and the Japanese Miracle: The Growth of Industrial Policy, 1925–1975.* Stanford: Stanford University Press.

Ohmae, Kenichi. 1995. *The End of the Nation State: How Regional Economics Will Soon Reshape the World.* New York: Simon and Schuster.

Pempel, T. J. 2000. *Regime Shift: Comparative Dynamics of the Japanese Political Economy.* Ithaca: Cornell University Press.

Polanyi, Karl. 1944. *The Great Transformation.* New York: Farrar and Rinehart.

Transparency International. www.transparency.org.

Resources for Further Study

Friedman, Milton. 1962. *Capitalism and Freedom.* Chicago: University of Chicago Press.

Gilpin, Robert. 2000. *The Challenge of Global Capitalism.* Princeton: Princeton University Press.

Globalization 101: A Project of Levin Institute. www.globalization101.org.

Heilbroner, Robert. 1985. *The Nature and Logic of Capitalism.* New York: Norton.

Keynes, John Maynard. 1935. *General Theory of Employment, Interest, and Money.* New York: Harcourt Brace.

OPEC Annual Statistical Bulletin. 2006. www.opec. org/library/Annual%20Statistical%20Bulletin/in-teractive/FileZ/Main.htm.

Rapley, John. 1996. *Understanding Development: Theory and Practice in the Third World.* Boulder, Colo.: Lynne Rienner Publishers.

Regional Economic Outlook, Sub-Saharan Africa. 2007. Washington, D.C.: International Monetary Fund.

Siebert, Horst. 2005. *The German Economy: Beyond the Social Market.* Princeton: Princeton University Press.

Wilber, Charles K., and Kenneth P. Jameson. 1995. *The Political Economy of Development and Underdevelopment.* New York: McGraw Hill.

Woo-Cumings, Meredith. 1999. *The Developmental State.* Ithaca: Cornell University Press.

PART II

POLITICAL SYSTEMS AND HOW THEY WORK

COUNTRY CASES IN PART 2

Chapter	Brazil	China	Germany	India	Iran	Japan	Nigeria	Russia	UK	US
6. Political Institutions: Governing	●		●	●		●		●	●	●
7. Political Institutions: Participation and Representation			●	●		●				●
8. Authoritarian Institutions		●			●		●			
9. Regime Change: Coups, Revolutions, and Democratization	●	●				●		●		

Country	Current Head of State	Formal Name of Government	Type of Government
Brazil	President: Luiz Inacio Lula da Silva	Federal Republic of Brazil	Federal republic
China	President: Hu Jintao Premier: Wen Jiabao	People's Republic of China	Communist state
Germany	President: Horst Koehler Chancellor: Angela Merkel	Federal Republic of Germany	Federal republic
India	President: Pratibha Patil Prime Minister: Manmohan Singh	Federal Republic of India	Federal republic
Iran	Supreme Leader: Ali Hoseini-Khamenei President: Mahmoud Ahmadinejad	Islamic Republic of Iran	Theocratic republic
Japan	Emperor: Emperor Akihito Prime Minister: Yasuo Fukuda	Japan	Constitutional monarchy with parliamentary government
Nigeria	President: Umaru Musa Yar'Adua	Federal Republic of Nigeria	Federal republic
Russia	President: Dmitri Medvedev Premier: Vladimir Putin	Russian Federation	Federation
United Kingdom	Queen: Queen Elizabeth II Prime Minister: Gordon Brown	United Kingdom of Great Britain and Northern Ireland	Constitutional monarchy with parliamentary government
United States	President: George W. Bush	United States of America	Federal republic

A black South African woman reads as she waits to vote in the country's first post-apartheid election in 1994.

Administrative Divisions	Most Recent Constitution	Significant Political Parties	Type of Suffrage and Age of Emancipation	Legal System
26 states and 1 federal district	October 5, 1988	7	Compulsory between 19–70; voluntary between 16–18 and 70 and older	Code law
23 provinces, 5 autonomous regions, 4 municipalities	December 4, 1982	1	Universal, 18 years of age and older	Code law
16 states	October 3, 1990	5	Universal, 18 years of age and older	Code law
28 states and 7 union territories	January 26, 1950	4	Universal, 18 years of age and older	Common law
30 provinces	December 2–3, 1979 (revised 1989)	0	Universal, 16 years of age and older	*Sharia* law
47 prefectures	May 3, 1947	3	Universal, 20 years of age and older	Code law
36 states and 1 federal territory	May 5, 1999	3	Universal, 18 years of age and older	Mix of common and *sharia* law
46 oblasts, 21 republics, 4 autonomous okrugs, 9 krays, 2 federal cities, 1 autonomous oblast	December 12, 1993	4	Universal, 18 years of age and older	Code law
England has 34 counties, Northern Ireland has 26 district council areas; Scotland has 32 unitary authorities; Wales has 22 unitary authorities	unwritten	3	Universal, 18 years of age and older	Common law
50 states and 1 district	September 17, 1787	2	Universal, 18 years of age and older	Common law

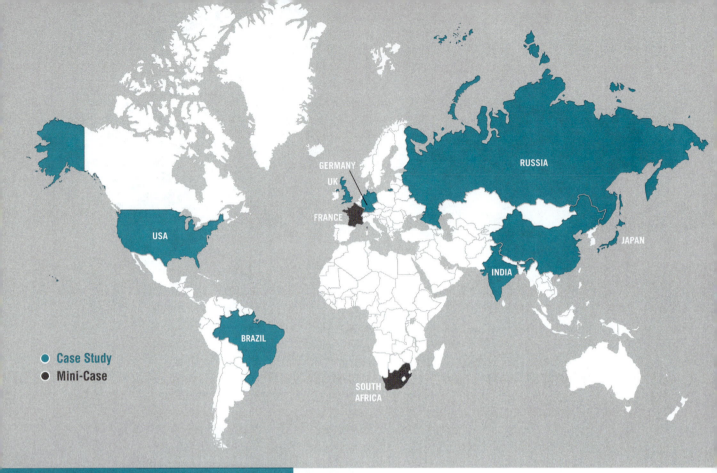

Case Study

Mini-Case

Who Rules?

- A democracy must limit the power of its executives to provide accountability. Which institutional choices best ensure accountability to citizens and how?

- How much power should a minority have in a democracy? How do different democracies seek to guarantee that minorities are protected from possible majority tyranny? Do some institutional choices seem to guarantee this better than others?

What Explains Political Behavior?

- Do institutional structures affect how political leaders act?

Where and Why?

- Which variables would be most helpful to explain why an institution that works in one setting might not work the same way in another?

POLITICAL INSTITUTIONS:
Governing

Americans are taught from a young age the importance of the three branches of government—executive, legislative, and judicial—and how essential their separate but equal status is for democracy. While these are certainly not the only political institutions that matter to a sophisticated understanding of politics, they are nonetheless among the most important. Most modern states, and virtually all democratic ones (the United Kingdom is the major exception), have written constitutions that define the formal powers of their governmental institutions. As we've noted, however, written formal powers do not always translate directly into actual power. The social, cultural, and historical contexts in which formal institutions exist can have significant bearing on how institutions function in practice. On paper, a president in one country may have a similar set of powers to a president in another country, but what each can achieve in fact might vary greatly between the two specific contexts. The actual power of particular institutions often changes over time as well, as changing socioeconomic and cultural factors give greater resources to one or another institution, or an occupant of a formal position helps strengthen or weaken that institution. The first questions we must ask, then, are: How institutionalized are the various branches of government of a particular state, and to what extent do they function as set out in the constitution that created them?

As we explore the answers to these questions, we can start to answer the other key questions that make the study of institutions important in democracies, which is the focus of this and the next chapter. The first question is part of the larger question of who rules: Do certain institutional arrangements achieve greater **political accountability**, meaning the ability of the citizenry to directly or indirectly control political leaders and institutions? Argentine political scientist Guillermo O'Donnell (1999) uses the terms vertical and horizontal accountability to analyze the extent to which the power of key state institutions is under democratic control. **Vertical accountability** refers to the ability of individuals and groups in a society to hold state institutions accountable, whereas **horizontal accountability** refers to the ability of the state institutions to hold one another accountable. The latter represents indirect control on the part of the citizenry in that particular institutions implicitly act on behalf of the citizenry to limit the power of and thereby control other institutions or leaders. For instance, an elected legislature in a democracy presumably should have enough power vis-à-vis the executive branch to limit what the executive can do, to ask him to justify his actions, and ultimately to punish him if he acts in ways unacceptable to the state's constitution or majority opinion in the country. Similarly, the court system may have the power to rule legislative or executive actions unconstitutional, which preserves the basic system of government against politicians' attempts to abrogate it. Horizontal accountability is the main interest of this chapter, as we examine the relative power of governing institutions in relation to each other. We examine vertical accountability in greater detail in the next chapter, looking at institutions of participation and representation.

Note that only one of the basic branches of government, the executive, is essential to a modern state as we defined it in chapter 2. Modern states are sovereign entities that administer territories and people; therefore, an executive power and accompanying bureaucracy are essential to their existence. The **executive** is the chief political power in a state. The position is filled through elections in a democracy and typically is embodied in the single most powerful office in the government, referred to as a president or prime minister in most countries. The modern state, however, also includes a bureaucracy, a large set of lesser officials whose function is to implement the laws of the state, as directed by the executive. We explore both executive powers and modern bureaucracies in this chapter.

The executive is essential, but a legislature with autonomy from the executive is an important institution in the democratization of the modern state even if it is not crucial to the state itself. Similarly, a judiciary is essential for the state to punish crime and enforce property and contract rights, but it need not have a political role independent of the executive, although it may well be beneficial for democracy if it does. The process of democratization is in part a matter of creating mechanisms through which the power of the executive can be limited. In democratic theory, the **legislature** makes the law and the **judiciary** interprets it. The power and autonomy of each, however, varies significantly.

Many political scientists see forces in the modern world as strengthening the executive branch. The contemporary state has far more and far more technically sophisticated functions to carry out than in earlier eras, and over the course of the twentieth century, this meant a general upward trend in the size of the bureaucracy that the executive branch leads. Legislators often leave the more technical decisions implied in particular laws to bureaucrats in the affected areas because the legislators feel they lack the technical competence to make those decisions. All of this gives greater resources and therefore greater power to the executive and the bureaucracy, which makes issues of control of the executive even more paramount. Some political scientists also worry about limiting the role of the judiciary, seeing wealthy democracies in particular as moving increasingly toward a "judicialization" of politics in which courts and judges replace elected officials as key decision makers.

A second crucial question in democracies is how much power to give to the majority that, at least in theory, rules. Democracy implies majority rule, but how much power the majority has over any dissident minorities is a fundamental question in the process. Some formal institutions give the representatives of the majority far greater power than do other institutions. The United Kingdom (UK) and United States stand in sharp relief on this issue and illustrate the range of available options. As we discuss below, the British parliament has the legal right to pass any legislation it pleases, which gives the majority party tremendous powers. British constitutional and political tradition does limit the exercising of these powers, but few formal limits exist. In contrast, the U.S. Constitution divides and thereby limits power significantly. Even when the same party controls both houses of Congress and the presidency, its power is limited by the ability of the Supreme Court to declare laws unconstitutional and by the various powers reserved specifically for state governments. Both countries are democracies, but they address the question of how formal institutions should protect minorities from the will of the majority quite differently, and each set of formal institutions provides a somewhat different answer to that question, as we demonstrate throughout this chapter.

A third question is often asked in response to concerns about accountability: What is the potential trade-off between accountability and popular control of the government and effective governance? If the institutions of a particular regime strongly limit each other, and the citizenry as a whole has many, effective means of holding political leaders accountable, does this limit the ability of the government to make effective policy? In terms of the United States, does robust horizontal and vertical accountability produce gridlock? We consider this question in both this chapter and the next.

We begin with the relationship between the executive and legislative branches, which, more than anything else, distinguishes different kinds of democracies. We then examine the roles of the judiciary and the modern bureaucracy and their relationships to the executive and legislative branches. We also look at the question of federalism and the extent to which the overall power of the state is centralized in national institutions or dispersed to subnational units of government, which can be another means of achieving accountability. In each of these sections, we discuss the broad debates in political science and then turn to one or more case studies to see how the institutions actually work in different contexts.

INSTITUTIONS: EXECUTIVES AND LEGISLATURES

The executive is indispensable to any state or regime and fulfills two very important roles. First, as **head of state**, the executive is the official, symbolic representative of a country, authorized to speak on its behalf and represent it, particularly in world affairs. Historically, the head of state was often a monarch, and this continues to be the case in the UK and Japan. Second, as **head of government**, the executive's task is to implement the nation's laws and policies. The two parts of the executive function may be filled by one individual or two, but both are essential to any regime. Legislatures are less ubiquitous because authoritarian regimes can dispense with them. They are, however, crucial to democratic regimes because a legislature's very democratic function is to debate public policy and pass laws. The executive and the legislature are often discussed separately because their functions are different. Here, we discuss them together, because in our view the relationship between the executive and legislature is one of the key variables that distinguishes different models of democratic government. These models are usually described by the terms **parliamentarism**, **presidentialism**, and **semipresidentialism**. The very terms, and the fact that one is defined by the title of the executive and another by the title of the legislature, suggest that the interaction and connection of the two types of institutions is significant to the function of each.

Parliamentarism: The Westminster Model

Another reason for discussing the executive and legislature together as a system rather than as separate institutions is that the oldest model of democratic government does not separate the two. The Westminster, or parliamentary, model of government is based on British parliamentary democracy. Countries that adopt this model often separate, as the British do, the two functions of the executive. They have a "nonexecutive head of state" who embodies and represents the country ceremonially. Countries lacking a hereditary monarchy typically replace the monarch in this function with an elected head of state who, somewhat confusingly, is often called the "president." In most cases, this president's role, like the queen's in Britain, is small and ceremonial. Countries tend to elect esteemed elder statesmen or women who gracefully perform the ceremonial role while leaving all important executive functions to the head of the government, usually called the **prime minister (PM)** (in Germany, the chancellor). In some cases, the constitution gives the head of state significant but rarely exercised legal powers, which means that "real" power on a day-to-day basis lies with the prime minister, but in moments of high tension or conflict, the head of state may intervene.

The prime minister's relationship to the legislature is really the key distinguishing feature of this model. This individual is not only the executive, but also a member of the legislature. In fact, the PM is the leader of the majority party or leading coalition party in the legislature. He or she is not elected separately to executive office, but rather is named after the legislative election determines the dominant party. Citizens cast one vote for a party or individual, depending on the electoral system, to represent them in parliament; the majority in parliament then names the prime minister. In practice, when citizens vote for parliament, they know who the PM will be because their vote for their preferred **member of parliament (MP)** or party is indirectly a vote for that party's leader to serve as PM. As a result, the prime minister relates to the legislature in a rather interesting way in that, as an MP, the PM serves in a sense at the pleasure of parliament. Should a parliamentary majority lose confidence in the party leader, members

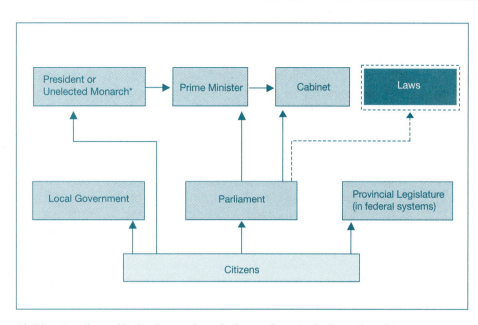

* In this system, the president's only power is nominating a parliamentary leader as prime minister.

Note: Up arrows indicate elections. Down or horizontal arrows indicate nomination or appointment. Hash-mark arrows indicate which body is responsible for formally passing and signing legislation.

FIGURE 6.1
Typical Parliamentary System

can cast a **vote of no confidence** that forces the prime minister to resign. At that point, the leading party in parliament can choose a new leader who will become PM, or the resigning PM will ask the head of state to call new parliamentary elections.

A prime minister is in a somewhat different relationship with parliament depending on whether his or her party has a clear majority in parliament. If not, the prime minister will head a **coalition government**, in which at least two parties negotiate an agreement to rule together. A vote of no confidence is far more likely in a coalition government: if one party in the coalition is unhappy with a PM's policies, it can leave the coalition, causing the coalition to lose its majority.

On the other hand, parliamentary systems typically do not have fixed terms of office, and while the parliament can oust a prime minister, a PM can similarly dissolve parliament and call for new elections. In Britain, for example, the maximum term allowed between elections is five years, but a PM can call earlier elections to take advantage of an electoral opportunity for his or her party. Lastly, the prime minister appoints the other ministers (what Americans call "secretaries") to the cabinet, but given the close executive relationship with parliament, these individuals cannot be whomever the prime minister pleases. The cabinet, especially in a coalition, serves as a check on the PM. Cabinet ministers must also be MPs, and in a coalition government the prime minister must consult with the other parties in the coalition about the distribution of "portfolios" (cabinet seats). Normally all parties in the coalition, and certainly the biggest ones, get some representation in the cabinet.

So, just how democratic is the Westminster system, the original model of modern representative democracy? In theory, it is extremely democratic, because it makes the legislature, the elected body of the people, supreme. The PM, after all, is essentially nothing more than the most important MP. In practice, the answer is far more complex. First, much depends on the electoral system used to select the legislature. In multiparty systems, parliamentarism may indeed promote negotiation, coalition-building, and representation of a wide range of views in the cabinet. However, as we describe more fully in chapter 7, a majoritarian electoral system such as Britain's that produces a "supermajority" for one party obviates this advantage: the PM may be an unusually powerful executive, because he or she is guaranteed a legislative majority as long as the majority party supports his or her leadership. Some critics also argue that the modern world, particularly the rise of television and other media and the growing importance of national security, has strengthened the hand of the PM. Campaigns have become more personalized and focused on the party leader who will become PM rather than on the party as an institution, and security issues tend to require more secrecy and private consultation and less discussion with party members or with the parliament in general. These observers suggest that modern prime ministers are much more than first among equals within their cabinets in that they have much more power and more agenda-setting prerogatives than the classic Westminster model suggests. If this is true, then they are more similar to presidents—but presidents who always have a legislative majority. This leads some critics to say that parliamentary systems vest too much power in the hands of a single individual, which threatens accountability. Instead, they advocate for the separation of powers characteristic of presidentialism.

CASE STUDY Parliamentary Rule: Britain and India

Britain and India are demonstrative of how very similar governing institutions can function dramatically differently in different social and political contexts. As a British colony, India adopted Britain's Westminster model almost completely, with the biggest difference being that India is a federal system. Differences in the party systems and the socioeconomic and cultural contexts of the two countries influence how the model functions in practice.

Britain's prime minister is often called the most powerful democratic executive in the world. The power of the office derives not just from its formal functions but also from the nature of Britain's parties and the strength of British institutions. Like the United States, Britain has two major parties (Labour and Conservative) that alternate in power: one or the other wins a majority of legislative seats in virtually every election. This means that coalition governments are very rare.

Like many former colonies, India adopted and modified its institutional structures from those of its colonial power. India's parliamentary democracy, though not without problems, has proven remarkably enduring. Members of Parliament gathered for this group photo in 2005.

Unlike parties in the United States, British parties are highly disciplined in the legislature, meaning that MPs almost always vote in support of their party's position on legislation. This is partly an effect of the parliamentary system itself. Ambitious MPs want to become cabinet ministers, and these positions are controlled by the head of the party, so loyalty to the party leadership is essential for these ambitious politicians. As head of the majority party, then, the PM can usually get legislation passed with ease.

As previously mentioned, the PM's formal powers include appointing the approximately twenty cabinet ministers who run the individual departments of government and whom the PM is supposed to consult before making major decisions. By tradition, the PM's power is checked by the cabinet and the practice of **collective responsibility**, which means that all cabinet members must publicly support all government decisions. A cabinet member who cannot do so is expected to resign. Since cabinet members are themselves senior leaders of the majority party and MPs, this constitutes an informal legislative agreement to policies prior to their formal introduction in Parliament.

Many argue that the cabinet's role has declined over the last generation and that PMs have begun to look more presidential. The two most important PMs of the last generation, Conservative Margaret Thatcher

(1979–1990) and Labourite Tony Blair (1997–2007), both centralized decision making to an inner circle of advisers and paid less attention to input from the cabinet as a whole. This reflected their personalities as strong leaders and their popularity. More than most PMs, they became charismatic figures in their own right, and their campaigns looked more like U.S. presidential campaigns, with a great deal more attention paid to the personality and individual attributes of the party leader than is traditional in Britain. And as long as these two powerful PMs were so personally popular, they could pursue the policies they desired; their cabinets and parties went along because they also benefited from the popular support showered on the PM. As Thatcher's and Blair's popularity waned, however, both faced increasing resistance, showing that democratic control still exists in the British system.

Britain's PMs and Parliaments serve a maximum of five years, after which the PM must call a general election for a new Parliament (neither MPs nor PMs face a limit on how many terms they can serve). Parliament can remove a PM with a vote of no confidence, but that is extremely rare. A more common means of removing unpopular PMs who refuse to call a new election early is for the majority party to replace them. The PM is the leader of the majority party, and the MPs of that majority party can vote to replace the party leader at any time they wish. As Margaret Thatcher lost popularity in the late 1980s but refused to change her policies or call a new election, Conservative MPs, fearing their party's future was sinking along with her popularity, voted to replace her with John Major, who immediately became PM. Britain had a new chief executive without holding a general election, a perfectly legitimate step in a parliamentary system. Similarly, Tony Blair left office without holding an election, albeit still on his own terms. He ran for a third term in 2005, but promised that he would not serve a full term and would instead turn power over at some point to his heir apparent, longtime chancellor of the exchequer (equivalent to the U.S. secretary of the Treasury) Gordon Brown. Blair was losing popularity mainly due to his support of Britain's participation in the war in Iraq, but gained reelection in part by agreeing to organize a smooth transition to a new leader. Though he seemed reluctant to fulfill this pledge after the election, growing pressure from within his own party led him to retire in mid-2007. Once again, the British chief executive changed hands without a single citizen voting.

With the growing power of the PM, what powers does Parliament have? In Britain's **bicameral legislature**, the lower house, the House of Commons, has virtually all legislative power. The older upper house, the House of Lords, consists of members known as "peers" appointed by the PM and aristocrats who inherited their positions. (In 1999 the Blair government ended the institution of "hereditary peers," allowing only a small minority to remain in office until further reforms. Since then, the government has proposed making the Lords either wholly or partially elected, with no hereditary peers.) The only significant power held by the House of Lords is to act as a final court of appeal for individual cases, though only a handful of cases ever reach that point. The Commons, though, retains considerable power. As noted above, even the most powerful PMs must take account of the views of their party's MPs in the Commons, especially if the PM's popularity is waning.

Parliament also serves an important watchdog function. The PM must attend Parliament weekly for Question Time, a very lively, not fully rehearsed, televised debate among the major politicians of the day. During Question Time, the PM is expected to respond to queries from MPs and defend the government's policies. In addition, MPs from both the ruling and opposition parties have a right to question all cabinet ministers about the activities of their departments, and the cabinet members must respond to these questions personally in Parliament, giving a public airing of issues of concern, large and small. The house recently took a step closer to resembling the U.S. Congress when it created more committees that hold hearings on proposed legislation. In the British system, the fate of legislation introduced by the government (the cabinet) is rarely in doubt, but the committees allow MPs to investigate the implications of proposed laws more thoroughly, and at times the ruling party will allow legislation to be amended if committees identify problem areas.

Even with this change, the British parliament does not modify legislation nearly as much as the U.S. Congress, but the executive branch still must pay attention to the opinions of the majority party MPs, and both houses of Parliament provide a forum for active, and at times closely watched, public debate over major issues. The prime minister's formal powers may allow him to ignore all of this, but his political survival requires that he attend to it closely; informally, Parliament remains an important check on even the most powerful PM.

In form, India's parliamentary system differs little from its British predecessor and counterpart. As in any parliamentary system, the prime minister and the cabinet are the key executives and decision makers, but in India there is also an indirectly elected president. The president's duties are similar to those of the British monarch, that is, acting as official head of state and carrying out various official functions "on the advice of the Prime Minister"—in fact, almost always doing what the prime minister says. The office is not completely for show, however. In India's multiparty system, no single party has won a majority of seats in Parliament in the last twenty years. This means that the president's power to ask a party leader in Parliament to form the next government can sometimes be important. When a coalition government collapses, the president must decide whether to ask a different party to attempt to put together a new coalition or call a general election. He usually follows the advice of the departing PM, but on occasion, if he thinks he has political support, he can make an independent decision. India, in contrast to Britain, is a federal system (see details below under federalism section) in which each state has its own parliamentary system, and the president, on recommendation of the PM, has the power to declare "President's Rule" in any state facing a political crisis. This was initially intended as an emergency measure only, but prime ministers Indira (1966–1977, 1980–1984) and Rajiv (1984–1989) Gandhi used it for partisan purposes: they would have the president declare President's Rule in a state ruled by an opposing party to force a new election that their Congress Party would try to win and often did.

Despite few formal differences, the role and power of the Indian prime minister and Parliament are significantly different from the British model, mainly due to differences in the number of parties in the two countries. Like Britain and most parliamentary systems, India's parties are highly disciplined, in the sense that MPs almost always vote with their party. The PM rules with the cabinet ministers, who at least in theory represent and are leaders of their fellow MPs, so the most important decisions happen when policy is formulated in the cabinet, not once that policy is introduced as formal legislation. Unlike Britain, India has never had a two-party system: one party dominated the government for the first forty years after the nation's independence from Britain, but no party has been able to imitate this feat, which has necessitated the formation of coalition governments.

This initially dominant party, the Indian National Congress (INC), ruled nearly continuously from independence in 1947 until 1989. An opposition coalition won power only once, from 1977 to 1980, over this entire period. The country's first prime minister, Jawaharlal Nehru (1947–1964), was a hero of the nationalist movement for independence and a deeply popular and respected figure. His cabinet consisted of leaders of the major factions within the ruling party and served as the actual governing body, debating policy as a cabinet is expected to in a parliamentary system. Shortly after his death, his daughter, Indira Gandhi, was selected to lead the INC and therefore became PM. She desired independence from the faction leaders within the party, and with this goal in mind, achieved much greater centralized control of the INC and, consequently, the government. Her cabinet ministers were not leaders of major factions in the party but were instead lesser-known MPs loyal only to her, and she ruled on the advice of an inner circle that did not include most of the cabinet. Her son, Rajiv Gandhi, ruled in an even more centralized manner, appointing and dismissing cabinet ministers on average every seven weeks.

The INC lost its dominant position after 1989 in part because of a corruption scandal that tarnished Rajiv Gandhi's image. Every government since has been a coalition of one large party and a number of smaller ones. This has profoundly changed the role of the PM. He remains the central executive and by far most im-

portant leader in the country, but all PMs since 1989 have had to make compromises with other parties in order to form a government. This has necessitated the creation of groups of ministers, which consist of representatives of various parties in the coalition, to meet to hash out policy in particular areas, a time-consuming and often fruitless effort. Most PMs since 1989 have had less central control, as they must continually compromise with their coalition partners, and if one small party decides to vote against the government, it can call a vote of no confidence and remove the PM entirely. A partial exception to this norm was Narasimha Rao (1991–1996). An INC PM who ruled with a coalition of other parties, he attempted to centralize power in his personal office, the Prime Minister's Office, while maintaining a coalition government. His rule was plagued by corruption scandals, including allegations that he bribed four MPs of a small party to support his government to maintain his power: centralization of power in a coalition government had its costs. He survived a full five-year term, but the INC then saw its biggest electoral defeat in its history. For all of this, Indian PMs remain quite powerful, but without the ability of any one party to win a majority, coalition government has been essential, and often unstable. This shift from one-party dominance is clearly seen in the number of PMs India has had: in its first thirty years of independence (1947–1977), the country had only three PMs; in its second thirty years (1977–2007), it had twelve, only three of whom served full terms.

The rise of coalition government has made small parties who negotiate membership in these coalitions quite important. This has not meant that Parliament as a whole has begun to play a more assertive role. Indeed, Parliament passes fewer laws now than it did under the dominance of the INC, and MPs spend far less time there. Parties are more important for their votes in putting a coalition government together than they are for their legislative activity, and most of the 544 MPs are focused more on their states than on the national government. Many of the small parties that are potential members of coalition governments are state-level parties with little support outside a particular state or region, so the political fortunes of many MPs are tied to their role in state-level politics more than they are to the national Parliament. As political malfeasance has increased in India, being an MP has also become a means of gaining access to corruption opportunities, as the case of PM Rao suggests. MPs are available to support their party, whether voting to enter a coalition government or oppose such a union, but don't do a great deal of legislating. While the British parliament in recent years has taken a slightly more active role in monitoring and attempting to check the PM, the Indian parliament seems to be doing less. Coalition government in India is a check of its own sort, though, that Britain has rarely had.

WHERE AND WHY Parliaments and Presidents

How many parliamentary and presidential countries are there, and where are they located? While parliamentary systems are more common globally, presidential systems historically have dominated in the Americas. Semipresidential systems are rarer, but are concentrated in Eastern Europe and Francophone Africa (see Map 6.1). This pattern suggests that timing and history—especially colonial history—affect countries' institutional choices. As former British colonies throughout the world gained independence after World War II, most adopted the institutions they saw in their colonizer, the "Mother of Parliaments." Former French colonies such as Côte d'Ivoire gained independence after Charles de Gaulle's Fifth Republic established a semipresidential system in France, and many adopted semipresidential constitutions. Latin American countries, in contrast, gained their independence much earlier (most during the 1820s or so) than the British and French colonies. They had no democratic institutional example to take from their Spanish and Portuguese colonizers, but they did have one from their regional forerunner in achieving independence, the United States. Taking it as a model, they wrote presidential constitutions.

Colonialism does not, of course, explain the European patterns, but we can note that as European countries replaced hereditary monarchies with democratic systems, they tended to follow but modify the British idea. Most revised and tinkered with their constitutions over time and some even had lapses in democracy, but today most have a modified "Western European" parliamentary system that differs from that of the British by using proportional representation rather than first-past-the-post (see chapter 7) to choose the parliament. Recently democratic Eastern European countries have tended to choose one of the two Western European models: parliamentary or semipresidential systems.

Colonial heritage played an important role in what democratic institutions newly independent countries chose in much of the world. Today, as political scientists ponder which institutions are "best" for newly democratic countries, this colonial legacy has become an important part of the debate. Institutions are notoriously difficult to change. Scholars may recommend a particular type of institution as superior for a new democracy, but such fundamental changes are quite rare.

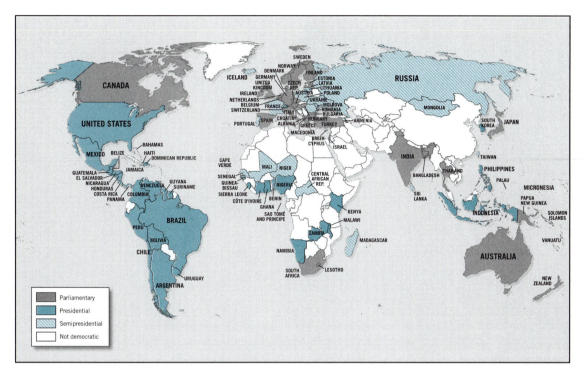

MAP 6.1
Three Major Types of Democracy

Source: Data are from William Clark, Matt Golder, and Sona Naderichele Golder,
Principles of Comparative Politics (Washington, D.C.: CQ Press, 2009).

Presidential Systems: The Separation of Powers

Presidentialism needs little introduction for American students, because the most famous and enduring example of this system is the United States. In a presidential system, the roles of head of state and head of government are normally filled by the same person, who is given the title of "president." The crucial, defining aspect of a presidential system, however, is not this fusion of executive roles. Rather, it is the concept of **separation of powers**. The Founders of the country argued that the functions of the executive and legislative branches should be distinct and separate, and everything about any presidential system reflects this choice, no matter how the particulars of any specific constitution may differ. This means that the executive and legislative branches are elected separately in their own (though possibly concurrent) elections, and the president must be independently and directly (or nearly directly) elected.

Presidential election processes can and do vary somewhat; for example, the U.S. president is elected indirectly by the Electoral College, but that institution is

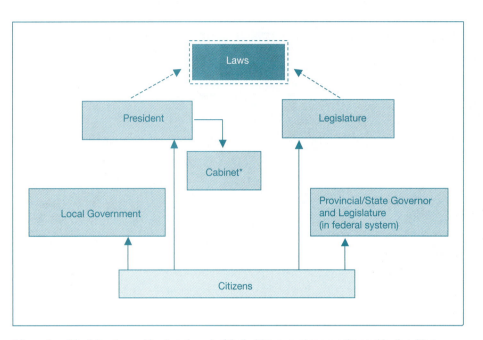

* In most presidential systems, at least one branch of the legislature must approve the president's cabinet members, but cabinet members do not come out of the legislature itself.

Note: Up arrows indicate elections. Down or horizontal arrows indicate nomination or appointment. Hash-mark arrows indicate which body is responsible for formally passing and signing legislation.

FIGURE 6.2
Typical Presidential System

bound to follow the popular vote closely. Some countries elect a president by plurality; others use a two-round system to achieve an absolute majority. No matter how the elections are administered, the important thing is that the president's legitimacy as head of state and government derives from an electoral process that legitimizes him or her as the nation's choice. Similarly, the legislature's legitimacy arises from the direct election of the representatives, who should therefore reflect the popular will. Even if the presidency and legislature are controlled by different parties, each is legitimized independently by the electoral process, and creating laws requires the agreement, in some way, of both the president and a majority in the legislature.

Presidents and their legislatures have a hard time interfering with each others' time in office. Presidents serve a fixed term, whether four years, such as in the United States, Brazil, Chile, and Argentina, or longer, such as six years in Mexico. During that fixed term, it is very difficult for a legislature to remove the president from office. Most countries make provision for some kind of impeachment process, but this requires extraordinary measures and can only be justified in extreme circumstances. Barring such a situation, no matter how much legislators, including members of the president's own party, disagree with the president or question his or her competence or policy, they cannot remove the executive from office. Similarly, legislators also have fixed terms. In a bicameral legislature in a presidential system, terms may be different for each house, and in any legislature elections may be periodic, with only a portion of the legislature being renewed in any particular election, but regardless of the details, a president may not tamper with a legislature's sessions by forcibly shortening or lengthening them.

Lastly, the separation of powers is clear in the president's powers of appointment. Although presidents may need the consent of the legislature, they are largely free to appoint their own cabinet ministers or secretaries. They may, and in the case of the United States, must, appoint individuals who are not drawn from the legislature; indeed, the individuals chosen may not even have any legislative or electoral experience. They may also appoint people from any party they wish. Their appointments need not reflect the composition of the legislature in any way: a president whose party is a minority in the legislature does not legally need to include cabinet officers from the majority party. Once appointed and confirmed by the legislature, the officers serve at the president's pleasure and their activities can only be minimally interfered with by the legislature.

In all presidential systems the president and a majority in the legislature must both support a policy for it to become law, though different systems differ in the specific division of powers between the two branches. Who initiates policy changes or budgets, who can veto or preempt legislation and how, who can declare war or approve foreign policy decisions in general—these details vary from country to country. Nonetheless, in all presidential systems the crucial concept of separation of powers has potentially positive and negative aspects. These became a source of hot debate in the 1990s, as formerly communist or authoritarian countries in Eastern Europe, Latin America, and Africa considered what kind of institutional arrangements would best serve their nascent democracies. Supporters of presidentialism saw many advantages. The Founders of the United States believed that the separation of powers would provide checks and balances that would diminish the concentration of power and the potential for its abuse in any one part of the government. Without a doubt the separation of powers makes the development of policies an iterative process with give and take among the branches by slowing down the legislative process, a form of horizontal accountability.

There is also some advantage to having a head of state and government whose direct election provides democratic legitimacy that can be seen as reflecting the national will. Whatever divisions exist in the legislature, the executive can arguably act as a unifying force for the country. Fixed terms can also be an advantage since they provide a timeline for the development of policy and accomplishment of objectives that allows legislators and the executive to think in the long term rather than worrying the government will fall imminently, providing greater predictability and stability. All of this, supporters argue, allows presidentialism to achieve effective governance while simultaneously maintaining accountability.

Political scientist Juan Linz (1990), however, argued that presidentialism has many potential disadvantages. He saw the separation of powers as leading to what he called "dual legitimacy." Since both the legislature and the executive are independently and directly elected, each has legitimacy. With such strong, independent claims to representing the national will, conflict is often just below the surface. What happens when they clash or dramatically disagree? Linz thought that since neither had a higher claim to legitimacy, there could be no democratic resolution. He also argued that the direct election of the president leads to other problems, including the creation of a breed of chief executives with a "winner-take-all" mentality who would overemphasize their national mandate and be less willing to compromise. Majoritarian electoral systems (see chapter 7) and presidential systems in highly divided societies are particularly problematic in this regard. In addition, direct election of the president could increase the chances of a political renegade or destabilizing outsider being elected, and because the executive is separate from the legislature, there is little incentive for a president to consider the composition of congress or to reflect the divisions of the popular vote in the composition of the cabinet. Linz believed all of this could foster an antidemocratic, domineering presidential style that threatened accountability and legitimacy. Comparable to arguments regarding the influence of modern PMs, his thesis argued that the nature of the office and its personalization would unduly strengthen the president relative to the legislature. Lastly, Linz claimed that presidentialism is too inflexible: fixed terms mean that any serious problem for which a president might need to be removed—or even a president's death in office or resignation for benign reasons—could provoke a political crisis. Inept presidents can be removed only at peril, and in many countries, fixed terms and no option or opportunity for reelection mean good ones must go after a relatively short fixed term.

Defenders of presidentialism have agreed with Linz's point about the potential for such problems to arise in a presidential democracy, but they argue that whether these factors become problems or not depends on a great many other variables unrelated to presidentialism per se. Moreover, it has proven very difficult to disentangle failures of presidentialism from these other variables. Parliamentary systems do have a better numerical track record of democratic stability, but how much of this can be attributed to the institutions? Skeptics note that since almost all presidential systems have been in Latin America, regional or cultural factors rather than presidentialism may be the problem. On the other hand, the number of stable parliamentary democracies is high in part because of Britain's many small, relatively homogeneous island former colonies having chosen parliamentarism. So, which is more important to stability: parliament, or a small, socially homogeneous population? In the end, Linz's critics argue that presidential institutions per se are not the problem. After extensive quantitative analysis, political scientist Jose Antonio Cheibub concluded that the society, not the institution, is the problem. Presidential systems "tend to exist is societies where democracies of any type are likely to be unstable" (2007, 3). The following case studies also illustrate the strengths and weaknesses of presidential systems in widely differing contexts.

CASE STUDY Presidentialism: The United States and Brazil

Most countries in the Western Hemisphere have presidential systems, although the socioeconomic and political contexts of these systems vary widely, as the cases of the United States and Brazil show. While the formal rights and duties of each branch of government are different in the two systems, the informal power of the presidency varies much more because the office is set in very different political systems. In the United States, the office of the president was one of the more controversial parts of the Constitution when it was written. Many leaders, most notably Thomas Jefferson, feared that a single executive would inevitably become authoritarian, mimicking the British monarch from which the colonists had just won liberation. These fears might surprise contemporary Americans, for the office as originally designed was far more modest than what it has become. The president's main powers are: 1) approving or vetoing legislation passed by Congress, and Congress can override a veto if a two-thirds majority votes to pass the legislation; 2) appointing cabinet secretaries and Supreme Court justices, as well as lower-level political appointees in the bureaucracy and federal judges, subject to the Senate's approval; 3) serving as head of state and commander in chief of the armed forces; and 4) entering into treaties and declaring war, again subject to Senate approval.

On their own, these powers are modest by modern standards. The early presidents were certainly important, but they were not the central focus of national politics that the president of the United States has become today. Many of the most well-known presidents are so recognized because they expanded the powers of the office. Ironically, this all began with Thomas Jefferson, who successfully proclaimed the right of the president to expand the country via the Louisiana Purchase. Starting with Andrew Jackson, the president became the de facto head of his party, giving him greater influence over Congress. In the twentieth century, Franklin Roosevelt created vast new social programs that increased the size and reach of the federal bureaucracy over which the president presides, and as the United States became a world superpower, the

Brazil's "worker" president, Luiz Inácio "Lula" da Silva, was reelected to a second term and was enjoying high popularity ratings when this photo was taken in 2008. It was unclear, however, whether his Workers' Party would find a strong candidate to succeed him in the 2010 elections.

president's powers in foreign policy and war correspondingly gained importance as well.

The U.S. president in modern times has become the symbol of the nation, the undisputed leader of his party, and the chief initiator of legislation as well as its chief implementer. The office has retained the symbolic legitimacy of all presidencies as the sole office for which every citizen votes, the embodiment of majority will, even though the individual selected by the Electoral College isn't always the individual who won the most popular votes, as occurred in the 2000 election between Al Gore and George W. Bush. While legislation formally starts in Congress, in practice this body looks to the president for major legislative initiatives, because as the leader of his party who sits atop a vast technocratic bureaucracy, the president and the cabinet are in a better position politically and technically to formulate complicated legislation. Certainly compared to parliamentary systems, members of Congress still initiate legislation, but most legislation of consequence has the support of the president. The president's position as head of his party and chief fund-raiser also gives him great influence over legislators in his party. This is especially true when a president is popular: members of his party want to be closely associated with him and often yield to his desires to gain his support in the next election.

Individual legislators may vie for the president's approval, but the U.S. Congress has substantial powers as well, and it certainly does not always yield to the president. Because it is independently elected, it jealously guards its autonomy from the executive branch. The U.S. House of Representatives and Senate have perhaps the most extensive and expensive staffs of any legislature in the world. Committees and subcommittees are crucial in investigating, amending, and passing legislation. Individual members have great freedom to introduce legislation compared to most legislatures in the world, and it's entirely possible that individual legislation will become law if it gains the support of the chairs of key committees or subcommittees. Few proposals make it through Congress without significant changes, however, which is in sharp contrast to the British parliament, where the dominant party typically passes bills as written by the PM and the cabinet. Most observers argue the U.S. Congress is the most powerful in the world, not only because it legislates on behalf of the most powerful country but because of its autonomy from the executive branch.

A direct result of the separation of powers between two powerful branches of government is the constant concern of contemporary American politics, that is, gridlock, or the seeming inability to pass major legislation. The United States has only two major parties, but these parties are relatively weak in the sense that individual legislators are not beholden to party leaders, and they vote as they choose on each piece of legislation. Ideological similarities mean that members of the same party usually vote the same way, but individual members of Congress frequently go against their party's wishes. This alone can occasionally produce gridlock,

but it is much more likely when one party controls the presidency and the other controls Congress, a common outcome of the U.S. presidential system. What this means is that one of the president's main jobs has become trying to get his legislation passed, either by cajoling members of his own party to support him or by negotiating and compromising with the opposing party in Congress, especially when it is in the majority. The failure of this process produces gridlock.

When not trying to negotiate the maze of political compromise, the U.S. president, as head of the executive branch, oversees a bureaucracy of thousands of people. Most are permanent civil servants, but several hundred at the top of the bureaucratic hierarchy serve at the president's pleasure. This gives the president great influence over the implementation of laws once they pass through Congress and are signed into law. Because no legislation can foresee and include every conceivable detail of implementation in today's increasingly technocratic society, the chief executive is given great latitude to enforce laws. For most of the nation's history, this power has been relatively uncontroversial; under President George W. Bush, however, this executive power became quite a bone of contention, particularly in regard to issues of national security. Critics charged that a variety of actions taken by Bush in the name of national security were violations of citizens' basic rights to due process and privacy, and they believed Bush overstepped the president's constitutional authority. Such conflicts have resulted in various court cases: in the United States and most presidential systems, the court system is charged with resolving disputes between the executive and legislative branches.

The fears of Thomas Jefferson and his followers were partly justified: the presidency of the United States is a very powerful office. The separation of powers in the presidential system, particularly in the context of relatively weak parties in the United States and the separate election of members of Congress, certainly limits what presidents can do. Presidents' leadership of their party and control over foreign policy and hundreds of key appointments in the executive branch give them far greater powers than many of the authors of the Constitution envisioned, however. This divided power in the context of a very old democracy with well-established institutions and only two main parties produces a system that is often seen as slow to make policy, but one that is nonetheless well institutionalized, a crucial context for effective relations between the separate branches in a presidential system.

Yet presidentialism can look very different when transplanted to different geographic, social, and institutional settings, as the example of Brazil shows. As in most of Latin America, Brazil's democratic regimes have always been presidential. The current system dates to a constitution approved in 1988. Brazil's president has more extensive formal powers than his U.S. counterpart, but a legislature with many weak political parties and the most decentralized federal system in the world make these powers substantially less effective than they appear on paper. Successive presidents have managed to use incentives and growing discipline within the major parties to strengthen the presidency and govern more effectively than was the case fifteen or twenty years ago.

Unlike in the United States, Brazil's president is directly chosen in a two-round election: if no candidate wins an absolute majority on the first vote (only one candidate, Fernando Henrique Cardoso, has won on the first ballot, in 1994 and 1998), a second vote takes place two weeks later between the top two candidates. Originally, the president could serve only one five-year term. Constitutional amendments subsequently reduced the term to four years so it would coincide with legislative elections and then allowed one reelection, and the last two presidents, Cardoso and Luiz Inácio "Lula" da Silva, both were reelected to second terms. Presidents otherwise have the typical powers of the office in a presidential system: head of state and government, commander in chief of the armed forces, and appointment powers. In Brazil they also have several unusual powers: 1) the authority to issue "provisional decrees" (PDs) that become law for thirty days unless the National Congress approves them permanently; 2) a line-item veto, meaning a president can eliminate individual measures in a bill sent from the National Congress without vetoing the entire law; and 3) monopoly over initiation of all legislation involving the budget.

The context in which Brazilian presidents must operate is a multiparty system with many fragmented parties. Because of Brazil's electoral system (which we discuss in detail in chapter 9), politicians have little incentive to form broad, inclusive parties to get elected or to follow party leaders once they are in the National Congress. Both houses of Brazil's bicameral legislature, the Chamber of Deputies (the lower house) and the Senate (the upper house) include numerous parties. After the 2006 election, the Chamber of Deputies included twenty-one parties, the biggest of which had only 17 percent of the seats. The president's party was the second largest in the chamber, with 16 percent of the seats. The only way for presidents to get their legislation passed in this system is to build coalitions among several parties, which can be done in several ways. In the last few elections, several parties have supported the two major presidential candidates, a result of pre-election negotiations regarding sharing power after the election. The president then shares power mainly by appointing members of parties supporting him to his cabinet and other appointed offices. Presidents essentially put together coalition governments like those in parliamentary systems, although the weakness of Brazil's parties means presidents still can have difficulty getting legislators to vote the way the party leadership wants.

Presidents can also use their line-item veto to negotiate with individual legislators to gain their support for particular items. As in the United States, Brazilian legislators engage in "pork-barrel" politics that include specific spending projects for their home areas in the national budget. This is the contemporary continuation of a long Brazilian tradition of patronage politics in which elected officials bring home government resources to help their areas as a primary means of gaining support. The president's line-item veto, however, allows him to decide which of these individual items to keep and which to eliminate, and he can exchange his approval of a legislator's pet project for the latter's support on a crucial piece of legislation.

The first president directly elected under the 1988 constitution, Fernando Collor, whose party had only 3 percent of the seats in the Chamber of Deputies, used none of these methods to build coalitions. He instead ruled largely through PDs, issuing 150 of them in his first year in office. Often, when one expired, he would simply reissue it the next day, essentially making it last as long as he pleased. Brazil's Supreme Court never ruled against this practice, despite its dubious constitutionality. When he continued to ignore the National Congress and failed to solve Brazil's long-term problem of hyperinflation, however, he lost support and was ultimately forced to resign over a corruption scandal. Subsequent presidents recognized the need to include the National Congress, and used the various negotiation strategies outlined above to pass legislation.

Overall, however, the powers of Brazil's president remain limited. Major presidential proposals often fail to pass the National Congress, and of those that do, virtu- ally all are modified. Each piece of legislation requires extensive horse trading, not only with party leaders but also with individual legislators looking for favors. Lula, the current president, is head of the Workers' Party, which is by far the most united and ideologically driven party in the country, but its small share of seats in the National Congress has made compromise with other parties a constant part of Lula's governing effort. Very slowly, however, the Brazilian presidency and parties are becoming stronger institutions as the possibility of presidential reelection and limits on PDs give incen- tives for greater cooperation between the branches of government. Governance, though, remains a slow and difficult process in a presidential system with weak and fragmented parties. Brazil's federalism also weakens the power of the presidency, a subject we return to below.

Semipresidentialism: The Hybrid Compromise

The pros and cons of two extreme alternatives led to the creation of compromise, intermediate systems. One such compromise is semipresidentialism, which splits executive power between an elected president and prime minister. The president is elected directly by the citizens as in a presidential system, but the cabinet is responsible to the prime minister, who is the leader of the majority party or coali- tion in parliament, as in a parliamentary system. The parliament can force the cabinet to resign through a vote of no confidence, but the president has the power to dissolve parliament and call a new election. For a complex arrangement like semipresidentialism to be successful, the powers and duties of the president and PM usually must be spelled out clearly in the constitution. For example, the presi- dent may be given power over military decisions (as in Sri Lanka) or foreign policy (as in Finland), whereas the prime minister typically concentrates on domestic policies. The specific division of powers varies greatly, however, and is not always clearly delineated.

Semipresidential systems also work most smoothly when the president and prime minister are elected from the same party. Critics of semipresidentialism, however, argue that when this happens the system gives too much power to the president. She or he not only has the power and legitimacy that comes with direct election like in the presidential system, but also the authority to dissolve the legis- lature at will through the PM. This makes it far less likely that the president will face a hostile legislature than is the case in presidential systems. **Cohabitation**, as the election of president and PM from different parties is called, produces more checks and accountability. If voters elect a majority to the legislature in opposi- tion to the president, dissolving the legislature immediately to call a new election would simply irritate voters; the president may be forced to accept the results and

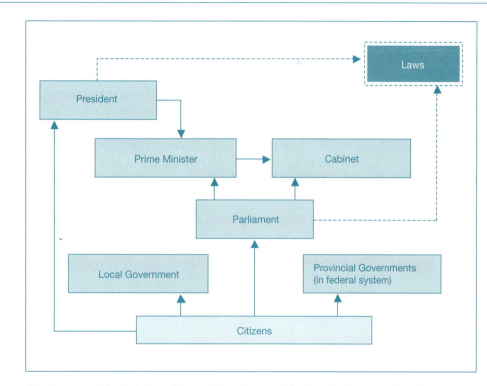

Note: Up arrows indicate elections. Down or horizontal arrows indicate nomination or appointment. Hash-mark arrows indicate which body is responsible for formally passing and signing legislation.

FIGURE 6.3
Typical Semipresidential System

live with cohabitation and the limits it imposes. However, cohabitation can also produce gridlock and inability to legislate effectively, as in a purely presidentialist system.

Supporters of the system argue that in divided societies, semipresidentialism combines the best of both worlds to create a legitimate (via direct election) and powerful executive who can govern effectively while allowing for the possibility of

MINI-CASE France's Semipresidentialism

The many and deeply divided parties of France's Fourth Republic (1945–1958) parliamentary system resulted in a series of unstable coalition governments that made the country famous for political instability, frequent changes in government, and little ability to "get things done." In 1958 Charles de Gaulle proposed that France replace this fractious system with a new constitution, and the "Fifth Republic" became the world's first semipresidential system.

To overcome the problems of the Fourth Republic, de Gaulle and his supporters envisioned a system with coexecutives, a president and prime minister, but a system in which the president would play the dominant role. The president (de Gaulle, of course)

In May 2007, France had a new president, Nicolas Sarkozy (left) and prime minister, François Fillon. Both are members of the conservative party UMP, perhaps indicating that recent reforms intended to reduce the likelihood of cohabitation have succeeded.

would first and foremost symbolize and unify the contentious nation, embodying what de Gaulle called its "spirit," as its directly elected leader. Since France has a two-round voting system, the president can achieve a high degree of legitimacy, having been elected by a majority in either the first or second round. (Since 1962 presidents have been directly elected; prior to that year they were chosen by an electoral college.) The president also has specific duties under the constitution: the president appointed his coexecutive, the prime minister, and also could dissolve the legislature. This meant that the president had a direct tie to the legislature, which avoided some of the potential conflicts inherent in purely presidential systems because he had a powerful ally and liaison to bring the legislature into line. The president, elected for seven years,

would also provide some institutional continuity if the legislature were dissolved.

The creators of the semipresidential system assumed that the same party would win the presidency and a legislative majority. So long as it did, its institutional arrangements would give the president, as head of the majority party who also appoints the PM, unparalleled power to govern. And this worked as intended until the 1980s, when for the first time the president was from one party and the majority of the legislature from another. This necessitated what the French humorously call cohabitation, in which the president must compromise with the legislature by appointing a PM from the majority party in the legislature, rather than from his own party. A compromise had to be worked out regarding the specific powers of the president and the PM, since the constitution does not draw clear boundaries on all types of issues. In practice, this compromise has been that the president has power over foreign policy while the PM and the legislature, the Assemblé Nationale, control domestic policy.

The experience of cohabitation has caused France to modify the original Gaullist system in several important ways. The president's term has been reduced to five years, which coincides with the length of legislators' terms of office, so presidential and parliamentary elections now coincide. Through these efforts, France has attempted to reduce the likelihood of cohabitation. Even with its flaws, France's semipresidential system has proven enduring and adaptable. It continues to evolve as cohabiting presidents and prime ministers work out new understandings of their roles and relationships and French politicians continue to tweak the system's rules to maintain its effectiveness.

a coalition government in the PM and cabinet that helps ensure compromise and accountability. Perhaps for this reason, many former French colonies and a number of post-Communist democracies in Eastern Europe have tried some form of semipresidentialism. The requirement that both the president and legislative majority must agree on the PM and cabinet provides plenty of representation of the popular parties in the government while reducing the possibility of constant instability. Critics argue that, like presidentialism, semipresidentialism may encourage a strong executive to overstep democratic bounds and become too powerful for an effective democracy. That said, the French, who pioneered the system, have shown its durability, retaining it with some modifications for about the past fifty years. How well does it work in other contexts? Post-Communist Russia provides an example.

CASE STUDY Russia: Semipresidentialism in a New Democracy with Weak Institutions

Russia is the largest country in the world with a semi-presidential system, and certainly one of the most important. Its current government demonstrates the worst fears of the system's loudest critics, fears that in a regime with weak institutions, a powerful presidency can be dangerous to democracy by allowing one official to achieve overwhelming powers. This is not inherent in all semipresidential systems, as the Mini-Case on France demonstrates, but it is a cautionary case of the problem of a strong presidency in a new democracy with weak institutions.

The Russian constitution adopted in 1993 created a semipresidential system with an exceptionally strong presidency. The president is directly elected to a four-year term, with a maximum of two terms possible. He must be elected by an absolute majority: if no candidate wins a majority in the first election, a second is held between the top two candidates. The president appoints the prime minister with the approval of the parliament, the *Duma,* but if the *Duma* votes against the president's candidate for PM three times, it is automatically dissolved and new elections are called. What this means is that unless the president's opponents in the *Duma* think they will gain from an election, they will be very hesitant to oppose his nominee. The president also appoints all cabinet members, and these do not need to be approved by the *Duma.* Neither the PM nor the rest of the cabinet need be members of the *Duma,* and the vast majority have not been. The Russian system, then, does not link the president and parliament via the PM and cabinet as fully as the original French model. This frees the president to appoint anyone he pleases to the cabinet, regardless of which party controls parliament. Furthermore, the president has direct control over several key ministries (Foreign

Are two chief executives better than one? Dmitry Medvedev (left) was Vladimir Putin's prime minister and succeeded him as president in 2008. Putin then became Medvedev's prime minister, leading people to ask who was really in charge.

Affairs, Defense, and Interior) and the Federal Security Service, successor to the KGB; in these areas, his authority bypasses the PM and the cabinet altogether. Perhaps most important, the president can issue decrees that have the force of law and cannot be vetoed by the *Duma* or challenged in court, which gives him the power to rule without legislative support. A constitutional amendment in 2000 also gave the president the power to appoint and dismiss all governors of Russia's eighty-nine regions (see the section on federalism below), who in turn appoint half of the members of the upper house of parliament. The *Duma* can vote no confidence in the prime minister but must do so twice to remove him from office. It can also impeach the president by a two-thirds vote, but it has only attempted this once, in 1999, and failed.

Two of Russia's post-Communist presidents, Boris Yeltsin (1991–2000) and Vladimir Putin (2000–2008),

IN CONTEXT Semipresidential Systems

Semipresidentialism spread with the wave of democratization in the 1990s. Political scientist Robert Elgie (2006) broadly defines semipresidentialism as any system with an elected president and a prime minister accountable to a parliament, and classified 32 electoral democracies as semipresidentialist systems in 2004.

- Ten were in Eastern Europe and the former Soviet Union.

- Eight are former colonies of 2 semipresidential European countries, France and Portugal.

- Seventeen semipresidentialist democracies are in Europe, 8 are in Africa, 5 in Asia and the Pacific, and 2 are in Latin America.

- Freedom House rated 23 semipresidentialist countries "free" in 2004.

- It rated 9, including Russia, as "partly" or "not free" in the same year.

- Elgie found that most of these 9 had very strong presidents and weak prime ministers.

His final prime minister was Putin, whom he anointed as his successor as president; Yeltsin actually resigned as president prior to the 2000 election to let Putin run as the incumbent.

Putin, a former KGB agent and leader, would prove to be a much stronger president than Yeltsin ever was, winning 53 percent of the vote in the first-round election in 2000. In the 2003 *Duma* election, his followers organized a new party, United Russia, which won control of parliament. He had complete control of the *Duma* for the rest of his presidency: it passed every major bill he submitted. He used his powers of decree and control

used the powers of the presidency quite differently. Yeltsin was the hero of the post-Communist revolution, having led the opposition to an attempted military coup in August 1991 that resulted in the demise of the Soviet Union, and he was elected president of Russia when it was still part of the Soviet Union. He was the architect of the 1993 constitution; his rule, however, was quite chaotic. Winning only 36 percent of the vote in the first-round election in 1996, he did go on to win a majority in the second round. Not being a member of any political party meant he was unable to marshal strong support in favor of his reforms. For most of his presidency, his chief opposition was the former Communist Party, which had a plurality (but not a majority) of seats in the *Duma* from 1995 to 2003. Yeltsin fought many battles with a hostile parliament and often enacted law by decree. This course of events came to a head in 1999, when the Communists attempted to impeach him on charges of illegally prosecuting a war against the breakaway region of Chechnya and engaging in corruption. He appointed seven prime ministers over his tenure, and more than two hundred different cabinet ministers.

over the prosecution of corruption to eliminate many of the "oligarchs" who had arisen under Yeltsin and come to control major sectors of the economy, replacing them with supporters or taking direct state control of some companies. He also severely restricted nongovernment sources of media. After winning the 2004 election with more than 70 percent of the vote, he reformed the constitution to also gain effective control over the country's regional governments. In September 2007 he appointed Victor Zubkov as his new prime minister, and at one point it appeared that the relatively unknown Zubkov might be Putin's heir apparent as president, but Putin later threw his support behind Dmitry Medvedev, who took the oath of office as president in May 2008. Putin used the already powerful presidency in Russia's semipresidential system to amass greater power, so much so that most analysts argue Russia is no longer a true democracy but instead is a semi-authoritarian regime, which we examine in detail in chapter 9. The Russian case, then, raises the worst fears about an excessively strong presidency in a semipresidential system, but in the context of weak institutions in a new democracy.

JUDICIARY

The judiciary is the least studied branch of government in comparative politics, which is unfortunate since it is becoming more important in many countries. On a daily basis, the job of the judiciary is to enforce a state's laws. Its more important political role, however, is interpreting those laws, especially the state's constitution. Most democracies have some version of **judicial review**, the right of the judiciary to decide whether a specific law contradicts a country's constitution. This authority, vested in unelected judges, is clearly a potential means to limit majority rule and achieve horizontal accountability, but it also raises a fundamental question: Why should unelected officials have such power? New democracies have often had to build new judicial institutions, and the weakness of these has become a major concern in comparative politics. In this section, we discuss judicial review and its relationship to democracy, the judicialization of politics, and the question of judicial autonomy and institutional weakness.

Two systems, common law and code law, emerged in modern Europe and spread to most of the world via colonialism. **Common law** developed in the United Kingdom and was adopted in most former British colonies, including the United States (it is sometimes referred to as Anglo-American law). Under common law, judges base decisions not only on their understanding of the written law but also on their understanding of past court cases. When a judge finds a law ambiguous, he or she can write a ruling that tries to clarify it, and subsequent judges are obliged to use this ruling as precedent in deciding similar cases. This is known as the principle of *stare decisis*. **Code law** is most closely associated with the French emperor Napoleon Bonaparte, who codified it in what became known as the Napoleonic Code. (It is also known as continental, or civil, law.) Under code law, which has its origins in ancient Roman law and was spread in modern Europe via Napoleon's conquests, judges may only follow the law as written, interpreting it as little as necessary to fit the case. Past decisions are irrelevant, as each judge must look only to the existing law. Like common law, code law spread globally via colonialism, especially to former French, Spanish, and Portuguese colonies. As is readily evident, the common law tradition is more accepting of interpretation of the law by judges, while code law relies on more detailed legal codes and leaves less to interpretation.

The two systems logically led to different kinds of judicial review. Common law countries, such as the United States, usually have decentralized judicial review: the same courts that handle everyday criminal cases can also rule on constitutional issues and can do so at any level. If a constitutional question begins in a lower court, it can be appealed upward, ultimately to the highest court. Code law countries usually have centralized judicial review: a special court handles constitutional questions. Another important distinction between these types of judicial review is the question of who can initiate cases. In some countries, including the United States, only an individual who has "standing"—someone who has actually been negatively affected by the law in question—can initiate a case. In others, certain public officials such as legislative leaders or the president can call on the courts to

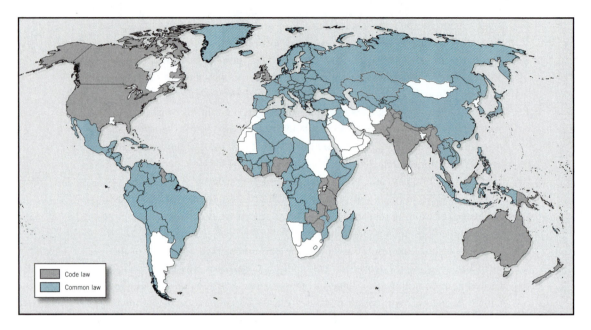

MAP 6.2
Code versus Common Law Countries

make a constitutional ruling even before the law is fully in effect. The length of appointments to whatever court handles judicial review is also important. Some countries have lifetime appointments; others limit judges' terms.

Code law and common law countries both have hierarchical court systems through which cases can be appealed, but such systems in code law countries tend to be more specialized. Judicial decision making in code law countries primarily involves knowing fairly detailed laws, the code, which is why many such countries have separate court systems for criminal and civil cases, separate courts for labor disputes, and a separate court for constitutional questions. In contrast, common law countries have fewer and more general courts. Federal systems (see the section on federalism below) in both kinds of countries often have court systems divided along federal lines: each state or province has its own court system that is usually overseen by a federal system.

The fundamental question about judicial review in a democracy is why judges, who are typically not elected and therefore not subject to vertical accountability, should be allowed to make decisions with major political consequences. Proponents argue that the difference in democratic legitimacy between judges and elected officials is one of degree, not kind, and it may well be far less sharply defined than often assumed. First, legislatures and executives are never perfectly representative or accountable, so the difference between them and the judiciary may be less than it first appears. Second, the judiciary's horizontal accountability to executives and legislatures can be seen as an indirect source of democratic accountability. Judges are typically appointed by elected officials, so their stands on issues reflect the ideas of those officials and, consequently, the ideas of the majority of the populace who put those officials into office. Robert Dahl, one of the foremost scholars of democracy, argued in a widely read 1957 article that U.S. Supreme Court justices are part of political coalitions just as elected officials are and that they reflect the same political divisions that divide elected officials.

Advocates of judicial review also argue that even if the judiciary is an imperfect democratic institution, it plays several crucial roles. It provides a check on executive and legislative power, and it is itself a mechanism of horizontal accountability. In the United States, many argue as well that judicial review exists to protect minority rights that might be trampled by a legislature or executive acting on majority opinion. In practice, however, most studies have shown that courts are more likely to rule in favor of those in power than on behalf of marginalized or oppressed minorities. And Stuart Chinn (2006) has argued that under some circumstances, the judiciary can support *majority* beliefs that might otherwise go unheard. Chinn contends that in a two-party system, parties shy away from issues that provoke strong minority reactions, even if the majority moderately favors action on the issue. For instance, suppose that most citizens favor abortion rights but don't feel strongly about them, while a more vocal minority strongly opposes abortion. Neither political party will gain an electoral advantage by acting on abortion rights, because it won't be a decisive vote-getter among the majority, but it will strongly antagonize the minority. In cases in which neither party acts on an issue, a court's ruling may do what the political parties did not.

However one answers the questions raised by judicial review, it is certainly becoming more widespread, a process that Tate and Vallindar call the "judicialization" of politics. They argue that it is "one of the most significant trends in late-twentieth and early-twenty-first-century government" (1995, 5). There are exceptions: the UK is one of the few democracies in the world that has no system of judicial review, and Japan has judicial review but under the long-dominant ruling party, the highest court has rarely had the temerity to rule against the party that appointed all of the judges. When large numbers of authoritarian governments adopted new constitutions in their move toward democracy in the 1980s and 1990s, these included some type of judicial review, although like their long-standing democratic counterparts, the strength and importance of these systems vary.

Under any legal system, new or old, the judiciary must constitute a strong institution if it is to carry out its function properly in a system of horizontal accountability. This requires **judicial independence**, the belief and ability of judges to decide cases as they think appropriate, regardless of what other people, and especially politically powerful officials or institutions, desire. Judicial independence is important to the daily working of criminal and civil courts because judicial systems that lack it are weak institutions in which corruption is common, with judges accepting bribes to decide cases in a particular way or refusing to rule against powerful individuals.

Judicial independence is also crucial for judicial review and the courts' role in deciding constitutional questions. Judges at the highest level must be able to decide cases as they believe the law requires, regardless of the desires of leaders of the other branches of government. This can be difficult. A recent study of post-Communist countries found that even where judicial review is well established in the constitution, high courts use it rarely and warily, in part because they lack legitimacy and therefore do not believe themselves to be strong enough to withstand pressure from more powerful officials. Given that the judiciary lacks both military and financial resources, legitimacy is crucial to its institutional strength: without widespread support and acceptance on the part of other officials and the general populace, the judiciary has little power. James Gibson and several colleagues (1998) found that judiciaries typically gain legitimacy only over time, as the populace comes to understand their role more fully and is satisfied with key court decisions. As we will see in the case study below and in the next chapter, the institutional strength of the judiciary in new democracies, and therefore judicial independence, is often a problem.

CASE STUDY The Judiciary: Germany and Brazil

Germany and Brazil illustrate the role of judicial review, the judicialization of politics, and the problem of judicial independence in even the most well-established democracies. Both countries use code law and therefore have multiple court systems, in addition to a specialized constitutional court. Germany has three branches to its court system. The Special Constitutional Court, simply referred to as the Constitutional Court, is the country's highest court and handles constitutional issues exclusively. The Federal High Court is the final court of appeal for all criminal and civil cases. The administrative court system includes a labor court, social security court, and finance court that deal exclusively with these areas of law. And because Germany has a federal system, the separate states (*Lander*) have their own court systems as well.

The Constitutional Court is the main court of political interest and is widely considered one of the most powerful courts in the world. The two houses of Germany's parliament together choose the sixteen members of the court, who serve single, twelve-year terms. The court is divided into two "senates," each of which hears particular kinds of cases. Both senates have the right of judicial review, but unlike common law countries each senate can hear cases not only from individuals who think a law is unconstitutional (referred to as "constitutional complaints") but also from particular political institutions that can seek a constitutional ruling before a law is implemented (called "abstract judicial review"). The federal government, one-third of the legislators in the lower house of parliament, or *Lander* governments can bring a law directly to the Constitutional Court for judicial review. If the court finds a law violates the constitution, it can declare that law invalid, send it back to parliament (at the federal or *Land* level) for a particular revision to make it constitutional, or rule that it must be interpreted in a particular way to fit the constitution.

Most observers argue that Germany has seen a significant judicialization of its political process. Because both common citizens and key political groups

Germany's sixteen-member Constitutional Court is widely considered one of the most powerful in the world. The court meets in Karlsruhe in southern Germany, a deliberate choice meant to emphasize its independence by keeping it separate from other national institutions based in the capital of Berlin.

can take a constitutional question directly to it, the Constitutional Court is overworked. Its caseload increased dramatically in the 1980s and 1990s, and the great majority of cases these days are constitutional complaints by individual citizens. While only about 2 percent of these cases have been successful, they represent an important constitutional right to German citizens. In contrast to the U.S. Supreme Court, the German court must consider all cases brought before it. As the number of cases has risen, the court has adjusted its procedures to better cope. To that end, three-judge panels rule on most cases, and as long as each panel unanimously rules against a complainant (saying the individual's rights were not violated), the case does not have to go to the full court.

Requests for abstract judicial review have been more successful and more politically important. Scholars have calculated that from 1951 to 1990 the Constitutional Court dealt with about 40 percent of all "key decisions" in parliament and invalidated about 5 per-

cent of all federal laws (Landfried 1994, 113). This process is the heart of the judicialization of German politics. Taking a question to the court has become a fairly regular move of last resort for opposition politicians: about two-thirds of all cases of abstract judicial review have been brought to the court by either the opposition in the federal parliament at the time or a *Land* government controlled by an opposition party. In a parliamentary system with strong party discipline like Germany's, opposition parties rarely win legislative fights, and they instead try to use the strong provisions for abstract judicial review as an alternative means of policymaking. Inclusion of the court has become so common that the majority party now uses it as well, asking the court to make rulings on laws that the party would like to pass but that are politically unpopular, because if the law is written the right way, the majority party can get the court to rule a particular way, and this allows the party to blame the court for the unpopular decision that it wanted in the first place.

Germany unquestionably has one of the world's strongest states with strong institutions. Even in this context, though, the question of judicial independence arises. The Constitutional Court long had one of the highest approval ratings of any political institution in the country; however, after a couple of controversial decisions in the mid-1990s involving reunification with East Germany and abortion, that approval dropped precipitously. A recent study by Georg Vanberg (2005) argues that in spite of Germany's strong institutions, the court itself thinks strategically in making its decisions. Vanberg argues that to enhance its institutional strength, the German high court wants to ensure its decisions are obeyed. Using rational actor analysis, he concludes that since the parliament is unlikely to defy or reverse a court ruling through new legislation if public opinion strongly supports the court's decision, the court is more likely to overrule other branches of government when the judges believe public opinion is on their side. Even in Germany, with one of the strongest constitutional courts in the world, the judiciary's institutional strength and therefore independence depends in part on its popular legitimacy. Vanberg argues that this means judicial review fits within the broad norms of democracy: the court actually follows popular opinion more often than not, even though it's not elected.

While not one of the world's strongest judicial systems, the system found in Brazil's relatively young democracy has nonetheless achieved what many have not: a degree of judicial independence that has actually curbed executive and legislative power. Independence, however, has not necessarily brought legitimacy or effectiveness, and many observers argue that it has harmed policymaking while encouraging growing judicialization of the political process. Judicial independence, judicial review in a code law system, and weak institutionalization have combined to produce Brazil's unusual situation. Judicial independence was enshrined in Brazil's 1988 constitution in great detail. The document set forth a complex judicial system with constitutional protection for its autonomy in most personnel, budgetary, administrative, and disciplinary areas. The system is headed by the Supreme Federal Tribunal (STF), the equivalent of the U.S. Supreme Court, which hears constitutional cases. Under the STF is the Supreme Justice Tribunal, the court of final appeal for nonconstitutional cases. Judges to these highest courts are appointed by the president, with approval of the Senate (the upper house of the legislature).

Judges in the two levels of federal courts below these are appointed by the judiciary itself based on criteria of merit. Most serve life terms up to seventy years of age. As is typical in code law countries, in addition to these constitutional and criminal courts, separate codes (and courts) exist for labor disputes, military issues, and elections. This system is replicated in large part within each state of Brazil's federal system, resulting in a total of approximately 16,900 judges in hundreds of separate courts throughout the system.

Initially, Brazil's top judges seemed hesitant to use their independence vis-à-vis the president, for example, permitting Fernando Collor to rule via the dubious use of emergency decrees. By 1992, though, the court had gained confidence, and its rulings helped lead to Collor's impeachment on corruption charges, a watershed event in the four-year-old democracy. The top courts have since ruled against a number of major political leaders, both on constitutional questions and on corruption charges, most recently in a massive corrup-

tion scandal involving several close aides of President Lula da Silva. This independence enhances horizontal accountability vis-à-vis the executive, but has also left few restraints on the judiciary. Carlos Santiso argues that while Brazil's judiciary serves an important function in horizontal accountability, its own lack of vertical accountability has become a major problem. Virtually all observers view the judiciary as slow, inefficient, and corrupt. Scandals involving judges have sometimes gone unpunished, many courts have a backlog of cases stretching out for years, and Brazilian judges are some of the most highly paid in the world. All of this has meant that "[p]ublic contempt for the judiciary has reached unprecedented levels" (2003, 177).

Part of the problem with the huge number of cases is the system of code law and judicial review established in the constitution. Constitutional cases can come to the STF either on appeal from lower courts or directly from key political actors, including most government agencies, national business or labor organizations, state governments, and political parties. Without *stare decisis,* lower courts ignore precedent and higher court rulings, and this means that cases that would be resolved in principle in a common law country still require trial in Brazil. Political leaders and groups have taken advantage of this situation by increasingly judicializing Brazilian political issues. If they cannot win in a state legislature or at the federal level, they take a case to court, making a constitutional argument if possible. They can start at a lower court and work their way up the system, or go directly to the STF, which gives them the right to "jump the queue." Cases on appeal from lower courts must then wait. Just initiating a case can often bring significant publicity to a group's pet cause.

Judicial independence has also made it difficult to clean up corruption or reform the parts of the system that almost everyone agrees aren't working. Brazil has long been one of the most unequal societies in the world, and Brazilians widely believe that all branches of the government favor the wealthy over the poor. Stories abound of wealthy people bribing judges to ensure court decisions go their way. Even without this, the courts are widely seen as partial and subjective: the poor are more likely to be brought to court, more likely to be convicted, and more likely to be sentenced to long terms in Brazil's overcrowded and often violent prisons. All of this demonstrates that even with independence, Brazil's judiciary remains weakly institutionalized, and its continuing problems seem likely to keep its legitimacy limited. Judicial leaders have successfully fought against reforms of this system since its creation in the early 1980s.

In December 2004, the legislature did pass some minimal reforms that legalized *stare decisis* in certain instances to reduce the number of cases in the courts and created a National Judicial Council composed of both top judges and nominees outside the judiciary to oversee the budget and administration of the courts. While this reform is still in its early stages of implementation, it represents a clear effort to bring some horizontal accountability to the courts to try to resolve the worst problems independence without accountability and institutionalization has created.

The German and Brazilian cases demonstrate how similar formal institutions can function quite differently in different settings. Code law and abstract judicial review put tremendous strain on the court systems in both countries, particularly at the top, and encourage the judicialization of politics. The stronger overall institutional setting of Germany, though, seems to be able to offset some of the problems Brazil faces. Some would argue that the German court is too involved in politics, but none question its integrity. Judicial independence has been an important achievement in Brazil's relatively young democracy and has helped the country start to resolve the widespread corruption found throughout the state, but it has not helped eliminate corruption within the judiciary itself.

BUREAUCRACY

Chapter 2 identified a bureaucracy as one of the key characteristics of a modern state. All states have an executive branch that includes a bureaucracy of some sort. The ideal modern bureaucracy, as originally envisioned by one of the founders of modern sociology, Max Weber, would consist of officials appointed on the basis of merit and expertise who would implement policies lawfully, treat all citizens equally according to the relevant laws, and be held accountable by the elected head of the executive branch. This ideal is an important component in the full development of an effective modern state; as we noted in chapter 2, a state (whatever type of regime it has) will have greater capacity to rule its territory and people if it has an effective bureaucracy. A bureaucracy in this modern sense is also a key component of liberal democracy, recruiting officials according to merit and administering policies according to law, treating citizens equally, and insulating bureaucratic officials from the personal and political desires of top leaders. On the other hand, bureaucracy can also be a threat to democracy, and so bureaucrats themselves must be held accountable. Who will prevent them from abusing their independence and autonomy? Because they are not elected, vertical accountability doesn't exist, meaning horizontal accountability becomes very important.

Bureaucracy can limit the executive in a number of ways even as it enhances a state's capacity. Prior to modern reforms, state positions in most societies were based on political patronage: leaders appointed all officials to suit the leaders' interests. (China was a major exception—Confucian ideas of merit in that country go back millennia.) Professionalization involved recruitment based on merit and a reduction of political patronage. It also came to include technical expertise on the part of bureaucratic officials, which political leaders often have to rely on to make decisions in an increasingly complex world. Knowledge and expertise are key sources of bureaucrats' independent power. Modern bureaucracies developed into formal, hierarchical organizations in which career advancement, at least ideally, was based on performance and personal capability rather than on political connections. While nothing ever exists in perfect form, the development of the modern bureaucracy both limited the power of the executive and raised questions about who would control the new bureaucracy itself to ensure that it maintained its professional standards and equal treatment of citizens.

Bureaucratic professionalization keeps the bureaucracy at least partially insulated from the personal and political whims of political leaders, but it raises the question of how the political leadership will hold the bureaucracy accountable. This fundamental problem can be understood as a **principal-agent problem**: the principal (the elected or appointed political leadership in the executive or legislative branches) assigns an agent (the bureaucrat) a task to carry out as the principal instructs; the problem is how the principal makes sure the agent carries out the task as assigned. Bureaucratic agents might well have strong incentives to deviate from their assigned tasks. Rational-choice theorists argue that bureaucrats, whatever their professionalization, are as self-interested and rational as any other actors. Their interests, usually expanding their sphere of influence and the size of their organization to enhance their own prestige and salary, guide their actions. This inevitably produces inefficiencies as bureaucrats expand the size of the bureaucracy, and it might distort the principals' purposes as well. Self-interest can also lead to corruption, as bureaucrats exchange favorable treatment of political leaders or ordinary citizens for favors.

Numerous solutions to this problem have emerged over the years. In every state the political leadership of the executive branch selects a certain number of **political appointees** to head the bureaucracy. These appointees serve at the pleasure of the president or prime minister and, among other things, are assigned the task of overseeing their respective segments of the bureaucracy. Different countries allow different numbers of political appointees: the United States typically allows six or eight for each significant department in the federal government, whereas two is more typical for each ministry in the UK. (The United States uses the term "department" to designate the major agencies of the government, whereas most of the world uses "ministry" to mean the same thing, harkening back to the religious influence on the early modern state.)

The power that political appointees have over professional bureaucrats is limited by the legal means through which the latter are hired and paid and earn career advancement; bureaucrats, however, must answer to political appointees within those legal limits. In democracies, **legislative oversight** is another key means of horizontal accountability in which members of the legislature, usually in key committees, oversee the working of the bureaucracy by interviewing key leaders, examining budgets, and assessing how successfully a particular agency has carried out its mandate. Often, citizens use the judicial system to try to achieve accountability by taking individual officials or entire agencies to court, arguing that they have either failed to carry out their duties or have done so unlawfully.

None of these measures can work perfectly, in large part because principals can never know exactly what their agents within a bureaucracy are doing, especially as technocratic knowledge becomes more and more important. For most of the twentieth century, governments relied heavily on professional socialization to help maintain standards. They recruited people who had been trained to abide by key professional norms of neutrality and legality, and they believed they could count on most of these recruits to behave in the general "public" interest as they had been trained. Some states, such as France and Japan, went so far as to recruit almost exclusively from one key educational institution to provide great prestige and professional status to those who were able to gain admission.

Rational-choice theorists, however, argued that training could not overcome the inherent incentives in the bureaucracy and self-interest. Following this line of argument, the **New Public Management (NPM)** movement arose. The movement first emerged in the United States and UK in the 1980s and was associated with President Ronald Reagan and Prime Minister Margaret Thatcher. NPM advocates contended that the inherent inefficiencies in the public bureaucracy required radical reforms to make it operate more like a market-based organization. This involved privatizing many government services so that they would be provided by the market, creating competition among agencies and subagencies within the bureaucracy to simulate a market, focusing on customer satisfaction (via client surveys, among other things), and flattening administrative hierarchies to encourage more team-based activity and creativity. The ideas of NPM became widely popular and were implemented in many wealthy democracies, though to varying degrees. Some countries, such as the UK and New Zealand, cut the size of their bureaucracies quite extensively via NPM, while others, including Germany and Japan, implemented it very slowly and partially. In those countries that adopted it more extensively, it had major effects in terms of reducing the size of the government, though debate continues as to whether it improved bureaucratic performance in general; in other countries, its effect was far less despite much discussion of the new approach.

As with all institutions and organizations, however, no example in the real world quite matches up to the ideal. Bureaucracies can become weak like any other political institution. When they do, officials no longer administer policies according to law, but instead do so according to their personal interests. This means that political elites may be able to use the bureaucracy to pursue personal or financial interests of their own, citizens may be able to gain favors from the state via bribery, and bureaucrats themselves may steal from the state.

Where the state and its institutions are generally weak, reform requires not only making the bureaucracy more efficient but also strengthening it as an institution. When bureaucratic rules and norms are extremely weak, corruption and massive inefficiency are likely (O'Dwyer 2006). Corruption exists in all societies and infects all bureaucracies, but the extent and type vary from state to state and regime to regime. A recent study of new democracies in Eastern Europe found that where political party competition is strong but institutions are weak, parties use patronage to compete; they create "runaway states" in which the size of the bureaucracy expands rapidly but the state's capacity does not improve.

Bribery and rent-seeking are two other primary types of corruption in bureaucracies. In the least institutionalized bureaucracies, citizens often have to bribe officials to get them to carry out the functions they are mandated to do. The principals—the political leadership—may not be interested in encouraging the bureaucracy to function effectively because they benefit from their own ability to purchase favors from bureaucrats, or they may have simply lost all ability to control their agents in the bureaucracy, often because of very low bureaucratic salaries. To supplement these low salaries, officials seek bribes before they will carry out the most menial functions, such as issuing a driver's license, providing basic medicine, or building a school. **Rent-seeking** is the gaining of an advantage in a market without engaging in equally productive activity; this usually involves using government regulations to one's own benefit. In weakly institutionalized bureaucracies, businesses may be able to gain favorable access to the state via bribing officials to grant them exclusive monopolies over certain sectors of the economy or exclusive rights to import certain items, thereby reaping huge profits for little effort. The case studies below demonstrate both the power and limits of bureaucracy and the complex issues that arise when bureaucracy weakens.

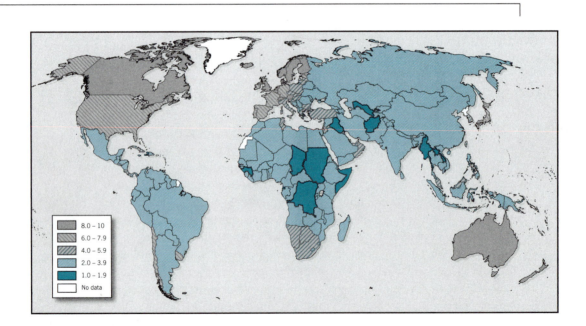

MAP 6.3
Annual Corruption Scores, 2007

Source: Transparency International CPI Scores, 2007.

CASE STUDY Bureaucratic Control and Corruption: Japan and India

All states have bureaucracies, but in some states they have played a greater political role than in others. Japan and India are two such cases, both justifiably well known for bureaucracies that played pivotal roles in their early economic and political development. They both emerged from World War II with unusually strong bureaucratic organizations: Japan's was just about the sole surviving institution from its prewar government, and India's developed out of British colonial rule. They both were intimately involved in setting economic policy, in particular from the 1950s to the 1970s. Unfortunately, they have both also been weakened by corruption over the last twenty years that arguably has had a negative impact on economic well-being and the legitimacy of their democratic governments more broadly.

In 1988 Japan's Liberal Democratic Party (LDP) was enjoying the approach of its fortieth year of uninterrupted power. The Japanese economy was booming, thanks in part to Japan's long-standing tradition of a highly professionalized, elite bureaucracy. While this bureaucracy was capable of collaborating closely with business and politicians to implement far-sighted and beneficial economic policies, critics worried that there was too little oversight. Their fears came to pass when the political system was shaken by revelations of the "Recruit scandal," so called because it transpired that the Recruit Corporation, a real estate and telecommunications firm, had engaged in "insider trading" by offering advance shares of a subsidiary about to go public to politicians who then profited handsomely. In addition to the seventeen members of the *Diet* (Japan's parliament) involved in the scandal, another thirty were found to have received "special favors" from Recruit. The entire cabinet resigned, and although the corruption involved many parties, the scandal was an important factor in the LDP's first electoral loss in 1993. Bureaucracy had helped the LDP grow and maintain power, but bureaucratic corruption also helped bring it down.

The Japanese bureaucracy was the only major political institution to survive the post–World War II U.S. occupation largely intact. This gave it a tremen-

Minister for Administrative Reform Yoshimi Watanabe responded to corruption scandals in Japan's bureaucracy by announcing new rules regarding *amakudari* in 2007. Beginning in 2009, government agencies are to phase out assisting retiring bureaucrats land new jobs. Critics called the new rules "toothless" and said the entire system needs to be overhauled.

dous advantage vis-à-vis other institutions in the new democracy. Like France, Japan's top bureaucrats are recruited primarily from one place: the Faculty of Law at the University of Tokyo. From the 1950s through the 1970s, the unwritten rule was that the top graduates of that school would enter the elite corps of the bureaucracy to begin their ascent to the top. The fifteen ministries were very hierarchically organized and insulated from external pressure. As a "class" moved up the bureaucratic ladder, those passed over for promotion would take early retirement. By the time the group reached the top rung, one of their number would be appointed to a top post and the rest would retire to leave him as the sole senior manager.

Early retirement and limited political oversight were facilitated by the common practice of **amakudari**, or the "descent from heaven," and rigid **iron triangles** among business, politicians, and key bureaucrats. Under *amakudari,* retiring civil servants gained lucrative positions in the businesses they previously regulated. Among other things, this gave bureaucrats an incentive to maintain favorable conditions for and relations with key corporations in their regulatory area. The term "iron triangle" was coined in reference to the United States, but the phenomenon is even stronger in Japan. Key bureaucrats, business leaders, and politicians cooperate to set policy in their area to their mutual interest. In a classic example of corruption expert Michael Johnston's "influence market" (2005), businesses give generous contributions to top politicians in exchange for the politicians securing favorable treatment from key bureaucrats, who grant the favors because they will eventually be working in the businesses themselves. This system was central to the success of Japan's developmental state outlined in chapter 5.

The power of Japan's bureaucracy was unusual for a democracy: it controlled key information and expertise used to guide the growing economy and was a source of highly prestigious employment. The prime minister only made two or three political appointments in each ministry, for a total of fewer than fifty appointments (as compared to several hundred that a U.S. president makes), giving him little executive oversight. Combined with little legislative oversight due to the iron triangles, the bureaucracy was left with great power vis-à-vis the other branches in Japan's democracy. At the height of its power, most major legislative initiatives began not with the prime minister or the legislature, but rather in the relevant bureaucracy. Interestingly, this power did not result in the further growth of the bureaucracy. Though it retained great regulatory powers in the economy, the number of officials as a percentage of all employment in the country was and remains the lowest among wealthy democracies, undoubtedly in part because of bureaucrats' ability to gain lucrative posts upon early retirement.

Admirers of the developmental state argued that this centralized and powerful bureaucracy played a positive role in Japan's economic success. Lack of oversight and the incentives of the iron triangle and *amakudari,* however, let corruption get out of control,

provoking scandals that significantly reduced the prestige and probably the power of the bureaucracy. Such scandals had long occurred in Japanese politics, but the Lockheed scandal of the 1970s that involved the bribing of top officials, including the prime minister, and the Recruit scandal described above took corruption to a new level. Prior to these, most Japanese knew that corruption was fairly common but thought it did not affect the top echelons; these scandals destroyed that belief and led to fundamental changes in the electoral system (see chapter 7). Combined with the economic stagnation of the 1990s, the scandals also diminished the prestige of the bureaucracy in general. At the height of the bureaucracy's power in the 1960s, forty-three top university graduates competed for each top bureaucratic position; by the 1990s only eleven did (Pempel 2000, 160). Business stagnation made *amakudari* more difficult, and the prestige of the bureaucracy plummeted.

Changes to Japan's bureaucratic system have long been proposed but have seldom succeeded. The 1993 electoral reforms, a direct response to the worst scandals, seem to have had little effect on the role of money in the election process (see chapter 7). The ideas of NPM filtered in from the United States and UK but also had relatively little impact, because neither Japanese bureaucrats nor politicians had significant interest in reforming a system from which they all benefited. And given the small size of Japan's bureaucracy, some of NPM's analysis clearly did not fit the Japanese case, but during the 1980s Japan did privatize a few state-owned companies, including the railway system. A reformist prime minister, Junichiro Koizumi, entered office in 2001 with bold proposals for reform, but few became law (see chapter 5). Australian political scientist Aurelia Mulgan (2002) argues that the bureaucracy's continued power prevented acceptance of many of his reforms, and some of the reforms he did pass were favored by particular sectors of the bureaucracy, especially the Ministry of Finance.

The relative power of the bureaucracy today, however, remains much disputed. A number of scholars disagree with Mulgan, arguing that the position of the bureaucracy has been significantly reduced as Japanese policymaking has become significantly more pluralistic over the past decade. The bureaucracy remains more powerful than in most wealthy democracies, but it has become more internally divided, which has allowed more voices within and without to have an effect on key questions in Japanese politics. If nothing else, this trend seems to point in the direction of at least somewhat greater accountability.

In the case of India, the level of accountability is only one of the things critics point to as needing improvement. The bureaucracy in any postcolonial developing state like India faces many demands. It not only implements state policies and helps mold economic growth, similar to the Japanese model, but also is often assigned the task of furthering "development" and helping to end poverty, as well as serving as a link between the highly educated, literate officials of the central state and the mostly poor, illiterate, rural populace. India's bureaucracy has certainly been assigned all of these roles at one time or another. Its evolution and current status is heavily influenced by the country's development efforts, from import-substitution industrialization (ISI) and central state planning in the 1950s–1970s to neoliberal reform since the 1990s. It expanded dramatically under ISI, taking on numerous developmental tasks, but since the 1990s it has been asked to reduce its role in line with neoliberal policies to do less but do it more efficiently. The combination of development policy and the pressures of political competition have produced the corruption that seems to be an endemic problem today. Indeed, although India has become a "hot" new economy, growing rapidly and emerging as a leader in a number of fields, such as software development (see chapter 10), most business leaders note that one of the biggest problems facing expanded economic growth is an inefficient and corrupt bureaucracy.

Like all postcolonial states, India's bureaucracy developed first under colonial rule, in this case from the British-created Indian Civil Service (ICS). Initially staffed only by British colonial officials, the ICS was nearly half Indian by the time of Indian independence. The British called it the "steel frame" of their Indian colonial empire, and they saw it as the crucial link between themselves and the majority of the population. As in all colonies,

the ICS served not only to implement laws but also as the eyes and ears of the colonial state, keeping order over the often "restless natives." At independence, the ICS lost nearly half its staff when the British officers nearly all went home and most Muslim officers migrated to the newly formed Pakistan. It subsequently was renamed the Indian Administrative Service (IAS), and many of the nationalist leaders who had criticized the ICS as a key component colonial oppression embraced the IAS as a crucial element of their new state.

The IAS kept virtually all of its colonial organization, recruitment, and training structures in place, with the obvious exception of the body now being composed only of Indians. It was designed to provide an elite cadre of bureaucratic officials who would link together India's diverse federal system. Its members are recruited nationally from top universities through an extensive examination process, trained for their service for more than a year, and then assigned to a state. They typically spend their career working in that state, though they are rotated to the central government in Delhi, the national capital, occasionally. In this way, a nationally recruited bureaucracy with knowledge of the central government works in and for the state governments, providing a bureaucratic bridge between the two levels of government that few federal systems have. The extensive recruitment and training were designed to produce a group of officials with a common understanding and professional norms designed to integrate the country's administration. Below the elite IAS, India has more than twenty national civil service groups and each state has its own as well, which amounts to a huge bureaucracy that the IAS is supposed to integrate and to some extent coordinate.

India's bureaucracy has been profoundly influenced by the country's evolving development policies, which it is supposed to implement. The government of the first prime minister, Jawaharlal Nehru, pursued a version of ISI with unusually extensive state involvement. Central development planning was seen as essential, with the state creating specific targets of growth in various sectors and often initiating specific projects to achieve them, all of which the bureaucracy was to implement. As with most ISI efforts, this involved the creation of state-owned enterprises, often via nationalization of private entities such as major banks. The bureaucracy expanded accordingly: the public sector accounted for 10 percent of GDP in 1960 but 27 percent by 1987, where it has remained, more or less, ever since. Virtually all economic undertakings required some sort of government permit, available only from the bureaucracy. The system's critics came to refer to as the "license raj." Beginning in 1991, this model began to change with the shift in the direction toward the neoliberal economic development model. That model called for a reduced and more efficient bureaucracy that freed business from unnecessary regulation and ensured the rule of law via an uncorrupt and competent administration. India's bureaucracy has certainly not fulfilled that role completely. While it has not expanded significantly since the late 1980s, it hasn't been reduced significantly either, and the level of corruption has changed relatively little.

Corruption has long been a problem in India, but it became much worse over the years, at least until recently. From the colonial era on, most Indians would tell you that you often had to pay a small bribe to get something accomplished at a government office. That kind of petty corruption, however, was just that: small and limited. By the 1970s and 1980s, it had become much more serious and extensive. Several factors explain this transformation. First, the ISI and development planning model of the first three decades after independence put bureaucrats in key positions from which to demand bribes. As the state regulated more economic activity, more people had to get licenses for what they wanted to do. Each license and each form that required a stamp of approval held the potential for a bribe. Second, civil servants' wages declined over the years, giving them an incentive to look for other sources of income. The IAS, in particular, was a service of great prestige, with some of the highest wages in the country, and it attracted the best university graduates who were trained to be professionals in their field and were well paid to uphold those standards. Then civil service wages at all levels was effectively frozen for thirty years, lowering their real value dramatically. By the 1980s, even the IAS was no longer a very high-prestige career; the most ambitious people pursued careers in the private sector, and those in the civil service increasingly took bribes to supplement their income.

The most important impetus to large-scale corruption, however, was undoubtedly politicization of the bureaucracy. As political competition increased in India's democracy, politicians at all levels wanted bureaucrats to grant favors to them and their constituents, and bureaucrats who refused often found themselves transferred to an unpleasant assignment in a remote village. This type of political pressure on the bureaucracy began in earnest under Prime Minister Indira Gandhi in the late 1960s and 1970s, and it continued and expanded under her son Rajiv, in the 1980s. Increased party competition after the demise of the Congress Party's rule in 1989 (see chapter 7) only exacerbated the problem. As political leaders were increasingly able to have bureaucrats moved, the latter had little choice but to yield to many of their demands. The result, especially combined with declining bureaucratic wages, was an ever weaker civil service. Corruption exploded at the top of the political system in the late 1980s and 1990s and helped end two governments over allegations of involvement by the PM in large-scale bribery and kickback schemes. These were only the most dramatic examples of a growing and continuing problem throughout the civil service and political system.

Influenced in part by NPM and aid donors' growing concern over corruption, India has pursued numerous civil service reform efforts over the years. These have included the creation of various government watchdog agencies, some decentralization efforts, and an attempt to strengthen elected local governments to take over some of the functions of the bureaucracy. None of these has been wholly successful. The bureaucracy, its critics contend, remains an overly hierarchical organization more concerned about procedures than outcome that continues its long-standing participation in corruption. The number of public scandals over corruption has certainly increased over the years, indicating growing public concern and perhaps making it a little more difficult for politicians and civil servants to do just as they please. These efforts are having some effect. Transparency International, a global anticorrup-

WHERE AND WHY Explaining Corruption

Political corruption—the illegal use of political office for personal or political gain—is universal, but its extent varies widely from one society to another and over time. The United States in the nineteenth century was widely known for its corruption. Today, it remains more corrupt than many European countries, but far less corrupt than most of the world. What explains the differing levels of corruption across different eras and countries? Political scientists have used the full array of theories to try to understand and explain this.

Many have looked at political culture, arguing that corruption is greater where societies lack shared values about the importance of the public sphere, placing personal, family, or kin interests above those of the society as a whole. Others have noted that greater corruption is found in postcolonial societies, and they contend that the lack of legitimacy of a postcolonial state that has no firm roots in the society leads people to think the public sphere is available to gain from as you can. Nigerian sociologist Peter Ekeh (1975) argued that in Africa, two "publics" exist: a more "primordial public" that includes ethnic, religious, and community identities in which people feel reciprocal moral responsibility toward one another, and an amoral "civic public" involving the state, which people feel no obligation toward and therefore take from freely.

Michael Johnston, one of the foremost scholars of corruption, uses a structural approach in his 2005 book, *Syndromes of Corruption: Wealth, Power, and Democracy* to argue that the type and extent of corruption varies systematically with the type of state and regime. In wealthy, established democracies, the primary type of corruption is what he terms "influence markets," in which corporations use access to politicians, usually via generous contributions to campaigns and parties, to gain preferential access to and treatment from key economic bureaucracies. In democracies in which the overall level of institutionalization is weaker, typically in middle-income countries, political competition is both more intense and the outcome less certain. In these countries, "elite cartels" emerge in which key political and business leaders form networks to gain control of the government and systematically use it to their joint political and financial benefit.

In middle-income countries that have recently become democracies, institutions are even weaker and political competition more intense, uncertain, and personal. Under these conditions, "oligarchs and clans" form whose members scramble for spoils in the system. This is likely to occur where a recent economic liberalization has also occurred, such as in Russia, one of Johnston's primary examples.

In the least institutionalized (and often poorest) states with personalized or neopatrimonial rule, corruption often takes the form of the "Official Mogul," a strongman who uses the resources of the state as he pleases to favor his political allies and punish his enemies. The extent of the problem and the possible remedies for corruption vary, Johnston argues, across these four types of countries, though corruption is an important issue in all of them. Where it exists, even in modest proportions, it undermines the capacity of the state and the democratic ideal of equal citizenship, two areas in which the modern bureaucracy is crucial.

tion nongovernmental agency, ranked India sixty-sixth out of eighty-five countries in terms of corruption (with 85 being the worst), with a score on its corruption perception index of 2.9 (with 10 being the best) in 1998. By 2007 India was number 72 out of 179, a much higher ranking relative to others, with a score of 3.5. While not a dramatic change, it does indicate progress.

Bureaucracy in poor and developing societies ought to fulfill all the roles that it does in any other state. However, it also is asked to take on the additional roles of ending poverty and linking the government elite to the poor populace. As the Indian case demonstrates, bureaucracies have been heavily influenced by the shifting models of development policy over the years. India is not unusual in seeing more corruption come from ISI and greater political competition: somewhat weak postcolonial bureaucratic institutions become much weaker in the face of strong incentives for corruption on the part of civil servants, political leaders, and ordinary citizens. The neoliberal model, to the extent that it has reduced the role of the bureaucracy in the economy, is likely to improve the situation, as it has in India, but only very slowly; the wheels of bureaucracy, whichever way they spin, spin slowly.

FEDERALISM

So far, we have only considered governmental institutions at the national level. In every country, of course, they exist at lower levels as well, though their role and autonomy vis-à-vis the national government vary widely. The most important distinction is between unitary and federal systems. In **unitary systems** the central government has sole constitutional sovereignty and power, whereas in federal systems the central government shares constitutional sovereignty and power with subunits, such as states, provinces, or regions. Local governments exist in unitary systems, but they derive their powers from the central government, which can alter them as it pleases. In federal systems, some subnational governments have constitutionally derived powers separate from the central government that can only be changed via change to the constitution itself, which generally is difficult to do.

The first modern federal system was the Dutch Republic of the United Provinces in what is now the Netherlands, but the best-known early example is the United States. Both states originally were contiguous units within larger empires that declared independence and banded together. In the case of the United States, separate and sovereign states—the original thirteen British colonies—came together to form a federation only after a looser union, a confederation, failed to produce a viable central state. Political scientist William Riker (1964) provided a now classic rational choice explanation of how American federalism emerged, showing how it was the result of a bargain among self-interested leaders of separate states who were motivated primarily by military concerns—protecting themselves from external threat.

Australia and Switzerland are other examples of federalism arising from separate states coming together to form a new state. Most modern federations, however, arose in exactly the opposite way: through states trying to remain together, often after colonial rule, as our case study of India below demonstrates. In some cases, such as India, federations arose via democracy and implicit bargaining between regional elites and the central government. In other cases, such as Russia, authoritarian rulers imposed federalism to help them rule a vast, heterogeneous territory. As the Russian part of the case study below indicates, imposed federalism seldom provides the stability or strong institutions of negotiated federalism.

While federal systems are a minority of the world's governments, they include most of its geographically largest countries. As the Country and Concepts table for this chapter shows, in our set of case studies, Brazil, Germany, India, Nigeria, Russia, and the United States are all federal systems; the exception is China. This is not accidental. Larger countries tend to adopt federal systems in part to provide some level of government closer to the populace than the national government can be. Providing a relatively local form of government in a large state is one of the primary purposes of federalism, but there are at least two others.

A second purpose is limiting the power of the majority by decentralizing and dividing governmental power. Federal systems usually have bicameral legislatures, with the second (usually referred to as the upper) house representing the interests of the states or provinces. They also have some sort of judicial review to settle disputes between the levels of government. Both institutions limit the power of the executive and the majority controlling the lower (and always more powerful) house of the legislature.

Lastly, federalism is often a means to protect the interests of and create subnational governing structures for religious or ethnic minorities. States use this federal solution when minorities are geographically concentrated in particular regions. When regional minority communities feel threatened by other groups' control of the national government, a federal system that creates separate states or provinces with clear ethnic or religious majorities can help ease concerns, for while these minority groups cannot control the central government, they can control the state in which they are a majority, and thereby limit the power of the central government over them. This explains the choice of federal systems in some relatively small states, such as Belgium, a state created in 1830 as a buffer against potential French expansion. Federalism there has been used to ensure some measure of self-governance for both French- and Dutch-speaking citizens. Despite its prolonged existence as a nation-state, regionalism in Belgium remains so strong that a 2007 crisis provoked by the inability to form a parliamentary majority sparked predictions that the country (composed of only three regions,

IN CONTEXT Federalism

Federalism is an unusual institutional choice: only 24 of 193 countries have a federal system. Those 24, however, account for 40 percent of the world's population. In addition:

- Seven are among the world's 10 largest geographically, and 6 are among the world's 10 largest countries by population.

- Seven of the world's 10 largest electoral democracies by area are federal, as are 5 of the 10 largest democracies by population.

- Federal countries average 0.55 on an index of ethnic fractionalization, where 0 is perfect homogeneity and 1 is highly fragmented; the world average is 0.48.

- Five federal countries are geographically fragmented, composed of 2 or more islands, or of a peninsula and at least 1 island.

Source: Based on data from Forum of Federations (www.forumfed.org), Fearon 2003, and Freedom House (www.freedomhouse.org).

one of which is the capital district) would break in two. The case of Nigeria in chapter 4 shows the complexities of using federalism to protect and respond to the concerns of ethnic minorities. Nigeria went from three regions at independence to thirty-six states today as it tries to accommodate ethnic minorities by creating states for them to govern. While this has helped mitigate ethnic conflict, it has done nothing to ease growing religious tensions, showing that federalism can be helpful in resolving ethnic or religious conflict but is no panacea.

MINI-CASE South Africa

The South African transition from apartheid to democracy in the early 1990s was a classic case of a minority demanding federalism as protection from the majority. The white minority, led by F. W. de Klerk and the National Party, knew that Nelson Mandela and his African National Congress (ANC) would win a democratic election, so they bargained with Mandela and the ANC to create a federal system that would limit the ANC's power in the national government. Some whites called for the creation of an officially "white" province but that was rejected by de Klerk and his party in favor of a system that gave distinct powers to the nine provinces created under the new constitution. In the first election, de Klerk's party was able to win control of the government of one of these provinces, as was another anti-ANC party, which limited the ANC's power.

Proponents saw the call for a separate white province as an example of another purpose of federalism: creating subnational governments for religious or ethnic groups. Typically, federalism is used for this purpose when such groups live in a more or less clearly identified region of a country. This was a problem with the South African proposal: whites did not and do not live in a particular region, and those calling for a "white" province wanted to encourage whites who wanted to remain separate from blacks to move to "their" territory. To many South Africans, this seemed an attempt to create a sort of reverse apartheid. In the end, most South Africans—both black and white—saw the call for a "white" province as racist and illegitimate and were content with the federal system's structure as a sufficient protection for minority rights.

A key determinant of the extent to which federalism limits majority power and provides accountability is the relative power and autonomy of the national and subnational governments. This, in turn, depends on the specific powers set out for each level of government in the constitution, the resources each level of government controls, and the composition and relative strength of the upper house in the legislature. The constitutions of all federal systems lay out the powers of both the central government and the states or provinces. Military, foreign, and monetary policies are always placed under the authority of the national level, as they are essential to the sovereignty of the modern state and a modern economy. States or provinces typically have power over education, transportation, and sometimes social services (at least partially). In more decentralized systems like the United States and Brazil, states also have separate judicial systems that handle most criminal law.

The real power of each level of government, however, depends not only on formal powers ordained by the constitution but also on the resources it has. Two key questions and battles in any federal system are how much each level of government can collect in taxes and how much it can spend. The power of taxation is particularly important as it gives subnational units autonomy from the central government that would not exist if the lower levels were wholly dependent on the central government for their revenue. In the most centralized unitary states, such as the UK and Ireland, the central government collects more than three-quarters of total government revenue; in the least centralized, such as Germany and Switzerland, the central government collects less than a third. Similarly, the central government in some unitary systems is responsible for around 60 percent of all expenditures, whereas in decentralized federal systems it is responsible for as little as 30 percent.

As mentioned, the upper house in a federal legislature is weaker than the lower house, which is usually designed to represent the individual voter. The upper house, such as the U.S. Senate or Germany's Bundesrat, represents the state or provincial governments. Its power and composition help determine the extent to which federalism limits majority rule, and its powers can be quite sweeping, as in the case of the U.S. Senate, which must approve all legislation, or much more limited, as in Germany's Bundesrat, which can only delay bills unless they directly relate to the *Lander*. Because states or provinces are typically of different sizes, smaller ones are often overrepresented in the upper house. In the U.S. Senate, every state has two seats: in 2000, the twenty least populous states had just over 10 percent of the U.S. population but elected 40 percent of the senators; the most populous state, California, had about 15 percent of the national population and had only two senators. Given that Senate legislation requires the approval of 60 percent of the house on important issues, the representatives of just over 10 percent of the population can stop legislation, an unusually severe restriction on majority rule. The ratio of representation of the smallest states to the largest in the United States is about 66 to 1. The same ratio in Germany is only 13 to 1; this ratio, combined with the weaker powers of the Bundesrat, show clearly that German federalism does not restrict majority rule nearly as much as American federalism does.

Most federal systems today exist in heterogeneous societies; part of their purpose is to give some local autonomy to ethnic or religious minorities. While all of the issues outlined above apply to these federal systems, other factors also come into play in preserving ethnic minority autonomy. The United States is an example of a **symmetrical federal system**: all states have the same relationship with and rights in relation to the national government. In contrast, many federal systems in ethnically divided societies are **asymmetrical**: some states or provinces have special rights or powers that others don't. These special relationships are often negotiated individually between the leaders of a particular group and the central government, sometimes at the end of or under the threat of civil war or demands for secession (complete separation from the country). A recent comparative study concluded that federal systems on the whole do help accommodate ethnic and religious divisions, which results in less conflict than occurs in unitary systems with heterogeneous populations. However, the study also found that federal systems work best where there has not been a history of severe repression of one group over another; in such cases, even the best designed federal institutions may not be able to overcome the tensions and lack of trust between a particular regionally based group and the central government (Amoertti and Bermeo 2004).

In recent years, the sharp division between federal and unitary systems has been blurring. The most decentralized federal systems have become somewhat more centralized as these federal governments use their revenue power and constitutional authority to override state prerogatives in areas such as civil rights, education, and even the drinking age. (Since the 1980s, the U.S. federal government has enforced the mandatory minimum drinking age of twenty-one by denying transportation funding to states that refuse to abide by it; therefore, all states do.) In unitary systems, such as the UK, some decentralization has taken place, often termed *devolution*, because it devolves power from the center to the regions or subnational units. A British parliamentary report comments that this differs from federalism because parliamentary sovereignty means that devolution of power is reversible. The "devolved" institutions in Scotland, Wales, and Northern Ireland also remain subordinate to the British parliament. Interestingly, Britain is an example of "asymmetrical devolution," since each region has its own set of devolved responsibilities and there is no common pattern (Leeke et al. 2003). In France, which had one of the most centrally controlled unitary systems, new regional governments with limited powers were created in the 1980s. All governments, both democratic and authoritarian, struggle with how much power to give subnational units of government and how much to retain in the center. In a democracy, this has crucial implications for the power of the majority and the preservation of minority rights, as the case studies below demonstrate.

CASE STUDY Federalism: Brazil, India, and Russia

Brazil, India, and Russia provide us with three distinct models of federalism: each represents differing degrees of centralization, symmetry, and institutionalization. Brazil, like the United States, is a case of exceptional decentralization that stringently limits what the majority in control of the national government can achieve; critics argue that the system was so decentralized that it harmed effective governance, at least until reforms were made in the 1990s. Decentralization makes state governors, and even mayors of the largest cities, more powerful than virtually all members of the

National Congress, though recent reforms did achieve somewhat greater centralization. India, in contrast, is a much more centralized federal system in which the center, especially under the continuous rule of a dominant party, controls state governments rather tightly. Also in contrast to Brazil, India is an example of a federal system that arose in part to ameliorate and contain the effects of linguistic and religious diversity. Russian federalism is also formally centralized and exists in part to contain ethnic differences, but shows the limited ability of federalism if federal institutions are weak.

Like the United States, Brazil is a case of decentralized, symmetric federalism. The power of states, and of their governors in particular, can severely limit national policymaking, though the balance between central and subnational power has ebbed and flowed over time. Brazil's overall federal structure also is similar to that of the United States, with twenty-six states, each with an elected governor and legislature. Federalism in the country dates back to the era of Portuguese colonialism, and it has never been based on ethnic or racial divisions. Rather, the Portuguese divided their vast and lightly populated South American colony into separate units, each under the informal control of local landowning elites. The emperor, however, maintained central control. At independence, local elites reacted against the empire's centralization by creating a very decentralized federal system and giving themselves great power at the local level. Although they never completely abandoned federalism, Brazil's authoritarian regimes (1930–1945 and 1964–1985) did recentralize control, whereas each new democracy, including the current one established under the 1988 constitution, reasserted local control via decentralized federalism.

The 1988 constitution spells out the powers of the states in great detail. They are guaranteed a share of national tax revenue, control over their own state banks, and very little oversight from the federal government. The upper house in the federal legislature, the Senate, is composed of three senators from each state. Given the exceptionally unequal populations of the states, each vote for a senator in the least populous state is worth 144 votes in the most populous, which is more than double the disparity found in the U.S. Senate. Like the United States, the Senate must pass all legislation, meaning that senators representing 13 percent of the population can block any legislation. Even the lower house, the Chamber of Deputies, favors the less populous states, because no state's delegation can be smaller than eight seats or larger than seventy. Since the population differences between the most populous and least populous states are much greater than this, the lower house does not provide equal representation of each citizen, as it does in most federal systems.

The greatest powers, however, are reserved for state governors. Brazilian politics have long revolved

Brazil's Law of Fiscal Responsibility, part of an effort to reform its extremely decentralized federalism, was passed in 2000 to reduce the government's deficit by cutting patronage, including the padding of the payroll of the civil service. This postal worker tore a copy of the Brazilian constitution to protest a clause requiring retired civil servants to make pension contributions.

around the use of patronage to build a political following, and much of that patronage is in the hands of state governors. National political parties have always been quite weak, in part due to Brazil's electoral system (see chapter 9); in reality, they are collections of separate state parties controlled via patronage by governors and other local elites. Members of the Chamber of Deputies, and even senators, aspire to be governors or mayors of large cities in their home states as these positions have more influence and power than the national legislature. This structure emerged at the end of Brazil's military regime, in reaction to the centralization of the authoritarian period, and understandably, it made central policymaking extremely difficult.

Brazil's primary problem in the 1990s—massive inflation and debt—was connected to the power and influence of these state governors. Much of this debt was held by banks owned and controlled by the twenty-six states, and governors used these banks as sources of patronage. They also had the power to force the federal government to bail the banks out if they got into financial difficulty, so that by the mid-1990s, Brazil's states were facing bankruptcy because of their irresponsible spending.

President Fernando Cardoso negotiated the following agreement with the governors: the federal government would bail out the states in exchange for the states agreeing to privatize the state banks. Cardoso also was able to shift some spending to the states and increase federal tax revenue. He combined these reforms with a constitutional amendment that allows both the president and all governors to be reelected. Previously, like officials in most of Latin America, Brazil's executives could only serve one term, so governors used their one term to gain as much patronage from the state's resources as they could. The possibility of reelection gave them a longer-term stake in successful reform and also allowed them to run for reelection in support of the widely popular Cardoso. After reelection, Cardoso succeeded in passing the Law of Fiscal Responsibility in 2000, which limits the amount states can spend on salaries and employees (a key form of patronage) and prevents the federal government from bailing out the states in the future, effectively limiting governors' resources for patronage. Brazilian federalism remains one of the most decentralized in the world, but over the past decade the pendulum has shifted slightly back in the direction of centralization, facilitating more coherent policymaking at the national level.

Like Brazil, the origins of India's federalism lie in the colonial era. The British colonial government put modern India together from literally hundreds of separate states, ruling some areas of India directly and others via various agreements with hundreds of local rulers. After independence, the new constitution recognized various categories of states and "union territories" with various powers. While most states today have the same basic powers, the central government has bargained with regional groups to create new states to enhance regional loyalty to the center. In some cases this has meant giving certain states greater autonomy and power than others. The designers of India's constitution specifically said they were not creating states along linguistic or ethnic lines, but over time that is primarily what has happened. A major commission in the 1950s led to the creation of new states drawn mostly along linguistic lines. In the northeast, six new states were eventually created along ethnic lines as well, and

each of these has greater power and autonomy than the other states, including respect for local customary law and religious practices. (One of these states, Sikkim, had been a separate country that India successfully added to its territory after agreeing to a distinct set of powers for it as a state.)

India's constitution created an unusually centralized system of federalism. States do not write their own constitutions; each is under the authority of the same central constitution, which includes a parliamentary government with a chief minister who is the state-level equivalent of prime minister. The national government, however, has the right to create, eliminate, or change state boundaries as it pleases. It can also declare President's Rule in a particular state, under which the state government is dismissed and the prime minister in effect governs the state directly until he or she calls a new state election. This was to be implemented only in cases of severe emergency, such as a political crisis in the state, but as noted earlier in the chapter, it was regularly used for political gain. The constitution also sets out clear lists of responsibilities and taxation powers for the national and state governments: states control issues such as public order, health, agriculture, and land rights. The national government has the greatest taxation ability, as the states' only significant taxing ability is a sales tax on goods. An upper house, the *Rajya Sabha,* exists to represent states but has very limited power, in that it has no significant effect on legislation or the composition of the national government.

The extent to which this centralized constitutional arrangement has limited majority rule has varied over time. When the Indian National Congress (INC—see chapter 7 for more details) was the sole dominant party and controlled the national government between 1947 and 1977, it had tremendous power. INC prime ministers in the 1970s and 1980s used President's Rule to dismiss state governments that disagreed with them or resisted their directives. The national government's control over taxation has also given it great power, which has expanded over time. In 1955–1956, Indian states could finance an average of 69 percent of their expenditure, with the rest coming from the national government; by 2000–2001, this was down to 49 percent (Rao and Singh 2005, 172). The power of the purse has given the central government great control over the policies of the states.

The greatest limitations on the center have come from changes in the Indian party system. Even in view of the limited power of the states, India's ethnically based federalism has helped create a number of state-level parties, especially in the south. These parties dominate the politics in their states but have little influence or support elsewhere. As we detail in chapter 7, since 1989 national governments have always been coalitions between a major national party and several state-level parties. The state parties have used this situation to bargain with the national parties for greater state autonomy, protecting their states' interests vis-à-vis the majority party in a way that neither the upper house nor other elements of the Indian constitution can provide. This, perhaps, is beginning to achieve some degree of institutional autonomy for state governments, and horizontal accountability vis-à-vis national institutions.

Despite the centralization of the system, India's federalism has managed to keep most ethnic and linguistic conflict within democratic bounds. Atul Kohli, one of the foremost scholars of Indian politics, argues that India has used federalism to contain conflict when national leaders have been willing to compromise with regional groups and political institutions were strong (2004). In the 1950s and 1960s, Prime Minister Jawaharlal Nehru used the creation of states to appease movements, such as the Tamils in the south, who demanded greater autonomy for their linguistic groups. In the 1970s and 1980s, Prime Ministers Indira and Rajiv Gandhi were less willing to compromise with regional forces, partly because they had less national political support. Since 1989, coalition governments and a 1994 ruling by India's Supreme Court have limited the ability of prime ministers to declare President's Rule or pursue other centralizing activities in respect to states.

Although they have weakened over the past several decades, India's major political institutions remain strong enough for political leaders to make compromises that mean something. If state leaders can successfully bargain for certain powers, they have state institutions under their control that can make more or less effective use of those powers. Therefore, it is reasonable for them to assume that central authorities will adhere to the bargain struck, in contrast with our last case, Russia.

Russian federalism dates back to the expanding Russian Empire, but its more recent antecedent is federalism under the Soviet Union. Officially, the Soviets created the largest federal system in the world, consisting of fifteen separate soviet "republics," of which Russia itself was only one; numerous smaller divisions also existed within the Russian Republic. Soviet federalism was elaborate, but absolute control by the Communist Party gave the republics and smaller political units no real autonomy. Local rulers, appointed by the central party, were able to run their governments more or less as personal fiefdoms, but they could not challenge or question central authority if a conflict between the center and the region arose. Federalism in any real sense cannot exist in an authoritarian system as centrally controlled as that present under Soviet communism. The collapse of the Soviet Union involved the separation of the fifteen republics into fifteen sovereign countries. The Russian Republic became a federation, though new and weak institutions have made it a rather ineffective one in terms of horizontal accountability vis-à-vis the center and effective governance.

The Russian constitution of 1993 created an asymmetrical federal system with eighty-nine subnational units ranging in size from republics to two federal cities (Moscow and St. Petersburg). The status of republic is given to areas deemed ethnically non-Russian. The boundaries of these, however, are rather arbitrary. At the time of the constitution, the titular ethnic group constituted a majority of the population in only seven of the twenty-one republics. For example, in 2002 Karelians were only 9 percent of the population of the Karelia republic, Udmurts were 29 percent of Udmurtia, and Khakas made up 12 percent of Khakassia. Republics do have noticeably more power than other federal units, including more power over state property and trade. The constitution, though, gives by far the greatest powers to the central government, reserving only a handful of powers for joint national-local control, and no powers are reserved exclusively for subnational governments.

The central government also has the greatest taxation powers: in 2001 it collected 85 percent of all revenue. The constitution and a federative treaty signed the year before were efforts on the part of Russia's first post-Communist president, Boris Yeltsin, to gain control over a chaotic situation in which numerous territories were declaring themselves republics or even claiming complete sovereignty in the aftermath of the 1991 collapse of the Soviet state.

While Russia appears to be a highly centralized system, its operation in practice has been less so. Chechnya's demand for independence from Russia encouraged all the republics and even some smaller units to push for greater autonomy. Chechnya has long been a sore spot for Russia. Stalin forcibly removed its mainly Muslim population to Siberia in the 1950s, and its demand for independence led to two wars between Russia and Chechen rebels. Today, it remains under Russian rule, under the control of a Russian-backed government with little popular support and continued rebel opposition.

No other large-scale violence has occurred in Russia's federal system, but the Chechen conflict nonetheless prompted the central government to find ways to accommodate demands for local autonomy. Between 1993 and 1998, demands from various republics and other subnational units led Yeltsin to sign separate bilateral treaties with more than half of the country's eighty-nine separate governments. In the case of Tatarstan, the republic gained the power to make separate treaties with foreign powers. This essentially allows it to pursue its own foreign policy, especially in economic areas, as long as these policies don't conflict with Russian foreign policy. While the laws of each of the federal units are supposed to comply with the national constitution, a recent study found that more than half violated that rule, some quite intentionally. Given that until 2004 each republic was governed by an elected president and elected legislatures, Kathryn Stoner-Weiss (2004) argues that these local officials "[are] the undisputed boss of any given region."

Russian presidents have attempted to overcome these centrifugal tendencies by various means. Before the constitution was signed, Yeltsin created the position of presidential representative to be the "eyes and ears" of the Russian president in each of the eighty-nine federal units. However, he left the powers of these representatives rather vague; many became active in local corruption while doing little to assert greater central authority. Vladimir Putin, Yeltsin's successor, reorganized this office, establishing just seven presidential representatives over superdistricts that together covered all the federal units. The constitutionality of these new representatives, who seem to be a new layer of government in Russia's federalism that is not in the constitution, has been questioned by many. Nonetheless, they have succeeded bringing republic and other subnational laws more in line with the national constitution.

In 2004 Putin introduced a second round of reforms that allowed him to appoint governors and up to half of the upper house of parliament, thereby further centralizing what was already a centralized system of federalism. This was part of his effort to transform Russia from a weak democracy to a semi-authoritarian state in which he and his allies had an effective monopoly on power. Federalism under the chaotic democracy of the 1990s was institutionally weak and fragmented by an extreme asymmetry based on Yeltsin's individual deals with the republics and other subnational regions, but it was federalism nonetheless. As we noted earlier, it's difficult to have real federalism without democracy; even the semi-authoritarian rule of the sort Putin created requires enough centralization that any significant federalism is a threat the ruling elite will want to eliminate, as happened in Russia.

CONCLUSION

As our final case study shows, institutions that are structurally the same can exist in very different social, economic, and political contexts. The same type of institution can even exist in both democratic and authoritarian regimes. For instance, a recent study classifies twenty-three countries as nonelectoral democracies with semipresidential systems, the same as the number of semipresidential countries classified as free electoral democracies (Elgie 2006). It's difficult to imagine what semipresidentialism looks like in practice in a country that's not an electoral democracy, just as it's difficult to imagine how federalism would work effectively there, but in fact, Russia today is an example of a country with both institutions that as of 2007 was not classified as a democracy by Freedom House. Comparativists can never assume that the presence or absence of a particular institution implies something about a country's politics, but rather they must examine how a particular institution functions in a given country.

Political scientists and policymakers, however, want to know whether some institutions are more conducive to certain outcomes than others. They hope to learn from experience whether particular institutions strengthen democracy, promote a better balance of power, or protect the rights of minorities. We can see blueprints of how institutions might achieve such ends in principle. For example, judicial review should check the executive and protect minority rights, and federalism should have a democratizing effect by decentralizing power. Analysis of institutions in the abstract can only take us so far, however. We need to look for patterns of where particular types of institutions exist and how they correlate with things like executive use or abuse of power, protection of civil rights, or efficient and honest policymaking.

Asking these kinds of questions often leads us to note that some types of institutions appear to function better in certain contexts than in others. We've already referred to the debate about why presidentialism, which seems to work quite well in the United States, seems to be more trouble-prone elsewhere in the world. Political scientists comparing institutions across countries want to know whether political culture, economic or other structural conditions, or other variables affect the way a particular institution works. They may also conclude, as Cheibub (2007) did regarding presidentialism, that in some contexts the institutional choice doesn't matter much to outcomes. Rather than one institutional structure being "better" than another, it may be that in some contexts no institution is able to function effectively or overcome the barriers to consolidating democracy, for instance.

Our cases also suggest that wholesale change of institutions is difficult and extremely unusual. Countries certainly seem prone to follow what they know, as the examples of Britain's former colonies suggests. Nonetheless, political scientists continue to debate the merits of various institutional choices and the context for their effectiveness, because historic occasions for choice do arise, and countries want to learn from each other's experiences. It's rare for a country to decide as France did that a complete change of structures is in order, but countries transitioning to

COUNTRY AND CONCEPT Snapshot of Governing Institutions

COUNTRY	EXECUTIVE-LEGISLATIVE SYSTEM	JUDICIAL SYSTEM		FEDERAL SYSTEM	BUREAUCRACY Corruption[1] (scale of 1-10; 10 = least corrupt)
		Type of legal system	Right of judicial review		
Brazil	presidential	code law	Yes	symmetric federalism	3.5
China	NA	code law	No	unitary	3.5
Germany	parliamentary	code law	Yes	symmetric federalism	7.8
India	parliamentary	common law	Yes	assymetric federalism	3.5
Iran	semipresidential (authoritarian)	Islamic *shariah*	No	unitary	2.5
Japan	parliamentary	code law	Yes	unitary	7.5
Nigeria	presidential	common law and *shariah*	Yes	symmetric federalism	2.2
Russia	semipresidential	code law	Yes (but weak)	assymetric federalism	2.3
United Kingdom	parliamentary	common law	No	unitary	8.4
United States	presidential	common law	Yes	symmetric federalism	7.2

[1] Transparency International, Corruption Perception Index, 2007.

democracy face this choice as they write new constitutions. Brazil, for example, seriously debated switching to a parliamentary system in the 1990s, although it ultimately rejected this option. More common is tinkering to improve a system at the margins: borrowing anticorruption policies to improve the bureaucracy's functioning, for instance, or delegating more authority to regions within a unitary system. Countries may rarely be able to change things completely, but they constantly adjust institutions in an effort to achieve their ends, whether these are greater stability and central control or greater representation and more local democracy. Sometimes such change comes about at the behest of a leader, as when De Gaulle developed semipresidentialism to strengthen his control over an unruly political system. Democratic participation can also result in change, however, as people strive to make their voices more clearly heard. We examine institutions and avenues of participation in the next chapter.

Key Concepts

amakudari (p. 233)
assymetrical federal system
  (p 241)
bicameral legislature (p. 208)
coalition government (p. 205)
code law (p. 223)
cohabitation (p. 218)
collective responsibility (p. 207)
common law (p. 223)
executive (p. 202)
head of government (p. 203)
head of state (p. 203)
horizontal accountability (p. 202)

iron triangles (p. 233)
judicial independence (p. 225)
judicial review (p. 223)
judiciary (p. 202)
legislative oversight (p. 230)
legislature (p. 202)
member of parliament (MP)
  (p. 204)
New Public Management (NPM)
  (p. 231)
parliamentarism (p. 204)
political accountability (p. 201)
political appointees (p. 230)

presidentialism (p. 204)
prime minister (PM) (p. 204)
principal-agent problem (p. 230)
rent-seeking (p. 232)
semipresidentialism (p. 204)
separation of powers (p. 211)
stare decisis (p. 223)
symmetrical federal system
  (p. 241)
unitary systems (p. 238)
vertical accountability (p. 201)
vote of no confidence (p. 205)

Works Cited

Amoretti, Ugo. M., and Bermeo, Nancy. G. 2004. *Federalism and Territorial Cleavages.* Baltimore: Johns Hopkins University Press.

Cheibub, Jose Antonio. 2007. *Presidentialism, Parliamentarism, and Democracy.* New York: Cambridge University Press.

Chinn, Stuart. 2006. "Democracy-Promoting Judicial Review in a Two-Party System: Dealing with Second-Order Preferences." *Polity* 38, no. 4: 478–500.

Dahl, Robert. 1957. "Decision-Making in a Democracy: The Supreme Court as a National Policy-Maker." *Journal of Public Law* 6: 279–294.

Ekeh, Peter. 1975. "Colonialism and the Two Publics in Africa: A Theoretical Statement." *Comparative Studies in Society and History* 17: 91–112.

Elgie, Robert. 2006. "A Fresh Look at Semipresidentialism: Variations on a Theme." *Journal of Democracy* 16, no. 3 (July): 98–112.

Freedom House. 2007. Democracies. www.freedomhouse.org.

Gibson, James, et al. 1998. "On the Legitimacy of National High Courts." *American Political Science Review* 92, no. 2: 343–358.

Johnston, Michael. 2005. *Syndromes of Corruption: Wealth, Power, and Democracy.* New York: Cambridge University Press.

Kohli, Atul. 2004. "India: Federalism and the Accommodation of Ethnic Nationalism." In *Federalism and Territorial Cleavages*, ed. Ugo M. Amoretti and Nancy G. Bermeo, 281–300. Baltimore: Johns Hopkins University Press.

Landfried, Christine. 1995. "Germany." In *The Global Expansion of Judicial Power,* by C. Neal Tate and Torbjörn Vallindar. New York: New York University Press.

Leeke, Matthew, et al. 2003. *An Introduction to Devolution in the UK.* Research Paper 03/84, 17 November. House of Commons Library.

Linz, Juan. 1990. "The Perils of Presidentialism." *Journal of Democracy* 1, no. 1 (Winter 1990): 51–69.

Mulgan, Aurelia. 2002. *Japan's Failed Revolution: Koizumi and the Politics of Economic Reform.* Canberra, Australia: Asia Pacific Press.

O'Donnell, Guillermo. 1999. "Horizontal Accountability in New Democracies." In *The Self-Restraining State: Power and Accountability in New Democracies,* ed. Andreas Schedler, Larry Diamond, and Marc F. Plattner, 29–52. Boulder, Colo.: Lynne Rienner Publishers.

O'Dwyer, Conor. 2006. *Runaway State-Building: Patronage Politics and Democratic Development.* Baltimore: Johns Hopkins University Press.

Pempel, T. J. 2000. *Regime Shift: Comparative Dynamics of the Japanese Political Economy.* Ithaca: Cornell University Press.

Raor, M. Gopvinda and Nirviker Singh. 2005. *Political Economy of Federalism in India.* Oxford: Oxford University Press.

Riker, William. 1964. *Federalism: Origin, Operation, Significance.* Boston: Little, Brown.

Santiso, Carlos. 2003. "Economic Reform and Judicial Governance in Brazil: Balancing Independence with Accountability." *Democratization* 10, no. 4 (November 2003): 161–180.

Stoner-Weiss, Kathryn. 2004. "Russia: Managing Territorial Cleavages under Dual Transitions." *Federalism and Territorial Cleavages,* ed. Ugo M. Amoretti and Nancy G. Bermeo, 301–326. Baltimore: Johns Hopkins University Press.

Tate, C. Neal, and Torbjörn Vallindar. 1995. *The Global Expansion of Judicial Power.* New York: New York University Press.

Vanberg, Georg S. 2005. *The Politics of Constitutional Review in Germany.* Cambridge, UK: Cambridge University Press.

Resources for Further Study

Cappelletti, Mauro, Paul J. Kollmer, and Joanne M. Olson. 1989. *The Judicial Process in Comparative Perspective.* Oxford: Clarendon Press.

Fearon, James. 2003. "Ethnic and Cultural Diversity by Country." *Journal of Economic Growth* 8: 195–222.

Forum of Federations. www.forumfed.org.

Frederickson, H. George, and Kevin B. Smith. 2003. *The Public Administration Theory Primer.* Boulder, Colo.: Westview Press.

Graber, Mark A. 2005. "Constructing Judicial Review." *American Review of Political Science* 8: 425–451.

Herron, Erik S., and Kirk A. Randazzo. 2003. "The Relationship between Independence and Judicial Review in Post-Communist Courts." *Journal of Politics* 65, no. 2: 422–438.

Mainwaring, Scott, and Matthew Shugart, ed. 1997. *Presidentialism and Democracy in Latin America.* New York: Cambridge University Press.

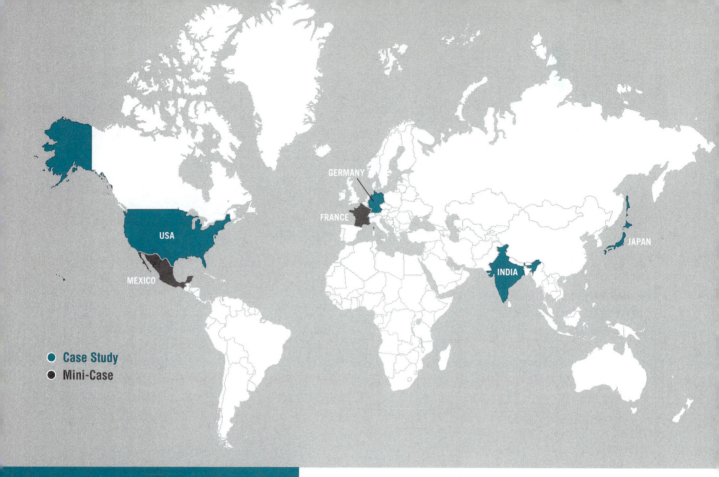

● **Case Study**
● **Mini-Case**

Who Rules?

- Do some types of institutions in democracies give greater power to political elites and others greater power to average citizens?

- How do formal and informal institutions affect the representation of ethnic, gender, religious, and other groups?

What Explains Political Behavior?

- Why do people join political parties and participate in other kinds of political activity?

- How do different types of institutions affect the extent and type of representation and participation of average citizens?

Where and Why?

- When and where do different types of informal institutions develop? Are there clear patterns for when and where particular types of formal institutions (party and electoral systems) develop as well?

POLITICAL INSTITUTIONS:
Participation and Representation

This chapter examines the institutions that shape political participation and interest representation in democracies. Virtually all regimes allow some degree of participation and representation, if only because these play a valuable role in shoring up legitimacy, or at least the appearance of it. Regimes differ dramatically, however, in the degree to which they seek to control and limit both. Democratic regimes all claim to value and promote widespread participation and representation, but differ significantly in regard to the "best" ways to promote citizen involvement and fair and accurate representation of interests. In general, democratic regimes face the problem of stimulating and channeling participation and representation, whereas authoritarian regimes are more interested in constraining or co-opting it. Because participation and representation are vital to and hallmarks of democratic regimes, we discuss the relevant institutions in these regimes first. In chapter 8, we make comparisons with the same kinds of institutions in authoritarian regimes.

We might imagine that the biggest problems regarding participation and representation occur in nondemocratic regimes seeking to suppress or severely limit these activities, but democratic regimes face their own participation problems. Although no regime wants unstructured, unfettered participation, democratic institutions need to help citizens overcome **collective action problems**. Rational actor theorists argue that most people most of the time have no rational reason to participate in political activity, including voting, because they cannot influence the outcome of the process to any significant degree. Expending time or money to work toward any political goal is irrational, given the huge number of citizens and therefore the correspondingly small impact of each individual. This means that members of the elite, with their much greater direct access to key decision makers, have a greater incentive to participate, which presents obvious problems for a liberal democracy based on the alleged equality and participation of all citizens. Institutions of participation and representation provide channels through which individuals might find it worthwhile to participate, whether alone or with like-minded people, to represent their views to or in the government. How these institutions overcome collective action problems is the final major question we address in this chapter.

A country's formal political institutions—electoral systems and political parties and party systems—reveal much about how that country defines and how much it values participation and representation. **Electoral systems** are formal, legal mechanisms that translate votes into control over political offices and shares of political power. Different electoral systems provide distinct incentives to individual voters and even influence voter turnout. They also affect political parties and their leaders, which in turn affect voter choice and influence. Political parties are associations that seek to formally control government. In democracies, parties seek to control the government via elections and are limited in what they can do once they gain control. They also serve as a component in **interest aggregation**, bringing together a number of discrete interests into a coalition of broadly shared interests, which enhances the power of individual votes by aggregating them and potentially overcomes the collective action dilemma. The number of parties and each one's respective strength as an institution constitute a **party system**. Electoral systems influence party strength and number and are crucial to understanding how individual parties function and what constraints on and opportunities for citizen participation they provide. Understanding electoral systems, parties, and party systems helps us understand how broadly and inclusively a country promotes participation and which interests and groups receive more representation and which receive less. They also help us answer the question we already posed in chapter 6: Is there a trade-off between effective policymaking on the one hand and active citizen participation and representation on the other?

A great deal of participation and interest representation also occurs in civil society, the sphere of organized citizen activity between the state and the individual family or firm that we discussed in chapter 3. Today, the term "civil society" typically connotes interest groups, particularly in democracies. These associations of individuals attempt to influence government, and most claim to represent clearly defined interests that their members share, such as protecting the environment, advancing civil rights, or representing various industries. They are formally organized, though their degree of institutionalization varies widely. They also are often regulated by the government and have to follow rules and procedures to be recognized as legitimate. Well-institutionalized interest groups are visible, have relatively large and active memberships, and have a significant voice in the public policy area or areas in which they are interested. Less institutionalized groups are less effective, and their legitimacy as representatives on various issues is often questioned. Similar to parties, interest groups join together like-minded individuals to achieve a goal, but interest groups do not seek formal political power.

When citizens perceive formal institutions as providing inadequate representation or opportunities for political participation, they may choose to participate in groups or activities outside of them. Such nonformal participation often occurs through **social movements**. Like interest groups, these are part of civil society, but unlike them, social movements have a loosely defined organizational structure and represent people who have been outside the bounds of formal institutions, seek major socioeconomic or political changes to the status quo, or employ non-institutional forms of collective action. Perhaps the best-known of these in recent history is the American civil rights movement of the 1950s and 1960s. In the 1960s, social movements arose throughout Western democracies that were aimed at changing women's status, protecting the environment, and opposing war. These movements brought a new generation of activists into politics, changed significant elements of Western societies, and fundamentally altered the way citizens have engaged in politics ever since. Sometimes social movements generate formal interest groups, but rarely does an interest group or broader movement become a political party. An exception is the European "green" movement, which eventually produced Green Parties with representation in a number of European legislatures.

A second type of informal participation is undoubtedly the most widespread: patron-client linkages. Like all informal participation, these are most important where formal institutions are weakest or most restrictive. This means that they are usually most important in authoritarian regimes, but they certainly exist in democracies, and are quite important in some, as the following cases studies on Japan and India demonstrate.

Here, members of the German Green Party demand greater use of solar and other alternative fuel sources. The party grew out of Germany's environmental movement, going from social movement to interest group to political party, and it was part of the governing coalition from 1998 to 2005.

Patron-client politics sound very undemocratic, or at least threatening to democracy, to Westerners. However, in the absence of other effective means of participation and representation, forming a relationship with a patron may be the best option available for having a voice and getting government help.

We now turn to an examination of each of the major institutions, formal and informal, that structure and constrain participation and representation in modern democracies: electoral systems, parties and party systems, and interest groups and social movements.

FORMAL INSTITUTIONS: THE ELECTORAL SYSTEM

Electoral rules and practices shape political participation by prescribing who votes, when, and by what mechanisms. They are also a means of representation, because while all types of regimes have executives and bureaucracies, electoral systems are a hallmark of democratic regimes. A truly democratic electoral system enfranchises a large portion of the population and permits a variety of choices.

Democracies differ, however, about what best promotes the voice and representation of their citizens, and each chooses rules that give some individual citizens a voice while limiting the voice of others. The clearest examples are rules for enfranchisement. No democracy permits every citizen to vote: in the past, women, certain racial and ethnic groups, illiterates, and nonproperty holders were groups that were commonly excluded. Countries still differ about the age at which citizens acquire their democratic "voice" and rights: historically, most chose the age of twenty-one. A global trend toward lowering the voting age emerged in the 1970s, and today most countries confer the right to vote at age eighteen. Lively debates occasionally still erupt about whether the age should be lower (Great Britain considered lowering it to sixteen in 2004, and Austria became the first EU country to lower the age to sixteen in 2007) or higher (Iran raised its previously uniquely low voting age of fifteen to eighteen in 2007). Brazil, Cuba, and a few other countries have set their voting age at sixteen.

In almost all elections, enfranchised citizens vote for people who will represent them, rather than vote directly on policy. This raises a key issue in all electoral systems: How are votes aggregated and counted? Countries make quite different decisions about what "good" representation looks like when they make this basic decision. One common way is to represent people by where they live: a country may divide its national territory into geographic units and give each unit one or more representatives. So even if you didn't vote for your representative and you disagree with him or her, that representative is still expected to work for you (as U.S. representatives often do by solving Social Security problems or writing letters of nomination to service academies). More important, your most vital needs and interests are assumed to have been aggregated into those of your district.

In contrast, some countries elect their legislatures nationally, and representation comes from the representatives of the party voters supported, though they may be from another part of the country. Voters' views and needs have been aggregated into those of the party they support. In this case, what's important is that beliefs, rather than personal or regional interests, are represented. Rarely do democratic countries choose to represent specific groups within society rather than or in addition to geographic districts or parties. However, after an ethnic conflict, for instance, a country may decide it needs to ensure special representation for ethnic minorities. Several African countries have legally reserved seats in parliament specifically for women to ensure that they are represented.

Thinking about the dramatically different options available can lead us to ponder interesting normative questions about good representation. On what basis do we wish to be represented, and with whom do we share our most important political interests or views? Each electoral system discussed below answers these questions differently. The answers affect participation as well, making these answers crucial decisions in any democracy.

In addition, electoral institutions often have other important effects on governance. Their impact on the party composition of legislatures and the relationship between ruling legislative and executive parties mean that they interact with other institutions to affect the stability and effectiveness of a government. Familiar examples of gridlock in American politics or the legendary instability of Italian parliamentary regimes after World War II illustrate this. These problems do not result from presidential or parliamentary systems per se, but rather from the ways these institutions interact with the electoral system. Systems that encourage many, fragmented parties provide representation of diverse views in the legislature but may make effective government difficult because of the instability of coalition governments in parliamentary systems or the gridlock of different parties controlling the executive and legislative branches in presidential systems.

Single-Member Districts: "First-Past-the-Post" and Majoritarian Voting

Americans borrowed the idea of the **single-member district** from Great Britain. In both countries, each geographic district elects a single representative. Whoever gets the most votes—a **plurality**—becomes the district representative. In a race with multiple contestants, the winner can be elected with a relatively low percentage of the vote total: 30 percent or so is not uncommon. This system is often called **"first-past-the-post"** (**FPTP**) because, as in a horse race, the single winner merely needs to edge out the next closest competitor. Some countries vary this system by requiring the winner to gain an absolute *majority* of the votes rather than a plurality. In **majoritarian systems**, if no candidate wins an absolute majority (50 percent plus one), a second election takes place between the top two candidates to achieve a majority win.

First-past-the-post can give constituents a strong sense of identification with their representative, even if they did not vote for that person. This may explain why most Americans famously dislike Congress but love their own representative. They may feel the member is "from" their district or constituency and therefore understands them and their needs. In other ways, however, FPTP may not be good for representation and participation. First, many votes are wasted, especially in plurality systems with multiple parties. Perhaps only 30 or 35 percent of voters actually favored the winner, so the votes of the majority of the voters were arguably wasted, because their preferences and views may not be represented at all. It is a "winner-take-all" system in which the winner does not necessarily reflect the preferences of the majority of the people. This may be one reason that voter participation tends to be lower in countries with FPTP than elsewhere. Voters—especially those who prefer minor party or weaker party alternatives—may have less incentive to overcome the collective action problem and find it a waste of time to vote at all.

Second, this problem can be compounded by the under- or overrepresentation of particular parties. Consider a case in which a third party wins a significant share of the votes in many districts, but a plurality in only one or two: it won a lot of votes, but only gets a couple of seats in the legislature. Conversely, if a large number of candidates from a particular party win by a very small plurality in their districts, that party's vote in the legislature will be inflated. The number of its representatives will suggest an overwhelming national consensus, when in fact the party may not have even won a majority of the vote nationwide. Table 7.1 gives an example from Great Britain's 2005 election, in which the two major parties won similar vote shares, but very different numbers of seats. Does this constitute a good representation of the voting public? According to proponents of FPTP it does, but others argue that the voice of a large segment of the electorate is ignored. On the other hand, a supermajority may promote efficient, stable policymaking by allowing decisive legislative action. This is one reason some proponents prefer FPTP, despite its wasted votes, to the primary alternative, proportional representation.

TABLE 7.1 **Results of the 2005 UK Parliamentary Election**

Party	Total Votes	% Votes	% Seats	Seats
Labour	9,562,122	35.3	55.2	356
Conservative	8,772,598	32.3	30.7	198
Liberal Democrat	5,981,874	22.1	9.6	62

Source: http://news.bbc.co.uk/2/hi/uk_news/politics/vote_2005/constituencies/default.stm.

Proportional Representation

Proportional representation (PR) differs from FPTP in almost every conceivable way. In PR, representatives are often chosen nationally rather than on the basis of single-member districts. Alternatively, a country adopting PR may create large electoral districts and give each district multiple representatives. What this means is that either a national legislature is simply divided on a purely proportional basis or multiple representatives for large districts are allocated proportionally according to the vote in each district. So, for instance, a party that gains 25 percent of the national vote receives a quarter (or very nearly a quarter) of the seats in the legislature. There usually is some sort of cut-off line, though: in most PR systems a party must cross a minimal electoral threshold—for example, 3 or 5 percent of the vote—to gain representation in parliament. Any parties that cross that threshold can be certain that they will be represented. As Table 7.2 demonstrates for the 2006 Swedish parliamentary elections, a PR system translates each party's share of the votes into almost exactly the same share of legislative seats.

If voters are not choosing among individuals running for a single seat, whom or what are they voting for and who ends up in the legislature? The answer re-flects a very different view of representation from FPTP, because in PR systems, the voter is usually voting for a *party*, not an individual. In **closed-list proportional representation** (the version of PR most dissimilar to FPTP), each party presents a ranked list of candidates for all the seats in the legislature. Voters can see the list and know who the "top" candidates are, but when they vote they are actually voting for the party. This means that if party X gets ten seats in the legislature, then the top ten candidates on the party list occupy those seats.

TABLE 7.2 Results of Sweden's 2006 Parliamentary Election

Parties and Coalitions	Votes %	Total Seats %
Swedish Social Democratic Party (*Arbetarepartiet-Socialdemokraterna*)	34.99	37.2
Moderate Party (*Moderata Samlingspartiet*)	26.23	27.8
Centre Party (*Centerpartiet*)	7.88	8.3
Liberal People's Party (*Folkpartiet Liberalerna*)	7.54	8.0
Christian Democrats (*Kristdemokraterna*)	6.59	6.8
Left Party (*Vänsterpartiet*)	5.85	6.3
Green Party (*Miljöpartiet de Gröna*)	5.24	5.4
Sweden Democrats (*Sverigedemokraterna*)	2.93	±0

Source: http://electionresources.org/se/riksdag.php?election=2006.

Another variant of PR is called **open-list proportional representation**. In this version, voters are presented with a list and may actually mark the ballot for the particular candidate of their choice. When the votes are counted, each party receives a number of seats based on the total number of votes cast for all candidates from that party. The seats are then awarded to the top individual vote-getters within the party.

PR assumes that voters primarily want the ideas and values they share to be represented. Voters, in theory, feel they are represented by the party they support and its actions in the legislature, regardless of the geographic origins of individual legislators. This has some obvious advantages over FPTP. First, there are very few wasted votes, because even very small parties can gain some seats. To the extent that voters feel represented by a party, they can be assured that someone in the legislature is there to give voice to their views—although realistically, smaller parties

WHERE AND WHY Women in Power

On January 4, 2007, Rep. Nancy Pelosi, a Democrat from California, became the first woman elected Speaker of the U.S. House of Representatives. Her election came only about six weeks shy of the eighty-fifth anniversary of the passage of the Nineteenth Amendment (February 22, 1922), which gave women in the United States the right to vote. Americans are used to considering themselves rather progressive when it comes to women's rights, but one reason the first election of a woman Speaker took so long was that not many women are found at high levels of government in the United States. In 2008 only 16.8 percent of representatives and 16 percent of senators were women.

Those numbers put the United States slightly below average on a global scale, which in 2008 was about 18.2 percent of female elected representatives in national legislatures (lower house or single house). Americans can take heart at being close to average, but in fact the country lags well behind twenty-two countries where women comprise 30 percent or more of lower or single house legislatures, and another forty-six where they account for 20 percent. What explains these disparities in how many women achieve power at the national level?

An initial hypothesis might come out of political culture, because regional breakdowns seem to suggest that it plays a role. The famously progressive Scandinavians elect the most women (41.4 percent); followed by the Americas (21.6 percent); Europe, excluding Scandinavia (19.3 percent); Asia (18.4 percent); sub-Saharan Africa (17.2 percent); the Pacific (13.4 percent); and the Arab states (9.7 percent). These figures might be interpreted to suggest that countries with longer histories of feminism and more secular societies are culturally more receptive to electing women. When we look at particular cases, however, we can ask whether this pattern holds up. For example, why does the United States lag behind the Americas' regional average? Why does it elect fewer women than Bolivia, Ecuador, or Costa Rica—all countries that enfranchised women later than the United States and have arguably less "feminist" cultures?

An alternative and persuasive hypothesis is that election of women is a case in which institutions matter. Overall, proportional representation systems are more conducive to electing women than are majoritarian systems. Of the more than sixty countries above the world average in 2007, only eight used a first-past-the-post electoral system, and thirty-seven FPTP countries elected less than the average percentage of women legislators. More evidence to support this hypothesis comes from countries that use semiproportional, or mixed, electoral systems. Data from Germany and New Zealand in the mid-1990s, for example, show that the percentage of women elected from single-member districts was around the U.S. average, whereas the percentage elected from PR lists was closer to Scandinavian levels.

Why would PR systems be more conducive to electing women? First, the more women are nominated, the more they win. Since PR systems require parties to submit lists of candidates, sometimes for multimember districts, more women are nominated. Second, a party may be under some inherent pressure to include at least some women on its list, since an all-male (or even overwhelmingly male) list would invite voter scrutiny and possible (negative) reaction. Finally, a quota system (a national requirement that parties run a certain percentage of women candidates) is easier to implement in a PR system than in a single-member district system, especially one as decentralized as that found in the United States. When a country uses a quota to increase the number of women nominated, more are elected. In fact, one reason the regional average for the Americas is higher than the U.S. average is that a number of Central and South American countries adopted PR systems, quotas for women, or both when they returned to democracy in the 1990s after periods of military rule. Increased representation of women may not be an intended effect of a PR system, but it is an example of how institutional choices can matter to political outcomes.

Source: Inter-Parliamentary Union, "Women in National Parliaments," World Classification Table, www.ipu.org/wmn-e/classif.htm. Based on figures for lower or single house.

can usually only impact policy significantly when they act in coalition with larger parties. Second, perhaps because fewer votes are wasted, participation rates in PR countries are higher, as Figure 7.1 shows. Proponents of PR argue that elections are therefore more democratic and more broadly representative, since larger percentages of voters participate. PR systems also tend to elect women and members of ethnic or racial minorities more frequently than FPTP systems do, as party leaders often feel compelled (in some countries they are required to by law) to include women or minority candidates on their party lists.

Of course, the system has its critics who point to the "indirect" nature of PR elections: voters don't really choose individual representatives, even in an open-list system. And in a closed-list system, party officials are the ultimate arbiters of a candidate's fate because they created the ranking. In addition, while representation of a broad range of parties in a legislature can be seen as a plus, opponents argue that in practice it often becomes a negative. Small parties, as noted above, often have little voice anyway, unless they join coalitions, but small extremist parties can gain inordinate power if they are able to bargain to be key players in these coalitions. Israel was for many years a classic example of this: small, religious parties were crucial for establishing coalitions in its parliament, the *Knesset*, and influenced policy far beyond their numbers because of their advantageous bargaining position. Coalitions can be hard to form in such a fragmented environment, and where they do form, they may be unstable. PR, therefore, is often criticized as leading to governmental instability and ineffective, fragmented policymaking.

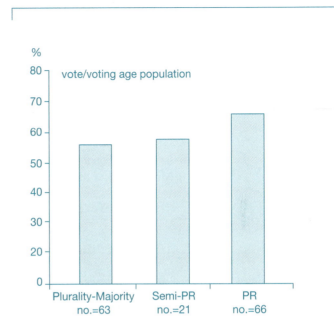

FIGURE 7.1
What Affects Turnout?

Source: International Institute for Democracy and Electoral Assistance, "What Effects Turnout?" Figure 24, www.idea.int/vt/survey/voter_turnout8.cfm.
Note: no. = number of elections

Semiproportional, or Mixed, Systems

Given the plusses and minuses of FPTP and PR, it is not surprising that some countries, most notably Germany and Russia, have chosen to combine the two. The resulting hybrid is called a **mixed**, or **semiproportional, representation system**. A mixed system combines single-member district representation with overall proportionality. Voters cast ballots for a representative from their district, and the winner is the individual who gains a plurality. At the same time, voters are also asked to vote for a party list. The legislature is then composed by first awarding seats to all the district representatives; the party lists are then used to adjust and add members until each party gets approximately its proportionate share of the vote. So, for example, a very small party that crosses the 5 percent threshold might send one or two representatives from its list to the legislature even though none of its candidates for individual district seats was elected. On the other hand, a large party that narrowly sweeps quite a few seats might gain only a few more from its list when proportional representation is factored in. At the end of the day, the party composition of the legislature looks much as it would had it been chosen based strictly on PR, but each district is also guaranteed its own, individual representative, as in a single-member FPTP system.

Mixed systems therefore share some of the advantages of FPTP and PR systems. Because there are few wasted votes, participation rates tend to be slightly

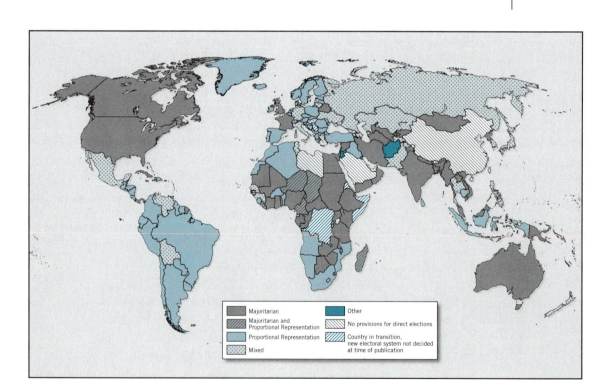

MAP 7.1
World Electoral Systems

Source: Data from Richard W. Soudriette and Andrew Ellis, "Electoral Systems Today: A Global Snapshot," *Journal of Democracy* 17, no. 2 (April 2006): 80–81.

higher as in PR (see Figure 7.1), yet citizens are also guaranteed a personal representative to whom they can appeal. In addition, the single-district component of semiproportional systems tends to reinforce the dominance of a couple of large parties that find it easier to win a significant number of individual seats. Small parties also form and are represented, but the dominance of a couple of major parties facilitates coalition formation and stability.

Summary

Majoritarian systems give preference to representation based on geography, as opposed to representation based on ideology that PR systems favor. Geographical representation means citizens can know specifically who "their" representative is and hold him or her accountable at election time. PR systems, on the other hand, represent ideological divisions in society. Given the importance of ideological beliefs in influencing how people vote in modern democracies, PR systems may well represent more important social divisions than majoritarian systems do. PR systems, however, do not give citizens a specific person who is "their own" representative. This is only one of the trade-offs the choice of electoral system entails. It can also have an important impact on two other formal institutions, political parties and party systems.

FORMAL INSTITUTIONS: POLITICAL PARTIES AND PARTY SYSTEMS

American political scientist E. E. Schattschneider wrote that "modern democracy is unthinkable save in terms of the parties" (2003, 1). Parties perform important functions for any democracy, from mobilizing citizens to participate in the political process to recruiting and training political elites and organizing governments to providing strong opposition. As we noted in the definition, parties not only seek political office, they also perform the function of aggregating interests by collecting coalitions of like-minded or at least politically compatible supporters. This helps clarify and simplify voter choice, which facilitates representation. Political scientists compare parties and party systems based on their ideologies, internal organization, and the number of parties in a system. These differences have important implications for where and how citizens can participate in a party system and the extent to which diverse interests are represented in a legislature.

Political Parties

Party organizations and their respective relationships to their members vary widely. One of the foremost scholars of parties, French political scientist Maurice Duverger (1969), distinguished between cadre and mass parties. **Cadre parties** are collections of political elites who choose candidates and mobilize voters to support them. They have very small memberships, often start among elected politicians rather than in the broader society, and have memberships restricted to carefully selected elites personally known to current members. **Mass parties**, in sharp contrast, recruit as many members as possible who expect to have some control, from whom the parties gain financial support, labor, and votes. Many parties began as cadre parties catering to a small political elite in the nineteenth century or earlier, but Duverger argued that mass parties would become universal in wealthy industrialized society.

All parties in democracies must mobilize citizens to support them. How can they overcome the classic collective action problem—why should the average citizen choose to participate? Most people would answer that citizens join parties because they agree with their ideas: they join for ideological reasons. This is often the case, but it's certainly not the only reason. People also join parties to gain direct material benefits. The party machines in early twentieth-century U.S. cities, for example, offered preferential treatment for jobs or business contracts with city governments to party members. Most political scientists argue that material incentives are more typical in new democracies in which parties are relatively weak and in relatively poor economies that lack economic alternatives. In contemporary, postindustrial wealthy democracies, ideological reasons are most common. Joining a party can also come almost automatically from being a member of a particular group, as in the case of ethnically or religiously divided societies in which each group has its own party, or in the case of the Labour Party in Britain, which most union members automatically join via their union membership.

The size of their membership and the reasons citizens join them are important in determining the institutional strength or weakness of a country's parties. The relationship among members, political candidates, and campaign resources (mainly money) is also essential. Mass and cadre parties that offer members formal mechanisms to select candidates are likely to be stronger than those that select candidates outside formal party structures. Candidates are likely to be very loyal to the interests and demands of the party members who formally selected them and provided the bulk of their campaign resources, and a party's legislators are more likely to vote as a block in support of official party positions, as they do in Britain. In contrast, candidates in the United States raise most of their own campaign funds and gain the party nomination via a primary election of all registered voters in the party, not just formal party members who have paid dues and attended meetings. This means that candidates in the United States are much more independent of demands made by party leaders and members and that they act accordingly once in office; U.S. parties are less unified and weaker than many of their European counterparts for this reason.

Klaus von Beyme (1985) created the classic categorization of European parties based on their origins and ideologies. The most important of these are: Liberal, Conservative, Socialist/Social Democratic, Communist, Christian Democratic, Right-wing Extremist, and the Ecology movement. The origins and ideologies of these parties reflect the social and economic changes that characterized nineteenth-century Europe. For example, Conservative parties originated as cadre parties interested in defending the traditions and economic status of the landed elite against the liberals, who pressed for expanded rights for the bourgeoisie and the growth of market economies. Socialists and communists, meanwhile, tried to create mass parties to represent the interests of the emerging vast, but as yet disenfranchised, working class. The following text box explains each of von Beyme's categories in more detail.

These European ideologies influenced parties throughout the world, though each country has its own variations, including parties based on social divisions and ideas other than those derived in Europe. In Latin America, as in Europe, cadre parties emerged in the nineteenth century that pitted some type of Conservative Party favoring the landholding elite against liberals favoring reforms in the interest of industry and urbanization. Later, Socialist parties emerged as well. With industrialization, parties expanded their mass membership to some extent, though in many countries they remained rather weak, due in part to authoritarian (usually military) interruptions to the democratic process. Military governments banned or severely limited the freedom of political parties and eliminated elections, at least for a while. Parties had to reemerge and rebuild whenever democracy was restored.

Von Beyme's Categorization of Political Parties

CONSERVATIVES arose in the nineteenth century to represent the landed aristocracy and other rural supporters who opposed economic reform and industrialization. They favor a strong state, nationalism, and preservation of the status quo. In the late twentieth century they increasingly accepted free market ideas, coming closer to the ideology of the Republican Party in the United States.

CHRISTIAN DEMOCRATS emerged in the nineteenth century to represent Catholics in predominantly Protestant countries, but the party now appeals to Protestants as well. Their Christian ideologies led to a centrist position between Socialists and Conservatives on social welfare, combined with very conservative positions on social and moral issues.

LIBERALS emerged in eighteenth- and nineteenth-century Europe to represent the growing bourgeoisie interested in expanding their political rights vis-à-vis the aristocracy, a largely unfettered market, and limited social programs. These are the parties of classic liberalism described in chapter 3. Von Beyme classified both major U.S. parties as liberal.

SOCIALISTS/SOCIAL DEMOCRATS emerged in the nineteenth century from the working class and championed political rights for workers, improved working conditions, and expanded social welfare programs. After World War I, most Communists split off from the Socialists to align themselves with the Soviet Union and participated in elections only as a means to power. Most Socialists became Social Democrats who were still committed to representing workers' interests but also to electoral democracy. By the 1970s, "Eurocommunism" emerged, an ideology of Communist parties that retained the goal of eventually achieving a communist society but in the meantime worked within the electoral system to gain power and expand social welfare policies, often in alliance with Socialist parties.

EXTREMISTS of many types operate at both ends of the ideological spectrum. Right-wing extremists include European nationalist parties that began emerging in the 1980s. They believe in a strong state, articulate an ideology based on the concept of "national character," and want to severely limit immigration and instill "traditional values." Left-wing parties include ecology movement parties, such as the German Greens (see the German Case Study in the body of the text). They emerged out of the environmental social movement of the 1970s to try to gain representation for environmental issues in the legislature. They often support Socialist parties but with a stronger environmental commitment, even at the expense of economic growth or jobs, something Socialists typically are unwilling to sacrifice.

Populism developed as a distinct and powerful movement and ideological basis for parties in the mid-twentieth century in much of Latin America. Populists proclaimed a vaguely socialist ideology and gained support from urban workers. They also, however, were often close to the military and championed a strong sense of nationalism and a strong state, at times undermining democracy altogether in the name of state strength. Their policies were often based on a form of clientelism—populist rulers rewarded urban supporters with government services and infrastructure—rather than a systematic shift toward a more socialist society. Material incentives, then, remained an important reason to support populist parties, which in many countries were and remain weak.

Parties emerged as part of the nationalist, anticolonial movement in Asia and (especially) in Africa in the last decade of colonial rule. These were mass parties from the start, but often remained very weak, in part because they were so new. In addition, their only ideology was anticolonialism because their members did not agree on much else. Many, in reality, were collections of disparate leaders, each with a following based on patronage and ethnic identity, so that their deep factional divisions were not based so much on ideology as on personality or identity. After independence many of these parties fragmented, inviting military intervention. Alternatively, one faction would gain control, create a one-party state, and eliminate democracy. Either outcome eliminated real party competition by destroying or emasculating most parties. These would eventually reemerge in the 1990s as very weak institutions in new democracies, a subject we turn to in chapter 9.

Party Systems

Individual parties exist in party systems, which are categorized by the number of parties and their strength. By definition, democratic party systems include at least two parties, but there is variation beyond that. At one extreme is the **dominant party system**, in which multiple parties exist but one wins every election and governs continuously. In such a system, free and (more or less) fair elections take place following the electoral rules of the country, but one party is popular enough and dominant enough to win every election. In South Africa, for instance, the African National Congress, Nelson Mandela's party that led the struggle for liberation from the racist apartheid regime, has won each of the three subsequent elections, gaining a larger share of the vote in each. (It garnered just short of 70 percent in the 2004 election.) Numerous opposition parties do exist, and they have some seats in the legislature and are allowed to compete openly in the elections, but the ANC remains overwhelmingly popular. Such dominance can mean that the line can be thin between a dominant party system and a semi-authoritarian regime in which the dominant party maintains power not only via its popularity but also via manipulation of the electoral system and government resources and intimidation of other parties.

MINI-CASE Mexico

Like the ANC in South Africa, Mexico's PRI (Institutional Revolutionary Party) benefited from its connection to historic events to become the country's overwhelmingly dominant party. Whereas the ANC led the struggle against apartheid, the PRI was established and consolidated from an earlier "party of the revolution" by Lazáro Cárdenas, the great general of the Mexican Revolution who would later become president. (Cardenas dubbed it the PRM, or Party of the Mexican Revolution. His successor altered it slightly by eliminating military representation and renamed it the PRI in 1946). The PRI's corporatist structure—three sectors represent peasants, labor, and the "popular" sector—made it an ideal umbrella party, and it claimed legitimacy by representing the ideals of the revolution. With the support of the most organized sectors of the population and a high degree of legitimacy, the party quickly consolidated power, and it did not lose its grip on that power for more than fifty years.

As time went on, observers began to wonder if the PRI's ostensible popularity was the hallmark of a dominant party like the ANC or Japan's LDP or a sign of disguised authoritarianism. By the 1970s and early 1980s, it was clear that the PRI could no longer claim to be the dominant party in a democratic system, if it ever had been. Political scientists dubbed it a semi-authoritarian regime, arguing that although it never depended on outright authoritarian measures it certainly manipulated the system undemocratically. The PRI's main rival, the more conservative PAN (National Action Party), repeatedly boycotted elections and called for other protests against electoral fraud. There is no doubt that electoral fraud was responsible for the highly inflated vote counts of PRI presidents, and presidential elections, though contested, always resulted in a PRI landslide. For thirty years, PRI presidents were elected with near unanimity. In 1976 the PRI garnered 98.7 percent of the vote for president; even in 1982, two years into the economic crisis precipitated by Mexico's external debt, the PRI candidate won with a surprising 71.2 percent of the vote. Indeed, it was not until later in the 1980s that the PRI lost its first state governorship.

The extent to which the PRI manipulated the system became clearer as the PAN and other political forces pushed it toward gradual reform. By the late 1970s, the PRI had been pressured to reform the country's congress by allowing a certain number of seats for opposition parties that would be allocated on the basis of proportional representation. Soon, the party legalized some small political parties on the left as well in an attempt to dilute the opposition. As electoral competition increased, however, the extent of the electoral fraud became clearer. In 1988 Mexicans were stunned by a controversial election. The PRI candidate won with the lowest percentage to date (about 50 percent of the vote), but many people believed that a candidate from the left, Cuauhtémoc Cárdenas (son of PRI founder Lazáro Cárdenas) was the actual victor. At the same time, the PRI vote count was an obvious admission on the part of the party that its dominance was slipping.

The PRI hung on to the presidency through one more election, but its days of maintaining power through covert manipulation were over. Forced to truly compete, its real weakness became apparent. In

After the PRI lost its dominance, PAN candidates came to the fore in Mexican politics. Here, PAN chair and current president of Mexico Felipe Calderón speaks at a June 2008 press conference.

2000 for the first time in seventy-one years, the elected president was not from the PRI. He was Vicente Fox of the PRI's old rival, the PAN, which narrowly repeated its electoral victory in a contested election in 2006 in which the Democratic Revolution Party (PRD) alleged fraud. The PRI candidate came in third in that election, with less than a quarter of the vote, which was down from around 50 percent in the 1988 and 1994 elections, and down even from the approximately 36 percent the PRI candidate gained in 2000 loss.

Overall, Mexico's history shows how fine the line between dominant democratic party and semi-authoritarianism can be. Was there a time when the PRI was legitimately the dominant democratic party? Early in its history, carrying the cachet of the revolution and its legendary founder, its dominance may have been real (though allegations of fraud and intimidation date even to that period). As its support eroded over its many years of rule, however, the undemocratic basis of its dominance became increasingly clear.

In a **two party system**, only two parties are able to garner enough votes to win an election, though more may compete. The United Kingdom (UK) has long had such a system. In the nineteenth century, the Conservatives and Liberals vied for control, and one or the other always won. With the rise of labor unions, the Labour Party emerged and eventually became stronger than the Liberal Party, which did not win an election after 1922 and merged with the Social Democrats in the 1980s. Since the 1920s, the Labour Party and the Conservative Party have been the only two parties able to win a majority in a national election; a small but viable third party has always survived, though never ruled. In the United States, no third party has had significant representation in government since the Republicans first emerged in the 1850s. Third parties, such as Ross Perot's Reform Party during the presidential campaigns of the 1990s, arise to compete in particular elections, but never survive more than two elections as a political force of any significance.

In the oddly named **two and a half party system**, two large parties win the most votes but typically neither gains a majority, which requires a third (the "half" party) to join one of the major parties to form a legislative majority. The classic case, which we review below, is Germany. Finally, **multiparty systems** are those in which more than two parties could potentially win a national election and govern. Some of these, such as Italy, are similar to the two and a half party system in that two of the parties are quite large, and one of these large parties almost always wins the most votes, but neither is able to win a majority. This requires the large parties to form coalitions with any of several smaller parties in order to govern. In still other multiparty systems, three or four relatively equal parties regularly contend for power, with a legislative majority almost always requiring a coalition of at least two of them.

How and why did these different systems emerge and change over time in different countries? The explanations offered have usually been either sociological or institutional. Sociological explanations put forth that a party system reflects the society in which it emerges so that parties arise to represent the various interests that develop as self-conscious groups in particular societies. For instance, sociological theorists argue that the United States does not have a Socialist Party like those found in most European countries because labor unions have always been relatively weak in the United States and have not adopted socialist ideas. This difference, in turn, can be explained by the multi-ethnic nature of the immigrant society found in the United States or by the "frontier hypothesis," which advocates that socialism never developed because of expanding economic opportunities on the U.S. frontier. Further, Germany has a Christian Democratic Party and France does not because Catholics were a self-conscious minority in nineteenth-century Germany—overwhelmingly Catholic France did not need such a party, but the German Catholic minority did.

Sociological explanations of party systems argue that in societies with a wide array of strongly held interests, a democracy will produce a multiparty system to represent those interests. Institutionalists, on the other hand, argue that the broader institutional setting, especially a country's electoral system, greatly shapes both the number and strength of parties. Political leaders will respond rationally to the institutional constraints they face by creating the types of parties that will help them gain power in the system in which they operate. One such classic institutionalist argument is known as **Duverger's Law**, named after Maurice Duverger, who contended that the logic of electoral competition in FPTP electoral systems results in the survival of only two parties in the long term. Multiple parties are unlikely to survive because all political parties must gain a plurality (or majority if required) in a particular district to win that district's legislative seat. The successful parties will be those whose members realize their parties must have very broad appeal. Relying on a small, ideologically commited core group will yield no legislative seats. Over time, ambitious politicians realize the way to electoral victory is through the already established major parties rather than through trying to create a third one.

In contrast, PR systems create an incentive for small, focused parties to emerge. The German environmental movment was able to create a successful Green Party because even with a narrow focus the party could get enough votes to cross the minimum threshold and gain seats in parliament. Conversely, the UK does not have a strong Green Party because such a party cannot compete for a meaningful number of seats with Labour Party and the Conservatives. As mentioned above, semiproportional systems tend to produce a couple of dominant parties (they usually win the FPTP individual seats), but also allow for the emergence of smaller parties in the proportional voting.

MINI-CASE France and the Shift toward a Two-Party System

Maurice Duverger's native France provides a classic example of Duverger's Law at work, though the country's two-round system and multiparty heritage has meant that even there the law has not worked perfectly. Political instability plagued France's Third (1871–1940) and Fourth (1946–1958) Republics. Both suffered from constantly changing governing coalitions that each typically lasted only a few months. The country under both regimes was deeply divided along ideological lines. Every election put numerous parties into parliament, producing the unstable coalition governments. A crisis at the end of the Fourth Republic led to the creation of the Fifth Republic in 1958 (see Mini-Case on France in chapter 6), with its semipresidential system designed to end the instability. It has been quite successful in this regard, though not only because of the semipresidential system—a new electoral system has also had a significant impact.

The prior republics had PR systems, which facilitated the election of numerous parties into parliament. The constitution of the Fifth Republic created not only a strong presidency but also a two-round, majoritarian electoral system. For both legislative and presidential elections (after 1962), a first-round election would be open to all registered parties. The country was divided into single-member legislative districts similar to FPTP systems. If a candidate for a legislative district (or nationally for the presidency) wins a majority of the votes in the first round, he is duly elected. If not, a run-off election is held two weeks later between the top two candidates in the first round, producing a majority winner. This allows all of France's numerous parties to contest the first-round election. In each district in which a second round takes place, the losing parties usually support the candidate ideologically closest to them.

The result of this system was the creation of two "families" of ideologically similar parties, one on the left and one on the right, pledged to support each other in the second-round elections. In some cases, if they knew a particular candidate was very strong in a particular district, other candidates within a party fam-

ily might agree not to contest the first round to ensure the stronger candidate's victory. By the 1970s, each party family consisted of two significant parties, the Communists and the Socialists on the left and the Gaullists (political descendants of the Fifth Republic's founder, Charles de Gaulle) and Centrists on the right. Within each family, the two major parties were almost equally represented in the National Assembly, producing four major parties.

The first shift away from this came in the 1980s and 1990s, as the Communists became less popular, and the Socialists won the presidency for the first time in 1981. By 1988 the Socialists had nearly 90 percent of the seats won by the left as a whole. They still governed in a coalition with the Communists but were overwhelmingly dominant in that relationship. On the right, the two main parties survived longer, but once the Gaullist Jacques Chirac became president in 1995, his movement also became dominant, gaining nearly 90 percent of the seats controlled by the right. By 2007 the two largest parties, the Socialists on the left and the Gaullists on the right, controlled 88 percent of the seats in the National Assembly, compared to only 56 percent in 1973.

France's two-round electoral system has allowed numerous smaller parties to survive, though their share of real power has declined substantially. Smaller parties use the first round to gain the support of their ideologically committed followers, often as a form of protest vote against the two major parties. The most notable recent example was the far-right (most say racist), anti-immigrant National Front, whose presidential candidate shocked the country and the world by coming in second in the first round of the 2002 presidential election. (He won only 18 percent of the vote in the second round.)

Indeed, the major party families have seen their share of the vote in the first round of legislative elections decline over time as more people vote for small parties outside the mainstream. The logic of the majoritarian system, however, has meant that the two largest parties have come to control the lion's share of the legislative seats and have the only viable presidential candidates. While the smaller parties continue to exist and gain some legislative seats, Duverger's Law has mostly worked in his own country: the shift from PR to a majoritarian system has come close to producing a two-party system. This has helped provide much greater political stability than France had under earlier regimes, but some would argue it has diminished real representation of the country's ideologically diverse citizenry.

Summary

Parties and party systems have important implications for democratic rule. Duverger's model of the mass party has long been viewed as the most democratic, with its large membership base that has an active voice in party policies and candidate selection. Cadre parties, on the other hand, are sometimes able to gain people's votes as well. Is it somehow less "democratic" if a party led by a small elite gains widespread support among voters? Does it matter whether citizens are more involved in the daily workings of the party, or is approving or disapproving party actions via the ballot box enough? Cadre parties also tend to have more coherent ideologies that all members and leaders must abide by to maintain party status. A cadre party may allow less participation internally but be able to control its elected legislators more easily, thereby allowing easier policymaking. On the other hand, mass parties allow great internal participation, but perhaps at the expense of clear policy positions.

The number of parties influences both the type of parties that exist and the choices voters have. Majoritarian systems tend to encourage two party systems rath-

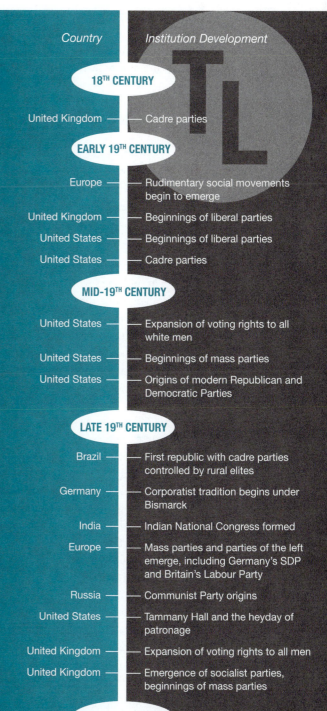

TIMELINE Political Institutions

Country	Institution Development
18TH CENTURY	
United Kingdom	Cadre parties
EARLY 19TH CENTURY	
Europe	Rudimentary social movements begin to emerge
United Kingdom	Beginnings of liberal parties
United States	Beginnings of liberal parties
United States	Cadre parties
MID-19TH CENTURY	
United States	Expansion of voting rights to all white men
United States	Beginnings of mass parties
United States	Origins of modern Republican and Democratic Parties
LATE 19TH CENTURY	
Brazil	First republic with cadre parties controlled by rural elites
Germany	Corporatist tradition begins under Bismarck
India	Indian National Congress formed
Europe	Mass parties and parties of the left emerge, including Germany's SDP and Britain's Labour Party
Russia	Communist Party origins
United States	Tammany Hall and the heyday of patronage
United Kingdom	Expansion of voting rights to all men
United Kingdom	Emergence of socialist parties, beginnings of mass parties
EARLY 20TH CENTURY	
Brazil	Populist political leaders and parties
China	Origins of Chinese Communist Party

Early 20th Century (continues)

er than the multiparty systems more likely under PR. In two party systems citizens must compromise their interests with others within large parties before they elect representatives, rather than electing a representative of a relatively small and carefully defined party who will then compromise with representatives of other parties after being elected. The former may produce less diverse viewpoints in the legislature, but it also means that two (or relatively few) broad parties will govern, probably making governing easier and perhaps policy more coherent. Multiparty systems, on the other hand, give more formal voice to diverse opinions in the legislature but can produce unstable coalition governments. How is this trade-off best made?

CIVIL SOCIETY

Interest groups represent their members' views in particular areas of public policy and provide formal institutions through which participation and representation can occur. If they are effective in carrying out these functions, a particular political system is more responsive and inclusive. Political scientists therefore investigate the internal organization of interest groups, the resources at their disposal, their overall institutional strength, and their relationships to the governments they try to influence. We examine the key questions of who rules within these organizations, how much power these organizations have in different political systems, how accurately they represent those on whose behalf they claim to work, what explains differences in their behavior and strength from one country to another, and what causes them to change over time.

Modern interest groups emerged in the nineteenth century alongside mass electoral democracy. In Europe this was also a period of rapid industrialization, and labor unions and business associations quickly came to be the most important interest groups. Associations representing the dwindling farming community also emerged to champion its concerns. Labor, business, and agriculture became the key "sectoral" categories of interest groups, that is, they represented the three key sectors of the economy. As the bulk of the citizenry became more involved in the political process, other interest groups emerged as well, including groups focused on expanding participation rights for women and racial minorities. In postcolonial countries, similar groups emerged. In Latin America, unions and business associations arose with the beginning of industrialization in the late nineteenth century. In Asia and Africa, trade unions developed under colonial rule as colonial subjects began to work for wages and started to organize. Unions became important in the nationalist struggles for independence in most countries.

No matter their origin or cause, the formal and informal relationships interest groups have with government are crucial to how they operate and how effective they can be. The two major democratic models of government–interest group interaction are known as "corporatist" and "pluralist." Although this is the same word we introduced in chapter 1 as one of the major theories to answer the question "who rules," here, **interest group pluralism** means a system in which many groups exist to represent particular interests and the government remains officially neutral. Under a pluralist system in this sense, many groups may exist to represent the same broad "interest," and all can try to gain influence: the government does not give preferential access and power to any one of them to be the official representative of that particular interest. The Unites States is the primary model of this pluralist system. The Chamber of Commerce exists to represent business interests, but so does the National Association of Manufacturers, the National Realtors Association, and myriad other groups. Washington, D.C., contains literally thousands of interest groups, sometimes dozens organized around the same issue, all vying for influence over decision makers. This is repeated, on a smaller scale, in all fifty state capitals. The government of the day may listen more to one than another of these groups on a particular issue, but no official and enduring preference or access is given to one over others. Even when one large organization speaks on behalf of most of a sector of society—such as the AFL-CIO for labor—it is a loose confederation of groups whose individual organizational members can and do ignore positions and policies of the national confederation if they choose to, and alternative groups have the right to organize as best they can.

The major alternative to interest group pluralism is corporatism. Unlike pluralism, which exists only in democracies, corporatism has more democratic (**societal**, or **neocorporatism**) and less democratic (**state corporatism**) variants. We discuss the latter in chapter 8. Neocorporatism is most common in

Germany	Origins of National Socialist (Nazi) Party
Japan	Taisho Democracy with electoral competition, 1912–1926
Russia	Russian revolution; Soviet Communist Party becomes ruling party
United Kingdom	Labour replaces Liberals as second major party
United States	Progressive movement (social movements such as temperance, women's suffrage); early interest groups such as Sierra Club, League of Women Voters

MID-20TH CENTURY

Brazil	New Republic; rapid industrialization and expansion of labor unions
Brazil	Military rule and state corporatism with limited party competition 1964–1985
Germany	New social movements, including Greens, antinuclear, women's movements
Germany	Electoral system created
India	Mass nationalist parties and independence
Iran	Competitive elections; Mossaddeq elected prime minister in 1951, later overthrown
Japan	Electoral system created
Japan	Origins of Japan's LDP
Nigeria	Mass nationalist parties and independence
United States	New social movements, including civil rights, antiwar, women's; new interest groups arise, including NOW, EarthFirst!, PETA

LATE 20TH CENTURY

Brazil	Transition to multiparty democracy, 1985–1989
Brazil	Presidential victory of strong, programmatic party, the PT, 2002

northern Europe, where strong **peak associations** bring together numerous local groups to represent the major interests in society, and government works closely with them to develop policy, but no legal restrictions exist to prevent other groups from arising. Germany is a key example, examined in greater detail in the case study at the end of this chapter. In such a neocorporatist system, these peak associations maintain their unity and institutional strength via internal mechanisms that ensure local organizations will abide by the decisions of the national body. By negotiating binding agreements with them, the state in effect recognizes them as the official representatives of their sectors. Unlike state corporatism, however, no individuals or groups are required to belong to these associations, and they maintain internal systems of democratic control. Dissatisfied members may try to change the association's policies or found alternative organizations, but most do not pursue this option because membership in the main body provides direct access to government.

Both pluralist and neocorporatist models have benefits and costs. Pluralism allows greater local control and participation, in that any individual or group is free to start a new organization. However, many national organizations have limited control over their local affiliates, so local members can work internally to move their local organization in whatever direction they wish. Because the state does not officially recognize any one group, there are fewer incentives for large organizations to maintain unity. This decentralization, however, may limit their institutional strength and overall power in national politics. France is well-known for its weak labor unions, for instance, in part because its two largest unions (one communist and one Catholic) are deeply divided over ideology. Interest groups gain power vis-à-vis the state due to the resources they can bring to bear on the government. More centralized organizations have more resources and can legitimately claim to speak on behalf of more citizens. This increases their potential clout in democratic systems, although critics point out that no government treats each kind of group equally, at least in a market economy. Following the argument we laid out in chapter 5, business interests are crucial for the well-being of the economy; therefore, the government in any market economy, even in the most pluralist systems, will pay more attention to business interests than to others, no matter how effectively others organize. In this case, other groups such as labor might be better off under neocorporatism in which they are united in one large, strong organization.

Because neocorporatist associations are so large and united, they typically have more direct influence on government than any single national association in a pluralist system. The disincentives to creating new organizations, however, and the power that government recognition provides to the elite leadership of the peak associations, make them seem less participatory. The incentives against starting alternative organizations are so strong that the vast majority of relevant constituents conclude it is wiser to participate within the confines of already established entities than to start new ones, no matter how dissatisfied they may be. A crucial question in these systems, then, is the degree of democratic control *within* the peak associations. If an institution has strong mechanisms of internal democracy, such as open elections for leadership positions and constituent participation in setting organizational policies, its leaders can legitimately claim to represent members' views. If the institution does not, it may have significant access to government and subsequent influence, but it may not really represent its members' views democratically.

Established interest groups also may not change quickly enough to reflect changes in even the most pluralist of societies. Well-established institutions provide powerful means for participation and representation, but because they are deeply entrenched they tend to change relatively slowly. What we now call social movements arose in the 1950s and 1960s out of discontent over this inertia. In much of the Western world, growing numbers of citizens, particularly young "baby boomers," came to feel that their governments, political parties, and interest groups were not providing adequate forms of participation or representation of their interests. All major political institutions, inside and outside of government, were viewed as organs through which the elite ruled and served their own interests. Established interest groups were overwhelmingly controlled by white men. And so, new social movements arose first among those challenging the status quo, including racial minorities, women, antiwar activists, and environmentalists. These have since been joined by many other groups, most recently those in the antiglobalization movement that proclaimed itself to the world in 1999 in protests and riots in Seattle.

Social movements are distinct from interest groups in that they are more informal, pursue participation outside the bounds of formal institutions, and tend not to have single and officially recognized leaders. Leaders may emerge, as Martin Luther King Jr. did in the civil rights movement, but they neither lead nor speak for a single unified organization that controls the entire movement. Others may propose other courses of action, as Malcolm X did during the civil rights movement. Yet these informal, uncoordinated social movements, and the underlying social changes they represented, profoundly changed Western societies. Women entered public life to a degree never before seen. Minorities united to get

China	Emergence of very limited civil society under state corporatism
Germany	Reunification of East and West Germany, rise of Green Party, and expansion of number of parties from 3 to 5
India	Rise of religious parties
India	End of Congress Party dominance, replaced by coalition governments, from 1989 onward
India	Rise of lower caste movements and parties
Iran	Elections, some with parties, under Islamic Republic, from 1980 onward
Japan	Electoral reform from SNTV to semiproportional system, only election loss for LDP, 1993
Nigeria	Transition to multiparty democracy, though with seriously flawed elections, 1999
Russia	Fall of Communism and birth of new parties, 1991
Russia	Reduction of party competition under Putin, from 2000 onward
United Kingdom	Continued dominance of centrist, mass parties
United States	Continued dominance of centrist, mass parties

many segregationist and discriminatory policies overturned and also were able to enter public life to a much greater degree. Today, environmental concerns are on national political agendas everywhere, and in the age of global climate change, environmentalists are making progress putting it on the agendas of international political, social, and corporate institutions.

As these movements have succeeded, they have changed, however. Some of their members have founded or joined formal interest groups, such as the National Organization of Women, or even political parties, such as the German Greens. When successful social movements cross over into the sphere of formal institutions, new social movement groups often emerge to replace them with new and more challenging agendas. In the environmental movement, for example, the institutionalization of groups like Friends of the Earth as interest groups has left the role of social movement open to new challengers like EarthFirst!

Some political scientists see these social movements as symptomatic of the problems that have come to be associated with participation and representation in wealthy democracies in the last two decades. Robert Putnam, for example, has decried a decline in **social capital**, that is, social networks and norms of reciprocity. He sees such capital as crucial to democracy and economic growth. Developed in the context of Italy and later applied to the United States in a widely read article and book, both titled *Bowling Alone* (2000), Putnam's argument is that even apparently "nonpolitical" organizations in civil society create social networks and mutual trust among members that can be used for political action. The demise of traditional membership-based organizations such as local parent-teacher associations and, yes, bowling leagues, undermines the ability of citizens to trust and cooperate with one another, which hinders their ability to engage in collective action in a democracy. Most research in this vein has focused on the United States, but scholars note that since the 1970s public opinion polls throughout Europe, North America, and Japan have shown a decline in levels of trust in government, political parties, and virtually all other political institutions. The extent to which this is true varies across countries, but the trend is similar virtually everywhere.

Russell Dalton and others propose a sociological explanation: the decline in the traditional social divisions based on class and religion, increased access to education, and the growing importance of the media have combined to produce the marked drop in membership in and loyalty to political parties since the 1950s, and especially since the 1980s (Dalton and Wattenberg 2000). This declining partisanship has resulted in lower voter turnout in most countries; increased electoral volatility in that voters switch parties more frequently from one election to the next; more single-issue voting, especially on such postmaterialist issues as the environment or abortion; and greater focus on the personality of individual candidates rather than on parties and policy platforms.

Parties have responded by changing how they conduct campaigns and how they relate to their members. In almost all countries, parties today have fewer members than in the past, though in some cases the members who remain have been given a greater role in choosing candidates and setting policies. Parties have also tended to narrow their ideological differences, as they can no longer rely on a core of committed partisan voters and must instead try to attract the growing number of uncommitted voters, highly educated individuals who tend to be in the ideological center. Overall, fragmentation and individualization of the electorate has weakened parties as institutions. They remain important legislatively, but no longer represent core groups, which Dalton and others argue, weakens democracy.

Much debate focuses on the impact of mass communication on democracy and democratic participation and representation. Do television, the Internet, portable cellular devices, and the like foster democracy or hinder it? While Putnam and Dalton fault mass media for undermining civil society, Pippa Norris (2002) reaches less dire conclusions. Using different data sets and dividing countries on the basis of wealth, she concluded that while party membership has declined in wealthier countries overall, and that this is tied to the presence of television in particular, it is questionable whether representation and parties as institutions actually are weakening. In countries without mass communication, building effective and representative parties by necessity must depend on face-to-face communication and campaigning, which is not easy. Communication (and therefore representation) improves in countries with nearly universal access to television, telephones, and the Internet.

Moreover, while levels of trust have declined, involvement in political activities has not. What it has done is shifted to social movements, in other words, to new and important, but informal and unstable, forms of participation. Citizens may participate in them and perhaps influence government successfully, but they move relatively quickly among different issues and different movements, not developing strong ties with any particular group. The U.S. organization MoveOn! is an example: tied together mainly via the Internet, communication among members is almost exclusively based on e-mail. Such relatively new communications media encourage electronic letter writing and petitions, phone call campaigns, and local demonstrations, though there are no formal local branches with official membership lists or regular meetings. Given her findings, Norris questions whether the changes she and others have observed are undermining democracy.

As usual in comparative politics, there are no certain answers about trends and what they mean. Nonetheless, the questions raised are profound. All agree that, in wealthy democracies at least, the ways in which people participate in local community groups and larger political institutions are changing significantly and that trust in political institutions has declined markedly. What effect does this have on the health of democracy? How much participation must take place and in what forms if a democracy is to thrive? What kinds of institutional connections must exist between the political elite and the citizenry for the former to represent the interests of the latter? How much involvement and influence do average members need in political organizations—whether interest groups or parties—to ensure that those institutions represent their members well? Do new, less formal, and less stable forms of participation adequately replace mass membership organizations such as trade unions and the mass membership parties common in the early and mid-1900s? Keep these questions in mind as we examine participation and representation in four of our case study countries below.

Political scientists are also concerned about the strength and effectiveness of civil society in postcolonial countries. They closely observe newly democratic countries to see whether civil society is becoming stronger and growing in ways that will contribute to democratic consolidation. Why? Authoritarian rule usually weakens civil society; sometimes it is banned completely. In some countries, organized civil society becomes so weak that people turn exclusively to what undoubtedly is the most widespread form of informal political participation: patron-client linkages. Where other options are few, individuals may seek to attach themselves to a powerful patron in the system to gain access to resources or power, or to at least have influence over some area of government via their relationship to their patron. Because patron-client linkages are most important where formal institutions for participation are weakest or most restrictive, we discuss them more extensively in the next chapter on authoritarian regimes. It is important to remember, however, that patronage and patron-client relations played an important part in the early growth of many political parties and party machines in countries we now consider quite democratic, including the United States. Our case studies show that many, if not all, countries have or had some elements of patron-clientelism. In newly democratizing countries, patronage networks may carry over from nondemocratic to democratic regimes. Will they weaken with time and anticorruption measures, as they seem to have done in more established democracies? This is one of the comparative historical questions political scientists try to answer.

Western aid donors who want to strengthen democracy spend money trying to build up alternatives to patron-client linkages within civil society by strengthening the weak associations that authoritarianism and state corporatism often undermined. Much of this money goes to **nongovernmental organizations (NGOs)**. While all interest groups are nongovernmental, today the term NGO is mainly used to refer to volunteer organizations working to make countries more democratic or to provide assistance with development. These include church-based organizations, youth groups, professional associations, human rights groups, anticorruption groups, and groups working to improve the lives of orphans or street children and build health clinics. Aid agencies want to strengthen these groups as institutions to provide for the well-being of people in poverty and help create an educated and active citizenry in new democracies.

Unfortunately, the legacy of weak institutions and weak states has undermined much of this effort, especially in Africa. With the exception of religious organizations, NGOs in Africa are mostly new organizations based around a small, elite leadership that is dependent on external donor funding. Because they do not need to rely on their own members for resources, the level of internal democracy and connections with ordinary citizens found in these organizations are often quite limited. In Latin America, where democracy has generally been more institutionalized and has a longer history, NGOs tend to have stronger roots in society and don't face such problems to the same extent as their African counterparts.

The most successful cases are organizations that have developed some legitimacy. These groups are a voice for their constituencies and causes and have had some influence on government in part because of their ability to publicize their government's activities globally. Many political scientists see these groups as a hopeful sign of the growth and development of stronger civil societies able to articulate and represent citizens' interests in new democracies with authoritarian pasts.

CASE STUDY The United States: Evolution of a Two-Party, Pluralist System

Americans complain frequently about "gridlock" and partisan division, the seemingly inherent inability of the two parties and the various governing institutions to pass laws to solve problems. This gridlock, however, reflects the exceptionally participatory nature of the American institutions of participation and representation, even if many citizens these days fail to take advantage of the opportunities the system provides. The United States is the classic case of a two-party, first-past-the-post electoral system and a pluralist interest group model. The decentralized nature of the U.S. federal system of government is a crucial context for understanding how the country's system of representation and participation functions. The system allows unusual variation from state to state in the institutions of participation and representation and provides numerous points of entry for groups seeking to influence government at various levels. The FPTP system and decentralization have resulted in two broad catch-all parties that are relatively weak in terms of party discipline and have become weaker in recent decades. Americans vote more frequently and for more offices than just about any citizens in the world: they typically have the opportunity to elect people to anywhere from six to twelve offices and judgeships at each of three subnational levels of government—municipal, county, and state—plus five national offices. In contrast, British voters typically elect one local representative, one MP, and one EU MP, and that's it. Yet, ironically, the United States also has among the world's lowest voter turnout rates.

The numerous points of access to government allow for considerable interest group influence, though in a pluralist system in which literally thousands of groups compete for attention. Historically, Americans joined groups in large numbers to take advantage of

Republican vice president Dick Cheney and Democratic House Speaker Nancy Pelosi await the president's State of the Union speech in January 2008. The two parties have completely dominated American electoral politics since 1860, but Congress provides many avenues for interest groups to gain access to the legislative process.

the access they gained to government's ear, but in recent years, the United States has been the site of declining participation and social capital, though the extent and nature of this issue remains hotly debated, as we touched upon above. Arguably, the U.S. model provides exceptional citizen access to elected officials at numerous levels, which should reflect the potential for a high degree of participation. This is mediated, however, by weak parties and a pluralist interest group system that critics say limit the real ability of organized citizens to influence the system. Critics also argue that this fragmentation can result in gridlock, in which little effective policymaking occurs.

The U.S. Constitution is silent on the details of an electoral system. The president was to be elected by an Electoral College, not directly by the populace,

IN CONTEXT FPTP

- In 2005 47 countries used "first-past-the-post rules" for their legislative elections.

- These countries included the Bahamas, Canada, Jamaica, Kenya, Pakistan, and Zambia.

- The vast majority of countries using FPTP are former British colonies.

- In 2005 no country in continental Europe used FPTP.

Source: International Institute for Democracy and Electoral Assistance, Table of Electoral Systems Worldwide, www.idea.int/esd/world.cfm.

which is still the case today. The Senate originally was appointed by state governments to represent their interests. This left only the House of Representatives to be elected directly by the people. The individual states had the task of designing their own actual electoral systems. Following the well-established British model, almost all adopted a FPTP system with single-member districts. And as suffrage was expanded over the decades, voter turnout initially increased accordingly.

State law continues to determine the type of electoral system used to choose political officials, though it has since been modified by constitutional amendment and significant court cases. These days, electoral districts for congressional and state legislative seats must be very close in size so that equal weight is given to each vote. State legislatures, however, are left to determine the exact boundaries of these districts, including those for Congress: the standard practice has become to draw the lines to provide a reasonably clear majority for one party in each district, with the total such districts for each party more or less matching its share of the voters in that state. This helps protect incumbents of both parties. Since a constitutional amendment in 1920 determined that senators were to be popularly elected, the boundaries of their electoral districts, the state boundaries, are fixed, regardless of population. This results in overrepresentation of small states and underrepresentation of large ones, which is reflected in the Electoral College as well.

Most Americans probably think of the current two-party system as a permanent fixture, as much a part of the U.S. political system as the Constitution and three branches of government. In fact, the Democratic and Republican parties did not coalesce until the election of Abraham Lincoln in 1860, and they, as well as the two-party system, have evolved significantly since then even though the two parties remain in place. The earliest parties were cadre parties that emerged as factions in the first few Congresses. One of these, the Jeffersonian Republicans, led by the "Virginia dynasty" of Thomas Jefferson, James Madison, and James Monroe, created what was really a dominant party system from 1800 to 1824: this faction controlled the presidency throughout this period and in the early 1820s controlled 187 of 213 seats in the House and 44 of 48 seats in the Senate.

Andrew Jackson and Martin Van Buren, both of whom would serve as president, founded what would become known as the Democratic Party in the 1820s. It emerged out of divisions in the old Jeffersonian Republican Party. As the franchise expanded to include all white men regardless of property ownership, members of Jackson and Van Buren's faction recognized the need for a party to organize and register more voters, and so they created the first party based on mass membership and appeal. Their opponents responded in kind, creating the Whig Party. This ushered in the first real two-party system, from Jackson's election in 1828 to Lincoln's in 1860.

The new mass parties greatly increased participation at the polls: turnout among the adult white male electorate increased from just over 25 percent in 1824 to 56 percent in 1828 and up to almost 80 percent by 1840. The Whigs split in the 1850s over the issue of slavery, with the Republicans emerging from the conflict on the side of abolition. Victory in the Civil War subsequently ushered in a long period of Republican dominance at the national level: only three Democrats would win the presidency between 1860 and 1932.

The election of 1932 proved another decisive turning point as Franklin Delano Roosevelt forged his New Deal coalition of trade unions, Southern Democrats, and farmers in response to the Great Depression. This would give the Democrats political ascendance, if not complete political domination, until the election of Ronald Reagan in 1980. Starting in the 1960s, the New Deal coalition came under increasing strain from sharp ideological differences between Northern liberals and younger members in the antiwar and civil rights movements and white Southern Democrats, most of whom opposed the shift by the national party toward favoring civil rights. By the 1990s, this ideological conflict had resulted in a wholesale shift of Southern political loyalty from the Democrats to the Republicans, producing the current era of sharp partisan differences and unusually even political division between the two parties.

As discussed above, in a wealthy society such as the United States, party loyalty is based primarily on ideology. The early parties, however, were based not just on ideology but also on the material benefits of patronage. Until the early twentieth century, most government employees served at the will of elected leaders. When power changed hands at any level of government, a bureaucratic purge took place as the incumbent's appointees were removed and the new victor's people were placed in office. In the late nineteenth century, urban politicians mobilized and politically controlled large numbers of new immigrants through what came to be known as political machines. These large, patronage-based parties provided jobs and public services to new citizens and voters in exchange for their loyalty. Opposition to these patronage practices resulted in the Progressive movement in the early twentieth century that eventually led to the creation of a professional Civil Service whose members would be selected by merit and not subject to removal after each election. While some patronage jobs still remained, these reforms drastically reduced their numbers and forced parties to shift their focus toward building support based on ideology, rather than material incentives.

Along with suffrage and the political parties, candidate selection has also evolved over time. Originally, party caucuses that consisted of existing officeholders, such as members of Congress and state legislators, selected a party's candidates. The elitism of this system came under fire in the Jacksonian era, and the major parties shifted to a convention system in which local par-

ty groups nominated delegates to the state level; these, in turn, nominated delegates to national conventions where candidates were selected for national office.

The patronage machines gained great influence in the convention system: it was often said that candidates were selected in smoke-filled back rooms through haggling and bargaining. Reformers of the Progressive era reacted against this urban machine control by creating the direct primary: all voters registered in a party would select the candidates by direct vote. By 1915 all the states had some type of direct primary elections for at least some offices. This has since produced the era of the long primary contest, especially at the presidential level, which is unique to the United States. Candidates spend months—now more than a year—campaigning among voters for their party's presidential nomination.

Even with these reforms, party leaders still maintained significant influence over candidate selection. They controlled the selection of a majority of the delegates sent to conventions, and rules allowed these delegates to switch their votes so that they could influence which candidates were selected. A series of reforms in the Democratic Party starting in the late 1960s weakened the influence of party leaders, and consequently, the delegates they selected. As this last institutionalized influence the national party leadership had over candidate selection came to an end, the nomination came to depend entirely on winning the popular vote in the primaries. National party organizations have lost virtually all direct control over the process; instead, they have come to play a supporting role by providing candidates services during campaigns and spending their own money for part of the campaigns, even if they do not directly control who the candidates are or what they say.

The party system in the United States has been an unusually enduring two-party system for well over a century. The FPTP electoral system encourages this stability in that it gives the major parties strong incentives to incorporate any new group or interest that emerges, including third parties. Party stability, however, does not necessarily signal party strength. At their height, mass parties in the United States were the main institutions through which citizens got involved in politics. They incorporated white male immigrants into the democratic system, and they did the same with women once they gained the right to vote. Parties used substantial material incentives to gain support, so partisan identification was very strong, and party leaders controlled most of the power within the organizations. Primary elections, local funding of most candidates, and mass communication have weakened this centralized power of the parties, however, because a great deal of the political participation that currently takes place is no longer channeled through or controlled by them. Voter turnout is relatively low for an established democracy and has declined, which supports the hypothesis that FPTP discourages voters.

The pluralist system of interest groups in the United States has been the venue of much political participation, especially since the early twentieth century, though concerns about declining social capital have been on the rise since the 1980s. Despite this, the United States historically has long been perceived as a country of joiners and associations. The French social commentator Alexis de Tocqueville famously observed in the 1830s, "Americans of all ages, all stations in life, and all types of dispositions are forever forming associations.... [A]t the head of any new undertaking, where in France you would find the government or in England some territorial magnate, in the United States you are sure to find an association" (1969 reprint, 513). Political scientist Theda Skocpol (2003) has meticulously documented the extent of what she terms "translocal but locally rooted membership associations" from the early nineteenth century to the mid-twentieth century. These local groups and clubs involved citizens in meetings, social gatherings, and community betterment. Over time, many of these formed state-level and national associations, uniting their groups and paralleling the structure of the U.S. federal system of government. And like much of the politics of this time, these were gender segregated and exclusively white affairs, though they often included members from across religious and class divisions. Whereas many did not have specific political agendas, some certainly did, notably temperance organizations, women's organizations, and antislavery societies. They all actively pursued local community improvements that included working with government at various levels. Yet while these associations undoubtedly helped build a wealth of social capi-

tal, it's safe to say that most of their members did not view them as primarily political; consciously political activity was still primarily the purview of political parties in an era of mass membership parties and high levels of partisan identity.

Modern interest groups with political agendas would arise in the Progressive era, as partisan loyalty began to decline. Disenchantment with the corruption of party politics led activists to create organizations independent of parties. One such group was the Sierra Club. Created in part to block the building of a dam in California and to protect Yosemite National Park, it ultimately expanded to become the country's largest environmental organization. These new groups engaged in a new activity called lobbying, in which they spoke directly to legislators to influence how they voted, and they also began working directly with the newly created Civil Service to influence the executive branch of government. In many ways these large membership associations were like many others that had come before, but they behaved differently, focusing explicitly on particular political issues as their central concern, with direct influence over government one of their primary purposes. Thus began the modern era of the pluralist interest group system in the United States, with literally thousands of groups free to organize when and how they pleased.

Skocpol argues that this system of mass membership organizations began to change, starting in the mid-twentieth century, into what she calls "managed advocacy" groups. Groups now rely on members for financial support and their occasional phone calls, e-mails, or presence at rallies to influence government, and they no longer have active local branches that bring members together on a regular basis. According to Skocpol, this shift has harmed the country's social capital, as citizens no longer work actively together in face-to-face situations. This decline has coincided with declines in partisan loyalty, in trust in government in general, and in voter turnout, and citizens do not seem to support or participate in the key institutions of the political system to the extent they did prior to the 1960s.

Other scholars, however, have looked at the same trends and questioned Skocpol's concerns, pointing out that some types of political activity have held steady or even increased. For example, political activity now occurs via Internet mobilization because groups no longer need formal membership lists or local branches to organize nearly spontaneous rallies or e-mail campaigns. Americans also volunteer more than ever before and join small groups such as self-help groups at higher rates than in the past. New forms of activities have arisen to replace, at least in part, those that have declined. The open question is whether these new forms are as effective at facilitating participation and representation and building social capital as those of the past. Research on this important question is really just beginning.

Today, some of the country's thousands of organizations, such as the National Rifle Association or the AARP (formerly the American Association of Retired Persons), are still mass membership organizations, though they do not have the active local branches that organizations in the past had. Other groups are much smaller, with small but committed membership bases and professional staffs in state capitals or in Washington, D.C., to provide analysis of and lobbying for specific issues. They have multiple entry points into the political process, and spokespersons have the opportunity to talk to members of Congress, permanent civil servants in relevant departments, and political appointees of the current president. They may write legal briefs to participate in relevant court cases. If they cannot get their ideas approved via legislation, they may try getting approval in the courts, or vice versa. The United States arguably provides more points of entry to the system than almost any other. In combination with the reality of the country's relatively weak parties, which leave legislators free to vote how they please, this makes its political system one in which organized citizens can actively attempt to influence the political process on an almost daily basis, not just during elections.

Logically, all of this seems like it should increase participation, but as we've seen, it's not clear that it actually does. Critics argue that this decentralized, pluralist system also makes governing difficult because constant compromise makes it nearly impossible to implement significant changes to the status quo, as one group or another will successfully block it in the legislature, the executive branch, or the courts. Americans increasingly worry about gridlock, often partisan in nature, preventing any coherent policies from being enacted. Whether this gridlock is a price worth paying to have the exceptional level of access provided to organized groups is a question Americans continue to debate.

CASE STUDY Germany: Neocorporatism under Threat

In the 2005 election, the two major parties in Germany nearly perfectly split the electorate but gained only 70 percent of the vote, their lowest combined total ever. After weeks of negotiations, the two major parties, for only the second time since World War II, joined forces to create a "grand coalition" to govern over what seemed to be a divided and increasingly alienated citizenry. Germany's democracy provides an example of a two and a half party system with relatively strong political parties; an unusual, mixed electoral system; and a neocorporatist interest group system. For much of its history, many political scientists saw the country as a model of effective policymaking in a democratic context; in recent years, however, unusually strong social movements inspired by seemingly alienated citizens and the economic effects of globalization have raised serious questions about both its effectiveness and the adequacy of its institutions of participation and representation.

The instability of Germany's first democracy, the Weimar Republic (1918–1933), profoundly influenced the post–World War II system the Allies helped create in West Germany. Parties were central to the new democracy, and were explicitly recognized in the Basic Law, West Germany's constitution, which required the creation of a legal code for their organization and an

Chancellor-designate Angela Merkel of Germany's CDU celebrates with the leaders of the CSU and SDP, the members of her new "grand coalition" government, in November 2005. The coalition became necessary because the election results had been so close, with the major parties' total share of the vote dropping to just 70 percent for the first time since World War II.

adherence to this code to support democracy. The major parties that eventually developed out of this were a large Christian Democratic group, the Christian Democratic Union/Christian Social Union (CDU/CSU—the CDU is primarily a northern and Protestant group, whereas the CSU is primarily Catholic and based in Bavaria in the south), and the Social Democratic Party (SPD), which was the dominant party prior to the Nazi era and reemerged after the war. The third, the "half" party, is the liberal Free Democrat Party (FDP), which lies ideologically between the two major parties. The mixed PR system adopted in the Basic Law encouraged the rise of this party system, but so did other factors. The conservative nationalists of the Weimar era were completely discredited by their association with Hitler, so no other conservative parties arose to challenge the CDU/CSU on the right. The Basic Law limited free association by insisting that all parties had to support democracy to prevent the rise of a new Nazi or other nondemocratic party. In the mid-1950s, the government took two smaller parties—a "radical right" party and the Communist Party—to the Constitutional Court, arguing that since neither believed in democracy they should be banned: the court agreed and ruled that both be dissolved.

Initially, the CDU/CSU under Konrad Adenauer was the dominant party, ruling continuously from 1949 to 1969, usually with the support of the FDP. Then the SPD moderated its ideology in 1959, giving up the official goal of nationalizing industry and creating a truly socialist economy and instead accepting the basic parameters of Germany's social market economy (described in chapter 5). This shift helped increase its electoral appeal: by 1965 the party was successful enough to enter into a coalition government with the CDU/CSU, and in 1969 it became the biggest party, forming a government with the FDP. What this proved is that the party had become ideologically flexible enough to support either of the major parties to gain a share of power. Since that time, power has shifted back and forth between the two major parties, almost always in coalition with the FDP or, more recently, the Green Party. The SPD's moderation and the willingness of the CDU/CSU to support the social market economy significantly reduced the ideological differences between the two major parties.

At the same time, German neocorporatism reached its zenith. The German Trade Union Federation claims to represent 85 percent of the unionized workforce. Via codetermination (see chapter 5) in the social market economy, its members constitute close to half of the board members of Germany's 482 largest firms. Business is represented by three organizations: the BDA represents the largest industrial groups, the BDI other large and medium-size firms, and the DIHT small businesses. From the 1950s through the 1970s, these organizations worked closely with the major political parties and the government at each level to set wage and social policies. Most members of parliament (MPs) on key committees were members of one of these key interest groups, and many worked professionally for them before entering politics. SPD MPs often had strong union backgrounds, and CDU/CSU MPs had business connections, though labor and business associations had members in and maintained close contact with both parties, especially the party in power at any particular time.

Political scientists and policymakers saw this model of stability and neocorporatism as a great success into the 1970s. Underlying it, however, were trends that would raise serious questions about the key aspects of the system. The popular discontent with the "new Germany" that emerged in West Germany in the 1950s and 1960s came from several sources and became quite apparent by the late 1960s. A student movement opposed to the Vietnam War and German rearmament and advocating a more neutral stand in the Cold War rocked the country starting in the mid-1960s. Members of this movement also criticized what they saw as a growing consumer culture, the creation of a society focused solely on economic growth and consumption that they viewed as inhumane. Growing unemployment affected both would-be middle-class college students and working-class young adults alike. All of this discontent culminated in widespread protests in 1968, which the CDU/CSU government, with SPD support, effectively and forcefully put down.

The demise of this movement led young political activists to pursue several different paths. Some withdrew from politics, at least beyond the local level, to start communes, cooperatives, and squatter settlements in abandoned buildings. These individuals pursued various alternative lifestyles and by and large turned their backs on national political action. Others tried to reenter the SPD and reform the party from within, to shift it further to the left. Still others turned to violence, creating a series of small terrorist organizations responsible for a number of bombings in the early 1970s before ultimately being defeated by the state.

Some activists from the middle class formed what came to be known as "civil action groups." These were small, local groups of usually not more than thirty people focused on petitioning local government to better people's lives in a variety of areas, such as building new schools or cleaning up pollution. Members continued to engage politically, but they were no longer willing to participate only through the major interest group associations or the major parties. By 1979, 1.5 million Germans were participating in at least 50,000 such groups. In the mid-1970s, some of the groups that focused primarily on the environment came together to form a national association to begin pushing environmental issues at the national level. This new movement, along with growing women's and antinuclear movements,

was a key pillar of the "new social movements" in Germany. Like in the United States, the feminist movement emerged out of the student movement of the 1960s, as women demanded more access to education, employment, and power. A strong antinuclear movement grew in the 1970s in opposition to U.S. plans to base nuclear weapons on German soil and plans by the German government to increase the country's dependence on nuclear energy.

These new social movements trusted neither major party, which they saw as nearly identical, too committed to economic growth rather than environmental protection, and too supportive of the United States and rearmament rather than peace and neutrality. By 1980 the Green Party had evolved out of these groups. In 1983 it became the first new party since 1949 to break the 5 percent barrier and gain seats in parliament, reducing SPD support in particular. After falling below 5 percent in the next election, the Greens rebounded, gaining more than 7 percent in 1994 and entering into government after 1998 with the SPD, creating what came to be called the "red" (socialist)—"green" alliance that ruled until 2005, when a new grand coalition of the CDU/CSU and the SPD was formed under newly elected chancellor Angela Merkel. And so it was that Germany came to be home to an exceptionally active array of new social movements; its electoral and party system based on mixed PR allowed and encouraged these diverse activists to create their own party, which ultimately gained a share of governmental power. Activists most critical of the system, however, were not necessarily happy with this outcome, which is an example of a classic trade-off facing any participants in democracy between pure principles and compromise in the name of gaining influence or power.

The other major shift in the German party system was reunification with East Germany in 1990. The East German Communist state had a one-party regime, of course. An outpouring of new parties emerged as this regime collapsed. The West German electoral system covered the entire reunited country, and initially, the major parties in the west reached out and worked with like-minded parties in the east to gain support there. Ultimately, they absorbed the eastern parties. The

CDU/CSU was initially the most popular party in the east because its leader, incumbent chancellor Helmut Kohl, had championed German unity after the fall of the Berlin Wall and promised to transfer large sums of money from west to east to improve the eastern economy. Continuing high unemployment and low incomes in the east, however, slowly eroded his support; as a result, the SPD did quite well in the east in the 1998 and 2002 elections, which it won at the national level as well.

The exception, interestingly, was the former ruling Communist Party, which re-created itself as the Party of Social Democracy (PDS) and positioned itself ideologically to the left of the SPD to champion in particular the poorer and heavily unemployed East Germans. Its association with the country's Communist past resulted in it gaining only 2.4 percent of the party vote in the first joint election in 1990, but it has since gained seats in parliament as its individual candidates have won some of the elections in particular districts in the east. Over time it has expanded its appeal, winning 21 percent of the eastern vote by the 1998 election, though falling below the 5 percent threshold for national representation in 2002.

At the same time that the new social movements, new parties, and reunification were altering the landscape of party politics, economic problems were threatening neocorporatism. The neocorporatist model in West Germany developed in the 1950s and reached its zenith in the 1970s after labor unions gained new power from a series of strikes in the late 1960s, the union-aligned SPD came to control the government, and the codetermination laws were put in place. The ability of the peak associations of business and labor to control their member organizations to enforce collective wage agreements was key to the operation of this model. In the 1980s, these key associations began to weaken as globalization began to increase unemployment. To encourage more employment, government and employers agreed to reduce the work week to thirty-five hours in 1984, and in exchange the unions allowed greater flexibility in setting working conditions within firms. As control of working conditions became more localized, local unions had less reason to obey the dictates of the peak associations, which weakened the ability of the latter group to speak on the behalf of all workers.

These trends accelerated in the 1990s as global competition heated up. Facing rising costs from exporters elsewhere in the world, smaller businesses began leaving the employers' association, which meant that central agreements covered fewer businesses. Some business leaders began to campaign openly for a shift to a more neoliberal economic model. The decline of traditional manufacturing, meanwhile, caused union membership to plummet by four million during the decade. The peak associations for both business and labor were speaking for and able to enforce central agreements on a shrinking share of the private sector, and this further weakened the neocorporatist model.

Politicians responded by distancing themselves from these associations: the long tradition of SPD politicians coming from the unions and CDU/CSU politicians coming from business association and churches changed drastically. Far fewer members of parliament from both parties were members of or worked in the key associations, and more of them developed career paths as professional politicians, staying in elected office rather than returning to work for the interest groups. In the face of these changes and continuing high unemployment, neither the CDU/CSU government prior to 1998 nor the SPD/Green government from 1998–2005 was able to negotiate new binding agreements with business and labor for fundamental reforms in the face of globalization. Both governments ultimately tried to impose these reforms unilaterally, without the support of the peak associations, and both failed to get them fully implemented and lost power.

The SPD government's failed attempt to reform the economy in the new millennium alienated its traditional "left" and working-class voters while failing to attract more pro–free market voters. Indeed, a former SPD leader, Oskar Lafontaine, split with the party, taking its more leftist members with him, and ultimately joined forces with the PDS. The result was the closely divided 2005 election. The CDU/CSU won slightly more votes than the SPD, but the results were so close that the parties ultimately negotiated a grand coalition (as they had in 1966–1969) to govern together. The new chancellor, Angela Merkel, was the leader of the CDU, the first woman to lead the country, and the first East German to do so since reunification. More than anything else, though, this most recent election confirmed prior trends: declining support for both major parties, seeming inability of either party to reform the German social market economy in response to globalization, and growing popular disenchantment. When voters were asked on election day which party would be most likely to solve future economic problems, 48 percent said "none of them."

CASE STUDY Japan: A Dominant-Party System, Weak Civil Society, and Electoral Reform

Japan has been a stable, wealthy democracy since its emergence from U.S. occupation after World War II, but its institutions of participation and representation are quite different from those of most wealthy democracies. From the full establishment of its democratic system in 1955 until 1993, a single party ruled Japan in a dominant party system. Japan's economic crisis in the early 1990s changed that: the ruling party was removed from power, and the electoral system was changed dramatically. Japanese democracy has also been characterized by a rather weak civil society and limited participation, though that may be changing: since the government liberalized its regulations over civil society, many new groups seem to be springing up and demanding greater voice in the policy-making process. On the other hand, Japan's legendary effective governance may be declining. Arguably, since the crisis of the early 1990s, participation is increasing while the various governments seem unable to solve the fundamental economic problems facing the country.

The Liberal Democratic Party (LDP) has dominated Japanese politics since its first election in 1955. Despite its name, ideologically it is a conservative party that supports the interests of business and economic growth, with state intervention as necessary, to rebuild a strong nation and economy. Its creation was in part an effort to establish a strong anticommunist party, and it had active U.S. support. The party guided the creation of Japan's phenomenally successful development model we outlined in chapter 5, winning a majority of the legislative seats in every election to the *Diet,* Japan's parliament, from 1955 to 1993, and always gaining a plurality (though after 1963, rarely a major-

ity) of the national vote. Its great economic success allowed it to provide benefits to large segments of the population, including the rapidly growing urban middle class, and this also helped maintain its popularity.

This also wasn't all that difficult given that the only significant opposition was the Japan Socialist Party (JSP), which at its height of popularity in the 1950s gar-

Japanese prime minister Shintaro Abe, second from left, meets with leaders of Japan's three major business associations in 2007. Japan's ruling LDP has always had very close ties with business. The party and business are two of the three points of the "iron triangle," the close relationship among the ruling party, business leaders, and top bureaucrats that guides most major policies.

nered no more than 35 percent of the vote, dropping below 30 percent throughout the 1960s and even lower since. A small Japan Communist Party (JCP) continued to exist but it too got very few votes. In 1964 a Buddhist movement, Soka Gakkai, founded another opposition party, *Komeito,* that came to occupy an ideological middle ground between the LDP and JSP and maintains the loyal support of the relatively small religious organization.

In addition, the LDP benefited from Japan's unusual electoral system. Until 1993 the country had an electoral system based on geographical representation and plurality voting. Rather than the FPTP system outlined above, however, Japan used the highly unusual **single, nontransferable vote (SNTV)** in multimember districts. The country was divided into 130 electoral districts, but each district simultaneously elected 2 to 6 (depending on the size of the district) members of parliament. (The *Diet* had just over five hundred members.) A voter could vote for only one candidate, and parties could not transfer that vote to any other candidate. Each party, therefore, ran several candidates in each district. The winning candidates (several in each district) often had only 15 to 20 percent of the vote in their district. Added to this, district lines were drawn to favor rural areas, giving them greater weight in the electoral system than their numbers of voters warranted: some rural districts had a four-to-one advantage over urban districts, meaning each rural vote was equal to four urban votes. This gerrymandering was intentional and was meant to provide strong rural support for the conservative, anticommunist LDP. Like any other plurality system, the SNTV system gave the winning party a larger share of seats in the legislature than its share of actual votes.

So even as LDP's popularity declined and it won an absolute majority of the national vote only twice between 1967 and 1990, it always maintained majority control of the *Diet* and therefore the government.

In addition to its majoritarian bias, the electoral system encouraged the creation of factions within the LDP. (To be fair, these arise in virtually all dominant parties.) These factions were based not on ideology, but rather on the loyal, patron-client networks that emerged within the LDP for campaign purposes. In each district, a winning party had to put forth several candidates who would draw votes from different groups of voters so as not to dilute the support of each individual candidate. To gain the resources to compete not only against other parties but also against other candidates in the LDP, potential candidates would become loyal members of a faction. Each faction was led by a patron, who was a leading national party (and often government) official who provided campaign funds. To make sure no single candidate became too popular, taking too many votes away from the party's other candidates in the same district, each candidate also developed a local voter mobilization machine, called a *koenkai,* which consisted of area notables and leaders of important area groups who could deliver votes. A candidate then promised the factional leader that he could use his *koenkai* to deliver a certain percentage of the vote in a district if the patron would provide the necessary campaign financing. As a result of this networking, five major factions emerged in the LDP in the 1950s, each based around personal loyalty to key leaders. Over time, these factions became informally institutionalized, complete with leadership battles for succession. Locally, *koenkai* were often informally institutionalized as well: an entire local machine may transfer its loyalty from a retiring candidate to a new one, sometimes the original candidate's son. At both the national and local level, factional battles within the dominant LDP became the most important political contests.

The 1990 economic crisis outlined in chapter 5 fundamentally changed this dominant party system and resulted in a reform of the electoral system as well. It didn't help the LDP that the crisis came on the heels of growing corruption scandals within the

IN CONTEXT SNTV

- The SNTV voting system used in Japan prior to 1993 is one of the world's rarest electoral systems.

- Currently, only four countries use SNTV: Afghanistan, Jordan, Pitcairn Islands, and Vanuatu.

- SNTV systems have the lowest average turnout of any electoral system, just 54 percent.

- SNTV encourages better representation of minority parties and independent candidates than simple FPTP systems because SNTV elects multiple candidates in the same district.

Source: International Institute for Democracy and Electoral Assistance, Table of Electoral Systems Worldwide, www.idea.int/esd/world.cfm.

party. Patronage politics of the type practiced within the LDP require a great deal of money. Quite simply, loyalty is based on rewards. These rewards took the form of such governmental largesse as infrastructure improvements (and awarding the construction contracts for these to local supporters). Although this sort of "you scratch my back and I'll scratch yours" behavior is common in many countries, Japanese politicians were also expected to attend local events such as the weddings and funerals of their supporters and provide generous gifts. Japanese elections, not surprisingly, soon became the most expensive in the world, in spite of the fact that candidates were not allowed to advertise on television and the length of campaigns was strictly limited. Candidates required huge amounts of money for patronage, money that came from the patrons in their factions. These patrons, in turn, gained these huge sums via corrupt deals that provided kickbacks from large businesses in exchange for government contracts or exceptions to the developmental state's strict regulations. As the economy and therefore the popularity of the LDP began to slip, citizens and the media began to question this system. The first major corruption scandal broke in the 1970s, and others were exposed at a growing pace in the 1980s. The biggest, known as the Recruit Scandal, was uncovered in 1988–1989 and led to the forced resignations of several major political leaders.

With popular support for the LDP already waning due to corruption and scandals, the final straw was the economic crisis, which the government did not seem to know how to fix. Perceiving imminent electoral disaster, several major LDP leaders left the party in 1993 to form new opposition parties, though these did not differ ideologically from the LDP. Some formed a coalition government after the 1993 election that would ultimately exclude the LDP from power for the first and only time since its founding.

In response to popular outrage at the corruption scandals amidst economic disaster, the new government passed a fundamental reform of the electoral system, creating a mixed system in which three hundred seats in the *Diet* would be elected in single-member districts and two hundred via open-list PR. To that end, the country was divided into three hundred single-member districts and eleven large PR districts; candidates could simultaneously run in both. Reformers believed this new system would reduce the role of money (and therefore corruption) in the electoral system and limit the power of the LDP. Neither outcome seems to have come to pass. The LDP regained power, though this time in a coalition government (as would be expected in a partially PR system with multiple parties), in 1996, winning 239 of 500 seats (up from 223 seats in its 1993 loss). It remained the ruling party in coalition governments from 1996 to 2005, at which time it once again won an outright majority of seats in the *Diet.* Following the logic of electoral systems, the dominant LDP has won far more seats in the single-member districts (219 in the 2005 election) than in the PR districts (only 77 of 180 in 2005), and opposition parties have fared better in the PR seats.

A new array of opposition parties has emerged from the instability in the party system of the early 1990s. The largest of these parties, with 133 *Diet* seats after 2005, is the Democratic Party (DP), a combination of some of the groups that formed after members left the LDP in the early 1990s that now pursues a slightly more centrist ideology than the LDP. The *Komeito,* now renamed the Clean Government Party, still exists and has thirty-one seats. The JSP, renamed the Social Democratic Party, has not fared well despite the changes in the electoral system. It and the JCP currently have only seven and nine seats, respectively, in the *Diet;* the left in Japanese politics appears to have lost virtually all its support, with the centrist DP the only currently viable opposition to the LDP.

The economic crisis and new electoral system also helped produce a new style of national candidate. In 2001 Junichiro Koizumi was the first person to win the presidency of the LDP, and therefore the right to become prime minister, without the support of any of the major factions within the party. He instead appealed directly to the local voting members of the party, advocating a reformist agenda that attempted to solve the decade-old economic crisis. This successful effort led to his victories in the parliamentary elections of 2001, 2003, and 2005. In each of these campaigns, Koizumi ran a populist national campaign much more like a presidential campaign in the United States than anything ever seen in Japan. As required by party rules, he resigned as president of the LDP and, subsequently, prime minister of Japan in 2006, and was replaced by Shinzo Abe, a member of an established LDP faction but nonetheless a politician who also made more mass popular appeals than LDP leaders prior to Koizumi. Abe, however, proved to be an unpopular leader. When the LDP lost a mostly symbolic election for Japan's weak upper house of parliament in 2007, he was forced to resign as PM. (It was an election for the upper house only, as if in the United States we were to have a separate election just for the Senate.) He was replaced by Yasuo Fukuda in September 2007.

Unlike the LDP, Japan's civil society has always been considered rather weak by political scientists. Is this weakness a product of Japanese culture and history or of institutional arrangements? Business was certainly very well represented and served during the period of unquestioned LDP dominance. Most major business interests were represented in the *Keidanren,* a single organization closely associated with and supported by the ruling party in a rather neocorporatist manner. At least as important, though, were the connections between key bureaucrats and major political leaders and individual businesses. A major business interest, a relevant bureaucratic agency, and key members of the *Diet* would form an iron triangle, a three-sided cooperative interaction that served the interest of all involved but kept others out of the policy-making process. Iron triangles still exist in many countries, but Japan was particularly well known for them. They allowed privileged business interests, especially the large conglomerates known as *keiretsu* (see chapter 5), personal access to and influence over governmental decisions, but excluded other interests. In addition, they fuelled the corruption that Japan would become famous for in the 1980s and 1990s. Business interests shifted as globalization came on to the scene, and the economic crisis set in because those larger businesses that became increasingly active in global trade needed less from the government in terms of special favors and regulations. Accordingly, they reduced their unquestioned support of the LDP, a factor that led to the LDP splits in the early 1990s. Even with the introduction of all of this, however, business remains the organized interest with the greatest access to and influence over the central government.

Japan's rate of unionization has always been lower than those found in most of Europe and, like those of other wealthy nations, has declined in the face of globalization since the 1980s. Two major union organizations existed until their merger in 1989. The larger of the two, which represented public sector workers, was fiercely critical of the LDP and was long the backbone of the major opposition party, the JSP. Yet as union membership declined and workers prospered under Japan's economic miracle, support for the "left" withered, leading to the merger and the creation of a new group, called *Rengo.* The group actually fielded its own candidates in the first elections after the merger, arguing that no major party could defend workers adequately. Despite its efforts, by the mid-1990s its members increasingly supported the LDP or the DP, contributing to the socialists' rapid electoral decline. Throughout this process, however, unions never had great influence over government policy because they were unable to gain the power to alter the LDP's conservative economic policies.

In addition to unions, Japan has a pluralist interest group system but one that is tightly regulated by the bureaucracy, as is the economy as a whole. To gain legal status, organizations in civil society must have the approval of a relevant ministry, and the government has used these regulations to limit the scope of interest groups. Many environmental, women's, senior citizen, and religious groups exist, as in other pluralist systems (more than four hundred thousand were legally recognized in the late 1990s), but the vast majority are local, with few professional staff and little expertise or influence. Political scientist Robert Pekkanen (2006) characterizes Japan's interest groups as having "members without advocates." In the United States, nearly 40 percent of all research reported in major newspapers comes from civil society organizations; in Japan only about 5 percent does. Instead, the government itself is the major source of reported research.

This civil society weakness, however, may be changing. In 1999 the government passed a law creating an official Non-Profit Organizations (NPOs) category. This significantly liberalized the regulations on civil society and provided tax breaks for financial support to many of them. More than twelve thousand NPOs were officially recognized by 2003 (Pekkanen 2004,

374). The new law gives civil society organizations much greater autonomy from the government and ruling party than in the past. The LDP supported it, in part, because the traditional campaign machines were not delivering votes as easily as they used to, and the party saw NPOs as possible new bases of electoral support. Whether this gives Japan's civil society significantly greater autonomy and influence than in the past is yet to be determined. The trends suggest that participation is increasing: more parties now compete for power, coalition governments have become common, and civil society seems to be on the rise. What is not clear is the extent to which this has resolved the problems in the electoral system that produced patronage politics or the inability of the government to find effective policies in the face of economic crisis.

CASE STUDY India: From Dominant Party to Multiparty Democracy

India is regularly heralded as "the world's largest democracy," which it certainly is. It is also a fascinating case study of democracy in a poor, exceptionally heterogeneous, postcolonial society. Critics initially argued that it was only partially democratic, with severe limits on real political alternatives or effective participation. The growth of multiple parties and coalition governments in recent years, along with the rise of interest groups representing the poorest segments of society, now suggest greater participation and representation. For three decades after independence, India had a dominant party system similar to Japan's. The ruling party used broad-based support in an FPTP electoral system to win every election from 1947 to 1977. At the time, many political scientists believed this dominant party system was the only thing stable enough to preserve democracy in such a diverse and poor country. Since 1977, however, viable opposition parties have emerged, which has created a multiparty system in which coalition governments have become the norm and power changes hands regularly and peacefully. Prior to this, India's dominant party ruled via patronage and contained numerous internal factions, similar to the way things were done in Japan; eventually, competition among them led to the party's split and the rise of viable opposition. And as in most postcolonial societies, the most politically influential interest groups are not those based on the key economic sectors of business and labor as they are in more industrialized societies; rather, they are based on identity groups.

The Indian National Congress (INC) led India to independence and became the country's dominant,

Two boys, members of India's *dalit* (formerly known as "untouchable") caste, return home from private school. India's constitution outlawed untouchability, but the *dalit* community has had to organize its own interest groups and parties to demand improved treatment. While large numbers are still poor, increasing numbers of *dalits* are now able to gain access to an education and become professionals.

ruling party. With a secular and social democratic ideology, the INC under the charismatic leadership of the Mahatma Gandhi and Jawaharlal Nehru dominated Indian politics for four decades. Nehru served as prime minister until his death, succeeded two years later by his daughter, Indira Gandhi, who led the country from 1966 to 1984 (except for 1977–1980) and was in turn succeeded by her son, Rajiv Gandhi, from 1984 to 1989. To achieve this continuity of leadership and to unite the nationalist movement, the INC became a very broad-based party. While proclaiming a transformative ideology of social democracy, its electoral success, in fact, rested on long-established hierarchies based on caste and wealth. It mobilized support primarily via local Brahmin elites, many of them landowners, who effectively controlled the votes of millions of local peasants. Like the LDP, the INC became a giant patronage machine, sharing the benefits of government in exchange for rural support. Because India uses a FPTP electoral system (adopted from its British colonizers), the INC never had to win an outright majority of the vote to control a majority of seats in parliament. In the first two decades it polled between 45 and 47 percent of the national votes, and that number dropped to around 40 percent later in its period of dominance, but because its support was geographically widespread, it still won a majority of the legislative seats.

It also didn't hurt that the INC's opposition was fragmented into numerous parties, most of which had significant support only in particular regions. The enduring opposition came from two ideological alternatives: communism and Hindu nationalism. The Communist Party of India (CPI) has existed since independence, but split in the 1960s between those supporting the Soviet Union and those supporting communist China. The CPI continued to follow Soviet policies of depending on the urban working class for support, while a breakaway faction, the CPI(M) (for Marxist), adopted the Maoist idea of organizing the peasantry in the countryside. The CPI(M) became the stronger party and controlled two state governments for many years.

Hindu nationalism dates back to the late nineteenth century. As the INC became stronger and fully secular, Hindu nationalists called for a Hindu conception of the Indian nation, one based on the three pillars of geographical unity of all of India, racial descent from Aryan ancestors, and a common culture with Hindu roots. Since independence, Hindu nationalists have joined various political parties, with their greatest strength in the northern, Hindi-speaking region of the country, where both Hinduism and caste identities are strongest. Beyond these two ideologically distinct

opposition groups, a variety of regional or state-level parties existed, some controlling state governments at times but none gaining more than a few percent of the vote in national elections through the 1970s.

Given its splintered and regionalized opposition, the most important political battles in India's dominant party system, as in all such systems, were among factions within the ruling party. The INC depended on patronage to local elites, who became increasingly corrupt and less willing to follow dictates from the center. This was particularly true after Nehru's death when his daughter Indira tried to assert her own authority over the party in the late 1960s and faced stiff resistance from local Brahmin leaders who wanted to maintain their own control over local party affairs. Before the 1971 election, she broke with many of them as she demanded greater loyalty to her and the central party leadership. The result? A number of regional elites left the party and formed a separate party—Congress (O), as opposed to Indira's Congress (I). In 1971 she launched the largest campaign in Indian history with the slogan *garibi hatao* ("abolish poverty"), trying to appeal directly to the poor peasantry with promises of improved programs, and the support of these millions of individuals won her a massive victory.

After the election, she greatly centralized control of the party in an attempt to control factional battles and ensure that one of her sons would succeed her by appointing virtually all key officials rather than allowing local elites to do so. Local elites increasingly resented her very personalized and centralized rule. Facing questions in court about the legitimacy of her elections and growing resistance from powerful local Brahmin, she declared emergency rule in 1974, suspended most civil rights, threw political opponents in jail, and essentially ruled as a dictator for three years, the only interruption to India's democracy since independence.

These factional battles played themselves out as major changes in other types of political participation also were taking place. As in most postcolonial, primarily rural countries, the most important groups in civil society are not trade unions and business associations. Certainly both exist, but they are rather weak institutions. The unionized workforce is a very small percentage of the population. Both unions and business at the time depended on access to the sole ruling party as the only real way to influence government because threatening to shift support to the opposition is not a credible option in a dominant party system in which no viable opposition exists.

Peasant movements existed as well. In the 1970s, a violent movement known as the Naxalites was active in the northeastern region of the country, following Maoist doctrine that favored aiding the rural poor. Its followers were ultimately defeated by military intervention. A peasant movement that worked within the democratic process by focusing on immediate economic concerns like crop prices also had become active by the 1970s, and other groups arose as well at about the same time. A budding women's movement emerged, focused first on issues of rape, domestic violence, and dowry. Initially tied closely to the communist parties, it later gained greater autonomy. An environmental movement, at times connected to the women's movement, continues to grow in importance, focusing on deforestation, water pollution, and the Bhopal incident, in which an entire area was severely harmed by a chemical explosion at a factory. While all of these groups remain quite active, none is a mass movement in the larger context of Indian politics.

Of much greater importance are groups that originally emerged to champion ethnic, religious, or caste interests. They came out of and appealed to the poor, rural majority, but ultimately have come to speak for many urban citizens as well. Numerous movements also arose around ethnic identity, based in India primarily on language. This was particularly true in the non-Hindi-speaking south of the country, where individuals demanded greater recognition and autonomy in India's federal system. In the end, a major government commission created additional states, drawn largely along linguistic lines, to appease these groups (see chapter 6).

Religious-based movements proved to be much more explosive. The best known of these was an initiative for Sikh independence in the state of Punjab on the border with Pakistan. Much of this movement took the form of a Sikh political party, the *Akali Dal,* which successfully sought the creation of a separate Punjab state as a Sikh homeland. Elements of the movement, however, wanted the Punjab to become a separate Sikh country, like Pakistan was for Muslims. These elements used the Sikh Golden Temple in the Punjabi capital of Chandigarh as a base from which they conducted terrorist campaigns against those they viewed as opponents, in particular Hindu nationalists. In 1984 Indira Gandhi ordered the military to invade the Golden Temple, militarily defeating the Sikh movement; a Sikh bodyguard assassinated her in retaliation a few months later.

The largest and most recently active religious movement remains Hindu nationalism. While its main pillars do not refer to religion as such, they assert a national identity tied to what the movement's followers see as the Hindu cultural heritage of all Indians, a position vociferously opposed by Muslims and Sikhs. The primary organization of this Hindu nationalism movement is the *Rashtriya Swayamsevak Sangh* (RSS), founded in 1925. It became a militaristic—many say neofascist—organization that trained young men for nationalist struggle, rejecting Gandhi's nonviolence and his mobilization of the lower castes. From the start, its primary supporters were educated, middle-class Brahmins, particularly in the northern regions of the country. After being fairly quiescent during the period of INC dominance, the RSS reemerged strongly in the 1980s. Its greatest cause became the mosque and proposed Hindu temple in the northern city of Ayodhya. Hindu nationalists had long agitated, with no success, for the destruction of a mosque built on the site of the mythical birthplace of Lord Rama, one of Hinduism's most important deities, where they wanted to build a temple. By 1990 the RSS had begun a march to the site with thousands of followers to destroy the mosque and begin building the temple. The government, citing India's secular principles, militarily repulsed this effort, which led to violence across northern India in which hundreds of Hindus and Muslims died. Another march in 1992 was also put down, but only after RSS supporters had invaded the site and destroyed the mosque; the site remains in that condition to this day. Occassional violent conflicts between Hindus and Muslims have occurred ever since, as religion has replaced language as the most volatile basis of political divisions in India, producing some religiously based groups in civil society that are willing to use violence to get their way, a continuing threat to the country's political stability.

The most common elements of Indian civil society, however, long have been based on caste. The Indian caste system is an exceptionally complex social hierarchy that has changed dramatically over the past century. At an abstract level, virtually the entire society is divided into four large *varna,* or castes; in reality, there are literally thousands of subcastes at the local level with more specific identities. Traditionally, most of the distinctions among castes were based on occupation: certain castes performed certain types of work. Along with these economic distinctions came strict social practices, such as not eating dinner with, drinking from the same well as, or marrying a member of a caste beneath you. At the bottom of this hierarchy were the so-called untouchables, now known as *dalits.*

The introduction of technological change, access to education, and urbanization has changed the economic basis for caste divisions markedly. Brahmin landlords no longer control land as completely and thoroughly as they once did, many of the lower caste occupations no longer exist, and growing numbers of people of all castes have moved to cities, taking up new occupations at various levels of education and compensation. Nonetheless, caste remains very important. A 1999 survey found that 42 percent of Brahmins worked in "white collar" professional positions or owned large businesses, as opposed to only 17 percent of middle castes and 10 percent of *dalits.* Conversely, less than 4 percent of Brahmins worked as agricultural laborers, as opposed to 35 percent of *dalits.*

Although the Indian constitution legally banned "untouchability" at independence and the INC promised to improve the lot of the *dalits* and other lower castes, the data show that their position in society remains rather poor. Electoral politics led them to organize to fight for their interests. These associations started in the colonial period, developed rapidly after independence, and have expanded further since the 1980s. Starting in the 1950s, the government has pursued what Americans would call an "affirmative action" program (Indians refer to it as "positive discrimination") for *dalits,* which gives them preferential access to education and government employment to create a small

minority of educated and wealthier members of those castes. Those individuals typically have become the leaders of the *dalit* associations, using the resources and knowledge they have gained to help others.

Developing these associations has involved shifting the social construction of caste identity. Traditionally, specific caste identities were very localized, and people mainly thought of themselves in relation to other local castes above and below them. Leaders of caste associations have helped create a more "horizontal" understanding of caste, forging common identities among similar castes with different names in different locales. Perhaps not surprisingly, middle-caste farmers and *dalits* were the earliest and most active groups. These movements created a new type of interest group based on caste identity that parties had to respond to if they wanted to win elections.

Indira Gandhi faced intense domestic and international pressure to restore democracy during the emergency rule. Believing she would win an election because the economy was growing, she agreed to hold new parliamentary elections in 1977. The opposition formed a new party, the Janata Party, that combined an older Janata Party that had championed the interests of farmers with Hindu nationalists, dissidents from the old INC, and members of various state-level parties. The Janata achieved a stunning electoral upset, removing the INC from power for the first time in Indian history. Equally important, for the first time a clear regional division in party popularity emerged. The Janata swept the north, where emergency rule had been felt most severely, and the INC retained its strength in the south. The Janata Party, however, was not very adept at governing; it was forced to call a new parliamentary election in 1980, which Indira Gandhi and the INC once again won by a large majority, controlling two-thirds of the seats in parliament. The INC would go on to dominate the government again throughout the 1980s, first under Indira and after her assassination in 1984 under her son, Rajiv Gandhi, until 1989.

The mobilization of caste, ethnic, and religious groups, combined with the unpopularity of the neoliberal economic model the government started to adopt in the mid-1980s and growing corruption scandals, led to the INC's second electoral defeat in 1989. The government that replaced them was a coalition of several major opposition parties that had to combine forces to establish a parliamentary majority. This marked the beginning of a new, multiparty system in India and seemed to put a permanent end to INC dominance. All governments since have required parliamentary coalitions, with power alternating between INC-led coalitions and coalitions of its opponents. By the mid-1990s, the chief rival to the INC was the Bharatiya Janata Party (BJP), formed in 1980 as the primary Hindu nationalist party. Following its championing of the Ayodhya cause, among others, it became the dominant party in the major northern states, the so-called Hindi Belt where Hindi is the predominant language. Its championing of the Hindu nationalist cause, however, limited its appeal mostly to the north and the upper castes. To gain wider support, in the mid-1990s, moderate elements gained power within the party and modified some of its most extreme nationalist stances, including that on Ayodhya. The revised party platform also appealed to lower castes by promising more extensive social benefits. This helped the BJP win the 1998 election, forming a coalition government with numerous regional parties that remained in power until 2004.

As shown, since 1989, the Indian party system has shifted from a dominant party system under the INC to a fragmented, multiparty system. National government now requires a coalition, and most state-level governments do as well. Institutionalists expect India's FPTP electoral system to create a two-party system eventually, and many observers believed that was happening in the early 1990s when the INC and BJP became the only viable parties at the national level. The heterogeneous nature of the country; the ability of parties to gain office at the local and state levels; and the growing demands of caste, ethnic, and religious movements, however, have produced an extremely complex multiparty system instead. Both major parties have lost support to growing numbers of regional and state-level parties. In the 1977 election, the first INC loss, the INC and Janata together received 75 percent of the national vote. By the 2004 election, the two largest parties, the INC and BJP, won only 49 percent of the national vote. In 1980 six officially registered "national parties" and nineteen state parties contested the election; in 2004 there were still six national parties in the contest, but fifty-five state parties. In several northern states, a party led by and championing *dalits* became the BJP's chief rival and won several state elections.

Given all of this, a sociological explanation of party system evolution seems more appropriate: India's heterogeneous society has produced a fragmented multiparty system in spite of the country's electoral system. As we'll see in chapter 10, these coalition governments have also presided over a rapidly growing economy in the last decade that is quickly making India one of the world's major "emerging powers."

CONCLUSION

Citizen participation and representation are at the heart of democracy, which ideally gives each citizen equal voice and power. The reality, of course, is that no set of institutions can translate participation into representation and power in a way that treats everyone perfectly equally. Different electoral, party, and interest group systems channel participation and provide representation in different ways. The Country and Concept table shows that our ten case study countries alone include numerous combinations, each producing a different result in a different context. These institutions also interact with the governing institutions we outlined in chapter 6, creating yet more variation.

Many people see a key trade-off embedded in the institutions of participation and representation between opportunities for participation and representation on the one hand and effective governing on the other. Institutions that allow citizens numerous points of access to the legislative and executive branches, such as strong pluralist interest group systems, may well impede the ability of the governing institutions to pass and implement laws. Similarly, PR electoral systems that usually allow numerous, small parties to gain legislative representation arguably represent more distinct viewpoints, but the party coalitions that are then necessary to govern are often difficult to form and often prove unstable. The nature of the governing institutions may influence the effects of this trade-off. For instance, presidential systems already divide power between the legislative and executive branches; a PR electoral system is likely to further divide power among multiple parties in the legislature, though the president will still exist as a nationally elected figure from a single party. This could have quite different implications from PR in parliamentary systems in which the executive and legislative branches are fused, but prime ministers are only in power as long as they can hold together a party coalition in parliament.

How effectively each set of institutions allows participation and provides representation also depends on the nature of the society in which the institutions

COUNTRY AND CONCEPT Parties, Elections, and Civil Society

Country	Electoral System	Party System	Number of Significant Parties in Legislature[1]	Interest Group System
Brazil	open-list PR	multiple	7	pluralist
China	NA	one	1	state corporatist
Germany	mixed PR	two and a half	5	neocorporatist
India	FPTP	multiple	4 (in addition to dozens of minor parties)	pluralist
Iran	FPTP	none	0[2]	weak
Japan	mixed PR	multiple	3	pluralist
Nigeria	FPTP	multiple	3[3]	weak
Russia	closed-list PR	dominant	4	weak
United Kingdom	FPTP	two	3	pluralist
United States	FPTP	two	2	pluralist

[1] Data on number of parties in legislatures are from *Political Handbook of the World, 2007* (Washington, D.C.: CQ Press: 2007).

[2] Although political parties are permitted under the constitution, none were recognized following the formal dissolution of the government-sponsored Islamic Republican Party in June 1987, despite Tehran's announcement in October 1988 that such groups would thenceforth be welcomed if they "demonstrated commitment to the Islamic system."

[3] Parties participating in the 2003 elections.

operate. As the case of India demonstrates, social divisions can affect the number and type of parties as much or more than the electoral system does. Groups in civil society, whether organized along pluralist or corporatist lines, are likely to be more effective in wealthier societies where they can draw on greater financial resources and a more educated membership base. Thus there seems to be no simple answers to our questions about which set of institutions provides greater citizenship access and representation and which gives greater power to the elite.

Comparativists seek to understand how the different systems interact and work in different social contexts in part to provide a menu of useful choices for countries thinking about ways to improve their democracies. Such a fundamental choice, however, arises rarely, usually when a new democracy is being created, a subject we examine in chapter 9. Most of the time, countries use the systems they have inherited, either from a founding moment such as the writing of the U.S. Constitution, or, in the majority of countries that are former colonies, from their colonial masters. Former British colonies typically have some type of parliamentary system, while their neighbors who were French colonies usually have semipresidential systems. Every country, however, modifies each general set of institutions to try to fit its unique circumstances. Even many authoritarian regimes, which we turn to in the next chapter, use (and abuse) institutions of participation and representation to try to appear to have some sense of democratic legitimacy in their particular contexts.

Key Concepts

cadre parties (p. 263)

closed-list proportional representation (p. 259)

collective action problems (p. 253)

dominant party system (p. 266)

Duverger's Law (p. 269)

electoral systems (p. 254)

"first-past-the-post" (FPTP) electoral system (p. 257)

Hindu nationalism (p. 292)

interest aggregation (p. 254)

interest group pluralism (p. 273)

majoritarian systems (p. 257)

mass parties (p. 264)

mixed, or semiproportional, representation system (p. 261)

multiparty systems (p. 268)

nongovernmental organizations (NGOs) (p. 278)

open-list proportional representation (p. 259)

party system (p. 254)

peak associations (p. 274)

plurality (p. 257)

populism (p. 266)

proportional representation (PR) (p. 258)

single, nontransferable vote (SNTV) (p. 288)

single-member district (p. 257)

social capital (p. 276)

social movements (p. 255)

societal corporatism, or neo-corporatism (p. 273)

state corporatism (p. 273)

two and a half party system (p. 268)

two party system (p. 268)

Works Cited

Dalton, Russell J., and Martin P. Wattenberg. 2000. *Parties without Partisans: Political Change in Advanced Industrial Democracies.* New York: Oxford University Press.

de Tocqueville, Alexis. 1969, reprint. *Democracy in America.* Garden City, N.Y.: Doubleday Anchor.

Duverger, Maurice. 1969. *Political Parties, Their Organization and Activity in the Modern State.* London: Methuen Publishing.

Norris, Pippa. 2002. *Democratic Phoenix: Reinventing Political Activism.* New York: Cambridge University Press.

Pekkanen, Robert. 2006. *Japan's Dual Civil Society: Members without Advocates.* Stanford: Stanford University Press.

———. 2004. "After the Developmental State: Civil Society in Japan." *Journal of East Asian Studies* 4, no. 3: 363–388.

Putnam, Robert D. 2000. *Bowling Alone: The Collapse and Revival of American Community.* New York: Simon and Schuster.

Schattschneider, E. E. 2003. *Party Government.* New York: Transaction Publishers.

Skocpol, Theda. 2003. *Diminished Democracy: From Membership to Management in American Civic Life.* Norman: University of Oklahoma Press.

von Beyme, Klaus. 1985. *Political Parties in Western Democracies.* Aldershot, UK: Gower.

Resources for Further Study

Aldrich, John H. 1995. *Why Parties? The Origin and Transformation of Political Parties in America.* Chicago: University of Chicago Press.

Pharr, Susan J., and Robert D. Putnam. 2000. *Disaffected Democracies: What's Troubling the Trilateral Countries?* Princeton: Princeton University Press.

Putnam, Robert D. 2002. *Democracies in Flux: The Evolution of Social Capital in Contemporary Society.* New York: Oxford University Press.

Thomas, Clive S. 2001. *Political Parties and Interest Groups: Shaping Democratic Governance.* Boulder, Colo.: Lynne Rienner Publishers.

Ware, Alan. 1996. *Political Parties and Party Systems.* New York: Oxford University Press.

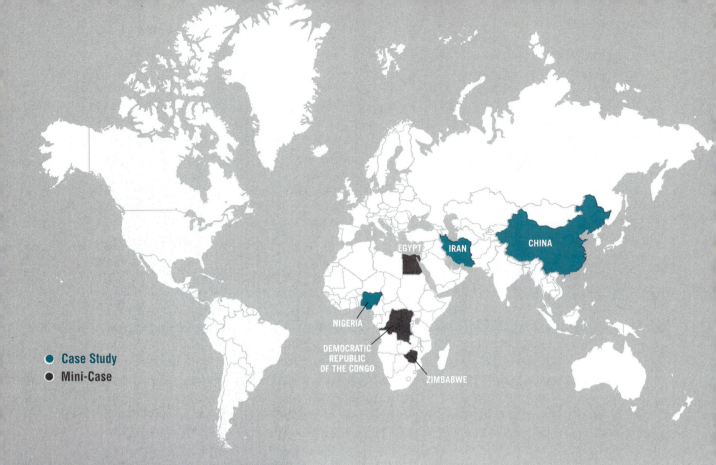

Case Study (Case Study legend — teal)
Mini-Case (Mini-Case legend — dark gray)

EGYPT IRAN CHINA

NIGERIA

DEMOCRATIC
REPUBLIC
OF THE CONGO

ZIMBABWE

Who Rules?

- Some authoritarian regimes disperse power more widely than others. What evidence would you examine to decide "who rules" and what limits executive power in an authoritarian regime?

What Explains Political Behavior?

- Why are patron-client networks so prevalent and important in authoritarian regimes? In what types of authoritarian regimes do they seem most important, and what might explain this?

Where and Why?

- Where do authoritarian regimes seem to become more highly institutionalized? What variables would explain where institutionalization is more likely to occur?

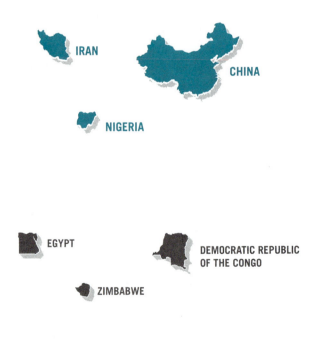

IRAN CHINA

NIGERIA

EGYPT DEMOCRATIC REPUBLIC
OF THE CONGO

ZIMBABWE

AUTHORITARIAN INSTITUTIONS

In the spring and summer of 2008, the world condemned the rulers of Myanmar and Zimbabwe, the first for refusing to let international aid reach typhoon victims, and the second for holding brutal and sham "elections" to legitimize the continued rule of octogenarian dictator Robert Mugabe. The military regime in Myanmar and the de facto one-party regime in Zimbabwe are just two of the more notorious authoritarian governments in recent history. In spite of the spread of democracy since the 1970s, authoritarian regimes remain an important component of modern political history. Indeed, only two of our case studies, the United States and UK, have not had authoritarian regimes in the modern era, and in both of these cases, "democracy" emerged very early and for many years was based on an extremely limited franchise, really a democracy only for wealthy white men with no political rights for the majority of the citizenry. Authoritarian regimes, in various forms and based on various ideological justifications, have been and most likely will continue to be of great political significance, and it behooves comparativists to continue to try to understand them as fully as possible. The Country and Concept table on page 339 shows how common and how varied authoritarian regimes are, just within our ten case studies.

In this chapter we address the following questions: To what extent do different authoritarian regimes limit executive power, and are these limits effective? In what ways and to what extent do these regimes allow participation, and does this participation have any real effect on accountability? Does the fact that these regimes allow far less participation than do democracies mean they provide more effective governance (the participation versus governance trade-off we examined in the last chapter in the context of democracy)?

Chapter 3 outlined the various ideological justifications for authoritarian rule—communism, modernizing authoritarianism, and theocracy. In addition, we described the variety of forms authoritarianism can take. Unfortunately for political scientists, there is no one-to-one correlation between political ideology and

WHERE AND WHY Authoritarian versus Democratic Rule

One of the biggest questions in comparative politics is why some countries developed democratic governments relatively early on that have endured for decades or even centuries, while others remain or became authoritarian. Is there something specific about certain kinds of countries that leads to one outcome or the other? Is there a distinct historical process that leads to one or the other? Are there countries that seem likely to remain authoritarian? We address these questions in the next chapter in the context of recent transitions to democracy, but what about earlier outcomes? Why did Britain develop a democracy as early as 1688, while Russia became communist, and Germany was authoritarian, with a brief and unstable exception, until 1945?

A prominent theory for many years relied on political culture. *The Civic Culture,* a famous work of comparative politics published in the 1960s that we mentioned in chapter 1, argued that some countries have cultures that value participation and expression of ideas and tolerate dissent, and others don't. A second long-standing argument was tied to the level of wealth: wealthy countries with large, educated middle classes become democratic; other countries don't. A third, and perhaps most influential, approach was Barrington Moore's *Social Origins of Dictatorship and Democracy* (1966). Moore set out to answer exactly the question we ask above, looking at Britain, Germany, and Russia, along with several other countries. He provided what many found to be a very convincing structural argument that was influenced by Marxist analysis and that focused on the structure of the transition from agricultural to industrial society. Take Britain: the main agricultural economic activity was wool production; British landlords drove peasants off the land and into the cities early on so that their sheep had a place to graze. Sheep take little labor, and wool producers did not need the state to help them control rural laborers since there weren't many. The displaced, unemployed peasants streamed into the cities and helped produce a cheap industrial workforce. Wool producers and traders wanted their freedom from government interference, and subsequently, they supported liberal ideas that argued for a reduction in the power of the king. They were joined by the rising bourgeoisie in industry who wanted political rights equal to those of the rural aristocracy.

In contrast, in Russia and China the peasantry remained on the land into the modern era, increasingly revolting against modernizing trends that harmed them. These dissatisfied peasants ultimately served as the basis of revolutionary movements that the communists came to lead. Lastly, in Germany, agricultural modernization involved grain farming that required large numbers of laborers. Landlords needed a strong state to help them keep labor on the land and under control. They were joined in their desire for strong government intervention by industrialists who the state supported to aid Germany's rapid industrialization. An alliance of rural elite, rising industrialists, and the state sought to repress workers in the name of rapid modernization, leading down the path to fascism. And so, in terms of democracy, Moore's famous aphorism, a key summary of the entire book, is "no bourgeoisie, no democracy."

form of the authoritarian regime. The oldest and most basic form is the personalist regime, in which one ruler concentrates power in his or her hands so extensively that government really becomes an extension of the ruler's personal decisions. The motto of the personalist regime might be Louis XIV's saying, "L'état, c'est moi" ("I am the state"). A personalist regime may claim that it is a modernizing authoritarian regime and that the leader's rule is crucial to development in the country, but in truth these regimes usually adhere to no real ideology and operate for the benefit of the leader and the leader's immediate circle. For example, the Somoza family, which ruled Nicaragua directly and indirectly from 1937 to 1979, claimed that their leadership and connections to the United States would help the country's economic development, but what they actually meant was that the family personally controlled much of the economic activity in Nicaragua for its own benefit, operating the country, as observers commented, like a "fiefdom."

Other authoritarian regime types have evolved more recently and disperse power at least somewhat more broadly. Military regimes often concentrate power in the hands of a group of upper-echelon military officers; chapter 3 discussed the bureaucratic-authoritarian regime, the highly institutionalized form of the military regime that evolved in Latin America in the mid-twentieth century. Some military regimes appeal very explicitly to modernization theory and claim that the military, with its technical training and rational structure, can best lead a country to development. Others may espouse more radical ideologies or none at all, claiming only that the military is the only institution capable of imposing and maintaining order and stability.

One-party regimes are also a relatively new form of authoritarianism. These have an ideological affinity to communism, because Communist parties claim an ideologically based monopoly on power as the only legitimate representative of the proletariat. Nationalist or other

Anastasio Somoza, dictator of Nicaragua from 1967 until 1979, was ultimately overthrown during a revolution. He, like his father before him, ran a classic personalist regime with virtually all economic and political power centered on him, his family, and his closest associates.

revolutionary parties may also evolve into one-party regimes that severely curtail competition and concentrate power in the hands of party elites. The revolutionary authority and charisma of parties or movements that have led a freedom struggle facilitate this transformation, whatever the party's ideology.

A key difference among types of authoritarian regimes is their level of **institutionalization**. By this we mean how much government processes and procedures are established, predictable, and routinized. In the least institutionalized personalist regimes, decisions truly can be made and implemented at the whim of the dictator. In other authoritarian regimes, the leader's power is still extensive, but it is somewhat curtailed by institutionalized checks. For example, the Brazilian military regime institutionalized a rotating presidency, with each branch of the military designating a president for an established term. Communist regimes have politburos and other mechanisms of high-level party consultation that may (or may not) force some discussion and consensus-building, at least among the party elites.

Authoritarian regimes may also develop institutions such as legislatures and even hold elections, and these provide some degree, however small, of citizen participation. Only somewhat institutionalized regimes can provide forms of participation that are predictable and seem like they might have some actual political effect; without these, citizens are extremely unlikely to engage in political activity except individually in their own self-interest (typically via patron-client networks) or when forced to do so as a show of support for the government. Depending on the level of repression of civil society, citizens may also organize into social movements in an attempt to force government accountability or change. Authoritarian regimes vary among themselves and also within one country over time in how much leeway they give civil society. The more freedom citizens have to organize, the more likely that they will be able to hold a nondemocratic regime at least somewhat accountable, even in the absence of the other institutions of democracy such as elections. The most personalist and least predictable regimes provide no secure means by which citizens can publicly participate or question the government, making it very unlikely any participation (except as noted above) will occur. In general, personalist regimes tend to be less institutionalized than either military or one-party regimes, but we must look closely at each case to confirm this. At times, what appears to be "military" or "one-party" may evolve into a more personalist regime, as, for instance, a highly charismatic leader accrues more power over time.

We now turn to how authoritarian institutions of government actually do or do not function. Authoritarian regimes include bureaucracies and judiciaries, and some even maintain legislatures or a system of federalism, but none of these institutions seriously limits executive power. Leaders rule via some combination of repression, co-optation, and efforts to appear legitimate. Yet while all authoritarian regimes severely limit participation, they vary in the ways and extent to which they do. Earlier chapters raised the question of whether a trade-off exists between participation and effective governance. If one does, we might then conclude that authoritarian governments are likely to be quite effective. Many observers have argued, for instance, that these governments are most capable of carrying out neoliberal economic reform effectively because they are insulated from popular opposition. As we will see, this isn't necessarily the case, as the type of authoritarian regime and its degree of institutionalization seem to matter more to effective governance than the level of participation. More institutionalized authoritarian regimes are likely to provide both greater participation and more effective policymaking.

GOVERNING INSTITUTIONS IN AUTHORITARIAN REGIMES

Virtually all authoritarian regimes recognize one supreme leader, even if he leads a larger ruling group, such as the politburo in a communist system or ruling junta in a military government. This **supreme leader** typically wields executive power with few formal limits. He is likely to consult with other top leaders and may be chosen by them, but he nonetheless contends with few of the constraints on power that an executive in a democratic regime must. In some regimes, the top leaders each informally control an important source of power, an institution, or a faction within the government, and the supreme leader must make sure he has sufficient support from such leaders before he makes major decisions. For example, in a military regime, the leader of each branch of the military might be informally consulted before an important policy decision is made. In more personalist regimes, even these informal limits often do not exist, however. The supreme leader, via repression and co-optation, has eliminated all alternative sources of power. All leaders become beholden to him and must do his bidding. Government in such cases (for example, in Haiti under Jean-Claude "Baby Doc" Duvalier from 1971 to 1986) becomes erratic, reflecting little more than the whims of the supreme leader.

While formal institutions will not limit authoritarian executive power to any great extent, they may help limit the power of any one individual vis-à-vis other key leaders, as well as make government more predictable than it is in less institutionalized regimes. Some regimes, like bureaucratic-authoritarian states, seem to have a relatively high degree of institutionalization from the outset. A military that itself has strong institutionalized norms, such as the Brazilian military that created the bureaucratic-authoritarian regime we outlined in chapter 3, is a hierarchical organization with a strong sense of organizational identity and purpose. In this type of regime, the strength of the military as an institution is reflected in a relatively institutionalized form of military rule. Yet military coups may also bring to power a charismatic individual who, at least initially, rules in a highly personalist way. Similarly, Communist and nationalist parties or movements might seem to be natural breeding grounds for more institutionalized regimes, and such regimes often do reflect the institutional structure of their origins. Communist parties, for example, often exist underground before taking power, and they have highly structured organizations, including politburos, committees, and cells, in addition to consultative and decision-making mechanisms. Even in these cases, however, authoritarian regimes can in practice be focused on an extremely powerful, charismatic leader with nearly limitless authority, at least for a period of time.

Institutionalization often emerges in an authoritarian regime as key leaders attempt to limit each other's power, sometimes in response to past experiences. While the Chinese Communist regime was well institutionalized on paper, Mao Zedong repeatedly attempted to undermine both party and state institutions to preserve his vision of a revolutionary government as well as his own power. His regime, particularly during periods such as the Great Proletarian Cultural Revolution, had as many hallmarks of personalism as of a Communist one-party state. Since his death, a more institutionalized authoritarian rule has slowly emerged in which a supreme leader is selected and solidifies his power with the understanding that the key institutions of the party will remain in place and the supreme leader will yield power in a decade or so to someone from the next generation of leaders.

Institutionalization can also arise in other types of regimes through elite struggles to share power. When a single, highly personalist leader strongly resists pressure to institutionalize shared power, the result can be his overthrow through a coup or revolution, as demonstrated by the fates of the Somozas of Nicaragua and Duvaliers of Haiti. In fact, the military—an institution we did not discuss with regard to democracies—is a key player in authoritarian regimes of all types for two reasons. First, it controls the guns, and so it is the most likely source of a threat to the ruling elite. Second, all authoritarian regimes rely to a significant extent on repression, and so they must have the support of and rely on the military to enforce their rule. To that end, they may take steps to ensure its loyalty: in personalist regimes, leaders often place close supporters, even family members, in key positions in charge of the country's security apparatus, including the military and police. In ethnically divided societies, they often place people of their own ethnic group, or even their own hometown, within the security apparatus to ensure its loyalty: Saddam Hussein in Iraq put not only his fellow Sunni Arabs in positions of authority in his extensive security apparatus, but also people from his home village. Personalist leaders also frequently create entirely new security organizations. Unable to rely on the loyalty of the existing military, they create personal, elite security forces loyal only to the executive. If a president has access to enough resources, his personal security force might be better paid and armed than the national army.

Even in more institutionalized regimes, military force is essential. One-party states incorporate key military leaders into the party leadership, make sure that loyal party leaders have control of the military, or both. After the 1979 revolution that overthrew Anastasio Somoza's personalist regime in Nicaragua, the new Sandinista regime insisted that the military (which replaced the Somoza-created, loyalist National Guard) remain under the control of the Sandinista army that had fought the revolution. The head of the army, Humberto Ortega, was not only a prominent Sandinista, but also the brother of Sandinista president Daniel Ortega.

Many authoritarian rulers also create vast networks of spies, both civilian and military, whose job it is to gather intelligence on who is opposed to the regime and what they plan to do to overthrow it. Security forces can then sweep in to arrest opposition members, throw them in detention without the benefit of a trial, or even execute them. The lack of institutional limits on the executive means liberal protections for individual rights are not secured, which gives the government a free hand to deal with opponents as it chooses.

No regime can rule indefinitely on the basis of fear alone, however. Force and fear can cow a population for a time, but eventually alternative leaders will challenge a ruler who uses nothing but the gun to rule. Authoritarian regimes therefore often develop institutional structures more to create a sense of legitimacy than for any actual function of governance. The relative predictability of a more institutionalized authoritarian regime can provide some legitimacy as the population comes to know what to expect from the regime and is willing, albeit hesitantly perhaps, to participate in its institutions.

Some regimes also use formal institutions such as legislatures and judiciaries to try to gain some modicum of legitimacy. The Brazilian military re-created an elected legislature, limiting participation to two parties—one officially supporting the regime and one officially opposed. The opposition, however, was severely restricted in what it was allowed to say or do in the legislature, whose powers were fairly nominal in any case. Overall, this was an attempt to gain some democratic legitimacy in a way that did not threaten the regime, similar to but not quite as open as contemporary semi-authoritarian regimes such as Russia. Many one-party states in Africa also preserve the presence of a legislature in an attempt to appear democratic and constitutional. That these bodies consist only of loyal members of the ruling party, who formally approve the executive's policy decisions, does little to enhance legitimacy, however. In some countries, such as Kenya, legislators can work on behalf of their constituents to gain resources for their home areas and use their access to government to gain direct benefits for themselves and their closest associates via corruption, as long as they do not seriously question the regime's top leadership.

Authoritarian regimes also exist that allow a degree of rule of law and autonomy for the judiciary, though this is always limited. Typically, judicial autonomy is permitted in nonpolitical cases of criminal law. By partially providing the political good of basic personal security to citizens who do not oppose a regime, that regime can attempt to gain a degree of legitimacy. Again, this is more likely in more institutionalized regimes. Even in these cases, regime leaders do not allow the rule of law to limit them in any fundamental way. Rather, they use the judicial system to condemn their opponents to jail or worse, reserving the right to remove judges as necessary to ensure that the executive will be done. And in many authoritarian regimes, the judiciary becomes quite corrupt as well. Regime leaders and other influential and wealthy people often bribe judges to rule in their favor; once this begins, more and more people recognize what "justice" actually requires, and corruption expands. The regime may formally preserve the rule of law, but in practice justice is based on wealth, power, and influence.

Many authoritarian regimes, both more and less institutionalized, also use elaborate public displays of support to try to gain legitimacy. They hold massive independence day celebrations, complete with throngs of cheering supporters and displays of military might to show their popularity and power. Participants typically have little choice but to participate, though doing so can often be of material benefit. When Mexico's Partido Revolucionario Institucional (PRI) ruled as a semi-authoritarian one-party state, supporters would be trucked in from the countryside to rallies in the cities, where they would enjoy free food, drink, and entertainment. Referring to authoritarian regimes in Africa, Achille Mbembe (1992) refers to such huge but empty displays of regime support as the "banality of power." In the most extreme cases of personalist rule, this becomes a **personality cult** that constantly glorifies the ruler and attempts to turn his every utterance into not only government fiat but also divine wisdom. Personality cults have arisen in an array of regimes, from Communist North Korea under the "Great Leader" Kim Il-Sung to Zaire under Western-supporting dictator Mobutu Sese Seko to "President for Life" Saparmurat Niyazov in post-Soviet Turkmenistan. Regimes with more elaborate ideological justification for their rule, such as Communist and theocratic regimes, also make extensive use of their founding ideologies to try to gain popular legitimacy, as the case of Iran below demonstrates.

The most extreme authoritarian regimes may be able to completely restrict civil society and meaningful participation, but all states require a bureaucracy. In an authoritarian regime, the question is the extent to which the bureaucracy is a strong and independent institution: in most cases, it is not. A more institutionalized regime is more likely to allow the bureaucracy to continue to function according to its own norms and procedures, though regime leaders will not hesitate to violate those norms when they believe it necessary. As with other institutions, a more personalist regime is likely to weaken the bureaucracy more thoroughly, as bureaucrats must obey the whims of the top leaders to keep their jobs, freedom, and sometimes, their lives.

A military regime faces a special set of considerations in regard to a civilian bureaucracy. After a military coup d'état, the military cannot possibly staff the entire state bureaucracy from within its own ranks. The regime compromises by making sure that military personnel are always in the positions of power in the executive; this usually includes all cabinet positions and often positions several levels below that as well. The civilian bureaucracy, however, continues to exist and starts carrying out the orders of the new regime. When these orders conflict with prior bureaucratic norms or laws, civilian officials have little choice but to follow the orders of their new bosses. In virtually all authoritarian regimes, as the autonomy of the bureaucracy wanes, the bureaucrats themselves are more likely to become corrupt. This is at least in part because as they see that few institutionalized norms remain and they begin to fear for their positions in the long term should they cross a higher official, they are more likely to begin to take bribes or steal directly from the government. Yes, the bureaucracy continues to exist, with many of the same civil servants in place, but it is likely to start acting less and less like an independent, rule-abiding institution.

Turning a blind eye to bureaucratic corruption has at least a short-term advantage for an authoritarian regime because opportunities for corruption can become a means of co-opting opposition. Co-optation, often via patron-client relations, is commonly used by authoritarian rulers to buy support. In more institutionalized regimes, this can take the form of formal appointments to key positions, such as top leadership positions in the sole ruling party, in exchange for loyalty. In addition to relatively high salaries and other perks of top office, officials in these positions have significant power over certain sectors of the government, economy, or society, and they often have the opportunity to engage in corrupt practices to their own benefit. The top leaders can thus maintain loyalty as long as enough resources are available. If this behavior is institutionalized it can become somewhat predictable and create greater loyalty further down in the system: lesser officials will remain loyal because they believe they can rise to higher and more rewarding positions, which can lead to somewhat predictable career paths within key institutions. In more personalist regimes, a similar process takes place but in a less institutionalized manner. The key leader alone puts people in positions of power in the state, the party, or any other ruling position. He may well change these frequently to ensure that no official has too much connection with or influence in any one organization because such an outcome could ultimately threaten the supreme ruler by creating an alternative power base for a potential rival.

MINI-CASE The "Politics of Survival" in Mobutu's Zaire

Zaire (now the Democratic Republic of the Congo) under the dictatorship of Gen. Mobutu Sese Seko (1965–1997) was a classic case of a corrupt, personalist regime in a weak state. Mobutu came to power via a military coup and created the formal structures of a one-party state, but his rule was very personalist. All power and all major decisions went through him, and personal loyalty and patronage were the key elements of political power. The state he took over had collapsed shortly after independence into a four-way civil war that became a significant episode in the Cold War in the early 1960s, ultimately involving the United States, Belgium, the Soviet Union, and China. With U.S. support, his coup and subsequent regime managed to pull the country together again but never did create strong institutions or a strong state. In fact, over time his regime severely weakened virtually all state institutions by following the logic of what political scientist Joel Migdal (1988) termed "the politics of survival."

On the surface, personalist leaders like Mobutu appear indomitable. In reality, these authoritarian leaders of weak states have limited power because they preside over weak institutions that can accomplish relatively little. One might think that this would lead them to try to strengthen those institutions to tighten their own grip on power. While this can happen, Migdal points out that it can be extremely risky for the dictator; indeed, more often than not a dictator in a weak state is driven to weaken rather than strengthen institutions.

Strong institutions are certainly sources of power but not necessarily for the supreme leader. He cannot directly control all of a state's institutions but must instead, like any national leader, rely on subordinates. Those subordinates who lead state agencies directly may well be the primary beneficiaries of the power that derives from strengthened institutions. An agency that can solve people's problems or provide valuable resources gains political support for those directly in charge, not only or even necessarily for the supreme leader, and so subordinates in charge of such agencies can easily become political rivals of the supreme leader. Migdal argues that this is why leaders of weak states often engage in practices that undermine the possibility of creating stronger institutions, including frequently shuffling their subordinates so that none becomes entrenched in any one position, appointing people personally loyal to them who may have little competence for the positions in question, and harassing subordinates by doing things like incarcerating them temporarily on trumped up charges.

Mobutu was a master of this kind of politics. He ruled first and foremost by patronage, creating a regime that many referred as a "kleptocracy," or rule by theft. He was personally quite corrupt, amassing an alleged five billion dollars over his three decades in power, and he allowed anyone he appointed to office to do the same. A government appointment was a license to steal whatever resources your position allowed you to access. Over time he increasingly appointed people personally loyal to him as well, especially in the all-important military. He even created several competing security agencies, the most important of which was a personal presidential guard staffed almost entirely with people from or near his home village. He shuffled cabinet members on a regular basis, and if he got angry with a cabinet minister, he was known to remove that individual from the cabinet to jail and then release him or her a few months or years later to return to the cabinet. A famous such case involved Nguza Karl-i-Bond, a top aide in Mobutu's regime. He was foreign minister and then head of the ruling party in the mid-1970s, but after being mentioned as a possible successor to Mobutu he was accused of treason in 1977, imprisoned, and tortured. A year later, Mobutu forgave him and restored him to the prominent office of state commissioner. Then in 1981 Nguza fled into exile in Belgium, denounced Mobutu for his corruption and brutality, and even testified against him before the U.S. Congress. In 1986, however, Mobutu once again forgave him, and Nguza returned to Zaire to a hero's welcome; shortly afterward he was named to the prestigious position of ambassa-

dor to Washington. Examples like this ensured that no one was secure in any position for too long and proved to all that Mobutu could take people from a top position to prison and back again in the blink of an eye.

"The politics of survival" (along with generous Western support during the Cold War) kept Mobutu in power for three decades but weakened all institutions in Zaire. Even basic infrastructure declined as the state's resources and capabilities collapsed. When Mobutu's neighbor and ally, Rwandan president Juvénal Habyarimana, was facing an armed insurrection in the early 1990s, Mobutu is alleged to have told him, "Your problem is you built roads. They are coming down those roads to get you." Mobutu did not make that mistake: Zaire's road network deteriorated to almost nothing under his rule. Nonetheless, rebel forces supported by the governments of Burundi, Uganda, and Rwanda (now composed of the rebels who overthrew Habyarimana) eventually forced the aging dictator out of power at the point of a gun.

Especially in cases where a single leader controls appointment to high offices and changes personnel frequently to protect his own power, authoritarian regimes are plagued by the question of succession. Electoral democracies provide a means of changing leadership on a regular basis; authoritarian regimes have no such procedure readily at hand. This means that each regime must create its own system for choosing new leaders. Again, the degree of institutionalization here matters greatly. Communist regimes, for instance, generally choose new leaders from among key contenders within the politburo. While the exact process is usually hidden from the general public, both regime leaders and citizens know that should a leader die, resign, or be forced from office, a pool of successors is available and top party leaders will collectively choose one from among their own. The Country and Concept table on page 339 illustrates the institutionalization of succession in the Soviet regime: it had seven different leaders while many other authoritarian regimes had only one, failing to survive their founder's demise.

Less institutionalized regimes typically have no succession system. Personalist leaders often rule for life or until they are forced out of office. The identity of their successor depends on how they are removed rather than on the presence of any formalized institutions of succession; the process thus lacks any predictability. Many personalist rulers will groom a successor as they age, all the while working to make sure that the potential successor does not become a threat to the ruler before the time to pass the baton arrives. In the most personalistic regimes, the leader grooms his own son to be his successor. The Somoza dynasty in Nicaragua

(1936–1979) began with Anastasio senior, who was succeeded by his son Luis, who in turn was succeeded by his brother (and head of the only military, the National Guard), another Anastasio. This was also the case in the regimes of "Papa Doc" (1957–1971) and "Baby Doc" Duvalier (1971–1986) in Haiti. Baby Doc was only nineteen years old when his father died and he became head of state. Should a personalist ruler die without clearly identifying a successor, a battle among key elites can emerge that causes the regime to crumble, often resulting in a military coup (or, in the past, external invasion) to reestablish order. Sometimes, as in the case of Nigeria, the death of a personalist ruler can be the opportunity for democracy to emerge anew.

MINI-CASE Succession in Egypt and Zimbabwe

Two of the world's longest ruling leaders illustrate the problems and perils of succession in authoritarian regimes: Egypt's Hosni Mubarak and Zimbabwe's Robert Mugabe. A November 1, 2007, *New York Times* article on Egypt started with a popular Egyptian political joke: President Mubarak is near death and is asked, "Mr. President, aren't you going to give a farewell speech to the people?" Mubarak answers, "Really? Why? Where are the people going?" The subject of succession has been taboo in the country for years. Mubarak rules over a classic semi-authoritarian regime that began in the 1960s under Gamal Abdel Nasser, who overthrew the monarch, King Farouk, and established what he called an "Arab socialist" state. Anwar Sadat succeeded Nasser upon the latter's death and opened the regime to the West and to greater internal political opposition. It never became a full democracy, but Sadat did allow much greater criticism and organization of opposition than any leader before or since. Then Vice President Mubarak assumed the presidency upon Sadat's assassination in 1981 so that, to date, succession in Egypt has always been via death or coup.

Mubarak has been Egypt's longest-serving ruler since the king. His regime allows elections for representatives to a very weak legislature, but ensures that the long-ruling National Democratic Party (NDP) wins overwhelming majorities. In the national elections in 2005, the NDP won 68 percent of parliamentary seats and Mubarak won 88 percent of the presidential vote in the first election in which he allowed any opposition for the presidency. (By far the largest opposition party

is the banned Muslim Brotherhood, whose members run for parliament as independents, though everyone knows their informal affiliation.)

In the 2011 election, Mubarak will be seventy-seven, and still the official party refuses to even discuss succession. (The government even threatened to detain a newspaper editor who wanted to report that Mubarak was ill.) Many observers believe Mubarak is grooming his son to succeed him in order to create a family dynasty, leading many to refer to Mubarak as the "modern pharaoh." Others, though, believe the chief of the secret intelligence service is his likely successor. No one knows for sure, no clear system is in place, and no one is allowed to even talk about this most sensitive of subjects.

Unlike Mubarak, Robert Mugabe helped lead his country to independence. As the leader and hero of Zimbabwe's nationalist movement, he amassed nearly unlimited power as president; however, since the late 1990s, his popularity has plummeted along with the nation's economy and opposition has mounted. He has been widely criticized in the West for encouraging landless peasants to invade white-owned large farms and taking over this property without compensating the owners. In many cases, the ultimate outcome of this has not been distribution of land to poor peasants but rather more acreage allotted to some of Mugabe's key political supporters, especially in the military. That military entered the civil war in neighboring Democratic Republic of the Congo in the late 1990s on behalf of its government, reportedly in exchange for the right to take whatever minerals it could get out of the mineral-rich country. The fortunes of military leaders were said to have benefited immensely from this process. Meanwhile, the Zimbabwean economy has become one of the world's worst. By 2006 it had the highest inflation rate in the world, and large numbers of Zimbabweans were trying to flee across their southern border into South Africa to escape economic hardship.

In response to a growing opposition movement, Mugabe has done nothing but repress rights further. He continues to hold elections for the parliament but ensures his victory, in part by flagrantly providing governmental largess in areas that vote for him and denying it to areas that don't. Opposition leaders are regularly beaten and arrested at rallies, and numerous journalists have been arrested and papers shut down.

Mugabe has also permitted formal presidential elections, though of course he has always won. By 2007, however, members of the ruling party had clearly begun trying to find ways to get rid of him. Many hoped he would say that his presidential term ending

in 2008 would be his last (he is well over eighty years old), which would have allowed the party to pick a successor. This would not have produced democracy, but it perhaps might have led to the smooth succession to a new supreme leader. Mugabe refused to do even this, however, announcing in March 2007 that he planned to run again in 2008, though for a shortened term of only five years.

When opposition candidate Morgan Tsvangirai won enough votes to force a second-round run-off in the 2008 election, officially sanctioned violence erupted against the opposition. Eventually the second round was held in June 2008, but violence and intimidation led Tsvangirai to withdraw, few people bothered to vote, and the world condemned the election as a sham. Mugabe began another five-year term as president. Zimbabwe's citizens suffer mightily at the hands of one of the harshest and most corrupt regimes in the world, and the perennial problem of succession seems likely to make their suffering continue until Mugabe leaves office via natural causes.

Some authoritarian regimes do have modest institutionalized limits on executive power, but this is almost always a matter of very limited horizontal accountability among the elite and the institutions they lead. For example, institutionalization may require a supreme leader to gain some degree of elite consensus before making major decisions. But this can also provide some level of predictability in the political system: key policy changes and the rise of new leadership develop out of an opaque but at least vaguely understood process among the elite. None of this, however, means average citizens have real representation or opportunities for participation. Vertical accountability, the ability of the citizenry to hold leaders directly accountable, is extremely limited, a subject we take up next.

ELECTIONS, PARTIES, AND CIVIL SOCIETY IN AUTHORITARIAN REGIMES

Elections, parties, and civil society are important to democracies in part because they help to overcome the collective action dilemma: they encourage participation and help channel and promote democratic representation. It should not come as a great shock that authoritarian regimes are not particularly interested in overcoming the collective action problem. In fact, they often go to great extremes to suppress any groups that might attempt to organize, seeing them as a threat. Many authoritarian regimes nonetheless create institutions that at least superficially resemble elections, parties, and interest groups, but these differ greatly from their more democratic counterparts, often in both form and function.

Perhaps the most surprising thing about authoritarian regimes is that quite a number of them actually go to considerable lengths to hold some kind of elections. Since elections are about that most democratic of values, representation, why do they bother? They bother because authoritarian regimes of all types have at least one common interest in promoting elections: attempting to enhance domestic and international legitimacy. The ascendance of more democratic regimes throughout the nineteenth and twentieth centuries led regimes of virtually every sort to try to argue that they represented or served their citizens. Authoritarian regimes see carefully contrived elections as a way to justify to both their citizens and the world community that they have "popular" legitimacy.

Just because it's called an election and looks like an election, doesn't mean that it *is* an election, however, at least not a valid one. A cynically minded government may simply use fraud to fix the electoral outcome. As Paraguayans remarked of their long-term dictator, Alfredo Stroessner (1954–1989), he won eight straight elections—sometimes with more than 100 percent of the vote. As discussed in chapter 7, Mexico's semi-authoritarian regime under the long-ruling PRI (Institutional Revolutionary Party) often won presidential elections with similar percentages until the 1980s. Alternatively, authoritarian rulers may try to create structures that will produce victory for an "official" party somewhat more subtly, as the Brazilian military regime did in the 1970s. This is easier said than done, however, because when an authoritarian regime allows any kind of "real" voting, people often find a way to express their views. Many Brazilians refused to vote for either of the two legally permitted parties, choosing instead to reveal the fraudulence of the system by casting blank or spoiled ballots or casting a write-in vote for "rice and beans."

Communist regimes have more clearly ideological reasons for holding elections, but elections of a specific type. Communist parties claim, after all, to represent at least some sectors of society: workers or workers and peasants. Born in the era of mass parties in Europe, Communist parties have some historical reasons for seeing elections as a way of "proving" their representational legitimacy. But because they also advocate democratic centralism (see chapter 3), and because they argue that "bourgeois democracy" characterized by one person–one vote is really biased in favor of the ruling class (capitalists), they can also claim that elections that don't look very democratic to liberal democrats are still fulfilling a representational function. Communist regimes often "stack" elections in such a way that ordinary citizens influence local elections only. The general electorate may get to participate in local block, neighborhood, or town elections, but then those representatives elect the next layer of representatives and so on up to the national parliamentary level. In addition, although nonparty candidates may be permitted at the local level, all candidates typically have to be cleared by the Communist Party before they can run. From the ideological perspective of communism, such an electoral system is quite consistent, because it permits popular participation, but also preserves the guiding role of the Communist Party, the only legitimate representative of the people. Whereas other authoritarian regimes—particularly personalist dictatorships—may dispense with elections altogether, any regime that emphasizes a party with an ideology—whether Communist or modernizing authoritarian—is likely to be drawn to elections. They provide a venue for "safe" participation if the elections are controlled, they may enhance legitimacy, and they also give the rulers a chance to gauge public opinion.

As these examples suggest, elections in nondemocratic regimes are usually tied to very limited party systems. If an authoritarian regime does not dispense with parties altogether, it may permit a one-party system in which legal opposition is proscribed or so severely restricted that no real competition is allowed. Other parties may be outlawed altogether, so that elections just become a referendum on the ruling party. Alternatively, a few weak, subservient token parties are permitted but can never win an election. The most extreme authoritarian systems use such obvious measures of intimidation, censorship, and manipulation of votes that parties and elections allow no real voice for opposition. Semi-authoritarian regimes, like Mexico under the PRI, may indulge opposition parties greater political expression so long as control of the government by the party is not in question (see Mini-Case in chapter 7).

Whether more or less restrictive, in a one-party system the official party is not really meant to perform the interest aggregation and mobilization functions it does in democracies, but it does play some real and important roles. The party is typically a vehicle for access to goods and jobs. In essence, it becomes a key mechanism for large-scale patron-clientelism, because material incentives may lead people to join and support the party and regime. In Stroessner's Paraguay, membership in the ruling Colorado Party was compulsory for government employees, and nearly a quarter of the population belonged. Mexico's PRI politicians operated on the basis of patronage, and those in rural regions in particular understood that votes for the PRI meant the potential for some goods for their communities. Similarly, membership in the Communist Party is usually a prerequisite for many types of jobs in any communist regime. These material incentives can help to diffuse opposition and even promote legitimacy. Communist parties also often promote political socialization of young people through party youth organizations so that they will have an ideological incentive to become members. Moreover, in communist regimes the party serves as ideological watchdog for the leaders. Party cells exist in all government agencies, communities, and major organizations, such as state-run companies. Their task in part is to ensure conformity with the party leadership's dictates.

Ironically, one-party systems tend to weaken the ruling party as an institution because the system lacks the competitive electoral environment that gives parties an incentive to build institutional strength. The only meaningful participation and competition takes place within the ruling party; therefore, all politically significant factions in society and their leaders must become part of the ruling party. Such parties show their weaknesses when forced to compete, as described in the Mini-Case on Mexico in the previous chapter. Similarly, the Soviet Communist Party was essential to all legal participation and paramount in government policymaking. It was, however, riddled with factions vying for influence and control. The fate of the Soviet and Eastern European Communist parties after democratization amply demonstrates their underlying weakness, in that most were able to gain only very small shares of votes in the first competitive elections. In postcolonial one-party systems, parties were often even weaker: they became empty institutional shells within which factions competed for power because of legal proscriptions on any alternative, but they had little unified purpose or identity. Parties in personalist and other authoritarian one-party systems will be either extremely strong, the sole route through which participation can occur, or will atrophy entirely.

Because what little participation that can occur must occur through approved regime channels, civil society in authoritarian regimes is extremely circumscribed and repressed. Indeed, often it hardly exists at all. Communist regimes such as the Soviet Union and China at their height were totalitarian, as North Korea remains today. What this means is the complete elimination of civil society, including interest groups. In such regimes, the ruling party "represents" all interests that it believes deserve representation. And on the face of it, some organizations may be present. Trade unions or youth or women's groups often nominally exist in Communist countries, but these "mass organizations" are always part of the Communist Party, as they are today in Cuba. They cannot be said to be truly part of civil society, which by definition is separate from the state.

Similarly, noncommunist regimes often use state corporatism to control interest groups. Remember that corporatism is the idea that each component (or interest) in society should be represented by one officially sanctioned organization. When a government legally mandates this, it is referred to as state corporatism because the state controls the interest groups and chooses the ones it wishes to recognize. A recent example was Mexico for most of the twentieth century under the PRI. The PRI claimed it was a revolutionary party representing the poor, and as such, it recognized and included within the party structure a single labor organization, a single peasant association, and a single association for "popular groups"—small businesses, women's interests, and various others. These groups were to represent their constituents within the party. Over time, however, they became increasingly corrupt and controlled by the elite at the top of the party hierarchy. The workers' organization, in particular, was very powerful within the party, and real wages rose in the economy for most of the PRI's long rule, even though the union did not publicly represent any workers' interests that contradicted official party policies.

The emergence of social movements within authoritarian regimes is often one of the first signs or sources of a democratic opening. In Latin America in the 1970s, labor-based social movements outside the confines of the official corporatist unions began challenging the status quo and ultimately forced authoritarian regimes to move toward redemocratization. Movements similar to those in the Northern Hemisphere also arose. Brazil, for instance, has active gay rights, Afro-Brazilian, and women's movements, many of which originated during the military regime. As the case of Brazil shows, however, most of Latin America also has a legacy of state corporatism under authoritarian rule in the twentieth century. This weakened the major interest groups and undermined their claim to legitimate representation of their constituents. The return to democracy in most of these countries over the last twenty years has allowed some of these groups to regain institutional strength and legitimacy and has allowed new groups to emerge. Neo-corporatist systems, however, remain fairly common.

In most of Asia and Africa, unions and other major interest groups arose with and were part of nationalist movements for independence. After independence, however, authoritarian regimes emasculated these organizations, often creating state corporatist systems in their place, in which the official interest groups were extremely weak institutions with little autonomy from government or ruling party control. With the spread of more electoral democracy since the end of the Cold War, interest groups and civil society more broadly have reemerged in most of these countries, but they face a legacy of extreme weakness. However, in some of the wealthier and more industrialized countries such as South Korea, powerful labor unions, for instance, exist and have considerable input in the political system. In many more, however, most interest groups remain very weak institutions.

The weak and curtailed formal institutions that are typical in authoritarian regimes leave patronage as one of the few, and perhaps the only, means through which individuals can participate in politics. By attaching themselves to a powerful patron, citizens can gain access to some resources or power or at least have influence over some area of government. Such influence would occur behind closed doors, of course, as authoritarian regimes severely limit public debate. As the patron gains power and position in the system, the clients gain also through special privileges and access to resources.

Such patron-client relationships are the primary means of political participation in virtually all sub-Saharan African countries. While myriad formal institutions exist, most citizens participate by attaching themselves to a patron. In Kenya's authoritarian regime (1963–1992), the long-time ruling party consisted of ethnically and regionally based factions headed by major patrons. The system allowed very limited public political debate, so political leaders gained support by directing government resources toward their home areas and providing individual support to their myriad clients. Clients got jobs in government or influence in local politics by attaching themselves to patrons who could offer them these benefits.

In the absence of other effective means of participation and representation, following a patron may be the best available option. A patron can represent a client's most immediate interests vis-à-vis the government. Weak and ineffective parties and interest groups mean citizens can't effectively pursue their interests via formal groups. The most likely way for them to get what they want from government is to support a patron who may provide it. The problems in this type of system, though, are numerous. First, its informality means no client is ever guaranteed anything: each individual has a unique and largely private relationship with a patron, who will try to maintain the client's loyalty in the long term, but who will not respond to every demand. Clients have no recourse unless an alternative patron is available (which is sometimes the case, but transferring loyalty is never easy or quick). Second, clientelism discourages citizens from organizing on the basis of collective interests. As long as citizens believe that following a personal patron is the most likely route to obtaining what they need from government, they have little incentive to organize collectively to change the government and its policies more broadly. This is especially true in authoritarian regimes that violently repress any significant organized political activity.

Summary

Participation in authoritarian regimes is extremely limited. More institutionalized regimes have allowed some formal participation, including elections with limited choices. Citizens are rarely content with these limited choices in the long term, however, because they do not give voters any real influence. Less institutionalized regimes typically grant little or no opportunities for participation. This means that parties and interest groups do not really serve the same functions they do in democracies, in which real political participation and competition exist. Given this, many citizens "participate" on a daily basis simply to survive and prosper individually through the use of patron-client networks. This allows the leadership of a regime to use co-optation to maintain adequate support, or at least prevent outright rebellion.

Rebellion, however, can and does happen. Social movements often arise in these situations outside the limited formal boundaries of legal participation. Larger movements for change that bring an entire regime into question also can emerge and produce fundamental regime change, a subject we examine in the next chapter. First, we need a better understanding of how actual authoritarian regimes function in our case study countries.

CASE STUDY China: From Communist to Modernizing Authoritarian Rule

In October 2007, the Chinese Communist Party (CCP) held the biggest event of its calendar, the Party Congress that happens once every five years. The elected congress publicly ratifies major policies and officially elects its top leaders, which the current leadership has already chosen. Analysts watch what happens at this event closely, and they look especially at any changes in the top leadership to try to understand the direction the country may be going. What they see, at least on the surface, is uniformity, with nearly unanimous votes on every issue and leader. But no one knows what goes on behind closed doors. The united face shown to the public is the product of months of jockeying among key leaders to get their people into top positions. When Hu Jintao, the supreme party leader, completes the second of his two five-year terms in 2012, one of the top leaders put into power with him in 2007 will almost certainly succeed him. This orchestrated changing of the

Hu Jintao, center, is president and supreme leader of China. Under China's regime, he rules in consultation with the top leadership centered in the Standing Committee of the Politburo, most of whom are also in top leadership positions in the state apparatus, such as the State Council, which serves as the president's cabinet. Hu's successor will almost certainly arise from among this group.

guard has added a level of regularity to China's political process that didn't exist under the regime's founder, Mao Zedong.

China's Communist regime has been in power since 1949 but has changed profoundly since Mao's death in 1976. Although it remains a one-party state under the unquestioned leadership of the CCP, more institutionalized rule has produced greater predictability within state institutions and the beginnings of what could become the rule of law. Communist in name, in practice, and in many of its ideological orientations, it has become a modernizing authoritarian regime by successfully encouraging capitalist development while maintaining a firm one-party hold on political power. This transition has allowed slightly more political participation in the system, which has led some observers to wonder if it is not on the way to becoming semi-authoritarian or even democratic.

This is a far cry from the early days of the regime. Communist rule under Mao developed into a full-blown personality cult by the late 1960s. Mao's rule, especially during the Cultural Revolution (1966–1976), undermined most institutions. The party, state bureaucracy, and other institutions still existed, but the regime was increasingly personalist, obedient to the whims of the aging Mao. The era is perhaps best captured by Chen Jo-hsi's short stories (1978) in which a young boy causes his parents great fear because he utters the phrase "Chairman Mao is a rotten egg." His parents also keep comic books with images of Mao away from the boy, because should he draw in them and accidentally deface a picture of Mao, the family would be in serious political trouble. These may sound like exaggerated tales written to make a point, but the threat of being seen as unpatriotic for even the most innocuous of actions was very real.

Upon Mao's death, the new leader Deng Xiaoping (1978–1989) joined others in trying to reestablish order and stable governing institutions under the authority of the CCP. These reforms were embodied in a new constitution in 1982 that was significantly amended in 1999. Among other things, the 1982 constitution abolished the position of party chairman, the position Mao had held and abused, but authority remains vested first and foremost in the ruling party, which fuses executive and legislative functions. As Figure 8.1 shows, each key governing institution has a parallel party institution. The National Party Congress is the official decision-making body of the party, and the National People's Congress is the equivalent of the legislature. Both institutions are ostensibly elected by provincial and local bodies, but in reality the higher organs choose virtually all the candidates or at least ensure that only candidates loyal to the ruling party are elected. For all of this, both institutions still have very limited power: they include several thousand members, and meet only occasionally (annually for the legislature and every five years for the Party Congress), doing little more than ratifying the decisions of the party elite. Real power lies in the party's Politburo and even more so in the smaller Politburo Standing Committee (PSC). The State Council and its Standing Committee are in effect the cabinet that actually runs the government, overseen by the Politburo and PSC.

Like all communist regimes, China's struggles with the relationship between the party and state institutions. Under Mao, membership in the top parallel institutions was nearly identical; today, overlapping membership continues but is by no means universal.

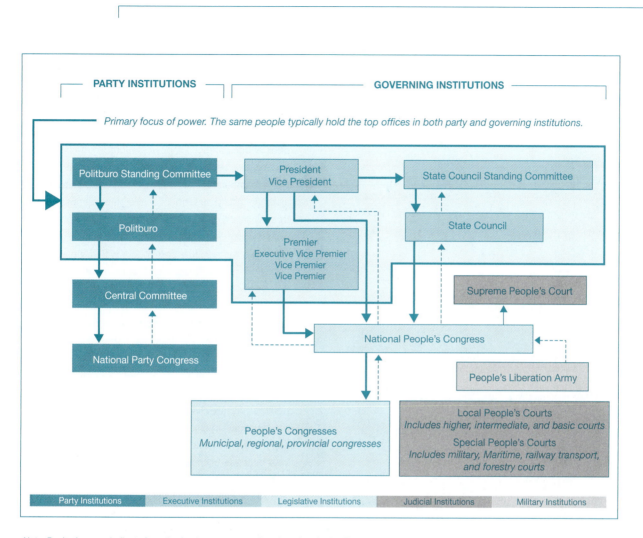

Note: Dashed arrows indicate formal selection process or direction of authority. Bold arrows indicate actual selection process or direction of authority.

FIGURE 8.1
China's Governing Institutions

The regime under recent leaders has tried to distinguish between the governing role of the State Council and the political oversight role of the Politburo and PSC. The ultimate authority of the party organs and their top leadership, however, remains unchallenged. There has always been one paramount leader, though he does not rule alone. While the workings of the Politburo and PSC are secret, all reports suggest that today a great deal of open discussion occurs within these highest organs of power. For instance, Deng shared formal powers with key colleagues. He was chair of the

crucial Central Military Commission (CMC) in charge of the military, but allowed allies to serve as general secretary of the party and as premier, the head of the State Council. More recently, top executive authority again has been fused in the hands of one individual: Hu is not only president, but also general secretary of the party and chair of the CMC.

IN CONTEXT The Decline of Communism

Number of one-party Communist states in 1975: 16

Albania	North Korea
Bulgaria	Poland
China	Romania
Cuba	South Yemen (People's
Czechoslovakia	Democratic Republic
East Germany	of Yemen)
Hungary	Soviet Union
Laos	Vietnam
Mongolia	Yugoslavia

Number of one-party Communist states in 2008: 5

China (in name only)	North Korea
Cuba	Vietnam (in name only)
Laos	

Sources: http://en.wikipedia.org/wiki/Single-party_state#
Former_single-party_states and http://en.wikipedia.org/wiki/List_
of_Communist_States.

Greater institutionalization has also become apparent in leadership succession, the perennial problem of authoritarian regimes. Upon Mao's death in 1976, a two-year battle among factions ensued that created a period of great turbulence. Ultimately, Deng and his allies emerged victorious, launching China on its current path of opening its economy to the world and reforming its institutions while preserving CCP rule. Deng anointed Jiang Zemin as his successor and systematically began transferring power to him in 1989, starting with the chairmanship of the CMC. In 2003 the transfer of power became regularized as Jiang chose Hu as his successor and duly appointed him to all three key executive positions (general secretary, chair of the CMC,

and president). Jiang became known as the "core of the third generation" of the leadership, and Hu is now the "core of the fourth generation." The 2007 Party Congress seems to have anointed Xi Jinping as the next heir apparent, electing him to the PSC, even though party observers say he was not Hu's first choice. He might not be the president's favorite, but he was selected because of support from prior leader Jiang, still a powerful force in the party, and on the basis of his own popularity with the party membership. All in all, China seems to have institutionalized a form of leadership succession that, while still opaque to outsiders, promises some predictability and stability: the new leader now "emerges" among key contenders within the PSC and other top institutions and, once agreed upon, is formally anointed by the leadership to create a smooth transition that is signaled some time in advance of the formal handing over of full power.

Even though the top leader has the fused power of all three important executive positions, he still does not rule alone, as may be inferred from Xi's ascension despite Hu's reluctance. Chinese politics has always been characterized by internal factionalism. Essentially the only reason Mao and Deng had greater power than current leaders was because of the respect they received as two of the revolutionary founders of the regime. Jiang and Hu do not command that kind of respect and therefore must negotiate among other key leaders to gain support for their leadership and policies. Jiang was known to be particularly good at factional infighting, putting his people into key positions and compromising with others. With Hu's elevation to the top leadership, two major factions have emerged: those with backgrounds in the party's youth league, through which Hu rose, who are supported by leaders from inland and poorer regions who back Hu, and those from the wealthier, coastal areas, collectively known as the "Shanghai gang," who support Vice President Zeng Qinghong, who was more or less forced to retire in 2007 (Li and White 2007). Such factional battles occasionally spill over into the larger legislative bodies; while the National People's Congress has never opposed the top leadership, since the early 1990s it has occasionally had some open debate, particularly within regional group meetings. Perhaps the best example of this was a debate over the controversial Three Gorges Dam, condemned by many environmentalists but seen as essential by the leadership for China's future energy needs. While the congress approved it, an unprecedented 77 members voted against it, and 664 abstained out of a total of nearly 3,000.

In addition to party leadership, the military has always been a crucial faction in Chinese politics. Both Mao and Deng retained great military loyalty because of their personal roles during the revolution. Even Deng, though, had to appease the armed forces at times. For example, the army refused to allow Deng to appoint one of his allies, Zhao Ziyang, to head the CMC in the mid-1980s, and when the top commander in Beijing refused to use his troops to disperse the student demonstrators in Tiananmen Square in June 1989, Deng had to call a meeting of all seven regional commanders and persuade the other six to back the move before the army would move in. After that Deng initiated major reforms of the military that Jiang continued. These have significantly professionalized the officer corps as well as improved its funding, reflecting China's rapidly growing strategic position in the world. The army remains an important faction behind the scenes, but for the moment the top leadership under Jiang and now Hu seem to have institutionalized effective civilian control over it, at least barring another crisis such as Tiananmen.

The judiciary has also seen significant institutionalization in the past two decades. Under Mao virtually no criminal justice system existed: criminal and political opponents were identified by Maoist loyalists and subject to local "people's courts." Little in the way of codified law existed and what did was not followed with any regularity. Significant changes have occurred since 1980 as part of the general post-Mao reform process and expansion of a market economy, though the Chinese legal system still does not include the basic rights familiar to Western citizens. A key institution is the Procurator, which exists to serve all levels of the court system. The Procurator combines the roles of prosecuting and defense attorney. He or she decides if a case should go to trial and provides the court with the relevant evidence. If a case does go to trial, conviction is almost certain. (Many minor offenses are resolved by informal community mediation.) A defendant can appeal a case once to a higher level of court. Trials are now supposed to be open to the public and most are, but the government still prevents the public from attending high-profile political cases. Civil law has been liberalized more extensively than criminal law, as the government has had to start the process of protecting private property rights and contracts to attract foreign investment. While the legal rights now in place are not fully implemented, Chinese law has made significant reforms in the direction of providing the basic legal framework capitalism requires. The Supreme People's Court, the country's highest court, has the right to interpret the law and the constitution but not to overturn decisions of the national congress. As always, the party remains supreme over all, including the judiciary.

As shown, China has significantly institutionalized its regime while maintaining ruling party control. One of the biggest threats to the party is the weakening of institutions via corruption. With the rise of a market economy that is now parallel with and increasingly replacing the state sector, opportunities for corruption have multiplied rapidly. State and party officials are in positions to gain bribes because of their control over regulation of financial services, key licenses for business activities, land use rights, infrastructure contracts, and government procurement. A new practice since the 1990s is *maiguan maiguan,* the buying and selling of government positions, especially at the local level in less-developed regions. In an extreme case, 265 local politicians in Heilongjiang Province, including the governor, were involved in the sale of government positions. The execution of Zheng Xiaoyu in 2008 for taking bribes to approve often dangerous medicines and accusations that same year that schools destroyed in the 7.8 magnitude earthquake that hit Sichuan Province were shoddily constructed because local officials took bribes have focused popular and global attention on corruption, but the problem is more pervasive than these high-profile examples illustrate. Between October 1997 and September 2002, an average of six thousand senior local officials were prosecuted annually for corruption (Pei 2007).

The party's Central Commission for Discipline Inspection is charged with ferreting out corruption within the party itself. In a five-year period from 1987 to 1992, it investigated nearly a million cases of corruption within the party and expelled more than 150,000 members. The odds of being convicted of corruption are not great, however. While 130,000–190,000 party members have been disciplined since 1982, only 6 percent have been prosecuted, and only half of those have been convicted. As a result, the risks of corruption remain low compared to the possible rewards (Pei 2007). The central leadership clearly recognizes the problem of corruption undermining the governing institutions it has built up since the 1970s, though, as always, the top leadership itself is beyond accountability, even though rumors of massive corruption among family members of the top elite are rampant. While these incidents have never been aired publicly or prosecuted, the widespread belief that corruption reaches the highest levels can only encourage those at lower levels to continue to participate in it themselves. It may well be the most serious institutional problem the regime faces.

China's Communist regime under Mao included ritualistic "participation" by the public in the form of token elections but also initiated spurts of greater participation in an attempt to, as Mao saw it, overcome the inertia of bureaucratic control of his "revolution." After each of these periods, the government would again clamp down on participation, because the uninstitutionalized participation was difficult to control and sometimes resulted in unwanted criticism of the government. The best known of these periods were the Hundred Flowers Campaign in the 1950s and the Great Proletarian Cultural Revolution. During the latter campaign, Mao encouraged young people and students to interrogate the party and government leadership. Mobilized "red" brigades spread across the country, uncovering "traitors" to the revolution who were sent to work camps or put to death. While this was clearly a form of political participation, it was one without any institutionalization or limits, other than absolute loyalty to Mao. The newly empowered young people in the red brigades often went beyond party control to attack teachers, neighbors, and even party officials. Many human rights abuses resulted and countless lives were ruined. As with other areas, the government after Mao's death was left to bring this spiraling mobilization under control.

For the average citizen, however, influencing government during Mao's era was much more informal and individual. CCP membership was the essential and the only formal route into the political process beyond the most local level. Such membership was also the sole road ambitious citizens could travel to political, social, or economic success. Yet fewer than 10 percent of citizens were party members, which meant that most people had to try to influence government in informal ways. With the complete ban on any independent organizations, citizens had little ability to demand such changes in government policy as legal protection for women or minorities, environmental protection, or many of the other issues on which the populace in freer countries typically lobby their governments. Individuals could only hope to gain a personal benefit or perhaps influence the way a policy was implemented locally.

As with most authoritarian regimes, patron-client linkages were crucial to this process. In China networks of personal supporters, including but not exclusively family, are known as **guanxi**. Before, during, and since the Mao era, the Chinese have used their *guanxi* to survive and attempt to prosper. At the height of the Communist system, the state controlled virtually the entire economy, including allocating jobs, houses, and other services. Appearing loyal to the regime was crucial to one's success in the system, but *guanxi* helped a great deal as well. Relatives and friends in the system could help get you a better job or apartment or keep you out of trouble with local authorities. Working the system in this way was essential to many people's survival. For the more ambitious, participation included becoming a member of and taking an active role in the local CCP apparatus in addition to using *guanxi* to help career advancement.

The rapid expansion of the market economy has forced the regime to open up the system of participation and representation at least slightly, making some political accommodations in terms of who can participate and how. This has involved co-opting new elites, allowing semicompetitive elections at the local level, and implementing elements of state corporatism to manage relations with the still limited civil society. One change has been a loosening in the Communist Party itself as it moves away from reliance on ideological and revolutionary credentials and toward more inclusion of people from many backgrounds who bring valuable skills and knowledge to the party. Throughout the Communist era, a debate raged over the role of "reds" and "experts." On one side were leaders, usually including Mao, who argued that those properly committed to revolutionary ideals (that is, loyal to Mao and the CCP) and from the proper "revolutionary classes" (the peasantry and proletariat) should constitute the core of the party and be given preference in participation. On the other side of this argument were those who favored party membership and participation for experts, or those intellectuals, scientists, and engineers who, presumably, could help modernize the country. Since the country's opening to the world market, the CCP has shifted significantly in the direction of the experts. Farmers and workers' share of party membership dropped from 63 percent in 1994 to 44 percent in 2003. Large numbers of scientists, engineers, and other intellectuals have joined the party, including many among the new fourth generation of the top party leadership. In 2001 the party leadership decided to allow private entrepreneurs into the party as well—the ultimate irony, including successful capitalists in a communist party (Dickson 2003).

While this has undoubtedly increased the expertise available for making decisions, its political implications are not clear. Given the development of liberalism in the West, we might expect that allowing intellectuals and especially entrepreneurs to enter the political system would expand democracy: the bourgeoisie, after all, was the class that helped create liberalism in Europe. Market economies, in precisely this way, are supposed to help produce and sustain liberal democracy. Political scientist Bruce Dickson (2003), however, has surveyed China's new entrepreneurs and found that their political attitudes do not suggest they will help create greater democracy because they share the concerns of other party officials about limiting participation to within the elite to maintain stability. The CCP so far seems to have

opened up the party to the intellectual and business elite without threatening its continued control.

Some observers see changes in the electoral laws as another attempt at co-opting potential opposition; others see it as the first real step in the direction of democracy. Over the course of the 1980s, the government revised the electoral law several times, first creating and then expanding the potential competitiveness of elections to rural village committees and township and county legislatures. China long had direct elections for these positions, but with only one candidate for each position who had been nominated by the party. By the early 1990s, the new system was in place. Now all these local elections can be subject to competition. Candidates can be nominated by the party, other local organizations, and any group of ten local citizens. The party, however, maintains great control, including final approval of those nominated.

Studies have shown that how this system actually works in practice varies greatly because local officials often severely limit the level of competition to ensure their own positions. Overall, however, most scholars see local elections as expanding participation and political openness. One survey in the late 1990s found that more than half of voters had attended a campaign event and nearly 20 percent had participated in nominating a candidate (Shi 2006, 365). Electoral turnout has varied widely, but in some places has been as high as 30 percent. A survey in Beijing found increasing participation in and acceptance of the legitimacy of local elections during the 1990s (O'Brien 2006, 389). In rural areas, voters have often used the elections to remove unpopular or unresponsive local officials. The government has also given slightly greater powers to local governments, though these are still quite limited. Ultimately, the central party can intervene as it pleases in local affairs, and official and public criticism of national policies remains virtually impossible. The top leadership, however, seems to want to encourage limited local participation and autonomy, as long as it remains within the parameters set at the center.

Under full Communist rule, the party completely controlled all interest groups. The All-China Federation of Trade Unions (ACFTU), for instance, was the sole legal union organization, with mandatory branches in any enterprise with more than a hundred employees. With the rapid expansion of private enterprises, the party has had difficulty keeping its monopoly on union organization, however. Citizens at all levels of society have become less dependent on the state, which in turn has less control over them. These increasingly independent citizens have taken the initiative to form various interest groups and NGOs (nongovernmental organizations), focused mostly on local, material grievances such as housing or working conditions. To control this, the government has created a registration system under which NGOs must gain official state approval, and the state approves only one organization of a particular type in each administrative area, in effect beginning a system of state corporatism. The state has also created its own organizations for policy issues it is particularly interested in: these are referred to by the Orwellian name Government Organized Non-governmental Organizations (GONGOs). An example is the China Family Planning Association, created to support China's one-child-per-family policy. Despite the restrictions the government puts on them, NGOs and interest groups have at times influenced the direction of government policy independently. Local branches of the ACFTU have successfully supported workers' strikes on a number of occasions, and the national organization helped get a five-day workweek approved.

Even though elections and civil society now offer opportunities for greater participation than in the past, pressure for more changes and informal opposition still exist, the most open and vocal of which have been successfully repressed by the government over the years. The most familiar case is perhaps the Tiananmen Square protest in 1989. It began in response to the death of Hu Yaobang, a popular party leader seen as a key champion of political reform who had recently been ousted from the party leadership. What started as a few hundred students gathered in protest mushroomed within a week to daily protests by two hundred thousand students that included demands to reevaluate Hu's career, free jailed intellectual dissidents, publicly account for party leaders' finances, permit freedom of the press, and provide greater funding for education (note that they did not demand full democracy with competitive national elections, as is often as-

serted). The government eventually agreed to negotiate with the students but gave little ground. With student interest waning and many returning to class, a group of three thousand began a hunger strike as a final effort to make their demands heard. This action garnered massive public support, as more than a million Beijing residents began to turn out to support the hunger strikers. Those who had undertaken the hunger strike finally got some minor concessions from the government and, facing serious health consequences, decided to end the hunger strike. That night, the government declared martial law in the city and tried to bring in the army. At least a million citizens, including many workers, poured into the streets, erecting barricades to prevent the army from entering, but by June 4, the army had successfully moved into Tiananmen Square. In the middle of the night it opened fire on the remaining student dissidents, killing between one thousand and three thousand students and civilians (sources vary considerably on this total, many state it as much higher). The military action sparked worldwide outrage and condemnation, and there were calls to break off trade and negotiations with the country to protest its violation of human rights.

More recently, the government cracked down on Falun Gong, a religious sect founded in 1997. It was legally registered as a religious organization, but in April 1999 the group organized a silent march of ten thousand followers in Beijing to protest a government article critical of the movement. After that, the government banned the organization and has since jailed thousands of its supporters.

This history of repression has successfully eliminated all large-scale protests for the time being, but many local protests continue. Tony Saich reports, "Hardly a day goes by in China without some workers' demonstration over lay-offs or unpaid wages, farmers' unrest over land issues or excessive taxes, or go-slows or stoppages being reported" (2001, 185). As this quote suggests, the vast majority of these continuing protests are not political but rather are in regard to local economic grievances. Reports abound of rural residents protesting and at times rioting over the abuses of a local official. These are typically against the imposition of illegal taxes and are designed to draw the attention of higher officials who local citizens believe will right the wrong. In addition, a number of illegal local unions are said to exist and actively support strikes in the private sector. Students and other urban dwellers also protest occasionally to attempt to change local laws or remove abusive local officials.

China has evolved from a classic Communist regime into one that is modernizing authoritarian. As it has done so, it has adjusted its Communist system of forced participation to legitimize the regime. The opening of the market economy has forced the party to allow greater participation, though it has done so in a way that has kept demands for fundamental reform effectively repressed. In April 2007, for instance, the party allowed some intellectual discussion of more democratic reforms in certain journals, but within very limited bounds. The co-opting of key elites into the ruling party, creation of state corporatist regulation of civil society, and repression when necessary have kept large-scale protest to a minimum since Tiananmen Square in 1989. Semicompetitive elections have allowed some real participation at the local levels of government, but nothing on a larger scale.

Even locally, reforms have been haphazard and partially implemented, though the best evidence suggests they have been expanded over time. All of this suggests that China may be evolving in the direction of a semi-authoritarian regime, but it is clearly not there yet. Semi-authoritarian regimes (see chapter 3) allow some actual public opposition and criticism to exist, but restrict this enough to ensure that the ruling elite maintain power. China's regime has not yet allowed even token public opposition to date. Democracy advocates within China and around the world hope the initial expansion of participation will ultimately yield greater pressure to push the regime toward real democratic reform, though that seems a long way off at this point. It is a characteristic it shares with Iran, our next case study. Both countries have been ruled by charismatic leaders surrounded by a personality cult who saw no reason to allow dissent, even if discussion and debate were permitted to a limited degree. And each country has been in the world eye for human rights abuses and incidents of corruption throughout the government.

CASE STUDY Iran: Theocracy with Limited Participation

The triumph of the Ayatollah Khomeini in 1979 in toppling the U.S.-supported regime of the shah of Iran, and the subsequent Iranian hostage crisis that helped push U.S. president Jimmy Carter from office, were singular events in modern history. They ushered in the world's first modern theocracy—a new type of regime that the West greatly feared. Radical Islam had emerged as a new force in world politics.

The Islamic Republic of Iran has survived for nearly thirty years and shows no signs of fundamentally changing in the near future. The regime has created a unique set of political institutions, based on the theocratic principles we outlined in chapter 3, but with significant participatory elements. The regime mixes appointed and elected offices to maintain the central control of the leading clergy while allowing some voice to other political forces within strict but somewhat flexible limits. Figure 8.2 provides an overview of these institutions, discussed in detail below. During its more open phases, Iran has come close to a semi-authoritar-

Ayatollah Ali Khamenei speaks in front of a portrait of the Islamic Republic of Iran's founding leader, Ayatollah Ruhollah Khomeini. Khamenei succeeded Khomeini upon the latter's death in 1989. Succession is often difficult in authoritarian regimes, but Iran's constitution gives clerical authorities the clear right and ability to choose a successor for supreme leader.

ian regime but has not quite moved into that category completely because the appointed clergy ultimately maintain legal power to do as they please: elected officials are allowed to pass laws and some public criticism is allowed, but the authority of the Shiite clergy is final. So despite its unique institutions, the Iranian government rules like many other authoritarian regimes, through a combination of repression and co-optation, simply with more than the usual efforts made at gaining legitimacy. Also like other authoritarian regimes, it has and will again face the problem of succession of its supreme leader. Similar to China, it also faces a question of whether it will become more democratic in the foreseeable future, as there is significant domestic pressure in that direction.

Khomeini's contribution to Islamic political thought is the position of supreme leader, who is always a respected member of the clergy. With one decree, Khomeini created the single most important position in the Iranian government, as this individual is both the legal and spiritual guide of the country. First occupied by Khomeini himself and since his death in 1989 by Ayatollah Ali Khamenei, the office has the power to appoint the heads of all armed forces, the head of the judiciary, six of the twelve members of the all important Guard-

ian Council, and leaders of Friday prayers at mosques. These powers mean that very little of significance can occur in Iran without at least the supreme leader's tacit consent. An Assembly of Experts composed entirely of clergy but popularly elected by citizens appoints the supreme leader and at least theoretically has the right to remove him, though so far it seems that the position has a life-time term of office.

The supreme leader shares executive power with a directly elected president in a theocratic version of a semipresidential system. Although the supreme leader has broader powers and is the legal head of state, loosely equivalent to the president in France (though with far more powers in reality, given the lack of real democracy in Iran), the elected president appoints a cabinet that the parliament must approve and can remove and runs the daily affairs of government, roughly similar to the prime minister in France. The president is selected via a majoritarian election, so if one candidate does not win more than 50 percent of the vote in the initial election, a run-off is held between the top two candidates. The winner can serve two four-year terms, which the last two presidents have done, each bowing out at the end of his second term.

Like other semipresidential systems, laws must be passed by the parliament and approved by the president. The Iranian system, however, strictly limits the freedom of these elected offices. The Guardian Council, consisting of six clergy appointed by the supreme leader and six lay leaders nominated by the judiciary and approved by parliament, must also agree to all legislation. Given that all of its members are either appointed directly by the supreme leader or nominated by his appointed judiciary, the Council of Guardians is a bastion of conservatism and clerical authority that preserves the theological underpinnings of the regime and the will of the supreme leader. It also must approve all candidates for elections at all levels and has repeatedly banned candidates it has deemed unacceptable for president, parliament, and local government councils. A second body, the Expediency Council, was added via constitutional amendment in 1989 to be an advisory body to the supreme leader. It has the power to resolve disputes between parliament and the Guardian Council, and its rulings are final. The supreme leader

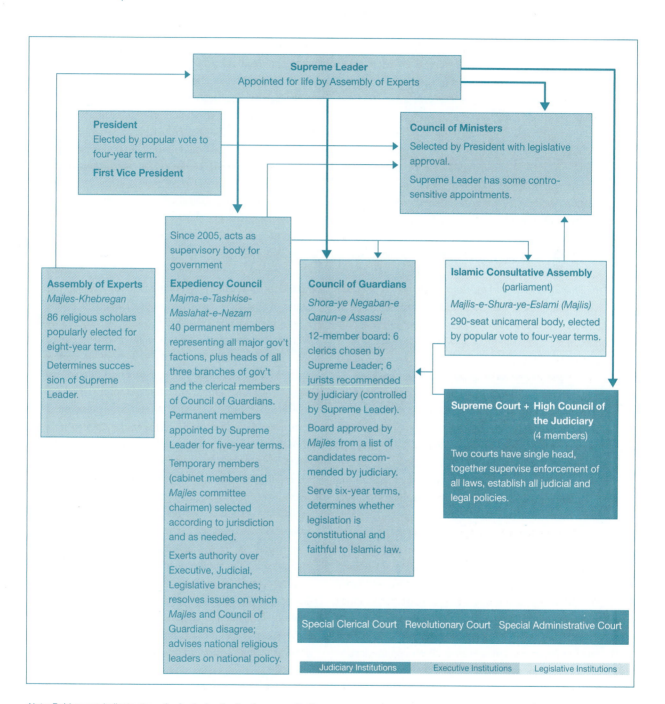

Note: Bold arrows indicate strength of actual authority of supreme leader.

FIGURE 8.2
Iran's Governing Institutions

appoints all of its members, so it is an additional way for him to make sure that the elected officials in parliament and the presidency do not pass laws he does not approve.

The dual executive has control over the bureaucracy, judiciary, and armed forces. Like many authoritarian systems, Iran has more than one army. The Revolutionary Guard was formed as the armed wing of the revolution. Khomeini maintained it after the revolution because he didn't trust the regular national army, an institution of the prior regime. The Revolutionary Guard has become a politically and militarily important organization. Along with the army, it successfully defended the revolutionary government in the Iran-Iraq War (1980–1988) and has since developed large commercial interests as well. Its members form a major political force, out of which emerged the current president Ahmadinejad. A large and ideologically loyal force for the theocratic regime, the clerical leadership takes good care of it in return for its continued loyalty—its annual budget is larger than those of all but a handful of government ministries.

The supreme leader appoints the head of the judiciary who in turn appoints all of the judges under him. The Guardian and Expediency Councils perform functions somewhat akin to judicial review in democracies, but the judiciary's role is strictly that of interpreter and enforcer of the Islamic legal code, the *sharia,* for criminal and civil cases. Other than nominating half of the Guardian Council, the judiciary has no major political role.

The Iranian bureaucracy has expanded by as much as 50 percent under the theocratic regime. Iran's massive oil revenue means that government spending represents a majority of the country's economy. The president is in charge of this large bureaucracy and appoints cabinet ministers to oversee it as well as the heads of various government agencies. Parliament must approve cabinet ministers. The supreme leader, of course, can and does exercise informal influence over both political and high-level technocratic appointments to the bureaucracy, further limiting the president's prerogatives. Throughout, the supreme leader has far greater powers, informally if not formally, than the elected president.

This importance of the supreme leader and his de facto life term leaves Iran with one of the classic problems of authoritarian rule: succession. Khomeini's popularity and power were based not only on the traditional legitimacy he enjoyed as Grand Ayatollah, one of a handful of the highest religious authorities in Shiite Islam, but also on his charismatic legitimacy as the leader of the revolution and spokesman for the "masses" against the hated regime of the shah. He and most other major political actors in the country did not believe any single person could fully replace him as the supreme leader, so to avert a potential crisis, Khomeini appointed a council to review and revise the constitution before his death. The amendments somewhat reduced the power of the state's religious authorities, but more important, they slightly eased the restriction on who could be selected as the supreme leader, eliminating the requirement that he come from only among the Grand Ayatollahs. This allowed a politically astute candidate, then president Ali Khamenei, to be selected as the new supreme leader. He was only a mid-level cleric, and in fact was raised overnight to the rank of Ayatollah (still below Grand Ayatollah) in an effort to give him greater religious authority. In reality, Khomeini and his advisers decided on political expediency, appointing someone who understood politics rather than an icon of religious authority. The other Grand Ayatollahs did not attempt to fight this because they had become increasingly disillusioned with the regime: while initially in favor of the revolution, most had taken an increasingly traditional position during the 1980s, divorcing themselves from active politics.

In contrast to the absolute authority of the supreme leader, the autonomy and strength of the parliament, the *majlis,* and the parties that compete to win election to it are severely circumscribed by multiple appointed positions and councils. The constitution gives the *majlis* significant power in the absence of interference from the Guardian and Expediency Councils: it must pass all legislation, and it can amend legislation. In addition, it must approve cabinet nominees and half the nominees to the Guardian Council, and it can investigate the executive's implementation of the law. It has used these powers repeatedly, exposing corruption in the bureaucracy and refusing to approve some of

Ahmadinejad's initial cabinet nominees because they were seen as incompetent. The power of the appointed clerics, however, always lurks behind the actions of the *majlis*. When the clerics disapprove of significant legislation, they don't hesitate to use their power to veto it and ultimately rewrite it in the Expediency Council.

Majlis elections are majoritarian in single-member districts, with a run-off if the top winner in the first round does not get more than 50 percent. They are held quite regularly, once every four years, and while none has been truly free and fair by standard democratic practices, the Guardian Council at times has allowed significant competition. The council is pivotal to the process because of its power to ban any and all candidates it deems as unsuitable based on their perceived loyalty (or, rather, lack thereof) to the ideals of the Islamic Republic. A pattern has emerged in which the Guardian Council cracks down on the subsequent election after any *majlis* election in which reformist candidates win a significant share of seats. Usually the council's actions include banning reformist candidates in significant numbers. So when reformists won quite a few seats in 1988, the council banned many of those victors in 1992 and 1996. In the 1997 presidential election, Mohammad Khatami, a reformist cleric who emerged as a spokesman for change, won a sweeping victory that many observers saw as the start of a major liberalization of the political system. Until 2000 there were too many conservatives in the parliament, however, for him to get any major reforms passed. In the 2000 *majlis* election, the Guardian Council did not prevent reformist candidates from running because of Khatami's popularity, and as a result, reformists won an overwhelming victory, clinching 80 percent of the vote. The new *majlis* passed major reforms involving greater freedoms of expression, women's rights, human rights in general, and market-oriented economic policies. The Guardian Council, however, vetoed many of these, arguing they violated *sharia.* By the 2004 *majlis* election, Khatami's failure to pass these major reforms had hurt his popularity, and the Guardian Council once again felt it was safe to clamp down. The reformist candidates elected in 2000 were banned from the new election, leading most reformists to call for a boycott. Conservatives won the election, but turnout dropped from nearly 70 percent to 50 percent.

Parties are quite weak institutions in contemporary Iran, but given the severe restrictions on the power of elective offices, this is quite understandable. The prerevolutionary regime of the shah was modernizing authoritarian and rarely allowed significant participation, so the country has no major history of parties. And despite the Islamic constitution's guarantee of a right to form parties, Khomeini banned them in 1987, claiming they produced unnecessary divisions. Reformist president Khatami successfully legalized parties again in 1998, which helped make the 2000 *majlis* election the most open and competitive since the revolution. Khatami's reformist supporters coalesced in a party called the Khordad Front that won the huge victory that year. The party brought together several newly formed parties, most formed around the leadership of a well-known reformer. Its opposition consisted of similar coalitions of supporters of Khomeini's original revolutionary ideals and of the continued dominance of the clerical establishment, each bringing together several newly formed parties as well.

Like parties, civil society is not particularly strong in Iran, but the period of reformist ascendancy—especially 1997 to 2004—saw an explosion of such activity when government restrictions were temporarily relaxed. Of particular note were media, women's, and student groups. Whenever the government has allowed it, the media has expanded rapidly in Iran. Leading up to the 2000 *majlis* election, many newspapers emerged and an exceptionally open political debate occurred. Since that time, religious authorities have again repressed newspapers, closing them down for criticizing the government too harshly and drastically reducing public debate.

Women have become an important organized force over the last decade. Ironically, in terms of women's position in society, the Islamic regime may well have been more "modernizing" than the earlier modernizing authoritarian regime. Women now constitute 62 percent of university students and a very successful birth control policy has lowered child bearing and population growth rates dramatically. Conservative clergy have resisted changes to laws regarding divorce, clothing, and other issues associated with religious observance, but have allowed significant socioeconomic changes in women's lives, and these have fostered women's organizations calling for even further change, a topic explored in chapter 12. All major politicians now court the women's vote during elections.

Intellectual critics and university students have repeatedly spoken out against the government and have repeatedly been repressed when they have spoken out too strongly. This came to a head in 1999, when some student leaders began to question the continued commitment to Islam as the key identity of the state, arguing for democracy and Iranian nationalism instead. Their arrest and the simultaneous closure of a reformist newspaper resulted in demonstrations across Iran's universities, a brutal police response, and violent student riots. Religious authorities successfully repressed the students but not without losing further legitimacy. Whenever the government has allowed it, civil society groups such as students, women, and the media have quickly emerged and voiced their complaints against the government, but they face government repression when those complaints go too far in the eyes of religious authorities. Iranian scholar Arshin Adib-Moghaddam (2006) nonetheless argues that a "pluralistic momentum" has emerged in Iran that no amount of repression can permanently eliminate.

Given the weak formal institutions of participation and the government's repeated repression of them, it is not surprising that patron-client networks are a crucial form of political activity as well as a key means used by the ruling elite to co-opt people to gain their support. Patron-client factions long predate the Islamic regime in Iran, but that regime has done little to eliminate them. Indeed, many scholars argue that they are essential to its continued rule. Government and quasi-governmental foundations have become key venues through which the nation's oil wealth is shared with regime supporters. For instance, the revolutionary regime established Islamic foundations to provide aid to the populace during and immediately after the revolution. Facing international pressure to adopt neoliberal economic policies, the government has privatized formerly government-controlled economic activities by giving these activities to foundations led by regime supporters. The foundations themselves often receive government funding, and some engage in commercial activity as well. One of the largest, the Imam Charity Committee, receives private donations in addition to the fourth largest share of the government's annual budget. It is controlled by conservative supporters of the clergy who use it to mobilize poor voters in favor of conservative candidates. Some of these foundations or their leaders engage in outright corruption, stealing oil revenues, and accepting bribes in return for access to key officials.

These patron-client networks mean that at the top of the political system the elite consists of numerous patrons, formally in one government position or another or well-placed in the leadership of a foundation, and informally leading a large number of clients who provide them political support. These factions, which can cross ideological lines, are crucial venues through which po-

IN CONTEXT Iran and the Middle East

In spite of its reputation as a "pariah state" in much of the West, Iran is above average in its region in terms of level of freedom, social well-being, and elections.

	Iran	Middle East Average*
Freedom House civil liberties score	6	5
Freedom House political rights score	6	5.2
Literacy rate	77	81.4
Number of national elections since 1980 (legislature)	6	4.47

Source: Data are from Freedom House (2007) and Electionworld database http://en.wikipedia.org/wiki/User:Electionworld/Electionworld.

* Averages exclude North Africa.

litical participation occurs. Indeed, President Khatami's reforms in the late 1990s and early 2000s were aimed in part at strengthening civil society to weaken the patron-client networks clerics and their supporters use as tools of co-optation.

Ideological factions exist as well, overlapping and at times crossing the factional divisions based on clientelism. David Menashri, an Israeli expert on Iran, argues that shortly after Khomeini's death three significant factions emerged among both clergy and secular politicians (2001). Conservatives supported adherence to pure Islamist ideals in terms of personal life and moral values and opposed interaction with the West, but they generally supported a market economy and private property. Radicals agreed with conservatives on religious and moral purity, but they supported Khomeini's revolutionary rhetoric in favor of significant state intervention in the economy, which is the economic policy the regime followed for most of the 1980s. Pragmatists, the third faction, were willing to moderate Islamic purity and open up more to the West as well as move in the direction of a market economy; these were the core of the reformists who supported President Khatami. These divisions are not always stable; various groups shifted alliances over the years in factional battles based on clientelist ties as well as various ideological disagreements.

The era of more open political competition and discussion and efforts at significant reforms of the theocratic regime definitively ended with the election of President Ahmadinejad. (Most Americans know him for his international defense of Iran's nuclear program and his questioning of the fact that the Holocaust oc-

curred.) Domestic, not international, issues dominated the campaign, and Ahmadinejad won the 2005 election based on a coalition of social conservatives and the poor, to whom he appealed with a populist campaign that promised more jobs, housing, and social spending. He also had the active support of the Revolutionary Guard, to which he once belonged, and some scholars now believe he may introduce an increasingly militaristic form of rule in which military institutions, especially the Revolutionary Guard, become more prominent.

Ideologically, Ahmadinejad is a radical who favors government intervention in the economy but social and moral conservatism. This combination quickly showed significant internal contradictions that seem likely to make the new president's rule difficult. For instance, social conservatives in the *majlis* have rejected some of his new economic policies, such as using more oil money to fund social programs for the poor. On the other hand, despite his socially conservative rhetoric, he has limited his reversal of earlier social reforms, knowing his youthful supporters would likely rebel. He has banned "Western and indecent music" from state-owned media but has only partially restored restrictions on women's attire and pursued other policies social conservatives favor. His very loud support for the continuation of Iran's nuclear program and his general anti-Western and, specifically, anti-U.S., rhetoric appeal to both halves of his coalition, which perhaps explains why he has been so vocal on these positions. Substantial domestic policy changes may well alienate one or another part of his coalition, but they can all unite behind him in support of his nationalistic rhetoric on the international stage.

Iran is the only fully developed Islamic theocratic regime in the world today. This gives it an unusual ideological justification and, at least initially, revolutionary and ideological legitimacy. After nearly three decades, however, it shows attributes of many other contemporary authoritarian and semi-authoritarian regimes: ruling via repression, co-optation, and efforts at legitimation. The clerical elite and their secular supporters in virtually all key positions have proven themselves quite willing to use repression through the denial of political rights to, the arrest of, and even the assassination of opponents who step beyond what they are willing to tolerate. The religious underpinnings of the regime's claim to legitimacy still seem to have real supporters among some of the population, including some reformers. That is, many Iranian reformers are not advocating the wholesale abandonment of the Islamic revolution and the adoption of a Western-style democracy so much as they are asking for democratic reforms within the Islamic framework.

The regime has presided over significant economic development, creating a much larger middle class and a more highly educated populace (especially among women) than existed at the time of the revolution. These changes led political scientist Michael McFaul to suggest that Iran is one of two countries in the world with "the best structural endowments for democracy that is still ruled by an authoritarian regime" (2005, 75). Iran's oil wealth, however, has allowed its elite to engage in large-scale efforts at co-optation as well, spreading governmental largesse via elaborate patron-client networks that help maintain their support, a common occurrence in our next case study, Nigeria. It, too, possesses great oil wealth. Unlike Iran, however, most of Nigeria's population has not seen their lives improve in any way because of this valuable resource.

CASE STUDY Nigeria: Weakening Institutions under Military Rule

Nigeria's military ruled the country for twenty-nine years, under seven military dictators, since independence in 1960. This history of military intervention is outlined in the timeline on page 335. While many observers viewed this military intervention positively in the 1960s and early 1970s, Nigerian military rule relied on a combination of repression, massive patronage, and attempts to gain legitimacy by promising a "return to democracy." As the economy declined under military rule, coercion became more and more common, and the military regimes became more personalist. In the 1980s and 1990s, three different leaders from the same regional military group consolidated their control over the government and its all-important oil revenues and used these revenues to engage in massive corruption and patronage to maintain their power. As this continued, Nigerian institutions grew weaker and weaker, so that by the 1990s the country was recognized as one of the most corrupt in the world.

Every Nigerian military government eliminated the country's legislature entirely: none attempted to use a legislature with even limited power to gain increased legitimacy. Instead, the military governments created executive councils to rule by decree. The top leader

Gen. Sani Abacha, Nigeria's most corrupt and brutal military leader, was in power from 1993 until his death in 1998. He used his control of the military to prevent a transition to democracy, despite widespread popular support for it. A transition finally happened shortly after his unexpected death.

took the title of president, head, or chairman, and the councils went under various names, such as the Supreme Military Council (1967–1975 and 1983–1985) or the Armed Forces Ruling Council (1985–1993). Under the first long-serving leader, Gen. Yakubu "Jack" Dan-Yumma Gowon (1967–1975), the council was somewhat consensual. As the military governments became more personalized over the years, however, the councils became mere rubber-stampers for the key leaders. Military governments typically appointed a mix of military and civilian leaders as cabinet ministers in charge of the various government ministries and agencies, and civilian elites in business, academia, and politics repeatedly proved themselves willing to work with a military government in exchange for the perks and power that came with cabinet positions. Military leaders used these positions to co-opt both military and civilian elites to ensure their loyalty, and not surprisingly, as oil revenues and corruption grew over the years, these positions became more lucrative and coveted. Each of the military regimes used such rewards as patronage to buy off at least some of its potential civilian opposition as well as ensure the loyalty of key military personnel to the top leader.

While the legislature was the only branch of government the military banned outright, it also severely weakened the judiciary, bureaucracy, and state governments. Yet many observers believe the Gowon government actually increased the power of the bureaucracy in that the elimination of elected officials ended the tense relationship between elected politicians and career civil servants that is inherent in a democracy. As was typical for the era, and in keeping with modernizing authoritarian rule, the Gowon government expanded the role of the state in the economy in the name of development. The "indigenization" decree of 1972 required Nigerian ownership of most investment, thus opening up lucrative opportunities for both civilian and military elite. Direct state ownership of enterprises expanded as well, giving more power and influence to key civil servants.

Up until Ibrahim Babangida's government in the late 1980s, top bureaucrats still maintained their permanent, professional status. Babangida changed this, however, with a decree that said the top civil servants in each ministry would be appointed by and leave of-

IN CONTEXT Authoritarian Rule in Sub-Saharan Africa, 1970–2000

Number of SSA Countries with One-Party Regimes

1970	1980	1990	2000
16	27	28	2

Number of SSA Countries with Military Regimes

1970	1980	1990	2000
9	15	13	4

Number of SSA Countries with Democratic Regimes

Freedom rating	1976	2006
Free	3	11
Partly free	16	23
Not free	25	24
Electoral democracies	—	23

fice with the cabinet ministers, which sharply reduced the distinction between top professional civil servants and political appointees. Growing corruption, as leaders throughout the system stole oil revenues, severely weakened the bureaucracy as an institution, and as corruption became rife throughout the government, civil servants no longer worked on the basis of clear rules and hierarchy. Instead, they increasingly gave jobs to their own clients, family, and friends; stole government funds for themselves; and engaged in nongovernmental businesses. All of this made clear bureaucratic control of the civil service impossible: orders were not followed, functions were not properly carried out, and the bureaucracy lost all respect from the citizens, who had to bribe civil servants to get anything done.

Nigeria's military governments did not eliminate the judiciary either, but like the bureaucracy, they severely weakened it. Civilian courts continued to exist, but decrees of the military governments were beyond any court's jurisdiction. Each military regime became more assertive than the one before in limiting individual rights, ignoring or undermining the courts, and repressing potential opposition. The first military leader, Gen. Johnson Thomas Umunnakwe Aguiyi-Ironsi (January–July 1966) declared that he wanted Nigeria to go on "as normal as possible," so his and Gowon's government interfered relatively little in daily governmental activities, including the judiciary. The later military governments, however, were another story. The Muhammadu Buhari government issued a series of decrees in 1984 and 1985 that severely undermined the judiciary, and military governments from that point on had the power to appoint judges. This was still to be with the advice and consent of a panel of judicial leaders, but the Supreme Military Council had ultimate appointment powers, and it could remove judges as well. The Buhari and Babangida governments (1983–1985 and 1985–1993, respectively) rewarded cooperative judges by promoting them and punished noncooperative judges by removing or at least not promoting them. In this environment, it is no surprise the courts did not challenge the military regimes. Sani Abacha (1993–1998) went even further, entirely eliminating the jurisdictions of many courts, eliminating *habeas corpus,* and arresting hundreds of political opponents in 1994–1995.

Even with all this control of the judiciary, the military still created separate military tribunals to try political cases, such as opposition politicians, coup plotters (Babangida faced coup attempts from disgruntled soldiers in 1985 and 1990), and leaders of local resistance movements such as the Ogoni movement discussed in chapter 4. With a weakened judiciary, individual rights had little protection. The Buhari government, in particular, took draconian measures against opponents. Coming into office with a claim of wanting to "clean up" the corruption of the elected leaders of Nigeria's Second Republic (1979–1983), Buhari used tribunals to try people accused of corruption. The accused had little ability to defend themselves and often faced the death penalty, and such uses of military tribunals grew over the years. We mentioned the most famous case in chapter 4: the 1995 execution of poet and political activist Ken Saro-Wiwa. Saro-Wiwa was leader of MOSOP, which campaigned peacefully for the Ogoni, who live in the oil-producing area of the country, to benefit more from the oil. Abacha, who was by far the most brutal of

Nigeria's rulers, accused Saro-Wiwa and several other MOSOP leaders of killing several Ogoni traditional elders, a charge that all independent observers believe to be false. Saro-Wiwa and the others faced a military tribunal with no public access to the trial and were convicted and summarily executed, which produced the greatest international outrage and protest a Nigerian government ever faced, including the withdrawal of U.S. ambassadors and those from major European nations as well as the removal of Nigeria from the British Commonwealth, a group of former British colonies. Despite this, Abacha's government would continue its rule for another three years, until his sudden death in 1998.

Nigeria's military rulers used federalism to reward supporters, divide potential opposition, and manage ethnic political competition, all while centralizing control of federal institutions. In 1967 General Gowon replaced the three existing political regions with twelve states—six in the north and six in the south—in an effort to reduce the conflict that division of the country into three large regions had caused (see chapter 4). This strategy worked to reduce conflict following the civil war (1967–1970), but it also began the process of centralization of power: the federal government became more powerful, and state governments were far less powerful than the governments of the larger regions had been prior to 1966. This shift of power to the central state was driven in part by rapidly rising oil revenues as world oil prices quadrupled in the early 1970s. The Gowon government used these revenues to fund the states, dividing them more equally than they had been before but nonetheless providing a growing percentage of all state revenues, thereby strengthening the central government's power in Nigeria's federalism.

Division into ever smaller states continued: Gowon added seven new states in the 1970s; General Babangida increased the total to thirty by 1991; and Abacha created six more, for a total of thirty-six, by 1998. State creation became a mechanism of patronage to reward supporters and divide opponents. Each new state required its own state government, which allowed for the local hiring of civil servants and for plum political positions to go to local government loyalists. State governors, who were military men, became famous for their corruption, using their state's share of oil revenue to feather their own nests and reward their own clients. In the southwest, where opposition to Abacha was strong, he created new states to divide his opponents, successfully pitting those who benefited from the creation of a new state against their would-be allies in neighboring areas. Throughout, Nigeria maintained a symmetrical federal system, but one run by the military with power increasingly centralized in its hands.

Nigerian rulers did not use limited elections or legislatures to enhance their legitimacy, but they did allow some political participation as part of a seemingly unending, Sisyphean process of "returning to democracy." All of the country's military rulers immediately promised a return to a democratic regime, and nearly all delayed taking action on this for as long as possible. Actual transitions to democratic rule occurred only in 1979 and 1999 (see chapter 9 for more details). One of the primary ways the military tried to gain some legitimacy was to create elaborate processes for writing new constitutions to prepare for a new democracy. This involved the creation of constituent assemblies in which politicians and leading members of civil society participated and the drafting of new procedures and electoral rules, among other things. The most open political activity took place within these assemblies, as old political alignments based on region and ethnicity informally emerged in the form of factions. In 1987 the Babangida government also allowed very restricted, "nonpartisan" local government elections, in which political parties from the prior democracy (1979–1983) informally participated.

In the process of preparing for a return to democracy, the military government would eventually have to allow political parties to reemerge, be officially registered, and begin campaigning. Olusegun Obasanjo's (1976–1979) government allowed this in the late 1970s, following the particular rules for party registration set down by the new constitution to try to ensure that the government had national appeal. Babangida (in 1989–1993) and Abacha (in 1995) interfered much more elaborately in the process of party creation. Babangida rejected all thirteen parties that sought registration and instead created two, whose platforms he

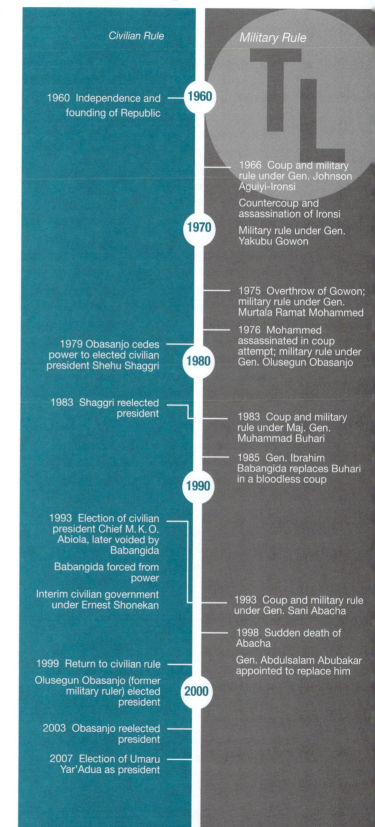

TIMELINE History of Military Intervention in Nigeria

Civilian Rule | Military Rule

1960 Independence and founding of Republic — **1960**

1966 Coup and military rule under Gen. Johnson Aguiyi-Ironsi

Countercoup and assassination of Ironsi

1970 — Military rule under Gen. Yakubu Gowon

1975 Overthrow of Gowon; military rule under Gen. Murtala Ramat Mohammed

1976 Mohammed assassinated in coup attempt; military rule under Gen. Olusegun Obasanjo

1979 Obasanjo cedes power to elected civilian president Shehu Shaggri — **1980**

1983 Shaggri reelected president

1983 Coup and military rule under Maj. Gen. Muhammad Buhari

1985 Gen. Ibrahim Babangida replaces Buhari in a bloodless coup

1990

1993 Election of civilian president Chief M. K. O. Abiola, later voided by Babangida

Babangida forced from power

Interim civilian government under Ernest Shonekan

1993 Coup and military rule under Gen. Sani Abacha

1998 Sudden death of Abacha

Gen. Abdulsalam Abubakar appointed to replace him

1999 Return to civilian rule

Olusegun Obasanjo (former military ruler) elected president — **2000**

2003 Obasanjo reelected president

2007 Election of Umaru Yar'Adua as president

wrote. Abacha allowed five parties to be officially registered, but all of them were pledged to support him for the presidency.

Civil society fared better under Nigerian military rule than did parties. The military governments of the 1970s interfered relatively little with civil society. By and large, labor unions and professional associations continued to operate as they had before, though this was in part because they did not challenge the regimes. The press also was unusually free for an authoritarian regime. The governments of the 1980s and 1990s, however, increasingly repressed civil society, as they did parties. When medical doctors went on strike to protest their working conditions and the government in 1984–1985, the Buhari government responded by banning all associations. Babangida reversed this when he came to power in an attempt to gain some initial legitimacy, but quickly changed course when the organizations opposed him, as when the Nigerian Bar Association actively opposed the use of military tribunals, preventive detention, and other restrictions on the rule of law and human rights. The Nigerian Union of Journalists tried to defend its colleagues jailed and detained in crackdowns on the press in the late 1980s and early 1990s.

Setting himself up for further criticism, Babangida's structural adjustment program that began in 1986 harmed far more Nigerians than it helped and increased poverty substantially, despite the country's massive oil wealth. Growing levels of poverty and unemployment fueled protests against the policies themselves and the military governments more generally. These were led by the Nigerian Labor Congress and the country's national student association. Abacha's even greater brutality and corruption inspired greater opposition, as several major democracy movements coalesced to oppose him, which we examine in greater detail in chapter 9.

Ethnic and religious associations also grew substantially in the 1990s. Nigerians increasingly saw the military rulers of the 1980s and 1990s (all of whom were Muslims from the North and all associated with the Kaduna mafia, a group of military men named after the northern city in which many of the members maintained homes) as centralizing political power in the hands of one ethno-regional and religious group. Christians in the southern part of the country voiced strong opposition to Babangida's 1989 decision to have Nigeria join an international group called the Organization of the Islamic Conference (OIC). In religiously mixed areas, violent conflicts broke out in several cities in the late 1980s and early 1990s as tensions rose. As discussed in chapter 4, new and more fundamentalist Islamic movements began to emerge in the northern region. Ken Saro-Wiwa and MOSOP became the best known ethnically based movement, but many others arose as well.

Nigerian political scientist Julius Ihonvbere argued in the mid-1990s that Abacha's crackdown on all efforts to establish democracy led many political activists to resort to ethnic political mobilization, producing "more than at any other time in Nigeria's history, a hardening of regional positions" (1994, 218). This legacy of growing religious and ethnic sentiment and organizations, some of which became violent, is one of the major obstacles to stability of Nigeria's young democracy, which we'll discuss in chapter 9.

Summary

Nigeria's military regimes became increasingly centralized, repressive, and corrupt over time. While those of the 1970s preserved some prior institutions and allowed civil society to survive more or less intact, later rulers centralized power in their own hands, reducing the strength of virtually all institutions. Predictably, corruption became a way of life in such personalized regimes of weak institutions, and patron-client networks became the main form of political participation and economic survival. Ihonvbere reports that by the early 1990s it was impossible to survive or make progress in the country without (1) belonging to a particular religion; (2) having connections with top military officers, their spouses, or traditional rulers; (3) coming from particular sections of the country; and (4) getting involved directly in one form of corruption or another (1994, 1).

Babangida used patronage to reward current and retired military personnel with appointments to public office and its lavish perks, giving military personnel, especially members of the Kaduna mafia, a greater presence in society than ever before. Oil revenue allowed rising government expenditures in such areas as construction, and contracts were awarded on the basis of connections and bribes, inflating costs and damaging the economy. Larry Diamond, one of the leading experts on Nigerian politics, argues that:

> Babangida degraded every institution he touched, and his fellow ruling officers followed his lead. Indeed, one of the most important legacies of Babangida's rule—with his lavish dispensation of cash, cars, contracts and kickbacks to the officer corp, as well as his license to use political appointments for personal accumulation—was the degradation of the military's own professionalism and institutional integrity, so that it increasingly became, like the politicians, a set of political actors, patrimonial ties, and factional alliances seeking after power, patronage, and wealth; another political party, but with an official monopoly on arms (1997, 471).

Abacha's regime was even more corrupt. Abacha himself stole $3 billion dollars from the Nigerian government in his five years in power (quite possibly setting a world record for the rate of theft of government funds), and gave license to his cronies to do the same. Military rule had descended by the mid-1990s into pure personal rule, in the uniform of military officers. The question we take up in the next chapter is if and how a new democracy can emerge from such a regime and what its prospects and problems are.

CONCLUSION

Nigeria illustrates the post-1990 wave of democratization, but a longer view of its history also reminds us that such trends are reversible. Unfortunately, authoritarianism is likely to remain a problem political scientists will need to continue to ponder. One question for the future may be whether each of the types of authoritarianism we have witnessed so far will continue to exist. In addition, the 1960s saw the development of the bureaucratic authoritarian state in Latin America, so it's reasonable to believe that new forms may develop in the future as well.

All authoritarian regimes, whatever their specific type, attempt to create some institutions, but the types of institutions and their viability vary greatly. And as this chapter has shown, all regimes have executives and bureaucracies, but personalist regimes in particular seem to have weakly developed institutions that place little restraint on the leader and his cohort and have little ability to create predictable lines of succession. In contrast, regimes that originate in the military or in a political party, whether communist or not, often seem to create more durable and somewhat more predictable institutions, although the case of Nigeria demonstrates that not all military governments further institutionalization. Authoritarian regimes may also create electoral institutions but do so for purposes quite different from the ones these institutions serve in liberal democracies. Rather, they are meant to validate and strengthen the regime, not encourage open and possibly challenging expression of public opinion. As a result, electoral institutions and parties in all types of authoritarian regimes are usually too weak to survive the demise of the regime. Some communist and revolutionary nationalist parties have survived such transitions, but usually in much weakened forms. Where parties do exist, however, their internal and often hidden politics may be a better clue to the distribution of power in the regime than the outcome of elections or the action of legislatures. What variables contribute to the creation of strong institutions in authoritarian regimes remains an intriguing question for comparativists.

It is somewhat surprising that authoritarians would bother to create electoral institutions at all, yet all types of authoritarian regimes from personalist to communist have done so. This may be because such regimes fear the free expression of public opinion and seek means to control or channel it. To that end, civil society is usually severely restricted in some way, and civic organizations may be outlawed altogether, subsumed into the state through corporatist structures, or permitted to exist but closely watched and kept within bounds set by the regime. Offering an electoral choice, even an up or down vote on the leader or a choice between two tightly controlled parties, may appear to the regime to be a sop that will help to limit demands for greater participation.

Similarly, because participation is so restricted, patron-client relations take on extraordinary importance in authoritarian regimes. While they also may exist in democratic regimes, they are often the only real channel for people to make their voices heard in an authoritarian regime. The less institutionalized the bureaucracy and other institutions, the more important patron-client linkages are likely to become to individual citizens. In addition, they serve the ruler's interest by creating an elite cadre of supporters, the patrons who are happy to enhance their power through access to state resources. Tracing their actions may help us answer the question "Who rules?" in some authoritarian regimes. More powerful individuals control more patronage, and on the other side, some clients are more powerful and thus more likely to have their requests attended to than others. Patronage networks may provide an entrée to the state in otherwise closed regimes, but it is one in which some politicians and some citizens are more equal than others.

Ironically, the weakness of institutions, patronage, and corruption that plague authoritarian regimes to different degrees often seems to undermine one of their typical rationales: the belief that only strong authoritarian rule can promote efficient and effective economic policy. Nearly every authoritarian regime has made some version of this claim. Some, like Mobutu Sese Seko in Zaire or Alfredo Stroessner in Paraguay, have cynically not acted on it at all. Others, like the Brazilian military or the Chinese Communist Party, have engaged in grandiose plans for development that they hoped would launch their countries into the future. The example of China in this chapter provides evidence of both effective and ineffective attempts at economic development at different times. So far, we might conclude that authoritarian regimes provide little evidence of a trade-off between participation and effective governance, perhaps precisely because of their tendency to develop weak institutions. We return to the question of whether authoritarianism is conducive to economic development in chapter 10.

COUNTRY AND CONCEPT Authoritarian Rule

Country	20th-Century Authoritarian Rule since Independence (years)	Regime Type	Number of Supreme Leaders	Average Length of Leader's Rule (years)	Cause of Regime Demise
Brazil	1930–1945	modernizing authoritarian	1	15	democratization
	1964–1985	military	5	4	democratization
China*	1927–1949	modernizing authoritarian	1	22	revolution
	1949–	communist/modernizing authoritarian	4	14.5	NA
Germany	1871–1918	modernizing authoritarian	2	23	war loss
	1933–1945	fascist	1	12	war loss
India	None	—	—	—	—
Iran	1921–1979	modernizing authoritarian	2	27	revolution
	1979–	theocratic	2	19	NA
Japan	1867–1945	modernizing authoritarian	3	26	war loss
Nigeria	1966–1979	military	4	3	democratization
	1983–1998	military	3	5	democratization
Russia	1917–1991	communist	7	10	democratization
	2000–	semi-authoritarian	1	8	NA
United Kingdom	None	—	—	—	—
United States	None	—	—	—	—

*China's republic (1912–1927) never consolidated an effective state.

Key Concepts

guanxi (p. 322)   personality cult (p. 308)
institutionalization (p. 303)   supreme leader (p. 305)

Works Cited

Adib-Mochaddam, Arshin. 2006. "The Pluralistic Momentum in Iran and the Future of the Reform Movement." *Third World Quarterly* 27, no. 4: 665–674.

Chen, Jo-Hsi. 1978. *The Execution of May Yin and Other Stories from the Great Proletarian Cultural Revolution.* Bloomington: Indiana University Press.

Diamond, Larry, Anthony Kirk-Greene, and Oyeleye Oyediran, ed. 1997. In *Transition without End: Nigerian Politics and Civil Society under Babangida.* Boulder, Colo.: Lynne Rienner Publishers and Ibadan, Nigeria: Vantage Publishers.

Dickson, Bruce J. 2003. *Red Capitalists in China: The Party, Private Entrepreneurs, and Prospects for Political Change.* New York: Cambridge University Press.

Ihonvbere, Julius. 1994. *Nigeria: The Politics of Adjustment and Democracy.* New Brunswick, N.J.: Transaction Publishers.

Li, Cheng, and Lynn White. 2006. "The Sixteenth Central Committee of the Chinese Communist Party: Emerging Patterns of Power Sharing." In *China's Deep Reform: Domestic Politics in Transition*, ed. Lowell Dittmer and Guoli Liu, 81–118. Lanham, Md.: Rowman and Littlefield.

Mbembe, Achille. 1992. "Personal Notes on the Postcolony." *Africa* 62, no. 1: 3–37.

McFaul, Michael. 2005. "Chinese Dreams, Persian Realities." *Journal of Democracy* 16, no. 4: 74–82.

Menashri, David. 2001. *Post-Revolutionary Politics in Iran: Religion, Society, and Power.* London: Frank Cass.

Migdal, Joel S. 1988. *Strong Societies and Weak States: State-Society Relations and State Capabilities in the Third World.* Princeton: Princeton University Press.

Moore, Barrington. 1966. *Social Origins of Dictatorship and Democracy.* Boston: Beacon Press.

O'Brien, Kevin J. 2006. "Villagers, Elections, and Citizenship in Contemporary China." In *China's Deep Reform: Domestic Politics in Transition*, ed. Lowell Dittmer and Guoli Liu, 381–404. Lanham, Md.: Rowman and Littlefield.

Pei, Minxin. 2007. "Corruption Threatens China's Future." Policy Brief 55 (October). Washington, D.C.: Carnegie Endowment for International Peace.

Saich, Tony. 2001. *Governance and Politics in China.* New York: Palgrave.

Shi, Tianjian. 2006. "Village Committee Elections in China: Institutionalist Tactics for Democracy." In *China's Deep Reform: Domestic Politics in Transition*, ed. Lowell Dittmer and Guoli Liu, 353–380. Lanham, Md.: Rowman and Littlefield.

Resources for Further Study

Clapham, Christopher. 1982. *Private Patronage and Public Power: Political Clientelism in the Modern State.* New York: St. Martin's Press.

Clapham, Christopher, and Ian Campbell. 1985. *The Political Dilemmas of Military Regimes.* Totowa, N.J.: Barnes and Noble Imports.

Mbembe, Achille. 2001. *On the Postcolony.* Berkeley: University of California Press.

Case Study
Mini-Case

Who Rules?

- Revolutions require massive support from a mobilized populace. What does the process and the regimes that result from it tell us about how much power the average citizen has in and after revolution?

What Explains Political Behavior?

- What seems to best explain why new democracies survive to move toward consolidation or revert back toward authoritarianism?

- Why does the military intervene in politics?

Where and Why?

- Revolutions are very rare events. What explains why they have happened only in certain places and at certain times?

- Does democracy's long-term well-being require a certain type of society, culture, or economy, or can it happen anywhere?

9

REGIME CHANGE
Coups, Revolutions, and Democratization

Fundamental political change has long been one of the primary interests of comparative politics. Major changes are dramatic events, long remembered in the country in which they occur and sometimes around the world. People rise up, peacefully protesting or even taking up arms to force governments to give up power, and new regimes are established with promises of a better world. Comparativists understand it as regime change, the process through which one regime is transformed into another. The last three chapters have examined political institutions in different kinds of regimes. We now examine how countries go from one type of regime, with its particular set of institutions, to another, and how that process influences the institutions of the new regime.

The end of the Cold War raised high expectations for positive political changes in the world. Francis Fukuyama (1992) termed the new era "the end of history" because he believed that the great political differences that had defined the twentieth century—the different ideologies and regimes we outlined in chapter 3—had ended for good. The new world he envisioned would be uniformly democratic and based on market economies. Many comparativists questioned Fukuyama's thesis from the start, but the terrorist attacks of September 11, 2001, definitively ended the "end of history." This is not to say that the 1990s were not a period of significant institutional and regime change, it's just that change was neither uniformly toward democracy nor the first of its kind in history. Comparativists have long studied regime change. Since the 1980s we have focused primarily on what Samuel Huntington (1991) has called the "third wave" of democratization. Earlier, however, the main focus was on military coups d'etat and social revolutions. All three remain important as the Country and Concept table at the end of this chapter illustrates, though this chapter gives greater attention to transitions to (and breakdowns of) democracy because of its greater contemporary relevance. First, though, we examine the older forms of regime change: military coups and social revolutions.

THE MILITARY IN POLITICS: COUPS D'ETAT

Military force is central to the modern state. All states must have a military and maintain effective control over it to maintain sovereignty. Americans generally view the military as an organization firmly under civilian control that should stay out of politics. And although in theory, the military is not involved in politics in a democracy; in practice, no military is completely apolitical. When President Bill Clinton sought to allow gays and lesbians to serve openly in the military early in his first term, he met fierce opposition from the military leadership that led him to reverse course and create a "don't ask, don't tell" policy. When congressional committees consider the U.S. defense budget, they hold hearings and listen to the advice of top military leaders, among others. These are both examples of the military engaging in political activity. A regime with effective control over the military, whether democratic or authoritarian, keeps such activities within strict limits: the military does not go beyond the bounds set by the civilian leadership. When it does, a constitutional or political crisis can arise. We now examine the most flagrant military intervention in politics: the coup d'etat, in which the military forcibly removes the existing regime and establishes a new one.

When American students are asked why the military does not stage a coup in the United States, the first answer is usually that the Constitution prevents it: the elected president is commander in chief and the military must obey him. But given that the Constitution is a piece of paper and the president one unarmed person, whereas the U.S. military is arguably the most powerful force on the planet, there must be more to it. And there is. A civilian regime, whether democratic or authoritarian, goes to great lengths to ensure that the military is loyal to the regime's ideals and institutions. The primary means it uses is instilling the appropriate values in the military leadership, either professional values specific to the military or more general values supportive of the regime and reflecting the broader political culture. Well-established democracies train military leaders carefully, in military academies such as the U.S.'s West Point or Britain's Sandhurst, in an attempt to instill professional values that portray the military as a prestigious and important profession with core values that must be maintained, including nonintervention in political affairs. Military officers and enlisted personnel, of course, come out of society as a whole, and a strong system of political socialization that ingrains democratic norms of respect for the major political institutions and elected offices helps build and maintain democratic legitimacy among the population at large, including present and future military personnel. Communist systems attempt to achieve the same ends via direct party involvement in the military, mandatory party membership for the military leadership, and, like democracies, a reliance on the party's efforts at political socialization in the broader society.

Less-institutionalized authoritarian regimes often lack these types of generally effective and systematic mechanisms. Instead, they rely on the creation of multiple military institutions (as mentioned in chapter 8) so that no single one becomes too powerful, or on informal ties of loyalty such as ethnic affiliations between the ruler and military personnel. Many African personalist rulers created a presidential guard from the same ethnic group or region as the president that was well-equipped and paid and personally loyal to the president as an individual patron. Its job was, in part, to protect him from his own national military.

Military coups occur when all such efforts fail or are overridden by other concerns among military leaders. Three major schools of thought exist to explain why coups happen. In the 1960s, when they became quite common in postcolonial countries, the dominant explanation focused not on the military itself, but instead on the societies in which the coups occurred. Samuel Finer, in his classic 1975 work, *The Man on Horseback,* made a political culture argument: countries with political cultures that do not highly value nonmilitary means of transferring power and civil society are more prone to coups. Samuel Huntington, focusing on the weakness of institutions, contended that "the most important causes of military intervention in politics are not military … but the political and institutional structure of the society" (1968, 194). Weak institutions and corrupt rule under early postcolonial leaders created political instability and often led to violence. The military, these theorists argued, intervened to restore order when civilian leaders had weakened the civilian regime via corrupt and incompetent rule. Most, including Huntington, were modernization theorists who argued that the military, with its training and hierarchical organization, was one of the few modern institutions in postcolonial societies. They believed the military could rule in the national interest, reestablishing order and restarting development.

A second school of thought looked not at society but within military organizations themselves. These theorists argued that a military engages in a coup in its own institutional interests such as getting larger budgets, higher pay, better equipment, and better tasks to perform (Huntington 1964; Janowitz 1964). When military leaders perceive civilian rulers as not adequately considering the military's needs, they may choose to intervene not in the national interest or because of prior misrule but rather to improve their own position. They may also instigate a coup in response to what they perceive as unjustified civilian intervention in military matters, such as appointment of top officers or assignment of inappropriate duties. Military leaders may see such interventions as a defense of their professional status vis-à-vis civilian leaders trying to get the military to engage in unprofessional behavior. In effect, the military is just another group clamoring for power and position within the government, but one with guns.

Samuel Decalo was the pioneer of the third major explanation of coups. Focusing on Africa, he argued that the first two schools of thought misunderstood the nature of many African (and perhaps other postcolonial) militaries and therefore misunderstood the motivations for coups. The typical African military, he said, was "a coterie of distinct armed camps owing primary clientelist allegiance to a handful of mutually competitive officers of different ranks seething with a variety of corporate, ethnic and personal grievances" (1976, 14–15). He saw the mistake of prior theories as that of viewing the military as a united and professional body concerned with national interests or its own. Instead, he saw African

WHERE AND WHY Coups in Africa: Colonialism or Contagion?

The major explanations for military coups could all apply to Africa, but the following map suggests other possibilities as well. What trends do you see in terms of where coups have happened most frequently?

Clearly, colonial background and region could have a role to play. Political scientists have long noted the tendency of former British colonies to have more stable and democratic regimes (see chapter 6 Where and Why: Parliaments and Presidents). The pattern in Africa suggests the same could be true for military coups. Former British colonies have clearly had far fewer coups than other African countries. But colonial rule was rather regional as well. West Africa, the region with the most coups (a total of forty-two out of eighty-five successful coups on the continent from independence to 2000), mainly consists of former French colonies, with only three former British colonies. Perhaps a regional explanation accounts for the pattern. Political scientists have long noted "contagion" effects: when a country of a particular type or in a particular region does something, other countries of the same type or in the same region often follow. A contagion may have swept West Africa that never spread as far as southern Africa. What could explain this? Several possibilities arise that a researcher could investigate: Does West Africa have distinct cultural differences? Did it go through a different process of decolonization that increased the likelihood of coups? Did it have distinct postcolonial political institutions that made coups more likely? (The last two questions, of course, lead back to colonial rule.) These are the kind of questions comparativists continue to try to answer to disentangle patterns of political behavior.

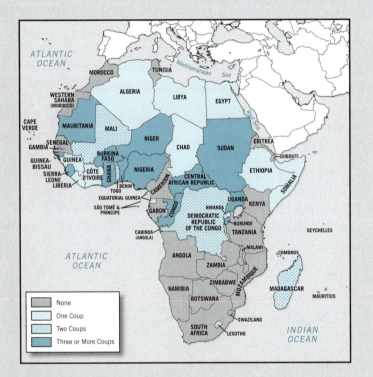

MAP 9.1
Coups in Africa

Source: Peter J. Schraeder, *African Politics and Society: A Mosaic in Transformation,* 2nd ed., New York: Thomas/Wadsworth, 2004, 203. Updates by the authors.

armies as riven with the same regional, ethnic, and personal divisions that characterize neopatrimonial rule in general. Decalo argued that most coups occurred because particular military leaders wanted to gain power for their own interests, those of their ethnic group or region, or those of their faction within the military. Coups were about gaining a greater share of power and, subsequently, government resources for the coup leaders and their clients.

Whatever the reasons behind them, different kinds of militaries and different kinds of coups clearly tend to produce different kinds of military regimes. Of greatest importance in determining the kind of regime is probably the institutional strength of the military itself, as we noted in chapter 8. A military that maintains a strongly hierarchical organization is less likely to produce a coup driven by individual or sectional interests like many of those that have taken place in Africa. Rather, an institutionalized military might instigate a coup to try to create order out of political chaos or a coup in the narrow interests of the military as an institution. The subsequent military regime is likely to be relatively institutionalized, predictable, and stable, if not necessarily legitimate. In addition, a coup carried out primarily in the interests of the military as an institution is likely to result in a shift of governmental resources toward military spending, which usually has deleterious economic effects for the society as a whole. A more personal coup is likely to produce a more personalist regime, far less institutionalized than the other options and more subject to countercoups or so-called palace coups in the future.

The three schools of thought on the causes of military intervention derive from major theoretical strands in political science: political culture, institutionalism, modernization, rational choice theory, and neopatrimonialism. As our case studies below demonstrate, it is often very difficult to discern which theory best explains a particular coup. Military leaders invariably claim that they intervened to save the nation from corruption and incompetence, and, as always in modernizing authoritarian states, to provide unity to pursue an effective development policy. The leaders portray the military as a modern and national institution intervening only out of necessity. Their subsequent rule often betrays them as having other motives, though knowing definitively why they intervened is still difficult: motives for intervention and subsequent actions are not always connected.

CASE STUDY Comparing Coups: Brazil and Nigeria

Brazil and Nigeria provide stark contrasts in the context of their coups, the nature of their militaries, and their postcoup regimes. They both demonstrate, however, the difficulty of explaining military coups. Political scientists have used both societal and institutional (within the military) arguments to explain Brazil's 1964 coup that ushered in the bureaucratic-authoritarian state, a crucial milestone in the country's political and eco-

nomic development. The Brazilian military has been involved in politics since the founding of the republic in 1889. It was instrumental in the governments of the first decade and emerged again as central under the fascist *Estado Novo* in the 1930s. Even during the country's democratic periods, the military has been politically influential; elected officials regularly consult with military leaders on a variety of policy issues, especially those touching on Brazil's rather broad concept of national security. When they believed the national well-being was at stake, military leaders were quite willing to privately get involved in politics, at least until the consolidation of Brazil's new democracy in the 1990s.

With U.S. assistance, the Brazilian military created an elite military academy after World War II, the *Escola Superior de Guerra* (ESG), or Superior War College, that came to play an influential role in the Brazilian military and elite politics in general. Its faculty developed what came to be known as the National Security Doctrine in the 1950s; this doctrine was then taught to students, who were not only high-ranking military officers but also selected senior civilian officials. Essentially, it envisioned national security as including both economic development and prevention of domestic insurrection. At the height of the Cold War, the ESG military intellectuals saw domestic Communist insurrection as much more of a threat than external aggression from another state. They also argued that strong economic development was essential to national security, as it would provide the economic basis on which overall national strength would depend. They came to distinguish between "national" policies, that is, their doctrine that they believed was essential for national well-being, and "government" policies, or those of the particular government of the day. Ultimately, the ESG's National Security Doctrine laid the intellectual roots for the 1964 coup and subsequent regime.

In 1961 President Jânio Quadros abruptly resigned and was succeeded by his vice president, João Goulart. From this moment on, elements in the military opposed Goulart. He was a leftist, seemingly intent on instituting such major reforms in Brazil's very unequal society as strengthening labor unions, pursuing land redistribution, and providing greater benefits to the urban working classes. For this reason, Goulart clashed with both the military elite and the National Congress, which was controlled by more conservative politicians. Some military officers tried unsuccessfully to prevent him from taking office in the first place; others retained their loyalty to the legal institution of presidential succession. Then as Goulart failed to get his policies passed through the National Congress and faced growing opposition within the military, he became more populist.

Gen. Ernesto Geisel is shown here being sworn in as Brazilian president in 1974. Geisel was the third president in Brazil's highly institutionalized military regime. His government began the slow liberalization process that eventually led to a return to democracy in 1989.

He requested, but did not receive, extraordinary powers from the National Congress to enact his reforms. To gain greater military loyalty, he replaced several senior officers who opposed him with others who were more supportive, meaning that the military itself became quite divided. Finally, in March 1964, he dramatically called for fundamental reforms that the conservative elite, both civilian and military, opposed. When junior navy officers revolted, demanding the right to unionize, Goulart supported them.

That night the military moved to take over the reins of government in a largely bloodless coup it dubbed the "Revolution." The regime it subsequently created was strongly institutionalized and based heavily on the National Security Doctrine. It did attempt to keep a veneer of civilian rule by preserving most of the prior constitution but also issued Institutional Acts that gave the military president the power to overrule the legislature and revoked many basic rights. Eventually, the party system was also restricted to two tightly controlled parties, one supporting the regime and one allowed to oppose it within strict limits. When popular opposition from students, workers, and the rural poor arose, the military leadership did not hesitate to use force. Brazil's military government may have been far less brutal than many in Latin America at the time, but it nonetheless jailed and killed opponents when necessary.

Several different explanations have been developed in regard to what happened in Brazil in 1964. The best known is Guillermo O'Donnell's concept of the bureaucratic-authoritarian state. O'Donnell (1979) argued that the coup came about because of economic contradictions that the democratic government could not resolve: if capitalist industrialization was to continue, it required a repressive government to force it on an increasingly restless population. Brazil's economic development model could advance no further than the industrialization that had occurred up to that point. Populism, the dominant way of mobilizing support in Brazil's democracy, had produced a growing working class that demanded a greater share of the benefits of economic growth, and the elite realized this would reduce the resources available for further investment. Further development therefore would require the "deepening" of industrialization with an investment in heavier industry that in turn would require a repression of wages. An elected government could not achieve this, so the military stepped in, under the auspices of its National Security Doctrine, to take the necessary steps.

Other analysts, however, have noted that the coup itself was caused just as much by Goulart's direct threat to the military hierarchy. By removing military officers who opposed him, and especially by supporting junior officers who wanted to unionize, Goulart was interfering with the autonomy of the military itself, or so a number of officers believed. Riordan Roett, another prominent scholar of Brazil, contends that the military remained divided over Goulart's economic policies but ultimately united in opposition to him because of what the leadership perceived as his threatening behavior toward both the autonomy of the military and the National Congress (1978). It is entirely possible, of course, that these two explanations dove-tailed, coming together to give the military the incentive and justification to intervene and set Brazilian politics on a fundamentally different course.

IN CONTEXT Military Coups in Latin America by Decade

Brazil's military coups and regimes (1930–1945) and (1964–1985) were part of a broader trend of coups and military rule in the region.

Of the 33 countries in the region:
8 had a military coup in the 1930s
4 had a military coup in the 1940s
7 had a military coup in the 1950s
5 had a military coup in the 1960s
7 had a military coup in the 1970s
3 had a military coup in the 1980s
4 had a military coup in the 1990s

Source: Political Handbook of the World, 2008, Washington, D.C.: CQ Press, 2008.

Nigeria represents a very different kind of military—one that is a far weaker institution—but still demonstrates the difficulty of understanding the motives for coups. The country has had six coups (see the timeline in chapter 8) and at least two failed coup attempts. Without exception, each of the military leaders came to power promising to serve only in a "corrective" capacity to end corruption, restore order, and revive the economy before handing power back to elected civilians. In reality, the military ruled for two very long periods (1966–1979 and 1983–1999) under multiple leaders and returned the country to democratic rule only after much domestic and international pressure, as we detail below. All the while, analysts have identified both societal and individual motives behind the actions of Nigeria's military. We focus here primarily on two of the six coups, those that overthrew democratic governments.

The first two military interventions happened six months apart in 1966. Nigeria's First Republic, its initial postcolonial democracy, had very weak institutions and grew increasingly chaotic from the time of independence in 1960 to 1966. The democracy and subsequent

IN CONTEXT Military Coups in Africa by Decade

Nigeria's history of military coups and regimes from the 1960s into the 1990s was part of Africa's continuing pattern of coups and military rule in the region.

Of the 50 countries in the region, there were:
1 military coup in the 1950s
23 military coups in the 1960s
24 military coups in the 1970s
18 military coups in the 1980s
19 military coups in the 1990s

Source: George K. Kieh and Pita O. Agbese, *The Military and Politics in Africa: From Engagement to Democratic and Constitutional Control,* Aldershot: Ashgate, 2002.

military governments were riven by increasingly intense ethnic rivalries. Numerical advantage gave the northern region control of the government at independence, in coalition with the main party of the eastern region. The government manipulated the 1964 national election and 1965 election in the western region to a considerable degree to ensure victory for itself and its allies. As a result, the situation in the western region especially became violent, as westerners felt the northern-dominated government had stolen control of their regional government. By late 1965 the national government had lost effective control over the western region, and general lawlessness was spreading throughout the country.

In January 1966 five army majors led a rebellion in an attempt to overthrow what they saw as an illegitimate national government. The coup attempt was only partially successful, but it led the head of the army, Gen. Johnson T. U. Aguiyi-Ironsi, to step in as the new leader. Both he and four of the five majors who attempted the coup were ethnic Igbos from the eastern region, and in carrying out the coup, they killed several important northern and western political and military figures but no eastern ones. Ironsi abolished all parties and ethnic associations, and he soon declared the end of Nigeria's fractured federalism, instead creating a unitary state in an attempt to bring the nation together. Many analysts viewed Ironsi as genuinely interested in national well-being, but northerners saw the coup and Ironsi's elimination of federalism as an attempt by the eastern, Igbo military elite to take and centralize all power for themselves. Certainly, easterners appeared to be at the core of the new regime.

Six months later, the northerners responded with a countercoup that brought Army Chief of Staff Yakubu Gowon to power. Gowon himself was from the Middle Belt in the center of the country and therefore technically not part of any of the major ethnic regions. He was backed, however, by northern military leaders intent on removing what they saw as an "Igbo" government. Gowon recreated a federal system, with twelve states replacing the former three regions, and restored the regional power-sharing represented by federalism. Eastern military leaders rebelled, proclaiming themselves the leaders of the independent Republic of Biafra. A three-year civil war ensued. Gowon received much credit for successfully ending the conflict and helping reconcile the nation afterward. As all of Nigeria's military leaders would do, he had from the start promised a return to democracy. By the mid-1970s, however, he and the military governors of the states were seen as increasingly corrupt, stealing from Nigeria's rapidly growing oil revenues and continually delaying the promised return to democracy. Ultimately, he was overthrown by other northerners who attempted to reduce corruption and did return the country to democracy in 1979.

That democracy would last until 1983, and in many ways, the events of that year can be seen as a repeat of those of 1965, though without the same ethnic conflict. The Second Republic government elected in 1979 and reelected in 1983 was again dominated by officials from the northern part of the country, and by 1983 it was both corrupt and malfeasant. Nigeria's economy was declining as the level of corruption seemed to be skyrocketing. Consequently, the 1983 election in which incumbent President Shehu Shagari was reelected was widely seen as fraudulent, though neither as fraudulent nor as violent as the 1964 and 1965 elections.

The coup weeks later came with little opposition. At first glance, it could also be explained as being motivated by the weakness and chaos of the civilian government and provoked by the weakness of political institutions. William Graf, a leading scholar of the era, argues differently (1988). In contrast to 1966, the coup leaders were not junior officers but rather the top military officials in the country, primarily from the north, which means that the coup was not ethnically motivated, in that both the perpetrator and main victim were northerners. Graf goes on to say that it instead was motivated by the desire of top officers to maintain their access to government resources and preserve the social status quo. He suggests that the top military officers took control because they saw the corruption of the civilian elite as excessive. These officers believed that corruption threatened to provoke an uprising within the military and perhaps within the broader society. (Rumors did abound that junior officers, with a more radical interest in fundamentally changing the Nigerian regime, were about to stage a coup.)

The new regime under Gen. Muhammadu Buhari created a harsh "War Against Indiscipline" in which many civilian political elites were convicted on fraud charges. By 1985 the northern military elite saw Buhari's campaign as pressing too hard and removing essential leadership from all levels of government and yet another countercoup occurred that brought Army Chief of Staff Gen. Ibrahim Babangida to power. Power remained, however, in northern hands, among what Nigerians refer to as the "Kaduna mafia" (see chapter 8).

Nigeria's two coups that directly overthrew democratic rule can be explained by societal factors that include the weakness of prior political institutions and increasing political and economic chaos. In both cases, the argument goes that the military stepped in to restore order in a situation in which stable democracy no longer really existed. However, the leaders of the coups had other motives, and both faced subsequent countercoups that brought to power northern military leaders who ruled for extended periods during which corruption grew and institutions weakened, as we discussed in chapter 8. As in the case of Brazil, understanding the precise motives for coups is difficult because all coup leaders claim to intervene in the national interest but the subsequent governments, especially in the case of Nigeria, belie those intentions, so other motives seem at least equally plausible. The biggest difference between the two countries, as we argued in chapter 8, is the level of institutionalization. Brazil's more institutionalized military entered politics with a clear ideology and was a strong enough institution to implement its vision, for better or worse, and it preserved some very limited civilian political participation in the process. Nigeria's far less institutionalized military reflected the country's ethnic and class conflicts and ruled in a far less institutionalized manner that ultimately undermined Nigeria's political institutions, and it engaged in at least as much corruption as the civilian officials it overthrew.

REVOLUTION

Military coups change governments and often regimes; revolutions change the entire social order. These are rare and profound events that mark major turning points in the life of not only the countries in which they occur but often world history. On the continent of Africa alone there have been more than eighty military coups since 1960, whereas only a handful of revolutions have occurred anywhere in the world.

Like so many terms in political science, scholars have debated endlessly how to define the term "revolution." The important point for our purposes is to distinguish revolutions from other forms of regime change. A revolution, then, is a relatively rapid transformation in the political system and social structure of a society that involves mass participation in extra-legal political action to overthrow the prior regime and usually includes violence. The major revolutions in the modern era have happened in France (1789), Russia (1917), China (1911–1949), Cuba (1959), Nicaragua (1979), Iran (1979), and the Eastern European satellite states of the Soviet Union—Bulgaria, Czechoslovakia, East Germany, Hungary, Poland, and Romania (1989–1990).

Political scientists distinguish among revolutions in several ways. One obvious way is based on the ideologies that inspire them: the liberal revolution of France, the communist revolutions of Russia and China, and the Islamic revolution of Iran. It seems obvious that these ideological differences are crucial, yet most scholars of revolution argue just the opposite. The ideological motivations and pronouncements of key leaders do not explain very much about revolutions. Typically, only the top leadership thoroughly understands and believes in the ideology in whose name the revolution is fought. Many participants have other motivations for joining the rebellion, and specific political circumstances must exist for revolutions to succeed. Ideology does help more in explaining the outcome of revolutions in that the subsequent regimes, as we discussed in chapter 3, arise out of the ideological commitments of the leadership, but it usually does not tell us much about why the revolutions happened in the first place.

A common distinction among revolutions is that between **revolutions from above** and **revolutions from below**. The classical revolutions before the 1980s are the main cases on which theories of revolution are based, and these are all revolutions from below. That is, in each the mass uprising of the populace to overthrow the government was a central part of the process. Some scholars argue that the revolutions to end communism in Eastern Europe, in contrast, were primarily revolutions from above (Sanderson 2005). The end of communism was certainly a revolution in the sense that the fundamental social and economic structures of the societies were transformed from communist to capitalist. Political changes were equally dramatic though varied more widely: some countries created fully democratic regimes even as others created new forms of authoritarian rule, though no longer communist. While the populace was certainly involved in the process, communism fell primarily because the political elite within the system abandoned it, choosing instead to create new systems. The outcomes were often negotiated among political elites, each with the backing of a segment of the populace. In contrast to revolutions from below, massive and violent uprisings did not occur and were not necessary, and except for the ill-fated Soviet coup attempt of August 1991, the old regime was not able to strike back violently against the revolutionary forces. These revolutions from above happened relatively peacefully and quickly. Several of them also produced liberal democracy, an outcome that no revolution from below has yet to achieve. We explore the Russian transition to democracy (and more recent movement to semi-authoritarian rule) in the section below on democratization.

As with military coups, comparativists have developed several theories to explain why revolutions occur and their likely outcomes. These theories focus on

Was the American Revolution Really a Revolution?

The careful reader might note that we did not include the United States in our list of major revolutions. This may well come as a surprise to American students accustomed to thinking of the "American Revolution" as a pivotal historical event. It certainly was the latter, but whether it was a revolution in the sense that comparativists use the term has been subject to extensive debate among political scientists and historians. Barrington Moore (1966) argues that the real revolution in the United States was the Civil War, which ended slavery as an economic system and established the dominance of industrial capitalism; in the slave-holding states in particular, this was the conflict that was the true social revolution. The crux of the debate is about whether the American war for independence and the founding of a new republic fundamentally transformed not just political institutions but society as a whole. It was clearly the first nationalist war to throw off the yoke of colonial rule, and it clearly established an unprecedented republic based on liberal ideals that, although far from perfectly implemented, was a crucial milepost on the long rise of liberal democracy.

Our definition of the term "revolution" follows conventional usage, which includes not just political change but fundamental social change as well. Scholars have long argued that the American war of independence did not really do this. It was led primarily by the colonial elite who did not envision or produce a major redistribution of wealth. Granted, they eliminated British rule and created a new republic based on the republican ideal of equality of all citizens, but they defined citizens very consciously and deliberately as white male property owners. Wealth was actually distributed less equally after the war than it had been before, and, arguably, slavery was more entrenched (Wood 1992, 115). Not only was slavery codified in the Constitution ratified in 1787, but it enjoyed a period of great expansion for several more decades. Indeed, the Constitution as a whole can be seen in part as an effort to limit the effects of egalitarianism, creating a powerful Supreme Court to protect individual rights (including, of course, property rights) from majority tyranny, an indirectly elected Senate to represent state governments rather than citizens, and an indirectly elected president.

The chief opponent of this view is historian Gordon Wood, and he puts forth his arguments with especial eloquence in his 1992 Pulitzer Prize–winning book, *The Radicalism of the American Revolution*. Wood argues that the American Revolution "was as radical and as revolutionary as any in history" (5). Though he readily concedes most of the points mentioned above, he argues that the egalitarian ideals of republicanism created not just a political but also a social and cultural revolution during and after the war. Republican thought did not deny the existence of all forms of superiority, but instead argued that superiority should not come from birth but from talent and reason. Some men (women were not included) would rise to the top as leaders of the new society based on their abilities, hard work, and the willingness of others to elect them to positions of leadership. These individuals would have to be not only white men, but also property owners who had the independence to speak and act on their convictions. Government was to thereby serve the public interest in a way a monarchy never did or could.

This egalitarian ideal spread throughout society, Wood contends, leading to further questions about the prerogatives of rank and privilege. He notes numerous changes to social and cultural norms, such as pressure to end many private clubs, the taking of the title "Mr." and "Mrs." previously reserved for the landed gentry, and the shift from reserving the front pews in churches for select families in perpetuity to selling rights to those pews to the highest bidders. As the latter suggests, the revolution caused commerce to expand rapidly as well: wealth became even more unequally distributed, but many new men gained it. This revolution of ideas and of the way men treated other men helped create a new society never before seen in which inherited status was illegitimate and leadership and high status was to be based solely on merit and election.

In the long term, the American Revolution clearly had a profound effect, especially its notion of equal citizenship. As Wood rightly notes, it went far beyond what its original Founders intended. But most of the political and social elite before the war of independence remained in that position after the war (the biggest exception was the significant number of Loyalists who emigrated either to Canada or Britain), and the ideals of equality, for all their grandeur, remained within the very restricted realm of white, male property owners for another generation. As Crane Brinton (1965) notes in his classic study of revolutions, the American Revolution (which he includes as one of his cases) is quite peculiar as well in its evolution and result: no reign of terror occurred as is so common in revolutions and an authoritarian state did not ultimately result. This isn't to say that it's a bad thing that these events didn't happen, but their absence, along with the other points above, raise questions about whether the first war of independence against European colonialism was also a revolution.

the economic structure of the old regime, psychological theories of motivation to revolt, the resources and organization of the revolutionary movements, and the structure and weakness of the old state institutions. The first theorist of revolution in the modern era was probably Karl Marx. As we explained briefly in chapter 3, Marx believed that social revolution was the necessary transition from one mode of production and society to another: most important, from capitalism to communism. Therefore, he thought the major revolutions of the future would be communist and would happen first in the wealthiest, most advanced capitalist countries. Events would show that he was clearly wrong about where, and therefore why, revolutions would occur. Most major revolutions since his death have been communist inspired, but they have not happened in wealthy capitalist societies or democracies, but instead in relatively poor countries with authoritarian regimes, most notably in Russia and China.

More recent scholars have used some of Marx's concepts to try to explain contemporary revolution but have focused mainly on the economic structure in rural areas and its effects on peasant farmers. Jeffrey Paige, for instance, argued that sharecropping, a particular type of agrarian economic system, tended to produce peasant involvement in revolution, whereas other economic systems produced more conservative peasant political participation (1975). Others have also focused on motivations for participation in revolution but from the perspective of social-psychological theories, which examine individual feelings to explain revolution. James Davies (1962) argued that revolution occurs at periods of rising expectations: people don't revolt when they are at their lowest point, but rather when things have started to get better and they want more. Ted Robert Gurr (1970) contended that relative deprivation explains revolution because people revolt when they feel deprived relative to what they believe they deserve. All these theories focus on the motivations of the populace to participate.

A later school of thought puts forth the idea that while motivation is important, it alone cannot explain when successful revolutions happen. Adequate resources in the hands of revolutionary groups, a weak and therefore vulnerable state, or both are also necessary. Charles Tilly (1978) suggests that the directly political dimension of a potentially revolutionary situation is important because not only must there be grievances against the government but also an organization must arise able to mobilize those grievances into a mass movement with sufficient resources to challenge the state. Theda Skocpol (1979) notes that a crucial ingredient for successful revolutions is a state in crisis that often has been weakened by international events, and she points to the effects of World War I on Russia as an example. A revolution can only happen where a state faces a severe crisis and lacks the resources to respond and where a mass uprising is in process. This conjunction of events, she argues, explains the major revolutions of the past as well as the infrequent outbreak of revolutions now and in the future. Revolutions may also be less frequent in the future because in the past they overthrew authoritarian regimes: the spread of democracy since the 1970s may mean revolutions are much less likely.

What about Terrorism?

Revolutions and coups bring to mind an image of armed men taking over a state, perhaps killing innocent civilians in the process. A more contemporary image of politically instigated violence is terrorism. An important question in the new millennium is the difference, if any, between revolution and terrorism. Is a revolutionary a terrorist and vice versa? Is "terrorist" just a term we now use for revolutionary? Both revolution and terrorism can be forms of what is today termed **political violence**, the use of violence by nonstate actors for political ends. We include the term "nonstate" in this definition simply to distinguish it from war or other efforts by states to secure their sovereignty or expand their power. We make no assumption or argument here about the ethical superiority or justification of one of these over the other, but we think it is useful to distinguish them analytically.

Despite both involving political violence, revolutions and terrorism have fundamental differences. The most important distinction is between ends and means. Successful revolutions result in a fundamental transformation of a society. They are usually violent, but not always. Their end, or goal, distinguishes them from other types of political movements or political violence. **Terrorism**, on the other hand, is a means. It can be defined quite simply as political violence targeted at civilian noncombatants. Some revolutionaries have certainly used terrorism and some terrorists have been revolutionaries, but neither is always the case. Revolutionaries by definition seek to overthrow an existing state.

On the other hand, leading scholar of terrorism, Martha Crenshaw (1981), long ago noted that terrorists usually have different purposes: the most common goal of an act of terrorism is to influence a broader audience, not the actual target of the violence. Revolutionaries aim at the state and attempt to overthrow it. Terrorists generally try to avoid the state and make no effort to overthrow it; they typically engage in acts of terrorism, whatever their long-term political goals, as a means of violence that does not directly confront the state.

Some terrorists may indeed be pursuing revolutionary aims, but many are not. Since 2001 the primary form of terrorism in the news is connected with radical Islamists, but many political groups, such as the Irish Republican Army (IRA) in Northern Ireland, have engaged in terrorism with nationalist, secessionist, or other quite secular aims that involve neither religious zealotry nor social revolution. Indeed, it is not completely clear how revolutionary the goals of al-Qaida and related groups are. They certainly seem to seek the establishment of a new type of society, though it is not completely clear how much they wish to take over existing states. Much of their ideology centers on the purification of the Islamic *umma,* the broad, transnational religious community. Some, such as the Taliban in Afghanistan, seem willing to mostly ignore the state, not build a new one once they have destroyed the old. This is in marked contrast to social revolutionaries, whose primary aim after the revolution typically is to build a new state. When an Islamist extremist attacks a Western target, it is not completely clear whether he or she seeks to undermine the existing social order (in Western or Islamic countries) or to force the West (especially the United States) to change its foreign policy or to encourage religious reform within existing Islamic societies. The aims may or may not be "revolutionary" in the sense of how the term is used in comparative politics.

Comparativists and others have used a wide array of theories to try to explain terrorism, particularly the motivation behind it. This debate draws on many of the ideas used previously to explain revolutions or social movements (see chapter 7). Scholars have argued that motivation for terrorism comes from psychological sources, relative deprivation or other types of alienation, structural inequalities, charismatic leaders, or ideological (including religious) beliefs. Others note that, like revolutions or social movements, terrorism requires resources and political opportunities to actually happen, regardless of individual motivations.

Terrorism, a concept that has been around for two hundred years, has become a "hot" new topic in international politics, but understanding it has largely come from long-standing theories in comparative politics. This reasoning, as well as the clear distinction between terrorism as a means and revolution as an end, supports thinking of both in the context of regime change, as comparativists have long done, rather than thinking of both as forms of political violence, regardless of their ultimate goals.

Aside from some of the former Communist countries of Eastern Europe, the general outcome of revolution has been fairly consistent: authoritarian rule. Postrevolutionary governments have taken various forms, based in part on the ideological beliefs of their revolutionary leaders, but none has become an enduring democracy directly after the revolution, even in France where many of the revolution's leaders were liberals. Scholars account for this by pointing out the extremely difficult political circumstances facing postrevolutionary governments. The entire regime and social structure has been overthrown, and so new ones must be created. Massive violence outside the control of the state is at the heart of most revolutions, and any new regime must attempt to recreate the state's monopoly on the use of force. Postrevolutionary societies are almost by definition deeply divided along ideological lines: the new leadership is committed to a particular ideological blueprint of what the new regime and society should look like, while many followers do not fully share this commitment. All of these factors lead postrevolutionary leaders to brook little dissent and to view almost any opposition as a threat to the goals of the revolution. As our cases below demonstrate, the immediate postrevolutionary situation often includes a diversity of viewpoints, but those who do not share the vision of the key leadership are quickly eliminated, and with them go the prospects for democracy, at least in the short to medium term.

The exceptions to this rule are some of the post-Communist revolutions from above (for example, those that occurred in the Czech Republic, Hungary, and Poland) that led to those countries becoming electoral democracies. The collapse of communism and its subsequent illegitimacy were so complete that the postrevolutionary divisions were not nearly as great as in classic revolutions. The populaces were also not as mobilized, and the revolutions from above were largely nonviolent. All of these elements made the compromise necessary for democracy more possible, though the failure to establish it in some of the post-Communist countries, including parts of Yugoslavia, Romania, and the Central Asian republics, indicates that a democratic outcome was by no means guaranteed (Sanderson 2005).

CASE STUDY Revolution: China and Iran

While political scientists have long debated the causes of revolutions, looking at actual revolutions suggests that they cannot be explained by any single factor. Several factors come together simultaneously to create the conditions for revolution in our case studies, perhaps explaining why revolutions have been such rare events. The outcomes are similar in the sense of producing authoritarian regimes, though these regimes are quite distinct because they are based on the differing ideologies of the revolutionary leaders.

The revolution in China in 1949 resulted from a combination of a sense of relative deprivation on the part of the peasant majority, the creation of a political organization (the Communist Party) that could mobilize popular discontent, and an extremely weak state. The first Chinese revolution, largely a revolution from

above, occurred in 1911 when the ancient empire finally fell (see chapter 1 for more details on this period). Since the Opium Wars of the mid-nineteenth century, however, the Chinese empire had been in decline. The peasantry, which constituted the great majority of the population, had long-standing grievances and a tradition of revolting against local landlords and other elites who became too repressive. During the late nineteenth and early twentieth centuries, though, the peasantry faced greater impoverishment than usual as the empire declined and lost control of much of its territory to Japanese and Western interests. A younger generation of elites increasingly questioned the traditions of and justifications for the old empire, given its inability to modernize the society or reverse the country's decline. The Empress Dowager Cixi tried to respond to this growing disenchantment and rebellion with reforms in the first decade of the twentieth century, including the creation of the first consultative assembly, a quasi-legislature, and the elimination of the Confucian system of government employment that was mostly restricted to the elite. Reformers, however, wanted far more radical change, and many wholly rejected Confucian traditions and argued for a Western and liberal society. Young military leaders in the provinces shared these sentiments and were the local leaders of the 1911 rebellion that created Sun Yat-sen's nationalist Republic of China.

The new republic failed to establish a democracy or hold the country together; regional warlords took over provinces and preyed on the local population while battling each other for territory. The plight of the peasantry only got worse. Chiang Kai-shek managed to reunite the country in 1927, but under a repressive authoritarian regime. A new generation of people educated in the post-Confucian era still clamored for change inspired by Western models, not only liberal ones but also communist. Members of the same young, educated elite who had championed nationalism and liberalism were the initial adherents to communism, with support from the newly established Soviet Union. The Communist Party became the principle military and political rival to the Nationalists in the 1920s. During the famous Long March (1934–1935), Mao Zedong gained control of the party and began implementing his major revision to Marxist revolutionary doctrine by focusing on the peasantry as a potentially revolutionary group.

At the end of the Long March, the Communists established themselves in Yenan in northern China, creating, in effect, a separate state from the Nationalists in Beijing. They began implementing their new society, including moderate land redistribution, careful distribution of consumer goods to ensure the survival of as many people as possible in difficult circumstances, and reduction in the usurious interest rates peasants paid to landlords. For the first time in a century, a significant segment of rural Chinese society saw their situation in life at least stabilize, if not improve, and they became the backbone of Communist Party support. Mao also built up the party in Yenan, including in it intellectuals, elites, and peasants. It became the central authority

This 1934 photo shows Chou En Lai, one of Mao Zedong's chief lieutenants who helped lead the Long March of 1934–1935. This event contributed to the victory of Mao's Communist Party in China's revolution in 1949. Chou, like Mao's successor Deng Xiaoping, came to represent "moderates" in the revolutionary government, often working against some of Mao's more radical policies.

in the "liberated" territory, an early version of the state he would create after 1949. The Communists' guerrilla tactics also proved effective and popular in regard to the Japanese occupiers during World War II, giving the Communists the mantle of defenders of the beleaguered nation.

After World War II, the final phase of the revolution broke out, a four-year civil war that the Communists won based on expanding support from the peasantry and effective guerrilla tactics against better-armed Nationalist forces that had Western support. Communist victory ushered in a new state that completely changed Chinese society: a full social revolution from below had occurred. And like other such revolutions, it resulted in an authoritarian state. Those who had supported the revolution but were not Communists, and even Communists who argued for alternatives to Mao's preferred policies, were quickly eliminated, creating the full-scale dictatorship that the People's Republic of China became.

The 1949 revolution certainly was based on grievances among the peasantry, including the disillusionment of seeing the 1911 revolution from above make their lives worse instead of better. But success also required political resources—a mechanism through which local peasant grievances and revolts could be channeled into a broader movement—and the Communist Party became that mechanism. It successfully overthrew a regime that had been weak from its inception in 1911 and had been weakened further by its humiliation at the hands of the Japanese in World War II. Deprivation, state weakness, and political mobilization had to combine to produce the Chinese revolution.

The Iranian revolution of 1979 that created the Islamic Republic is a stark contrast to the Chinese Communist revolution in terms of ideology, but it emerged from roughly similar circumstances. A sense of relative deprivation among many segments of the population despite a growing economy, a state weakened by at least the perception of a loss of international (especially U.S.) support, and a religious movement whose leader had become the symbol of the revolution combined to produce Iran's revolution. The movement, though symbolically led by the Ayatollah Khomeini, was not united under one organization like the Chinese Communist Party, which meant that after the revolution, numerous groups with differing ideologies competed for power. Khomeini and his religious followers simply proved the most popular and outmaneuvered other groups to assume complete control during the first year of the new government.

The shah of Iran's government had seemed a classic case of a modernizing authoritarian regime during the 1960s and 1970s. The shah consciously sought to modernize his society through his "White Revolution" by encouraging foreign investment, greater mechanization of agriculture, access to higher education, and secularism. Iran seemed to be taking its place among the modern nations of the world. The shah's policies, however, did not benefit everyone equally, favoring

larger over smaller enterprises, foreign over domestic investors, and urban over rural interests. Therefore, while economic growth and personal incomes rose noticeably on average, what the poor saw was the elite's conspicuous consumption, and they compared it to their own very meager gains. In rural areas, peasant farmers and nomadic pastoralists often lost land and income, and these trends accelerated after the 1973 quadrupling of world oil prices. This event brought Iran a glut of wealth but skewed its distribution even further and caused significant inflation that eroded the purchasing power of the poor. The elite who benefited became increasingly conspicuous, a target of resentment for the rest of society. Modernization of agriculture drove rural migrants to the cities; there they joined the long-standing bazaari groups, petty traders in Iran's traditional bazaars. Bazaaris felt threatened by modernization as well, as the shah encouraged Western shops and banks to open to cater to the growing urban middle class, which reduced the bazaaris' market opportunities (Clawson and Rubin 2005).

The bazaaris and recent urban migrants, along with students and workers, became key supporters of the revolution. Opposition to the shah had survived underground ever since the brief political liberalization under Mohammad Mosaddeq in the early 1950s (see chapter 2). Despite brutal and often effective repression at the hands of the shah's secret police, two guerrilla groups survived: the Fedayin and the Mujahedin. By the 1970s, both were divided along ideological lines among nationalists who wanted greater democracy, Marxists, and religious groups. While students gave much of their support to Marxists, the bazaaris saw their trade as part of Islamic traditional practice and tended to support religious leaders. Secular intellectuals wrote anonymous letters and circulated pamphlets calling for the overthrow of the shah. The Islamic clergy, the *ulema,* opposed the shah's Westernization policies as a threat to Islam. Exiled radical cleric Ayatollah Khomeini increasingly became the chief symbol of opposition to the regime, and even though the opposition groups supported varying ideologies, they all united in opposition to the shah.

A perception that the shah's regime was weak was a crucial element in igniting the actual revolution.

U.S. president Jimmy Carter enunciated a new foreign policy based on human rights, mentioning the shah's as one of the world's regimes that did not adequately protect these. While Carter nonetheless continued to support the shah, the mere mention of U.S. criticism was enough to make some opposition leaders believe that the United States would not support the shah if the people rose up against him. The United States had supported the regime for decades, including the regime's crushing of an attempt at greater freedoms under Mosaddeq in the 1950s, so even the hint of U.S. willingness to consider regime change inspired the opposition to act. In January 1978, the government wrote a newspaper article attacking Khomeini. The following day, theology students responded by organizing a large demonstration in the holy city of Qom. The shah's police responded with violence, and at least seventy people were killed. The religious opposition, joined by students and the bazaaris, then used the traditional mourning gatherings for those killed to organize greater demonstrations, and the government could not disrupt these proceedings due to religious strictures. By September 1978 a demonstration of more than a million people took place in Tehran, and the shah once again reacted with the use of force: more than five hundred people were killed. The government also declared martial law shortly afterward, shutting down universities and newspapers. This only led to greater opposition as the urban working class joined the movement by organizing strikes, including one in the country's crucial oil sector.

By December the shah tried to respond to the rising revolt by replacing his prime minister with one seen as more sympathetic to reforms, but this was not nearly enough change to satisfy the growing opposition. In January 1979 the new prime minister managed to get the shah to leave office "temporarily" and began dismantling his hated secret police. The opposition, though, demanded Khomeini's return from exile, which the government continued to resist before finally giving in on February 1. Khomeini immediately declared one of his supporters the "real Prime Minister," which the government rejected. The guerrilla groups and students mobilized their followers to invade prisons, police stations, and military bases on February 10 and 11 to take them over in the name of the revolution. After two bloody days in which hundreds more people were killed, the revolutionaries succeeded in gaining power.

Unlike the Chinese revolution, however, no single political organization had control of the movement. Khomeini was the charismatic and symbolic leader but one who also pledged to work with other forces, starting with his appointment of a secular prime minister and support for a secular president. The revolutionary forces that came to power included religious groups that followed Khomeini, secular liberal nationalists who argued for a democracy, and Marxists of various sorts. Over the course of the first year, Khomeini systematically put his supporters in charge of key institutions and called for an early referendum on the creation of an Islamic Republic. The population overwhelming approved this move, and the new constitution discussed in chapter 8 was put in place. Over the next few years, Khomeini and his religious supporters increasingly repressed the other factions of the revolutionary movement to take firm control and create Iran's authoritarian theocracy.

DEMOCRATIZATION

In 1972 Freedom House, a nongovernmental organization (NGO) that analyzes the level of political and civil rights in the world, classified forty-four countries as "Free," meaning they are functioning liberal democracies; in 1990 that number rose to sixty-one; and in 2006 it had grown to eighty-one. The third wave of democratization, the first two following each of the world wars, respectively, was a dramatic process. It included the "People Power" movement that overthrew the corrupt and brutal Philippine dictator Ferdinand Marcos, the fall of the Berlin

Wall, and the election of Nelson Mandela in South Africa, and it seemed the world's people were arising en masse to demand democratic rights. Without a doubt, democracy expanded, but the image of mass rebellion overwhelming dictators and establishing lasting democracy was, alas, overly simplistic. Comparativists have tried to understand the expansion of democracy by asking why countries become democratic, how they become democratic, what obstacles they face, how democratic they are, how likely they are to stay democratic, and how they can become more democratic.

Prior to the third wave, all but a handful of democracies were wealthy, Western countries. In the 1950s and 1960s, political scientists understandably argued that democracy could be sustained in only certain types of societies. Seymour Martin Lipset (1959) famously argued that democracies arise only in countries with reasonably wealthy economies and the large middle class that accompanies the presence of wealth. This middle class is educated and has its basic needs securely met, which means that political competition won't be too intense and that compromise, essential for democracy, is easier. In *The Civic Culture* (see chapter 1), Gabriel Almond and Sidney Verba argued that democracy can thrive only in countries with democratic political cultures, what they called civic cultures, that value participation but whose citizens are willing to defer to elected leaders so that these leaders can govern while in office. Others put forth that political developments had to occur in a particular sequence: a strong state and sense of national identity, for instance, had to emerge before a democracy could.

The third wave wreaked intellectual havoc on these theories as democracy began breaking out in all the wrong places. First southern European and then Latin American military dictatorships became democratic. Then the end of the Cold War unleashed a new round of democracy creation, first in the former Communist countries of Eastern Europe and then in Africa and parts of Asia. These were countries that were far too poor, that still faced questions about the strength of their state and national identity, and that seemed not to have democratic cultures, and here they were writing constitutions, holding elections, and establishing democracies. Almost out of necessity a new approach to the study of democratization emerged. Influenced by rational choice theory, a new generation of democratization theorists argued that democracy could emerge in any country if the major political elites came to see it as a set of institutions that could serve their interests, whether they or their followers actually believed in democratic principles or not. Well-institutionalized democracy provides all major political actors a degree of participation, protection from the worst forms of repression, and the possibility that they can gain power at some point. These features led self-interested political leaders to create democracies in countries that comparativists previously had seen as bound to be autocratic for years to come.

Basing their ideas mainly on the experiences of southern Europe and Latin America, this new type of democratization theorist argued that understanding elite dynamics and negotiations in times of crisis was crucial to explaining this new process, dubbed **transition to democracy**. When an authoritarian regime faced a severe crisis of some sort—economic downturn or succession were common crises out of which democracy could emerge—its leadership would split internally into **hardliners** and **softliners**. The former believed in repressing any opposition and preserving the status quo; the latter were willing to consider compromising with opponents as a means to survive the crisis. Simultaneously, the crisis would produce a surge in the activity of civil society, typically led by unions, religious authorities, or middle-class professionals, with these groups demanding fundamental political reforms. Civil society subsequently would often divide between **radicals**, who wanted immediate and complete democratization, and **moderates**, who were willing to compromise with the authoritarian government to make some gains. A successful transition to democracy was most likely when the softliners in the regime and the moderates in civil society could each gain the upper hand over their internal opponents and then negotiate with each other to establish new rules of the game. Some form of democracy, though often with limits, became a compromise on which both sides could agree (Huntington 1991).

Most theorists believed the ideal process involved a **pact**, a conscious agreement among the most important political actors in the regime and in civil society to establish a new form of government. Such a pact would usually be proceeded by **political liberalization**, or the opening of the political system to greater participation. This included legalizing opposition parties, lifting restrictions on the media, and guaranteeing basic human rights. The pact itself would ideally produce a new democratic constitution and be followed by a **founding election**. This would be the first democratic election in many years (or ever) and would mark the completion of the transition. Most theorists argued that the regime and civil society had to be of roughly equal strength for the transition process to produce a democracy: if the regime, especially the hardliners, was very strong it would control the process and if a democracy managed to result, it would have significant limitations. In Chile, for instance, the military under dictator Augusto Pinochet wrote a democratic constitution that reserved seats in the Senate and control of the central bank for the army. On the other hand, if civil society, especially its more radical elements, was too strong it would demand full democratization with no protection to members of the old regime, and this would likely produce a hardliner backlash that would crush democratization.

MINI-CASE Philippines

Over a period of four days in February 1986, the world watched as "People Power" brought about the fall of Philippine dictator Ferdinand Marcos and his replacement by his electoral rival, Corazon Aquino. To many observers at the time, it was a classic case of the people getting fed up with a dictatorship and bringing it down. As is often the case, though, it was an alliance of civil society and the military that brought

about the downfall of the regime, ultimately with U.S. support. Such an all-encompassing alliance against a detested dictator might bode well for future democracy, and indeed, so far formal electoral democracy has survived multiple elections in the Philippines. The country has not suffered a return to authoritarian rule, but ironically the very same civilian-military alliance that so effectively brought down the dictator has left its current democracy extremely weak and vulnerable twenty years later.

By 1986 Marcos's long rule was tottering due to loss of support across the board. First elected president in 1965, Marcos was reelected in 1969, but even at that early date his presidency was marred by corruption and the increasing use of violence to hold on to power. In 1972 he imposed martial law, suspended the constitution, and ruled openly like the personalist dictator he had become. His rule mirrored that of others, including the Somozas in Nicaragua, with rampant corruption, cronyism, and reliance on a small entourage of close trusted allies including his wife, former beauty queen Imelda Marcos, who became mayor of metropolitan Manila. The couple amassed a huge fortune, and their lavish lifestyle became legendary. Their ostentatious wealth, along with the notorious suppression of political opponents like Benigno Aquino, jailed for seven years and then exiled in the United States, won them few supporters. Opposition by two armed guerrilla movements, one communist and one Muslim, guaranteed the Marcoses U.S. support in the Cold War environment, however. Marcos also tried to use "show" elections to prove his democratic credentials. In 1981 he finally agreed to lift martial law and submit to a presidential election, but he rigged the rules from the outset by, among other things, setting an age limit that prohibited opposition leader Aquino from running. The opposition boycotted the election, which Marcos "won" with 88 percent of the vote. This only outraged the opposition further and led them to rethink their strategy. By 1983 Aquino was prepared to lead these forces in a nonviolent call for new elections. When he returned to Manila, however, he was gunned down as he exited his plane.

The Marcos-controlled media suppressed news of Aquino's assassination in the Philippines itself, but word spread through the largely Roman Catholic country in part through the Catholic Church's radio station. The nation mourned a martyr and, more important, began to organize in earnest. Business leaders, the Catholic Church, and housewives as well as workers and the poor became involved in a series of nonviolent demonstrations. An organization that had first emerged in the 1950s, NAMFREL (National Movement of Citizens

for Free Elections), was resurrected with financing from businessmen and personnel recruited by the church and the opposition parties. Marcos permitted another rigged election in 1984 for the National Assembly, but this time the opposition contested it. Marcos's party retained a majority, but the opposition won 30 percent of the seats in contrast to the 10 percent it had held previously. At least as important, NAMFREL poll watchers, many of them Catholic nuns, were able to report vote counts in many regions that clearly revealed the Marcos regime's widespread fraud. The obvious fraudulence and growing popular outrage led some members of the military to push for change, calling for Marcos to resign or be overthrown. They were also already upset that Marcos was undermining military professionalism by promoting officers based on personal loyalty to him. The United States, too, was becoming less supportive of Marcos's excesses and obvious fraud.

Marcos thought one more rigged election might shore up his position. He called a snap presidential election in 1986, believing that the opposition would not be able to unify or organize in time and that he could continue to use fraud and intimidation to gain a victory. The opposition, however, did not lose this historic opportunity. Catholic cardinal Jaime Sin brokered an agreement among the opposition to rally behind the candidacy of Corazon Aquino, widow of Benigno Aquino. Moreover, NAMFREL organized poll watchers to verify the official electoral commission's vote counts throughout the country. When the election came, Marcos announced victory, but things quickly began to unravel. Thirty members of the electoral commission walked out, stating that they had been asked to falsify vote counts. NAMFREL reported missing voter lists, people barred from voting, and the use of violence. People turned out at mass rallies to support Aquino. The Catholic Church supported Aquino. Perhaps most important and fatal to his circumstances, Marcos himself decided to move against the military men he knew were plotting against him, and this precipitated military resistance at two Manila bases. The renegade troops would not have been able to hold out long, but, remarkably, the Catholic radio station and the opposition mobilized the population to come out in support of the troops. Filipinos filled the streets of Manila, precipitating the defection of loyalist troops and much diplomatic maneuvering by the United States. Convinced at last that Marcos had to go, the United States facilitated his evacuation on the fourth day of the "People Power" demonstrations, and Corazon Aquino became president. Marcos's regime collapsed completely. In the end, his personalist regime had unified all of Filipino society, the military, and the United States against him.

This unanimity probably has helped the transitional regime survive so far, but it has not gone unchallenged. Corruption continues to plague the government. In 2001 another People Power demonstration forced President Joseph Erap Estrada from office. His obvious corruption and lavish lifestyle smacked too much of Marcos for most Filipinos' tastes. His successor, Gloria Maca-

pagal Arroyo, pardoned him to the dismay of many, and her government also came to be charged with corruption and massive electoral fraud. Most important, the military remains divided over its proper role. Ironically, some of the same military officers who helped oust Marcos in the name of professionalism then advocated a continued role for the military in politics. Aquino's presidency survived a number of coup attempts by those officers because more senior officers supported a return to political neutrality. Coup threats continue, however, with the most recent attempt, involving officers being tried for earlier coup attempts, thwarted in November 2008. For Filipino democracy, the alliance of People Power and the military has proved to be a mixed blessing.

Once the transition is complete, the obvious question is whether the democracy will last. Transition theorists developed the concept of **democratic consolidation** to aid in consideration of this question, but much dispute over the definition and utility of the concept has arisen. Intuitively, democratic consolidation is simply the idea that democracy has become widely accepted as the permanent form of political activity in a particular country: it has become "the only game in town," and all significant political elites and their followers accept democratic rules and are confident everyone else does as well. This is important, because democracy requires faith that in the future any significant party or group might gain power via an election. If some major political actors do not believe that, they might be tempted to use nondemocratic means to gain power in the present, fearing that their opponents will not give them a chance to win via free and fair elections in the future. Knowing when a country has reached the point of democratic consolidation, however, is quite difficult because how do we know that all the actors accept democracy unquestionably? Samuel Huntington (1991) argued that a country must pass the "two-turnover test" before we can consider it a consolidated democracy: one party must win the founding election and a different party must later win an election and replace the first. Only then, he stated, can it be known for certain that consolidation is complete. By this strict standard, West Germany did not become a consolidated democracy until 1969, India until 1980, and Japan until 1993, and neither South Africa nor Mexico qualify yet today.

Transition theorists looked for evidence of democratic consolidation because they feared democratic breakdown, the return to authoritarian rule. Relatively few countries that have completed a transition to democracy, however, have reverted to full-scale authoritarian rule. Instead, many have survived as electoral democracies without full citizen participation or political accountability or have become some type of **hybrid regime** that mixes elements of democracy with authoritarian rule. With these trends in mind, theorists since have examined **democratic deepening**, improvement in the quality of democracy, including the extent of participation, rule of law, and vertical and horizontal accountability. Guillermo O'Donnell (1994) argued that many Latin American regimes are **delegative democracies** in which free and fair elections take place but neither vertical nor horizontal accountability is strong enough to prevent the emergence of elected executives with nearly unlimited power. Others called these and similar regimes electoral (but not liberal) democracies or even **illiberal democracies** (Diamond 1996; Zakaria 2003).

Many scholars initially assumed that these regimes still qualified as democratic and were still in a process of transition, although rather prolonged ones. Others argued instead that these cases represented a new kind of hybrid regime, variously called semi-authoritarian, **competitive authoritarian**, or electoral authoritarian. Regardless of the label, these hybrid regimes allow the existence of formal opposition and some open political debate and hold elections to select the executive and legislative branches. These processes are so flawed, however, that the regime cannot be considered democratic in any real sense. Those in power manipulate the electoral process and harass or restrict opposition parties, civil society, and the media to such an extent that the opposition has virtually no chance of gaining control of the government, though it typically wins some legislative seats.

With the rise of delegative or illiberal democracies and hybrid regimes, crucial questions emerge: What causes transitions to democracy to produce these kinds of regimes? How can they make renewed progress toward democracy? Democratic transitions and new democracies face numerous obstacles, any of which can partially or completely derail the process. Among these, certainly, are economic development and political culture. While neither a particular level of economic well-being nor a particular political culture is essential for a transition to democracy, each is certainly beneficial to democratic consolidation and deepening. A recent quantitative study covering 135 countries from 1950 to 1990 found that while wealthy countries are no more likely to become democracies than poor countries, democracies in wealthier countries, once established, are much more likely to survive: "democracy is almost certain to survive in countries with per capita incomes above $4,000" (Przeworski et al. 2000, 273).

Cultural norms in favor of and past experience with democratic forms of participation undoubtedly are likely to strengthen democracy and accountability. Most scholars have assumed that ethnic fragmentation is likely to harm the chances of democracy; following the lessons of the school of sequential political development, they argue that ethnically divided societies have a weaker sense of national unity. Such divisions often become bitter political competitions for control of the state that threaten to go beyond democratic norms and institutions. A recent study by Steven Fish and and Robin Brooks (2004) across approximately 160 countries found no correlation between ethnic diversity and the strength of democracy, however.

Transition theorists have long worried that if democracy does not produce favorable policy outcomes quickly, a populace with limited attachment to core democratic values will reject democracy altogether rather than blame the particular party or individual in power. Many postcolonial countries going through transitions to democracy simultaneously go through neoliberal economic reform, which in the short term often causes economic decline before it brings benefits. Adam Przeworski (1991) contended that in such cases governments are well advised to pursue economic reform as quickly and thoroughly as possible rather than slowly and partially, because by getting through the worst of the economic crisis quickly, there is less chance that the populace will blame democracy for the crisis and start supporting nondemocratic alternatives. In her 2003 book, however, Nancy Bermeo examined the hypothesis that popular disenchantment undermines democracy, looking at the breakdown of democracy in Europe before World War II and in Latin America in the 1960s. She found that in these cases the populace as a whole did not reject democracy, but that key elites did in times of economic crisis; the military in Latin America, for instance, feared economic instability and ended democracy without widespread popular support.

Weak political institutions and civil society can also lead to democratic breakdown and the rise of hybrid regimes. The transition process in sub-Saharan Africa has not fit the model derived from Latin America and southern Europe very well because the African countries possess much weaker institutions and civil societies. Africa's neopatrimonial regimes systematically weakened almost all political institutions prior to the arrival of the "third wave" in the early 1990s just as severe economic crises in the 1980s as well as the end of the Cold War produced a wave of democratization efforts across the continent. Many new groups arose in civil society, demanding greater democratization, but in countries with miniscule middle classes these groups had limited resources and leadership, which made it difficult for them to hold governments accountable. The old authoritarian governments often did split, as transition theory suggests, but typically not between hardliners and softliners but instead between patrons leading competing ethnic groups. Continued poverty in that region means that citizens depend on this patronage for much of their well-being, and clientelism remains a primary form of political participation. Holding an open election does not substantially change any of this.

Michael Bratton and Nicholas van de Walle (1997) put forth the argument that African neopatrimonial regimes have a distinct logic of transition. During and after a formal "transition," political competition remains primarily about securing access to government to gain resources, except that now this is done via elections rather than military coups. Pacts almost never happen because parties are little more than temporary vehicles for shifting coalitions of patrons trying to gain power, and parties do not disagree ideologically and are not stable enough to provide the credible commitments pacts require. In the absence of pacts, incumbents typically do not liberalize their regimes completely, holding elections that are only partially free and fair. More often than not, they win those elections, and even when the opposition wins, it also often uses the reins of power in rather undemocratic ways. In the absence of a clear agreement for a new constitution and new institutions, whichever group is in power has access to important authoritarian means of staying there. The result is often the rise of lasting hybrid regimes. Freedom House ratings reflect this: eleven African regimes were rated as "free" and fourteen as "not free" in 2006, but twenty-three were "partly free," the designation given to a majority of illiberal democratic and semi-authoritarian regimes.

Not only weak institutions but also inappropriate ones can harm new democracies and create hybrid regimes. New democracies are often deeply divided societies, either ideologically or ethnically. The "perils of presidentialism" that Juan Linz (1990) identified are, he argued, particularly important in new democracies. Presidential systems, he suggested, lead to "winner-take-all" mentalities as parties compete for the presidency, which makes compromise unlikely and often produces policy deadlock as each captures one branch of government. He and others believe that parliamentary systems are more likely to survive in new democracies because they allow for coalition governments. Following Arendt Lijphart's consociational theory (1969), many comparativists argue that because new democracies are often deeply divided and competing elites do not fully trust one another or the new democratic institutions, power-sharing mechanisms are likely to help preserve democracy. Others disagree with all of these arguments, suggesting instead that presidential systems can provide both democratic legitimacy and stability by having a single head of state directly elected by a majority of the nation; advocates of this stance point out the stability of many Latin American democracies, virtually all of which have presidential systems.

Little empirical evidence strongly supports either side in this debate. Indeed, a recent study by Steven Fish (2006) used a new set of data that measured the strength of the legislative branch to argue that a strong legislature is the most important institutional ingredient in maintaining democracy, regardless of the kind of political system in place. In spite of the uncertainty in the scholarship in this field, it is clear that institutions can matter. If one faction in a deeply ethnically divided society captures a strong presidency, and political support is based on the patronage that control of the government provides, the temptation will be to keep control of that office by any means necessary. Opponents, recognizing this possibility, will compete fiercely to win the executive office for themselves, often resulting in bitterly divided and violent elections. An electoral authoritarian regime, in which one side wins and does what is necessary to maintain its power, is a likely outcome of this scenario.

Many comparativists initially saw hybrid regimes as simply "protracted" or "stalled" transitions to democracy. As they endured, however, the concept of stable hybrid regimes arose. The question remains of whether and when these regimes might give way to greater democracy. A number of theorists have tried to tackle this question. Most argue that the quality of whatever elections exist is important to the likelihood of further democratization. In regimes in which elections, while quite limited, nonetheless allow the opposition to win some share of power—a significant share of legislative seats for instance—further democratization is more likely. These regimes give dissidents within the ruling party incentives to defect to

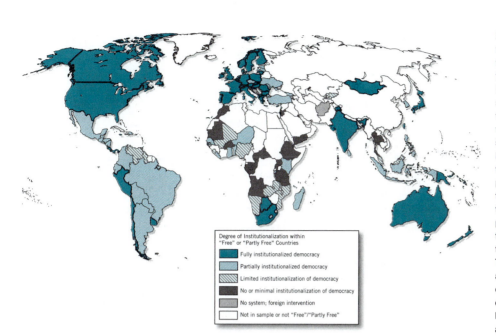

Degree of Institutionalization within
"Free" or "Partly Free" Countries

Fully institutionalized democracy

Partially institutionalized democracy

Limited institutionalization of democracy

No or minimal institutionalization of democracy

No system; foreign intervention

Not in sample or not "Free"/"Partly Free"

Note: The map shows Polity IV institutionalized democracy scores for 2006 for all countries rated as "free" or "partly free" on the Freedom House scale. The Polity IV institutionalized democracy score measures the degree of institutionalization of democracy within a state, with 10 being the highest degree of institutionalization and 0 being the least. Democracy is conceived as three essential, interdependent elements. First is the presence of institutions and procedures through which citizens can express effective preferences about alternative policies and leaders. Second is the existence of institutionalized constraints on the exercise of power by the executive. Third is the guarantee of civil liberties to all citizens in their daily lives and in acts of political participation. Other aspects of plural democracy, such as the rule of law, systems of checks and balances, and freedom of the press, are means to, or specific manifestations of, these general principles. Polity IV institutionalized democracy scores do not include coded data on civil liberties.

Note: Scores for "Civil Liberties" shown here are for "free" or "partly free" countries, according to Freedom House's 2006 report, on a scale of 1-10, with 1 being the highest degree of civil liberties. (Scores are shown only for those countries included in the Polity V data set.)

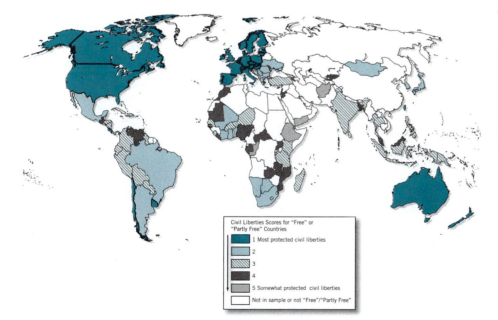

Civil Liberties Scores for "Free" or
"Partly Free" Countries

1 Most protected civil liberties

2

3

4

5 Somewhat protected civil liberties

Not in sample or not "Free"/"Partly Free"

MAP 9.2
**Third-Wave Democracies and
Governing Institutions**

the opposition because doing so is a viable means of maintaining a political career, which encourages splits in the ruling party. Just this type of situation helped produce greater democracy in the hybrid regimes of Mexico and Taiwan, for instance. Similarly, a real chance at some share of power encourages opposition coalitions, as does a majoritarian electoral system. Opposition fragmentation is likely to keep the incumbent hybrid regime in place in that a coalition is often essential for any real chance at electoral victory and regime change. When political leaders think an opposition coalition has a real chance to win, they become more likely to join it themselves, further strengthening its chances until a "tipping point" is reached at which a large opposition coalition emerges to win an election in spite of the incumbent's manipulation of the system.

Other experts look instead at particular circumstances within countries rather than institutional factors. William Case (2006) argues that the political skills of individual leaders are vital because leaders of hybrid regimes who can manipulate the electoral system subtly to keep opposition fragmented can maintain themselves in power much longer than those who are less skilled. Steve Levitsky and Lucan Way (2006) have argued that close connections with the West are most likely to produce further democratization in hybrid regimes. Given that most Western powers favor greater democracy, those countries with close ties to the West find such demands more difficult to resist than more isolated countries do. Any or all of these institutional or contextual factors could help produce changes in hybrid regimes. Most of these regimes are new enough that strong empirical evidence for how and when they might change does not yet exist. The question, though, is certainly at the forefront of contemporary thinking about future waves of democratization since the third wave produced a variety of processes of transition and regime types. We examine three distinct outcomes in our cases studies of Brazil, Russia, and Nigeria.

CASE STUDY Brazil: Model Transition and the Question of Democratic Deepening

Brazil has long been one of the world's most unequal societies. From the *coronelismo* of the late nineteenth century to the populism of the more industrialized mid-twentieth century, Brazil's elite has kept the masses under its control. Given this, January 1, 2003, was not your average day for poor Brazilians. On that day, they celebrated the inauguration of President Luiz "Lula" Inácio da Silva, a trade union leader who grew up in poverty with a fourth-grade education. The inauguration of the leader of the social democratic Workers Party (PT) seemed to herald the fruition of Brazil's new

democracy. His party, born out of the workers' struggle to gain the right to form their own unions and end military rule, was a new type of political organization in the country's history. It had been created from the bottom up rather than from the top down. Since gaining power, however, Lula's rule has disappointed many of his most ardent supporters. He has compromised on many key economic issues, following mostly neoliberal policies that provide stable growth and a generally beneficial business climate. These policies have partly been the result of the need to compromise with the many other political forces and parties in Brazil's fractious political system. Yet because many of his working-class supporters do not see these policies as having benefited them substantially, they have grown increasingly disenchanted, though he was still able to win reelection in 2006.

Democracy is certainly thriving, but weak political institutions continue to plague the country, raising questions about democratic deepening, accountability, and the rule of law. Despite such flaws and the questions they raise, Brazil's transition to democracy stands as one of the models of the process. A long and gradual transition, beginning in 1974 and not fully ending until 1989, eased the country from military rule and to democracy. While there were contentious moments along the way, the result was a new constitution and electoral democracy that has stood for twenty years and has included five presidential elections that have put four presidents in power from three different parties. By the basic measures of free and fair elections, free association and expression, and electoral turnover, Brazil is a consolidated democracy, and it achieved the status of "free" in Freedom House's rankings in 1986 after the first indirect election of the president. It dropped to "partly free" from 1993 to 2003, however, because its score in the "Civil Liberties" category dropped, due mainly to rampant and nearly unchecked police brutality. Since 2003 the country has once again achieved the status of "free," though problems of the rule of law and weak institutions remain.

Brazil's liberalization began in 1974 when a new military president allowed greater political rights within the limited electoral system under the military authoritarian regime. The official opposition party (the only one allowed) dramatically increased its share of the vote in legislative elections that year, undermining the status of the official ruling party. This inspired greater pressure for change, but while the military presidents in the 1970s favored some liberalization, they did not support democratization. Liberalization, however, just led to greater demands for real democracy. Some business leaders began calling for political reform, as did those leaders of the Catholic

A key element of any transition to democracy is successfully convincing the military to give up its formal and most of its informal political power. Many observers believe that Brazil's democracy had achieved this by the new millennium. While still boasting a large and relatively powerful military, Brazil's civilian leaders seem to have firm control over it to a greater extent than at any time in the country's history.

Church who were part of the liberation theology movement, which used church teaching to argue for greater justice for the poor. Then in 1978–1979, large strikes broke out in the industrial heartland of São Paulo;

IN CONTEXT Freedom in Brazil and Latin America

In 1990: Brazil's Freedom House Civil Liberties score was 3, compared to the Latin America average of 2.73; its Political Rights Score was 2, compared to the Latin America average of 2.42.

In 2006: Brazil's Freedom House Civil Liberties score was 2, compared to the Latin America average of 2.42; its Political Rights Score was 2, compared to the Latin America average of 2.15.

illegal unions rejected the complacency of the military's official unions and the corporatist system that had long guided Brazilian unionism. These massive strikes won workers the right to form their own unions and then their own party, the PT.

With growing demands for further liberalization, the military allowed direct elections for state governors in 1982. The opposition's victory in the largest states demonstrated the increasing popularity of democracy. Shortly afterward, the military announced that it would allow a civilian to be elected president in 1985, but only indirectly: he would be elected by the National Congress. The PT and other groups in the democracy movement responded with a massive "diretas já!" ("direct elections now!") campaign that mobilized hundreds of thousands of people in street protests to demand full democratization. Military leaders soon recognized the overwhelming popular support for the end of their rule and agreed to a pact that gave birth to full democracy: the National Congress and the indirectly elected president put in office in 1985 would write a new constitution that would result in direct elections for all offices in 1989.

The 1988 constitution created the presidential system we outlined in chapter 6. Brazil was unusual in that it had a full public debate about whether to switch to a parliamentary system or stick with a presidential one. The Constituent Assembly that wrote the constitution favored a parliamentary system, but the president and military favored preserving the presidential one. They compromised: the constitution was presidential but promised a national referendum in 1993 on which system to adopt permanently. The referendum engendered a rare (for anywhere in the world) public debate over the merits of each system, complete with often misleading campaign ads. In the end, voters supported the presidential system by a large margin.

The most interesting and controversial element of Brazil's new democratic constitution was the electoral system that has helped produce the extremely fragmented party system we mentioned in chapter 6. Brazil uses an open-list PR electoral system for the Chamber of Deputies, the lower and more powerful house of the National Congress. Each state is an electoral district that has a number of seats based on its

population, with a minimum of eight and maximum of seventy. Open-list means that individual candidates choose to run on a party's list, and a party has no control over who runs on its list. Voters can vote either for the party or an individual candidate. Within each district, a party gets the number of seats proportional to its total share of the vote, and then the individual candidates running in the party who get the most votes get those seats.

This system gives candidates an incentive to garner as many individual votes as possible to place them as high as possible among their party's candidates. It provides no incentive for candidates within the same party to cooperate. It doesn't matter whether candidates gain many votes within a particular area of a state or have more widespread but shallow support across that state as long as their total number of votes is as high as possible. Given the long-standing role of patronage in Brazilian politics and the decentralized federal system (as described in chapter 6) in which state governors are very influential, candidates understandably focus almost exclusively on local issues. Most are really representatives of particular areas or particular social groups in somewhat larger areas such as major cities, rather than party stalwarts. They are dependent on their own ability to mobilize supporters in their home areas and perhaps on important local leaders such as major city mayors and state governors.

The obvious result of this electoral system is weak parties. In fact, parties are so weak that between 1989 and 1995 one-third of legislators switched parties while in office: their party affiliation was a matter of convenience rather than an indication of ideological commitment. A national party organization has virtually no means of controlling who runs on its ticket; rather, a party is dependent on locally popular candidates to garner votes to add to its tally in a state. With the exception of a few major parties, most parties, like most candidates, are really local. They represent one region or sometimes are just vehicles in a region that will help a particular local candidate win an election. The electoral system has no minimum threshold of votes a party must get to gain representation in the chamber, so a locally popular candidate with a tiny fraction of the national total may well end up in office. And, yes, this produces many parties in the legislature—twenty-one after the 2006 election.

In addition, party leaders in the legislature have few means of influencing legislators' votes once they are in office. This is in part because the long-term career goals of most of these legislators focus on winning one of the more important local executive positions, such as mayor of a significant city or state governor. These positions ultimately have more clout in Brazil's system than individual members of the legislature, and are another reason for legislators' focus on local issues.

The degree and effect of this party weakness has been the subject of significant debate among scholars of Brazil. Initial assumptions in the early 1990s were that such weak parties inhibited the system's ability to pass coherent legislation, especially in the all-important area of economic reform. The economic reform efforts of the first directly elected president, Fernando Collor, a member of a tiny local party who ruled mainly via the president's power of issuing provisional decrees (see chapter 6), were unsuccessful and unpopular. Brazil's classic problem, inflation, remained out of control, which supported the argument that the political system was dysfunctional.

Research by Brazilian scholars Fernando Limongi and Argelina Figueiredo (2000), however, demonstrated that Brazil's parties were stronger than previously believed. The evidence collected showed that legislators voted with their parties to a higher degree than had been assumed, and this suggested that party leaders were able to marshal their troops in favor of their preferred policies. Several scholars have since questioned the argument, suggesting that final votes in the National Congress are not terribly important because many presidential proposals never make it that far because presidents drop them for lack of support from among the fractious coalitions. Political scientist Barry Ames (2001) supports the view that legislators' votes on controversial issues are explained not by the influence of the party leaders but instead by the characteristics and needs of constituents and the ability of legislators to gain patronage and resources for their home areas in exchange for their votes. Brazilian legislators are quite able to say "no" to their party leaders, and they do so regularly.

It does seem clear, though, that as weak as Brazilian parties were in the first few years of the new democracy, they have since gained some strength, even if they remain weak compared to those of many countries. Recent research suggests that legislators are increasingly voting as a bloc and that party switching has halved from what it was in the early 1990s. And though they are quite vague, the major Brazilian parties do have distinct ideological positions: they can loosely be grouped into "right," "center," and "left" parties (with several in each category). In recent presidential elections ideologically similar parties have formed coalitions to support the most popular candidates. The popularity of the last two presidents, Fernando Henrique Cardoso and Lula, has undoubtedly helped spur presidential coalitions—parties want to support a winner if possible. As Brazil's second directly elected president, Cardoso was successful at using his powers of cabinet appointment and control over patronage to negotiate major changes in economic policy to finally defeat inflation and initiate other significant economic reforms. And while he has faced challenges, Lula seems to be trying to continue this trend. The progress made by these individuals has made governing a little easier for these presidents and allied party leaders.

Another reason for somewhat stronger parties in recent years is the presence of the PT. Forged in the massive strikes of 1978–1979, the PT was a different kind of party from the start. From its first election in 1982, it refused to play by the rules of "politics as usual" in Brazil, insisting instead that it would recognize only those candidates it vetted as supporting its ideology. Because of its scathing critique of the corruption of the Brazilian political elite, it refused to cooperate, before or after an election, with any other party, even others on "the left." It also refused to use patronage to gain political support. Its long-timer leader, now President Lula, is a union leader who campaigned wearing blue jeans and using the working-class vernacular. He and the party, with their socialist policies and symbols, represented a grassroots critique of the entire Brazilian political elite.

The party's discipline and ultimate success in becoming a major influence by the 1990s led other parties to become somewhat more disciplined in imitation. Lula ran for president and came in second in the elections of 1989, 1994, and 1998, finally winning the presidency in 2002 and reelection in 2006. In the end, to win the PT did have to make some compromises. To reassure the upper and middle classes, the business sector, and even some workers who feared a president who was "uneducated," Lula donned suits when campaigning and improved his speech to sound more formal and educated. The PT dropped its opposition to forming coalitions, a crucial step in Lula's eventual election. Yet while it ultimately compromised, it remains one of the more disciplined parties in the country, and most observers argue it has positively impacted the institutional strength of its major competitors.

Lula's government is not without its faults, however. Despite its official stance against the same old–same old of Brazil's political system, it nonetheless has been plagued by corruption, another continuing problem for Brazil's young democracy. The country's patronage politics and weak institutions made it a bastion of corruption throughout the twentieth century, so much so that Transparency International's 1995 Corruption Perception Index gave it a score of 2.7 out of 10 (with 10 being the least corrupt), ranking it number 37 out of 41 countries surveyed. By 2007 it had improved notably, to a score of 3.5 and a rank of number 72 out of 179 countries. Improved yes, but this number still represents a significant corruption problem. The positive development is that high-level corruption has been exposed, and those officials involved have been forced from office. This began with the impeachment and resignation of the first elected president, Collor, in 1992 after he was accused of embezzling $23 million. It was the first time a Brazilian president had ever been constitutionally removed from office. This policy of nonpreferential treatment continued under Cardoso's presidency, when members of the National Congress caught discussing the taking of bribes to support changing the constitution to allow presidential reelection and members of Cardoso's cabinet caught discussing how to influence bidding on the privatization of the government's giant telephone company were all forced to resign. The most recent major scandal was under Lula: it seems the PT's compromises to win election led it into the corruption morass of Brazilian

politics. Several leading party members were forced to resign as a result, and Lula publicly apologized for corrupt campaign finance practices. These cases demonstrate the continuing problem of corruption in Brazil, but they also illustrate the first major steps for holding officials accountable for their actions.

Today few political scientists question the consolidation of Brazil's democracy, but many question its quality and degree of democratic deepening. Frances Hagopian (2005), in a major review of the quality of Brazil's democracy, argues that it has improved over time. The electoral system and the existence of multiple parties mean that citizens' views are represented relatively accurately. The system's effects on vertical accountability are ambiguous, however; the large, multi-member electoral districts make direct connections between citizens and particular legislators tenuous. Informally, though, the system encourages legislators to focus on their home areas, and this does enhance accountability.

Horizontal accountability has increased as major politicians have been forced out of office for inappropriate behavior, and the legislature has gained powers to investigate the executive that have helped expose corruption. Although the country's supreme court has increasingly ruled against the other branches, the weakest element is almost certainly the rule of law in general. Brazil's gross social inequality has long meant that the police treat citizens of different classes differently, and law enforcement, which is decentralized to the state level, regularly abuses the rights of the poor. Brazil's courts also are famous for favoring the wealthy who can afford the best legal help, and the prisons are reportedly full of prisoner abuse. So while Brazil's democracy increasingly represents citizens and the latter can hold politicians accountable in certain areas, equality before the law is far from being realized.

Brazil's civil society was instrumental in the initial transition process to democracy and remains quite active. Despite this, democratic deepening and participation remain a concern among observers. The country's exceptional social inequality, many argue, affects participation the same way it affects the rule of law: the poor, who are often black, are left out. Once again, the PT has been innovative in trying to overcome this problem. Starting in the city of Porto Alegre under a PT government, the party has instituted a "participatory budgeting" (PB) system in which citizens in neighborhoods meet to set their priorities for the annual budget. These groups elect representatives who meet at higher levels to produce a set of budget proposals for the city's officials to consider and enact. The system gives local citizens a voice and a means of higher level participation for more active citizens, who typically are members of local social movements or NGOs. Most observers credit the PB process with providing an avenue for greater participation for the poor.

Brazil's still young democracy is an example of a successful transition and consolidation, a transition very different from that experienced in Russia, our next case study. Indeed, the transition itself is considered a model for its relative smooth and gradual process, whereas Russia's has been seen more as a model for one step forward, two steps back. The institutions created in Brazil's 1988 constitution satisfied various interests involved, although they perhaps did not create the most coherent political system imaginable. The electoral system provides few incentives for strong parties to emerge, and the unusually decentralized federalism limits central power, again in sharp contrast to Russia, in which power has become more and more centralized under recent leadership.

Nonetheless, and in part because of these features, the power of the executive has been reduced from what it was during Brazil's earlier democratic regimes. The military is firmly under civilian control, and these days no one expects any significant intervention from that quarter. Accountability and even party strength seem to be rising, though weak institutions and corruption remain serious problems. Participation is undoubtedly greater than at any time in Brazil's history, and the prominence of the PT has allowed poorer citizens more access to government than ever before. This is not to say that problems do not remain: continuing inequality affects the quality of democracy, especially the rule of law. Effective governance continues to be hampered by a system that includes twenty-one rather weak parties in the National Congress. Compared to much of the third wave of democracies, though, including Russia, Brazil stands as a relative success case.

CASE STUDY Russia: Transition to Semi-Authoritarian Rule

As Russian president Boris Yeltsin climbed atop a tank in Moscow to stop a coup attempt in August 1991, it seemed freedom was on the rise in Russia. The coup was the last gasp effort of hardliners in the old Communist regime of the Soviet Union. The reforms of Soviet president Mikhail Gorbachev in the late 1980s had significantly opened the Soviet political system and economy, but demands for far greater reforms were in the air. With Gorbachev on vacation, elements in the military tried to roll the tanks into Moscow to restore the old system and prevent the possible breakup of the Soviet Union. Popular and international opposition, led by Yeltsin, forced the military to back down. By December the Soviet Union was dissolved. Fifteen new countries emerged, each expected to make a transition to democracy, with Russia by far the biggest and most important of these. The world's number two superpower appeared to be starting an unprecedented transition from a Communist state to one that was democratic and capitalist.

Russia's transition, however, has not been to democracy but instead to semi-authoritarian rule. In 1991–1992, Freedom House gave the country's political rights and civil liberties each a score of 3 on their 7-point scale, defining the country as "partially free." These scores deteriorated slowly over the next decade to 5, the low end of the "partially free" category. In 2005 its political rights score slipped to 6, marking it as "not free," where it has stayed. This slide from moving toward democracy to moving away from it is a result of weak institutions, an exceptionally strong presidency that has become autocratic in many ways, and the perverse effects of Russia's abundant natural resources.

Gorbachev's most dramatic reform was ending the Communist Party's claim to absolute power in February 1990. This was followed by legislative elections in March to the Congress of People's Deputies in Russia, still just one of fifteen constituent republics of the Soviet Union at that time. This was the first election to include non-Communist candidates since the Communist revolution. A year later, Boris Yeltsin was elected to the new position of Russian president, only two months before the coup attempt. With the dissolution of the Soviet Union, the Russian institutions became those of the newly independent state. Yeltsin was the elected president, and the Supreme Soviet, which had been the working body of the Congress of People's Deputies, became the legislature, but one that still had a Communist majority. This would lead to what would become a long-term battle between Yeltsin and his legislature, which we discuss below.

Yeltsin immediately began the country's transition to a market economy, using what came to be known as "shock therapy" to free prices from government control overnight and create the rudiments of a market economy. He claimed that the benefits of the new capitalist economy would be widespread, but the immediate effect was a dramatic increase in prices that left Russians with little means of support, especially those relying on government pensions for their livelihood. Shock therapy also included a rapid privatization of the government-owned economy by distributing vouchers to all citizens, who could then use them to

Boris Yeltsin stands on a tank on August 19, 1991, as the Soviet military attempts a coup d'etat to reverse the reforms initiated by the last Soviet leader, Mikhail Gorbachev. Yeltsin's actions helped convince military leaders to reverse course, which led to the peaceful dissolution of the Soviet Union on December 31, 1991, and the birth of an independent Russia.

purchase shares in former government-owned companies, but the poverty of the average citizens gave them an incentive to sell their shares to the companies' managers instead. More often than not the former Communist factory managers became the owners of the newly privatized businesses. To the average worker, it looked like not much had changed, until the owners had to fire much of the bloated workforce to compete in the new market economy. The economy declined 14.5 percent, and inflation ballooned to more than 1500 percent in 1992. Unemployment tripled from 1992 to 1998. Higher prices and massive unemployment sent Yeltsin's popularity plummeting, so that after the initial shock therapy, the government actually backed off of further market-oriented reforms, creating a hybrid economic system. A few spectacularly successful businessmen, especially in Russia's huge oil sector, emerged to control vast swaths of the economy. They became key allies of Yeltsin, a group that came to be known as the "Family" that in effect ran the economy and the government.

The early years of an independent Russia were as chaotic and difficult politically as they were economically. Yeltsin chose early on not to hold elections to help create a legislature with a more democratic mandate, because he feared that the unpopularity of his economic reforms would produce a legislature even more opposed to him. Faced with an increasingly hostile parliament, he ruled primarily by decree. In lieu of revising the constitution, he proposed the creation of the semipresidential system with an exceptionally strong presidency that we outlined in chapter 6. The legislature refused to ratify his ideas, leading him to disband it in September 1993. Legislators barricaded themselves in the parliament building, determined not to leave and voting to impeach Yeltsin. After a week-long standoff, Yeltsin called in the army to lay siege to the parliament building, forcibly ending the Soviet-era parliament.

In late September, large demonstrations against Yeltsin began in the streets of Moscow and became violent; fears of civil war were palpable. However, he subsequently held a referendum on the constitution, which passed by a narrow margin, and an election for a new legislature. In spite of these successes, Yeltsin continued to face opposition to many of his reforms in the newly elected *Duma* (parliament) and frequently had to use his powers of decree to govern in the absence of legislative support. Citizens also blamed him for the unpopular, brutal, and ineffective war in the breakaway region of Chechnya. He narrowly won a bid for reelection in 1996, but neither his popularity nor the economy ever fully recovered.

A primary reason Yeltsin and his policies lacked support in the legislature was that he refused to join a political party, trying instead to appear "above" partisan politics. His refusal to participate, in addition to the very weak powers of the *Duma,* resulted in weak parties overall. Some observers at the time saw a strong presidency and weak legislature as ensuring stability while Russian democracy "matured," but most now recognize this institutional arrangement as a flaw that undermined democracy. Parties are crucial to any democracy: they connect the citizens to the government via the legislature. Strong parties have clear ideologies and organizations that can mobilize voters, endure through numerous elections and leadership changes, and have a major impact on government in general. Russia's parties have none of these attributes. Because the legislature is so weak, party loyalty among both the elite and the citizenry is low. Power resides overwhelmingly in the executive branch, and until Vladimir Putin joined a party in October 2007, the chief executive remained distanced from them, so parties remain of limited consequence except as often temporary vehicles to gain election. They rise and fall with the popularity and shifting allegiances of major politicians.

Only seven of the thirteen parties in the first elected parliament in 1993 also had seats in the second parliament elected in 1995. That parliament included seventeen parties, only five of which returned after the 1999 election. The 1999 parliament included fourteen parties, only six of which survived into the parliament elected in 2003, which included twelve parties or coalitions, none of which were new. While some of these changes were in name only or were the result of the creation of new parties via the merger or the splitting of old ones, this trend nonetheless shows the lack of durability of Russian parties as institutions. Ironically, the biggest exception is the Communist Party, which has the clearest ideology and is an organization reputed to include five hundred thousand members. It has endured as a significant voice in the *Duma* throughout Russia's tumultuous post-Communist history and was the largest party in the *Duma* from 1995 to 1999. To date it is also the largest force in the *Duma* not allied with the executive.

Political scientists Hans Oversloot and Ruben Verheul (2006) argue that the most important party in Russia is the "party of power, the party that those around the president create to win as many seats as they can in the *duma,* insuring support for the president's proposals." This party changes from one election to the next: it was called Russia's Choice in 1993, Our Home is Russia in 1995, Unity in 1999, and United Russia in 2003. The newly wealthy owners of private industry around Yeltsin (known as "the oligarchs") tried to create and heavily funded parties of power in the 1990s but gained only a minority of seats in the 1993 and 1995 *Dumas*. While the largesse of the executive branch and the oligarchs attracted politicians looking for a share of that wealth, Yeltsin's lack of popularity prevented them from gaining an outright win.

Putin's greater popularity did allow his parties of power to win more handily, coming in second to the

Communist Party in 1999, but winning a plurality of almost half the seats in 2003. From that point, Putin's parties of power and their allies dominated the *Duma,* in sharp contrast to the status quo during Yeltsin's term in office. Putin did not have to rule by decree as Yeltsin did because the *Duma,* under the firm grasp of his parties of power, approved every major piece of legislation he sent it. Oversloot and Verheul note that the presence of these parties of power reverses the democratic relationship between party and state. Rather than a party gaining control of the state via an election to the legislature, those in charge of the state in the executive branch create a party to win an election and gain control of the legislature.

Putin, anointed as Yeltsin's successor in 1999, duly elected in 2000, and reelected with more than 70 percent of the vote in 2004, significantly centralized power and eliminated most vestiges of real democracy in Russia. In addition to increasing the powers of the presidency vis-à-vis the regions, he harassed and closed down most independent media, undermined independent civil society groups, and broke the informal power of the oligarchs who had arisen under Yeltsin. Many of these oligarchs quietly agreed to support him in exchange for his allowing them to continue their business practices. Others, including a major media magnate and the owner of Yukos, a huge oil company, tried to resist his power. Their economic empires were systematically destroyed, either by directly shutting down the media or, in the case of Yukos, by using charges of corruption to arrest the oligarch and seize his assets. Putin turned their assets over to his supporters to keep them under his tight control. Clearly, despite being Yeltsin's hand-picked successor, Putin turned against the "Family" early on. He ruled primarily via a group of former agents of the Federal Security Bureau (FSB), the successor to the KGB where he had spent most of his career. Members of this group sit in key ministries and agencies throughout the executive branch, have been appointed governors in several cases, and control important companies (Hesli: 2007, 145).

Putin also changed the electoral system. Under the 1993 constitution, Russia has a mixed PR electoral system similar to Germany's in which half of the *Duma* is elected via closed-list proportional representation and the other half via single-member districts. His most significant opposition in the *Duma* came not from opposition parties but from independent members, voted into office in the single-member districts. Putin first put a 5 percent threshold on the PR seats, requiring parties to get that percentage of the national vote to gain seats in parliament. Then he had parliament change the electoral system altogether to a purely closed-list PR system to eliminate independent candidates entirely. More recently, he passed a law increasing the threshold for representation to 7 percent to eliminate more small parties.

In October 2007, he officially joined the United Russia Party, his primary party of power and the majority party in the *Duma.* Constitutionally barred from running for a third term as president, Putin announced he was joining the party and would be a candidate for prime minister. He also hand selected Dmitry Medvedev, a relatively obscure bureaucrat without a major political following, to succeed him as president. Observers speculate that now that Putin is prime minister and staunch supporter Medvedev is president, Putin will either change the constitution to strengthen the office of PM and weaken the presidency or he will relatively soon resign as PM and begin a new term as president, having stepped out of office briefly and thereby becoming eligible to hold the office again. The legality of either would be subject to some question, but the courts have been unwilling to challenge Putin given his overwhelming power. Such an undermining of the intention of the constitution—to limit the president to two terms in power—would be the most blatant example of how he weakened or strengthened particular institutions to serve his short-term interests.

Putin's rule fully transformed Russia from a weak but fledgling democracy to a semi-authoritarian hybrid regime. Political scientist Steven Fish, one of the foremost experts on Russia, argues that this has occurred because of a weak legislature, limited economic reform, and a dependence on oil (2005). The weak legislature was a choice made by Yeltsin and his supporters to establish a strong presidency and has resulted in weak parties and the dynamics we describe above. Limited economic reform and massive oil production have led to large-scale corruption. Putin justified his actions against the oligarchs and reduction in civil liberties in terms of building a strong state and reducing corruption, though the evidence suggests he has achieved relatively little to that end. The worst elements of the weak state—widespread mafia activity in Moscow that characterized the mid-1990s—have been reduced but corruption overall remains a problem. Transparency International gave Russia a score of 2.4 (out of 10, with 10 being least corrupt) in 1999 in its annual Corruption Perceptions Index, and the country scored a 2.3 in 2007, its ranking virtually unchanged nearly a decade later. Oil revenues also mean the government can limit economic reform because rising oil prices in the last few years have given it ample revenue, allowing it to co-opt potential opposition in civil society and the political class by controlling who can engage in business and how. Weak institutions in the context of abundant resources and limited reform have turned a transition to democracy into a transition to semi-authoritarian rule.

Russia's parties of power and its oligarchs are in some ways similar to the patrons in Nigeria's political system. That country's politics continue to be based on patron-client ties amidst weak institutions, and democratizing in the sense of holding elections and allowing greater political freedoms has not changed these fundamental relationships. This reality has led those who capture power to do everything they can to keep it—at the expense of democracy itself—also in some ways similar to the power grab in Russia. And as in Russia, oil revenue has fueled corruption, which has helped ruling politicians maintain their power via patronage. Amidst these problems, however, Nigeria continues to hold elections, uphold basic freedoms of association at least partially, and strengthen some democratic institutions.

CASE STUDY Nigeria: Neopatrimonial Transition

Nigeria seemed to be making history in May 2007 when it held its third consecutive multiparty election and inaugurated a second elected president, the first time in the history of the country that the presidency changed hands via election. In fact, the election achieved far less than supporters of Nigerian democracy had hoped for when military rule ended in 1999 with the creation of a presidential and federal democracy. Domestic and international observers saw the 2007 election as deeply flawed, neither free nor fair: the prior president's party and his hand-picked successor won an overwhelming victory at all levels of government, and each of the three national elections (1999, 2003, 2007) was further from democratic norms than the one before. Throughout, Freedom House has rated Nigeria as "partially free," with scores of 4 out of 7 for both political rights and civil liberties most years.

The election of 1999 marked Nigeria's third attempt to return to democratic rule. The military had allowed elections in 1979, which created the Second Republic that ended in a military coup in 1983 (see chapter 8) amidst claims that elected leaders had expanded corruption and stolen the election. A second transition attempt occurred in 1993, when General Babangida allowed a carefully controlled election in which only two parties, both created by him, were allowed to run. The party he did not favor won, and so he annulled the election. This decision not only plunged Nigeria into its darkest period under Gen. Sani Abacha, but it also gave rise to a vociferous democracy movement. The 1999 democratic constitution was modeled almost exactly after the 1979 one and created a presidential system with an FPTP electoral system closely modeled after that of the United States. It has survived longer than any previous civilian government, and some of its institutions seem to function, but the electoral process and increasing domination of the ruling party have thrown doubt on the long-term prospects for consolidating Nigerian democracy.

As in much of Africa, democratic transition in Nigeria began with grassroots protests. The country's first human rights group, the Civil Liberties Organization, emerged in 1987. By 1991 a number of new human rights groups formed an umbrella organization, the Campaign for Democracy (CD), that became Nigeria's first large-scale civil society movement for democracy. This movement put pressure on Babangida to complete his "long transition program" that had started in 1985 and finally led to an election in 1993. Babangida's annulment of that election and the subsequent jailing of the rightful winner, Moshood Abiola, produced outrage in Nigeria and around the world.

That annulment of the long-awaited election motivated many new groups to join the democracy effort; in 1994 they formed a new umbrella group, the National Democratic Coalition (NADECO), that included former politicians, union members, students, and human rights campaigners of the CD. NADECO's breadth brought even greater pressure to bear on Nigeria's military government. Its first campaign was "Babangida Must Go," to be replaced by Abiola, the rightful winner of the election. Babangida did go, but only gave up power to a hand-picked "caretaker" government, which was over-

Nigeria's new president, Umaru Yar'Adua, inspects the guards after being sworn into office May 29, 2007. This was the first time in the country's history that power passed from one elected president to another, though Yar'Adua was handpicked to succeed President Olusegun Obasanjo and won an election that virtually all observers saw as highly fraudulent. Nigeria's democracy survives but without strong institutions guaranteeing truly free and fair elections.

thrown by Abacha a few months later. While amassing a fortune from corrupt control of oil revenue, Abacha severely repressed the democracy movement. Most NADECO leaders ended up in jail and (as discussed in chapter 4) the Ogoni leader Ken Saro-Wiwa and eight others were hanged in 1995.

Although Abacha claimed in 1995 that he was initiating a transition to democracy, it was a sham from the start. The five parties he allowed to register for what was to be the first election all proclaimed loyalty to him and only him. The real transition began only after his death in 1998. His successor recognized how discredited the military had become under Abacha's rule and immediately agreed to a transition and elections. The subsequent elections in 1999 were far from perfect, but most observers deemed them minimally adequate to start Nigeria's new democracy. The military elite of the Kaduna mafia put together what became the ruling party, the People's Democratic Party (PDP), and chose the military dictator who had shepherded the 1979 transition, Gen. Olusegun Obasanjo,

IN CONTEXT Freedom in Africa

In 1990: Nigeria's Freedom House Civil Liberties score was 5, compared to the Africa average of 5.06; its Political Rights Score was 5, compared to the Africa average of 5.56.

In 2006: Nigeria's Freedom House Civil Liberties score was 4, compared to the Africa average of 4.15; its Political Rights Score was 4, compared to the Africa average of 4.42.

as its presidential candidate. Obasanjo was credited with having revived democracy in 1979 and as actively opposing Abacha, spending part of the 1990s in jail. He also had become something of an elder statesman in Africa, with wide international respect, and in Nigeria's ethnically and religiously divided society, he benefited from being a Yoruba from the southwest. The long dominance of northerners under military rule and the annulment of the election of Abiola, a Yoruba, led all Nigerians to recognize that it was time for a president from the country's southern region.

And so the Kaduna mafia, a group of Muslim military leaders from the north that has controlled most of Nigeria's governments, picked a southerner whom it trusted, a former general himself, as its candidate. He faced only one opponent, another Yoruba, though his party faced two major opposition parties in the legislative races. The All People's Party (APP) was led by military officers and other "Big Men," wealthy patrons who provide funding and strongly influence candidate selection, who had been close to Abacha but not part of the Kaduna mafia. The Alliance for Democracy (AD) was based heavily in the southwestern region among the Yoruba. Ironically, Obasanjo won handily in most of the country except his home area among the Yoruba, who saw him as having sold out to northern military interests.

By the 2003 election, Obasanjo had gained significant support in his home area, so much so that while the AD continued to exist and won legislative seats in Yoruba states as well as one governorship, it chose not to select a presidential candidate. Its supporters mostly voted for Obasanjo, who won the 2003 election more easily than in 1999, as did his party. The only significant opposition came from the APP (now renamed ANPP), which increasingly became the party of northern leaders unhappy with Obasanjo. Its presidential candidate was Muhammadu Buhari, military dictator from 1983–1985, who had a reputation for being a devout Muslim and relatively uncorrupt. He and Obasanjo's hand-picked successor, current president Umaru Musa Yar'Adua, were the two major presidential candidates in 2007 as well. Yar'adua won 72 percent of the vote, and the PDP won a similar majority in the legislature. Though many parties existed, by 2007 only two had a real shot at gaining power, and of those, the ruling party was overwhelmingly victorious, though often via fraudulent means.

Political parties in Nigeria are not strong institutions with loyal supporters based on party ideology and symbols, but instead are based mainly on the support of key Big Men. In 1999 a rule that required parties to gain the support of 5 percent of the voters in three-quarters of the states meant that only the three parties were on the ballot. By 2003 the country's Supreme Court had invalidated this limit, and dozens of parties registered, "but most parties consisted primarily of the office staff at the national headquarters … and were typically centered on a Big Man who was funding the operations and running for president" (Kew 2004, 147). In 1999 the Big Men in all the parties were uncertain about the future of democracy, and so they tended to appoint deputies to run for office rather than running themselves. By the 2003 election, most Big Men had come to realize that democracy seemed likely to endure, and so they chose to run themselves for such positions as state governor. In the major parties, their deputies, after four years in office and significant corruption, had their own bases of support and refused to yield to their erstwhile patrons, which led to very expensive (winning a governor's office reportedly cost individuals at least $2 million) and often violent campaigns.

Elections are also institutionally weak in Nigeria. Former U.S. president Jimmy Carter was so upset by what he saw as electoral fraud in 1999 that he refused to endorse the results as legitimate, though ultimately his organization and other international election observer groups decided to accept the elections as minimally adequate, in part out of fear that not doing so would encourage yet another military coup. In 2003 and even more so in 2007, international and Nigerian observers saw the elections as increasingly fraudulent. In 2003 the elections were free and fair in about one-third of Nigeria's states, were "dubious" in another third, and completely fraudulent in the final third (Kew 2004). By 2007 observers for Human Rights Watch reported that "the elections were marred by extraordinary displays of rigging and the intimidation of voters in many areas throughout Nigeria" (Rawlence and Albin-Lackey 2007, 497). In quite a few states no elections took place at all: officials simply made up results in favor of the ruling party. Incumbent governors won in most states, whether they were members of the PDP or the opposition ANPP. Voter turnout was grossly inflated in many states in which the ruling party won, and observers saw officials openly stuffing ballot boxes in a number of cases.

While institutions of participation are extremely weak, Nigeria's experiment with democracy has produced some examples of institutionalization that have seemed to strengthen democracy. A key area is civilian control of the military. Military leaders of the Kaduna mafia backed Obasanjo for president in 1999, assuming they could then control him. In a number of areas, they were proven wrong. After becoming president, he quickly removed those northern generals most actively engaged in politics and replaced them with less politically active and more southern officers. While it is difficult to make certain predictions given Nigeria's history of military coups, Obasanjo seems to have established civilian control over the military, a first in Nigerian history. Indeed, some observers believe that elections have become so hotly contested and fraudulent because the stakes are so high: no one expects military intervention, so election is the sole means of gaining political power.

A second institution that has been strengthened is the Supreme Court. The new constitution created a National Judicial Council that has helped insulate the judiciary from pressures from elected officials. The Supreme Court has made several important rulings over questions of federalism that have long been of importance in Nigeria. In the area of federal versus state control over oil revenues, the Supreme Court ruled in some key cases in favor of the oil-producing states and in other cases in favor of the federal government, indicating a certain degree of autonomy from undue political pressure from either side. On the eve of the 2007 presidential election, it also ruled that Obasanjo's estranged vice president, whom the president had tried to prevent from running, could stand in the election. While this created havoc in terms of the ballots, since his name was not on them, the Court's ruling against an important issue for the sitting president was nonetheless another indication of its autonomy.

Perhaps the most important test of institutional strength for Nigerian democracy went against President Obasanjo. The 1999 constitution set a limit of two terms for the president, like the U.S. Constitution. Facing the end of his second term, Obasanjo launched a major campaign to revoke this amendment, an action that required Senate approval. Reportedly, he and his supporters were even trying to bribe senators, with offers as high as $750,000, to get them to vote in favor of the amendment. It became crystal clear, though, that the population overwhelmingly opposed the move, and the Senate voted it down despite all the pressure and inducements Obasanjo brought to bear. Some observers also argue that many of the elite quietly opposed Obasanjo as well. In a patronage-based system with oil revenue available, the presidency is very powerful and very lucrative. The political elite want that office to rotate, not be monopolized for too long by any one individual, so that other leaders and other groups have a chance at gaining its benefits. The result, in any case, was the preservation of an institutionalized limit on one individual's time in office, despite the power and wealth at his disposal.

Establishing a stable federal order in Nigeria has long been a contentious process, and it continues to be under the new democracy. The biggest issue is control of revenue from oil, which is located in a handful of southeastern states. Not surprisingly, these states argue that they should receive a larger share of the revenue generated from resources within their borders, while the federal government and other states argue exactly the opposite. The current formula gives 13 percent of all such revenue to the state of origin, meaning that the oil states receive far more money than non-oil states. Nonetheless, their leaders demand more, and their people remain among the poorest in the country. They benefit little from the oil revenues in large part because of the still massive degree of corruption found in Nigeria, including in the oil-producing states. The ethnic movements we discussed in chapter 4 arose and continue because of the population's failure to gain much from the oil on their land. In recent years, unfortunately, some of these armed movements have become armed gangs for hire to the highest bidder. Not infrequently they are armed thugs for politicians in the oil-producing states who serve as the violent wing of campaign teams.

The *sharia* controversy we described in chapter 4 is also part of the federalism question in Nigeria. The 1999 constitution allows states to set their own legal codes within national law, and Nigeria has long allowed dual civil law codes based on religion. The twelve northern states that have implemented *sharia* have expanded this to criminal law as well, setting off confrontations with Christian minorities in several of these states and opposition from the south in general. Long-standing northern and Muslim control of national politics has left southerners and Christians fearful of any further Islamic movements. And because of federalism, each state's version of *sharia* is slightly different: some states apply some Muslim laws to non-Muslims, and other states don't; some include the harshest penalties such as stoning, and others don't. So far, national courts have not revoked states' rights to implement *sharia* or insisted on a uniform version of it across all states.

All of these institutional problems in Nigeria are related to the overall weakness of the state. The country continues to be one of the more corrupt in the world, though it has made improvements. Transparency International's 1999 Corruption Perception Index ranked it number 98 of 99 countries surveyed, with a score of 1.6 on a 10-point scale (with 10 being least corrupt). In 2007 it was number 147 of 179 countries, with a score of 2.2. While still far below average, it nonetheless is an improvement. This is due in part to an anticorruption drive Obasanjo launched that received great praise in its early years. Unfortunately, it seems that before both the 2003 and 2007 elections, Obasanjo and his party in parliament were willing to use their anticorruption efforts for political purposes, targeting charges at their opponents and protecting their supporters. Continued corruption has made all state institutions weak, harmed the ability of the electoral commission to conduct proper elections, prevented people in the oil-producing states from benefiting from their oil, and led northerners to turn to *sharia* in the hope it will be less corrupt and more just than secular courts.

Summary

The Nigerian case demonstrates both the potential and severe problems of establishing democracy in a poor country when politics are based on patronage. The competition for office becomes all consuming and often violent, which undermines virtually all democratic norms of the "free and fair" choice of candidates. Corruption continues throughout the country with only slight change, weakening all state institutions and popular faith in democracy. Yet this fragile democratic regime seems to have brought the military under control: a coup seems less likely than at any time since the first one occurred in 1966. A few other key institutions—term limits and judicial independence—have been strengthened as well. Advocates of democracy in countries like Nigeria hope that these institutional gains will be the basis for further improvement and the slow establishment of a consolidated and relatively high quality democracy, though that seems quite far off in Nigeria's case.

CONCLUSION

Regime change is the high drama of comparative politics. Many of our most iconic political images are of regime change: from the "shot heard round the world" in 1776 to Boris Yeltsin standing atop a Soviet tank in 1991 to Nelson Mandela taking the oath of office in 1994. They are images of popular and charismatic leaders backed by the mobilized masses demanding a better world. There can also be less positive images, though, like that of a general seizing power as tanks roll into the capital. Of course, when examined systematically, regime change is more complex and less clearly positive or negative than it is often portrayed. It involves the destruction of an old regime (and sometimes a state) that is already weak and the attempt to create a new one that will be stronger and better. No matter how it is carried out or by whom, it is no simple process.

Military coups are probably the most common and quickest form of regime change. Troops can seize the capital for a variety of reasons: the military's sense that the nation needs to be "rescued," the military's own interests as an organization, or the more particular interests of individual leaders or groups within the military, and explaining any particular coup may require more than one of these ideas. Which explanation is most useful often depends on the nature of the military itself, especially its degree of institutionalization. Civilian regimes, from communist to democratic, have to worry about the possibility that those holding the guns will use them against the civilian order, regardless of what the constitution says. Institutionalizing norms of professionalism and loyalty to the civilian regime is crucial to keeping the soldiers in their barracks. When push comes to shove, they hold the guns on which the state and regime rely.

Revolutions are much rarer and more dramatic events, the stuff of which world history is made. A particular set of circumstances, then, must account for them, but it's not always easy to figure what those circumstances are. A weakened old regime and state seem essential, as strong states are strong enough to resist revolution, no matter how many people are involved. A strong revolutionary organization that unites and mobilizes people's grievances also seems vital. Revolutions are known by their leaders' ideologies, but that does not always explain the motivations of the masses supporting them. A seemingly united revolutionary front can often hide a disparate set of groups, past grievances, and future agendas. This makes building a new regime with strong institutions particularly fraught and unlikely to have a democratic outcome. As is so often the case in politics, those who fought for change do not necessarily get what they seek. While revolutions have been an essential part of world history, the relative lack of them over the last generation (with the unusual exception of the revolutions from above ending communism in Eastern Europe) has led many to speculate that the age of revolution may be over.

While revolutions have become less common, the last, slowest, and perhaps most complicated form of regime change has become much more common: democratization. The process of creating new democracies dates back centuries but has become much more common since the 1970s and especially since the mid-1980s. Again, iconic images like Nelson Mandela walking out of jail and Ferdinand Marcos fleeing the Philippines often inform popular understanding of this process. In truth, democratization almost always requires some sort of weakness or split in the old, authoritarian regime in addition to a mobilized populace demanding change. Getting the process started often seems difficult, as elements of the old regime typically cling to power as long as they can. Once started, however, completing the process becomes even more difficult. Consolidating a new democracy is an extremely challenging process. Major political groups often do not trust

COUNTRY AND CONCEPT Regime Change and Outcome

Country	Date	Type of Regime Change (20th century)	Outcome: Type of Regime	Length of New Regime (years)
Brazil	1930	Military coup	Neofascist	15
	1945	Democratization	Democracy	19
	1964	Military coup	Bureaucratic-authoritarian	21
	1985	Democratization	Democracy	23+
China	1911	Revolution from above	State collapse/warlord rule	16
	1949	Revolution from below	Communist	48+
Germany	1918	Democratization	Democracy	15
	1933	Fascist putsch	Fascist	12
	1950	Democratization	Democracy	57+
	1990	Democratization (end of East German state)	Democracy (expanded)	NA
India	1947	Democratization (end of colonial rule)	Democracy	60+
Iran	1921	Military coup	Modernizing authoritarian	58
	1979	Revolution from below	Theocratic	28+
Japan	1950	Democratization	Democracy	57+
Nigeria	1960	Democratization (end of colonial rule)	Democracy	6
	1966	Military coup	Personalist	13
	1979	Democratization	Democracy	4
	1983	Military coup	Personalist	16
	1999	Democratization	Democracy	8+
Russia	1917	Revolution from below	Communist	74
	1991	Democratization	Democracy	9
			Semi-authoritarian	7+
United Kingdom	None	NA	NA	NA
United States	None	NA	NA	NA

one another or the new and untried democratic institutions they have created, but democracy requires trust in both in the long run. For years comparativists believed that partly for this reason democracy would only survive in very specific kinds of countries. Yet while a propitious cultural or economic context is undoubtedly helpful, most scholars have shifted to the idea that it is at least possible to create a set of institutions that can function initially in an environment of limited trust, thus building trust over time as they work. A particular context may be nice, but it is not essential. The process, though, can be easily undermined by institutional breakdowns of all sorts. What seems to be an increasingly common result of these breakdowns, especially in the former Soviet Union and much of Africa, are hybrid regimes, part authoritarian and part democratic. The future of these regimes will have a major impact on the future of democracy around the world.

Comparative politics today focuses much more on democratization than on military coups or revolutions. We suggest, however, that the latter remain important topics of investigation. Military coups have certainly continued to occur in this era of democratization (a coup took place in Mauritania in August 2008 as the final editing of this book was taking place), albeit less frequently than in the past, and studying revolutions teaches us much about how people are mobilized into political activity of all types. While future revolutions will not necessarily look exactly like those of the past, ruling them out entirely seems a risky prediction. Understanding the motives of any actors who choose to use violence for political ends continues to be crucial.

Key Concepts

competitive authoritarian regime (p. 364)
delegative democracies (p. 364)
democratic consolidation (p. 363)
democratic deepening (p. 364)
founding election (p. 361)

hardliners (p. 361)
hybrid regime (p. 364)
illiberal democracies (p. 364)
moderates (p. 361)
pact (p. 361)
political liberalization (p. 361)
political violence (p. 355)

radicals (p. 361)
revolutions from above (p. 352)
revolutions from below (p. 352)
softliners (p. 361)
terrorism (p. 355)
transition to democracy (p. 360)

Works Cited

Ames, Barry. 2001. *The Deadlock of Democracy in Brazil.* Ann Arbor: University of Michigan Press.

Bermeo, Nancy. 2003. *Ordinary People in Extraordinary Times: The Citizenry and the Breakdown of Democracy.* Princeton: Princeton University Press.

Bratton, Michael, and Nicholas Van de Walle. 1997. *Democratic Experiments in Africa: Regime Transitions in Comparative Perspective.* New York: Cambridge University Press.

Brinton, Crane. 1965. *The Anatomy of Revolution.* New York: Prentice Hall.

Case, William. 2006. "Manipulative Skills: How Do Rulers Control the Electoral Arena?" In *Electoral Authoritarianism: The Dynamics of Unfree Competition,* ed. Andreas Schedler, 95–112. Boulder, Colo.: Lynne Rienner Publishers.

Clawson, Patrick, and Michael Rubin. 2005. *Eternal Iran: Continuity and Chaos.* New York: Palgrave Mac-Millan.

Crenshaw, Martha. 1981. "The Causes of Terrorism." *Comparative Politics* 13, no. 4: 379–399.

Davies, James. 1962. "Toward a Theory of Revolution." *American Sociological Review* 27: 5–18.

Decalo, Samuel. 1976. *Coups and Army Rule in Africa.* New Haven: Yale University Press.

Diamond, Larry. 1996. "Is the Third Wave Over?" *Journal of Democracy* 7, no. 3: 20–37.

Finer, Samuel E. 1975. *The Man on Horseback: Military Intervention into Politics.* London: Hammondsworth Press-Penguin.

Fish, M. Steven. 2005. *Democracy Derailed in Russia: The Failure of Open Politics.* New York: Cambridge University Press.

———. 2006. "Stronger Legislatures, Stronger Democracies." *Journal of Democracy* 17, no. 1: 5–20.

Fish, M. Steven, and R. S. Brooks. 2004. "Does Diversity Hurt Democracy?" *Journal of Democracy* 15: 154–167.

Freedom House. Freedom in the World. www.freedomhouse.org/template.cfm?page=15.

Fukuyama, Francis. 1992. *The End of History and the Last Man.* New York: Free Press.

Graf, William. 1988. *The Nigerian State: Political Economy, State Class, and Political System in the Post-Colonial Era.* London: J. Currey and Portsmouth, N.H.: Heinemann.

Gurr, Ted Robert. 1970. *Why Men Rebel.* Princeton: Princeton University Press.

Hagopian, Frances. 2005. "Chile and Brazil." In *Assessing the Quality of Democracy,* ed. Larry Diamond and Leonardo Morlino, 123–162. Baltimore: Johns Hopkins University Press.

Hesli, Vick L. 2007. *Government and Politics: Russia and the Post-Soviet Region.* Boston: Houghton Mifflin.

Huntington, Samuel P. 1964. *The Soldier and the State.* New York: Random House.

———. 1968. *Political Order in Changing Societies.* New Haven: Yale University Press.

———. 1991 *The Third Wave: Democratization in the Late Twentieth Century.* Norman: University of Oklahoma Press.

Janowitz, Morris. 1964. *The Military in the Political Development of New Nations.* Chicago: University of Chicago Press.

Kieh, George K., and Pita O. Agbese. 2002. *The Military and Politics in Africa: From Engagement to Democratic and Constitutional Control.* Aldershot: Ashgate.

Kew, Darren. 2004. "The 2003 Elections: Hardly Credible, but Acceptable." In *Crafting the New Nigeria,* 139–173. Boulder, Colo.: Lynne Rienner Publishers and the World Peace Foundation.

Levitsky, Steve, and Lucan Way. 2006. "Linkage and Leverage: How Do International Factors Change Domestic Balances of Power?" In *Electoral Authoritarianism: The Dynamics of Unfree Competition,* ed. A. Schedler, 199–218. Boulder, Colo.: Lynne Rienner Publishers.

Lijphart, Arendt. 1969. "Consociational Democracy." *World Politics* 21: 207–225.

Limongi, Fernando, and Argelina Figueiredo, 2000. "Presidential Power, Legislative Organization, and Party Behavior in Brazil." *Comparative Politics* 32, no. 2: 151–170.

Linz, Juan. 1990. "The Perils of Presidentialism." *Journal of Democracy* 1, no. 1: 51–69.

Lipset, Seymour Martin. 1959. "Some Social Requisites for Democracy: Economic Development and Political Legitimacy." *American Political Science Review* 53, no. 1: 69–105.

Moore, Barrington. 1966. *Social Origins of Dictatorship and Democracy.* Boston: Beacon Press.

O'Donnell, Guillermo. 1979. *Modernization and Bureaucratic-Authoritarianism: Studies in South American Politics.* Berkeley: Institute of International Studies, University of California.

———. 1994. "Delegative Democracy." *Journal of Democracy* 5, no. 1: 55–69.

Oversloot, Hans, and Ruben Verheul. 2006. "Managing Democracy: Political Parties and the State in Russia." *Journal of Communist Studies and Transition Politics* 22: 383–405.

Paige, Jeffrey. 1975. *Agrarian Revolution: Social Movements and Export Agriculture in the Underdeveloped World.* New York: Free Press.

Przeworski, Adam. 1991. *Democracy and the Market: Political and Economic Reform in Eastern Europe and Latin America.* Cambridge, UK: Cambridge University Press.

Przeworski, Adam, et al. 2000. *Democracy and Development: Political Institutions and Well-Being in the World, 1950–1990.* Cambridge, UK: Cambridge University Press.

Rawlence, Ben, and Chris Albin-Lackey. 2007. "Briefing: Nigeria's 2007 General Elections: Democracy in Retreat." *African Affairs* 106, no. 424: 497–506.

Roett, Riordan. 1978. *Brazil: Politics in a Patrimonial Society.* Revised Edition. New York: Praeger.

Sanderson, Stephen K. 2005. *Revolutions: A Worldwide Introduction to Political and Social Change.* Boulder, Colo.: Paradigm Publishers.

Skocpol, Theda. 1979. *States and Social Revolutions: A Comparative Analysis of France, Russia, and China.* New York: Cambridge University Press.

Tilly, Charles. 1978. *From Mobilization to Revolution.* New York: McGraw-Hill.

Wood, Gordon. 1992. *The Radicalism of the American Revolution.* New York: Knopf.

Zakaria, Fareed. 2003. *The Future of Freedom: Illiberal Democracy at Home and Abroad.* New York: W. W. Norton.

Resources for Further Study

Ackerman, Peter, and Jack Duvall. 2000. *A Force More Powerful: A Century of Nonviolent Conflict,* ch. 10. New York: St Martin's Press.

Casper, Gretchen. 1995. *Fragile Democracies: The Legacies of Authoritarian Rule.* Pittsburgh: University of Pittsburgh Press.

Dahl, Robert. 1971. *Polyarchy: Participation and Opposition.* New Haven: Yale University Press.

Diamond, Larry, and Leonardo Morlino. 2005. *Assessing the Quality of Democracy.* Baltimore: Johns Hopkins University Press.

Haggard, Stephan, and Robert R. Kaufman. 1995. *The Political Economy of Democratic Transitions.* Princeton: Princeton University Press.

Levitsky, Steve, and Lucan Way. 2002. "Elections without Democracy: The Rise of Competitive Authoritarianism." *Journal of Democracy* 13, no. 2: 51–65.

Morgenstern, S. N. 2002. *Legislative Politics in Latin America.* New York: Cambridge University Press.

O'Donnell, Guillermo. 1999. "Horizontal Accountability in New Democracies." In *The Self-Restraining State,* ed. A. Schedler, Larry Diamond, and M. F. Plattner, 29–51. London: Lynne Rienner Publishers.

Pinkney, R. 2003. *Democracy in the Third World.* Boulder, Colo.: Lynne Rienner Publishers.

Reynolds, Andrew. 2002. *The Architecture of Democracy: Constitutional Design, Conflict Management, and Democracy.* New York: Oxford University Press.

Schedler, Andreas. 2006. *Electoral Authoritarianism: The Dynamics of Unfree Competition.* Boulder, Colo.: Lynne Rienner Publishers.

PART III

ISSUES AND POLICIES

COUNTRY CASES IN PART 3

Chapter	Brazil	China	Germany	India	Iran	Japan	Nigeria	Russia	UK	US
10. Globalization, Deindustrialization, and Development	●	●	●	●	●		●		●	
11. Public Policy When Markets Fail	●	●	●				●		●	●
12. Policies and Politics of Inclusion and Clashing Values	●	●		●	●			●	●	●

Country	GDP (U.S. dollars at current prices in millions)*	GDP Dist. by Sector (percent of total)[†]			Official Development Assistance Received (US$ per capita)[‡]	Transnational Corporations[§]	
		Agriculture	Fishing	Services		# of parent corporations based in economy	# foreign affiliates located in economy
Brazil	1,346,927	9	37.3	53.7	1	165	3,549
China	3,286,881	12.8	46.6	40.7	1.3	3,429	280,000
Germany	3,302,252	1	30	69.1	0	5,855	9,193
India	1,136,921	19.6	27.1	53.3	1.6	587	1,796
Iran	314,334	10.9	41.6	47.5	1.5	46	57
Japan	4,395,398	1.6	28.9	69.5	0	4,563	4,500
Nigeria	151,312	33.1	44.4	22.5	48.9	...	171
Russia	1,284,698	4.8	38.4	56.8	0	...	1,176
United Kingdom	2,738,278	.9	24	75.1	0	2,360	13,667
United States	13,816,049	.9	22.1	77	0	2,418	24,607

* UNCTAD data, 2007
[†] UNCTAD data, 2006
[‡] Year varies

[§] Dates vary. According to the United Nations conference on Trade and Development (UNCTAD), "transnational corporations (TNCs) are incorporated or unincorporated enterprises comprising parent enterprises and their foreign affiliates." *Foreign affiliates* are enterprises in which an investor, residing in another country, has a "lasting interest in the management of the enterprise." Typically, investor interest in a corporation requires an equity stake ownership of at least 10% or its equivalent for an unincorporated enterprise.

As members of religious minorities, like this young French Muslim, attempt to gain more rights in civil society, battles wage on the front lines between church and state.

Telephone (mainlines per 1,000 people)**	Internet Users (per 1,000 people)††	Forest Area Change, 1990–2005 (thousands of sq. kilo.)‡‡	Births Attended by Skilled Health Personnel (percent of total)§§	Physician Density (per 10,000 population)***	Primary School Enrollment, % Female (percent of total)	Secondary School Enrollment, % Female (percent of total)	Tertiary School Enrollment, % Female (percent of total)
230	195	-423.3	97	121	47	52	56
269	85	401.5	98	14	47	48	47
667	455	3.4	100	34	49	48	...
45	55	37.6	47	6	47	43	40
278	103	0	97	9	54	47	51
460	668	-.8	100	21	49	49	46
9	38	-61.5	35	3	45	45	35
280	152	-1.6	100	43	49	49	57
528	473	2.3	99	23	49	49	57
606	630	44.4	100	26	49	49	57

** UN Human Development Report data from 2005 or 2006

†† UN Human Development Report data from latest year available

‡‡ UN Human Development Report data

§§ WHO data

*** WHO data

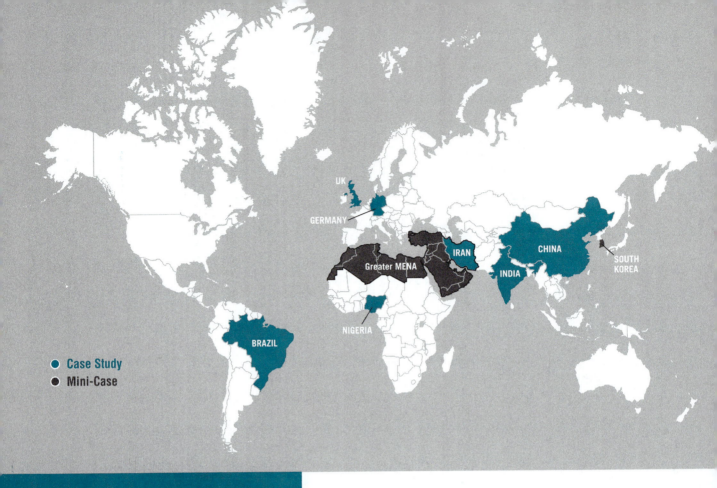

UK

GERMANY

Greater MENA

IRAN

CHINA

INDIA

SOUTH KOREA

NIGERIA

BRAZIL

● Case Study
● Mini-Case

Who Rules?

- How much has globalization eroded the power of states to make economic policy?

- If states no longer "rule" with regard to economic policy in a globalized world, who does?

What Explains Political Behavior?

- What explains the ability of states to pursue successful development policy in the context of globalization?

Where and Why?

- Has globalization produced similar responses and similar patterns of growth in particular regions, such as East Asia, Africa, or continental Europe? If so, what would explain such regional patterns?

- Why have some countries moved to liberalize their economies in the face of globalization much more than others?

BRAZIL

GERMANY

CHINA

NIGERIA

UK

INDIA

IRAN

Greater MENA

SOUTH KOREA

10

GLOBALIZATION, DEINDUSTRI-ALIZATION, AND DEVELOPMENT

On July 2, 1997, the government of Thailand was forced to "float" its currency, the *baht*. For more than a decade, the *baht* had been "pegged" to the U.S. dollar, meaning that the government adjusted the currency's value to maintain its value relative to the dollar. Up to that point, throughout the 1990s, the Thai economy had been booming, along with the rest of the countries that were part of what was known as the "East Asian Miracle." International capital poured into the country, factories opened, and the real estate market soared. Much of this activity, however, went through unregulated banks in a relatively weak state, which may be the reason why international investors began to doubt the stability and long-term prospects of the Thai economy, although this is still up for debate among economists. The famous venture capitalist, George Soros, was one of the first to sell his Thai currency, and as more investors sold, the government no longer could afford to trade dollars for the *baht* at the pegged value. Running out of money, the government had to adjust the rate downward, lowering the *baht*'s value against the dollar and other currencies.

If this sounds like a relatively small event, of interest only to the investors involved and a few economists, it wasn't. It set off an economic collapse as international investors began to fear that other countries in Southeast Asia would have to lower the value of their currencies as well. To beat the odds, investors sold their currencies rapidly, getting out of the currency market the way people get out of a stock market when they think it's about to downturn. That, unfortunately (but not surprisingly), caused the very crash they all feared. And this economic contagion spread rapidly from Thailand to Indonesia, Malaysia, the Philippines, and South Korea. As investors pulled out, real estate prices and company profits collapsed. Economies that had been booming went into steep decline, and unemployment soared. This financial downturn became the biggest loss of wealth in the world since the Great Depression of the 1930s, and it ultimately affected countries as

In 1997 Thailand's economy imploded when the government was unable to prop up the value of the country's currency, forcing currency exchanges like this one to shut their doors. The event led to a Southeast Asian financial crisis that produced the biggest worldwide loss of wealth since the Great Depression and raised fundamental questions about the value of globalization.

far away as Brazil, South Africa, and Russia, where investors also came to fear a collapse of emerging market economies.

The 1997–1998 East Asian financial crisis, as it has come to be known, showed the world how interconnected we all are. The technological and communications revolution associated with globalization allows currency to be exchanged daily and instantly on international markets. The flow of trade and foreign investment has rapidly expanded since the 1970s as the cost of communications and transportation has fallen, and the neoliberal economic policies we outlined in chapter 5 helped open national borders to trade, facilitating this expansion of global economic activity.

Three distinct aspects of this economic globalization can impact national economies and economic policies. Globalization has led to increased **trade**, the flow of goods and services across national borders: global trade in 2000 was more than four times what it was in 1970. **Foreign direct investment (FDI)** has expanded as well, as **transnational corporations (TNCs)** invest directly in productive activity around the world, and international investment (as a share of the global economy) has increased almost as much as trade. Finally and probably most important, **international capital flows** have expanded dramatically as the virtual elimination of barriers to moving money across borders and improvement in global communications have resulted in more than a trillion dollars crossing international borders daily. The impact of these trends in our case study countries are shown in the "Country and Concept" table at the end of this chapter.

Globalization has raised major questions about economic policy in both wealthy and poorer countries. As we discussed in chapter 5, the biggest of these questions is whether the state still matters: Are states still sovereign over their economies? Modern states, whatever the regime type, are expected to guide economic growth; even the most venal want leverage over the economy so they can benefit from it. Economic growth provides revenue to a state and legitimacy to a regime.

In the context of globalization, what policies can governments use most effectively to steer their economies beneficially? Does the rapid flow of capital and goods around the globe impede these efforts? Does globalization force different regimes and societies with different values to follow the same economic policies dictated by the need to attract global capital? To what extent do the multinational organizations that help manage the global economy—the World Trade Organization (WTO), the World Bank, and the International Monetary Fund (IMF)—dictate policies to individual countries, reducing governments' economic sovereignty? This chapter addresses these enduring questions, turning first to the wealthy industrial countries of the "global North." For them, the biggest issues are how to respond to the movement of manufacturing out of their countries and whether they can continue to maintain the level of social spending their citizens have come to expect, especially in Europe.

WEALTHY COUNTRIES: DEINDUSTRIALIZATION AND THE WELFARE STATE

The first globalization debate in the wealthy countries of Europe, North America, and Australasia (Australia, New Zealand, and Japan) was not about "globalization," a word that had not yet come into vogue when the debate took place in the 1970s. It was about "deindustrialization," especially in the United States. The countries that had long been known as "advanced industrial democracies" discovered that they were rapidly losing that industry, and their economies were making a transition to "postindustrial" society in which the service sector, high-technology endeavors, and research and design were replacing manufacturing as the core of the economy. In retrospect, this was the start of a wave of globalization that began in earnest in the 1970s.

As transportation and communication improved and liberal trade policies allowed industries to take advantage of lower production costs in developing countries, they began moving manufacturing plants out of the wealthy countries and exporting products back to the home markets. Hundreds of thousands of workers, long reliant on relatively well-paying and secure jobs in such industries as automobile manufacturing and steel, faced unemployment and bleak prospects. Not only did they lose their jobs, but other positions in the same field were not available: entire sectors shrank and moved overseas. Workers had to seek retraining in newly emerging fields or take lower-paying unskilled positions in sectors such as retail. Many of the new jobs paid less than the old ones and were less secure. Workers had to become more flexible, often working at multiple jobs for longer hours. Managers, meanwhile, reaped increasing salaries as their companies profited and expanded. The result in many countries has been growing inequality.

The abstract logic of globalization's effects on wealthy countries, then, seems pretty clear. As capital becomes more mobile and can flow around the globe, even wealthy governments must do what they can to attract it. They must maintain macroeconomic stability by keeping inflation low by restraining government spending and the money supply (following the monetarist principles we outlined in chapter 5). They must keep corporate taxes low so that businesses will want to invest, but if taxes are low then spending must be low as well, meaning that social welfare programs also have to be restrained or even cut. They must ensure that labor is flexible and relatively compliant and do what they can to keep labor unions from making too many demands because rigid contracts and rules that guarantee jobs or benefits for long periods discourage investment. And, of course, they must keep tariffs and other barriers to the entry and exit of capital at a minimum.

According to this perspective, which Colin Hay (2004) calls **hyperglobalization**, globalization tends to produce a **convergence** among the policies of wealthy countries. The distinctions among liberal market economies (the United States), European welfare states (Germany), and developmentalist states (Japan) and partisan differences over economic policy within each country tend to disappear as all of these governments, regardless of their past economic models or current ideological disposition, are forced to conform to the logic of attracting global capital. In the last decade, however, growing numbers of scholars have questioned this argument, noting that while changes are certainly occurring in the general direction Hay predicted, they are not happening very rapidly and are strikingly different in different countries. Empirical studies generally show this to be true for taxation, welfare spending, union power, and overall levels of inequality.

For this reason, many comparativists use institutionalist arguments to suggest that, at least for wealthy countries, national economic sovereignty will continue to exist: countries can and are choosing unique means to respond to globalization's demands. And while most agree that the forces of globalization apply pressure in the direction hyperglobalization theorists suggest, they believe that long-established political and economic institutions in specific countries heavily influence how these countries can and will respond, with different effects on their long-term economic well-being.

The most influential school of thought questioning hyperglobalization is known as the **varieties of capitalism approach**. This school of thought focuses primarily on business firms and how they are governed in terms of their interactions with government, each other, workers, and sources of finance such as banks and stock markets. Proponents distinguish two broad types of economies among wealthy capitalist countries: **liberal market economies (LMEs)** and **coordinated market economies (CMEs)**. LMEs, of which the United States and the United Kingdom (UK) are the primary examples, rely more heavily on market relationships, meaning that firms interact with other firms and secure sources of finance through purely market-based transactions. They know little about each others' inner workings, which leads them to focus primarily on short-term profits to enhance stock prices, a key source of finance. Their relationship to workers is also primarily via open markets: rates of unionization are low and labor laws are flexible, allowing firms to hire and fire employees with ease. The government's role is relatively minimal and is focused simply on ensuring that market relationships function properly through, for instance, fairly stringent anti-monopoly laws and rules governing stock exchanges to guarantee that all buyers are privy to the same information.

CMEs, by contrast, involve more conscious coordination among firms, financiers, unions, and government. Many firms and banks hold large amounts of stock in each others' operations, which gives them inside information on how these firms operate. This, in turn, encourages firms to coordinate their activities and establish long-term relationships in terms of finance and buying inputs. Firms are more able to focus on longer-term initiatives because financiers have inside information about the potential for long-term gains. CMEs tend to have stronger unions and higher levels of unionization, and worker training is focused within sectors of the economy and within related firms. The government is involved in negotiating agreements among firms and between firms and unions, and allows or even encourages the close relationships that might be termed "insider trading" or quasi-monopoly situations in an LME. Germany is a prime example of a CME. Japan's developmentalist state is usually classified as a CME as well, though with a smaller role for unions than is found in European CMEs.

Peter Hall and David Soskice (2001), who created this approach, coined the term **comparative institutional advantage**, as opposed to the standard comparative (economic) advantage, to help explain how these different kinds of economies respond to the pressures of globalization. They argue that the various institutionalized relationships in each kind of economy are complementary: the institutions work together to provide greater benefits than any single institution could alone. It's difficult to change one particular institution, such as corporate finance, without changing many others. Consequently, firms have interests in maintaining the institutions in which they operate, and they will be reluctant to change them in response to globalization. Firms in CMEs benefit from the various institutions that help them coordinate their activities, train workers, and secure employees' services over the long term. A more rigid labor market that does not make it as easy for workers to move from firm to firm, for instance, complements a training system in which firms invest in educating their workers for specific tasks: if workers could quickly move from job to job, the firms would lose the benefits of their training investment. In LMEs, by contrast, more flexible labor markets mean firms have little incentive to train employees: workers and the public education system invest in more general skills that workers can transfer from firm to firm, and firms don't have to invest directly in employee training.

The comparative institutional advantage of LMEs is in their flexible market relationships. In response to globalization, they tend to strengthen market mechanisms even more. Governments work to decrease union influence, provide broad-based education for an ever more flexible workforce, and increase the variety and efficiency of open-market sources of finance such as stock markets. LMEs, advocates argue, are more adept at making radical innovations in response to new opportunities. Management and workers all have few reasons for caution, as their long-term futures are not tied to a specific firm.

The comparative institutional advantage of CMEs is in adjusting but maintaining their coordination mechanisms in response to globalization. Firms do not simply abandon these countries because of the institutional advantages they would be giving up, advantages in which they have long invested. CMEs are better

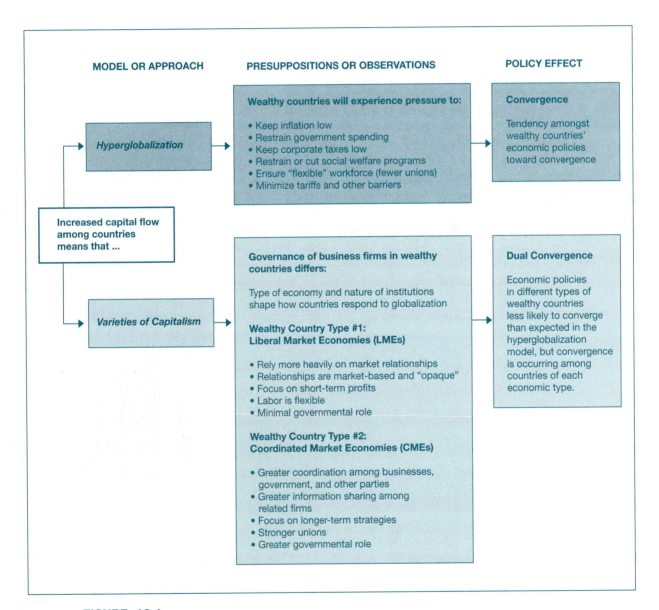

FIGURE 10.1
Globalization's Effects on
Economic Policies: Two Views

at marginal innovation than at radical innovation because they can and must co-ordinate activities across a number of firms and sectors, including training workers in specific skills. Management and workers have incentives to make marginal changes to improve the performance of the firm in which they have a long-term interest. CMEs tend to be more innovative in older industries, such as pharmaceuticals, than in newer industries, such as high-tech sectors. Indeed, firms in CMEs tend to transfer their branches that engage in more radical innovations to LMEs, where they benefit from the comparative institutional advantages LMEs offer. Hall and Soskice and their collaborators argue that rather than the convergence of all wealthy capitalist economies, globalization is encouraging greater specialization in LMEs and CMEs. A **dual convergence** is happening; that is, convergence is occurring within each type of economy, but the difference between the two types is at least as great as in the past and will probably become greater.

The varieties of capitalism approach has implications for contemporary welfare policies as well. Convergence theorists argue that governments will have to cut social spending as they cut taxes to attract global capital, whereas scholars using the varieties of capitalism approach argue that in CMEs business often supports social spending. Much of this social spending provides workers with security—pensions, health care, disability benefits—that helps them stay with a particular firm without fear of losing their jobs. Spending on industry or even firm-specific job training also benefits firms in CMEs. These scholars argue that large businesses in CMEs benefit from social spending, and so they do not insist on reducing it; rather, they tolerate higher taxes and spending to help secure a highly trained and productive workforce. LMEs, on the other hand, operate much as convergence theorists speculate they "should": greater labor market flexibility does not provide the same incentives found in CMEs, and firms are less willing to tolerate the high taxes necessary to maintain high spending, so social spending drops more precipitously in the face of globalization.

Scholars of welfare policy have argued from a variety of perspectives about the effects of globalization on social spending. Some come to the same conclusion as advocates of the varieties of capitalism approach but provide different explanations. Evelyne Huber and John Stephens (2001) argue that strong social democratic or Christian democratic parties and their class-based supporters helped create the most extensive European welfare states and continue to have significant power and ideological support today, which allows them to maintain most of the provisions of their welfare states despite the demands of global capital. Social spending and the partisan divisions that have occurred over it have declined in most countries but not dramatically (with the notable exceptions of the UK and New Zealand). These declines, proponents argue, are mostly attributable to rising unemployment caused by more rigid fiscal and monetary policies that many people see as imposed by globalization. In this sense, globalization has indirectly reduced the size of many welfare states, but not to a significant degree. Supporters of this theory also argue that political institutions matter, noting that countries with fewer "veto points" in their political systems and therefore faster decision-making mechanisms have changed welfare policies the most. Colin Hay (2004) goes a step further than others in questioning the effects of globalization, arguing that cuts in social spending have been caused not by globalization in general but by EU policies in particular. Most European countries are becoming less truly "global" in their economic interaction and more European focused as the EU expands, and the requirements to join the euro have become the main constraints on welfare spending.

Summary

The logic of globalization seems clear. Capital's greater mobility ought to give it greater power vis-à-vis immobile states and less mobile workers. Virtually all scholars agree that this has happened to some extent over the past thirty to forty years, but the changes may not have been and are not now as dramatic as initially asserted. The institutional, ideological, and cultural legacies of different models of state-market interaction in wealthy capitalist countries have not disappeared entirely. Unionization, taxation, social spending, and coordination efforts among businesses, unions, and governments continue to a noticeably greater extent in some countries than others. Two of the paradigmatic examples in the varieties of capitalism debate are our own case studies, the UK and Germany, to which we turn now.

CASE STUDY United Kingdom: Radical Reform in a Liberal Market Economy

The UK and the United States are the classic examples of LMEs for scholars using the varieties of capitalism approach. Prior to the 1980s, however, the UK had exceptionally large and active trade unions, and since World War II the country has had a far more extensive welfare state than the United States: while its social spending is below that of most European countries, it is well above the U.S. level. The UK, however, pursued the most radical economic reform of any major Western country in the 1980s under Prime Minister Margaret Thatcher. Her government profoundly reduced the role of the state in key areas via privatization of state assets and reduced the power of unions, as the varieties of capitalism approach would predict an LME would do in the face of globalization, though Thatcher did not significantly reduce overall social spending. Subsequent Conservative and Labour governments have not substantially changed the economy Thatcher created. The result in the new millennium is an economy with reason-

ably strong growth and low unemployment compared to its European neighbors, but with greater inequality across social classes and regions of the country.

The 1970s were a period of unparalleled economic crisis in the UK. Rising oil prices and global recession hit the country particularly hard, reducing growth and increasing inflation. Both Conservative and Labour governments tried but failed to respond in a way that improved the economy. As inflation grew, union demands that wage increases keep up became a key problem, as these wage increases would in turn fuel more inflation. About half of the British labor force belonged to a union, an unusually high level even by European standards. The government tried voluntary agreements a la corporatism to get unions to restrain their demands and thereby slow inflation. Unfortunately, the peak labor association, the Trade Unions Congress (TUC), did not have the power over its members that unions in corporatist systems do, and local unions repeatedly

Arthur Scargill, leader of Britain's National Union of Mine-workers in the 1980s, is joined here by an impersonator of then prime minister Margaret Thatcher. Scargill led the massive miners' strike in 1984–1985 that Thatcher decisively defeated as part of her effort to reduce the power of unions, a key element in her sweeping reforms of Britain's economy to make it more flexible and open to the global market.

ignored the voluntary restraints negotiated by the TUC leadership. In an LME such as the UK, neither unions nor business have a history of or incentive to negotiate lasting agreements to moderate wage increases, and so the result was a growing number of strikes. These culminated in the "winter of discontent" in 1978–1979, when the Labour government lost control and massive strikes occurred.

Out of this crisis rose a new manifestation of the Conservative Party, which Margaret Thatcher led to victory in the 1979 election. She won on promises of implementing a completely new approach to economic policy, unions, and the welfare state, very much along the same lines as Ronald Reagan, who was elected U.S. president a year later. Her first target was reducing the power of unions to create a more flexible labor force in line with the LME model. Over her first five-year term, Thatcher passed legislation through Parliament that made it far more difficult for unions to strike: they became increasingly liable for damages caused by striking workers, union leaders were forced to hold a ballot of their members before calling a strike, and secondary strikes (support for a striking union by mem-

bers of a different union) and closed shops (in which all employees must belong to the union) were made illegal. The culmination of this process came in a stand-off with the National Mineworkers Union in 1984–1985 over a strike against the state-owned coal companies; Thatcher ultimately defeated the union, which gave up its strike after gaining virtually nothing. This symbolized the end of an era of union strength in the UK. The number of strikes dropped dramatically from what they had been in the 1970s, and by 1995 union membership had dropped to a third of all employees from a full half of all employees when Thatcher was elected. As the LME model suggests, when facing global economic pressure, LMEs look to reduce labor costs and increase flexibility to compete more effectively, and this is precisely what Thatcher did.

The second area of major reform under Thatcher was privatization of state-owned assets. Since World War II, the British state, especially under Labour governments, had taken ownership of numerous large companies, including utilities, mining companies, auto manufacturers, and airlines, and many of these were far from profitable when Thatcher took power. She began selling off the state-owned companies to private investors—a process that continued through the 1990s—and her government ultimately privatized 120 corporations. Some became profitable private-sector companies; others simply went bankrupt. One immediate effect of this was increased unemployment as the unprofitable companies laid off workers in large numbers: unemployment rose from an average of 4.2 percent in the late 1970s to 9.5 percent in the 1980s (Huber and Stephens 2001, A11).

Thatcher's most popular policy was not privatization of state-owned companies but rather the selling of state-owned housing. After World War II, the British government dedicated itself to building public housing for the working class. By the 1970s the vast majority of the working class—typically union and Labour Party members—paid subsidized rents to live in publicly owned houses or apartments. Thatcher sold more than a million housing units, mostly single-family homes and mostly to the current tenants. This created a dramatically expanded class of homeowners who were no longer tenants of the state. Most political analysts argue it also shifted many of these individuals from Labour to Conservative voters and helped Thatcher win two unprecedented landslide reelections.

Prime Minister Thatcher was less successful at reforming monetary and fiscal policy. She came to power a committed monetarist, advocating a reduced government with lower budget deficits and tight monetary policy to eliminate inflation, and like all monetarists she put greater priority on macroeconomic stability than on achieving full employment, the long-term goal of the Keynesian consensus that had dominated British economic policy in earlier decades. In the early 1980s, her government successfully reduced inflation by reducing the money supply and budget deficit, in part through an unusual tax increase instituted during a recession in 1981, which deepened the recession but made it clear that fighting inflation was the top priority. The government relaxed monetary policy starting in 1986, however, to generate greater economic growth, again producing an inflation rate of 10 percent by 1990 (the first incidence if high inflation occurred in the mid-to-late 1970s). Thatcher also shifted the source of taxation, though this did not greatly lower the overall amount of revenue the government claimed from the economy. She reduced income taxes on individuals and corporations in the mid-1980s, compensating for this by raising Britain's national sales tax (the value-added tax, or VAT). The net result was an increased tax burden on lower-income groups and a lower burden on the wealthy.

Thatcher's inability to reduce the overall size of the government's budget was due in no small part to her failure to reduce social spending. After her election, she set out to radically reform Britain's welfare state, which centered on what the British call social security, that is, government payments given to the poor, unemployed, disabled, and others unable to make a minimally adequate income in the market. Her biggest reform to that end was to reduce the real value of social security payments and insist that the unemployed sought work while collecting social security. She also proposed dramatic changes to Britain's universal health system, the National Health Service (NHS), but its popularity prevented her from implementing most of these suggested reforms. She was only able to instill some market-

type mechanisms within the NHS, not fundamentally change the system as a whole (we discuss this more in chapter 11). In the end, her only revolutionary change to Britain's welfare system was the dramatic reduction in public housing.

Subsequent British governments have not fundamentally changed Thatcher's policies. Her immediate successor as PM was fellow Conservative John Major, who changed very few policies other than the unpopular poll tax proposal that had caused Thatcher's fall from power. The Labour government under Tony Blair (1997–2007) and Gordon Brown (2007–) also changed the British economic system relatively little. The most dramatic action Blair took immediately after becoming PM was to give autonomy to the Bank of England to set monetary policy as it saw fit, much like the Federal Reserve does in the United States. In the past, the PM and the cabinet had always controlled monetary policy; giving the bank autonomy clearly signaled to the world that the new Labour government would value macroeconomic stability at least as much as its Conservative predecessors. Other than that, Labour has invested more heavily in education and job training in a successful effort to lower the unemployment rate. The government has not, however, changed any of the fundamentals of the British LME.

Summary

Thatcher's reforms reshaped the British economy by making it a purer LME. The reforms were particularly dramatic not only because of the crisis the country faced at the time but also because the British parliamentary system allows a government great power in reorienting policy. The comparison with Ronald Reagan in the United States is interesting in this regard. Elected at around the same time and holding the same ideas as Thatcher, Reagan was not able to make nearly as sweeping reforms. While he pursued a similarly successful monetary policy to defeat inflation and also reduced the power of unions (though not as significantly as Thatcher), Reagan instituted no changes as substantial as Thatcher's privatization. The U.S. presidential system in which an independent Congress is often controlled by the opposition party, combined with a federal system that reserves considerable power for the states, limited what Reagan could accomplish.

Faced with a crisis induced by global economic forces, Margaret Thatcher reoriented British economic policy by reducing the power of unions and privatizing many state assets. This resulted in a more flexible labor market with more competitive wages; a higher percentage of employees now work at part-time jobs and far fewer are unionized. Britain's corporate ownership, like that of the United States, is dominated by large pension and insurance funds interested in short-term profitability, which is typical of an LME. This, and a more flexible labor market, has allowed British companies to enter new markets aggressively and relatively successfully. In the new millennium, the overall British economy has been strong, with growth rates of typically more than 5 percent, unemployment around 5 percent, and inflation rarely above 2 percent.

Inequality, on the other hand, increased more in Britain under Thatcher than in any other wealthy country during the 1980s, and this has changed little since. The share of the population living on less than half of the average national income increased from 9 to 25 percent under Thatcher and has since dropped only slightly (Ginsburg 2001, 186). Regional inequality has increased a great deal as well. Many of the unprofitable state-owned companies and older manufacturing firms were in the northern half of the country. Deindustrialization combined with Thatcher's reforms to hurt that region severely, causing increased unemployment and poverty, while the southern part of the country, especially London, has become one of the wealthiest regions in Europe. Britain remains a highly competitive LME that reformed dramatically to succeed in the globalization era, but not without imposing costs on some of its people.

CASE STUDY Germany: Struggling to Reform the Social Market Economy

In the era of globalization, political pundits have shifted from portraying the German social market economy as a singular success story of "high everything"—high productivity, high-quality goods, high wages, high taxes, high benefits—to the "sick man of Europe" unable to reform in the face of new economic realities. Following the hyperglobalization thesis, they argue that Germany must change its economic model to prosper under globalization. Scholars using the varieties of capitalism approach question this conventional wisdom, however; to them, Germany is a classic case of a CME whose institutions, though modified slightly, continue to function to its comparative institutional advantage. They argue that it has changed relatively little in the face of globalization and that it won't need to.

What seems beyond dispute is that German policies are moving in the direction of a more LME model, though moving rather slowly. Most reforms have been "tinkering" rather than "transformative" (Cox 2002). This is in part due to the dynamics of German political institutions: its bicameral legislature and federal

system give various forces the power to veto radical reforms of the sort Margaret Thatcher was able to enact in Britain's more centralized democracy. The most significant changes have come in corporate finance, where the German system has shifted noticeably in an LME direction. The nature of collective bargaining between employers and unions is also changing as large businesses respond to globalization, and this change is threatening to undermine the corporatist agreements that have kept wages high and labor unrest minimal over the years. Reforms to Germany's elaborate social welfare programs have been less dramatic, but they have begun to happen. Many analysts, though, argue that these changes have all been caused as much by the expense of reunification with East Germany and the constraints of EU membership as by the broader forces of globalization.

Globalization has had its biggest impact in Germany's corporate finance system. While convergence of German practices with the LME model has certainly not happened completely, German businesses have

A homeless person begs in the German city of Hamburg in September 2007, holding a sign that reads "Five years on the street This is Hartz 5—Thanks for alms." The controversial Hartz reforms were begun in 2003 as part of the German government's effort to reduce social spending and create a more flexible labor force to battle the chronic problem of unemployment that some blame on globalization.

taken advantage of globalization in ways that have altered the coordination of Germany's CME. With the rise of new global financial opportunities, large German businesses and the government have pushed for financial reform, including legal reforms to open the stock market up to global investors and the listing of German firms on global markets. Manufacturers have looked to these changes as providing new sources of finance, and banks see them as new areas of profit. The net effect in the 1990s was a sharp reduction of the share of firms' capital controlled by the banks that lent them money. Firms instead rely increasingly on global investors to purchase their stock, which means that they, like firms in LMEs, have had to become more concerned about anonymous shareholders' short-term interests in profits. Codetermination still operates, so unions still have a significant voice in corporate governance, but this has been reduced due to increased concern for shareholders' short-term returns.

Like codetermination, collective bargaining has also been affected by globalization and for similar reasons. Germany's model has always been based on peak associations of employers and unions being able to make and stick to wage agreements. These agreements kept wages high while providing stability and predictability. Globalization, though, has created divisions among German companies. The largest have invested significantly outside of Germany, including in the rest of the EU. In key sectors, notably pharmaceuticals, the most successful firms have noted the institutional advantages of LMEs such as the United States and UK and have relocated (or sold) their more innovative components to those economies, leaving the less innovative areas, such as chemicals and metal working, in Germany. In doing so, they have created globally linked production processes that are very sensitive to disruption. Because of this, they have become more willing to agree to high wages to avoid strikes or lockouts. Smaller businesses without international investments that are often in direct competition with manufacturers in other countries cannot afford these agreements, and they increasingly ignore agreements set between unions and the largest employers. Unions respond with more strikes at the local level in the smaller firms. The result has been a fragmentation of the corporatist agreements that used to govern wages: in 1990 less than 27 percent of all wage agreements were made at the level of the individual company; by 2000 this had increased to 39 percent, due in part to the much higher level (more than 70 percent) of local agreements in the former East Germany (Streek and Hassel 2003, 112). This coincided with the steep decline in membership in employers' associations and unions that we discussed in chapter 7.

High unemployment has long been the Achilles' heel of the German economy. The shifting bargaining system and continuing high unemployment in the former East Germany continue to plague Germany as a whole. Larger businesses continue to tolerate high wages, paid to highly trained workers, as the CME model would predict. The negative effect of this, though, has been very limited job growth as many lower-paying jobs move out of the country to elsewhere in the EU (especially Eastern Europe) and the rest of the world. High unemployment means fewer workers paying taxes, a financial problem for the country's general

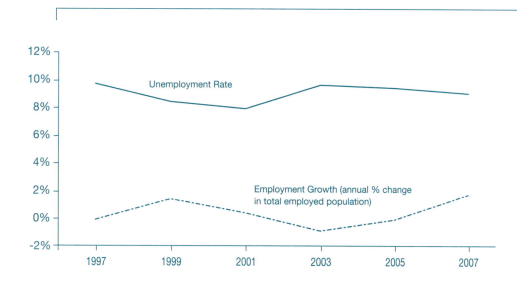

FIGURE 10.2

Employment Growth and Unemployment Rates in Germany, 1997–2007

social benefits that are mostly funded via payroll taxes. And while most wealthy countries face the problem of low population growth and aging populations, meaning fewer workers must pay for more retirees' benefits, in Germany the problem is particularly acute.

German governments came face to face with the reality of this problem in the early 1980s. From then through the late 1990s, they enacted reforms to the country's extensive welfare system to ease the financial constraints (see chapter 11), but while these efforts kept spending from increasing far beyond what the government could afford, they were not enough to reduce Germany's relatively high social spending. Similarly, tax reforms that favored business gradually began to be passed. From 1985 to 1995, corporate taxes' share of all taxes was cut in half, with most of the revenue compensated for by increases in payroll taxes on workers (Daly 2001, 88).

A number of analysts have noted that the relatively slow pace of reform in the German system is partly due to the nature of the country's political institutions. Its bicameral legislature and federal system give unusually strong powers to the upper house (not unlike those of the U.S. Senate), which has often been controlled by opposition parties. Any law that affects the state governments (which means most laws) must pass the up-

per house as well as the lower house, meaning that the system has a large number of veto points for the opposition to stop proposals. As early as the mid-1990s, Germany's third party, the liberal FDP, was calling for fundamental reforms of the economic system. These were opposed by one or the other of the major parties, as well as by unions and even some business interests that were content with preserving the status quo. Opponents were able to use one house or the other, as well as Germany's strong civil society, to successfully resist radical reforms.

Germany's corporatist system had long used tripartite agreements among government, business, and labor to set major social and economic policies to overcome the veto possibilities inherent in this system. Both the Christian Democratic government of Helmut Kohl (1982–1998) and the Social Democratic government of Gerhard Schröder (1998–2005) attempted for years to forge such agreements on pension, unemployment, and tax reform, but neither government was successful, and both ultimately instituted unilateral moves to reform the system. Schröder was the more successful with his Agenda 2010 reforms, in part because he argued that globalization required the German economy to become more competitive. While most analysts believe this really wasn't true—Germany's highly paid and

The grand coalition government of Christian Democrats and Social Democrats in place since 2005 under Chancellor Angela Merkel has reformed relatively little, though it has presided over a fairly robust economy. German export growth has been strong in the new millennium, and it regained its position as the world's largest exporter in 2003. Overall economic growth remains relatively weak but grew to 2.7 percent in 2006, and unemployment fell from a high of 11.7 percent in 2003 to 8.1 percent in 2006, which is still rather high, but definitely better.

IN CONTEXT Government and Growth in the EU

The government in Germany and in the EU as a whole consistently take in a larger share of the economy as taxes than does the United States (see chart A). Many economists predict this will hurt economic growth, but no clear pattern has emerged in recent years. As chart B shows, the EU grew faster than the United States in the first two periods, but the United States grew faster more recently.

A.
Total Government Tax Revenue
(% of GDP)

B.
Real GDP Growth Rate
(% change on previous year)

European Union   Germany   United States

Source: All data are from OECD and EUROSTAT.

productive workforce does not really compete against low-wage workers in poorer countries—the claim helped him push through the reforms he wanted. In addition, Germany's welfare system had long been based on the idea of providing income security for workers regardless of what happened in the market; Schröder argued that globalization required changes to this attitude if the economy was to rebound. Yet while he was able to get his reforms passed in 2003, he paid for these victories by narrowly losing the 2005 election.

Summary

In its core activity of high-quality manufacturing, Germany's CME seems to be holding its own in a globalizing world, but the overall economy continues to be plagued by low growth and persistently high unemployment. It has nonetheless withstood what some believe to be globalization's demand that all countries dramatically reduce the role of the state in guiding the economy. While it has certainly modified its CME, especially in the area of corporate finance, the key components remain in place, and most analysts now believe that the most important factors affecting the German economy are the costs of reunification and membership in the European Monetary Union (EMU), which requires it to limit its fiscal deficit, rather than the pressures of broader global forces. The German state willingly took on and even championed both of these initiatives, however; they were not forced on it by global forces.

DEVELOPMENT AND GLOBALIZATION

Globalization has clearly affected the ways in which wealthy and powerful states guide their economies. While most political scientists no longer subscribe to the hyperglobalization thesis that the state is now irrelevant, virtually all recognize that states have had to alter their economic and social policies to some extent in response to pressures from rapidly expanding global market forces. If this is true for even the relatively powerful and wealthy, could the hyperglobalization thesis apply to much poorer and less powerful states? Have they in effect lost economic sovereignty to the global market, or do its effects vary among them as well?

The world's relatively poor and powerless states are almost all postcolonial. Their economic and social policies, and debates about them, have long involved the goal of "development." Officially, their governing regimes seek to achieve economic growth to improve the lives of their people through industrialization and other forms of economic diversification. A key part of the debate over development, of course, has been not only how to achieve growth but also how the benefits of that growth are distributed to relieve poverty. The development debate we outlined in chapter 5—from import-substitution industrialization (ISI) to structural adjustment programs (SAP)—long preceded the contemporary globalization debate, but both end up addressing the same key question: How can states in developing countries use economic policies to help them navigate the global economy in ways that are most beneficial to their people? A key element in this debate is not economic but is instead political: What types of regimes are most willing to and capable of pursuing beneficial policies? The long-standing debates over economic and political development are now intertwined with the globalization debate as the countries in question are increasingly subject to the vicissitudes of the global market.

At the heart of these debates is the role the state can and should play in the development process, including vis-à-vis global markets. The reigning conventional wisdom is that the state should allow the market to operate more or less unfettered, following the logic of comparative advantage. Regardless of local circumstances, this maximizes the efficiency with which resources are used and therefore improves economic well-being overall. This is the core of the argument supporting the neoliberal development model and SAPs.

Since the early 1990s, however, scholars and practitioners have been raising a growing number of questions about this model. The World Bank, in particular, has articulated an agenda of "good governance," arguing that states need to have more of a role in reform than the neoliberal model allows. Focusing on the alleviation of poverty, the World Bank argues that states need greater capacity to effectively and efficiently provide the key requisites for capitalist development that we outlined in chapter 5—security, property rights, contract enforcement, and infrastructure—and essential services to the poor—particularly health and education—that will enhance human capital and development potential. This new focus, dubbed "pragmatic neoliberalism" by Dickson Eyoh and Richard Sandbrook in 2003, was distilled in each country in a document called a Poverty Reduction

Strategy Paper (PRSP), and following the precepts set forth in the PRSP has become pivotal to receiving funding from either the World Bank or the IMF. The World Bank, along with virtually all major Western development agencies, continues to support the basic principle that states should not distort markets (as they did under ISI), but it and many others now believe the state does have a role to play in simultaneously attracting capital and alleviating poverty.

The View from East and Southeast Asia

Any discussion of globalization and development today must start in East and Southeast Asia. The Asian economic miracle has been the primary development success story of the last generation, and the world has far fewer poor people today than a generation ago primarily because of the dramatic drop in poverty in Asia, especially in the four original East Asian "Tigers"—Taiwan, South Korea, Hong Kong, and Singapore—and, more recently, China. The Tigers have all become wealthy industrialized countries, and as they initiated the process of industrialization, inequality actually dropped, the only place in the world where that has happened. A famous comparison is South Korea and Ghana in West Africa: at Ghana's independence in 1957, it and South Korea had nearly identical per capita incomes and economies, both poor and mostly agricultural; today, South Korea is a member of the OECD (Organisation for Economic Co-operation and Development), the club of the world's wealthiest countries, with a per capita gross national income (GNI) of $17,690 in 2006, compared to Ghana's GNI of $510, which remains one of the world's lowest.

The Asian story has served, or at least interpretations of it have served, as the model for development policy throughout the world, especially before the 1997–1998 financial crisis. Its success was clearly based on **export-oriented growth (EOG)**, in contrast to ISI policies popular prior to the 1980s, and the neoliberal model was in part a reaction to the success of the four original Tigers. Their spectacular growth based on exports stood in sharp contrast to the growing problems ISI began facing in the 1970s. Neoliberal economists argued that if

Hyundai automobiles await export to South Africa. South Korea's phenomenal economic growth has been based on exports, making some of the country's biggest companies into household names around the world. The economic success of South Korea and the other Asian Tigers was a major reason global development agencies shifted their support from ISI to EOG in the 1980s.

exports produced success, then all countries should open up to the market, pursue their comparative advantage, and export as well and as much as they could.

The original SAP efforts based on neoliberalism assumed that the success in Asia was founded on getting the state out of the way of the market and allowing comparative advantage to work its magic. Further research clearly showed this was not always the case in the successful East Asian cases. Hong Kong, still under British colonial rule, certainly followed a *laissez-faire* policy of minimal governmental intervention, probably the most minimal on the planet. The other three Tigers, however, did not. In 1993 the World Bank published a major study, *The East Asian Miracle*, that distilled this research into a series of lessons learned that could be applied to policy elsewhere in the world. This study showed that the state had a greater role in the economic successes in East Asia than originally had been assumed. Taiwan and South Korea especially had developmental states similar to Japan's that guided industrialization. They used carefully targeted credit and subsidies and provided some protection to create new industries that could compete on the world market. The state guided investment into areas of comparative advantage, rather than simply allowing the market to send signals. These states did certainly follow neoliberal recommendations on fiscal and monetary policy, keeping inflation low and their currencies stable and realistically valued vis-à-vis others, which encouraged investment and exports. They had begun with ISI policies but had shifted their focus to EOG very early (in the 1950s and 1960s), and their success had also been based on a highly educated, literate populace able to utilize a high-quality education system. The 1993 study went on to suggest that a key component to all of this was a strong state, one in which key economic bureaucracies were insulated from short-term political pressures so that they could pursue solid, long-term policies. A strong state was necessary to make the often painful transition from ISI to EOG early on, as well as to guide the subsequent industrialization along channels that enhanced rather than diminished comparative advantage. This revised understanding of the East Asian miracle helped lead the World Bank and other development experts to recognize that the state still has a role to play in effective development.

MINI-CASE South Korea's Economic Miracle

Starting in the early 1960s, South Korea's economic development began to fully qualify as a "miracle." Its GDP per capita in 1963 was $100; less than fifty years later in 2005 it was $22,600, and the country boasted the world's twelfth largest economy. In 1996 it joined the Organisation of Economic Cooperation and Development (OECD), the leading group of the world's wealthy industrialized countries, only the second Asian country, after Japan, to do so. Like several of the East Asian miracle economies, it has achieved this level of growth and prosperity while maintaining a low level of inequality. A military government led the first phase of this spectacular growth from the early 1960s until the early 1990s. Following growing protests, especially on the part of labor unions, the country went through a successful transition to democracy, culminating in the 1992 election of the first civilian president in more than thirty years.

Like many others at the time, South Korea's economic policies in the 1950s focused on ISI. This allowed a rather weak, authoritarian regime to use extensive patronage, such as the granting of preferential protective tariffs, credit, or licenses, to maintain its power. The "miracle" began under long-term military dictator Park Chung-hee, who came to power in 1961. When the country faced a severe financial crisis, Park responded by creating what would become a famous institution, the Economic Planning Board (EPB), filled with economic technocrats who wanted to steer the country toward EOG. And a key difference between South Korea and many other developing countries at the time was the government's success in doing this. This was due in part to active U.S. support for the policy and tremendous U.S. influence: since the Korean War, the country had become extremely dependent on U.S. aid. The financial crisis made it difficult to secure funding from other sources, but the United States continued to provide it, further increasing dependence on the United States. U.S. influence wasn't the only factor, though. Park was also a nationalist who wanted a growing and prosperous country, and he came to believe that encouraging exports was the way to accomplish this goal.

Park and the EPB ultimately created a developmental state similar to Japan's. The military government nationalized the banking sector and used targeted and below-market credit to encourage firms to begin exporting, even as it repressed opposition from firms not favored by the new policies and from the labor sector. The result was the rise of the famous *chaebol,* Korean equivalents of the Japanese *zaibatsu* (see chapter 5). These massive conglomerates, often controlled by extended families, entered numerous markets around the world. The process began with a focus on light manufacturing that utilized Korea's plentiful and cheap labor force. The government then supported research and development and shifted credit policy to encourage investment in heavy industry in the 1970s, when the most successful *chaebol* grew by as much as 30 percent a year.

This model produced tremendous growth, but it also increased corruption and inefficiency, not unlike the experience in Japan. The growing *chaebol* became politically more powerful, and this growth rested in part on massive debt to government-owned banks. When smaller *chaebol* or less profitable segments of the big ones faced insolvency, the government made sure they didn't fail. By the 1990s, the largest of these *chaebol* had become successful transnational corporations (Hyundai, Samsung, Daewoo, Goldstar) and had begun to push for liberalization of the economy. Some liberalization occurred under the first civilian government in the mid-1990s.

For all of this, the 1997 Asian financial crisis did not spare South Korea. Its partly open economy and massive debt meant it fell victim to the contagion, but it recovered relatively quickly. The crisis produced the first negative growth in a generation, and the government had to accept an IMF bailout package that required further liberalization and significant changes to the developmental state model. This suggests to some analysts that globalization is now pushing the country toward a neoliberal system. In the wake of the crisis, the government has privatized much of the banking sector, refused to continue subsidizing insolvent branches of the *chaebol,* allowed its currency to freely float on the global market, and actively encouraged foreign investment. All of this has meant the virtual bankruptcy and sales of the assets of some of the *chaebol.*

These reforms, while dramatic, appear to be working relatively well so far. By 1999 South Korea's growth rate was back up to 7 percent, and the economy continued to grow at a rate of about 5 percent in 2007. The country remains a major exporter with a huge trade surplus, especially with the United States. Like other wealthy countries, South Korea now faces the problems of an aging population and financial constraints on its growing welfare state, but it still has high economic growth rates and quite low unemployment. The problems it faces are problems of success, those that come with being a wealthy, industrialized economy in the globalized era.

The 1997–1998 financial crisis shook the foundations of even this revised East Asian model. The massive loss of wealth in the region ultimately brought down the government of long-time dictator Suharto in Indonesia and threatened the political stability of other countries as well. The crisis originated and centered in the Little Tigers of Thailand, Indonesia, Malaysia, and the Philippines, rapidly growing countries whose industrialization followed behind the original four Tigers and which remain middle-income countries today (though South Korea and Hong Kong were severely affected as well). Their economic growth has been impressive and was booming in the 1990s prior to the crisis; indeed, they were generally seen as following the successful model of the original Tigers until the crisis erupted. They suffered a severe recession from the crisis, though by a decade later they had recovered and were growing substantially (at rates varying from a low of about 4 percent in Thailand to a high of more than 7 percent in the Philippines).

In spite of this recovery, the crisis and response to it profoundly affected the globalization and development debate. The IMF, whose job it is to help resolve such crises, blamed the lax financial regulations of the governments involved, and it insisted on cuts in credit and government spending to restore macroeconomic stability. This initially deepened the recession, producing the greatest criticism the IMF has ever faced about its role in the global economy. Critics of the IMF and globalization argued that the problem was unfettered global currency markets: fixed exchange rates before the crisis had seemed to guarantee investors a high return in the booming regional economies, so money had poured into these countries from around the globe, causing a massive "bubble" in their stock and real estate markets. When the bubble burst, investors sold rapidly, causing a market panic that the IMF then deepened with its orthodox neoliberal policies. Malaysia refused IMF help, instead pursuing policies that limited the market in the short term to restore stability, and it recovered more rapidly than the other countries, though some of the others subsequently caught up. The crisis reignited the debate about the benefits and costs of globalization, especially open financial markets, in even the most successful developing economies.

The crisis also raised new questions about the role of the developmental state. While analysts long recognized that the Little Tigers did not have developmental states as effective as those of Japan or Korea, they nonetheless saw them as roughly similar. The crisis revealed that the state's regulation of the financial sector in particular was very weak, even in Korea. Banks lent money for dubious investments, often to companies with which they had close, even family, ties, and when the crisis hit they rapidly sank into bankruptcy as their creditors could not repay the loans. Neoclassical economists argued that in spite of East Asia's rapid success, the state's role was not as beneficial as had been assumed. Many began to argue that economic growth would have been even more rapid without state credit and subsidies to key industries. They began calling for states that provided the classic regulations needed to protect against financial and corporate malfeasance, but not states that attempted to "guide" the market. Their opponents countered that the crisis showed the problem of rapid flow of investment in and out of countries open to the global economy, which suggested the need to put mechanisms in place to slow down the speed at which these transactions occurred and guide them into longer-term investments rather than short-term currency speculation. These critics suggested the international factors were to blame rather than the developmental state itself.

The focus on the state throughout the Asian miracle debates also raised a classic question of comparative politics: Do democracies or dictators produce better economic development? All four original Tigers achieved their early growth under authoritarian regimes, in marked contrast to the relative economic stagnation in Asia's democratic giant, India. In the 1990s, the two largest Tigers, Taiwan and South Korea, made relatively smooth transitions to democracies that continue to function today. Pundits and policymakers used this as evidence to argue that newly developing countries could not "afford" democracy, that less wealthy countries need authoritarian rule to guide successful development. Development would produce a growing middle class that, following a major stream of thought in democratization theory, will eventually demand and get democracy. Pushing democracy on a poor country will produce neither a healthy democracy nor economic development. The seeming failure of the Little Tigers brought this argument into question. There, as well as across Africa, authoritarian rulers seemed far less capable of guiding beneficial development, often preying on their people and economies instead in a form of corrupt "crony capitalism" that limits growth.

Political science research on this issue since the mid-1990s suggests that neither democratic nor authoritarian regimes are inherently more successful at producing development. What matters is the creation of a politically insulated economic bureaucracy with the competence to pursue successful policies and the ability to withstand immediate pressures to distort these policies in favor of one group or another (Evans 1995; Haggard and Kaufman 1995). In the most recent major study, Atul Kohli (2004) argued that democratic states are likely to be "middling performers" in development. Authoritarian regimes in strong states with a close alliance to a capitalist class have produced the rapid development success stories such as South Korea, whereas authoritarian regimes in weak, neopatrimonial states have proved the least successful, as in the case of Nigeria. Democracies, if they include strong bureaucratic and political institutions, may be reasonably capable of pursuing development and almost certainly do so in a manner superior to authoritarian regimes that rule on the basis of patronage and corruption.

MINI-CASE Where Are the Middle Eastern "Tigers"?

Ask comparativists to list the world's most rapidly industrializing, export-oriented economies, and they are likely to name a number of countries in East Asia, South Asia, and Latin America. Sub-Saharan Africa has noticeably lagged behind this trend, and it remains an overwhelmingly agricultural and very poor region. Perhaps surprisingly, the Middle East and North Africa (MENA) region has also been slow to produce export-oriented, industrializing economies. Although affected by the same trends of globalization, liberalization, and reform that have sparked export-oriented growth (EOG) booms elsewhere, the MENA region has produced only a few, rather tentative, "tigers" of its own. What explains this?

Some of the factors inhibiting the development of Tigers are regional. For instance, oil has been a blessing and curse to the region as a whole, which has been dependent on a product that is unlikely to be able to produce sustained development in the long term, especially given that it is a nonrenewable resource. In the short term, high oil prices provide governments with few incentives to attract other kinds of investment. Even non-oil–producing states have tended to rely on income from transfers of cash and remittances from the oil-rich countries. Second, long-term conflict, insecurity, and instability have led countries to allocate resources to military expenditures rather than to more productive economic and social uses. Third, the region has received relatively little long-term direct foreign investment outside of that from oil companies, partially because of the serious security concerns that have long plagued the area. The persistence of authoritarian regimes—encouraged by the oil-consuming major powers—may also create a barrier to greater integration into global economic and political processes.

Even without factoring in the presence of oil or the lack thereof, development potential of specific countries in the region varies greatly. Ziya Öniş (2003) suggests that there are at least five contrasting patterns of economic structure and development in the region. The very poorest countries, including Sudan and Yemen, are primarily agricultural. Their best economic hope is to develop any agricultural potential they can. A second set of countries includes Syria and Jordan, small, non-oil producers with few other resources. Öniş argues that their best hope for development is to invest in their human capital to create a basis for specialized export manufacturing. Small, oil-rich countries such as Qatar and the United Arab Emirates form the third category. With small populations and large, if sometimes unstable, revenues from oil exports, these states have often felt no incentive to industrialize. They may have weak links to their societies and feel little domestic pressure to develop the economy, in part because they can provide a high standard of living to their populations without necessarily making significant investments in development. A fourth group has made some headway toward industrialization. The "oil industrializers," including Iran and Iraq, have the strong natural resource bases and large populations that should permit industrialization. War, political instability, and mismanagement have stymied their attempts at following this path, however.

Only the final group of Turkey, Morocco, and Egypt constitutes those currently closest to tiger status. These three large, non-oil–producing countries have pursued export-oriented industrialization with varying degrees of success. Each has achieved moderately high growth rates and more stable growth than the rest of the region. Each enjoys a large population base, but at the same time population growth has diminished the impact of relatively rapid economic growth, spreading the benefits of that growth across a larger population.

Of the three, Turkey has perhaps the greatest claim to the title of Middle Eastern Tiger. In achieving this status, the country has benefited from a number of favorable conditions that set it apart from surrounding states. For instance, despite setbacks and limitations, Turkey experienced an early version of developmentalism and the early creation of a formally democratic regime beginning in the 1920s. By the 1960s, it was undertaking ISI and industrial deepening very similar to what was taking place in Latin America, whereas these activities began much later (not until the 1950s) in Egypt and Morocco. Later, when pressure to liberalize grew in the 1970s and 1980s, Turkey received substantial help from the OECD and other international organizations. Although it is not yet a member of the EU, Turkey's prolonged and extensive involvement with the body and its desire to attain membership have reinforced liberalizing policies and brought benefits that smoothed the path from ISI to EOG. Turkey has never achieved the extremely high growth rates of the East Asian countries, and direct foreign investment remains relatively low and income inequality relatively high. Nonetheless, the country's sustained, moderate growth and industrial deepening may give it a fair claim to being the Middle East's first tiger.

The View from Latin America

The Asian experience and model have had implications for development policy throughout the world. The major Latin American countries have faced many of the same issues, though with distinctly different outcomes. The neoliberal model and the IMF have probably influenced Latin America more than any other region. The debt crisis that began in Mexico in August 1982 and quickly spread to Brazil and Argentina paved the way for the first implementation of SAPs, and the 1980s became known as the "lost decade" in Latin America because of the severe economic downturn that followed the debt crisis and the start of neoliberal reform. Countries initiated market-oriented reforms at different rates, but all did eventually. Chile was the regional model of neoliberal reform, having begun the process under the dictator Augusto Pinochet prior to and without IMF insistence, and its economic success and later return to democracy became a model for neoliberal reformers in the region. Some countries, notably Brazil and Argentina, experimented with "heterodox" reforms in the 1980s and early 1990s by combining elements of the neoliberal model with continued state controls in key areas, but all of these efforts were ultimately unsuccessful. By the mid-1990s, most Latin American countries had engaged in extensive privatization of state-owned activities, reduction in trade barriers, and fiscal restraint.

The economic and political effects of these reforms have varied. Overall economic growth recovered in the early 1990s but slid again in the late 1990s and early 2000s. By 2004, however, it had recovered to healthy rates of more than 5 percent most years. The region has tremendous trade with and investment from the United States, and some years, its overall foreign capital inflow has surpassed East Asia's. It has been plagued, though, with repeated financial crises. The first major one since the full implementation of neoliberal reforms happened in Mexico in 1994 and required a major inflow of cash from the U.S. government. Brazil's currency and stock markets were hit by the contagion from East Asia in 1998, though not as severely as in Asia itself. Argentina, which had the highest growth in the region in the 1990s, experienced a spectacular financial crash in 2001–2002: like Thailand, it had pegged the value of its currency to the dollar, but investors no longer believed the Argentine peso was worth that much. In 2002 the economy shrank by more than 10 percent, and the country went through four presidents within a period of a few weeks as economic crisis produced political chaos. While the country has since recovered economically and politically and significant growth has returned, Argentina's crisis was only the latest in a series of such events, which has led Latin American governments to be very concerned about the perceptions of global investors.

High, but at times unstable, growth has not produced a large amount of change in levels of poverty or inequality. Latin America has long been the most unequal region in the world, due in part to unequal distribution of land dating back to the colonial era. Improved growth and export levels under the neoliberal model have not changed this. Poverty in 2005 remained at about 40 percent, well above the levels in East and Southeast Asia. The lives of many of the poor, then, have not improved substantially in spite of better economic growth, investment, exports, and employment.

Not surprisingly, this has helped cause a political backlash. Citizens in Argentina, Bolivia, Brazil, and Venezuela have elected leftist critics of neoliberal reforms in the new millennium. Some of these governments, such as those of Argentina and Brazil, have not fundamentally challenged neoliberal policies once in office but have attempted to institute greater social programs aimed at the poor. Others, most famously Hugo Chavez in Venezuela, have intervened in the economy in ways that seriously question the market model. The primary regional economic policy think tank, the Economic Commission for Latin America and the Caribbean (ECLAC), issued a major report in 2006 that called for a new model of investment in social policies if the region is ever to follow Asia in substantially reducing poverty. The major countries of Latin America are newly industrialized, middle-income countries, similar to those of Southeast Asia though, it seems, not benefiting as fully from globalization.

The View from Africa

Africa continues to be the site of primarily poor countries. Of 177 countries on the UN's Human Development Index in 2007, the lowest (meaning the least developed) 24 are African, and only 6 of the lowest 40 are *not* African. The continent has become the poster child of economic failure in the age of globalization and the subject of growing attention for everyone from global development agencies to private foundations to rock stars. Africa suffered the same debt crisis in the 1980s that afflicted Latin America and was also, in turn, subject to neoliberal reform. The neopatrimonial regimes of Africa, however, did not implement these reforms as thoroughly as did many Latin American countries. Because government employment was a chief source of patronage, cutting government services was a politically costly policy. Most African regimes were forced to do so to some extent to secure Western aid, but reform proceeded much more slowly than it did in Latin America.

By the millennium, though, most countries had finally implemented significant reforms. In doing so, they typically cut spending on the poor, the rural majority who had the least political clout to protest effectively, and African "reform-ers" preserved as much as possible the patronage positions available to wealthier and urban political supporters (Van de Walle 2001). Simultaneously, many of these states were making transitions to democratic or at least semi-authoritarian regimes. With political divisions across Africa based mainly on ethnicity, region, religion, and patronage rather than on class or ideology, democratization did not substantially affect reform efforts: neither democratic nor semi-authoritarian regimes have been more or less likely to implement neoliberal reforms than their authoritarian predecessors.

WHERE AND WHY Asian Miracle versus African Malaise

The spectacular economic success occurring in East Asia and the continuing stagnation and poverty of sub-Saharan Africa raise a classic "where and why" question for analysts of comparative politics: Why has East Asia been so successful while Africa has not? The facts are indisputable: from 1970 to 2000, sub-Saharan Africa's per capita GDP actually declined 0.2 percent per year, as East Asia's rose 5.7 percent per year during the same period. In the new millennium, Africa's growth has started to improve: in 2005–2006 GDP per capita grew 3.2 percent, but that still paled next to East Asia's rate of 8.6 percent. These differences in growth resulted in huge differences in overall wealth: in the 1960s, East Asia's GDP per capita was only 63 percent greater than Africa's; by the early 1990s this had increased to more than 500 percent. What explains this startling disparity?

The potential answers can be grouped into four broad categories: culture, policies, background conditions, and institutions. Many early development theorists of the modernization school believed cultural values influenced development. Ironically, in the 1950s many believed "Confucian values" in Asia prohibited successful development. More recent cultural theorists

now argue exactly the opposite, seeing Asian values as helping capitalism grow. In contrast, African values of tolerance for corruption and ethnic identification are seen as potentially harming development. The shift in evaluation of Asian values, in particular, demonstrates the problem with cultural theories of development. Indeed, at one time, many analysts thought predominantly Catholic countries would not develop as much as others, a position that few hold today given the great economic success of places like Spain and Chile.

The neoliberal development model argues that the policies of a government explain development success or failure. Advocates credit the early opening of East Asian countries to the market economy, which encouraged exports and investment, as the chief determinant of the region's success. African countries after independence, on the other hand, practiced ISI policies that restricted market access. They attempted to encourage industrial investment but did so at the expense of harming Africa's key export sector, agriculture. Extensive government regulation and intervention heavily taxed the agricultural sector to provide investment and lower food prices for urban centers. The result was rather inefficient investment and continued reliance on a narrow range of exports. Weak export production led African governments to take on increasing debt, which they couldn't pay back when productivity did not increase. There may be a light at the end of the tunnel, however: African policies have certainly become more market-friendly in the past two decades. Perhaps the noticeable growth in the new millennium is at long last a result of this, though Africa still does not include any economy growing as fast as most in East or even Southeast Asian countries.

Other analysts, such as Jeffrey Sachs, the former head of the UN's Millennium Development Program, argue that various background conditions limit African growth, and they suggest that these conditions explain why improved policies have yet to achieve as much success as they have in Asia or Latin America. Sachs (2005) points to geography, disease, and climate as key issues: low population densities, few good ports, long distances from major consumer markets, many landlocked countries, and the ravages of tropical diseases all reduce Africa's growth potential in the absence of major foreign assistance. Africa at independence also lagged behind Asia in human capital: the education and health levels of its people. Numerous economists have shown that Asia's relatively high levels of literacy underlie its economic success.

What are called "neighborhood effects" might help explain the difference as well. The success of the East Asian Tigers is in part due to the presence of an already rapidly growing industrial power in the neighborhood: Japan. In the 1960s Japanese capital began outsourcing labor-intensive production to nearby countries, starting with South Korea. As our Mini-Case above shows, Japan also served as a model for other Asian developmental states. For some, especially South Korea and Taiwan, their location at a Cold War crossroads meant they received massive levels of U.S. aid in the 1950s and 1960s—far greater in real terms than almost any country receives today. All of these factors potentially explain why good policies have made so much greater difference in Asia than in Africa.

The fourth and most recent explanation takes an institutionalist approach. Institutionalists in both comparative politics and economics argue that strong, market-friendly institutions are the chief cause of Asian success, and their absence in Africa explains the region's general level of stagnation. The core of the Asian developmental state model is strong economic institutions that encourage high levels of investment, which typically includes key government economic bureaucracies that guide policy. And even as Asian success cases include noticeable amounts of corruption, this corruption tends to occur at the top and be market-friendly: top government leaders benefit from kickbacks from successful capitalists in exchange for favorable government policies. In Africa, institutionalists argue, corruption harms investments and markets by exacting benefits at all levels and distributing them via vast patron-client networks. The level of corruption is generally higher, and its constant presence continually drains resources from investment. Patron-client networks are themselves a response to very high levels of risk, both political and economic. For the poor, rain-fed agriculture remains an extremely risky way to survive, and they use patrons in times of emergency to reduce their risk of complete failure. Patrons in positions of power subsequently search for sources of patronage, stealing government resources rather than investing in infrastructure and education. Lack of infrastructure and the political instability associated with Africa's neopatrimonial forms of rule make large-scale capitalist investment risky as well. African states thus do not build better infrastructure, and key institutions do not function according to clear rules. This heightens risk for both domestic and international investors, further limiting growth even when policies improve.

The striking difference between Asia and Africa cries out for explanation. Comparativists have suggested many plausible ones, outlined above. No single theory has, so far, been proven definitive. How might we as analysts go about sorting through these theories and finding evidence to show which is right and why?

The effects of the (often partial) neoliberal reforms have been even less impressive in Africa than in other regions. The debate over whether this is the result of the nature of the reforms themselves or the fact that African governments have only partially implemented them continues. In any case, economic growth throughout the 1980s and 1990s remained sluggish at best and was often negative in per capita terms. (Growth improved somewhat from 2000 to 2006, averaging 4.7 percent.) By the beginning of the new millennium, Africa's economic decline meant that it was less involved with globalization than at the time of its independence: its share of global trade and investment had fallen substantially. The only category in which it had gained was aid, of which it had gained the largest share of any region of the world. Such aid had declined substantially in the 1990s after the end of the Cold War, but it doubled on a per capita basis between 1998 and 2005, as the world's attention became more focused on the problems of African poverty.

Despite negotiating debt agreements and reform measures with the IMF and other Western donors, African countries continue to have debt problems because lack of economic growth has made it impossible for many to pay off their past debts. By 2005 a growing movement had convinced Western governments that Africa needed relief from its debt burden, most of which had been contracted and stolen by dictators during the 1970s and 1980s. The effort led to the creation of the World Bank and IMF's Heavily Indebted Poor Country (HIPC) initiative, which began forgiving the debt of poor (mostly African) countries in exchange for new economic reforms (following pragmatic neoliberalism). In 2005 the G-8, the world's eight largest economies, agreed to accelerate this process by fully relieving in a matter of a few years the past debt of the countries that had completed the HIPC process, and by 2007 this had substantially reduced the continent's overall debt. The result was a modest decline in poverty levels, from 47 percent of the population living on less than $1 per day in 1990 to 41 percent in 2004. In 2004 to 2007, the pace of Africa's economic growth quickened after several civil wars ended. While this was positive news, Africa remains the world's poorest continent. Neoliberal reform, while perhaps starting to show results very recently, has yet to produce a substantial African success story like Chile in Latin America or the Little Tigers of Asia.

Africa's continued poverty has inspired a host of theories and policy debates about what to do to alleviate the situation. In the new millennium, a vigorous debate about how to end poverty ignited passions and ideas to an extent not seen in decades in development circles. The United Nations launched the **Millennium Development Goals (MDGs)**, a set of targets to reduce poverty and hunger, improve education and health, improve the status of women, and achieve environmental sustainability, all fueled by a call for a large increase in aid. Economist Jeffrey Sachs (2005), the chief intellectual architect of the effort, has called for a massive inflow of aid, arguing that a large enough volume targeted the right way can end African poverty in our lifetime. He has even created his own nonprofit foundation, the Millennium Promise, that has established "millennium villages" in several African countries to demonstrate how his vision can work. But critics such as William Easterly (2006) point to Africa's long history as the world's largest aid recipient and yet its failure to achieve substantial development. Easterly argues that the result of misguided efforts such as Sachs's will be that "the rich have markets" while "the poor have bureaucrats." The former, he suggests, is the only way to achieve growth; the latter will waste and distort resources and leave Africans more impoverished and dependent on Western support.

In both Africa and the Middle East, a special concern is the blessing, or curse, of natural resource wealth, especially oil. Resource wealth ought to provide a government with the resources to build roads, schools, health clinics, and communications networks to foster economic development. Unfortunately, it often does just the opposite by creating incentives for massive corruption. In the most resource rich states, the government gains all the revenue it needs from exporting natural resources, meaning it doesn't need to bother with much general taxation of the economy, which gives it little incentive to try to improve the economy outside the key natural resource sector. This is most true for large oil producers. A perennial problem, even for the wealthiest states in the Middle East, is economic diversification outside of oil. Oil wealth often allows these states to ignore other kinds of economic development, as well as demands from citizens for political change. Our case studies of Iran and Nigeria demonstrate the problems and prospects such oil wealth provides.

Summary

Globalization and development clearly show large regional variation in their impact. East and Southeast Asia, in spite of the financial crisis of 1997–1998, have been globalization success stories, achieving rapid growth that quickly reduced poverty levels. China, one of our case studies below, is the latest and most dramatic entrant into this Asian success story. Latin American governments have pursued neoliberal reform more fully than Asian governments and have achieved substantial growth in recent years, though nothing compared to Asia, and continuing inequality has also meant that poverty has not declined very much despite significant growth. Africa, at least until about 2005, showed few signs of development and had actually been disengaged from the global economy, except as an aid recipient.

In all regions, global market forces have shaped and limited governments' economic policies, but governments have nonetheless had some room to maneuver. Malaysia rejected the IMF's proposed recovery plan after the crisis and has done quite well since. China, as we will see below, has also succeeded without full adoption of the unfettered market model, though it has adopted most of it. Latin America's relatively young democracies, including Brazil, have elected governments that question and modify the neoliberal model at least to some extent, while African governments have been able to limit reforms in the interest of their own political well-being. This mixed achievement has led development theorists and policymakers to modify the original neoliberal model that championed hyperglobalization, modifying it to recreate a role for the state. We examine the detailed contours of these trends in the following case studies.

CASE STUDY China: An Emerging Powerhouse

China's economic development has been unparalleled since its initial entrance into the world market. Its economy has taken more people out of poverty faster than any other country in history. Since economic reforms began shifting the country away from the communist-planned economy in 1978, the population in absolute poverty (living on less than $1 per day) has dropped from about 60 percent to 10 percent, and GDP per capita has increased sixfold. Economic growth has averaged between 8 and 10 percent for more than twenty-five years, and went above 10 percent in 2005–2007.[1] This is particularly impressive in comparison with the other big post-communist country, Russia, whose transition to a market economy produced economic decline throughout the 1990s; significant growth in Russia didn't emerge until the new millennium, fueled in part by rising oil prices, and still far below China's rate. And China's development path has certainly not been identical to that of the East Asian Tigers. It started from a fundamentally different place—a communist command economy—but key elements of the East Asian experience do help explain China's success: a strong authoritarian state that guided policy via gradual opening to the world, pursuit of EOG after a long period of internal focus, and the benefits of being in the East Asian region.

China's reforms emerged gradually starting in 1978 and the process continues, and remains incomplete, thirty years later. The first reforms were focused inward and on agriculture. Deng Xiaoping's first major economic changes were designed to give producers in state-owned endeavors an incentive to produce more efficiently. The "household responsibility system" converted many of China's collective farms into family-leased and -operated enterprises in which families could dispose of their surplus production on the open market. In six years (1978–1984), virtually all farming households had converted to this system, agricultural production was growing at an unprecedented rate of 7 percent per year, and per capita rural incomes increased by more than 50 percent. Shortly thereafter, the government signed contracts with state-owned en-

Chinese torchbearer Luan Xiuju in May 2008 in Hainan province was part of the massive lead-up to the Beijing Summer Olympics. In many ways, the games were China's "coming of age" on the global stage. Rapid economic growth since the 1970s has been heavily based on integration into the global economy, has made China a major world power, and has helped the country remove more people from poverty faster than any other country in history.

terprises (SOEs) that allowed these enterprises to sell their surplus production (after meeting state quotas) and retain part of the profits to reinvest in their plants. In rural areas, Town and Village Enterprises (TVEs), mostly owned by local governments, were given even greater freedom to produce what they could for a profit: their production rose fivefold between 1983 and 1988 (Qian 2007, 235–237).

At the same time, the government began to gradually open to the market, domestically and internationally. It created a "dual-track" market system in 1984 under which SOEs continued to sell their products at official state prices up to their official state production quota, but beyond that, they were free to sell at whatever market price they could get. Prior to reform, the government had set all retail prices. By 1985, 34 percent of retail commodities were sold on the open

---

[1] Exact data on long-term economic growth in China are disputed due to faulty data collection. The official figure for 1978–1998 was 9.7 percent per year, but the World Bank estimates the actual figure at 8.4 percent.

market, and that number gradually rose to 95 percent by 1999. Internationally, the state created four "special economic zones" (SEZs) in 1980 along the coast that were allowed to engage in external trade. They began to grow very rapidly, and in 1992 the government allowed many other cities to engage in external trade as well. Throughout the 1990s, the government gradually but systematically lowered tariffs on imports and freed up companies' rights to both import and export, a process which culminated in China's joining the World Trade Organization (WTO) in 2001. WTO membership requires further movement toward a market economy, including the creation of transparent and uniform laws governing property and trade. The result has been an explosion of international trade in and out of China: it increased fivefold between 1996 and 2005, with three-quarters of that expansion occurring after it joined the WTO (Qin 2007, 721).

The market had opened up to a large degree before China legally institutionalized private property. While private property, often in the form of foreign investment, existed in the SEZs more or less from the start, the SOEs and TVEs that increasingly produced for the market remained largely government owned until 1995. By then, the private sector had grown so quickly that the SOEs represented a rapidly shrinking share of the total economy. In 1995 the government announced the start of privatization, selling off the vast majority of SOEs to private investors. The process resulted in the laying off of at least twenty million workers in 1995 to 1997, but the growing economy was able to employ enough of these individuals that the layoffs did not cause widespread unrest (Qian 2006, 243). A decade later, the private sector constitutes 70 percent of the economy and the state-owned sector only 30 percent, mostly in utilities and natural resource production. The culmination of the move to private property came with a 1999 amendment to the constitution that recognized private enterprises as being on an equal footing with state-owned ones and then the 2001 invitation to private business leaders to join the Chinese Communist Party (CCP).

The role of the state in creating institutionalized incentives for greater efficiency and production has been crucial to China's economic success. This began with fiscal decentralization early in the reform period.

Local governments controlled many SOEs and what became TVEs under the command economy. By giving these businesses the right to keep a larger share of the revenue their enterprises earned, the central government gave them a strong incentive to produce beyond their state-mandated quota. A recent World Bank study (Winters and Yusuf 2007) argues that the institutionalization of Chinese Communist Party (CCP) rule that we delineated in chapter 8 was also essential. Local officials and would-be entrepreneurs needed to trust that the central government would follow through on its commitments to allow profits to stay within local enterprises and continue supporting the growing market. Given the history of Mao's capricious rule, it was not obvious at the dawn of Deng Xiaoping's era that the government would stick to its new commitments. The CCP gained credibility by institutionalizing its rule, assuring local party leaders and government officials that they would be promoted based on clear criteria tied in part to the success of their local enterprises and economy. As the system worked successfully over the first decade, it gained greater credibility. And when China invited increasing foreign investment in the 1990s, the greater institutionalization led investors to believe that continued political stability was likely. At the same time, the government began large-scale spending on infrastructure expansion and improvements, facilitating and showing its financial commitment to both domestic and foreign private investment.

China's economic success, measured in terms of economic growth, per capita income, and poverty reduction, is spectacular. That does not mean, however, that no problems exist. China faces growing global pressure, especially from the United States, to revalue its currency. (China's currency is the *Renminbi* [RMB], meaning "The People's Currency." The popular unit of RMB is the *yuan*.) It tied the value of the *yuan* to the U.S. dollar early in the reform process and has periodically raised its value relative to the dollar, but the state has never allowed its value to be determined solely by the market. This and a large amount of foreign currency from exports allowed it to survive the Asian financial crisis relatively easily; its rate of growth did slow because foreign investment and markets shrank, but it still grew at close to 8 percent a year (as opposed to recession—negative growth—for the Little Tigers). In July 2005 the government introduced a significant change in its currency, revaluing it upward and tying it to a combination (or "basket") of several currencies. Nonetheless, its low value relative to that of other currencies continues to favor its exporters, making Chinese goods cheaper on the global market than they would likely be if the currency were allowed to float to its global market value.

Domestically, China has experienced what most countries in the early stages of rapid industrialization do: growing inequality. This is in marked contrast to the Asian Tigers, which simultaneously grew and became more equal, rather than less. Inequality within rural areas, within urban areas, between urban and rural areas, and between provinces has grown substantially over the past thirty years. China's overall inequality as measured by the GINI Index is now slightly higher than that of the United States, a sharp increase from the Communist era. Rural areas actually gained wealth relative to urban areas when the TVEs were the fastest growing sector of the economy in the 1980s, but since the early 1990s, the urban-rural gap has grown considerably as foreign investment and manufacturing in coastal cities have exploded, and it now surpasses where it was before reforms started. Even though virtually all households have gained from the expanding economy, the wealthiest 20 percent in both rural and urban areas have gained far more than their poorer neighbors, and the booming coastal regions have become much wealthier than the distant interior provinces, which remain largely rural and poor. One result of this has been massive migration to the coastal cities in search of jobs, and while the state has long tried to regulate this movement, it has been only partially successful. Privatization

and migration from the countryside has produced considerable urban unemployment in recent years. Under Jiang Zemin, the government recognized this concern and officially shifted focus from maximizing growth to providing greater social services to improve the lives of the least fortunate. The economy, nonetheless, continues to grow at a record pace and the trend toward greater inequality so far has not been reversed.

Rapid industrialization has also produced massive environmental problems and demand for energy sources. China surpassed the United States to become the world's largest producer of greenhouse gases in 2007. It exploits huge domestic reserves of coal to fuel its growing industries, and the state-owned oil company has aggressively invested in oil exploration and production around the world, including in such controversial and unstable places as Sudan and Somalia. The country faced global condemnation for building the Three Gorges Dam and other massive dams on its many rivers, as millions of village dwellers were displaced against their will; sites of historical, religious and spiritual, and archaeological significance were lost; and thousands of square miles of land were inundated. Water pollution is a growing concern, raising global worries about the safety of the country's huge seafood export industry. The story is similar for air pollution: nine of the ten cities with the highest levels of air pollution in the world are in China. The environmental costs of China's rapid growth are massive externalities that are not included in the immediate market value of its production: future generations in China and around the world will have to pay these costs eventually to improve the environment. The government has begun to recognize the problem to some extent, a theme we will return to in chapter 11.

China's growth has been phenomenal. Opening itself to market forces has created the largest increase in wealth and decrease in poverty the world has ever seen. This did not result, however, from a rapid conversion to the neoliberal economic model. Russia, whose economy declined measurably in the first decade after the end of Communist rule, pursued the model much more aggressively; whereas China chose a much more gradual approach, slowly increasing incentives for public and private entrepreneurs to engage in production for a growing market. An increasingly institutionalized state provided investors with assurance that they would be able to keep their profits. The state also invested in expanding public infrastructure and continued the Communist Party's policy of educating the populace. Like most of the East Asian Tigers, an increasingly strong state guided its export-oriented growth. The country also benefited from its massive size and population, which gave it a huge labor force to draw on and a huge market to attract investors. Being in East Asia helped as well: Japan, Hong Kong (which Britain returned to China in 1997), and Taiwan are major investors in mainland China and buyers of Chinese exports. A strong state pursued wise policies, navigating the shoals of globalization exceptionally well, but in unusually favorable circumstances. India is the latest challenger to China as a rapidly industrializing economy. While it has not grown as quickly as China, in the new millennium it has become a very "hot" economy, and, in contrast to China, it has done so under a democratic regime.

CASE STUDY India: Development and Democracy

In a reversal of the typical pattern of globalization, India's giant software company, Infosys, invested $250 million in 2007 to purchase a Polish calling center, whose staff can speak and work with clients in half a dozen European languages. Infosys also owns calling centers in Mexico and China to serve regional clients in their languages. Bangalore, site of Infosys's headquarters, has become a major global hub for information technology, especially software development and calling centers. It's the high visibility element of India's recent broader success in dealing with globalization: the country's overall economic growth rate surpassed 7 percent in 2003 and 9 percent in 2005, averaging a very strong 6.4 percent from 1996 to 2006. Widely seen to be "on the move," India has become an increasingly important player in world economic affairs, the second Asian giant to rise via globalization, yet it is also home to the largest number of poor people in the world, with nearly one quarter of its population undernourished. India's development and continuing problems stem from a significant 1991 policy shift toward engagement in the global economy, though its success is based on foundations laid much earlier. Its gradually improving growth rate demonstrates the possibilities and perils of economic reform achieved by a democracy.

For its first three decades of independence, India pursued a classic policy of planned ISI, with self-proclaimed "socialist" goals. While the economy was based on the market, it was highly regulated, internally and externally. A number of major industrial sectors were reserved exclusively for government investment and control. Doing business required so many governmental forms and licenses that the system came to be known as the "permit, license, quota Raj." The extensive regulations were based on the idea that the government should guide the economy in the national interest and reflected standard development theory in the ISI period, but also they provided numerous sources of patronage for the dominant Congress Party and its supporters. The program certainly produced substantial albeit rather inefficient industrial investment, and in the 1960s the Green Revolution, with considerable public investment, dramatically increased agricultural production, especially of key grains for food consumption. While progress was made, growth remained sluggish, rarely surpassing about 3 percent per year, leading some observers to refer to a "Hindu rate of growth" that would never exceed about 3.5 percent—a cultural argument to explain limited economic success.

Political dynamics in India's democracy affected economic policies in a major way in the 1970s and 1980s. Indira Gandhi's break with the Brahmin leaders of the old Congress Party in 1969 (see chapter 7) and her appeal to the poor with the rally cry of *garibi hatao!* ("End poverty now!") led her to enact populist economic policies. In the 1970s, her government lowered public investment and increased fiscal deficits by refusing to raise taxes while simultaneously expanding government subsidies to various groups, all in a bid to maintain her political support. Growth was lower under her rule than it had been earlier, with little reduction in the country's level of poverty. Her fall from power in 1977 ushered in a period of increased political competition that drove a change in policy beginning with her return to power in 1980 and accelerating during her son's rule to 1989. Increased competition and the failure of populism forced the Congress Party governments in the 1980s to shift economic gears.

Many observers trace India's current high level of growth to the 1991 liberalization of the economy, but comparativist Atul Kohli (2004, 2007), a leading expert on India, argues that this success is based on earlier changes that were only partially liberal. Around 1980 elites within the ruling party and bureaucracy, influenced in part by the shift in global development thinking at the time, came to the conclusion that development policies needed to be much more pro-business to achieve economic growth. Indira appointed these individuals to key committees that developed a new, pro-production set of policies. The new government sharply curtailed limits on the size of private business and the sectors in which it could invest, reduced business taxes, liberalized the stock market, and passed laws to limit the ability of unions to strike. It also initially liberalized import restrictions, but domestic business opposition to having to compete with imports forced a reversal of this within a couple of years. Government also made new public investments in infrastructure, funding these mainly by deficit spending and going deeper in debt.

The result of this policy shift was a doubling of growth rates in the 1980s to about 5.5 percent. Kohli argues that while these policies only partially followed the new neoliberal development model pushed by the World Bank and IMF in the 1980s, they were very pro–domestic business. In a modest and gradual way, they paralleled those of the pro-business interventionist states of East Asia, especially in the use of targeted policies to encourage growth in the computer sector (Evans 1995). India's democracy did not allow the government to pursue

The headquarters of Infosys in Bangalore, India. The company has become a major transnational corporation, now outsourcing work to Eastern Europe and Mexico, among other places. India's economic policies have successfully encouraged massive growth in software and related services since the 1990s, centered in Bangalore, South Asia's version of Silicon Valley. Simultaneously, India is home to the largest number of poor and malnourished people in the world.

pro-business policies too thoroughly or at the complete expense of the poor majority of voters, but it nonetheless put economic policy in the hands of a group of pro-business elite able to guide policy to favor business over the poor in the interest of increasing growth.

More dramatic liberalization began in 1991 in response to economic crisis and opened the country much more to globalization. The growth of the 1980s had been partly fueled by debt, both public and private. The end of the Cold War and the first Persian Gulf Crisis of 1990–1991 produced a financial crisis for India that left it close to bankrupt, and it had to go hat in hand to the IMF to secure emergency funding. The coalition government (led by the Congress Party) that came to power in 1991 used the emergency to justify greater liberalization. The pro-business policies of the 1980s expanded, and the government implemented new policies to lower restrictions on imports, foreign exchange, and foreign investment. It also promised to reduce the size of the public sector and the fiscal deficit, privatize state-owned companies, and reform labor laws to further favor business. While these measures helped secure IMF support and were initially received favorably by the population, once the immediate crisis was over, opposition emerged. Like those of the early 1980s, these new policies had been initiated by technocrats in the key ministries; while the ruling party supported them, it made little effort to sell them to the populace as a whole. Farmers feared reduction in their governmental subsidies, government bureaucrats resisted the reduction in their power that a more open market would entail, and advocates for the poor feared the poor would fare even worse in a more open market. Business groups divided over the reforms: older businesses in what was called the "Bombay Club" opposed opening to the global market, fearing they wouldn't be able to compete, whereas new businesses in engineering and computing that were interested in exporting formed a new association that favored the liberalization policies. The latter were joined by a still small but rapidly growing urban middle class who held jobs in trading sectors such as computing software. The result of these political forces in India's democracy so far has been significant but partial reform and several electoral defeats for incumbent governments.

On the economic front, the reforms of the early 1990s did not really change growth rates. After the economy recovered from the 1991 crisis, growth resumed at about the same level as during the 1980s, around 6 percent. Its composition, though, changed substantially (Kohli 2007). To reduce the fiscal deficit, the government had curtailed public investment, while the reforms encouraged greater private investment, both domestic and international. To date, the greatest growth has come not in manufacturing but rather in services, including computing services: in 2007 India had two-thirds of the market in off-shore information technology services. Foreign direct investment increased measurably, as did the volume of trade.

Compared to the most open economies of the world, India remains only partially globalized; tariffs on imports were still at about 30 percent and only about one-quarter of the economy was involved in trading at the beginning of the new millennium (Kohli 2007, 105). Nonetheless, compared to the closed economy of prior decades, the country has opened a great deal. The promised reforms of drastically reducing government's role by privatizing state-owned companies, including banks, and reform-

ing labor laws never happened, but reform has been significant in India's democracy, albeit gradual, in part due to the politically contentious effects of those changes. Despite the very high growth rates of 2005 to 2007, a leading business advising company suggested in 2007 that "India's economic growth remains constrained by inadequate infrastructure, bureaucracy, labor market rigidities, and regulatory and foreign investment controls," and the group called that growth "unsustainable" unless further reforms take place (CountryWatch: India Country Review: Economic Conditions).

Despite India's impressive growth record since 1980, poverty remains a serious problem and inequality has grown. This is not to say that growth has not significantly lowered poverty, which stood at more than 50 percent in the 1970s, dropped to around 40 percent in the 1980s, and to 26–29 percent by the new millennium. Since the onset of the 1991 liberalization, sixty million people have moved out of poverty, although India still has the largest number of poor people in the world. Forty-three percent of children younger than five years of age were malnourished in 2000, only 61 percent of adults were literate in 2005 (up from 48 percent in 1990), and seventy-five out of every one thousand babies died in infancy (down from ninety-four in 1990) (Adams 2002; World Bank 1993).

A great deal of progress has occurred, but much remains to be done. Many of the poor remain in the agricultural sector. After rapid growth during the Green Revolution in the 1960s, agriculture has grown at a much slower rate than the rest of the economy since liberalization. It has also been regionally concentrated. The highly productive areas, notably the Punjab state on the Pakistani border, have seen tremendous growth in agriculture, while other states have stagnated. The same pattern appears for overall growth and poverty. A few states have grown very rapidly and reduced poverty quite significantly even as several others have seen little change. Some, most notably Kerala, have experienced only moderate growth but have invested heavily in social services, achieving very high literacy rates, low population growth, and high-quality health care. While these states have not seen the growth of the wealthier states, their residents live better than most Indians because of their committed public investments (Adams 2002).

India's recent opening to the global market has made it a major player in key sectors such as software and other technology services, but the agricultural sector has stagnated. Growth has been regionally uneven, which has meant that high levels of poverty remain in poorer areas, and overall inequality is increasing. By favoring domestic business in ways loosely similar to those of the East Asian development model and then opening further to global markets, the Indian government has helped produce an expanding economy that increased income per capita from $355 in 1990 to $585 in 2005. Whether that progress can be sustained and whether a greater opening to the global market will be required are major questions for the future. Brazil, although it is a much wealthier country, has had a similarly mixed experience with opening to the global market. Its new democratic regime struggled with economic policy in the early 1990s but since the mid-1990s it has been much more successful at achieving growth. Continuing inequality and poverty, however, have produced a political backlash that put a leftist labor leader into power in 2002, but it is not at all clear that global forces have or will allow him to alter Brazil's economic direction in any major way.

CASE STUDY Brazil: Does Globalization Allow a Different Path?

When working-class hero "Lula" and his Workers Party (PT) won the 2002 presidential election in Brazil, the poor celebrated it as the victory of one of their own who promised to provide them a better life, while the rich worried that the economy would be ruined. Both have been proved wrong. Lula's presidency has not substantially reversed Brazilian economic policy, which has been primarily neoliberal since the early 1990s. The economy, while not growing rapidly, is growing faster than it did in the 1990s, but Lula's promises to substantially redistribute wealth to the poor have been only partially realized. The question this raises is whether even a large, middle-income country like Brazil can greatly reorient its policies after it has been integrated into the global market. Both international and domestic economic pressures, as well as Brazil's fractionalized political system, have worked against such major changes.

Brazil's shift from ISI to a neoliberal policy more open to the global market began in earnest in the early 1990s under the first elected postmilitary president, Fernando Collor. His government reduced tariffs on imports from an average of 32 percent to 14 percent and began a process of privatization of Brazil's numerous state-owned enterprises that his successors contin-

ued, eventually selling off 120 companies worth nearly $90 billion. Collor's success at reorienting policies did not cover all areas, however; he was only particularly successful at reversing Brazil's seemingly perpetual problem of hyperinflation. Indeed, in 1993 and 1994, inflation was more than 2,000 percent. This was due in part to Collor's inability to control Brazil's long-standing problem of fiscal deficits, which the 1988 constitution compounded by giving states guaranteed shares of federal revenue and the ability to contract their own debt via state-owned banks.

Collor's impeachment and resignation in 1992 brought the short-lived government of President Itamar Franco to power, but more important, it brought Fernando Henrique Cardoso to power as finance minister. Cardoso and a team of economists created what came to be called the "*Real* Plan" to battle inflation. The key components of this plan were greater fiscal discipline via increased taxes and reduced spending, a tighter monetary policy via high interest rates, and a new currency (named the *real*) which was loosely tied to the value of the U.S. dollar. Brazil's past efforts at reducing inflation had mostly involved sudden and temporary price freezes and introductions of new currencies, on the theory that hyperinflation was primarily fueled by expectations: once started, everyone believed inflation would continue so they spent money quickly, buying things today because prices would be higher tomorrow, the effect of which was ever-higher prices. Cardoso's plan followed neoclassical economic orthodoxy that puts forth that inflation is caused by some combination of loose fiscal and monetary policy. The plan was spectacularly successful. Inflation fell from more than 50 percent per month in June 1994 to less than 3 percent by the end of the year. Annual inflation went from 2,407 percent in 1994 to 11 percent in 1996. Its success helped Cardoso get elected president in 1994 and continue his economic reforms.

Cardoso, however, was less successful at resolving government budgetary problems in the long term. Brazil's fragmented National Congress, patronage-based politics, and decentralized federalism prevented him from passing reforms to reduce government employment and the size of the civil service social security system, which meant that fiscal deficits continued. And his efforts to get the National Congress to amend the country's constitution to allow him to run for a second term as president also required significant concessions, usually in the form of government spending.

When the effects of the Asian financial crisis hit in 1998, Brazil tried to respond with both a fiscal tightening of the belt and extremely high interest rates. The National Congress blocked the former and the latter didn't work; by November 1998 Cardoso was forced to allow the currency to float freely, causing a devaluation of 40 percent. Circumstances also compelled him to accept a bailout package from the IMF that came with stringent demands for fiscal reform attached. In the mid-1990s economic growth had hit 5 percent, but the crisis reduced it to nearly zero in 1998–1999.

By 2002 Cardoso's economic policies were widely unpopular, despite his success at ending inflation eight years earlier. Growth remained sluggish, unemployment was increasing, and real wages were stagnant overall and declining for the industrial working class. Lula rode these grievances to electoral victory that fall. The Workers' Party (PT) had long championed a move toward a more socialist economic policy, though leaders often left such a policy vaguely defined. During the

Brazilian president Luiz Inácio "Lula" da Silva holds a sign reading "Food: a privilege for the few." Elected on a platform of reversing social inequalities, Lula started programs to that end but also had to maintain orthodox macroeconomic policies to reassure global markets that their capital is safe in Brazil, which his critics see as a contradiction. Lula's election raised questions about how much the electorate of a middle-income country can change economic direction in the face of globalization.

campaign domestic and international business leaders feared a PT government, so investment slowed and foreign capital dried up in anticipation of what might come. To ease these concerns, the PT wrote a manifesto stating that "social development," focused on reducing poverty and inequality, was crucial to the party but that this would be coupled with orthodox economic policies to keep inflation low and the government budget in surplus. Despite these reassurances, business remained uncertain after Lula's election.

In part to convince such skeptics, Lula appointed a well-known orthodox economist as finance minister and pledged that the government would actually surpass the IMF's goal for a low budget deficit via more efficient tax collection and continuing limits on government spending (the 1998 IMF package had forced the government to reduce the budget deficit in the late

1990s). To maintain international business confidence, Lula kept interest rates high and the budget deficit low. High interest rates, however, meant the government had to pay more on its past debt, leaving it very little money to spend on Lula's new social programs.

A leading scholar of the Brazilian economy, Werner Baer, argues the Lula government faces a "core dilemma": "the pursuit of a macroeconomic policy orthodox enough to win the approval of the international financial community and the achievement of a greater degree of socioeconomic equality" (2008, 167). Lula has tried to do it sequentially by first securing economic stability and business confidence and then focusing on social programs, but Baer suggests a fundamental incompatibility will persist: Brazil's orthodox policies to ensure international investor confidence in an open economy will prevent large amounts of social spending on the poor.

Lula's government has disappointed many of his most ardent followers. Ironically, the election of the "socialist" PT has pleased international business far more than it has the urban or rural working class as foreign investment into the country has been strong and inflation has been kept in check. Lula was reelected in 2006, despite corruption scandals in his party, but his popularity to date is not what it once was. Real wages in the industrial cities, the heart of his electoral support, remained stagnant through 2006, and unemployment

only dropped from 11 to 9 percent, while the GINI coefficient, which measures overall inequality, has declined only very slightly since 1989 (Baer 2008, 161–164). By the mid-2000s, however, poor people's incomes had begun rising more rapidly, indicating a reduction in inequality was underway. In rural areas, Lula has pursued less land reform than did Cardoso, even though the active landless movement, the MST, long supported the PT and expected major land reforms once Lula won. After a couple of years of patience, the group once again began illegal land invasions, a tactic they had used while opposing prior Brazilian governments.

Such problems and dissatisfied, impatient supporters are among the profound effects caused by Brazil's opening to the global economy over the past twenty years. The country has shifted a major share of its economy from public to private ownership, expanded exports dramatically, and finally beaten inflation and severe fiscal problems. Greater opening to the world economy, however, has produced a greater concentration of assets in both the industrial and large-scale agricultural sectors as well as greater output. Profits have increased relative to wages, and unemployment has increased from less than 5 percent in the 1980s to nearly 10 percent twenty years later as more efficient private industry has replaced less efficient SOEs that had employed more people but produced less (Baer 2008, 369–380).

Lula came to power in Brazil promising to change priorities, which meant not reversing the opening to the global market so much as substantially redistributing its rewards to the poor. While he has initiated commendable social programs (see chapter 3), maintaining international investor confidence has required economic policies that have given him few resources to redistribute. Investment and exports are up, but overall economic growth over his first term averaged only 3.35 percent. Without higher growth rates, the requirements of stable macroeconomic policies may continue to limit redistribution of wealth in what has long been one of the world's most unequal societies. Despite its transition over the last century from a poor agrarian society to a middle-income industrial exporter, 21 percent of Brazil's population still lived on less than $2 per day in 2004. In 2007 Brazil announced it had discovered a large offshore oil field that, when fully developed, could make it a major oil exporter. This could be good news, eventually providing the revenue needed to address the country's continued social problems. Oil, though, is often a very mixed blessing, as our case studies of Nigeria and Iran demonstrate.

CASE STUDY Iran and Nigeria: Struggling with the Blessings of Oil

Iran and Nigeria are different in many ways, but they share an important economic problem: dealing with the mixed blessings of massive oil wealth. For both, exporting oil is by far the most important role in and connection with their global economy. Despite their radically different kinds of government, oil wealth has provided revenue that rulers in both countries have used to enhance their political support, but these revenues have not encouraged efficient or wise use of resources to improve overall well-being. In recent years, both governments have made strides to reduce the role of government and improve the efficiency of their economies, though the current Iranian government under President Mahmoud Ahmadinejad has partially reversed that. In neither case, however, has oil wealth transformed their societies into wealthy countries.

Iran's unusual theocratic regime has not shielded it from the impact of globalization and the problems it brings to middle-income countries, but the revolution and oil have heavily influenced Iran's specific trajectory. The new revolutionary government nationalized many economic assets in 1980: many large private companies, including banks, became SOEs, and property confiscated from the shah's family and close associates was the source of the Islamic foundations (*bonyads*) that became a key part of revolutionary rule. The eight-year Iran-Iraq war in the 1980s pummeled the economy, which shrank nearly 1.3 percent per capita per year over the decade. The 1990s saw some improvement, with per capita growth of nearly 2 percent per year, but this was accompanied by annual inflation of more than 20 percent and growing unemployment, which reached 16 percent by 2000. The end of the war did help the poverty rate drop dramatically, however, from 36 percent in 1985 to less than 15 percent in 1992 (Saeidi 2001, 231). Throughout both decades, the country remained critically dependent on oil, which accounted for more than 80 percent of exports and anywhere from one-third to two-thirds of government revenue, depending on world oil prices.

The heavily state-controlled economy resembled other middle-income countries with ISI policies de-

A Boeing official presents a new 737 to the chair of Nigeria-based Arik Air in 2007. The company ordered two of the planes and a total of seven others of different models. Oil wealth and a somewhat revived economy under Nigeria's democracy in the new millennium have allowed some Nigerians to prosper, though the majority of the country remains mired in poverty. Oil continues to provide huge incentives for corruption, a situation the new government has improved but not fully resolved.

cades earlier. The Iranian government, though, intervened unusually extensively. Government-controlled banks set interest rates uniformly, trade barriers were quite high, and the government set multiple foreign exchange rates. The latter served to subsidize the SOEs and *bonyads* that had access to the more favorable rates. As we noted in chapter 8, the government budget provided large subsidies to the *bonyads* and to the SOEs as well, and lack of fiscal discipline played a major role in the high rates of inflation. Government subsidies and protection gave SOEs little incentive to operate efficiently: their losses from 1994 to 1999 equaled nearly 3 percent of the country's GDP (Alizadeh 2003, 273).

Facing growing economic problems, in the late 1990s the government under reformer President Mohammad Khatami attempted the first significant liberalization of the economy, belatedly responding to global trends and pressures. Iran's theocratic government even took advice from the bastion of Western economic imperialism, the IMF, in setting new policies. The most dramatic reforms were announced in 2000 in the Third

Five-Year Development Plan. This plan included implementing a unified and floating exchange rate, selling some government-controlled banks to the private sector (the government gave up controlling interest rates in the mid-1990s), and reducing import and export barriers, all designed to open the economy to greater global activity. It also called for significant privatization and the creation of an Oil Stabilization Fund (OSF) that would take in oil revenue when prices were high and save them to be spent when prices dropped. Neither of these reforms worked as envisioned. Privatization of SOEs has been quite slow and partial, in part out of fear of increasing already high unemployment, and the government has already used some of the OSF to, among other things, continue subsidizing *bonyads* (Amuzegar 2005). Overall, the reforms increased growth in the new millennium to around 5 percent per year and reduced inflation to less than 15 percent, but unemployment and poverty levels remained largely unchanged, and these partially successful reforms may have created a backlash that brought President Ahmadinejad and more populist economic policies to power in 2005.

Even with these reforms, Iran's chief interaction with the global economy remains its oil exports. In 2006 oil still accounted for 80 percent of exports. This means that Iran's overall economic well-being remains tightly wedded to the fluctuations in the global oil market. In fact, its economic growth is more closely related to oil revenue since the Islamic revolution than it was under the shah (Karshenas and Hakimian 2005). The 1980s, when the country fought a war and faced a declining world price for oil, were economically disastrous. The late 1990s and new millennium have been better, but primarily because of the high price of oil. Oil revenue is also of great political importance: it is still the key source of patronage that the regime depends on to fund the various Islamic foundations that are crucial pillars of regime support.

Despite its massive oil revenue, Iran's theocracy has faced many of the same challenges other middle-income countries in a global economy have navigated. Its attempt at state control of major assets resulted in inefficiency, inflation, and unemployment, though the regime has successfully lowered poverty levels. Khatami's attempt at more market-oriented reforms by moving slightly in a neoliberal direction was only partially successful, both in terms of changing policy and improving the economy. Subsequently, Ahmadinejad was elected president in 2005 on a pledge of reducing corruption and redistributing resources to the poor, returning to the revolution's promise of social justice, not unlike Lula's rise to power in Brazil. His first two years in office saw significantly increased public spending, buoyed by rapidly rising oil prices, and higher inflation, but the lives of the poor were not changed much. Throughout the upheavals of revolution, expanding state control, and recent partial liberalization, Iran has remained as dependent on oil as it was under the shah, and that dependence seems to be hindering further reform.

As in Iran, Nigeria saw a transition from one type of regime to another. When Olusegun Obasanjo took the oath of office as the first democratically elected president in Nigeria in nearly twenty years, he inherited a country that had endured one of the most corrupt dictatorships in the world under Sani Abacha (1993–1999) and an even longer legacy of corruption and lack of development that we outlined in chapter 5. Could a democratic government in what had been a corrupt, neopatrimonial regime navigate globalization, improve economic policy, and reduce corruption and thereby make better use of the country's oil wealth? Many analysts said it was highly unlikely: the political demands on a newly elected democratic government in a country long characterized by neopatrimonial rule would, if anything, increase corruption and undermine development policy further. Obasanjo's government was able to prove the skeptics at least partially wrong, however, for although most Nigerians remain mired in poverty, the democratic government has negotiated an improved position vis-à-vis the global economy and improved its development policy.

One of Obasanjo's key promises was that he would reduce Nigeria's level of corruption, ranked by Transparency International as the world's worst in 2000. To that end, he initiated a series of anticorruption measures that included the creation of a special agency to investigate and prosecute cases. An initial target was the return of the billions of dollars Abacha had stolen, some of which the new government was able to get back from various European banks. In subsequent years, and especially after Obasanjo's reelection in 2003, several major politicians in the new government also became targets of court cases. For the first time in Nigeria's history, political leaders faced criminal prosecution for stealing the country's wealth. The country became one of the first and most active participants in a new effort to increase transparency in accounting for oil revenue, with the first-ever independent audit of its oil sector completed in 2006.

In the run-up to the heated elections to succeed Obasanjo in 2007, however, the anticorruption campaign became more politicized. Obasanjo used the agency to target and eliminate potential opponents of his party and his hand-picked successor. Most notably, the agency targeted Atiku Abubakar, the sitting vice president with whom Obasanjo had split; Abubakar was charged with major counts of corruption (there is evidence that these charges had merit) and forbidden to seek office in the election. The overall results of the anticorruption campaign have been positive though not revolutionary. Nigeria improved in Transparency International's rankings from a score of 1.2 in 2000 to 2.1 in 2007, from dead last in 2000 to number 147 out of 179 countries in 2007. It remains a very corrupt country, but strides have been made.

Before all the political mayhem of the 2007 election, Obasanjo had entered office with tremendous domestic and international support. He used this in part to gain financial support from Western aid donors, but in turn he was required to make substantial progress on improving economic policy. This policy shift came, however, only in his second term. Despite its oil wealth, Nigeria was a heavily indebted country; like many other African countries. Abacha's rule had prevented it from participating in the HIPC debt-relief process in the 1990s, so it was not eligible for the major debt relief some African governments were set to receive by 2005. From the start of his term in office, Obasanjo campaigned internationally for a separate debt relief deal for Nigeria, in part based on the argument that corrupt military dictators had received and stolen much of the debt funds. His campaign succeeded after 2003 when he appointed a new finance minister, Ngozi Okonjo-Iweala, to help set more stable economic policies that convinced Western creditors that the economy was moving in a positive direction. In 2004 half of Nigeria's $36 billion debt was forgiven; by 2006 its overall debt had dropped to only $3.5 billion, less than one-tenth of what it had been two years earlier (Gillies 2007, 575). The government also brought inflation under control via tight monetary policy, stabilized government spending and the country's currency, and reduced various tariff barriers. Aid donors responded not only with debt relief but also with a massive increase in aid, from less than $200 million in 2000 to more than $6 billion in 2005. All this combined with rapidly increasing world oil prices to substantially improve Nigeria's global economic position.

Given Nigeria's long history of development failure, a much longer period of success is needed to fundamentally change people's well-being. Economic growth has been relatively strong—around 5 percent in the new millennium—and non-oil sector growth was an impressive 8 percent in 2005–2006, indicating the first significant development outside of oil in decades. More than 90 percent of Nigerians, however, still live on less than $2 per day, and the level of corruption—though improved—remains a serious concern. Nonetheless, its democratic government has started a process of reversing decades of corruption and ineffective development policy, at least slightly improving the country's position in the global economy.

Nigeria, like Iran, remains critically dependent on oil. Obasanjo's policies have started to show slight progress in reducing corruption and generating non-oil growth, but the reality remains that both countries' economic fortunes and global connections rest with oil. The 1980s were economically difficult in both countries because world oil prices plummeted; the new millennium has been much kinder because of record oil prices. In both countries, oil revenues provide crucial sources of patronage on which regime survival often seems to depend. Prior to democracy, Nigeria's military governments used this revenue in the most venal of ways, stealing much of it. Iran's Islamic government, while certainly not free from corruption, channeled oil revenue to political supporters but stole relatively little of it. Oil allowed both countries to avoid market-oriented economic reforms for a long time, but both finally began the process in the late 1990s. To the extent these reforms continue, the countries are likely to become more involved in the global economy, though for the time being that involvement remains nearly wholly focused on petroleum. Economically, globalization has had quite different results for major oil producers than it has for other middle-income and poor countries.

CONCLUSION

Globalization has certainly changed the context in which sovereign states, whether rich or poor, make economic policy. If nothing else, increasing cross-border flows of all types are much more difficult to monitor and control. A related and more important point is that the increasingly open global economy creates its own imperatives that make certain kinds of economic policy tools much less desirable, and for weaker states, perhaps also much less enforceable. Most important, the global imperative pushes rich and poor states away from the use of time-honored economic policies such as taxes, tariffs, and exchange rate control. In addition, states are under increasing pressure to utilize policies that will keep inflation and state spending low and labor flexible. For poorer states with debt burdens and balance of payments problems, the unwritten imperatives of globalization can be reinforced by the lending requirements of international financial institutions (IFIs) like the IMF. Wealthy countries in the euro zone face similar pressures to cut deficits, inflation, and the like to conform to EMU policy.

As our case studies suggest, however, states have not all responded to globalization in the same way. There is less convergence among policies and outcomes than one might expect. Among the wealthy, LMEs have intensified their openness to the market, but to varying degrees, whereas CMEs have also moved in that direction but have done so much more slowly while preserving some aspects of their older, statist policies. For these established states, it seems clear that long-entrenched institutions, the political cultures that reinforce them, and established political ideologies limit the extent to which states will bow to pressure for dramatic change—even to pressure as great as that from globalization.

Poorer countries have also moved in the general direction of economic liberalization, but whether this has been a blessing is not yet clear. While pursuit of export-oriented growth in East Asia has generated strong growth and reduced poverty, the East Asian model is based on strong state intervention, but in ways that favor rather than hamper exports. Neoliberal policies elsewhere have not always reduced poverty and have sometimes seemed to lead to repeated financial crises, at least in Latin America. Advice to the state to "get out of the way of the market" now seems to be moderating, suggesting that sovereign states do indeed have a role to play in generating growth, if only by creating the context of "good government" and well-developed human resources that will permit the market to generate solid growth. Poorer countries are much more susceptible to the vicissitudes of the global market as the repeated financial crises in these countries suggest, but this does not mean that these states are powerless. They can play an important role in creating a context, fostering growth and human development, and responding to those crises. Recent experience suggests that, within some parameters set by the global market and IFIs, they respond differently based on their own political histories, cultures, and institutions. The resurgence of Latin American populism suggests that just as in richer countries, old political ideologies, cultures, and institutional structures die hard. As for the question of whether democratic or authoritarian regimes produce more growth, our cases suggest that the real question is whether the regime's institutional structure enables the policymakers to follow sound economic policies. Some authoritarian states have clearly achieved this while others have not, and the same can be said for democracies.

States remain important actors on the global economic stage though globalization may have diminished the range of policy tools available to them. State sovereignty has never meant that states were insulated from the impact of the world economy, and today they remain capable of making (and do make) a range of choices in response to it. Though most are moving toward more liberal market economies, they nonetheless continue to make a range of economic policy choices that affect not only growth rates, but also the distribution of wealth and the well-being of their citizens.

COUNTRY AND CONCEPT Globalization, Deindustrialization, and Development

Country	Industry as percentage of GDP[1]		Stock of foreign direct investment (FDI) as percentage of GDP[2]		Exports of goods and services as percentage of GDP[3]		Imports of goods and services as percentage of GDP	
	1995	2005	1995	2005	1995	2005	1995	2005
Brazil	36.7	38.4	1.51	1.85	7.7	16.8	9.5	12.4
China	47.2	47.5	3.66	2.71	23.1	37.5	20.9	31.9
Germany	32.1	29.7	6.01	4.57	24	40.1	23.5	35.1
India	28.1	27.3	.20	.44	11	20.5	12.2	24.2
Iran	34.2	44.6	.08	.04	21.7	38.8	13.1	30.2
Japan	34.4	30.2*	1.21	1	9.2	13.4*	7.8	11.4*
Nigeria	46.7	56.8	.59	.35	44.3	53.1	42.2	35.2
Russia	37	38	.20	1.68	29.3	35.1	25.9	21.6
United Kingdom	32	26.2	7.23	8.27	28.3	26.1	28.8	30
United States	26.3	22*	19.4	15.87	11.1	10.1*	12.3	15.4*

Source: Stock of Direct Foreign Investment, 2006.
*2004
[1] Data on Industry as percentage of GDP are from World Resources Institute.
[2] Data on Stock of FDI are from FDISTAT, United Nations Conference on Trade and Development (UNCTAD).
[3] Data on Imports and Exports of Goods and Services as % of GDP are from World Resources Institute.

Key Concepts

comparative institutional advantage (p. 395)

convergence (p. 394)

coordinated market economies (CMEs) (p. 394)

dual convergence (p. 397)

export-oriented growth (EOG) (p. 406)

foreign direct investment (FDI) (p. 392)

hyperglobalization (p. 394)

international capital flows (p. 392)

liberal market economies (LMEs) (p. 394)

Millenium Development Goals (MDGs) (p. 416)

trade (p. 392)

transnational corporations (TNCs) (p. 392)

varieties of capitalism approach (p. 394)

Works Cited

Adams, John. 2002. "India's Economic Growth: How Fast? How Wide? How Deep?" *India Review* 1, no. 2: 1–28.

Alizadeh, Parvin. 2003. "Iran's Quandary: Economic Reforms and the 'Structural Trap'." *Brown Journal of World Affairs* 9, no. 2: 267–281.

Amuzegar, Jahangir. 2005. "Iran's Third Development Plan: An Appraisal." *Middle East Policy* 12, no. 3: 46–63.

Baer, Werner. 2008. *The Brazilian Economy: Growth and Development.* 6th ed. Boulder, Colo.: Lynne Rienner Publishers.

Country Watch. www.countrywatch.com.

Cox, Robert Henry. 2002. "Reforming the German Welfare State: Why Germany Is Slower than Its Neighbors: The Social Construction of an Imperative." *German Policy Studies* 2, no. 1: 174–196.

Daly, Mary. 2001. "Globalization and the Bismarckian Welfare States." In *Globalization and European Welfare States: Challenges and Change,* ed. Robert Sykes et al., 79–102. New York: Palgrave.

Easterly, William R. 2006. *The White Man's Burden: Why the West's Efforts to Aid the Rest Have Done So Much Ill and So Little Good.* New York: Penguin Press.

Evans, Peter B. 1995. *Embedded Autonomy: States and Industrial Transformation.* Princeton: Princeton University Press.

Eyoh, Dickson, and Richard Sandbrook. 2003. "Pragmatic Neo-Liberalism and Just Development in Africa." In *States, Markets, and Just Growth: Development in the Twenty-First Century,* ed. Atul Kohli, Chung-in Moon, and Georg Sørensen. New York: United Nations University Press.

Gillies, A. 2007. "Obasanjo, the Donor Community, and Reform Implementation in Nigeria." *The Round Table* 96, no. 392: 569–586.

Ginsburg, Norman. 2001. "Globalization and the Liberal Welfare States." In *Globalization and European Welfare States,* ed. Robert Sykes et al., 173–192. New York: Palgrave.

Haggard, Stephan, and Robert R. Kaufman. 1995. *The Political Economy of Democratic Transitions.* Princeton: Princeton University Press.

Hall, Peter Andrew, and David W. Soskice. 2001. *Varieties of Capitalism: The Institutional Foundations of Comparative Advantage.* Oxford: Oxford University Press.

Hay, Colin. 2004. "Common Trajectories, Variable Paces, Divergent Outcomes: Models of European Capitalism under Conditions of Complex Economic Interdependence." *Review of International Political Economy* 11, no. 2 (May): 231–262.

Huber, Evelyn, and John Stephen. 2001. *Development and Crisis of the Welfare State.* Chicago: University of Chicago Press.

Karshenas, Massoud, and Hassan Hakimian. 2005. "Oil, Economic Diversification and the Democratic Process in Iran." *Iranian Studies* 38, no. 1: 67–90.

Kohli, Atul. 2007. "State, Business, and Economic Growth in India." *Studies in Comparative International Development* 42, no. 1–2 (June): 87–114.

———. 2004. *State-Directed Development: Political Power and Industrialization in the Global Periphery.* Cambridge: Cambridge University Press.

Önis, Ziya. 2003. "States, Markets, and the Limits of Equitable Growth: The Middle Eastern NICs in Comparative Perspective." In *States, Markets, and Just Growth: Development in the Twenty-First Century,* ed. Atul Kohli, Chung-in Moon, and Georg Sørenson, 164–192. New York: United Nations University Press.

Qian, Yingyi. 2006. "The Process of China's Market Transition, 1978–1998: The Evolutionary, Historical, and Comparative Perspectives." In *China's Deep Reform: Domestic Politics in Transition,* ed. Lowell Dittmer and Guoili Liu, 229–250. Lanham, Md.: Rowman and Littlefield.

Qin, Julia. 2007. "Trade, Investment, and Beyond: The Impact of WTO Accession on China's Legal System." *China Quarterly* 191: 720–741.

Sachs, Jeffrey. 2005. *The End of Poverty: Economic Possibilities for Our Time.* New York: Penguin Press.

Saeidi, Ali A. 2001. "Charismatic Political Authority and Populist Economics in Post-Revolutionary Iran." *Third World Quarterly* 22, no. 2: 219–236.

Streek, Wofgana, and Anke Hassel. 2003. "The Crumbling Pillars of Social Partnership." *West European Politics* 26, no. 4 (October): 101–124.

Van de Walle, Nicolas. 2001. *African Economics and the Politics of Permanent Crisis, 1979–1999.* Cambridge: Cambridge University Press.

Winters, L. Alan, and Shahid Yusuf, ed. 2007. *Dancing with Giants: China, India, and the Global Economy.* Washington, D.C.: World Bank.

World Bank. 1993. *The East Asian Miracle: Economic Growth and Public Policy.* New York: Oxford University Press.

Resources for Further Study

Ferreira, Francisco H. G., and Michael Walton. 2005. *Equity and Development.* Washington, D.C.: World Bank; New York: Oxford University Press.

Garrett, Geoffrey. 1998. *Partisan Politics in the Global Economy.* Cambridge: Cambridge University Press.

Jha, Prem Shankar. 2002. *The Perilous Road to the Market: The Political Economy of Reform in Russia, India, and China.* London: Pluto Press.

Jones, R. J. Barry. 2000. *The World Turned Upside Down? Globalization and the Future of the State.* Manchester, UK: Manchester University Press.

Kohli, Atul, Chung-in Moon, and Georg Sørensen, ed. 2003. *States, Markets, and Just Growth: Development in the Twenty-First Century.* New York: United Nations University Press.

Rothstein, Bo, and Sven Steinmo. 2002. *Restructuring the Welfare State: Political Institutions and Policy Change.* New York: Palgrave/Macmillan.

Sykes, Robert, et al., ed. 2001. *Globalization and European Welfare States: Challenges and Change.* New York: Palgrave.

UN Millennium Project, www.unmillennium project.org/mv/mv_closer.htm.

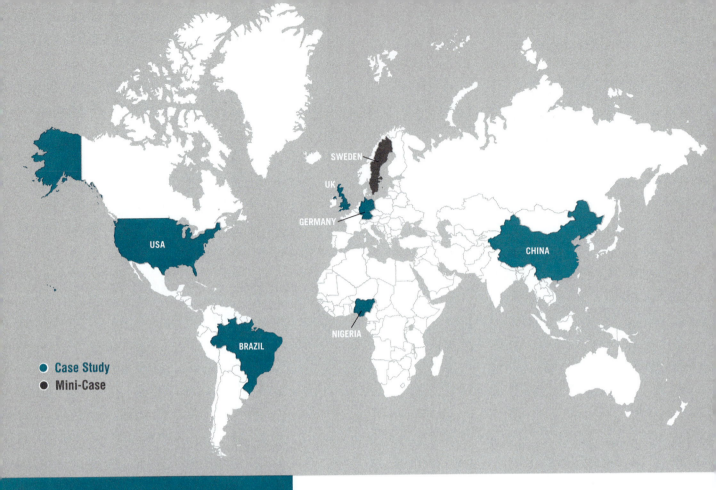

Who Rules?

- What do policy outcomes tell us about who has effective representation and power in a political system?

What Explains Political Behavior?

- Why did extensive welfare states develop in most wealthy countries after World War II?

- Why have many governments pursued significant reforms to welfare states in the era of globalization?

- Why do states intervene to protect the environment?

Where and Why?

- Why have extensive welfare states developed in certain countries and not in others?

- Where and why did more effective welfare and health systems emerge, and can the most effective ones be replicated in other countries?

PUBLIC POLICY WHEN MARKETS FAIL
Welfare, Health, and the Environment

As globalization expands the market economy, the issues raised in chapters 5 and 10 about the relationship between the state and the market loom ever larger. States must continue to provide the essential public goods that allow capitalism and the market to operate: security, property rights, contract enforcement, and some basic infrastructure. Chapter 10 showed that the current debate is over how else governments ought to intervene in the market in an effort to maximize the well-being of the citizenry. This chapter addresses three key areas that have long been subjects of debate in virtually every country: welfare, health care, and the environment. The common thread among them is the call for government to intervene in response to market failure.

Market failure occurs when markets do not perform their expected functions, which is usually because they fail to perform efficiently or they fail to perform according to other widely held social values. The primary justification for a market is efficiency: a well-functioning market maximizes the efficient use of all available resources, and the most common type of market failure occurs when unfettered markets do not achieve this. Chapter 5 presented externalities as a common cause of market inefficiency: if costs and benefits are not fully included in a market transaction, resources are not allocated efficiently. A key example is one subject of this chapter: environmental damage. Another common cause of inefficiency is imperfect information. Markets only maximize efficiency when buyers and sellers know the full costs and benefits of the transactions. In our technologically complex societies, this is often not the case. A pivotal example examined in this chapter is health care: its highly complex nature makes it difficult for buyers (patients) to know fully the benefits of possible purchases (remedies for illness or injury). That means consumers may purchase health care goods that they falsely believe will benefit them, and the waste of their money and their continued ill health are the costs of these inefficient transactions. Advocates of an unfettered market recognize market failures like these as something governments should try to correct, but exactly when such intervention is justified and how governments should respond remain controversial.

Market failure also results when markets fail to fulfill social values not inherent in the functioning of the markets themselves. Properly functioning markets maximize efficiency and therefore wealth generation, but as pointed out in chapter 5, markets do not lead to a particular distribution of wealth. They do not necessarily reduce inequality or end poverty, and the elimination (or at least alleviation) of these often is a widely held social value. Markets respond to those individuals or companies with resources (money or commodities) that can be exchanged for other resources, and because poor people have fewer resources they receive less from the unfettered market. Economists speak of "effective demand" in a market, meaning demand backed with money. There is often very little effective demand for food during a famine in a very poor country; government and international intervention in the form of emergency food aid is justified because of the social value of keeping people from starving to death. Similarly, poor, uninsured individuals who are very sick may have no effective demand for health care so the market will provide none, but government might choose to intervene to restore their health based on a value of preserving and extending life for all citizens regardless of their relative wealth. Governments develop what Americans typically call "welfare" policies in part to respond to market failures to distribute wealth in socially acceptable ways that reduce poverty, inequality, or both.

Citizens often call for government intervention when markets fail to fulfill important social values. These are the politically generated interventions we discussed in chapter 5. When markets fail to maximize efficiency, they undermine the central value of the market itself and create an economic justification for government intervention even in the eyes of the most neoliberal economists. Investigating welfare, health care, and environmental policy allows us to examine both kinds of market failures and how different governments have intervened to try to resolve them.

"WELFARE": SOCIAL POLICY IN COMPARATIVE PERSPECTIVE

A large number of Americans think of welfare as a temporary government handout to poor people. Being "on welfare" is a situation virtually all Americans want to avoid, as a certain moral opprobrium seems to go with it. Partly because of this, and partly because different countries relieve poverty in different ways, political scientists and other scholars of public policy usually prefer the term **social policy** to welfare. Social policy can have many goals, but the primary ones are reducing poverty and income inequality and stabilizing individual or family income. Citizens or states may intervene to reduce significant poverty, inequality, or economic insecurity—three things perceived as market failures. Most people view a market that leaves people in abject poverty, unable to meet their most basic needs, as violating important values. Similarly, when market distribution produces inequality that goes beyond some particular point (the acceptable level varies widely from one individual and society to another), many people argue that it should be reversed. Markets also inherently produce instability: in the absence of government intervention, capitalism tends to be associated with boom and bust cycles, as John Maynard Keynes argued. This instability can create severe economic insecurity for market participants, especially in the form of unemployment. Reducing this insecurity has been one of the main impetuses behind modern welfare states.

Various philosophical and practical reasons justify these types of interventions in the market. On purely humanitarian grounds, citizens and governments might wish to alleviate the suffering of the poor. States might also be concerned about social and political stability: high endemic poverty rates and temporary economic instability often are seen as threats to the status quo, including a state's legitimacy, and poverty is associated with higher levels of crime almost everywhere. Some Keynesians argue as well that reducing poverty and stabilizing incomes in the face of market fluctuations are economically beneficial for society as a whole because reducing poverty increases purchasing power, which stimulates market demand.

Opponents of social policy also disagree, criticizing social policy primarily for producing perverse incentives. Markets maximize efficiency in part by inducing people to be productive by working for wages, salaries, or profits. Neoliberal opponents of social policy argue that providing income or other resources for people whether they are working or not gives them a disincentive to work, which leads to underutilization of productive labor. This reduces efficiency and productivity, and ultimately, overall wealth. Critics also argue that financing social policy via taxes discourages work and productivity because higher tax rates reduce incentives to work and make a profit.

In liberal democracies, the debate over social policy has implications for citizenship. According to liberalism, citizens are supposed to be equal, autonomous individuals, yet in a market economy, citizens are never truly socioeconomically equal. As we saw in chapter 3, T. H. Marshall argued that social rights are the third pillar of citizenship because without some degree of socioeconomic equality, citizens cannot be political equals. Following this line of thought, when the market fails to create an adequate degree of equality, governments should intervene to provide it to preserve equal citizenship, even if this may conflict with the other element of liberal citizenship: autonomy. In all market economies, market participation is the primary means of achieving economic autonomy. The founders of liberalism believed only male property owners could be citizens because they were the only ones truly autonomous from others in their daily interactions: women and nonproperty owners were too economically dependent on others to act effectively as autonomous citizens. All liberal democracies have modified this position, but the fundamental concern remains. Many citizens in market economies view those who participate in the market—whether owning capital or working for a wage—as autonomous citizens. Welfare policies that provide income from nonmarket sources can then be seen as problematic. Traditional liberals argue that social policy thus undermines equal and autonomous citizenship by creating two classes of citizens: those who earn their income in the market and those who depend on the government (funded by the rest of the citizens). This argument typically makes an exception for family membership: an adult who depends on other family members who participate in the market is implicitly granted full autonomy and citizenship. Social democrats argue, to the contrary, that citizens should be granted full autonomy regardless of their source of income and that social policies that keep income inequality and poverty below certain levels are essential to preserving truly equal citizenship. Different kinds of welfare states are in part based on different values in this debate, as we will see below.

Whatever their justification, social policies can be categorized into universal entitlements, social insurance, and means-tested public assistance. **Universal entitlements** are benefits that governments provide to all citizens more or less equally, usually funded through general taxation. The only major example in the United States is public education. Education is an indirect component of social policy, because a greater level of education tends to reduce the chances a person will end up in poverty. All communities in the United States must provide access to public education for all school-age residents without exception, making it a universal benefit. Many European countries provide child or family allowances as universal entitlements: all families with children receive a cash benefit to help raise the children, and this allowance increases with the number of children and sometimes is adjusted slightly for household income. Universal entitlements by nature do not raise questions about equal and autonomous citizenship, even when individual citizens may choose not to take advantage of them—no one questions the equal citizenship of public versus private school graduates in the United States or those who do not have children and therefore don't get child allowances in the Netherlands. Critics, on the other hand, argue that universal entitlements are wasteful because much of the money goes to relatively wealthy people who do not necessarily need the benefits.

Social insurance provides benefits to categories of people who have contributed to a (usually mandatory) public insurance fund. The prime examples in the United States are Social Security, disability benefits, and unemployment insurance. In most cases, workers and their employers contribute to the funds while the individual is employed. Workers can then benefit from the fund when they need it: after retirement, when temporarily unemployed, or when disabled. Because only those who contribute can gain benefits, fewer questions arise about the beneficiaries deserving their benefits, even though there is usually only a very general relationship between the size of contributions and benefits. In fact, the average American retiree earns substantially more in retirement benefits than the total of his entire lifetime of contributions with interest, but to date that has never been a major political question in the United States, so it has no impact on questions of citizenship. (This may change, however, as the number or retirees increases in coming years.) In addition, by covering entire large groups of people—all workers or the spouses of all workers—social insurance is not seen as undermining equal citizenship because it covers things nearly everyone expects (retirement) or hopes to avoid (unemployment).

Means-tested public assistance is what most Americans think of as "welfare." Food Stamps, subsidized public housing, and Temporary Assistance to Needy Families (TANF) are examples found in the United States. These are programs that individuals qualify for when they fall below a specific income level. Some countries impose additional requirements for public assistance, such as work requirements or time limits, but income level is the defining characteristic. Means-tested programs target assistance only to the poor, in contrast to the broader distribution of universal entitlements or social insurance and so they are the most economically efficient means of poverty relief. Their disadvantage, though, is their impact on recipients' status as equal and autonomous citizens. Because only those below a certain income level can benefit, and benefits are typically financed from general taxation, recipients may be seen as somehow less deserving or not fully equal with other citizens who are paying the taxes. When people believe—even erroneously, as our case study of the United States shows—that recipients of means-tested assistance receive it continuously or at least for very long periods, that belief adds to the perception that such individuals are somehow less deserving or not fully equal and autonomous citizens.

The three types of social programs are often associated with particular kinds of benefits or groups of recipients. Workers are often covered by social insurance, for instance, while public housing is typically means-tested. This need not be the case, however; in theory, any of the three could be used for any type of benefit. For instance, unemployment insurance is fairly restricted in the United States, benefiting only long-term employees for only six to nine months, but such programs are more extensive elsewhere and less distinct from what Americans call welfare. Preschool is a universal entitlement in France but is means-tested via the Head Start program in the United States. Retirement benefits also could be means-tested so that when people no longer earn a market-based income, only those below a certain income level would qualify for benefits. This would target retirement benefits more efficiently on reducing poverty but might raise questions of citizenship common with means-tested programs, questions that retirees currently don't face in any country.

Different governments combine these three types of programs in different ways and levels of generosity, creating distinctive **welfare states**. The Country and Concept table later in the chapter gives some idea of the wide variety of combinations states use, especially in poor and middle-income countries. Evelyne Huber and John Stephens (2001), modifying the pioneering work of Gosta Esping-Andersen (1990), classify wealthy countries into three main types of welfare states: social democratic, Christian democratic, and liberal. **Social democratic welfare states** strongly emphasize universal entitlements to achieve greater social equality and promote equal citizenship. Governments typically provide numerous universal entitlements in a wide array of areas, including paid maternity leave, preschool, child allowances, basic retirement pensions, and job training.

They use high rates of general taxation to fund their generous social benefits and transfer more income from the wealthy to the poor (taxing the wealthy more and giving equal universal entitlements to all) than do the other types of welfare states. Social insurance programs also exist, such as employment-based retirement pensions, but these usually supplement the universal entitlements that are available to all. The primary examples of these social democratic welfare states are the Scandinavian countries.

MINI-CASE Sweden's Welfare State

Sweden's generous, redistributive social welfare state is a long-standing model of "the middle way" between capitalism and socialism. The Swedish Social Democratic Party was in power from 1932 to 2006, except for two brief periods in the opposition: 1976 to 1982 and 1991 to 1994. The party instituted the first elements of its welfare state in the 1920s. From the start, it established basic services such as unemployment benefits and retirement pensions as universal social rights of citizenship, in part to gain the support of the important Agrarian Party in the 1930s, when the country still had a large farming population opposed to tying benefits to wage employment. In the late 1950s, the party added extra benefits above and beyond the flat-rate universal ones. These additional benefits were tied to earnings and replaced as much as 90 percent of workers' wages when they were unemployed, disabled, or retired. In the 1970s, the social democratic government expanded services designed to induce women into the workforce, including the world's most generous maternity leave and sick leave policies.

The state then combined these benefits with very high tax rates on income (60 percent of the economy at their height in the 1970s), but used low corporate rates to encourage large-scale investment in export industries while maintaining one of the most open trade policies in the world. At its height in the 1970s, Sweden was the world's second wealthiest country, with robust growth, strong export levels by brand name companies such as Volvo, virtually no unemployment, and the world's most generous social services. Even after reforms in the 1990s, Sweden's social services

and taxes remain among the world's highest. Unemployment benefits still cover about 80 percent of wages and have virtually no time limit. The universal family allowance in 2001 was $138 per child up to sixteen years of age (higher for special needs children), and parental leave provides sixteen months of paid leave at any time during the first eight years of a child's life at 80 percent of full salary. Parents get ten paid "contact days" per year to spend time in their children's schools as volunteers, up to sixty days of benefits per year to care for sick children, and a daycare system that enrolls 75 percent of preschoolers, with more than 80 percent of the cost funded by the state (Olsen 2007, 147–151). To pay for this, government revenue remains more than half of the entire economy (compared to a little more than a third for the United States). In addition, more than 30 percent of all employees work in the public sector.

Sweden's model faced a crisis in the late 1980s and early 1990s. Declining traditional industry and growing interest by businesses in outsourcing combined with demographic changes to increase unemployment, inflation, and difficulty in paying for the state's extensive social services. When the Social Democrats lost the 1991 election, the newly elected Moderate Party government passed what was seen at the time as the most sweeping tax reform in the Western world, with the top rate on income tax dropping from 80 to 50 percent and the marginal rate on corporate taxes from 57 to 30 percent even as the entire system underwent a radical simplification (Huber and Stephens 2001, 242). Eliminated from the system was the strong incentive in favor of domestic investment in the old tax code, which allowed Swedish corporations to enter the global market more fully. Even with these changes, the tax reform, continued slow growth, high unemployment, and an aging population left government finances in dire straits by the mid-1990s.

Returning to power in 1994, the Social Democrats negotiated a series of reforms that led to the creation of a new index that tied retirement pensions to the levels of unemployment and economic growth and divided financing equally between employer and employee (previously, employers paid for virtually all of it). Similarly, the government reduced unemployment benefits from 90 to 80 percent of income. Unions did successfully resist an attempt to impose a three-year limit on such benefits (nine months is typical in the United States).

These were seen as unprecedented changes to Sweden's social welfare system, but it remains one of the world's most generous. By 2008, global economic growth and these policy changes had restored Sweden's growth to normal levels and reduced unemployment to about 5.5 percent, a rate below the European norm. Sweden's economic outlook was strong: the extensive welfare state has been modified but its main planks, including its exceptional generosity, remain in place in a robust economy.

Christian democratic welfare states primarily emphasize income stabilization to mitigate the effects of market-induced income insecurity. Their most common type of social program, therefore, is social insurance, which is designed to provide a relatively high percentage of a family's income when its market-based source of income is disrupted through unemployment, disability, or something similar. Benefits are usually tied to contributions to social insurance plans, and financing is mainly through employer and employee payroll taxes rather than general taxation. This means that redistribution is not as broad as under social democratic welfare states, and the emphasis is instead on income stabilization. Most Christian democratic welfare states also feature corporate models of economic governance; that is, social insurance programs tend to be administered by and through sectoral-based organizations such as unions, under the state's guidance. Germany is a prime example of such a state, which we explore below in detail.

Liberal welfare states focus on ensuring that all who can do gain their income in the market; these states are more concerned with preserving individual autonomy via market participation than with reducing poverty or inequality. They emphasize means-tested public assistance more than the other types of welfare states, targeting very specific groups of recipients for benefits. A great deal of government effort often goes into assessing who is truly deserving of support, which usually boils down to who is unable to work for a wage as opposed to who is unwilling. Their emphasis on ensuring that only the poor and truly deserving receive benefits often means that some poor people don't receive benefits, and the desire to provide incentives for people to work can mean that social benefits for the poor still do not raise them above the poverty level. But not all programs are means-tested in these countries; retirement benefits are typically provided via social insurance. The United States, which we turn to below, is a prime example of this type of welfare state.

WHERE AND WHY The Development of Welfare States

Why have three different types of welfare states arisen in different wealthy, industrialized countries? Comparativists have come up with numerous cultural, institutional, and structural (both economic and political) arguments to explain the origins of welfare states. An early economic theory is known as the "logic of industrialism" approach. It argues that as societies get wealthier they can afford to care for their remaining poor, and as industrialization grows groups harmed by it, such as the unemployed and the elderly, will organize to demand protection (Willemsky 1975). Peter Katzenstein (1985) proposed a different economic theory: openness to international trade led to greater welfare spending to ameliorate the increased uncertainty brought on by trade—the opposite of the convergence theory discussed in chapter 10, which argued that globalization decreased spending. These theories may explain in general why welfare states arose and expanded over time, but they are not very helpful in explaining why distinct types of welfare states emerged.

Cultural arguments have looked at differences in long-standing values among wealthy countries to explain the variation among welfare states. Anglo-American countries, they argue, have stronger liberal traditions emphasizing the importance of the individual and individual autonomy, which causes them to be more reluctant to encourage extensive government spending to help people via policy. Numerous surveys have shown, for instance, that despite upward social mobility being about the same in the United States and Europe, Americans are much more likely than Europeans to believe that people can work their way out of poverty if they really want to (Alesina and Glaser 2004, 11–12).

Other experts argue that religious beliefs influence welfare states: countries more influenced by Protestantism, especially Calvinism, see wealth as morally superior and have less sympathy for the poor, whereas countries with more Catholics are more generous due to their beliefs in preserving social and family stability. And a final cultural explanation focused on the United

States argues that racial divisions explain the country's particularly small welfare state: surveys show people (not only Americans) are less sympathetic to those of different races, and in the United States many whites perceive the poor to be primarily black or Hispanic, and as a result they are relatively unwilling to support policies to assist them. Two Harvard economists, Alberto Alesina and Edward Glaeser (2004), recently argued this was part of the explanation for the striking difference between generosity of social spending in the United States and Europe. Yet while these cultural explanations may help explain why some states are more generous than others, they still don't fully explain the rise of different kinds of welfare states.

Huber and Stephens (2001) combine a structural argument focusing on the political organization of social classes with an institutionalist argument to explain the rise of distinct types of welfare states, as well as their relative levels of generosity. They argue that welfare states primarily reflect the strength and political orientation of the working and lower-middle classes. In countries where working classes were able to organize into strong labor unions and powerful Social Democratic parties that were able to hold office for a long period of time, social democratic welfare states emerged. Countries with more Catholics that had stronger Christian Democratic parties that appealed to working and lower-middle classes successfully saw the emergence of Christian democratic welfare states. Where working classes were not strong enough to organize to gain political power, liberal welfare states emerged. Following their party ideologies, Social Democratic parties instituted welfare states with far-ranging social services, including ones that facilitated greater redistribution of wealth and the entry of women into the workforce. Christian democratic welfare states followed Catholic belief in decentralizing welfare payments to the local community and emphasizing social and family stability, rather than resource redistribution and women's participation in the workplace. Liberal welfare states believed in minimal support only for those deserving poor who were truly unable to work.

Huber and Stephens then went on to combine this argument with an institutionalist argument that regimes with fewer "veto points" in their constitutions developed more extensive welfare states. Federal systems, for instance, tend to produce less extensive social policies, as do presidential systems. The authors of the study also argue that once created, the welfare state tends to be self-perpetuating: both recipients and the middle-class bureaucrats who staff the social service agencies have an interest in preserving the institutions as they exist. Other institutionalists have argued that state bureaucracies themselves created the welfare state: Hugh Heclo (1974) contended that the central ideas for and differences between the Swedish and British welfare states were developed by bureaucrats first and were later championed by political leaders. Huber and Stephens reject this argument based on extensive quantitative analysis, but they do agree that once created (by parties and unions mobilizing the lower classes) the institutions tend to be self-perpetuating.

The study by Huber and Stephens is an impressive analysis of how and why the three types of welfare states arose, but the debate will continue. Cultural theorists might well argue that underlying values (Catholicism, solidarity) allowed the Social Democratic or Christian Democratic parties to organize the lower classes in the first place, in a way that is most unlikely in Anglo-American culture with its individualist orientation. Race theorists will continue to argue that the exceptionally low levels of social spending in the United States reflect racial divisions, and an interesting question is whether rising racial and religious diversity in much of Europe will have the same effect over time. Supporters of the hyperglobalization thesis we discussed in chapter 10 continue to support the idea that regardless of how the various types of welfare states arose, they will tend to converge toward the liberal model as the effects of globalization are fully realized, even if evidence of this has not emerged yet.

The different types of welfare states have created significantly different societies in terms of how much of the national income passes through government coffers and how much is redistributed from the rich to the poor. Table 11.1 provides data comparing the three types of welfare states. Social democratic welfare states clearly take the biggest share of the national economy as government revenue to provide their extensive social services, which is reflected in their high social expenditures, though the gap between them and Christian democratic systems seems to be narrowing. Government's overall share of the economy has shrunk in each of the types of welfare states, though social expenditures have only decreased slightly, suggesting that globalization has so far not hurt overall spending on social policy. At their height in the 1980s, social democratic welfare states redistributed more income than Christian democratic ones, with liberal welfare states redistributing the least. Similarly, social democratic welfare states facilitated greater female participation in the labor force via such policies as universal child allowances, paid ma-

TABLE 11.1 Comparison of Welfare State Outcomes

Year	Government Revenue (% of GDP)			Social Expenditure (% of GDP)			Redistribution Resulting from Taxes and Transfers (percentage reduction in GINI Index)
	1980	1996	2003	1980	1995	2003	1980s (various years)
Social Democratic Welfare State	50.9	56.5	39.5	22.2	28.1	26.6	41.4
Christian Democratic Welfare State	43.4	45.9	34.83	20.6	23.6	24.6	34.2
Liberal Welfare State	36.4	37.3	25.75	15.2	17.8	17.5	29.4

Sources: Government Revenue: 1980 and 1996: Huber and Stephens (2001), Appendix A.1; GDP Growth and Unemployment (pre 2003), Huber and Stephens (2001), Appendix A.11; Social Expenditure: OECD Dataset: Social Expenditure: Aggregate Data; 2003 data: OECD Statistics Portal and ILO (Unemployment); Redistribution: Huber and Stephens (2001, 109); Female labor: 1980 and 1994: Huber and

ternity leave, and subsidized preschool. Liberal welfare states, with their emphasis on work, achieve higher female participation rates than do Christian democratic states that built their welfare state around the male breadwinner.

The extensive social policies of the social democratic and Christian democratic welfare states, however, did not lower the rate of economic growth significantly at their height in the 1980s, though liberal welfare states seem to be growing faster recently. Similarly, more generous welfare states actually achieved lower levels of unemployment until recent years. These economic data suggest that while states have been able to maintain different levels of social policy in the face of globalization, the more generous ones may be paying a price in recent years in terms of economic growth and employment.

All welfare states have been under pressure to reform in the age of globalization. As we suggested in chapter 10, though, few countries have fundamentally altered their social policies. The aggregate data, however, hide reforms that have been occurring. Pressure on social expenditures comes primarily from demographic changes in wealthy countries: as populations age, fewer workers must somehow pay the benefits for larger dependent populations, particularly the elderly, and in Europe, the growing number of unemployed. While only a few countries have fundamentally changed policies (as the UK did under Prime Minister Margaret Thatcher in the 1980s), most have reduced benefits to some extent, and these changes have focused mainly on reducing the costs of the programs, however they are administered and however generous they were in the past. Governments have raised the minimum age at which people can retire, reduced the length of unemployment or other benefits and the percentage of salary that is replaced, changed the indexing of benefits relative to inflation to lower the real value of those benefits, raised employee contributions to social insurance programs, and removed guarantees of set benefits so that governments can reduce them in the future if necessary (Bonoli et al. 2000).

Women's Labor Force Participation (% of women in labor force)			GDP Growth (%)			Unemployment (% of civilian labor force)		
1980	1994	2004	1979–1989	1995–1997	2003	1980–1989	1995–1998	2003
69.3	72.2	75.1	2.3	3.3	1.25	4.6	8.1	6.2
47.2	58.2	63.4	1.8	1.7	.33	7.1	8.5	7.1
53.8	63	67.6	2.1	4.1	3	10.2	8.1	5.8

Stephens (2001, 136-137); Women's Labour Force Participation Rates for 2004, OECD Statistics Portal, http://stats.oecd.org/wbos/Index.aspx?usercontext=sourceoecd.

In poorer countries, neoliberal development strategies, bolstered now by the spectacular success of China, have long focused on achieving high economic growth as the best means of reducing poverty. The limited success of neoliberal strategies in other regions, however, led to the reemergence of social policy as an important issue in developing countries, especially those in Latin America, in the 1990s. A number of governments embraced programs for new social safety nets that would not only help ameliorate poverty among the poorest households but would also be an investment in human capital by helping provide better education and health for future workers. By and large, these programs are means-tested and target the poorest households to gain the maximum impact with very limited resources. Results have been mixed and the policies remain relatively modest in scope, but they nonetheless constitute a new development in social policies around the world. The case studies below demonstrate in greater detail the struggle governments have faced in trying to finance social policies in an era of globalization and shifting demographics.

CASE STUDY Germany: Reforming the Christian Democratic Welfare State

Otto von Bismarck pioneered social insurance, beginning the first programs of their kind in Germany in 1883. Most of the country's modern Christian democratic welfare state was not put into place until 1949, but it still relies primarily on social insurance to provide the bulk of benefits, paid for mainly by roughly equal employer and employee contributions. Following Germany's cor-

poratist model, the system is run by nongovernmental organizations overseen by employer and employee associations, with the state providing the legal framework and regulations. In the golden era during which the economy was growing rapidly and achieving close to full employment, the system provided relatively generous benefits and was self-financing. Structural chang-

Germany has begun giving out cash cards that allow recipients of the controversial Unemployment II benefit to withraw funds directly from an ATM. The benefit is part of the Hartz reforms, which were designed to reduce long-term unemployment benefits and have met considerable popular resistance.

es, including reunification, a lower rate of economic growth, higher unemployment, and an aging population have since brought severe financial constraints to the system, producing seemingly continuous reform efforts since the early 1980s. Both the Christian Democratic Union (CDU) and Social Democratic Party (SDP), however, continue to vary only marginally on their policy choices; before 2003 reforms by governments of both major parties only slightly reduced the generosity of the system. That year both parties supported a more fundamental change to unemployment benefits, though the other pillars of the system remain largely unchanged, and social spending remains unusually high (Siebert 2005, 114–136).

Prior to such recent reforms, the core social insurance system provided nearly complete income replacement for sickness, at least 60 percent of an unemployed worker's salary for up to thirty-two months, and a retirement pension that averaged 70 percent of wages. These benefits continue to constitute the great majority of German social spending. Those unemployed for periods longer than three years who had worked at least a year at some point gained unemployment assistance at about 53 percent of their most recent salary with no time limit, though adjusted for family and

other available support, and all of this was funded by general taxation. Those who had not worked a full year still received social assistance, a means-tested system that indefinitely provided a level of support to individuals to keep them above the poverty line. Originally, the system assumed a male breadwinner would support his wife and children, with the latter gaining benefits only through the former. In 1986 child benefits were added, including direct payments and tax breaks for children and government-paid contributions into social insurance for unemployed parents so that they could care for any children three years of age or younger. In the 1970s, maternity benefits of fourteen weeks that covered the full income of many women were added, and more recently up to three years of unpaid parental leave has been made available.

As the population aged and unemployment grew, financial constraints appeared on the horizon. The reform debate began in 1982 with the CDU government under Helmut Kohl and focused on strengthening support for the family via child benefits and reducing social spending somewhat, down from a high of more than 31 percent in 1975 to 28 percent in 1989, by increasing employer and employee contributions. Then German reunification in 1990 dramatically increased the costs of the system: unemployment rates skyrocketed in the former East Germany as the economy made the transition from a communist to a capitalist system, and massive transfers of funds from the former West Germany were essential to pay social insurance benefits to these workers. By the mid-1990s, social spending had exceeded its previous high of twenty years earlier.

The CDU government and then the SDP/Green government after 1998 responded to this financial pressure with additional proposals. While the SDP criticized the CDU government in the 1990s for making the system less generous, once in power the Social Democrats produced even more substantial reforms. In 2003 the SDP/Green government passed what became known as the Hartz reforms, part of a broader effort to modernize the economy known as Agenda 2010. Full unemployment insurance (set as a percentage of a worker's wage) was limited to only twelve months, after which a worker would be placed on "Unemployment Benefit II," which was set at a fixed level (not connected to past earnings) equal to the prior level of social assistance and funded in part by general revenue rather than contributions. The latter is now only for those classified as unable to work. Unemployed workers are also now required to accept jobs at only 80 percent of their prior wage levels, rather than being allowed to wait for positions equivalent to their previous ones. In effect, the long-term unemployment assistance has been eliminated, meaning workers now see a drastic reduction in their income after a year out of work (Vail 2004).

The primary goal of the Christian democratic welfare state in Germany has always been to ensure income stability throughout a person's life. Once securely in the workforce, or dependent on someone who is, citizens can count on relative stability for as long as needed, at a minimum of half of their prior salary. This system was far more generous than those of liberal welfare states but transferred much less income from the wealthy to the poor than did social democratic welfare states.

Facing years of financial constraints as the population aged and unemployment remained near 10 percent, the government even under the Social Democrats had to modify the system somewhat. Relatively generous retirement benefits remain, but the unemployment system now provides income stability for only a year. Implicit in this policy is the assumption common to liberal welfare states that everyone who wants to can find employment in a reasonable amount of time. Permanent support continues to exist but only at a level just above the poverty line. In the long run, the hope is that this will reduce social spending, which in 2003 was at 27 percent of gross domestic product (GDP), well above the OECD (Organisation for Economic Co-operation and Development) average of 21 percent. The new system makes Germany's Christian democratic welfare state notably more similar to a liberal welfare state, as a comparison with the United States will demonstrate. While more similar than they used to be, however, the two systems remain quite distinct. The In Context provides data on the ability of each system to reduce poverty from what the market alone would produce.

IN CONTEXT The German Welfare State

Germany spends an unusually large share of its economy on social spending, though not as much as Sweden. Both countries spend more and transfer more income to the poor than does the United States.

	Germany	U.S.	Sweden
Public Social Expenditures in 2003 (% of GDP)	27.3	16.2	31.3
Mean Social Transfers (% of pre-tax household income)	25.1	11.7	44.5
Market Income Poverty (pre-tax and transfer) in 2000 (% of population)	28.6	23.7	29.2
Disposable Income Poverty (post-tax and transfer) in 2000 (% of population)	8.2	17	6.4

Sources: Mean Social Transfers: Alesina and Glaeser (2004, 31); Public Social Expenditure: OECD (2008); Income Poverty: Smeeding (2005, Figure 2).

CASE STUDY The United States: Reforming the Liberal Welfare State

The *In Context* above shows that based on income earned in the market alone, the United States has a smaller percentage of people in poverty than Germany or Sweden, but taxes and government social programs lower the poverty rate by only about seven percentage points in the United States compared to twenty or more in the European cases. The end result is much less poverty in the latter than in the American liberal welfare state. Aside from Social Security, the large social insurance system for the elderly, most U.S. social programs are means-tested and many are restricted to certain categories of recipients. The United States only legislated unpaid parental leave in the 1990s, and in contrast to Europe, no national paid maternity or parental leave policy exists. Most European states heavily subsidize child care, in contrast to the small U.S. means-tested Head Start program and tax deductions for child care. Since 1996 poor people can still receive some income support for a maximum of five years, but they no longer have a legal entitlement to it beyond that unless they are disabled. The federal system also sets only minimum standards and allows state governments significant flexibility in implementing the main social programs, so benefits vary widely across states.

Modern social policy in the United States began in the Great Depression as part of President Franklin D. Roosevelt's New Deal policies. The Social Security Act of 1935 established the system and remains the country's primary social program. The most important manifestation of this program was the Social Security system of retirement pensions. This social insurance program is similar to Germany's but is administered by the federal government, not by nongovernmental organizations. Pensions are tied to individuals' previous earnings and are financed by mandatory employer and employee contributions. The Social Security retirement system became and remains the country's most successful antipoverty program, and while not as generous as most European pension systems, it nonetheless dramatically reduced poverty among the elderly. Prior to Social Security, the elderly had constituted the country's largest group of people in poverty, but now

Children attend a Head Start program in Hillsboro, Oregon. Publicly funded pre-kindergarten programs have expanded rapidly in recent years in the United States, funded mostly by state governments. The country's liberal welfare state provides only limited free or subsidized preschool, in contrast to the much more generous funding of these programs in most European welfare states.

this group has one of the lowest rates of poverty of any American demographic group, less than 10 percent in 2005. The Social Security Act also created Aid to Dependent Children (ADC), a program that provided cash grants to poor households with children present but no resident male breadwinner.

President Lyndon Johnson's War on Poverty in the 1960s produced the second major expansion of American social policy. During the unprecedented post–World War II economic boom and on the heels of the civil rights movement, the nation came to recognize that many nonelderly individuals remained in poverty. The War on Poverty augmented Social Security with Medicare, a health insurance program for the elderly, and Aid to Families with Dependent Children (AFDC, the descendant of ADC) became an entitlement, with each state legally obligated to indefinitely provide a minimum level of support, primarily to single mothers with resident children. Medicaid was created to fund health services for AFDC recipients, and the Food Stamps program provided vouchers for purchases by poor families. By 1975 the poverty rate hit a low of about 12 percent of the population, half of what it had been in 1960.

For all of this, the programs were not necessarily widely accepted. Whereas Social Security was regarded as an earned benefit, AFDC was controversial from the outset. Critics argued that its structure of indefinite, per-child payments to families headed by women created perverse incentives for the poor to divorce or have children out of wedlock, have more children, and become dependent on government payments. Levels of support also varied widely from state to state, with some states providing as much as five times the money that others did. In reality, half of AFDC recipients received benefits for less than four years, and the average household size of recipients dropped from 4.0 in 1969 to 2.9 in 1992, meaning an average of only 1.9 children per mother by the 1990s, below the national average of about 2.1 (Cammisa 1998, 10–17). Nonetheless, the perception of a perverse incentive structure persisted.

Reform proposals began as early as the late 1960s under President Richard Nixon, but they grew significantly in the 1980s under President Ronald Reagan. Reagan's 1980 campaign was based in part on fundamentally changing the welfare system, though with a Democratic-controlled Congress he never succeeded. Indeed, when faced with a financial crisis in Social Security, Reagan led a bipartisan effort to increase the mandatory payroll tax contributions to the system to restore solvency without substantially cutting benefits. Reagan did help pass a law that allowed state governments greater flexibility in implementing AFDC, including permitting them to demand that recipients work, a condition for receiving aid that many states began experimenting with.

President Bill Clinton got elected as a "New Democrat" in 1992 on a platform that included a promise to "end welfare as we know it," and when the Republicans swept into control of Congress in 1994, they made a similar pledge, setting the stage for major reform. Two years later, Congress, with Republican support and mostly Democratic opposition, passed and President Clinton signed the most important reform of social policy since the 1960s. The legislation ended AFDC as an entitlement to poor, single mothers and replaced it with a new program called Temporary Assistance to Needy Families (TANF). TANF eliminated the bias against households with fathers, limited recipients to two years of continuous benefits and five years over a lifetime, required virtually all able-bodied recipients to work to keep their benefits, and allowed them to keep a significant share of those benefits after they began working.

The creation of TANF changed social policy to a greater degree than reforms in almost any other country. Supporters believed it would reduce welfare dependence, encourage individuals to work, and lower poverty. Critics claimed it meted out harsh punishment to the poor, who would be cut off without the possibility of finding work that would lead them out of poverty. Numerous studies of the program's effects have been carried out without definitive conclusions. Part of the problem is that many factors besides social policy, the most important of these being overall economic growth, affect the poverty and employment rates for the poor. TANF was introduced in a period of rapid growth. Poverty and the number of AFDC recipients actually had started falling two years before TANF was enacted, presumably because of the strong economic growth that had started in 1992, so it is difficult to judge TANF's impact.

What is clear is that the number of people receiving benefits via AFDC and now TANF fell sharply, from a monthly average of more than five million households in 1994 to less than two million by 2005. Most of those leaving the rolls gained employment in the year they left the program, but only a minority worked the entire year. Most still work at part-time, low-paying jobs with no long-term job security or hope for advancement. Overall incomes among poor households increased through 2000, though the poverty rate dropped only slightly (Grogger and Karoly 2005; Slack et al. 2007). Since 2000, as economic growth has slowed down, TANF rolls have continued to shrink though the number of recipients working has also started to fall and poverty levels had risen slightly by 2007. Welfare reform seems to have moved many poor people away from dependence on the government, but it has neither substantially improved their overall well-being nor reduced the nation's poverty rate, which remains by far the highest among wealthy countries.

The American liberal welfare state has accepted entitlement to permanent benefits only for the elderly and the disabled. All other programs are means-tested, and the most important, TANF, is strictly limited in terms of how long people can use it and what they must do (work at whatever job is available) to get it. Social policy, both creating and reforming of programs, takes place in the United States only at times of unusual crisis or consensus: the Great Depression, the tumultuous 1960s, and the politically volatile 1990s. The decentralized American system, with its weak political parties, means that major changes occur only in such unusual circumstances. The American federal system also means that social policy on the ground, in terms of who benefits and by how much, varies greatly from state to state. The liberal welfare state tolerates much higher levels of poverty than other types of welfare states in exchange for encouraging participation in the workforce at whatever level of remuneration possible. In poorer countries like Brazil, the poor have long been left pretty much on their own to survive, or not, in the market. Only relatively recently have middle-income countries like Brazil began to think seriously about social policy to alleviate at least some of their extensive poverty.

CASE STUDY Brazil: Starting a Welfare State in a Developing Economy

At his first presidential inauguration in 2002, former metalworker Luiz "Lula" Inácio da Silva famously declared, "If, by the end of my term of office, every Brazilian has food to eat three times a day, I shall have fulfilled my mission in life" (Hall 2006, 690). Despite being the largest economy in South America and one of the largest in the world, Brazil continues to be home to great poverty and inequality. In the last two decades, however, the country first expanded its pension system for the elderly and more recently created means-tested programs that, while still quite small, represent a new and important effort to adopt distinct social policies aimed at alleviating poverty. As it industrializes, the country faces the same set of social policy options as wealthier states but does so with far fewer resources and less effective bureaucratic institutions to implement the policies. In this context, it is moving in the direction of creating a liberal welfare state focused primarily on means-tested programs in practice, in spite of lofty language in the constitution and recent legislation that suggests it will provide universal benefits.

For most of the country's history, Brazilian economic policy focused on achieving growth, the result of which was its becoming one of the most unequal societies in the world. Its populist tradition meant most assistance to the poor came from government or private in-kind contributions, such as food baskets. Populist politicians also helped the poor with programs like housing projects to gain political support. As in many countries, the first systematic government social policy focused on the elderly. The pension system implemented earlier in the twentieth century was expanded significantly after the adoption of the 1988 constitution institutionalizing democratic rule. Until the 1990s, the pension system covered a small percentage of the population: civil servants, whose pensions were paid for by the government, and formal sector private employees, whose pensions came from mandatory contributions. This left out the large share of the population that works in the informal sector: most agricultural workers and those in unofficial and quasi-legal small businesses that are not officially recognized and don't pay taxes. The new constitution established a right to a minimum income for all

A Brazilian family, recipients of the *Bolsa Família* program, watch President Lula on TV. The *Bolsa Família* program has become the largest social program of its kind in Latin America. Along with rapid economic growth under Lula, the program has helped moved millions out of poverty and reduced Brazil's high levels of inequality.

elderly people. In response, the government expanded the existing pension programs and created new ones for those not already covered. The major new policies are noncontributory and financed primarily via general taxation. One covers anyone over a certain age who can prove past employment in the agricultural sector. The other is means-tested, distributed to any elderly person in a household with a monthly income less than one-half the minimum wage. Both provide a set benefit equivalent to the national minimum wage. While slightly less than half the population contributes to the pension system, 90 percent of the elderly now receive benefits from the combined programs, an unusually high number for Latin America. The result has been a dramatic reduction, indeed a near elimination, of poverty among the elderly (Lavinas 2006, 110).

The biggest criticism of this pension system is its inequality. The contributory and civil service systems still constituted more than 90 percent of all benefits in 2002, and half of the recipients were in the top 10 percent of households in terms of wealth. The new systems have expanded rapidly, but they remain quite limited in terms of total resources, which is part of the reason why Lula's first and largest reform was to the pension system for civil servants. He and his advisers argued that the generous benefits went to mostly middle-class civil servants (a small proportion of the popu-

lation) and that reducing the program's cost would free up resources for social programs for the poor. He was eventually able to get the National Congress to pass a reform that increased the retirement age, required civil servants in the middle-income and above levels to contribute to their pension system, and reduced the generosity of the pensions. In the long run, it is predicted that this will save the government a great deal of money, but it has freed up very little immediate funding.

Lula's pledge to end hunger led to the creation of his signature program, *Bolsa Família* (Family Grant), early in his first term. The program consolidated and expanded several programs from the 1990s to provide food and cash grants through various channels. It targeted poor and "very poor" households in the exceptionally poor northeastern region, with those in the very poor group receiving larger grants. The largest single component of *Bolsa Família* is *Bolsa Escola* (School Grant), which provides grants to poor parents who guarantee they will send their children to school and utilize children's health services. Local social service councils were created to oversee implementation of the program, an attempt to reduce corrupt and political selection of recipient households. Anthony Hall (2006) reports that all of this has been successful where implemented, but the councils only function in two-thirds of municipalities. In the rest, the mayor's office is typically involved in recipient selection, with benefits often going to political supporters. Both the World Bank and the Inter-American Development Bank support *Bolsa Família*, providing about one-quarter of its funding. Overall, it has been relatively successful, reaching forty-four million people by 2006 and tripling the average benefit (Baer 2008, 402). The popular program was reportedly a major reason for Lula's strong electoral showing in his 2006 reelection, particularly in the northeastern region, where one-third of all families receive benefits.

Bolsa Família has become the largest social assistance program in Latin America and is clearly a major innovation in the development of the welfare state in that region and in developing countries in general. The World Bank and other international financial institutions (IFIs) have come to support means-tested and carefully targeted social programs, which they see as alleviating the poverty that continues in the region despite the implementation of neoliberal economic reforms. Indeed, in Brazil, *Bolsa Família* has helped reduced poverty and inequality significantly: from 2001 to 2006, the wealthiest 10 percent of the population saw its income increase by 7 percent, but the income of the poorest 10 percent increased by 58 percent. Critics, however, argue that far more expansive policies are needed, including the transferring of assets (especially land) to the poor and the provision of guaranteed and universal benefits. In fact, a leader of Lula's Workers' Party (PT), Eduardo Suplicy, led a successful effort to have Brazil's National Congress pass a law in January 2004 that provides a universal entitlement to a minimum income for all residents. The law, however, allows the government to implement it by focusing first on the neediest and includes no time limit by which the new right must actually be made real (Lavinas 2006).

Summary

Social policy emerged as countries industrialized and became relatively wealthy; poverty was no longer the norm. The continued presence of poor people became for many citizens an unacceptable outcome of the market economy that had provided wealth for the majority. For the poorest countries, such as Nigeria, poverty remains the norm and no real social policy exists. Middle-income countries like Brazil, however, are beginning to ask the same questions as citizens of wealthy countries: How can social policy help reduce poverty? In part because dependence on government support has implications for democratic citizenship, governments in wealthy countries have made different choices about how and how far to pursue poverty alleviation via government programs, creating distinct types of welfare states. Some mainly use universal entitlements to provide extensive and largely equal benefits to all, emphasizing values of equality, while others use means-testing to target assistance only at the poorest, reflecting values about the importance of ensuring as many people as possible are "making it on their own" in the market economy. All welfare states reflect such differences in values, as well as differences in moral assessments of those who require assistance. Our next area of government intervention, health care, is characterized by greater value consensus around the world about the importance of extensive government involvement, though exceptions do exist to this consensus, including the United States.

HEALTH CARE AND HEALTH POLICY

Much of the world has adopted the idea of health care as a social right of all citizens regardless of their position in the market. Wealthy countries have the resources to make market interventions in an attempt to realize this concept, but all countries except the very wealthiest lack the resources to make it a reality. A few countries, including the United States, do not embrace health as a social right, but nonetheless still claim the provision of the best health care possible to the largest number of people as a legitimate political and social goal.

Social values are not the only reason for policy intervention in health care markets, however. Market failure takes distinct forms in health care that are based on health care's unique nature. The key problems in the health care market are very high risk and poor consumer information, and both produce inefficiency and misallocation of resources. High risk is the biggest factor driving the dynamics of the health care market and government intervention in it. People will do almost anything—pay any price or undergo any procedure—to restore their health when it is seriously threatened. On the other hand, healthy people don't need much medical care beyond annual check-ups and preventative care. Demand for health care in a pure market is episodic: most individuals demand little health care except when sick, and then they demand a great deal. Those who lack the resources to pay for care when sick may face severe harm or even death. Insurance is the typical solution to high-risk markets. It spreads risks across many people so that the healthy help subsidize the sick and in turn are subsidized when they face illness. Paying smaller, regular premiums more or less fixes the cost for each individual in the insurance pool, so catastrophic illness does not mean catastrophic bills. This principle also is true of homeowner's or auto insurance. Government or private companies can provide insurance as long as a relatively large group of people with diverse risks pools its resources to cover the emergencies of each member when such emergencies arise.

Although insurance is a potential market-based solution to high risk, it creates its own potential market failure: **moral hazard**. Moral hazard occurs when someone does not bear the full consequences of his actions in a transaction, which gives him an incentive to overuse a beneficial resource. In health insurance, this results from the disconnect between paying a fixed premium for health care and the costs of the care itself. If insurance covers the full cost of the care, the individual has no incentive to economize its use because his costs (the insurance premium) will not change as a direct consequence of his greater use. Many insurance systems pay medical providers for each procedure, which gives providers an incentive to oversupply procedures just as the patient has an incentive to overuse them. The obvious results are excessive (and perhaps unnecessary) medical procedures and rising costs. Governments intervene in health care in part to attempt to limit the effects of the moral hazard inherent in an insurance system.

Another market failure, poor information, compounds the problem of overuse. Patients generally rely on medical professionals to know what procedures or drugs are needed to get well. Concerned about getting well, even most highly educated patients will readily agree to their doctor's recommended treatment, especially if they are insured and face relatively little direct cost. Transactions are unlikely to be efficient, because the lack of information compounds the likelihood of unnecessary procedures. In addition, a completely unregulated market with poor information can produce the iconic image of nineteenth-century American medical quackery, the "snake-oil salesman," a charlatan selling false remedies to desperate people. To avoid this, virtually all governments regulate both pharmaceuticals and medical practitioners.

Health Care Systems

Wealthy countries have developed three distinct types of health care systems to address the problems discussed above. These serve as models for poorer countries as well, though the latter are severely limited by lack of resources. The earliest and still most common system in wealthy countries is **national health insurance (NHI)**. In an NHI system, the government mandates that virtually all citizens must have insurance, and NHI countries typically allow and encourage multiple, private insurance providers while the government provides access to insurance to the self-employed or unemployed who do not have access via family members. Since the government mandates the insurance, it also regulates the system in some way, setting or at least limiting premiums and payments to medical providers. In many NHI systems access to health care is not specific to a particular employer, so workers can keep their insurance when they switch jobs. Germany pioneered this system in the late nineteenth century and continues to use it today, as do many other European countries and Japan. Few poor countries attempt to implement such a system because many of their citizens simply cannot afford insurance, although some do use a limited NHI system for wealthier segments of the population, such as civil servants or employees of large corporations.

A **national health system (NHS)** is the second most common type of health care system in wealthy countries and the most common type worldwide. NHS is a government-financed and -managed system that is frequently called a **single-payer system**. The government creates a system into which all citizens pay, either through a separate insurance payment (like Medicare in the United States, but for everyone) or via general taxation. The classic example of this type of system is the United Kingdom (UK), which established its NHS after World War II. In the UK and most NHS countries, the majority of medical professionals work directly for the government, which implicitly controls the cost of medical care via salaries as well as the provision of equipment and drugs. In some such systems, including Canada, the government runs a single-payer system but medical professionals work for private organizations or are self-employed and are paid for services by the government. Most poor countries have an NHS through which the government provides most medical care via hospitals and local clinics, and doctors are government employees. With limited resources, however, clinics and doctors are few, and many people lack access to or must wait long periods for what is often low-quality care.

The third system, a **market-based private insurance system**, is the least common. Although NHI and NHS countries typically permit some private insurance as a supplement for those who can afford it (and, indeed, it is usually the chief source of health care for the rich in resource-starved poor countries), the United States, Turkey, and Mexico are the only OECD countries that rely on private insurance for the bulk of their health care. In the United States, citizens typically gain insurance through their employment, and medical care is provided mostly by for-profit entities such as private clinics and hospitals and self-employed doctors. A variety of government programs might exist in market-based systems to cover specific groups without private insurance, such as the poor, noncitizens, the unemployed, and the self-employed. Market-based systems, though, do not guarantee access to health care to all citizens, and even in the wealthiest of these countries a noticeable minority lacks any insurance.

Common Problems

Almost all countries face a common set of problems regardless of the system they choose. The most evident of these are rising costs (especially in wealthy countries), access to care, and growing public health problems. In addition, as part of cost containment, all countries and systems make decisions about how to ration care: who will get it, when, and how much.

Wealthier countries are perhaps most concerned with cost, because health care costs tend to rise faster than those in other sectors of the economy as wealth increases. This is because wealthier people demand more and better care, and improved but often expensive technology emerges to help provide that care. Wealthier countries also have relatively low birth rates and high life expectancies, so the proportion of the population that is elderly increases over time and an older population incurs greater health care costs. A 2007 OECD study showed 2005 health expenditures in member countries varied from a high of 15.3 percent of GDP in the United States to a low of 6 percent in South Korea, with the average being 9 percent. From 1995 to 2005, health expenditures in OECD countries grew at an annual average of 4 percent, well above overall economic growth. People in almost all wealthy countries use more and more of their income for health care, regardless of the system in place.

Wealthy countries choose several means to try to control costs depending on their health care systems, though some methods can be used by any system. A key factor is the size of insurance pools. Larger and more diverse pools of people lower costs because a larger number of healthy people (especially young adults) cover the costs of those (often the elderly) who use health care more heavily, and this lowers premiums for everyone. NHS and NHI systems that group most or all of a country's citizens into one insurance pool gain a cost-saving advantage. In market-based systems, on the other hand, the risk pools are much smaller (usually the employees of a particular company) so costs tend to be higher. Governments in these countries spend less tax revenue on health care than in the other systems, but society as a whole may still spend more on health care overall via private insurance premiums and direct fees. The 2007 OECD study found, for instance, that the United States and Switzerland, the two countries with the lowest share of government expenditure on health, had the highest overall health costs as a share of GDP.

Other cost-saving measures focus on limiting the effects of moral hazard and can be used under any system. For example, paying doctors on a capitation, or per patient basis, rather than for each procedure prescribed, creates an incentive to limit unnecessary procedures. Critics, however, argue that this gives providers an incentive to underprescribe, which endangers patients' well-being. A second strategy, "gatekeepers," also may be used to limit patients' demands for expensive treatments. For example, such a system might require patients to consult their general practitioner before they consult a specialist, which may limit unnecessary visits to expensive specialists. Health Maintenance Organizations (HMOs) in the United States used both capitation and gatekeepers extensively in the 1990s to try to lower health care costs. A third approach is requiring patients to make copayments, small fees to cover part of the cost of each service used. Copayments change patients' incentives by making them pay more out-of-pocket rather than just having funds deducted automatically from their paycheck. If kept to moderate amounts, copayments can theoretically discourage unnecessary or frivolous procedures; if set too high, however, they may discourage poorer patients from getting medically necessary procedures.

There is clearly a potential trade-off between cost containment and achieving a healthy population. Meeting all demands for health care instantly might produce

COUNTRY AND CONCEPT Welfare, Health, and the Environment

Country	Welfare System	Social Spending (% of gov. expenditure)	Life Expectancy	Infant Mortality (deaths per 1,000 births)
Brazil	Liberal	—	72.5	26.7
China	Liberal welfare state emerging: social insurance for pensions and unemployment; means-tested programs for others in urban areas	—	73.2	7.9
Germany	Christian Democratic	56	79.1	4.0
India	Minimal: small means-tested programs, such as food subsidies and rural employment	—	69.2	32.3
Iran	Mixed: social insurance for retirees; state-funded means-tested programs; Islamic charity via *bonyards* (Islamic foundations)	—	70.9	36.9
Japan	Employment-based, with additional means-tested government programs	46	82.1	2.8
Nigeria	None	—	47.8	93.9
Russia	Social insurance for pensions; other benefits targeted to particular groups (in-kind until 2007, cash since)	—	65.9	10.8
United Kingdom	Liberal	48	78.8	4.9
United States	Liberal	43	78.1	6.3

Source: Social Expenditures data are from OECD. Health Care Spending: OECD and WHO data for most recent year available. See www. oecd.org/dataoecd/46/36/38979632.xls and www.who.int/whosis/data/Search.jsp?indicators=[Indicator].[HSR].Members. CO_2 Emissions data from World Resources Institute, using International Energy Agency (IEA) data. Original source is CO_2 *Emissions from Fuel Combustion (2006 edition).* Paris: IEA. Available at http://data.iea.org/ieastore/default.asp.

the healthiest population, but it would be prohibitively expensive and would aggravate moral hazards. No government ever does this; instead, all choose to ration health care in some way, though they may not perceive it as such. NHS countries can control costs most directly simply by limiting the overall health care budget, the salaries of medical providers, purchases of new equipment, or drug prices. The result can be relatively low-cost but sometimes limited care. The limits most typically take the form of patients waiting for certain procedures rather than getting them on demand. An NHS country must ration care by setting priorities on which services to provide more quickly and which, such as elective surgery, to delay. Waiting lines are longer in systems, including Britain's, that simply have fewer doctors per capita, another cost-saving measure. NHI countries can set insurance premiums and medical payments as well, but usually don't do so as universally as NHS countries, though Germany has experimented with greater regulation

Health Care System	Public Expenditure on Health (% of total expenditure on health)	Per Capita Total Expenditures on Health (int'l dollars, PPP)	Annual CO_2 Emissions (million metric tons of CO_2)	Global Share of CO_2 Emissions (%)
NHS, plus much private financing and some private insurance	44	755	311.5	1.2
NHI emerging, plus much private financing and some private insurance	39	315	3,958.41	13.7
NHI	77	3,250	844.75	3.4
NHS, plus much private insurance, direct financing, and NGO provision of health services	19	100	1,066.10	4.4
NHI	56	677	352.01	1.2
NHI	82	2,498	1,247.14	4.7
NHS, plus much private financing and NGO provision of health services	31	45	51.59	0.3
NHI	62	561	1,556.45	5.9
NHS	87	2,597	540.75	2.2
Market-based insurance	45	6,350	5,720.51	22.5

in recent years. Some countries, including the United States (the only wealthy country in this category), provide insurance only to a segment of the population, who thereby have access to fairly extensive care; those without insurance have very limited or no access to care.

The data in the Country and Concept table suggest that the form of rationing does not make a substantial difference among wealthy countries. Those with the lowest costs, such as Britain, do not have significantly lower health outcomes overall, measured in terms of key data such as infant mortality or life expectancy. For poorer countries, where the problem is not so much cost containment as it is the availability of minimally adequate resources, lower costs do seem related to lower-quality health. Access is a much greater problem than rising costs for the very poorest countries, where limited resources mean a much smaller number of doctors, hospitals, and clinics per capita. Even though individuals may be nominally covered by a government health plan, they simply cannot access health care if facilities and providers are not available, and the poorest countries cannot afford to expand their health care networks. While many have NHS systems, as the Country and Concept table demonstrates, most health care funding still comes from private financing, often direct payments to providers without even the benefit of insurance. As a result of limited access and costs too high for the poor majority, preventable and easily treatable diseases continue to shorten life spans and cause debilitation and loss of income and productivity in much of the world.

The third type of problem is public health concerns. These are common to all countries, but vary greatly between rich and poor. In the poorest countries access to enough food and clean water remain public health issues. Without access to clean water, diseases continue to plague much of the population, and significant numbers of people are malnourished, which further exacerbates the effects of the water-borne contagions as immune systems are weak and resistance consequently low. The health effects in terms of core indicators such as infant mortality and life expectancy are clear in the Country and Concept table: compare the data for wealthy countries such as the United States, UK, or Japan with poorer countries such as India or Nigeria.

The wealthiest countries face a different kind of malnutrition: obesity. The highest rates of obesity are found in the United States and Mexico and now include more than 30 percent of the population. Obesity rates are rising in almost all wealthy countries: food is relatively inexpensive compared to our incomes, so we overconsume it.

Other public health issues resulting from affluence—alcohol and tobacco consumption—have seen positive change recently. Rates of alcohol use in the OECD declined by 15 percent from 1980 to 2005, while rates of tobacco use declined by more than 20 percent from 1990 to 2004 (OECD 2007). Active public health education programs, along with legal limits on alcohol and tobacco consumption, reaped impressive results in many wealthy countries. Unfortunately, alcohol and tobacco consumption rates are increasing in many poorer countries, as their populations become wealthier and as alcohol and tobacco producers actively market in developing countries as their traditional markets shrink.

Lastly, globalization has produced a new set of public health concerns that cross borders as physical interaction among populations, including migration, increases. These include the expansion of sexually transmitted diseases (especially HIV/AIDS) and insect-borne diseases such as Lyme disease, West Nile virus, and malaria. Increased importation and exportation of products and international travel have also led to the global spread of such conditions as salmonella, foot-and-mouth disease, and SARS. Public health issues such as these lower overall well-being and raise health care costs. They are best dealt with via preventative measures such as education campaigns and infrastructural projects, including providing birth control measures and controlling insect populations, that are public goods, and which therefore, are inherently government responsibilities. With increasing globalization, what happens in one country increasingly affects others, meaning that the makers of health care policy in one country might be well advised to assist the citizens of other countries as well as their own.

IN CONTEXT Health Care in Wealthy Countries, 2005

Different health care systems in our case study countries have significant differences. Costs, in particular, vary dramatically, while outcomes are rather similar. Access to doctors, hospitals, and technology depends on how each country chooses to spend its health budget.

	Germany	United Kingdom	United States	OECD Average
Costs				
Health care expenditures per capita ($)	3,287	2,724	6,401	2,759
Health care expenditures per GDP (%)	10.7	8.3	15.3	9
Public share of total health expenditures (%)	77	87	45	73
Physicians' remuneration (ratio to GDP per capita)	3.7	3.8	4.4	—
Outcomes				
Life expectancy at birth (years)	79	79	77.8	78.6
Infant mortality rates (per 1,000)	3.9	5.1	6.8	5.4
Childhood measles vaccination rate	91.5	91.4	91.5	91.5
Access				
Practicing physicians (per 1,000 pop.)	3.4	2.4	2.4	3
Acute care hospital beds (per 1,000 pop.)	6.4	3.1	2.7	3.9
MRI units (per million pop.)	7.1	5.4	26.6	9.8
Wait time for nonemergency/elective surgery (% more than four months)*	6	41	8	—

Source: OECD 2007.
*2005 Commonwealth Fund International Health Policy Survey of Sicker Adults.

CASE STUDY Germany: Pioneer of Modern Health Policy

As noted earlier, Germany's Otto von Bismarck created the first modern, national health care system. He did so as part of his effort to use social policies to calm labor unrest and weaken worker sympathy for communist movements and demands for democracy. The 1883 Sickness Insurance Act created the world's first modern health insurance program, the basic system which Germany still uses today. Germany's NHI system is corporatist in both organization and management and relies heavily on professional and patient associations to implement it under the overall regulation of the state. It provides very generous benefits, including dental, hospital, and preventative care and even rehabilitative health spa treatments, primarily through a network of sickness funds financed by payroll taxes shared by employers and employees. Cost control has been a major issue (though less so than in the United States), which has resulted in a series of reforms introducing limits on overall costs and increased competition within the system. As the previous In Context feature shows, Germany has achieved average to above average health outcomes among wealthy countries, but it has done so at above average costs.

The sickness funds are nonprofit organizations run by boards of employers and employees. They are connected to employer, profession, or locale and are autonomous from the government in setting most of their policies and prices, though the services they must offer are uniform across the country. They negotiate services and payments with regional physician associations: doctors who wish to participate in the system, which is about 95 percent of them, must be members of their regional association and abide by the negotiated agreements. All but the wealthiest Germans must belong to a sickness fund; in this way, Germany has long achieved universal coverage. The unemployed must belong to a fund as well, the costs of which are covered by federal and local governments, and by law these individuals must receive the same benefits as all other members. The wealthiest individuals may opt out of the system and purchase private insurance, though about two-thirds of them choose to join a sickness

A patient pays his ten euro (about sixteen dollars) copay at a dentist's office in Bremen, Germany. While dental benefits have long been standard in Germany's NHI system, modest copays for many services have become a means of cutting down costs in recent years.

fund anyway. More than 90 percent of the population uses the sickness fund system. Residents can also purchase supplemental insurance to give them greater choice in where and how they are treated, and about 10 percent of members do so (Adolino and Blake 2001, 225; Green and Irvine 2001, 57).

Until 1997 employment status determined which fund a German belonged to. In that year a reform allowed Germans to choose their sickness fund and change it annually, introducing competition among funds. This reduced the number of sickness funds from 1,200 in 1985 to around 300 in 1998, as competition has pushed most out of the market (Green and Irvine 2001, 57). Nonetheless, German patients have exceptional levels of choice among sickness funds and, once they've selected a fund, among doctors. The German system has not traditionally had gatekeepers, and patients are free to go to any physician in any specialty. Some sickness funds have been allowed to experiment with using general practitioners as gatekeepers or creating networks of providers like HMOs in the United States, but few have done so.

Despite nearly universal coverage, equity has been a continuous concern, especially for the Social Democratic Party. Some sickness funds have unusually high numbers of poor and unhealthy members or are in unusually poor and unhealthy regions, meaning their members must pay more for care than members of funds with wealthier and healthier members or in wealthier and healthier regions. A 1992 reform attempted to resolve this by creating a compensation system through which money is transferred from wealthier sickness funds to poorer ones. As costs have risen in recent years, relatively young, healthy, and wealthy people have increasingly opted out of this system altogether, taking the lowest cost members out of the sickness funds, which raises premiums for everyone else. This becomes a particular burden in already poor funds. Reforms legislated in 2007 for the first time legally mandated that all citizens have insurance, but as mentioned, the wealthy can purchase private insurance instead of joining a sickness fund. The SDP argued for eliminating the option of purchasing private insurance to provide greater equity by forcing all citizens to join a sickness fund, but Chancellor Angela Merkel's Christian Democratic Party did not support the proposal.

Cost containment has long been a major issue in the German system. The key relationship in the system is between the sickness funds and the regional associations of physicians; these negotiate agreements on how the physicians will be paid. In the early twentieth century, physicians were paid on a capitation basis but a 1950s reform demanded by doctors allowed a shift to fee-for-service payments. This led to the first spurt of cost increases and the first major reform of the system in 1977, which established a classic corporatist solution: national negotiations among the sickness funds, physicians' associations, and the government to set targets for annual expenditure growth. The targets were tied to increases in wage levels so that, in theory, health care costs would rise with wages, not faster. Yet by 1986 players recognized that the negotiated targets were not adequately constraining costs, so a further reform introduced a cap on expenditures. Each year, sickness funds and physicians' associations negotiate a binding cap (with government intervention if they cannot agree) on cost increases tied to general wage increases of people in that sickness fund. Each sickness fund pays the physicians' association a lump sum based on the cap multiplied by the number of patients the association serves, giving the doctors an incentive to police their own expenditures. As a result of this plan, German health care costs rose much more slowly in the 1980s than those in many countries, including the United States. Reforms in 1989 and 1993 went further, extending the expenditure cap system from physicians to hospitals and pharmaceuticals, and doubling many patient copayments. The 1997 reform allowing patients to choose which sickness fund to join has created much greater competition, presumably lowering costs, as well as creating larger pools in each fund since the number of funds has dropped by three quarters in twenty years.

Despite these reforms, cost remains a major concern for Germans in the new century. An aging population and expensive technological innovations continue to increase the cost of health care. Germany's extraordinarily high number of doctors and hospital beds per capita (see the In Context above) give patients tremendous choice and little wait time for treatment, but they also cost a great deal. A reform in 2004 increased copayments again and shifted a greater share of total costs onto contributions from employers and employees. The government passed a more radical reform in 2007 that fundamentally changed the financing of health care to try to increase competition and improve equity. Rather than each sickness fund establishing its own rates for member premiums, the new system creates a single nationwide premium schedule tied to workers' incomes. The new national fund then distributes the premiums plus general tax revenue to sickness funds on a per capita basis, adjusting for the wealth and health of the membership of each fund. Individual sickness funds can give rebates to their members if they can provide services at a cost lower than what they receive from the national fund, or they charge members additional premiums if necessary, and this encourages efficiency as the funds compete for members.

Germans continue to debate two major issues in their health care system: equity and costs. Numerous reforms have tried to increase competition within the system to lower costs. The Christian Democratic government has put in place a system that partially decouples insurance premiums from local wages. The SDP, on the other hand, would like to incorporate the privately insured into the public system to gain their financial support as well as achieving greater equity.

The liberal Free Democratic Party, on the other hand, continues to argue for an even more radical shift to a market-based system.

Germany has long been a model of the NHI system, but one that continues to struggle with higher than average costs. Bismarck established it before physicians were a major political force in German politics, so they provided little effective opposition to the state intervening in their market. Decades later, as they became a political force of some influence, the system was modified to their benefit, putting pressure on costs. Reform efforts continue to work within the corporatist tradition and the German Christian Democratic welfare state, adjusting the regulation and organization of the major associations to try to improve outcomes with relative equity. Germany, like all wealthy countries, will continue to struggle with a health care sector that consumes an ever larger share of national income, though Germans have a system that achieves unusually high levels of care, coupled with widespread patient choice and universal coverage. This is in sharp contrast to the UK's NHS that controls costs quite effectively, but as the In Context above demonstrates, does so by forcing patients to wait longer for nonemergency surgery than in the United States or Germany.

CASE STUDY United Kingdom: Reforming the NHS

Like Germany, the United Kingdom is a pioneer of health care. It created the earliest and most universal NHS as part of the Beveridge Plan, written during World War II as a vision of a more egalitarian postwar society. The NHS was based on four key principles: health services would be universal, comprehensive, free to the patient, and financed by general tax revenue. With minor exceptions, the NHS has worked that way ever since, though both Conservative and Labour governments have made significant reforms in the last twenty years. Again, Britain achieves health outcomes that are about average for wealthy countries at lower than average costs. As the In Context shows, this is achieved in part by having fewer doctors and less technology, and most important, by rationing nonemergency care via long waits.

The NHS traditionally functioned like one giant managed care system: it signed contracts with general practitioners (GPs) in each region of the country to deliver primary services to patients. Each region served as one giant insurance pool, with about half a million patients in each. And GPs still are paid on a combination of fee-for-service and capitation basis as originally established, while British patients still sign up with the GP of their choice, usually in their neighborhood, who provides basic care and functions as a gatekeeper, referring them to a specialist or hospital as needed. The NHS regional and district health authorities still receive national government revenue to provide hospital and specialist services, and most services (except for some pharmaceuticals) are free to the patient at the point of service, having been paid for by general taxes. Waiting times for seeing GPs are very low, but waiting times for specialists and nonemergency hospital stays are among the world's highest.

No one can opt out of the NHS, but patients can purchase private supplemental insurance that allows them to see private doctors and get hospital services without the long waits of the NHS. As Britons have grown wealthier and, like citizens in all wealthy countries, have demanded more health care, a growing number supplement NHS coverage with private insurance. Patients can go back and forth between the two, using the NHS for routine illnesses and private insurance for procedures that have long waiting lines in the NHS system or for elective procedures.

Britain alone among the wealthy countries has not had its health policy driven by an overriding concern with rising costs since the 1980s. The NHS allows the national government to control costs directly: it simply sets the annual overall budget, thereby limiting the system to a certain expenditure level. Through the 1990s, this resulted in Britain spending far less than most wealthy countries on health care: in the mid-1990s it spent barely half what the United States did as a share of its GDP. It also had significantly fewer doctors and hospital beds per capita. As part of reform efforts to improve the system, the Labour government pledged in 2000 to significantly increase health care spending, resulting in Britain partially closing the gap in terms of money spent and doctors available, as reflected in the previous In Context table. Despite its ability to control costs, health care reform has been a major political issue since the 1980s. The NHS has always been and remains very popular with British citizens, but there are those unhappy with the long wait times for certain procedures and lower quality care, both byproducts of cost control structures.

The NHS as originally structured had no internal incentives for efficiency. The Conservative government under Margaret Thatcher in the 1980s initiated a debate and a major study about how to reform the system to improve efficiency. The result was a reform plan in 1990 that introduced elements of competition within the NHS. The idea was never popular, but Thatcher used her majority in Britain's parliamentary system to pass the reform anyway. The reform created large purchasers and sellers of health care. GPs with large practices (five thousand patients or more) were given their own budget by the NHS that they used to purchase specialist and hospital services for their patients.

The UK's low number of doctors and hospital beds per the general population translate into long wait times and delayed procedures. In an attempt to reduce this gap and improve care availability, Britain recently gave Stephen Inns (shown) and fewer than one hundred other pharmacists permission to prescribe drugs for patients and provide basic care without relying on a doctor. The move is part of the country's attempt to expand its health system by allowing medical professionals like nurses and pharmacists to treat patients.

Those who negotiated better deals would be likely to get more patients and earn more money. Similarly, hospitals gained the ability to manage their own affairs. Rather than being run by the regional health authorities, hospitals would sell their services to GPs and to the regional health authorities. Hospitals were still public entities but could increase their revenue by providing the best services at the lowest cost.

The results of this bold experiment were mixed. Wait times did drop and there were signs of improved efficiency, but the benefits mainly went to patients of the GPs with the largest practices in the wealthiest areas. The Conservative government also kept overall funding low, so improvements in wait times and quality of care in general were not dramatic. Indeed, unhappiness with the state of the NHS was one reason the Labour Party under Tony Blair swept into office in 1997.

Labour campaigned on a platform of reversing the market-based incentives that the 1990 reform had introduced into the NHS. In reality, in a series of reforms starting in 2000, the Labour government modified rather than eliminated the new system. The main reform was to group physicians into regional associations that would purchase services for patients. This kept an element of competition but eliminated the different deals GPs in the same area provided their patients. By 2005 three hundred GP associations managed 75 percent of the NHS's total spending. The Blair government also

pledged to significantly increase funding to hire more doctors (many of whom came from other countries) and reduce wait times in hospitals. Finally, the reforms introduced new regional authorities to assess the quality of each hospital. Higher quality hospitals were given greater operational freedom and financial bonuses. The Labour government ultimately embraced the Conservative idea of managed competition within the NHS but reformed it to achieve more egalitarian benefits, greater overall funding, and incentives to improve not just efficiency but quality of services.

In contrast to corporatist and federal Germany, Britain's NHS produced a unitary and centralized system of health care. The NHS, one of the world's largest bureaucracies, has always been one of the country's most popular government programs. It has allowed the government to keep costs under control but has done so at the expense of quality and timeliness of service, or so its critics claim. Britain's parliamentary system has allowed recent governments of both parties to enact significant reforms more easily than either Germany or the United States. These reforms have focused on reorganization to encourage improved efficiency and quality of service. The Labour government coupled this with sharply increased spending in the new century to provide Britons with health care quality closer to that of other European countries. The United States, in contrast, remains the only wealthy system in the world with a primarily private health system that, as the In Context above shows, achieves slightly below average outcomes at much higher than average costs.

CASE STUDY U.S. Health Policy: Trials and Tribulations of the Market Model

The United States spends more on health care—both as a dollar amount and as a share of its total economy—than any other country in the world. The data above suggest these large expenditures produce health outcomes comparable to, albeit slightly below, those in other wealthy countries. The United States possesses considerably more medical technology than most countries as the data on MRIs implies, but this has not translated into better relative health. Costs have led to the term "crisis" being associated with United States health care policy at least since the early 1970s, yet

government policy has been slow to change. Since the inception of the private insurance system in the mid-twentieth century, proposals have existed for creating a national, universal system similar to those in each of the other wealthy countries but have never been enacted, probably due to Americans' general aversion to government intervention and the political system's openness to influence by lobbying groups.

The first major effort at a national mandate for insurance occurred in the 1950s and the most recent in the early 1990s, with several in between, but none has ever become law. Most health insurance in the United States is tied to employment. This is similar to Germany and other systems, but unlike most, the United States does not mandate insurance. Today, more than 60 percent of the population is covered by employment-based private insurance, with another 25 percent or so covered by government programs for particular categories of people. The remaining 15 percent or so have no health insurance and rely on their own resources or free care from mobile clinics, community outreach programs, or hospital emergency rooms, which are required by law to provide aid to anyone who walks in, though many do not. The uninsured have very limited access to care. Most are near poverty but are not recipients of official welfare funds, work part-time jobs that do not provide insurance benefits, or are self-employed.

The American private insurance system became widespread during World War II, when wage freezes prevented employers from luring employees with higher wages; instead, they competed by offering more generous health benefits. After the war, the government encouraged this system via tax incentives: health benefits are not taxable income. The system gives advantages to large employers and their employees because each employer negotiates insurance rates as a company; larger companies create bigger risk pools and therefore can get lower premiums and better coverage. The authors of this textbook, for instance, had the best health coverage of their lives when they were very low paid teaching assistants in graduate school: their salaries were low, but because they taught at a state university they were state employees receiving the generous benefits a very large employer (the entire state government) provided. Now, they have much higher salaries teaching at a small liberal arts college but not nearly as generous health benefits from an employer of only about five hundred employees.

Extensive government health programs only began in 1965 with the creation of Medicare and Medicaid. Medicare provides health insurance to retirees who receive Social Security (the disabled were later added as recipients as well), and Medicaid is a means-tested program that provides coverage to most recipients of the country's primary social program (now TANF). In 1997 the State Children's Health Insurance Program

Health maintenance organizations (HMOs) expanded rapidly in the 1990s. Employers, the main purchasers of health care in the American system, switched to HMOs in large numbers to try to control costs, and cost increases were reduced for a few years, but restrictions on care caused protests like the one shown here in California in 2000. Costs began increasing rapidly again in the new millennium, returning health care to the national agenda in the 2008 presidential campaign.

(SCHIP) was created to provide insurance for poor or low-income children. The combination of SCHIP and an expansion of Medicaid coverage reduced the percentage of low-income, uninsured children from 22.3 percent in 1997 to 14.9 percent in 2005 (CBO 2007, 8). President George W. Bush vetoed legislation in 2007 that would have expanded the popular SCHIP to cover more of the nation's children, arguing that it created too much government involvement in health care. Overall, even in America's largely private system, government spending on health is more than 40 percent of total health spending (though that remains the second lowest level in the OECD), largely due to the expensive Medicare program for the elderly, who utilize more health care products and services than other groups. Both Medicaid and SCHIP, like most social policies in the United States, are implemented by individual states, which have some flexibility in the funding and services they provide. Because of this, the levels of benefits vary widely from state to state.

Health costs became a serious political issue in the 1970s, but it was in the 1980s that costs rose at alarming rates, reaching an annual inflation rate of nearly 20 percent by the end of that decade. This led even large corporations to start demanding some type of intervention to bring costs under control, and health care reform became a major issue in the 1992 presidential campaign. After his election, President Bill Clinton appointed his wife, Hillary Clinton, to lead a task force to propose a major reform to the system. By late 1993, the result was a plan that focused on "managed competition." This plan would have set up funds similar to Germany's sickness funds across the country and encouraged them to compete for clients among employers. Coverage would be mandatory and could travel with the employee from one job to the next, and those not employed would be covered by various federal programs and still be part of the funds. A year of raucous debate, however, produced no reform, though the SCHIP did emerge three years later out of the debacle.

Judith Feder and Donald Moran (2007) argue that until political leaders accept the fact that universal coverage combined with cost containment will require limits on the already insured, no fundamental reform will be possible. In the meantime, and in absence of national policy reform, employers (the primary purchasers of insurance packages) began reforming the existing system to lower costs via a large and rapid switch from fee-for-service insurance to HMOs and related groups that try to hold costs down by capitation and gatekeeper rules. The share of privately insured Americans in fee-for-service plans dropped from 70 percent in 1988 to 14 percent in 1998. As a result annual cost increases dropped from 18 percent in 1990 to less than 4 percent by 1996, removing health care costs from significant political concern for a time as the country entered the new millennium (Graig 1999, 22–35).

The ability of managed care to keep costs under control seems to be limited, however; while costs as a share of GDP actually shrank slightly from 1993 to 1998, from 13.7 to 13.5 percent, they have since risen again. In 2006 health care constituted 16 percent of the economy and this number is projected to reach 20 percent by 2015 if no significant reforms take place. By the 2008 presidential election, rising costs had once again put health care on the national political agenda. The major Democratic candidates proposed enhanced government programs to better cover the uninsured, even as Republican candidates put forth plans that favored market-based solutions such as the Health Savings Account, a system in which patients would have insurance primarily for catastrophic expenses and would set aside money for day-to-day health care in a tax-free savings account, paying those costs themselves.

Summary

The American political system's openness and weak parties have made significant health care reform difficult. Members of President Clinton's own party proposed several different reforms to challenge the president's, including a proposal for a single-payer NHS. Republicans opposed any significant expansion of the government's role, and the insurance industry lobbied Congress hard to resist major reforms as it launched a massive national media campaign against Clinton's proposal, branding it "socialized medicine." Many analysts point to American political culture as an explanation for why the country still has no universal health care system: Americans generally distrust "big government" and anything that can be labeled "socialist," making major government interventions in the economy relatively rare. Employer-based health insurance emerged as an industry initiative in the labor market during World War II, and the most recent significant reform, the shift to managed care plans, also came out of the private sector. Aside from the creation of Medicare and Medicaid in the 1960s, government reform efforts essentially have come to naught. Medicare, Medicaid, and SCHIP have expanded coverage, though they have not achieved the universal coverage found in most wealthy countries, and these programs have done little to rein in costs, which continue to be the highest in the world and are growing rapidly.

Summary

Like social policy, distinct health care models have arisen in wealthy countries, providing different levels of government involvement in trying to ensure all citizens have access to adequate health care. No society can afford to provide every type of care instantly to everyone who demands it. Within this limit, the "bottom line" of any health care system is, presumably, to produce the healthiest possible population at the lowest possible cost. Based on this formula, both NHI and NHS systems seem to fare better than purely market-based ones, probably because of the unique aspects of the health care market we discussed above. All wealthy countries, though, face a common set of problems, regardless of what type of system they have: rising costs due to an aging population and demand for more and better care, perverse incentives for both consumers and producers of health care that make it difficult to find ways to maximize efficiency, and growing public health problems associated with wealth such as obesity and heart disease. Poor countries are in a starkly different situation: their biggest problems are lack of resources for health care of whatever type and the presence of massive public health problems associated with poverty, such as high infant mortality and preventable communicable diseases such as measles. Some of these public health problems arise from environmental problems, a subject to which we now turn.

ENVIRONMENTAL PROBLEMS AND POLICY

Global warming (climate change) is only the latest and largest environmental problem confronting governments around the world. The modern environmental movement and environmental policies developed in the 1960s and 1970s, though some environmental concerns, especially preservation of natural spaces, are much older. Environmental issues became a significant policy issue later than either health care or welfare, perhaps in part because the environment, in contrast to the other two, is a classic postmaterialist concern. Environmental preservation tends to become a more widespread social value as wealth rises and other material interests are met. Early industrializers in Europe and the United States weren't too concerned about environmental degradation until the 1960s, when people began to look at the effects of long-term pollution from the new context of economic security. Today, increasing wealth and security in some more recently industrialized countries also seems to be stimulating interest in clean air, water, and other environmental concerns. Globalization simply has added a new dimension to the problem.

Environmental damage is also an exceptionally clear case of market failure in the form of externalities. No form of pollution is without cost. When a factory pollutes a river with sewage, people downstream get sick and need costly health care while fish and other aquatic life die, raising the cost of fishing and reducing ecosystem diversity, further destabilizing the river and surrounding area. Vehicle exhaust produces cancer-causing smog that results in the need for millions of dollars of health care annually, and most people consider clean air and water beneficial, so they pay an implicit cost any time it is fouled. Polluters rarely pay the cost of their own pollution: whatever is produced costs less than it would if its true cost was internalized in the production process. The market will therefore devote more resources to that undervalued product than it ought, creating inefficiency. Meanwhile, other people bear the costs of the pollution produced.

Many environmental goods are inherently public and often free. Unregulated use of free goods like air, water, or public land can lead to the **tragedy of the commons**. This is an old idea: if free public grazing land exists in a farming area, all farmers will use it to graze their herds and none will have an incentive to preserve it for future use; collectively, they will likely overgraze the land and destroy it so that they all lose out in the end. In wealthy industrial countries, a more current example is clean air, a completely "common" good we all breathe and pollute. Without a collective effort to limit use and abuse, no individual has the incentive or ability to preserve it, so it's likely to be overused and perhaps ultimately depleted. The free market grossly undervalues (at zero cost) a valuable public good.

National governments have been grappling with market interventions to compensate for environmental externalities, trying to avoid the tragedy of the commons, for most of the past century. Recently, globalization has raised new, international challenges in this process. Globalization has spread not only industrialization but also environmental damage. Industrialization always increases the pollution of previously agrarian societies. In addition, many observers also fear that the dynamics of global competition will produce a "race to the bottom," as countries use lax environmental rules to attract foreign capital. Many argue that wealthy countries are not only outsourcing factories and jobs but pollution as well. The quality of the air and water around Pittsburgh has dramatically improved as the city's steel industry has declined, while China, now the world's largest steel producer, faces a rapidly growing pollution problem. Opponents of this race to the bottom thesis argue that as globalization helps produce wealth it will help lower pollution because, as described above, wealth and environmental concern seem to increase in tandem. Whichever argument proves to be more accurate in the long term, it's clear that the countries rapidly industrializing now also face dramatically expanding environmental problems. This is clearest in Asia, as our case study of China shows.

Also tied to globalization are what many term "third generation" environmental problems of a new type: these problems are global and therefore require global responses. Air and water pollution have always crossed borders, but this new type of concern is distinct: the source of the pollution matters little because the effects are truly global. The major example is global climate change. The mining and burning of fossil fuels—full of previously trapped carbon—has pumped excess carbon into the atmosphere. Virtually all scientists now agree that this has increased the entire planet's ambient temperature by an estimated 0.7 degrees centigrade (1.3 degrees Fahrenheit) since the dawn of the industrialization age in the nineteenth century, and the pace is accelerating. The 2007 United Nations Human Development Report (UNHDR) focused on climate change, recommending that the world endeavor to keep the temperature increase in the twenty-first century to no more than two degrees centigrade. Current projections, if no changes are made, go as high as a five-degree centigrade rise. This may not sound like much, especially if you live where the winters are long and cold, but it is greater than the change from the last ice age to our present climate. The effects would be catastrophic in terms of rising sea levels flooding coastal areas around the world and severe drought, especially in the tropics, which are already relatively poor areas even without the loss of current available resources that drought and flooding would bring.

Developing countries have long struggled to achieve **sustainable development**: economic development that can continue over the long term. Development always involves increased use of resources, but if nonrenewable resources are being used quickly, the development won't be sustainable. As demand for food and land increases, for instance, farmers and ranchers clear forested areas throughout the tropics. This gives them nutrient-rich soil on which to grow crops and graze cattle, as well as valuable wood to sell on the global market, but tropical rainforest soils are thin and are quickly depleted when put to agricultural use. After a few years, new land must be cleared as the old is exhausted. The result is rapidly disappearing forests and development that is unsustainable in the long run. Deforestation also increases global warming because trees absorb and retain carbon. Farmers' and ranchers' rational response to growing global demand for agricultural products, then, has created unsustainable development in the countries in question as well as global warming. Globalization-induced pollution of air and water and rapid use of nonrenewable resources make the goal of sustainable development ever more challenging for many poor countries.

Most analysts agree that environmental damage is an externality that must be addressed, but a vociferous debate thrives on the uncertainty nearly always present in these types of issues. Scientists can rarely tell us exactly what a particular form or amount of pollution will do. Like health problems, the best we can do is predict likely outcomes. The top climate scientists in the world won the Nobel Peace Prize for their 2007 Intergovernmental Panel on Climate Change Report, but even their most certain predictions were termed "very likely" (90 percent certainty) or "likely" (66 percent certainty) outcomes of climate change. Similarly, we know that air pollution causes lung cancer but we can't predict with absolute certainty how many cases it will cause, let alone which individuals will be affected. Environmental policy everywhere has to be based on **risk assessment** and **risk management**. Risk assessment tells us what the risks of damaging outcomes are, and risk management is policy used to keep those risks to acceptable levels. The costs of reducing risks must be weighed against the potential (but always uncertain) benefits.

Much of the debate, of course, is over what level of risk is "acceptable." In recent years, the European Union (EU) and its member states have employed the **precautionary principle**, which emphasizes risk avoidance even when the science predicting the risk is uncertain. This principle lies behind the EU ban on genetically modified organisms (GMOs) in food. With limited scientific evidence on whether GMOs are harmful or benign, the EU errs on the side of caution, banning them until the science is clarified. The United States, especially under the administration of George W. Bush, erred more toward reducing the costs of environmental fixes: the United States currently allows extensive use of GMOs in the absence of greater scientific evidence of harm.

How do governments respond when they decide that environmental damage is an unacceptable risk? Several approaches exist. The oldest is known as **command and control policies**, which involve government regulation. These were the first type of policies most wealthy countries enacted in the 1970s. Based on assessments of health and other risks, a government simply sets a level of pollution no one can surpass. Businesses must reduce production or find ways to produce the same goods with less pollution. At least in the short term, this is likely to raise production costs, partially internalizing the costs of pollution control. Command and control policies require governments to set very specific limits on many pollutants from many sources and to inspect possible polluters to ensure they are following the regulations. Both of these tasks are expensive, leading many analysts to argue for what they see as more efficient means of pollution control in the form of incentive systems.

The best known incentive system is the **cap and trade system**, in which a government sets an overall limit on how much of a pollutant is acceptable from an entire industry and issues vouchers to each company that gives it the right to a certain number of units of pollution. The individual companies are then free to trade these vouchers. Companies that face high costs to reduce their pollution levels will be interested in buying additional pollution rights, while those who can more cheaply invest in new and cleaner technology will sell their rights. In theory, pollution is reduced in the most efficient way possible and at the least cost. Government agencies must still determine the overall cap on pollution, but the market allocates that pollution.

Critics point out that cap and trade can result in high levels of pollution at particular sources: if you live down river from the factory that purchased a large number of pollution rights, your water will be particularly polluted, while the water in other locations serving other populations gets cleaner. This problem can be corrected by setting a maximum allowable level of pollution rights for any single source, limiting the market in pollution rights to ensure people in particular spots do not pay the costs for the rest of the country's cleaner air and water. Simply taxing pollution directly is another way to provide an incentive to reduce it without dictating specific levels from specific sources. Both cap and trade and taxation systems require the government to set an overall cap or tax at a level that will reduce pollution by the desired amount. While perhaps less complicated than specifying pollution levels from each source, it is still a complex and uncertain task.

Tax or cap and trade systems attempt to set a direct cost on pollution, forcing polluters to internalize an externality. A similar goal is embedded in policies to control use of what otherwise could be free goods such as public land and the minerals under them to avoid the tragedy of the commons. User fees on public land exist to limit use of it for ranching and other activities so that the overuse inherent in free public goods does not occur. Similarly, governments can charge for access to minerals, including oil, under public lands. Given that minerals and fossil fuels are nonrenewable, their depletion contains an intergenerational externality: future generations will pay the price of finding alternatives to the finite resources current generations use. Many economists argue that this justifies government intervention to tax mineral extraction, raising the internal cost of their production. In practice, many governments, including that of the United States, pursue exactly the opposite strategy, subsidizing mineral exploration and development in order to maximize production and lower consumer costs in the present. Cheaper minerals and fuels spur economic growth, which all legitimate states strive to achieve. Oil production, in particular, is also seen as a matter of national security, as each state tries to reduce its dependence on other states for this most crucial of commodities. These policies, however, encourage rather than discourage the tragedy of the commons in nonrenewable resources.

The complexity of environmental regulation is magnified at the international level but the policy options are similar. Global warming became a well-known concern in the 1980s, but the first significant international effort to respond to it was signed at the major international environmental conference in Rio de Janeiro in 1992, and this was only a voluntary agreement for countries to adopt goals of reducing their carbon output. Growing scientific consensus and continued negotiations led to the signing of the Kyoto Protocol in 1997, which included mandated targets for developed countries: they would reduce their carbon emissions by an average of 5 percent below their 1990 levels by 2012. The protocol left each country to determine how it would meet the targets. The vast majority of the nations of the world signed the protocol, but full implementation required several additional agreements, and it came into force only in 2005. U.S. president Bill Clinton signed it but never submitted it to the Senate for ratification, knowing it would fail. His successor, President George W. Bush, repudiated it entirely. While it is now in effect, having gained the acquiescence of more than 140 countries, without the participation of the United States—the second largest producer of greenhouse gases after China—it is likely to have limited effect.

Most of the controversy around Kyoto is the differential treatment of developed and developing countries. The wealthy industrialized countries have been producing significant amounts of greenhouse gases since industrialization began two centuries ago. Because these gases do not dissipate, the wealthy countries have produced the vast majority of the total greenhouse gases to date. The United States alone is estimated to account for nearly 30 percent of the total since 1840 (UNDP 2007, 40). The large, rapidly industrializing countries, however, are quickly catching up in terms of their annual output of greenhouse gases: China overtook the United States as the single largest contributor in 2007, beating forecasts that it would achieve this dubious distinction by 2012. Still, the developing countries, led by China, argue that the wealthier countries will long remain the main source of the total excess carbon in the atmosphere and can afford the costs of reducing their emissions. Moreover, denying countries now industrializing the right to pollute will doom them to inferior status forever, and the wealthy countries remain by far the heaviest emitters of greenhouse gases per capita: China and India produce a lot because they have so many people, but each Chinese or Indian citizen produces a small fraction of what the average American does. The developed countries, especially the United States, argue that mandatory limits must apply to all to be fair and effective. They argue that all nations that contribute to global climate change must adopt mandatory limits. Inarguably, someone must pay the costs of this ultimate externality of industrialization; the political and normative debates are over who it will and should be.

The Kyoto Protocol does not specify how countries should reach their targets. The United National Development Programme (UNDP) 2007 report on climate change attempted to push the debate forward by suggesting that the world adopt a carbon tax or a cap and trade system to reduce emissions. The EU has already instituted its own international cap and trade system that allows European companies to continue emitting large quantities of greenhouse gases if they instead invest in reducing emissions elsewhere in the world. Because many factories in the developed world use older technology, it's cheaper to reduce emissions in developing areas than in Europe. Given that global climate change is just that—global—it doesn't matter where emissions are reduced as long as they are. The EU system has been criticized for adopting caps that are too high, allowing a windfall profit to certain European companies without substantially reducing overall emissions. The UNDP, however, endorses the basic principle of creating a global incentive system to reduce emissions. A cap and trade system would allow this to occur where it is most efficient.

Of the three policy areas we discuss in this chapter, the environment is the easiest area in which to justify government intervention in markets. Environmental damage is clearly an externality that should be internalized for efficient allocation of resources and long-term sustainability across societies. This has become particularly clear and urgent in the face of global climate change, which threatens to wreak havoc on the lives of millions in the relatively near future. A number of clear policy choices exist as well. Their implementation, however, has been limited and slow. Different policies internalize costs in different ways, often resulting in different people paying those costs. Both within individual countries and on a global scale, individual polluters and national governments strive to minimize the costs they will have to pay. Our three case studies of three large countries who are major polluters—the United States, China, and Nigeria—illustrate the debates well.

CASE STUDY The United States: Pioneer that Lost Its Way?

April 22, 1970, the first Earth Day, marked the coming of age of the environmental movement in the United States. The now annual event emerged out of the fervor of the 1960s and represented a strikingly broad consensus in the country: environmental problems were important and the government should do something about them. From 1965 to 1970 the number of people saying the quality of their air and water was a serious issue went from less than a third of the population to nearly three quarters; in May 1969 only 1 percent of people mentioned pollution as one of the "most important" problems facing the country, but by May 1971 that number had risen to 25 percent (Layzer 2006, 33). A decade of rapid expansion of the government's role in protecting the environment began, making the United States a pioneer in this field. The decentralized U.S. political system and shifting ideological trends in the country, however, meant that further progress was mixed. By the new century, the U.S. government stood nearly completely alone in its opposition to the Kyoto Protocol. The United States had gone from pioneer of environmental policy to the chief opponent of the biggest environmental legislation of the new century.

The major U.S. environmental policy that pre-dates 1970 was the protection of public lands for recreational and ecological purposes, starting with the national park system in the early 1900s under Theodore Roosevelt and continuing through the creation of pristine wilderness areas where no development is allowed, starting in 1964. The landmark legislation of the early 1970s included the creation of the Environmental Protection Agency (EPA), the Clean Air Act (1970), the Clean Water Act (1972), and the Endangered Species Act (1973). The decade ended with legislation dramatically expanding protected land, with the addition of 102 million acres in Alaska. These were all command and control policies, setting specific regulations for allowable levels of pollution from individual sources and protecting specific species and plots of land. Coming from a broad bipartisan consensus, they established the United States as a pioneer in environmental protection, generally seen as well ahead of most European countries.

Former U.S. vice president Al Gore at the premier of his movie, *An Inconvenient Truth,* in Hong Kong. Gore and the Intergovernmental Panel on Climate Change (IPCC) jointly won the Nobel Peace Prize for their advocacy of solutions to global climate change, including the Kyoto Protocol which the United States refused to ratify.

Ronald Reagan's election as president in 1980 began a reversal of this environmental trend. Reagan's neoliberal economic ideology of small government led him to argue for a reduced government role in the environment. With environmental protection still relatively popular, he did not try to reverse the legislation of the 1970s; instead, he significantly reduced funding to the EPA and other environmental agencies and appointed opponents of government intervention to key environmental posts who rewrote regulations to reduce their impact on business. By mid-decade, Congress began resisting some of these policies. The most significant congressional reversal was the Superfund Act (1986), which requires that thousands of toxic waste sites be cleaned up over several decades. Ironically, Reagan's open opposition to environmental protection seemed to strengthen the environmental movement in civil society, leading to growing concern about the environment by the end of the decade. One result was a major amendment to the Clean Air Act in 1990, which for the first time included a cap and trade system focused on one particular pollutant: sulfur dioxide, a key ingredient in acid rain. The cap and trade system has significantly reduced this pollutant nationwide, at an estimated cost only half of what a similar reduction under the older command and control model would have incurred (Freeman 2006, 206).

The 1980s also saw the emergence of a new element in U.S. environmental history in the form of the **environmental justice movement.** It began in 1982, in Warren County, the poorest county in North Carolina, in which 65 percent of residents were African American at the time (three times the state average). Buoyed by EPA approval, a waste disposal company proposed locating a toxic waste facility in the county. The poor residents organized demonstrations once they got wind of the idea, and the environmental justice movement began. Focused on environmental damage in particular locales, members initially argued that poor and, especially, black or Hispanic neighborhoods are much more likely to be sites for polluting industries and toxic waste depositories. The movement has grown significantly since, setting out a clear set of principles at a major conference in 1991. While research results depend on how the researchers define "neighborhood" or "community," it seems that across the United States black and Hispanic citizens are more likely to live in areas where air and water pollution exceed legal limits and toxic chemicals are produced or stored (Ringquist 2006).

Bill Clinton's election in 1992 with noted environmentalist Al Gore as his vice president gave environmental advocates hope that the policies of the Reagan/Bush years of the 1980s would be reversed. By the end of the decade, however, environmentalists had mixed assessments of the Clinton administration, noting some significant successes but also major failings; overall, they were disappointed relative to their expectations at the outset. A key issue was global warming. Both Republican and Democratic presidents had agreed to voluntary reductions in greenhouse gas emissions, but continued to resist mandatory targets, including the Kyoto Protocol. President George W. Bush repudiated the treaty entirely and pursued an energy policy that provided greater incentives for fossil fuel exploration and development. The United States is estimated to spend about $100 billion per year—half the world's total—on fossil fuel subsidies, encouraging rapid use and therefore depletion of these nonrenewable resources, and more global climate change (Hempel 2006, 305).

The country remains the only major country not to give final approval to Kyoto.

Despite what environmentalists see as setbacks, U.S. policy has produced a much cleaner environment. The greatest success has been in air pollution. Between 1970 and 2003, production of the six key ingredients in air pollution dropped by 51 percent in spite of significant population growth and even greater economic growth. The only exceptions were a slight increase in nitrous oxide (a secondary ingredient in acid rain) and carbon dioxide, the key greenhouse gas. Surveys of water quality at the turn of the century indicated that 61 percent of rivers and 55 percent of lakes met acceptable standards for clean water, though destruction of wetlands by development continues at about fifty-eight thousand acres per year. By 2004 the Superfund Act had cleaned up, or was in the process of cleaning up, 61 percent of the "National Priorities" list of toxic waste sites (Kraft and Vig 2006, 21–24).

Environmental success in the United States seems to require a broad popular consensus. The American political system provides numerous opportunities for interest groups to influence policymaking. The nature of Congress, especially the Senate, makes it particularly easy for groups to get legislation vetoed. Rational choice scholars have noted that environmental legislation often provides diffuse benefits to many people and high costs for a few (typically businesses), and the latter are often able and highly motivated to block such legislation. Environmental legislation succeeds only at times of generally high concern among the broader public that leads legislators to override the veto efforts of a few key players. As a result, U.S. policy has a "stop and go" character, with occasional great advances followed by periods of reversal or stagnation. Some legislation, such as fossil fuels subsidies, work in reverse: they provide huge benefits to particular actors and diffuse costs (via taxes to pay the subsidies) to the general population. These types of policies have endured in the U.S. system despite what most economists see as their clear encouragement of externalities and therefore inefficiency and environmental damage. The U.S. political system produced both the pioneering legislation of a generation ago and the limits on actions more recently, especially in regard to global climate change.

CASE STUDY China: Searching for Sustainable Development

As the 2008 Summer Olympics approached, commentators around the world began to question whether Beijing could really host the games adequately, not because of a lack of infrastructure or resources, but because of the quality of the air the athletes would be breathing. Global concern was certainly not misplaced. In 2007 China was home to sixteen of the twenty most polluted cities in the world, and even after the government instituted a policy to remove half of the city's 3.3 million vehicles from highways daily, banned three hundred thousand aging vehicles found to be especially heavy polluters, encouraged commuters to return to using the bicycles once so ubiquitous across the country, opened three new subway lines and set up numerous new bus lines, some athletes still bowed out of some competitions, citing fears of asthma attacks and physical stress (CNN 2008; ABC News 2008).

Since 2002, however, the "fourth generation" of Chinese leadership has made a significant commitment to environmental protection, exemplified in the October 2007 addition of the "Scientific Development Concept" to the nation's constitution, which President Hu says will "[combine] the development of the economy with the protection of resources and the environment" (Johnson 2008, 93). The Chinese government has passed an impressive array of environmental laws and signed numerous international environmental treaties, but protecting the environment still is in conflict with the country's rapid economic growth, and the laws are weakly enforced at the local level.

China's environmental degradation and problems are breathtaking, no pun intended. Besides urban air pollution, 30 percent of the nation's water is unfit for human or agricultural use, almost 90 percent of the country's grasslands and forests are suffering degradation, and the Yellow River now dries up before it reaches the ocean, becoming an open sewer instead (Morton 2006, 64–65; Ho and Vermeer 2006). Severe soil erosion and the expansion of the Gobi Desert are rapidly reducing arable land, and increasing consumption and declining supply of water have hurt crop production and threaten the sustainability of China's rapidly growing cities. The

A runner wears a mask to protect himself from the smog as he runs past the new National Stadium built for the 2008 Summer Olympics in Beijing. China's rapid industrialization has produced dramatic environmental problems, including several of the most polluted cities in the world. Chinese authorities took numerous measures, such as banning some vehicles and shutting down factories, to try to clean the air for the Olympics.

result of all of this is skyrocketing health problems: air pollution is estimated to cause four hundred thousand deaths per year, and cancer rates increased by 19 percent in urban areas and 23 percent in rural areas between 2005 and 2007. To meet its soaring energy needs, the government is building the infamous Three Gorges Dam on the Yangtze River, the largest project of its kind in human history. While it will reduce China's dependence on coal for electricity, helping to clean the air, the dam forcibly displaced more than one million people and the reservoir it has created has inundated both agricultural and pristine forest land.

The Chinese government has passed a host of environmental laws, dating back as far as 1956. The Communist government under Mao, however, put little real priority on environmental concerns. Marxist ideology favored production over all else, and the country's rigid Communist political system allowed no environmental movement to emerge as it did in many countries in the 1960s and 1970s. Environmental issues were included explicitly in the earliest legal reforms that were part of Deng Xiaoping's opening of the Chinese economic system in 1979, when the government amended the constitution to include environmental protection as one of its explicit duties. A number of laws specifying protections of and standards for such things as air and water quality were enacted over the 1980s and 1990s. This culminated in 1998 when the State Environmental Protection Agency (SEPA) was raised to ministerial rank.

SEPA is currently the key agency governing environmental protection in China, and while it has an energetic leader and has been a bureaucratic advocate for the environment, it has had limited ability to enforce China's environmental laws. It has offices throughout the country to monitor local conditions but is dependent on local governments for most of its funding and staff at the local level. Local government leaders are rewarded in China's system primarily for their ability to further rapid economic growth, so they have had virtually no incentive to slow growth in favor of protecting the environment. Consequently, they have not taken SEPA concerns seriously. Most environmental damage starts at the local level as household pollution, so the unwillingness of local leaders to enforce environmental laws has undeniably hampered the effort. SEPA has avoided cuts to its staff that most central state bureaucracies have endured as the government has tried to reduce its size in recent years, and the central government came close to doubling funding for environmental protection from 1995 to 2005 (Chan et al. 2008, 297). Unfortunately, the Chinese Academy for Environmental Planning reported that between 2001 and 2005, only half of state funding for environmental protection was actually used for that purpose. Local government officials diverted most of the rest to corrupt purposes or simply to other governmental tasks they considered more important.

The policies that have been enforced have mostly been command and control, though recently SEPA has begun to experiment with market-based policies as well. The two major policies are fines for excessive polluting from individual sources such as factories and requisite environmental impact assessments (EIAs) for new industrial projects. The fines, however, are quite small, and many firms find it cost-effective to pay them and keep polluting, even when the rules are enforced. An initial market-based experiment was SEPA's 2006 introduction of the concept of a "green GDP" in several major cities, in which an estimate for the cost of environmental damage is subtracted from the cities' annual GDP increase. The organization found that environmental damage cost 3 percent of the cities' total GDP. The intent behind this was to introduce a measure by which local government officials could be held accountable: the central government could use this measure, instead of simple GDP growth, as the chief means of evaluating local officials' performance. SEPA initially announced that it would expand this green GDP to the entire country the following year, but local governments successfully resisted this effort; to date, there has been no follow-through on the experiment (Johnson 2008, 95–97). SEPA has also experimented with some taxes, such as the "chopsticks tax" on wood products to slow deforestation, and taxes on yachts and luxury cars that consume high amounts of fuel. Most of its efforts, however, remain command and control, and given that SEPA is charged with monitoring the pollution level of three hundred thousand factories and other pollution sources, it has a tall order to meet for a bureaucracy with only a few hundred employees directly working for it.

Recent years have seen an increase in interest in environmental matters that some analysts see as the start of real change in China's attitude toward the environment. From 1995 to 2005, SEPA approved all but two new industrial projects. In 2005 it began a highly publicized process of rejecting greater numbers of projects and insisting that all relevant projects actually produce an EIA prior to approval. In what came to be known as "environmental storms," SEPA suspended thirty projects in early 2005 and greater numbers in early 2006 and 2007. In 2006 it rejected a total of 110 proposed projects, and by October 2007 it had rejected a further 187. Beyond publicity, it's not completely clear how much these decisions matter in the long run. Among the rejected were thirteen dam projects suspended in 2005 pending their producing EIAs. The latter were duly produced, but by a firm closely connected to the hydroelectric firms building the dams. At least four of the dams were subsequently approved. Enforcement of environmental regulations has increased in recent years, but by how much remains unclear (Johnson 2008, 97–99).

The suspension of the dam projects in 2005 came about in part because of campaigns by environmental nongovernmental organizations (NGOs). With the limited political opening taking place in China, the number of environmental NGOs and protests has expanded significantly. Concern about the environment among Chinese citizens was evident as far back as the 1970s, but it has taken an organized form only since the mid-1990s, as the government has allowed some NGOs to function. The first two environmental NGOs were registered in 1994 and 1996. By 2005 there were an estimated 1,000 to 2,800, with no more than 20 percent of them officially registered with the government. Most are urban-based, and as many as half are student organizations. This trend is reflected in local protests as well: in 2005 there were fifty-one thousand environmental protests across the country, an increase of 30 percent over the previous year. The government often tolerates environmental NGOs and local-level protests, because top officials often see them as pushing recalcitrant local officials to enforce environmental policies better while doing little harm on the national level. Indeed, the government has started its own environmental GONGOs (government organized nongovernmental organizations) as well. If NGOs criticize the broader policies too severely, though, the government is certainly willing to crack down, which includes jailing leaders and trying them for crimes against the state. In May 2007, students used cellular phones to mobilize between seven and twenty thousand people to protest construction of a petrochemical plant. The authorities stopped the construction but also attempted to publicly discredit the organizers of the protest, which seems to have been larger than they were comfortable accommodating (Chan et al. 2008).

Internationally, China is best known for its successful opposition to any mandatory limits on production of greenhouse gases for developing countries. It has ratified the great bulk of international treaties, but jealously guards its sovereignty, implementing only those with which it agrees. By 2007 it had started discussions about setting targets for major cuts to greenhouse gases, far beyond what Kyoto called for, but these currently remain unofficial. The country has also become an active participant in Kyoto's global carbon market, becoming the biggest seller of carbon credits to the rest of the world (India is second). Regardless of its policies, though, China's environmental problems impact the world. Its pollution has had major effects in neighboring countries, including Myanmar and North and South Korea. Indeed, on some days, experts estimate that as much as one quarter of the soot in Los Angeles originates in China.

Summary

China's rapid industrialization and massive size have made it one of the largest polluters in the world, though on a per capita basis it remains a modest one. After decades of nearly complete neglect of environmental protection, the fourth generation of leadership has significantly raised official emphasis on doing better. Its efforts are supported by a rapidly growing network of local and national environmental groups, but while progress has clearly been made, the fundamental conflict between rapid economic growth and environmental protection remains unresolved. SEPA has become stronger but is still relatively weak vis-á-vis many other government ministries, especially at the local level. Fundamental changes of direction, such as the idea of the green GDP, continue to be successfully resisted. As China continues to grow and be integrated into the global economy, its environmental policies will become crucial not only to its own well-being but to that of the planet as a whole.

CASE STUDY Nigeria and Oil: A Question of Environmental Justice and Sustainable Development

The Niger Delta in southeastern Nigeria is the world's third largest wetland and its largest freshwater mangrove swamp. It is also a major oil-producing region, one of the biggest suppliers to the United States. Demand for fuel wood and extensive desertification in the north, mainly caused by deforestation of nearly one million acres per year, are among the numerous environmental concerns Nigeria faces, but the best known issue, and one with global implications, is the impact of oil production. This not only causes serious environmental damage to a fragile ecosystem but has also generated local responses, including the rise of ethnic militia and the kidnapping of Western oil workers. Inhabitants of the region believe they receive very few benefits from the oil drawn from their homeland while paying most of the environmental costs. Their protests raise profound questions about environmental justice and sustainable development, both locally and globally, in the context of a weak state with little effective environmental policy.

A 2006 UN development report clearly catalogs oil's negative environmental impact in Nigeria. The region is dotted with nearly 1,500 oil wells, about 4,000 miles of oil pipelines, and 4 refineries. To ease transportation through the large wetlands, oil companies have dredged numerous canals, depositing dredge material on the banks. Both the oil wells and the canals have severely hurt the local fishing industry by disrupting the fragile freshwater ecology, in some cases allowing saltwater to enter. With most of the pipelines above ground, oil spills are more common than in most oil-producing areas: nearly seven thousand occurred between 1976 and 2001, though the annual rate of spillage dropped slightly from 2001 to 2004. Spills are caused not only by human and equipment failures but also by sabotage. The desperately poor people of the region frequently break into the pipelines to gain access, in particular, to refined gasoline to sell on Nigeria's active black market. Between 10 and 15 percent of daily production is lost to illegal "bunkering," the stealing of oil and gas.

Flaring gas is much more common in Nigeria's oil fields than in most oil facilities around the world. This is just one of many environmental problems caused by oil production in the Niger Delta in southeastern Nigeria.

Gas flaring, an element of oil production everywhere, is worse in Nigeria than almost anywhere in the world. Natural gas is found wherever oil is, but given the expense and difficulty of storing and transporting it, if it cannot be piped to consumers immediately it is often burnt off at the well. The poverty in West Africa means there are few paying customers for gas, so an estimated 75 percent of Nigeria's gas is flared, sixteen times the world average. Gas flaring causes significant air pollution, which surpasses national and international standards in the region in spite of its poverty and lack of industry compared to most areas with air pollution. Acid rain is also a problem. Given its poverty, Nigeria produces relatively little greenhouse gas, but gas flaring from oil wells represents a major component of Nigeria's greenhouse contribution.

The environmental damage caused by oil production in the Niger Delta represents a massive set of external costs not factored into the price of the Nigerian oil purchased on the global market. In the absence of effective environmental policies either to control the pollution or internalize its cost, local people pay the price. Nigeria's exceptionally weak and corrupt state, unfortunately, has virtually no environmental policy. An excerpt from a 2006 UNDP report sums up the situation well:

> The oil companies, particularly Shell Petroleum, have operated for over 30 years without appreciable control or environmental regulation to guide their activities. The Federal Environmental Protection Agency did not come into being until 1988, and all the environmental quality standards on emissions and effluent discharge, and the laws requiring an environmental impact assessment for every major project, did not come into effect until the early 1990s. By that time, the Niger Delta environment had suffered much damage at the hands of the oil companies. Even now, it is doubtful whether the Government's environmental monitoring agencies can adequately control the activities of the oil companies (81).

Even with new environmental laws in place since the 1990s, Nigeria's corruption-riddled government rarely enforces them effectively or wants to. Oil companies, for instance, are supposed to compensate individuals harmed by oil spills and an elaborate set of compensation benefits exists in law. In practice, local people often receive less than they are due, and redressing the problem requires going to court, something impoverished local people do not have the resources to do (Ikporukpo 2004).

Niger Delta inhabitants do not believe they are benefiting as much as they should from the oil wealth. As Nigerian scholar Chris Ikporukpo (2004) points out, they have raised a question of environmental justice: most of the benefits of oil go to global oil consumers and recipients of government revenues elsewhere in Nigeria, while delta inhabitants absorb the environ-

mental costs. In Nigeria's ethnically divided political system, this sentiment has taken a mostly ethnic form. Local leaders have mobilized people in opposition to the oil companies and the central government by arguing that their ethnic group has been discriminated against. The most famous example is the Movement for the Survival of the Ogoni People (MOSOP) led by the poet Ken Saro-Wiwa. MOSOP published an Ogoni Bill of Rights in 1990, claiming that thirty billion dollars of oil wealth had been pumped out of their land and that they had received virtually nothing in return, had no representation in the federal government, and had been left with land that had become an "ecological disaster." The military government in the 1990s responded brutally to this effort, ultimately hanging Saro-Wiwa and eight other Ogoni leaders in 1995 to international condemnation.

Since the destruction of the mostly peaceful MOSOP, numerous violent movements have arisen. They have initiated armed attacks on oil company workers, oil installations, and government soldiers. This has included kidnapping and holding for ransom Western oil company employees, as many as two hundred in 2007. Sabotage of oil installations and safety concerns for workers have at times lowered Nigerian production, with a noticeable impact on world prices. Ethnic militias have also turned on each other, fighting for control of land that may contain oil or might generate compensation claims for oil spills. With the return to multiparty elections in 1999, local politicians unaffiliated with the ethnic movements have hired and used members of some of the militias for their own partisan purposes, harassing and intimidating political opponents during campaigns. After the elections, they often end their patronage of the militia groups, leaving the latter to hire themselves out to the next bidder. In a weak state that cannot provide a strong sense of security, such militias for hire often arise, whatever their original purpose might have been. The federal government has repeatedly used military force, both under the military government and the democratic regime since 1999, to oppose the ethnic militias.

The grievances of the local inhabitants focus on not only environmental problems directly but also on the disbursement of oil revenues the government collects. In all federal systems, tensions arise over what share of revenue from natural resources each level of government should receive. Nigerian law originally gave only about half of all oil revenue to the federal government, but when world prices rose dramatically in the early 1970s the military government declared all natural resource wealth to be the property of the central government and increased its share of the revenue generated from it. By the 1990s, states in the Niger Delta received only 3 percent of the total revenue. The new democratic constitution improved this significantly, guaranteeing states 13 percent of oil revenue, a position they have maintained since, though many local leaders call for at least 25 percent.

Over a period of many years, the federal government has created various development agencies that it claims are meant to meet the development needs of people in the delta. Under the military governments these were fraught with corruption and led by people from outside the region. The last of them, the Oil Mineral Producing Areas Development Commission (OMPADEC), was established in 1992. It received a total of $135 million in oil revenue to repair environmental problems and enhance development in oil-producing regions. When the democratic government came to power in 1999, it disbanded the military's last effort at such an agency after discovering that the OMPADEC had given construction contracts to numerous firms

that had stolen the money and that it could not be traced, that the organization was deeply in debt, and that it had completed virtually no actual work. The new government created yet another new development agency for the region, the results of which remain to be seen (Ikporukpo 2004, 335–337).

Summary

Nigeria and its oil is a case of severe environmental problems in the context of a weak state that cannot or will not intervene. Local people, mostly impoverished, absorb the bulk of the externalities of oil production, even as the benefits go to others in Nigeria who make use of oil revenue in the form of government services, corruption, and new roadways and export the oil to consumers worldwide. The political response has been, in a sense, an environmental justice movement with motivations similar to those in the United States. In Nigeria, however, the movement has faced a weak and, until recently, military state, and as a result it has taken an ethnic and sometimes violent form. The return of democracy has not fundamentally changed the situation: it has improved revenue sharing in Nigeria's federal system, but that revenue still has not reached many of the people who actually pay the cost of oil production. The Nigerian case demonstrates some of the worst possibilities of environmental externalities in the absence of effective state intervention.

Summary

Pollution is a classic example of market failure, and one that has now gone global. Government intervention initially tried to impose specific limits on pollution to create cleaner air, water, and land. More recently, market-based policies have emerged that promise to achieve similar results at lower costs. All attempt to internalize the externality that pollution of any sort represents. This means the costs of various production processes shift, with some people bearing those costs and other benefiting, which leads to major political battles in every country over who exactly is going to pay the costs, how, and when. Climate change is only the latest, and arguably biggest, of these environmental battles. It has the added problem, and perhaps potential benefit, of being truly global, requiring a global solution that has little to do with locale. But it still raises the same questions that all environmental issues do. In most environmental issues, including especially climate change, one of the players in the game is future generations, who lack political clout now. The outcome of these battles may tell us much about "who rules." Assuming they are self-interested, whoever they are, they are likely to avoid paying the costs, at least until others can convince them that something has to change for all to survive and for greater efficiency and wealth to be achieved.

CONCLUSION

This chapter has examined three areas in which most states choose to intervene in economic markets: poverty reduction or social welfare, health care, and the environment. State intervention in each has its own rationale, but in all three, market failure of some sort offers a reason for the state to modify pure market outcomes. States don't seem to intervene just on the economic basis of recognition of market failures, however. The market failures described, such as the externalities associated with pollution, long predate state intervention in the wealthy, industrialized countries. Normative and political motivations also need to be present for a state to mobilize to implement new policies in these areas. For instance, the Great Depression in the United States helped bring the value of reducing poverty to the fore and led to the birth of the welfare state, while in Britain it was the postwar consensus on rebuilding a new and more equitable society that produced social and health policy. Similarly, wealthy industrial countries have led the way in environmental intervention, a classic postmaterialist value. Middle-income and rapidly industrializing countries may be attempting to join the bandwagon, but in the very poorest countries it's difficult to argue convincingly that resources are something to be conserved rather than depleted to meet immediate human needs.

In general, wealth seems to raise the prospect that countries can and will act effectively on value consensus in these areas. In wealthier countries, social and institutional structures provide important clues to timing and implementation of policies. For example, many European countries concerned about gaining the support of workers implemented welfare policies in advance of the United States and UK, where labor was not as well organized. Parliamentary democracies also seem to be able to implement policies in a more holistic and cohesive fashion than the divided powers and many veto points allowed in, for example, the United States. Analyzing the connections between institutional structure and policy outcomes may also tell us a great deal about who has power in these particular issue areas.

Welfare and the need for adequate health care may be more widely held values than environmentalism, but poorer countries simply lack the resources to intervene effectively in these areas. They also face quite a different set of problems: rather than creating mechanisms for appropriate distribution, they may first need to find the resources (doctors, clinics, clean water) before they can worry about equitable distribution. When resources and social consensus permit, they may look at the wealthier countries to see whether there are practical models to be followed.

Would they be better off with command and control or cap and trade policies, NHI or NHS, or more market-based health care? As more countries develop policies in these areas, they will no doubt examine the effectiveness of earlier models and ask whether social and institutional conditions would allow them to replicate these policies. Most policy instruments, such as social insurance, command and control, or cap and trade, can be used by anyone, but a country's particular institutional structure and the relationship between the state and important social groups may make it more feasible to adopt and implement a particular set of policies.

Globalization, too, will have an impact on future policies in all countries. If hyperglobalization theorists are correct, then wealthy states will converge toward more market-based policies and poorer countries, rather than choosing among models, will be forced to do the same. We can't know yet whether this will happen. For now, our cases show a persistence of diverse models, but a trend toward at least limited reform in all. At least as important, truly global health and environmental problems, especially, may require new types of global policy solutions. States may increasingly have to interact with one another to hammer out effective and feasible policy solutions to problems, implementing these solutions across borders. The normative, political, and economic issues associated with working out such new global policies will be significant, as the example of the Kyoto Protocol suggests, but global problems will increasingly demand states' attention in the twenty-first century.

Key Concepts

cap and trade system (p. 470)

Christian democratic welfare states (p. 441)

command and control policies (p. 470)

environmental justice movement (p. 474)

liberal welfare states (p. 441)

market-based private insurance system (p. 454)

market failure (p. 435)

means-tested public assistance (p. 439)

moral hazard (p. 453)

national health insurance (NHI) (p. 454)

national health system (NHS) (p. 454)

precautionary principle (p. 470)

risk assessment (p. 469)

risk management (p. 469)

single-payer system (p. 454)

social democratic welfare states (p. 439)

social insurance (p. 438)

social policy (p. 436)

sustainable development (p. 469)

tragedy of the commons (p. 468)

universal entitlements (p. 438)

welfare states (p. 439)

Works Cited

Adolino, Jessica R., and Charles H. Blake. 2001. *Comparing Public Policies: Issues and Choices in Six Industrialized Countries.* Washington, D.C.: CQ Press.

Alesina, Alberto, and Edward Glaeser. 2004. *Fighting Poverty in the U.S. and Europe: A World of Difference.* Oxford: Oxford University Press.

Baer, W. 2008. *The Brazilian Economy: Growth and Development.* 6th ed. Boulder, Colo.: Lynn Rienner Publishers.

"Beijing: Cars come off roads for Olympics." 2008. www.cnn.com/2008/WORLD/asiapcf/06/23/pollution.olympics.ap.

"Beijing Traffic Cut to Help Clear Air for Olympics." 2008. http://a.abcnews.com/International/wireStory?id=5411374.

Bonoli, Giuliano, Vic George, Peter Taylor-Gooby. 2000. *European Welfare Futures: Towards a Theory of Retrenchment.* Cambridge, UK: Polity Press; Malden, Mass.: Blackwell Publishers.

Cammisa, Anne Marie. 1998. *From Rhetoric to Reform? Welfare Policy in American Politics.* Boulder, Colo.: Westview Press.

Chan, Gerald, Pak K. Lee, and Chan, Lai-Ha. 2008. "China's Environmental Governance: The Domestic-International Nexus." *Third World Quarterly* 29, no. 2: 291–314.

Congressional Budget Office. 2007. *The State Children's Health Insurance Program.* Washington, D.C.: Government Printing Office.

Esping-Andersen, Gosta. 1990. *The Three Worlds of Welfare Capitalism.* Princeton: Princeton University Press.

Feder, Judith, and Donald W. Moran. 2007. "Cost Containment and the Politics of Health Care Reform." In *Restoring Fiscal Sanity 2007: The Health Spending Challenge*, ed. Alice M. Rivlin and Joseph R. Antos. Washington, D.C.: Brookings Institution.

Freeman, A. Myrick, III. 2006. "Economnics, Incentives, and Environmental Policy." In *Environmental Policy: New Directions for the Twenty-First Century*, ed. Norman Vig and Michael Kraft, 193–214. Washington, D.C.: CQ Press.

Graig, Laurene A. 1999. *Health of Nations: An International Perspective on U.S. Health Care Reform.* Washington, D.C.: CQ Press.

Green, David G., and Benedict Irvine. 2001. *Health Care in France and Germany: Lessons for the UK.* London: Civitas: Institute for the Study of Civil Society.

Grogger, Jeffrey, and Lynn A. Karoly. 2005. *Welfare Reform: Effects of a Decade of Change.* Cambridge: Harvard University Press.

Hall, Anthony. 2006. "From *Fome Zero* to *Bolsa Família:* Social Policies and Poverty Alleviation under Lula." *Journal of Latin American Studies* 38: 689–709.

Heclo, Hugh. 1974. *Modern Social Politics in Britain and Sweden.* New Haven: Yale University Press.

Hempel, Lamont C. 2006. "Climate Policy on the Installment Plan." *Environmental Policy: New Directions for the Twenty-First Century,* ed. Norman Vig and Michael Kraft, 288–331. Washington, D.C.: CQ Press.

Ho, Peter, and Eduard B. Vermeer. 2006. "China's Limits to Growth? The Difference between Absolute, Relative and Precautionary Limits." *Development and Change* 37, no. 1: 255–271.

Huber, Evelyne, and John Stephens. 2001. *Development and Crisis of the Welfare State.* Chicago: University of Chicago Press.

Ikporukpo, Chris O. 2004. "Petroleum, Fiscal Federalism, and Environmental Justice in Nigeria. *Space and Polity* 8, no. 3 (December): 321–354.

Johnson, Tom. 2008. "New Opportunities, Same Constraints: Environmental Protection and China's New Development Path." *Politics* 28: 93–102.

Katzenstein, Peter. 1985. *Small States in World Markets: Industrial Policy in Europe.* Ithaca: Cornell University Press.

Kraft, Michael, and Norman Vig. 2006. "Environmental Policy from the 1970s to the Twenty-First Century." In *Environmental Policy: New Directions for the Twenty-First Century,* ed. Norman Vig and Michael Kraft, 1–33. Washington, D.C.: CQ Press.

Lavinas, Lena. 2006. "From Means-Test Schemes to Basic Income in Brazil: Exceptionality and Paradox." *International Social Security Review* 59: 103–125.

Layzer, Judith A. 2006. *The Environmental Case: Translating Values into Policy.* Washington, D.C.: CQ Press.

Morton, Katherine. 2006. "Surviving an Environmental Crisis: Can China Adapt?" *Brown Journal of World Affairs* 13, no. 1 (Fall/Winter): 63–75.

Olsen, Gregg M. 2007. "Toward Global Welfare State Convergence? Family Policy and Health Care in Sweden, Canada, and the United States." *Journal of Sociology and Social Welfare* 34, no 2: 143–164.

Organisation for Economic Co-operation and Development (OECD). 2008. *OECD Factbook 2008: Economic, Environmental and Social Statistics.* http://ocde.p4.siteinternet.com/publications/doifiles/10-02-02-g1.xls.

———. 2007. *Health at a Glance 2007.* Paris: OECD Publishing.

Ringquist, Evan. J. 2006. "Environmental Justice: Normative Concerns, Empirical Evidence, and Government Action." In *Environmental Policy: New Directions for the Twenty-First Century,* ed. Norman Vig and Michael Kraft, 239–263. Washington, D.C.: CQ Press.

Siebert, H. 2005. *The German Economy: Beyond the Social Market.* Princeton: Princeton University Press.

Slack, Kristin Shook, et al. 2007. "Family Economic Well-Being Following the 1996 Welfare Reform: Trend Data from Five Nonexperimental Panel Studies." *Children and Youth Services Review* 29: 698–720.

Smeeding, Timothy. 2005. *Government Programs and Social Outcomes: The United States in Comparative Perspective.* Luxembourg Income Study, Working Paper 426.

United National Development Programme. 2007. *Human Development Report 2007/2008: Fighting Climate Change: Human Solidarity in a Divided World.* New York: UN Press.

———. 2006. *Niger Delta Human Development Report: Abuja, Nigeria.* New York: UN Press.

Vail, Mark. I. 2004. "The Myth of the Frozen Welfare State and the Dynamics of Contemporary French and German Social-Protection Reform." *French Politics* 2, no. 2: 151–183.

Willemsky, Harold. 1975. *The Welfare State and Equality.* Berkeley: University of California Press.

Resources for Further Study

Donaldson, Cam, et al. 2005. *Economics of Health Care Financing.* New York: Palgrave.

Goodin, Robert E., et al. 1999. *The Real Worlds of Welfare Capitalism.* Cambridge: Cambridge University Press.

Organization of Economic Cooperation and Development (OECD). www.oecd.org.

World Health Organization. www.who.org.

Case Study

Mini-Case

Who Rules?

- When values and identities such as religion and gender clash, what does the outcome tell us about who rules?

What Explains Political Behavior?

- What role does globalization play in increasing group demands for recognition and inclusion?

- How do culture, institutions, and rational choice shape the particular demands of identity groups in different countries?

Where and Why?

- What might explain why different types of secularism have developed in different countries? How have differences in secularism affected religious conflict and state responses to challenges from religious groups for inclusion?

12

POLICIES AND POLITICS OF INCLUSION AND CLASHING VALUES

Over the past fifty years, numerous groups have demanded greater inclusion in their societies and the political process, raising a host of new policy issues. These groups include the ethnic, racial, and religious groups we discussed in chapter 4 as well as groups demanding changes to policies toward gender and sexual orientation. In many countries, these have been part of the new social movements we mentioned in chapter 7. The demands of these movements have raised fundamental questions about equal citizenship and how to reconcile clashing moral values. States throughout the world have created new policies of one sort or another to try to address their concerns, and globalization has meant that even states with very little open political space or only weak demands for change have nonetheless felt pressure to address at least some of these issues.

The policy debates that these groups have raised return us to issues we have examined in several prior chapters. Chapter 4 argued that identity-based groups desire some combination of recognition, autonomy, representation, and participation. In this chapter, we add improved social status to this list. The groups that have made these demands do so in part to achieve what members see as truly equal citizenship, and better social status is seen as part of that. Their demands for inclusion raise questions about what equal citizenship should really look like. Although equal citizenship is certainly not an ubiquitous value, it is a core value of liberal democracy that has spread significantly since World War II and is powerful enough that virtually every government today must justify itself as either a democracy or a critique of it. Formally or informally excluding particular groups of citizens from the political sphere threatens this fundamental value. Including them, however, can cause clashes with other groups with equally strong and opposing values. While few people or governments question the legitimacy of equal treatment of all citizens regardless of ethnic or racial identity, doing the same for women, homosexuals, or transgender individuals often conflicts with deeply held religious beliefs or long-standing cultural practices. Even when the principle of equal citizenship is not questioned, major controversies arise over what the state must and can do to help ensure equal status and what "equal treatment" even means.

As we discussed briefly in chapter 4, identity groups make a distinct set of demands. The first is usually for recognition. They want the state and the rest of society to recognize them as distinct with particular sets of legitimate concerns. This usually includes the provision of legal rights equal to (or perhaps greater than) those of all other citizens. While the last vestige of legalized racial discrimination was eliminated with the end of apartheid in South Africa in 1994, legal discrimination against women, especially in areas of property ownership and family law, remains fairly common, and legal discrimination against homosexuals is the norm in most of the world. Members of ethnic or religious groups also sometimes seek autonomy to control their own affairs, either in a particular region where they are in the majority or over areas of their lives influenced by cultural traditions or religious beliefs, such as family law and property rights. A third demand that virtually all groups make is for representation and participation, essentially the right to participate fully in the political process. This is initially a simple legal matter of ensuring basic political rights, but it often becomes more complicated and controversial as groups question whether they are truly being allowed to participate on an equal footing with other citizens and whether institutional changes are necessary for them to achieve that equality. A final demand that we add in this chapter is the demand for better social status. Virtually all groups that mobilize to make demands for inclusion on the basis of identity begin in a socially marginalized position: they are typically poorer and less educated than the average citizen of a state and may be socially segregated as well. Harkening back to T. H. Marshall's ideas of the social rights of citizenship (see chapter 3), they argue that they need better education and economic positions and greater respect from and acceptance in society as a whole. How to achieve those improvements has proven quite controversial in many countries.

Equal citizenship is not the only value involved in policies of inclusion. Demands for inclusion often produce confrontations among competing values. Historically, demands for racial or ethnic equality gave rise to such conflicts: many white supporters of apartheid in South Africa and Jim Crow laws in the southern United States believed deeply that whites were superior to blacks and that racial mixing would threaten the well-being of society as a whole. In the contemporary world, most such conflicts are between religious or cultural beliefs, on the one hand, and claims for equality across genders or sexual orientations on the other. The recent controversies over gay marriage in the United States and Europe are just the latest in a long history of clashes of deeply held values. Ironically, successful assertion of demands from one group can come into conflict with those of another, as well as with concepts of equal citizenship, as our case study of India below demonstrates.

The questions these policies raise are so profound and so central to liberal democracy that numerous political philosophers have developed arguments in recent years centered on which policies of inclusion should be pursued and why. Most of this debate has taken place in the context of democratic theory: normative theories about how democracy ought to work. It has clear implications, though, for any modern state, all of which grapple with the demands of mobilized groups asking for greater inclusion in the political process. At the heart of the debate is the question of individual versus group rights. Liberal democracy in its classic formulation is based on individual rights and the equal treatment of all citizens. As we saw in chapter 3, it took the better part of two centuries to implement this idea in basic legal terms before even getting to most of the contemporary issues liberal democratic regimes face over what true inclusion ought to mean.

Some theorists argue, however, that individual rights, no matter how fully respected, will never allow full inclusion of culturally distinct or socially marginalized groups. Social or cultural differences mean that legal equality cannot produce real inclusion for these individuals as truly equal citizens. More must be done, usually in the form of rights for specific groups or preferential policies that target the distinct needs and weak social position of particular groups. Theorists making these arguments support policies of several types: 1) recognizing and actively supporting the preservation of distinct cultures, 2) granting some degree of governing autonomy to particular groups, 3) reforming representative institutions such as electoral systems and political parties to enhance or guarantee participation and office-holding for members of particular groups, and 4) actively intervening to improve the socioeconomic status of distinct groups, usually via government intervention in the market. Opponents argue that any such group rights or preferences undermine the norm of equal citizenship, serve to perpetuate a group's distinct and therefore unequal position, and threaten the common identity and bonds on which citizenship and national identity must be based.

Two of the most prominent advocates of group rights and preferences are political theorists Will Kymlicka (1995) and Iris Marion Young (2000). Both argue from within the tradition of liberal democratic theory, but they suggest that in certain circumstances group rights are not only justified but are essential to achieve full inclusion of all citizens. Kymlicka argues that minority cultures must be recognized and granted certain collective rights because the individual autonomy on which liberal democracy is based entails freedom to choose among various options in life, and those options can only be understood within the context of a particular culture. Culture gives individuals the means to understand the world and their role in it, providing them with the means to choose how to act and what to believe. For this reason among others, people deeply value their cultures and are justified in doing so.

Kymlicka goes on to contend that collective rights for minority cultures are justified "to limit the economic or political power exercised by the larger society over the group, to ensure that the resources and institutions on which the minority depends are not vulnerable to majority decisions" (1995, 7). This is particularly true for minority groups that are part of preexisting cultures incorporated into larger states, such as Native Americans in the United States; these groups not only deserve protection within the larger society but also, if they wish, merit some degree of autonomy from that society to preserve their culture. Even for immigrants and other minority groups, though, Kymlicka favors specific types of cultural support and protection, arguing that most people find it very difficult to fully cross cultural barriers, and without recognition and protection for their distinct culture they will not be able to participate completely in the larger society and make the choices on which democratic citizenship depends. He and coauthor Wayne Norman argue for **multicultural integration** rather than assimilation. The latter, as practiced in the United States and elsewhere, has as its goal the eventual submersion of the distinct cultures of immigrants in favor of the creation of a common culture shared by the whole society with corresponding political attitudes and practices. Conversely, multicultural integration

> does not have the intent or expectation of eliminating other cultural dif-
> ferences between subgroups in the state. Rather, it accepts that ethno-
> cultural identities matter to citizens, will endure over time, and must be
> recognized and accommodated within [political] institutions. The hope
> is that citizens from different backgrounds can all recognize themselves,
> and feel at home, within such institutions (2000, 14).

Young offers a different approach to justifying similar rights for various groups, although she focuses not on identity and culture, but rather on what she terms structural social groups, or groups of people who share a structural position and therefore similar experience in social and political institutions. A structural position can be based on economic position, physical attributes, or a variety of other factors. Structural groups can therefore overlap with cultural groups but are not the same thing. She argues that collective rights or preferences for such groups are justified in the interests of justice and greater democracy. Democracy, she suggests, should have as one of its primary goals the seeking of justice. Achieving this requires a democratic debate that includes all important perspectives on relevant issues in a form of what is termed **deliberative democracy**, that is, democ-racy which asks citizens not only to assume their rights and minimally participate through voting but also to engage actively in democratic discussion in the effort to build a better society.

Deliberative democracy, Young argues, is enhanced and justice is more likely to be attained when all important social perspectives are included in the discussion, and groups in structurally marginalized positions are typically not included unless governments intervene to ensure they are. Her goal is inclusive democracy:

> Inclusion ought not to mean simply the formal and abstract equality of all
> members of the polity of citizens. It means explicitly acknowledging social
> differentiations and divisions and encouraging differently situated groups
> to give voice to their needs, interests, and perspectives (2000, 119).

This stance leads her to favor adjusting political discussion and debate to recognize and value the forms of communication that marginalized groups, such as women or speakers of different languages, are often more comfortable using. She also suggests that if a history of discrimination or current practices prevents members of marginalized social groups from being elected or appointed representatives in political institutions, some reform to ensure that they can enter such positions is warranted. This could take the form of rules for how parties select candidates, reserved legislative seats for particular groups, reserved positions on appointed boards for particular groups, or the drawing of electoral districts to increase the likelihood that members of particular groups will be elected.

Critics of group rights make several arguments in response to Kymlicka, Young, and others. The classic liberal position is that only individuals can have rights, and all individuals should have them equally. This implies support for government policies of nondiscrimination, but it does not justify giving any rights or preferences to members of particular groups who would then receive treatment different from that given to other citizens. Once legal equality is achieved, individuals are and should be free to pursue political participation as they desire and are able. The state should not intervene in any way in either cultural or social differences, which, even if acknowledged to exist, are beyond its rightful purview.

Indeed, proponents of civic nationalism (see chapter 4) fear that group rights will undermine political stability and democracy, both of which, they argue, require a common identity, a shared set of values, or both. Nationalism underlies the development of the modern state and of democracy, and each state is given international legitimacy as a representative of "a people." A sense of commonality, then, is essential to domestic and international legitimacy for all states. Civic nationalists see group rights and preferences as divisive and fear that acknowledging and accommodating them will preserve differences rather than encourage commonality and that this will ultimately undermine political stability and make democratic discussion difficult because of a lack of common values.

A third, but similar, strand of criticism of group rights comes from proponents of deliberative democracy who suggest that the goal of democratic discussion should not be the representation of particular interests and bargaining among them but instead should be the achievement of a collectively defined common good. Giving special rights or preferences to particular groups will encourage them to pursue their own interests, and others will respond in kind, diverting attention from the common good. Lastly, all liberal theorists ask to what extent group rights can and should be supported if those groups pursue goals contrary to a state's liberal ideals: Should a religious group that explicitly opposes equal rights for men and women not only be allowed to participate in the political process but be given specific preferences?

These theoretical arguments lie behind the many concrete policy debates that face contemporary states. These debates take different forms in different societies, depending on which groups have demanded inclusion, how they have done so, and the nature of the regime, but while many of the overtly political goals of representation and participation seem relevant only in democracies, even leaders in authoritarian regimes face pressure to include women and members of various religious or ethnic groups in positions of authority. We examine the most controversial contemporary debates in this chapter, those involving religion, gender, and sexual orientation.

RELIGION: RECOGNITION, AUTONOMY, AND THE SECULAR STATE

Religion is both the oldest and, in a sense, newest basis for questions of inclusion and clashing values. As we noted in chapter 3, religious divisions within Christianity in early modern Europe led to civil wars and the emergence of liberalism. Eventually, secular states became universal in Western societies that, at least in theory, relocated religion into the private sphere. The secular state reached its zenith after World War II and the onset of independence of numerous secular states across Africa and Asia. In the past generation, however, and with renewed emphasis since the terrorist attacks of September 11, 2001, religion has again become a major issue in both Western and postcolonial societies. As we noted in chapter 4, religious groups typically seek recognition and autonomy, though individual members of those groups may also seek to participate in politics and achieve greater social status, ambitions which they may feel have been hindered by society's lack of respect for their religious beliefs.

The vast majority of the world's states are officially secular, with most of the exceptions being in the Middle East. Secularism, however, takes many different forms in principle, and its implementation does not always match those principles. The key relationship is between the state and organized religious groups such as churches and religious associations. In liberal democracies, few question the right of citizens to practice any religion they choose in the private sphere (with the possible exception of religious practices that break other kinds of laws, such as those against drug use or polygamy). Religious groups may organize, build houses of worship, and do charitable work as they desire. Controversies arise over what role, if any, the state should play in this process and what role, if any, the religious groups should play in secular politics and policy (see Country and Concept table on pages 528–529).

That said, several approaches to secularism exist today. The version most familiar to Americans views the state as neutral about, and not opposed to, religion: the state does not actively support religious activities such as religious schools or charitable work, but it does not oppose them either. Religious perspectives in secular politics are treated the same as any other perspectives, with the state (at least in theory) as a neutral arbiter that does not choose sides in the debate. This form of secularism stems from the earliest days of the United States, when thirteen colonies with different predominant branches of Christianity (in many cases, officially recognized by the state) had to find a way to live together. They believed that the example of the English civil war just over a century earlier illustrated the price paid by a state that was not neutral. Recent controversies in the United States have therefore involved actions that seem to question this neutrality, such as the posting of the Ten Commandments in courtrooms or public school classrooms, or requiring children to pray in school or learn about creationism in addition to or instead of the theory of evolution. Other controversies implicate the state in actively supporting religion, such as President George W. Bush's faith-based initiatives; policy of government funding for the charitable work of some religious groups; advocacy of abstinence programs in classrooms in lieu of sex education courses; or incentives for individuals to marry rather than have sexual relations, and possibly children, out of wedlock.

A more absolute version of secularism developed in societies whose political origins lay in a battle to separate the state from a single, dominant religion. France, Turkey, and Mexico are all examples of this. The French and Mexican revolutions and the establishment of the modern state in Turkey after the demise of the Ottoman Empire each involved the creation of a secular republic independent of the politically powerful Catholic Church in France and Mexico and the Islamic caliphate in Turkey. The result was what the French call *laïcité*, a secularism advocating that religion should play no part in the public realm. The state is not neutral toward religions but rather is actively opposed to any religion having a role in the public sphere. Private religious practice remains acceptable, as long as it is kept private. Religious references in political discourse, while not illegal in most cases, are nonetheless considered inappropriate by most political elites. In practice, not all of these societies have enforced this doctrine strictly: in France, for instance, the state supports many Catholic schools as long as they follow central state educational guidelines. Controversies arise in this type of secularism when a religious group seeks a public role for its religious beliefs, as the case of Islamic girls wearing veils in France and, more recently, in Turkey demonstrates.

MINI-CASE Islamic Headscarves in France and Turkey

France and Turkey share a similar take on secularism: a strict version that separates religion and state, with religion viewed as a private matter to be kept out of the public sphere as much as possible. France is at least nominally largely Christian, but is home to the largest Muslim population in Europe, most of whom are immigrants from North Africa. Turkey is largely Muslim. These shared characteristics have led to a shared conflict: both countries have faced considerable controversy over young women wearing Islamic headscarves to school. The issue aroused such passion in both countries in part because each state's sense of national identity includes its particular conception of secularism; any questioning of it threatens national identity itself. A 2004 law in France attempted to resolve the controversy, but has not laid it to rest, while in Turkey, the issue threatens to bring down the current government, perhaps even sparking a coup d'etat.

The French concept of secularism, or *laïcité*, became law in 1905 after a century of controversy over the public role of the Catholic Church. The law represented a triumph of the secular Republic over the church, and it seemed to resolve religious tensions. That is, until October 1989, when the principal of a junior high school in a Paris suburb expelled three Muslim girls for wearing the *hijab,* the Muslim headscarf, in school. This immediately became a major national controversy that pitted defenders of *laïcité* and feminists who viewed the headscarf as a form of oppression against defenders of religious freedom and multicultural understanding. The case was initially resolved in about a week, with the girls allowed to wear their headscarves to school as long as they took them off in class. Ten days later, though, the girls demanded the right to wear them in class as well, reigniting the firestorm. The government determined that religious symbols could be worn in schools unless "by their nature ... or by their ostentatious or protesting character ... [they] disturb the order or normal functioning of public services" (Fetzer and Soper 2005, 79). In effect, the national government left it to local schools to decide on a case-by-case basis.

As a consequence, dozens of Muslim girls were expelled from school and denied a public education. The few Muslim families that could afford lawyers inevitably filed lawsuits that led to a clarification of the ruling in 1997, a clarification that stated that simply wearing the headscarf was not "ostentatious," and a school had to have a clear justification for each individual case of expelling a girl from school. The debate continued into the new millennium, arising more vociferously whenever a particularly dramatic case occurred and intertwining with France's broader debate about the place of Muslims in French society, assimilation, French national identity, and preservation of cultural and religious distinctiveness. In 2003 Conservative president Jacques Chirac finally appointed a commission on laïcité that recommended completely banning the wearing of all "conspicuous religious symbols" in schools. After heated debate, the French parliament passed a law to this effect in 2004, and since then, more Muslim girls have been banned from school for wearing the hijab. Critics contend that this is an anti-Muslim attack on religious freedom, since students have long worn small crosses and yarmulkes to school without incident. Supporters argue that the law was essential to the preservation of a secular republic under the threat of encroaching Islamist ideology and to the preservation of French gender equality. French Muslims themselves are divided over the issue. A tiny fraction of them wear headscarves regardless of the law. They split almost evenly in opinion polls for and against the 2004 ban.

In Turkey, like France, secularism is also tied deeply to national identity. Kemal Atatürk founded the modern Turkish state after World War I based on an explicit campaign to modernize and Westernize the country in part by eliminating the role of Islam in the former seat of the Muslim caliphate and Ottoman Empire. The secular elite ran the country's bureaucracy, judiciary, and military, and whenever Muslim parties, which opposed Westernization and called for Turkey to recognize its place in the Muslim Middle East, gained too much power, they were banned or the military carried out a coup to reorganize the government entirely.

The first Islamic party to lead the government came to power in the 1995 election in a coalition government. It was banned after two years in office and its leaders arrested, but new Islamic parties kept arising. Most recently, the Justice and Development Party (JDP) was formed in 2001 by the popular, charismatic mayor of Istanbul, Tayyip Erdoğan. In contrast to past parties, the JDP radically modified its call for an end to Westernization. While preserving its embrace of Islamic principles on social issues, it also supported globalization, economic modernization tied to the West, and Turkey's application to join the EU. This garnered it greater support than prior Islamic parties, and it won the 2002 election with 34 percent of the vote, by far the largest share in Turkey's multiparty system. It has been the ruling party since, winning the 2007 election with 47 percent of the vote, and Erdoğan has served as prime minister since 2002.

The wearing of headscarves in Turkey is controversial in part because they were associated with the Islamist movement there long before they became an issue anywhere in Europe. The JDP came to power promising to allow them to be worn more widely, including in universities, but it did not pass legislation to that effect in its first five years in power. Any such law would have faced a certain veto from the president, Ahmet Necdet Sezer, a strong secularist from another party, and the constitutional court, which ruled in favor of preserving the ban in 2005. The election of a JDP leader, Abdullah Gül, as president in 2007, however, changed the equation. Indeed, one of the biggest controversies in that presidential election was the fact that Gül's wife wears a headscarf (as do Erdoğan's wife and daughters). With a JDP president, Erdoğan passed a law in February 2008 that lifted the long-standing ban on Muslim headscarves in public universities, with JDP members promising the ban on them in all public offices would be lifted soon. The secular elite reacted swiftly. There were pro-ban demonstrations in the streets, and the constitutional court ruled in June 2008 that the new law was unconstitutional. More ominously for the JDP, the public prosecutor filed a case asking that the party and seventy of its top leaders be banned from office for violating Turkey's secular principles. The lifting of the headscarf ban was a key piece of its evidence. The constitutional court was set to rule on the case in autumn 2008.

It may seem odd to many Americans that a simple headscarf would provoke a major political crisis on two continents, but that is because secularism in the United States more readily allows religion into the public sphere as long as the state remains neutral among religions. French and Turkish secularism, and more important, their sense of nationalism, has long envisioned a much more strictly secular public sphere, a vision that rising Islamic sentiment is challenging.

A third variant of secularism sees the state as neutral among but willing to support religions that it recognizes as important elements in civil society. Germany is the classic model of this type. Following its corporatist tradition, Germany since the end of World War II has officially recognized various Judeo-Christian faiths, the leaders of which register with the government to gain recognition. The state even collects a tax on their behalf to help fund them, and they help administer some of Germany's extensive welfare programs. Controversies in this type of secular state involve deciding which religious groups gain recognition and how they have to be organized to do so. Most Sunni Islamic sects, for instance, are nonhierarchical, which means that each mosque is independent, and this has raised questions in Germany about if, who, and how the state should recognize Muslim groups the way it has Judeo-Christian ones. (Several pilot programs have been instituted in recent years to address this situation.) As with the other models, states do not always implement this type of secularism fully. Indonesia, which is 90 percent Muslim, officially allows freedom of religion and the state legally recognizes Islam, Catholicism, Protestantism, Hinduism, and Buddhism. In 2008, however, the government yielded to pressure from Islamists to ban a small Islamic sect known as Ahmadiyah, which does not believe Mohammed was the last prophet, a central tenet of mainstream Islam.

WHERE AND WHY Explaining Policy Differences toward Muslims in Europe

Increasing Muslim immigration to Europe has made the place of Islam in these primarily secular and historically Christian societies a major issue in policy circles and in comparative politics. Islam now constitutes the third largest religion in Europe after Catholicism and Protestantism, and as Muslims have settled in the region, their demands for the right to build mosques that look like the mosques in the countries they came from, to establish Muslim schools, to have women wear veils in public, to have their religious holidays as official holidays, and to have their religious teachings included in secular school curricula have echoed across the continent. European states have responded in various ways, and political scientists have developed a spectrum of theories to explain this variation in policy response. Joel Fetzer and Christopher Soper (2005) outline several of these.

Some explanations have focused primarily on Muslim groups themselves, using social movement theories to explain success or failure in getting policies adopted. Resource mobilization theory argues that the success of any social movement depends on how many financial and organizational resources it has. Muslim groups, these theorists suggest, are often decentralized and financially weak, meaning that most have had limited success at convincing European states to change their policies. Those that are somewhat wealthier and more hierarchically organized have been more successful. A second social movement theory argues that the political opportunity structures best explain success. For instance, German immigration laws mean far fewer Muslims have gained citizenship than in Britain, so British Muslims have the opportunity via citizenship to have greater influence in the state. Similarly, the more centralized political system and parties in France mean Muslims have had to focus on national-level politics, whereas in Britain local government is a more important political arena so Muslims have been able to use that to win some policy battles at the local level.

Other scholars look at the state itself, rather than at the Muslim groups, to explain response to Muslim demands. One focus has been on ideology. In France the core ideological concept of *laïcité* has meant that the state has been unwilling to support Muslim schools or allow Muslim symbols and teachings in public schools as any such move would violate the core principle of the secular state. Fetzer and Soper argue that the most important explanation of all, however, is the legacy of past church-state relations. Germany's formal recognition of several religious groups has led Muslims there to ask for the same, to become part of the system, and to organize themselves in a manner that allows the German state to work with them. Germany's long-standing church-state relationships have shaped not only the government's response to the Muslims, but also what Muslim groups have requested. Similarly, the presence of the official Church of England and the tradition of teaching religion in both religious and secular schools have meant that Britain has been willing to include the study of Islam in its secular school curriculum and has been more willing to fund Muslim schools than has France.

As is often the case, more than one theory presents a plausible explanation of why states enact the policies they do. Combining several often results in the fullest explanation. The ideas developed for studying response to Muslims in Europe might also be useful for explaining other states' responses and policies toward religious groups and their demands, beyond Europe and involving religious groups other than Muslims.

The primary models of secularism arose first in Europe and North America, but most postcolonial states are also officially secular. They do make various accommodations of religions though. On the whole, perhaps the biggest difference between African and Asian states, in particular, and European states is that postcolonial societies are much more religious, as the Country and Concept table indicates for most of our case study countries. Like the United States, religious expression in the public sphere is widely accepted. Most African states have Christian majorities, and while many of them do not discriminate against Muslims, political leaders nonetheless openly practice Christianity and make religious references in public discourse. Similar patterns exist in majority Muslim states. Some of these make no pretence of being secular: in Saudi Arabia, the regime's legitimacy is tied closely to its support of Islam, and key clerics play important rules in establishing laws on personal behavior that follow their interpretation of *sharia*. In contrast, a number of other majority Muslim states, such as Syria and Egypt, maintain a strict secularism, especially via-á-vis Islamist groups that are the most powerful domestic threats to these regimes.

In demanding recognition and autonomy, religious groups worldwide have challenged the secular state in all its forms. In seeking recognition and autonomy, they are typically interested in gaining official status in countries where that is important, including the teaching of their religion in schools, establishing and gaining support for their own parochial schools, gaining legal recognition of their religious holidays, using religious symbols and ideas in the public sphere, and being allowed to practice their own religious law in personal and family matters. Some of these simply require the state to include a new religious group in policies it already pursues toward other religious groups. Other groups, though, ask for more. They ask that the state to be less secular in one way or another or that it set policies preferential to their religion over others. All of these demands have provoked debates in various countries in recent years. We investigate some of them in two quite distinct case studies of secular states grappling with religious demands: the United Kingdom and India.

CASE STUDY United Kingdom: Religious Challenge to Multiculturalism

London is without question one of the most racially, culturally, and religiously diverse places on earth. After centuries of relative homogeneity, Britain since World War II and decolonization has been the recipient of large-scale immigration from its former colonies in the Caribbean, South Asia, and Africa. The 1960s gave witness to Conservative member of Parliament (MP) Enoch Powell's thinly veiled racist call for the end of immigration to preserve the white Briton heritage and well-being, on the one hand, and the adoption of an official policy of **multiculturalism,** on the other. Britain's multiculturalism policy

> encouraged cultural groups to create their own organizational structures, to safeguard their customs and religious practices as they saw fit, and to introduce an awareness of and celebration for Britain's cultural pluralism into the state education system (Fetzer and Soper 2005, 30).

Crowds of children await Queen Elizabeth II on a street in London's East End. Immigration has made the city probably the most culturally and racially diverse in the world, which has raised major questions about what it means to be a Briton, and this debate has been especially acute around the question of religion, focusing on the role and demands of Britain's large Muslim minority.

Until very recently, however, this policy was focused almost exclusively on race and culture, not religion. Antidiscrimination laws on the basis of race became national policy in the 1960s, but it was not until December 2003 that the government made discrimination on the basis of religion illegal. Since the 1980s, British Muslims have increasingly sought inclusion as a religious group, and this has included calls for recognition, support, and some degree of autonomy. They have sought greater inclusion of their religion in school curricula, funding for their own schools, and rights to practice their faith publicly without discrimination.

Britain's unusual immigration history produced the challenges it faces today in dealing with religious diversity. From 1948 to 1962, citizens of the Commonwealth (the former British colonies) could immigrate to Britain and automatically gain rights equal to those of British citizens. At first it was mostly young men who immigrated to work in Britain's labor-short, postwar economy with the intent of saving money and returning home. Starting in 1962, British immigration policy made it much more difficult for Commonwealth citizens to immigrate, based on explicit fears that too many nonwhite immigrants were arriving. This dramatically reduced the arrival of new migrant workers, but the mi-

grants already in the country retained all of their rights, including the right to bring their families to join them, which actually led to higher numbers of immigrants than before 1962. For the first time, Britain was host to a number of immigrants from their former colonies who were complete families and who intended to stay. By far the largest number of these came from South Asia, and many of them were Muslim. Muslims now represent more than 8 percent of Britain's population and have founded more than one thousand mosques and many educational associations (Fetzer and Soper 2005, 46–48). Some of these institutions receive funding from Muslim countries such as Saudi Arabia and Libya and may therefore follow the theological teachings of those countries, but not all do.

Britain's policy of multiculturalism was put in place in this context. The 1976 Race Relations Act created the Commission on Racial Equality (CRE) whose job it was to improve race relations and battle racial discrimination. By the 1980s, a "black" political movement had grown that attempted to group all people who were not white under one political and racial umbrella to gain greater political strength. While championed by prominent political activists, the common identity was only visibly popular among people of Caribbean descent. It was far less clear whether many Africans and South Asians accepted "black" as their personal identity. By the end of the decade, though, it became increasingly evident that most Muslims did not. The event that made clear to all that religion, not race, was becoming the most important identity for Britain's Muslims was the controversy over Salman Rushdie's novel, *The Satanic Verses.* Rushdie is a British, Pakistani novelist who was already well-known in literary circles when he published his controversial novel in 1988. Many religious Muslims of various sects were offended by the novel's portrayal of the Prophet Mohammed and his family, and Iran's Shiite Ayatollah Ruhollah Khomeini, among other leaders, issued a *fatwa* condemning Rushdie. Large-scale protests broke out across Britain, and numerous Muslim organizations united to demand that the book be banned. This produced a major political backlash in the name of free speech that a large number of non-Muslim blacks readily joined. Many Muslims concluded from the experience that their interests diverged from those of the black community, even though virtually all Muslims are also racial minorities.

Muslim organizations were well established long before the Rushdie affair, however: the first umbrella organization, the Union of Muslim Organizations, began in the 1970s, and the Council of Mosques was established in the 1980s. The political prominence of such organizations grew substantially in the 1990s, as Muslims came to identify with their religion more than with their ethnicity or race. Yet this did not mean that most of them supported an Islamist ideology that questioned the legitimacy of the secular state. To the contrary, most of Britain's Muslims follow the Hanafi school of Sunni Islam, which respects the *ulema* (clerics) and *sharia* (Islamic law) but also the sovereignty of the secular state. They practice their religion, including its laws, within the confines of the secular state. Individually, Muslims are very active politically. Most are British citizens, and in Britain immigrants from the Commonwealth have the right to vote. Indeed, Muslims are registered to vote and vote at higher percentages than white Britons. Given that most Muslims live in urban areas (40 percent in London alone), many have been elected to local urban offices.

Such activity has not produced complete satisfaction of all their demands. Muslim associations seek recognition and the right to religious equality. A key area of dispute has been education. The Church of England (also called the Anglican Church in the UK or the Episcopal Church in the United States) is by law the country's official church and faith. This means relatively little now, but it has left an important institutional legacy in church-state relations. The British education system, even in public schools, includes religious instruction. Historically, this meant the teaching of Anglican beliefs. As Britain became more secular in the twentieth century, however, religious instruction increasingly came to be a nondenominational, vague Christian message that focused more on basic moral beliefs than on doctrine. The Anglican Church runs many schools, especially at the primary level, and it receives state funding to do so, with the requirement that these schools must teach the same national curriculum as public schools. Muslim parents placed their children in these highly regarded church schools, but increasingly resented the Chris-

tian elements of the education. Since the 1980s, the government has encouraged local school authorities to include religious instruction that reflects their community. This has meant including Islamic instruction in areas with heavy Muslim populations, though this process has been a long and slow one that has required significant agitation by Muslims at the local level. Local *ulema* have been actively involved in urging and assisting schools to incorporate Islamic education (Fetzer and Soper 2005, 39–42).

The heavily secular nature of British education, however, has become a growing concern to many Muslims, who responded by creating a movement to found separate Muslim schools. The movement began in the 1970s, and by 2003 there were an estimated ninety-eight Islamic schools across the country (Fetzer and Soper 2005, 44). A few of these started petitioning the government for funding parallel to that received by Christian and Jewish schools in the late 1980s. This met with resistance from secularists, who sided with Muslims on the need for parity but wanted to achieve it by ending funding for all religious schools. After initial government resistance, the Labour Party government elected in 1997 changed course, officially approving the UK's first state funding for Muslim schools. These institutions must comply with the established national curriculum just like all other religious schools, but as of 2005, only five Muslim schools had received funding (Modood 2006, 44).

Like all religious groups, British Muslim organizations have worked to achieve government recognition in various areas of everyday life. They were less successful in areas other than education until quite recently. Despite the clear rise of religion as an identity of importance, especially among Muslims, British multicultural policy continued to focus only on race and culture, reflecting Britain's increasingly secular society. (Nominal Christians are so secular that most estimates suggest there are more religiously observant Muslims than religiously observant Anglicans in Britain today.) This is reflected in the fact that it was not until the 2001 census that people were asked what their religious affiliation, if any, was: prior to that, estimates of Muslims or Hindus were based on the census's racial and ethnic information. Discrimination in employment on the basis of religion was made illegal in 2003, and then only because EU provisions that Britain had agreed to in 1999 required this legislation. In October 2007, the CRE, which had become an important source of information and policy on multiculturalism, merged with commissions on gender and disability to became the Equality and Human Rights Commission, with a mandate to work "to eliminate discrimination, reduce inequality, protect human rights and to build good relations" on the basis of not only race, gender, and disability but also "age, sexual orientation and religion or belief, as well as human rights."

This new recognition of religion as an important category for inclusive citizenship comes in the shadow of the September 11, 2001, attacks on the World Trade Center and the Pentagon in the United States and, more important for British Muslims, the July 7, 2005, London subway bombings. Responding to both, the Labour government enacted new Terrorism Acts in 2001, 2005, and 2006 that give the state much greater latitude to investigate and detain, without charges, citizens or foreigners suspected of being or assisting terrorists. The most controversial of these is the 2006 law, which allows detention for twenty-eight days without charges being filed and makes such activities as publishing terrorist materials and training terrorists illegal. Many British Muslims feel threatened by these new laws. Indeed, between September 2001 and September 2004, 664 people had been held in detention without being charged or given a trial, almost all of them Muslim (Modood 2006, 46–47). Without a doubt some British Muslims are sympathetic to al-Qaida and other similar Islamist extremist organizations: the perpetrators of the 2005 subway bombings were almost all native-born British Muslims, not immigrants. Yet the great majority of British Muslims believe in nonviolent versions of Islam, and they condemn terrorism even as they protest Britain's participation in the invasions of Afghanistan and Iraq.

Summary

Since the 1980s British Muslims have become a significant political force. They have used Britain's multiculturalism policy, which long ignored recognition on the basis of religion, to include Islam in school curricula and to start gaining state funding for Muslim schools. Individually, many have become active participants in the political process. Others, especially young second- and third-generation Britons, have become increasingly alienated. Bangladeshis and Pakistanis, who constitute three-quarters of Britain's Muslims, remain the poorest demographic group in the country. Their children also perform more poorly in school than other groups. Residential segregation continues to predominate in most British cities. In this context, a minority of young Muslim Britons have become attracted to more radical versions of Islam, a problem that will continue to challenge the British government as it attempts, belatedly, to recognize and work to include Muslims as full citizens.

CASE STUDY India: Secularism in a Religious and Religiously Plural Society

On February 27, 2002, a train full of Hindus returning from a pilgrimage to a disputed Hindu temple unexpectedly stopped in a small town in Gujarat, a western state in India and the birthplace of Mahatma Gandhi. A Muslim mob set the train on fire, killing fifty-eight passengers. In response, Hindu nationalists called for a massive protest, which the government supported. This protest quickly became a rampage against Muslims and their businesses; as many as 2,000 Muslims were killed and 150,000 displaced, and for three days the police failed to act to stop the violence.

This was only part of the most recent round of major religious violence in India, the world's largest and officially secular democracy. Religious divisions led to the partition of India and Pakistan at independence, which left India with a population which is more than 80 percent Hindu but which has numerous religious minorities, including about 10 percent of the population that is

Muslim. After partition, religion was not a major division in India's secular democracy for two decades, but since the 1970s it has become an increasingly important issue and has led to significant conflicts. India has seen major debates over what exactly secularism should mean, especially in the area of personal law governing marriage, divorce, and inheritance, and these debates have pitted the idea of equal citizenship for all individuals against the idea of community rights to practice a religion and observe specific religious laws.

British colonial rule had to deal with India's religious diversity from its earliest days. To avoid conflict, the British mostly allowed religious leaders of various groups to implement their own laws locally, and in the nineteenth century the colonizer helped codify religious laws into written and more uniform codes. As Britain accepted the idea of Indian independence and the nationalist movement took center-stage, the issue of religious divisions grew. The Indian National Congress, the main nationalist movement of Mohandas Gandhi and Jawaharlal Nehru, believed itself to be democratic and secular, and it rejected the claims of the Muslim League for special status for Muslims based on their religious identity and community. This ultimately led to the partition of India and the creation of Pakistan. As Indian leaders debated the country's new constitution in the 1940s as partition loomed, most recognized that religious divisions could be quite explosive to the new country. All major leaders in the National Congress agreed that some sort of secular state was essential, but various ideas of what secularism entailed arose and continue to be debated today.

Three ideas of secularism have competed throughout India's history: the state as modernizer working to reduce the influence of all religions, the state as neutral arbiter among religions, and the state as protector of religious minorities against the Hindu majority. Much of the top leadership of the nationalist movement, the educated elite, saw religion as backward and standing in the way of modernization. Nehru, India's first prime minister and scion of its leading political family, was a self-defined agnostic. For him and much of his cohort, secularism meant that the state worked to reduce the influence of religion in public life, encouraging instead an equal and secular citizenship and national identity.

Bodies of Hindu pilgrims are laid out in Gujarat on September 24, 2002, victims of anti-Hindu violence. This was the most recent major outbreak of Hindu-Muslim violence, a recurring problem in India, especially since the early 1990s. Both the rise of the Hindu nationalist party, BJP, and the growing global Islamist movement have raised religious tensions that have long simmered in India's secular but religiously plural state.

Most recognized, however, the reality that the country was very religiously observant and divided.

Ultimately, the constitutional statutes regarding the place of religion in the operation of the state were based on the idea of equal respect for all religions. In Hindi the term used for secularism literally means "religious neutrality." The Indian state, then, in a fashion similar to that of the United States, is supposed to be a neutral arbiter among faiths. Specifically, the constitution prohibits "discrimination on grounds of religion, race, caste, sex, or place of birth"; a state-mandated religious tax (à la Germany); and state-mandated religious education in state-funded schools. For the most part, religious organizations were left the authority to mind their own affairs, though within limits. Article 26 of the country's constitution "provides freedom to manage religious affairs, subject to public order, morality and health," and Article 25

> provides for freedom of conscience and free profession, practice and propagation of religion subject to public order, morality, and health. It confers on the state the right to regulate or

restrict any economic, financial, political, or other secular activity which may be associated with religious practice (Rao 2006, 53–54).

These clauses respect the right of religious groups to practice their faiths but also grant the state the ability to limit these practices when it deems necessary.

As in all states, these somewhat ambiguous principles have been put into practice in varying ways over the years in different states in India's federal system. The state does not allow religious education in publicly financed schools, but it does allow and even aids religious schools that have religious curricula. Given the decentralized nature of both Hinduism and Islam, the government has also intervened at times to facilitate interactions with religious organizations or has informally recognized certain groups as representing these religions. The southern state of Tamil Nadu, for instance, helps administer Hindu temples and their large endowments, with prominent members of the government on the boards of directors of the temples as well. These temples own half a million acres of prime agricultural land and manage great wealth, making the happiness of their membership politically important to the state.

Uncertainty over Islamic law led to the creation of the All India Muslim Personal Law Board (AIMPLB) in 1973 to oversee the implementation of *sharia* in personal law. In 2005 further disputes led to the creation of the All India Shia (Shiite) Personal Law Board and the All India Muslim Women's Personal Law Board, the latter an Islamic feminist effort to interpret *sharia* in ways that support expanded rights for women.

As these last examples suggest, personal law, as it is known in India, has been an arena of great religious conflict. The constitution recognizes the rights of religious groups to follow their own law in areas of marriage, divorce, and inheritance, but it also promises to work toward an eventual "uniform civil code" applicable to all, again reflecting a compromise between those who accepted the continued role of religion in the state and those who thought secularism should mean ultimately reducing religion's position. The first battleground in this area was Hindu law. At independence, a debate was already underway over a Hindu Code Bill that would reform Hindu law to outlaw polygamy for

Hindus and grant women greater rights to divorce and inheritance. Opposition was significant and focused especially on enforcing monogamy, sanctioning divorce, and giving women equal rights to property (even though the constitution prohibited discrimination on the basis of sex). A compromise bill passed in 1955 finally gave limited and unequal rights to women but still excluded agricultural land, the most important form of wealth in the country, from the laws allowing women to inherit.

The biggest battle over personal law and religion occurred in 1986. Shah Bano, a seventy-three-year-old Muslim woman divorced from her husband of more than fifty years, went to court to seek financial support from him because a law in the criminal code, which applies to all citizens regardless of religion, requires husbands to provide for their former wives as a means of preventing vagrancy. Under Muslim law, however, a husband is not usually obligated to support his wife for more than three months after divorce. The case went all the way to the country's Supreme Court, which ruled that the state's criminal code overrides Muslim personal law and, therefore, Shah Bano's husband had to support her. This seemingly innocuous personal case led to large-scale protest and intense political drama. The AIMPLB launched a campaign against the ruling that included a demonstration of half a million people in Bombay, numerous conferences attended by tens of thousands of people, and even a thirty-five-thousand-strong women's protest. In response, secular liberals and women's movements launched counterdemonstrations and demanded further reforms directed toward fulfilling the constitution's promise of a uniform civil code.

The case pitted individual equal rights of citizenship directly against communal rights of religious law and practice. After some hesitation, the Congress Party government chose the latter side, introducing the Muslim Women's (Protection of Rights on Divorce) Bill in parliament in February 1986. The vociferous debate was closely watched across the country, and it took place mainly in terms of the communal rights of a religious minority versus universal equal rights: few MPs raised questions of gender justice. The bill passed, making an exception for Muslims to the criminal code's requirement for maintenance after divorce: the communal rights of the religious minority had won out.

The Shah Bano case also occurred in the context of rising religiously inspired participation in electoral politics. Although a small minority, Muslims in India participate actively in party politics. Where they constitute a sizable group, they often support a Muslim-identified party such as the Muslim League, a re-creation of the party that helped create Pakistan; this strategy works where Muslims make up around a third of the electorate. Where they are a smaller minority, they choose a secular party they hope will support their interests, though these are usually dominated by Hindu politicians. While it was dominant, the ruling Congress Party received the most Muslim votes, which partly explains its support for the Muslim Women's Bill. Since the Congress Party's decline in the late 1980s, Muslims also have supported state-level and ethnic parties.

They also actively debate leadership of the community in civil society, which has led to what are now three separate boards seeking to regulate Islamic personal law. Muslim traditionalists, including members of the AIMPLB, defend existing Islamic law even as modernizers seek to reinterpret Islamic law and practices in a way they see as supporting equal citizenship. A growing Islamic feminist movement, a rising phenomenon throughout the Muslim world, seeks to justify expanded women's rights not on secular grounds of universal human rights, but rather on an interpretation of *sharia* that they argue is consistent with the tenets put forth in the Quran. They argue that Islamic law can justify a woman's right to initiate divorce, as well as severe restrictions on polygamy and a woman's right to negotiate a prenuptial contract that includes provisions for maintenance after divorce and inheritance.

Growing Muslim movements are in part a reaction to the growth of Hindu nationalism and its party, the Bharatiya Janata Party (BJP) (see chapter 7), which was the ruling party from 1999 until 2004. The BJP's ideology, *Hindutva,* is based on a claim that Hinduism lies at the core of Indian national history and identity. Most Hindu nationalists do not claim that Muslims have no rights in India, but they do argue that Muslims and others must recognize the cultural influence and centrality of Hinduism to true Indian nationalism. The party actively opposes what it sees as "appeasement" of Muslims and other religious minorities and instead calls for a uniform civil code and the end of quotas reserving educational and civil service positions for Muslims or other minorities (an Indian form of affirmative action). Hindu Nationalists reject official secularism, arguing it is a Western import of little relevance to deeply religious India and that it has been used as an excuse to pander to religious minorities and thereby divide the nation: "According to the BJP, India will emerge as a strong nation only when it becomes a cohesive *Hindu Rashtra,* a Hindu nation-state" (Rao 2006, 76). They favor assimilation rather than recognition and support of minority rights. At the state level, BJP governments have actively worked to rewrite Indian textbooks to remove what they see as bias in favor of the Muslim role in the country's history. While in power at the national level, however, the party moderated these views substantially and did not pursue the uniform civil code. Despite this partial moderation, the Hindu nationalists have caused significant fear and opposition among Muslims.

Summary

India's battle over secularism and the role of religion raises the classic questions about equal citizenship and clashing values that have arisen in the West, but it does so in very different circumstances. Faced with a religious and religiously divided population, the founders of India's democracy agreed to a secular state but defined that state as a neutral arbiter among religions rather than a supporter or opponent of any. Recognizing religious groups' rights to follow their own laws, however, has pitted communal rights against individual rights of equal citizenship. So far, the state has mostly sided with the preservation of minority rights to religious practice and law, and the state's official secularism stance does not seem to be increasing or reducing the role of religion. Indeed, religious movements seem stronger now than at any time since independence. These movements among Hindu and Muslim groups (as well as other small religious groups such as Sikhs) have raised even more challenges to Indian secularism, the survival of which some see as threatened.

Summary

Secularism has long been seen a part of modernity and therefore the modern state. In reality, however, religion continues to play a prominent role in many parts of the world. Political conflicts over it emerge primarily where multiple religions exist within the same state. Officially secular states find it nearly impossible to be truly neutral among religions, and religious minorities argue the state should not be completely neutral but instead should work to protect their threatened interests. Doing so in the name of cultural respect raises fundamental questions about values, often pitting individual rights as understood by liberals against group rights aimed at cultural preservation. These debates have affected Western states, many of which seemed headed toward complete secularization just a decade or two ago, as well as more religious postcolonial states and societies. Neither of our case studies seems to have found the perfect set of policies to satisfy all sides in these debates. Religion and religious divisions, it seems, are becoming more, not less, relevant to modern politics. As is so often the case, these battles about the place of religion and religious values centrally involve the role of women and women's rights, a subject to which we now turn.

GENDER: THE CONTINUING STRUGGLE FOR EQUAL SOCIAL STATUS, REPRESENTATION, AND PARTICIPATION

The women's movement and changes in women's position, activity, and status have been the most dramatic social and political revolution of the last generation, especially in wealthy countries. The number of women in the workforce in wealthy countries, in professional positions, and in higher education has skyrocketed since the 1960s. Jeane Kirkpatrick wrote in the early 1970s in her classic study of the United States, *Political Woman*:

> Half a century after the ratification of the nineteenth amendment, no woman has been nominated to be president or vice president, no woman has served on the Supreme Court. Today, there is no woman in the cabinet, no woman in the Senate, no woman serving as governor of a major state, no woman mayor of a major city, no woman in the top leadership of either major party (1974, 3).

With the exception of the presidential nomination (and Hillary Rodham Clinton came close to that in 2008), all that has changed. While women still make up a small percentage of each of the offices Kirkpatrick mentions, they are present in noticeable numbers, and many other countries outstrip the United States in percentage of women in high offices.

The contemporary women's movement in the West emerged out of the tumultuous 1960s. Initially, women's rights and feminism were seen as exclusively

Western concerns of little relevance to the rest of the world, especially the poorest countries. In many postcolonial countries, though, the women's movement has expanded greatly since the 1980s, often in conjunction with the democratization process we discussed in chapter 9. This expansion was marked by major United Nations conferences on women in 1985 in Nairobi, Kenya, and in 1995 in Beijing, China. Women in many postcolonial societies struggle to gain equal legal status with men in areas of family law, a victory now mostly won in wealthier countries, and, like women in wealthier countries, they also demand greater social status and a more extensive role in the political process.

The women's movement and feminist theory have raised fundamental political questions. We noted in a text box in chapter 4 that gender is a distinct identity category in part because women themselves often are used as markers of identity. Particular notions of gender roles frequently help define what it means to be a member of a particular nation, ethnic group, race, or religion, so when women challenge traditional gender roles they implicitly challenge the validity of other identity groups to which they belong. Women demanding recognition of gender as a distinct category of concern have thus come into conflict not only with nationalists in the West, but also with postcolonial nationalists who demanded national unity to throw off colonial rule, male revolutionary leaders who demanded unity to achieve the revolution, and leaders of racial or ethnic groups who demanded unity to overcome oppression. Women's movements and feminist theory have threatened all other groups at one time or another.

As they challenged other groups in many societies, feminists also debated among themselves what their full agenda ought to be. Liberal feminists focus on gaining equal rights with men as their main goal, and they tend not to challenge social or political norms beyond that, accepting existing political and economic systems but demanding equal treatment within them. Many feminist theorists, though, demand more than just equal treatment in legal, political, and economic contexts. Most have come to believe that major social and political institutions need to change if women are to make full use of legal equality. Carole Pateman (1988), for instance, questions the terms of equal citizenship itself, contending that citizenship as typically conceived is inherently male and patriarchal, with its greatest expression being military service. She argues for a new conception of citizenship that values women's lived experience that places motherhood, for instance, on the same moral level as military service. Women in racial or ethnic minorities and in the Global South, on the other hand, have criticized the global women's movement as too focused on concerns exclusive to white women in wealthy countries, arguing successfully over the last two decades for an expansion of feminist theory and political demands to recognize the distinct needs of women of color and poor women.

Still other feminists point to more practical concerns: key aspects of welfare states such as health care and access to contraception and affordable child care have been recognized as essential to achieving women's full political and economic participation. Even where broad equality has been achieved, much of society, including many young women, still assumes that women will (and should) be the primary caregivers for children, and this frequently impacts their economic and political lives. Studies show that even in families where women work (though still often do not earn) as much as men, they continue to provide the bulk of child care and unpaid household labor, creating what has come to be known in the United States as the "second shift." In response, feminist activists increasingly are calling for a change in social assumptions, perceptions, attitudes, and discourses as essential to full realization of the equity that is now legally theirs in many countries.

Women's demands for inclusion have also raised a fundamental question about what is and ought to be "public" and "private." Much political debate in all societies is restricted to what is deemed public, with private matters left to the individual, family, and religious institutions. Each society defines for itself, however, what is public and what is private, and the women's movement has successfully pressured many societies to redefine these boundaries to make formerly private concerns into public ones. In most societies, including those in the West, men's treatment of their wives was a private concern: verbal, physical, and sexual abuse, as long as it did not go as far as murder (and sometimes even when it did), was typically ignored and considered a private, family matter. The women's movement has changed this in many societies by arguing that abusive relationships within the private sphere of the family violate fundamental rights and impede women's ability to participate fully in the public sphere. And so, concerns that were once private have now become public. Women's demands continue to question and at times shift the public/private boundary in many societies, especially in areas of legal status and relationships within families.

Women have gained recognition as a group with legitimate concerns and basic political rights equal to men in many societies: they are allowed to vote and, at least in theory, hold elective office. Their social and legal status, however, is less uniformly equal to men's. Women's groups worldwide have sought greater access for women to education and participation in the labor force at all levels, and while they have not achieved full parity, women have made tremendous gains in a wide variety of societies. While many people in the West have an image of Western women as having achieved nearly equal status with men even as women in postcolonial countries continue to be mired in oppression, in many postcolonial countries, this image no longer applies. The gender gap in educational access and attainment has narrowed substantially in most Latin American and African countries and in some Asian ones as well over the last two decades, although, as is true everywhere, professional status and labor force participation rates lag behind education. The Country and Concept table provides several measures of gender equality for our case study countries, showing that some postcolonial societies are not that much more unequal in gender terms than are wealthier countries.

Concerns about achieving greater social and economic status have led women to demand reproductive rights and state support for child bearing and rearing. Because women bear children and in all societies continue to do the bulk of child rearing, advancement and improvement in these areas are essential to improving their social status. Women's movements have successfully championed the spread of access to contraception in much of the world, and birth rates have fallen significantly in most countries over the last generation. Legalized abortion remains a controversial subject, with women successfully leading efforts in many societies to support it even as moral objections, often from women themselves, keep it illegal in quite a few others and disputed in most. Women in approximately sixty countries currently have access to legalized abortion.

Women, especially in wealthier countries, have also demanded greater state support for child bearing and child rearing to facilitate their participation in the labor force while still allowing them to have children. This has included paid and unpaid maternity leave, paid and unpaid paternity leave (for fathers to help with child rearing), and access to affordable and high-quality child care. State responses to these demands have broadly mirrored the types of welfare states outlined in chapter 11. Social democratic welfare states provide more generous maternity leave and greater access to child care, and women's labor force participation is highest in these societies. Christian Democratic welfare states are generous but their ruling philosophy remains based primarily on the male head of household model, and these societies have lower labor force participation rates for women. Liberal welfare states, though providing relatively ungenerous benefits, are in the middle on women's labor force participation, reflecting the emphasis of these states on work.

A key target of women's groups worldwide has been the achievement of legal status equal to that of men in areas of family law, including rights in regard to custody of children, land, and inheritance of family property. These gains have been achieved in virtually all wealthy countries but not in all postcolonial countries. In many of the latter, women still face various legal inequities vis-á-vis men that prevent them from independently owning land or inheriting property; in some cases, women are even restricted from having independent access to banking and travel. And while virtually all countries have active women's movements working toward these goals, women in most developing societies remain poorer and less educated, on average, than in wealthier countries, so their movements lack the resources that have helped wealthier women achieve many gains. Women in the poorest countries, though, often have powerful potential allies in international development agencies such as the World Bank that have come to recognize that women, especially in rural areas, play a crucial role in development. Educating and employing women has been shown to lead to dramatic increases in use of contraception and reduced birth rates, and helping women obtain better incomes demonstrably improves the education and health of children, as women on average are more willing to spend their income in those areas than are men. Development agencies therefore support efforts to educate women and improve their legal status as part of a broader development effort. Local and international nongovernmental organizations (NGOs) also actively champion greater rights and resources for women to enhance development; a primary form of this in recent years has been microfinance loans to women to start their own local businesses.

MINI-CASE Women in Saudi Arabia and Kuwait

Women's rights to equal citizenship remain in dispute in many countries around the world, though in no area are the disputes and gender disparity greater than in the countries in the Persian Gulf region. Saudi Arabia and Kuwait are two countries that have seen repeated struggles over the issue of women's rights. Despite their many similarities and official adherence to Islamic law, the status of women in the two countries is different, though in ways that would not be predicted from the history of women's inclusion in citizenship in the West.

Both of these Persian Gulf kingdoms base their laws on Islam, but each interprets that law somewhat differently. The two countries share laws regarding women's rights in marriage, divorce, and inheritance that give men much greater freedom than women. They differ, however, in that Saudi law effectively defines women as legal minors, who have virtually no adult rights. This means that they are not allowed to travel, work, study, marry, receive medical treatment, legalize a contract, or testify in court without the permission or accompaniment of a close male relative, usually a father or husband. Women exist legally under what is known as "male guardianship" at all times. In addition, Saudi Arabia has created a system that critics have dubbed "sexual apartheid," complete gender segregation in all public facilities. Universities, most offices, shopping malls, restaurants, and other such places are strictly segregated by sex. In recent years, "women only" shopping malls and hotels have been built. In contrast, Kuwaiti women have greater freedom on a day-to-day basis. While they do not have full freedoms in the area of marriage and divorce, they are allowed to drive, travel, and dress as they please. Sex segregation has not been nearly as consistent, though it is growing. A rising Islamist group in parliament successfully pushed to resegregate public universities in 2003, which had been integrated since the 1970s.

In both countries, however, women have become increasingly prominent in the economic and educational arenas. As in Iran (see our case study in this chapter), women now form a majority in both countries' higher education systems. In Kuwait there are two-and-a-half times more women than men in higher education, in Saudi Arabia one-and-a-half times more. This does not necessarily translate into higher income however. First, in these oil-rich states, a college education is not always necessary for a high income: men often simply go to work in business after secondary school. Second, Islamic versions of the "glass ceiling" exist that limit women's advancement. In Saudi Arabia, in particular, it is illegal for women to work in any position in which they will come into regular contact with unrelated men. This leaves them working more heavily in the public sector, as teachers of girls, and out of sight of the general public. Saudi women earn only 16 percent of the income Saudi men do; in contrast, Kuwaiti women earn 35 percent what Kuwaiti men do. In 2006 women constituted 42 percent of the Kuwaiti workforce, making the country the highest-ranking Arab state in this respect.

While some women seem willing to live with these restrictions, both countries certainly have budding women's movements. Saudi Arabia's women's movement is still having difficulty getting legal recognition for its organizations. In Kuwait, in contrast, an active women's movement emerged in the 1960s and, among other things, successfully resisted the imposition of wearing of the *burqa,* the full-body Islamic covering common in the region: in urban Kuwait, wearing the *burqa* has long been the exception rather than the rule. This is in sharp contrast to Saudi Arabia, where it remains the norm and is legally enforced by "morality police" who have virtually unlimited power to harass or arrest women who show any body part in public.

In Kuwait, the main goal of the women's movements since the 1970s has been gaining the right to vote. Kuwait's parliament has greater power than most in the region; the emir still must approve its laws, but he tries to support the parliamentary majority whenever possible to maintain his popularity. A major women's push for the right to vote failed in 1999, but a renewed effort succeeded in 2005. In the 2007 parliamentary elections, Kuwaiti women voted and ran for office for the first time. They constituted a majority of the electorate and helped put an opposition coalition into power (though one that included a conservative Islamic party, so the new government is not set to expand women's rights further). None of the handful of women candidates for parliamentary seats won, but since 2000 a total of three women have been appointed to cabinet positions. In contrast, the most immediate focus of the much smaller and weaker Saudi women's movement is gaining the right to drive. In 2008 a major Saudi cleric argued that under certain circumstances women driving would not violate Islamic law. Saudi women are hopeful that they will at last gain this long sought after right, though sexual segregation continues unabated in other areas.

The image of the fully clad woman in black is one of the first that comes to the minds of many Westerners when they think of the Persian Gulf or of the Middle East in general. That image has some validity, especially in Saudi Arabia. Kuwait, however, is only one of several examples of Middle Eastern countries where that image is inaccurate. While women have not achieved the Western feminist goal of fully equal citizenship anywhere in the region, they are much closer in some countries than in others. Even in Saudi Arabia, one of the most restrictive states in terms of women's rights, women have made economic and educational gains within sexual apartheid, and a budding women's movement is demanding more.

Women's movements have also focused on improving the representation and participation of women in the political process, even in countries that are not fully democratic. As we noted in chapter 7 (see Where and Why: Women in Power), proportional representation (PR) electoral systems tend to produce higher numbers of women representatives, as do multimember district systems. Scholars use the term "descriptive representation" to indicate representation of people who look like you and have similar life experiences. Jane Mansbridge (2000) argues that such representation is particularly important when social inequality results in particular groups of citizens not trusting their elected representatives who hail from a different group, when communication among members of different groups might be difficult, and when unforeseen issues arise between elections. For instance, gender inequality may make many women not trust or feel comfortable communicating honestly with their male representatives. Furthermore, when a new issue arises that did not exist at the time of the last election, citizens may want representatives from their social group who have had similar experiences to make decisions that will reflect their perspectives. For all these reasons, women's movements have worked to improve the percentage of women in political office at all levels. Many countries have women's groups whose primary purpose is to train and fund women candidates. In a number of countries, including France, Nepal, Rwanda, South Africa, and Uganda, women's groups have successfully campaigned for quota laws that either require parties to ensure that a certain percentage of their candidates are women or reserve a certain number of legislative seats for women, elected in a separate vote from the rest of the legislature. Overall, though, women remain severely underrepresented relative to their proportion of the population in all but a handful of countries: in 2007, women constituted an average of just over 18 percent of members of parliaments around the world (Inter-Parliamentary Union, 2008).

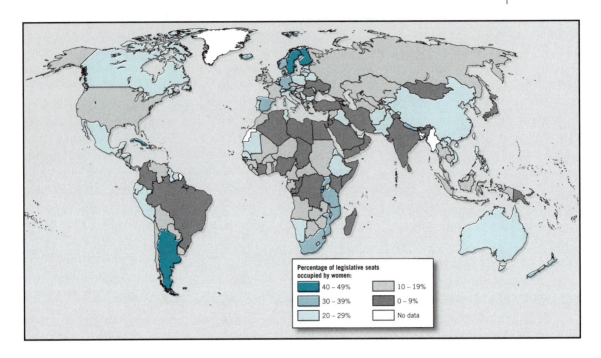

Source: Inter-Parliamentary Union's Women in National Parliaments, www.ipu.org/wmn-e/classif.htm.

Note: Percentages are for lower and single houses only. Data for upper houses, where available, can be found at the source Web site above. South Africa's estimate does not include the thirty-six special rotating delegates appointed on an ad hoc basis; all percentages given are therefore calculated on the basis of the fifty-four permanent seats. For Kuwait, no woman candidate was elected in the 2008 elections. Two women were appointed to the sixteen-member cabinet sworn in June 2008. As cabinet ministers also sit in parliament, there are two women out of a total of sixty-five members.

MAP 12.1
Women in Legislative Seats Worldwide

Even in countries where women have achieved quite substantial gains, they have not achieved full parity with men. Nowhere are women fully equal with men in terms of professional status, wages, or political representation. We examine these issues in two countries that have faced significant changes in the last twenty years, countries that most people do not think of as having women's movements of import: Russia and Iran. These countries demonstrate the ubiquity of the global women's movement and the questions it has raised.

CASE STUDY Russia: Women through Social and Political Transformation

Russian women, like Russian men, have lived through dramatic and at times traumatic social, economic, and political change since the end of the Cold War. The state and regime they grew up under imploded, an older state (Russia) was recreated, the state's social and economic systems were transformed almost entirely, and a new regime (some would argue two regimes) emerged. The Soviet Union left an unusual legacy for women's role in society. Soviet women were heavily involved in the labor force and highly educated before their contemporaries in the West or postcolonial societies, and the Soviet Union at times attempted to counter traditional cultural norms about gender roles, though with mixed results. Yet Soviet women had no history of autonomous political action, in spite of some formal "representation" in the centralized Soviet political system. In the new Russia, women have nearly complete legal rights in all areas, but in practice these are often not enforced. They continue to face cultural and social constraints to their full participation in society and politics, but they remain nearly equal to men in their participation in the economy and superior to men in their educational achievement. Neither of these achievements, however, has translated into equal wages and incomes. A growing women's movement emerged in the 1990s, but Vladimir Putin's elimination of much of Russia's autonomous civil society severely curtailed it after 2000.

Even as the Soviet Union claimed to favor full gender equality, this was always ideologically subordinated to the needs of the proletarian revolution and in practical terms it was secondary to the needs of building a stronger state and economy. Early Soviet laws gave women more freedoms than most societies at the time. For example, by the 1920s, women had gained the right to marry whom they wanted and divorce when they wanted, own their own property separate from their husbands, inherit property, keep their own surnames after marriage, refuse to move with their husbands, and have abortions paid for by the state. As Josef Stalin created a more centralized dictatorship in the 1930s he declared the "woman question" closed and women

Feminists protest the celebration of International Women's Day in Moscow in 2006. The banner reads "Flowers— today, shackles—everyday?" Like women in many countries, Russian women achieve at higher levels than men in the educational system but still command significantly lower wages, and continue to provide the bulk of household labor and child-rearing.

to be completely "liberated." Facing a falling birth rate, he made abortions illegal to encourage more children but also encouraged women to expand their participation in the labor force because of a labor shortage. By the 1960s, women's participation rate in the labor force was nearly equal to men's, abortion was again legal and widely available, and women were rapidly catching up to men in the educational system.

The state continued to face a demographic dilemma that only grew worse after the end of communism: it encouraged women to participate in the labor force to increase production but at the same time Russian women were having fewer and fewer babies. To counter this, the Soviet government instituted generous and widely available child care as early as the 1920s and later added quite generous maternity leave: a total of 112 days at full pay. Economic reform in the late 1980s under Mikhail Gorbachev, the Soviet Union's last Communist leader, led to the first recognized official unemployment policy under the Soviet system. With fewer workers needed and the birthrate continuing to fall, the Communist state in its last years shifted to a more traditional attitude. In the words of Gorbachev:

> Over the years … we failed to pay attention to women's specific rights and needs arising from their role as mother and home-maker, and their indispensable educational function as regards children … women no longer have enough time to perform their everyday duties at home—housework, the upbringing of children and the creation of a good family atmosphere … we are now holding heated debates … about the question of what we should do to make it possible for women to return to their purely womanly mission (quoted in Racioppi and See 1995, 824).

This would be a harbinger of things to come in terms of cultural attitudes, though not of actual shifts in the work done by women.

The transition to a market economy after the dissolution of the Soviet state produced dramatic economic decline for most of the 1990s. Men and women alike suffered from this, but most observers see women as losing more. The full legal rights equal to those of men that they had under Soviet rule were preserved in the new 1993 constitution, but the effects of economic and cultural change nonetheless harmed women's position. Women continued throughout to equal men in their participation rates in employment, and both suffered unemployment at about the same rates as the Communist economy made the transition to a market-based system. Women, however, faced much longer periods on the unemployment rolls than men, who gained new jobs more quickly. In the early 2000s, as the economy began to rebound, men and women benefited about equally in terms of gaining new jobs. Women's wages, however, have always been and remain below men's: they were on average 70 percent of men's at the end of the Communist era, and by 2003 this number had dropped to 64 percent despite women's higher education levels on average. Women receive lower wages and are in less prestigious positions even in fields where they predominate, such as education and public

service. The biggest cause of the wage gap, though, is the shift of women out of high-paying sectors, such as finance and industry, since the end of the Soviet era. Women now constitute more than 60 percent of the employees in low-paying fields like education and public service and only about 30 percent in the high-paying sectors (Roschin and Zubarevich 2005, 7–17).

The transition to a market economy has unquestionably affected other aspects of women's working and personal lives. Women increasingly end up in part-time employment, which further lowers their income relative to that of men. They are also overrepresented among Russia's poor, in part due to the large numbers of impoverished and elderly widows, as Russian women's life expectancy is thirteen years longer than men's (seventy-two versus fifty-nine years), one of the largest gaps in the world. (The reasons for this gap are the subject of much debate; the factors include much higher male rates of tuberculosis, industrial accidents, suicide, and alcohol and drug abuse.) The Soviet system of state-sponsored preschools shrank dramatically as funding dried up in the 1990s, causing attendance to drop as well: in the late Soviet era, as many as 84 percent of children three years of age and older were in child care institutions; by 2000 that number had fallen to only 47 percent. Families, including extended families, have been forced to make up the difference. The Soviet Union's relatively generous maternity leave policies were preserved and even extended, and a "parental leave" for either parent was instituted as well, to be used until a child reaches eighteen months of age, though it only provided $17 per month in the 1990s, when the poverty level was about $200 (Teplova 2007). Welfare benefits were widespread, but provided very little income, forcing most women to continue working at least part-time. Like women in the United States and elsewhere, Russian women continue to work the second shift as well: in the mid-1990s they were employed an average of thirty-eight hours per week, compared to forty-three hours for men, but women also did an average of thirty hours per week of household chores and child care whereas men did only fourteen hours per week (Roschin and Zubarevich 2005, 20).

Russian women did not sit idly by in the face of these challenges. An active women's movement arose in the early 1990s, supported by Western donors interested in developing Russia's new civil society. The Soviet Union had allowed only official and therefore state-controlled women's organizations to exist, so no autonomous civil society groups were permitted until the reforms of the late 1980s. New women's organizations mushroomed in the early 1990s, with three hundred registered by 1994 and two thousand by the end of the decade. Many of these were small and poorly funded groups that did not survive long, but a few became important centers for gathering information and publicizing issues of concern to women. The most prominent of these groups began under the leadership of highly educated, professional women, and not all automatically adopted all aspects of Western feminism, though their emphasis on better working conditions, welfare support for women, and greater political representation were quite familiar to feminists worldwide. A division emerged within the movement between those who had been members of the official state-sponsored organizations of the Soviet era who focused more directly on making practical gains in women's immediate well-being, self-consciously "feminist" groups critical of the former Soviet organizations that sought extensive changes in social and cultural attitudes toward women. Other women's groups focused on broader issues such as the environment or peace, particularly in opposition to the war in the Russian province of Chechnya. While the movement gained strength in the early 1990s, by the end of the decade, such divisions and lack of resources had noticeably weakened it. Under President Putin it declined further like most autonomous organizations in Russian civil society (Racioppi and See 1995).

Even at its height in the 1990s the movement had limited success placing women in decision-making positions. The powerless Soviet legislature had a quota that ensured one-third of its members were women. This quota was eliminated at the time of the first competitive election for the Russian (as opposed to Soviet) parliament in 1990, resulting in only 5.4 percent of its members being women. The successor to the official Soviet women's organization, the Union of Women of Russia, formed a political party, Women of Russia, to contest the 1993 legislative elections. The party suc-

ceeded in raising women's numbers in the lower house of parliament, gaining 8 percent of the seats, and women overall constituted 13.6 percent of all members (higher than in the United States at the time), a significant accomplishment given the context. By the next election in 1995, however, many women were disillusioned with the party's failure to provide any concrete benefits, and it failed to gain the 5 percent of votes necessary to be allotted seats in parliament. The total representation of women in that parliament fell to 10 percent, with a further decline to less than 8 percent in the 1999 election. This trend was reversed in elections in the new millennium: the 2007 election (in the far less powerful legislature under then president Putin) produced a lower house in which 14 percent of members were female, tying Russia for eightieth place with Guinea-Bissau on a global list (Inter-Parliamentary Union 2008).

Despite possessing full legal rights, Russian women continue to face attitudinal barriers to full participation in society. Social attitudes about women's roles seem to have become somewhat more traditional since the end of Communist rule. While a majority of both men and women expect women to work for a wage and think that is fine, and a majority of women want a fulfilling career, a majority of both genders also think that the man should be the primary breadwinner in the family. A 2002 study found the persistence of many traditional stereotypes of ideal male characteristics being strength, intelligence, and the provision of material security, whereas ideal female characteristics were appearance, loving children, and housekeeping skills (White 2005, 431). These attitudes are apparently reflected in the economy as well: women have reported discrimination in hiring by men who prefer them to stay in the home as, well as incidents in which they were forced by employers to sign contracts promising not to get married or have children because businesses fear having to pay maternity leave.

While the new Russian state has preserved full legal rights and fairly extensive benefits for women, including maternity leave, it has done little to counter the underlying attitudes and norms that continue to limit the progress of women. Both President Boris Yeltsin and President Putin established government agencies ostensibly meant to improve the status of women, but neither accomplished much. Overall, the state provides little support for ending discrimination against women. A recent United Nations report summed up the situation:

> There have been two distinct phases of policy formulation and implementation [about women's issues in Russia]. The first stage, in the 1990s, gave an appearance of activity, but tended to be limited to words.... [In] the second phase, dating from the turn of the Millennium, the state has given up both declarations and actions. Gender issues have effectively dropped out of the Government's socioeconomic priorities (Human Development Report 2005, 60).

Putin's crackdown on women's organizations along with the rest of civil society and his complete control of the legislature elected in 2007 suggests that little will change in the foreseeable future, even under the leadership of Dmitry Medvedev, a Putin supporter handpicked to succeed Putin to the presidency in 2008.

CASE STUDY Iran: Social Gains, Political and Cultural Restrictions, and Islamic Feminism

In 2003 Iranian human rights lawyer and feminist activist Shirin Ebadi won the Nobel Peace Prize amidst great adulation from much of the world but condemnation from the Iranian government. Three years later, a large group of women planned a demonstration in Tehran to protest discrimination against women. Police arrived and broke up the demonstrators before they really got started, arresting forty-two women and twenty-eight men. These actions launched a new wave of women's activity against laws they felt were discriminatory under the Islamic Republic. In response, the government under conservative President Mahmoud Ahmadinejad began a new crackdown in 2007 on public morality, especially women's public appearance. Over the course of a year, "chastity police" arrested hundreds and harassed thousands of Iranians, mostly women, for not abiding by a particular interpretation of Islamic teachings about what women can do and how they can appear in public. This is only the latest battle in a long-standing dispute over women's rights in Iran, and while the Iranian government certainly does not treat women equally in cultural and political areas, it has nonetheless allowed and often even encouraged significant social and economic gains. This has created a contradiction, as educated and employed women demand greater equality and the government continues to deny it. The women's movement leading this effort includes not only secular

A woman wearing brightly colored clothing is stopped by the "chastity police" in Tehran in June 2008. President Ahmadinejad's government has increased enforcement of Iran's strict dress code for women, reversing some liberalization that the women's movement had gained earlier in the decade. Iran has pursued policies that have encouraged women to gain greater education, have fewer children, and work more, but has resisted the women's movement that was the seemingly inevitable outcome of these changes.

feminists opposed to the Islamic regime but also Islamic feminists who argue for an interpretation of Shiite Islamic teachings that grants greater gender equality than the Islamic Republic so far will accept.

Under the shah's modernization program of the 1960s and 1970s, women were encouraged to reject their traditional roles and appearance in order to "modernize" along Western lines. The effort had a significant effect in urban areas, but far less of an impact in rural locales. Like the rest of the shah's policies, however, it increasingly came to be seen as imposed by a dictator doing the West's bidding, and women were active participants in the 1978–1979 Islamic revolution that created the Islamic Republic. Like all revolutions, the political forces that brought down the shah included groups with quite disparate ideologies united in their opposition to the old regime (see chapter 9), and women were active in virtually all of these groups: secularized women in the secular forces of students, professionals, and traders and religious women in the Islamist groups. The revolutionary process itself, though, regardless of ideology, gave women an active role (not as leaders) that brought them into the political arena in larger numbers than ever before.

As the Islamist clerics under the Ayatollah Khomeini consolidated their power in 1979–1980, however, one of their first acts was to reverse the shah's Family Protection Law that had Westernized much of the country's family law: the new regime eliminated women's right to divorce while giving men nearly an unlimited right to leave their wives; required women to wear the *hijab,* the Islamic veil, in public; forced women out of the legal profession and restricted them from several other professions; banned contraception; and segregated the education system. Many secular and Islamist women who had been active in the revolution felt betrayed and protested these changes, including hundreds of thousands who took to the streets in March 1979 to protest mandatory veiling, but their protests proved fruitless.

During the 1980s most of the social gains women had made since the 1960s were at least partially reversed: women's employment levels dropped, their political participation was minimal (only 4 women out of 270 MPs were elected to the first parliament after the revolution), and without access to contraception they bore more children. At the same time, the Iran-Iraq War (1980–1988) pushed women into the public sphere in other areas as the war effort required a great deal of volunteer work that women took up, especially with so many men fighting the war. The absence of men also gave women an opportunity to enter school at all levels to an unprecedented degree, which the government encouraged as part of a large literacy campaign. Indeed, gender segregation of schools increased girls' enrollment, as conservative parents were more willing to send their daughters to all-female schools. Any critical political activity was still severely repressed, however, especially in light of the war, but women found new paths to enter the public arena and education system.

With the war over the government set out to improve the country's weak economy by pursuing an economic liberalization program throughout the early 1990s. Yet the various restrictions put on women's economic roles after the revolution came into direct conflict with economic growth. Spurred by a renewed women's movement and facing economic necessity, the government partially reversed various laws restricting the advancement of women. Over the course of the decade, most restrictions on what women could study and where they could work were eliminated, and the government reintroduced and actively supported contraception to reduce the birth rate and it mandated maternity leave. Women were also allowed to reenter the legal profession in any position except that of courtroom judge. Fertility rates dropped, women advanced through the educational system, female literacy increased dramatically, more women chose not to marry, and the age at the time of a woman's first marriage increased (Bahramitash and Kazemipour 2006).

By the new millennium the results of these actions were quite significant. From the time of the revolution to 2002, women's life expectancy increased from fifty-eight to seventy-two years, their illiteracy rate fell from 69 to 31 percent, the percentage of women still single in their early twenties increased from 21 to 54 percent, their fertility rate dropped from an average of 6.5 live births to 2.7, the gap between men and women in age of marriage and level of education dropped dramatically, and starting in 2000, women surpassed men to become the majority of entering university students

(Bahramitash and Kazemipour 2006). In 2008 women had become so prominent in medical education that the government passed a regulation that medical fields had to have a student body that included at least 30 percent of each gender to ensure a place for men.

As these dramatic social and economic changes were taking place, an active women's movement re-emerged that involved both secular and Islamic feminists. The latter asserted their right to interpret the holy texts (*ijtihad*) as placing an overall emphasis on gender equality, and they used the Prophet Mohammad's wives and daughters as examples of women actively involved in the public sphere. They argued that

> [t]rue Islam ... combined equality of opportunity for men and women to develop their talents and capacities and to participate in all aspects of social life, because it acknowledged women's maternal instinct and their essential role within the family (Paidar 1995, 241).

These feminists rejected what they saw as Western society's sexual objectification of women and the individualistic assumptions of much Western feminism, but they nonetheless argued for a place of equality within Iran's Islamic society.

As the broader reform movement grew in the 1990s (see chapter 8), the women's movement became even more active. This was clear in the growing role of women's NGOs. To date, there are only an estimated twenty NGOs, but they have been very active in providing services and education for women, especially in urban areas (Alaedini and Razavi 2005, 69). Women also have started numerous publications whenever press restrictions are partially eased, the best known of which has been *Zanan* (*Women*), which became a major forum for both secular and Islamist women to present their arguments.

Despite severe cultural and legal restrictions on women, the Islamic constitution gave them full rights to participate in politics, except for being barred from holding the office of the president. Prior to 1991, only clearly identified Islamist women had been elected to parliament. In 1991 secular women activists were added to their ranks, and women's numbers peaked in the 1996 election at fourteen MPs. From the start of the Islamic Republic, most of the small number of

IN CONTEXT Women in Iran and the Middle East

Improvements in the status of women in Iran since the late 1980s have made it roughly equal with the average of other Middle Eastern states on a variety of measures of women's well-being and equality, and well ahead of the regional average in reduced fertility rate.

	Gender-Related Development Index (2005)	Gender-Empowerment Measure (2005)	Fertility-Rate (births per woman, 2000–2005)	Ratio of Female to Male Income	Ratio of Female to Male Adult Literacy (2005)	Ratio of Female to Male Secondary Enrollment (2005)	Ratio of Female to Male Tertiary Enrollment (2005)	Percentage Female Seats in Parliament
Iran	0.750	0.347	2.1	0.39	0.87	0.94	1.09	4.1
Rest of Middle East	0.769	0.372	3.2	0.31	0.83	0.98	1.53	7.9

Source: United Nations Development Report 2007/2008, http://hdr.undp.org/en/statistics/data.

women MPs worked actively in support of achieving greater equality for women. In the area of family law, women were granted slightly more rights to divorce, including the indexing of the traditional payment a man must make to his wife when divorcing her to take inflation into account, and greater rights over guardianship of children, which came with child allowances from the government. Such legal victories, though, have remained relatively few and minor.

The height of the reformist movement under President Mohammad Khatami (1997–2005) saw relatively limited legal changes beyond those already mentioned, but the severity of the cultural restrictions on women's public actions lessened. The reformist governments of the 1990s and early 2000s did not enforce the rules about veiling and public segregation of the sexes with the zeal that earlier governments had or subsequent governments have. As we noted in chapter 8, the Islamic Republic has a long history of the clerical elite allowing reform efforts to expand and then clamping down on them when they go beyond what the conservative clerics find acceptable.

The election of President Ahmadinejad was the end of the Khatami-led reform effort. While Iranian women made unprecedented social and economic gains after 1988, their movement to achieve greater legal equality and cultural freedom achieved far less. Ahmadinejad's renewed efforts to restrict women and segregate them in public has included not only the crackdown since 2007 but also banning numerous women's (and other dissident) publications and Web sites and expanding the gender segregation of public amenities, including buses, taxis, and even telephone booths. In 2007–2008 more than one city built "women only" parks behind high walls within which women could enjoy being outside and exercise without being veiled. Economic needs and the women's movement to date have combined to achieve significant social and economic gains for women, though these gains have been far less in the legal, political, and cultural spheres. Nonetheless, an active women's movement continues, one that is not only secular and feminist but also Islamic and feminist that is trying to use the powerful religious symbols and ideas to reinterpret women's place in the Islamic Republic.

Summary

The women's movement has fundamentally questioned and challenged conventional liberal notions of modern citizenship as well as all other forms of identity. It has been the most successful domestic and international social movement of the last half century, changing mores and policies in many countries. While it has arguably achieved the greatest success in wealthy democracies, its effects have been felt everywhere, as our case studies demonstrate. Our case studies and much other evidence point to a broad trend of women achieving great gains in the educational sphere that have translated only partially into gains in the economic sphere. While women are working for wages far more frequently than they used to in virtually every country in the world, they work for less money and in less prestigious positions than men. Similarly, while they have made substantial gains in political power in many countries, especially in parts of Europe, they are nowhere equal to men in the political sphere. These continued shortcomings raise fundamental questions about whether our understanding of citizenship, common social attitudes, and major institutions have to change before women will truly achieve equal citizenship in its broadest conception. In addition to raising all these questions, the feminist movement has been intimately connected with the rise of the "gay rights movement," to which we now turn.

SEXUAL ORIENTATION: ASSIMILATION OR LIBERATION?

What is commonly known as the "gay rights movement," the demand for inclusion in full citizenship for people of all sexual orientations, challenges social norms at least as much or more than the women's movement with which it is interrelated. The movement for equality based on sexual orientation faces a unique set of challenges compared to the other movements discussed in this chapter and chapter 4. Its primary demand has been for public recognition; once this is achieved, other demands include full legal equality and open representation and participation in the political process. Recognition is especially central to the movement because homosexual activity has been hidden through most of human history. Homosexuals are able to hide their identity in a way women or minorities typically cannot. Throughout history and around the world, people have engaged in homosexual activity but have hidden it because of social and political discrimination and criminalization. In this context, being publicly recognized and "coming out" as gay or lesbian is the first crucial political act and demand. Literal recognition, in the sense of no longer having to hide, is essential.

A major debate within the gay rights movement has long been how to identify the group(s) and whom to include. The matter of definition is not simple. Indeed, the term "homosexual" itself first appeared in print only in 1869. Prior to that, most people were well aware of the fact that individuals of the same sex had sexual relations, but this was thought of as a practice not as a category of people. Given the strong social and financial pressure to marry in virtually all societies, much homosexual activity took place and continues to take place among individuals married to members of the opposite sex. Only in the last century have people come to think of themselves as homosexuals and, more recently, as "gay" or "lesbian."

But even with this social construction of an identity category, the name and exact boundaries of the group and movement have shifted over time. Originally referred to as "homosexual," by the late 1960s the group had adopted the term "gay and lesbian" in some countries, in part because "homosexual" had been a term used by psychiatrists to classify the practice as a mental disorder. By the 1980s, though, it was becoming clear that not all people who were not heterosexual identified themselves as gay or lesbian. Sex research has long shown that sexual preferences do not fit into absolute categories but rather extend along a continuum, from sole preference for the opposite sex on one end and for the same sex on the other, with a range of variation in between. Eventually, the categories "bisexual" and "transgender," meaning people who do not identify clearly with either major gender, were added to produce "lesbian, gay, bisexual, and transgender" (LGBT), the most common current designation in the United States. Recently, some activists and theorists have adopted the word "queer," formerly considered quite derogatory, as an affirmative term to include the entire LGBT group or sometimes as an addition to the label, as in LGBTQ.

In addition to these definitional debates, the LGBT community has debated the terms on which they should try to gain inclusion. Like the women's movement, members are divided over the extent to which they should simply seek equal rights within the existing system or seek to transform the norms within the system. Those who favor an assimilationist approach seek equal civil and political rights but generally are willing to adopt the cultural norms of mainstream, heterosexual society: for instance, they favor same-sex marriage, the expansion of a heterosexual institution to include them. The **liberationist approach**, on the other hand, seeks to transform sexual and gender norms, not simply to gain equal rights with heterosexuals but also to liberate everyone to express whatever sexual orientation and gender identity they wish in order to gain social acceptance and respect for all regardless of their conformity to preexisting norms or institutions. Those favoring a liberationist approach question the importance of same-sex marriage because they question the entire idea of marriage as a patriarchal, heterosexual institution that they would like the freedom to move beyond. They certainly favor equal rights, but they seek much greater change than that, calling for a new "sexual citizenship" (Bell and Binnie 2000).

In terms of rights, members of the LGBT group are unusual in the sense that they secured basic political rights as individuals long before civil rights, because as individuals they could vote or run for office like any other citizen, as long as they kept their sexual orientation private. As a group, though, they were unwelcome until quite recently in all modern societies. They could not proclaim their identity publicly in most countries because of laws criminalizing their behavior. Repeal of such laws therefore became one of the movement's first priorities. Beyond decriminalization of their behavior, they have worked for passage of antidiscrimination laws that prevent government, employers, educators, and adoption agencies from discriminating against them on the basis of sexual orientation. Those who favor same-sex marriage do so in part because they see the right to marry as part of equal civil rights because in all societies, marital status comes with legal benefits of some sort, usually involving taxation, inheritance, employment benefits, and control over major health decisions. The movement's political success remains greater than its success in the area of civil rights in a number of countries, however; while active gay rights movements engage in the political process in wealthy democracies without restraint, in most countries they have still not achieved equal civil rights in terms of antidiscrimination laws, marriage, and other related areas.

States have responded to these movements in various ways. On the whole, the movements have clearly been more active and influential in wealthier countries. In well-established democracies, LGBT movements have been able to use their political rights to demand full civil rights but only with partial success. The biggest issue of recent years has been same-sex marriage. A handful of states have granted complete rights to marry, starting with the Netherlands in 2001 and subsequently Belgium, Canada, Norway, South Africa, and Spain. A number of others have instead legalized domestic partnerships or civil unions of various types that grant many but not all the rights of marriage. When first enacted, civil unions in France became surprisingly popular with heterosexual couples even though they were intended primarily for gay and lesbian couples: given France's strict divorce laws, many straight couples preferred a civil union to marriage.

Fewer postcolonial societies have active LGBT movements. Higher levels of religiosity and cultural traditions in many of these societies mean greater social opposition to public proclamation of homosexuality, as the Country and Concept table demonstrates for our case study countries. In a number of countries, however, active gay rights movements do exist. Indeed, South Africa became the first country in the world to include sexual orientation in its constitution as a category protected from discrimination. In 2005 a South African court interpreted this to apply to marriage, making it one of the first countries in the world with legalized gay marriage. Fledgling LGBT movements elsewhere in Africa, such as in Zimbabwe and Kenya, however, face much greater popular and legal resistance, and in many postcolonial countries, homosexual activity remains explicitly illegal. However, one of our two case studies, Brazil, is an example of a postcolonial society with an active LGBT movement that has had some notable policy successes. We compare it with the United States, the country that has been at the forefront of the LGBT movement for a generation now, though the U.S. government has not responded with pro-LGBT policies as quickly as a number of other governments around the world.

CASE STUDY The United States: Birthplace of a Movement but Limited Policy Change

The modern gay rights movement was born in New York City in 1969 at the famous Stonewall riots. New York police raided a popular gay bar, the Stonewall Inn, on June 28, setting off five days of sometimes violent defense of the bar and attacks on the police. While a small gay rights movement had existed since the 1950s, the Stonewall event led to a rapid expansion across the country and then around the world. The movement has had greater success at the state and local level than at the national level in the American federal system, which has left a patchwork of laws and rights across the country. This limited success has been due in part to the growth of an equally active antigay rights movement centered in conservative religious groups, with greater strength in some areas of the country than in others.

The first gay rights movement was the Mattachine Society, founded in Los Angeles in 1951. Known as the

"homophile" movement, its main goals were to unify homosexuals, raise their and others' consciousness of their existence and numbers, and lessen discrimination against them. The movement quickly divided over assimilationist versus liberationist strategies, with the former becoming the dominant group through the 1960s. While branches opened in a number of major cities and the movement won a couple of important court cases on discrimination in employment, it remained a small effort. William Eskridge describes the effects of Stonewall on this fledgling movement:

> Literally overnight, the Stonewall riots transformed the *homophile movement* of several dozen homosexuals into a *gay liberation movement* populated by thousands of lesbians, gay men, and bisexuals who formed hundreds of organizations demanding radical changes (1999, 99 emphasis in original).

A month after Stonewall, the Gay Liberation Front was formed, and soon thereafter a more assimilationist Gay Activist Alliance emerged, once again reflecting division in the movement.

By the 1980s this social movement had grown exponentially, with the assimilationist forces forming several major interest groups, including the Human Rights Campaign (HRC), the National Gay and Lesbian Task Force (NGLTF), and the Lambda Defense and Legal Education Fund. These and other groups lobbied Congress and state legislatures for legal changes, pursued court cases, and funded gay candidates for office, as well as straight candidates who supported their cause. The birth of the HIV/AIDS crisis, which primarily affected the gay male population in its early years, gave new impetus to a more social movement orientation among other activists. Believing that neither the government nor the mainstream gay rights groups were adequately addressing the epidemic, new groups emerged that demanded greater attention as well as greater freedom to express their sexuality publicly. The best known of the HIV/AIDS groups was the AIDS Coalition to Unleash Power (ACT UP), formed in 1987. It and other groups fought for greater funding for AIDS research and drugs and initiated the practice of occasional marches on Washington, the first of which was held in 1979, to demand broader gay rights in general. ACT UP also sought to recruit racial minority members, whose absence from the broader movement (similar to their absence from the early women's movement) had been notable and a source of criticism and weakness.

The LGBT movement, both the assimilationist and liberationist strands, has become a significant component of American civil society, as has opposition to it. Members' success in establishing themselves as a political force to be reckoned with, however, has not been matched with complete success in achieving their policy objectives. Legal battles have become a major area of policy action, given that a central issue in this battle is civil rights and because of the role of the American judicial system in making policy in this area. The pre-Stonewall movement focused narrowly on particular cases of egregious discrimination, winning some court cases that restricted police from harassing

The annual Gay and Lesbian Pride Parade passes the original Stonewall Inn in New York's Greenwich Village in 1989. A 1969 raid on the Stonewall, a gay bar, ignited the modern gay rights movement in the United States, which then spread to much of the world. Despite being the home of the modern movement, policies in the United States are not as supportive of the gay rights movements as are those of a number of other countries.

patrons of gay bars or closing these businesses simply because they catered to gays and lesbians, as well as a few cases of employment discrimination for gay people fired from government employment, including the military, even with exemplary service records. All of these rulings were by lower courts and their reach was relatively narrow. Police harassment of gay bars, for instance, continued unabated, using sodomy and other laws as legal justification. The first Supreme Court decision of note ruled in favor of the Mattachine Society's right to transmit its magazine through the mail; the U.S. Post Office had banned its distribution via the mail on the grounds of obscenity even though it was simply a newsmagazine addressing gay issues.

LGBT legal activists believed the Supreme Court had set the stage for a federal repeal of all sodomy laws in the 1965 *Griswold v. Connecticut* decision that legalized the use of contraception by married adults on the grounds of a "right to privacy" implicit in the Constitution (a right also used in 1973 to legalize abortion in *Roe v. Wade*). In 1986 the Court heard *Bowers v.*

Hardwick, in which a Georgia man had been arrested in his own bedroom for having sex with another man. In a 5-4 decision the Supreme Court ruled that the right to privacy did not apply, in part because no long-standing tradition of respecting privacy in the case of homosexual relations existed, in contrast to the case for married couples. Finally, in the 2003 case of *Lawrence v. Texas,* the Court ruled 6-3 that sodomy laws were unconstitutional for violating the right to due process, explicitly reversing its 1986 decision.

Other legislative and legal battles have not been as successful. While twenty states have laws protecting against employment discrimination on the basis of sexual orientation and another twelve do the same for state employment, the federal government has never passed such a law, even though legislators first introduced this legislation in 1974. Currently titled the Employment Non-discrimination Act (ENDA), the bill has continuously been introduced and has passed in the House of Representatives but has fallen short in the Senate. Its latest version includes protection not only on the basis of sexual orientation but also gender identity, which includes transgendered people already protected in some states.

Another area of only partial success has been the right of members of the LGBT community to serve openly in the military. When President Bill Clinton came to office, the movement thought—based on statements made during his campaign—that it had a champion for its concerns, and he was the first president to meet with leadership from the major groups in the White House. Nonetheless, facing nearly certain opposition from Congress and from the military, Clinton chose not to insist that the military allow gay men and women to serve openly but instead created a "don't ask, don't tell" policy under which the military quit inquiring about sexual orientation but gay soldiers could also not reveal their orientation. Discharges based on sexual orientation, however, have continued, though at a slower pace than before the policy. In the 1980s, approximately 1,500 soldiers were discharged annually due to homosexuality; since the policy went into effect in 1993 that number has been cut approximately in half (Servicemembers Legal Defense Network 2008).

The biggest current issue in the United States and much of the wealthy world is legalization of same-sex marriage. The mainstream, assimilationist organizations in the American movement have fought for this right in terms of American civil rights laws, arguing that restricting marriage to a man and woman discriminates against homosexual individuals. The LGBT movement has successfully convinced numerous urban municipalities and (as of 2008) nine states (Hawaii, Vermont, Massachusetts, California, New Jersey, Connecticut, Maine, Oregon, and Washington) and the District of Columbia to legalize some type of domestic partnership, civil union, or marriage to give same-sex couples most of the rights of married couples. The first court case to question a state's refusal to grant a same-sex couple a marriage license was in 1993 in Hawaii, but it ultimately resulted in the state passing a constitutional amendment banning same-sex marriage and writing a law allowing civil unions. The case produced a nationwide campaign against same-sex marriage, however, that led to state laws and constitutional amendments explicitly restricting marriage to a union between a man and a woman, and a federal law, the Defense of Marriage Act in 1996 (passed by Congress and signed by President Clinton), did the same. More than thirty states now have explicit limitations, many written into their constitutions, that define marriage as between a man and a woman. Following state Supreme Court rulings, Vermont legalized same-sex civil unions in 2000; Massachusetts became the first state in the nation to allow gay marriage, but only for its residents, in May 2004; and California joined it in June 2008, though a ballot measure to change the constitution to once again ban this was pending after the court ruling. The movement's efforts, therefore, have succeeded only in a handful of states and have produced a backlash that may make same-sex marriage less likely than it once was in most states.

Summary

The United States was the clear birthplace of the LGBT movement and continues to have one of the most active movements in the world. Strong opposition from Christian conservatives, a stronger political force in the

United States than in any other wealthy country, and the decentralized, federal system has resulted in the movement gaining only partial success, however. While it has clearly gained recognition of the group as a politi-cal force and, for most people, legitimate interest group in American politics, it has only partially succeeded at changing policies, mainly via litigation.

CASE STUDY Brazil: LGBT Rights in a New Democracy

In 2006 São Paulo, Brazil's largest city, hosted the big-gest gay pride parade in world history, and it remains the biggest annual gay gathering on the planet. Al-though it is the world's largest predominantly Catho-lic country, Brazil has a long history and reputation of being relatively open about sexuality in general. While it has long had a well-established LGBT community, this community only became an open political move-ment with the start of the transition to democracy in the late 1970s, and it didn't fully develop into a viable political force until the 1990s. Like the United States, the Brazilian movement went through years of contro-versy over how to define itself. It has succeeded in get-ting policies that are more inclusive of LGBT rights than most states, especially in comparison to most post-colonial states, but these are by no means complete. The movement continues to work to achieve policies to eliminate discrimination on the basis of sexual orien-tation, to establish same-sex marriage or at least civil unions, and to reduce violence against members of the LGBT community.

The first explicit Brazilian gay rights group, *Grupo Somos* (We Are), formed in São Paulo in 1979. It was preceded in the 1960s by mostly apolitical homophile groups not unlike those in the United States before Stonewall. *Grupo Somos* emerged at the same time that major pressure on the military regime for political opening of the country began (see chapter 9). By the early 1980s about twenty LGBT groups existed, but many of these did not survive more than a few years as these initial groups were plagued by divisions over the inclusion of lesbians and transvestites. Both of these groups went on to form separate organizations at vari-ous points: lesbians in the 1980s and transvestites in the 1990s. Until 1992 the major annual meeting of the

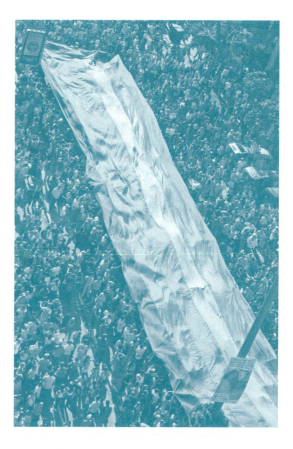

São Paulo's ninth Gay, Lesbian, Bisexual, and Transgen-der parade was held in 2005. The city annually hosts the world's largest parade, drawing as many as two million participants and spectators. Brazil has one of the most active LGBT movements in the postcolonial world, and pushed by the movement, the country now supports nu-merous benefits for homosexual couples though has not legalized civil unions or gay marriage.

movement was called the Brazilian Meeting of Homo-sexuals; in 1993 this became the Brazilian Meeting of

Lesbians and Homosexuals; in 1998 the Brazilian Meeting of Lesbians, Gays, and Transgenders; and finally in 2005, the Brazilian Association of Lesbians, Gays, and Transvestites was founded, bringing all the major groups under one umbrella. (In Brazil the movement is known usually by the label GLT rather than LGBT; the active transvestite community did not accept the "transgender" label.)

The movement's growth, despite its divisions, has been quite impressive and was initially helped and inspired by the post-Stonewall movement in the United States and Europe. It also benefited from the political opening in the early 1980s as the country began the transition to democracy. The leadership of the union-based Workers' Party (PT) (see chapter 9) rhetorically embraced gay rights activists and their cause at the first PT convention in 1981, though opposition from some Catholic activists in the party continued. The AIDS crisis first hurt and then strengthened the movement in the 1980s. Initially, AIDS hit the gay male population the hardest, as it did in the United States. As awareness grew, however, infection rates among gay men dropped significantly. Simultaneously, and in part as a result of active pressure from the movement, Brazil developed an AIDS prevention and treatment policy that became a global model of success. Many AIDS NGOs with ties to the gay rights movement arose in the 1980s. By the 1990s, the World Bank and other international donors were funding some LGBT groups that were helping implement the National AIDS Program. In 2006 Juan Marsiaj noted that "[t]he size and diversity of the Brazilian GLT movement make it the largest and one of the strongest of its kind in Latin America" (172).

In 1823 Brazil became one of the first countries in the world to eliminate antisodomy laws. While homosexual activity is not illegal, antidiscrimination laws are still only partial. The gay rights movement worked hard to get "sexual orientation" included in the 1988 constitution's antidiscrimination clause but was unsuccessful in its efforts. A constituent assembly wrote the constitution, and those members from leftist parties supported the effort unanimously but most centrist and right-wing members voted against it. Two states, however, included the language in their state constitutions.

A national antidiscrimination law focusing on discrimination by commercial enterprises and government offices passed the National Congress in 2000. By 2003 three states and more than seventy municipalities, including the country's two largest cities, had passed some type of antidiscrimination law.

Attempts to legalize civil unions and same-sex marriage have not been as successful, and current efforts focus primarily on establishing legal civil unions. In contrast to the United States, the federal government controls marriage law in Brazil. The PT introduced a bill in the National Congress in 1995 to legalize civil unions nationwide but it has languished there ever since. Court cases have expanded the rights of same-sex couples, however, in a number of important ways. Using the constitution's antidiscrimination clause, which does not list "sexual orientation" specifically but does mention at the end of its list "and other forms of discrimination," the federal high court ruled in 1998 that a gay man deserved to inherit the property of his partner of seven years. The court went on to rule in 2000 that same-sex partners in a "stable union" should be treated as married couples in the social security and public pension systems. In the most important of these cases, the state government of Rio Grande do Sul legalized civil unions after a case on the issue was argued in the state court in 2004. In 2008 the movement's hopes increased further when President Luiz Inácio "Lula" da Silva of the PT said publicly he would do all he could to see that a hate crimes law against homophobia and a civil union law are enacted.

Despite achieving only partial success, Brazil's LGBT community has actively engaged in the legislative process, focusing more attention in that arena than the movement has in the United States. Much of the activity has taken place within the PT, which became the governing party in 2002. In 1992 a gay and lesbian group was officially formed within the party to pressure elected members to support LGBT causes. Over the next decade it grew to the point where it was hosting annual national meetings, though ultimately it fell apart due to internal divisions. Nevertheless, it helped spur PT legislation in numerous state and local governments, but it continues to face opposition from PT members with strong traditionalist ties to the Catholic Church. And in June 2003 LGBT activists in the National Congress convinced the lower house to convene a National Seminar on Affirmative Politics and Rights of the Gay, Lesbian, Bisexual, *Travesti* (transvestite), and Transsexual Community. The seminar brought together legislators, bureaucratic officials, and LGBT activists to discuss LGBT rights issues, and out of it grew the Parliamentary Front for Freedom of Sexual Expression, whose eighty-five members convinced the PT government to create and fund a program explicitly aimed at combating homophobia nationwide.

Summary

The LGBT community in Brazil enjoys significantly greater rights than it did during the 1980s and more than those allowed to LGBT communities in many countries. Arguably, it has been more successful than the United States movement that helped inspire it. The transition to democracy, which emphasized expanded rights for all even though "sexual orientation" was explicitly rejected for inclusion in the new constitution, set a political context in which Brazilian policy has shifted significantly. While the state has not yet legalized civil unions, let alone same-sex marriage, Brazilian same-sex couples in practice have rights nearly equal to married couples in many important social and policy areas, and they certainly have these rights more uniformly throughout the country than do same-sex couples in the United States. In terms of recognition, the first and most important goal of the LGBT movement, Brazil has achieved a great deal. The LGBT community is widely known and celebrated, especially via São Paulo's gargantuan gay pride parade. Opposition from both traditionalist Catholic and evangelical Protestant movements continues, but all indications are that the Brazilian political system has expanded its definition of equal citizenship to include LGBT members in such a way as to affect permanent change.

Summary

The LGBT movement has raised, if anything, more profound challenges to conventional social mores and institutions than the women's movement. Sexual orientation is unique as an identity category due to the ability of homosexual and bisexual individuals to "hide" their identity relatively easily. This has meant that as individuals they have long had basic political rights that women, racial, and other minorities often had to fight for. As a group, however, they were repressed and forced to hide until quite recently. They remain the group least frequently given recognition, respect, and rights by states around the world. Like feminists, gay rights activists raise fundamental questions about core institutions such as marriage, not only who ought to be included but also how it should be defined and whether it should exist. Some simply want inclusion into existing institutions, but others want more fundamental institutional and attitudinal changes. Our case studies are two countries that have had unusually active movements, yet their policies continue to allow certain areas of discrimination based on sexual orientation. This is in part caused by the fact that the goals of the movement conflict with deeply held values based on cultural or religious traditions that accept group membership and behavior only within the bounds of heterosexual practice. In this sense, the LGBT movement raises the same questions about citizenship and inclusion that we have discussed throughout this chapter.

CONCLUSION

Identity groups always pose challenges to the modern state. As we saw in chapter 4, under some circumstances ethnicity, race, or religion can challenge the very conception of a nation. At other times, religion, like gender and sexuality, poses a different kind of challenge to modern states: issues of inclusiveness and equal citizenship. In liberal democracies, such challenges cut to the heart of one of the defining characteristics of the regime. These demands for inclusive citizenship can also raise challenges when they clash with the demands of other identity groups. States must then resolve the question of which group's demands to meet. This can be particularly difficult when, for instance, women or gays demand individual civil rights in the name of equality, while a religious, ethnic, or other minority group claims a conflicting right to respect for its cultural practices. This is a difficult challenge for democracies that pride themselves on respecting minority rights and cultural pluralism but also wish to promote individual equality.

When groups make new demands or conflicts arise between identity group demands, what determines the policy outcome? As our cases suggest, many factors are at work in this decision-making process. First, it is important to recognize that the demands of similar groups in different countries are not always the same. For instance, our cases on women's rights show that not all women's groups have adopted Western feminist demands or rationales for women's rights. Islamic women's groups and others throughout the non-Western world have developed their own sets of demands that only partially overlap those of European and North American women's movements. Thus, states are responding to different sets of demands from the start. Second, the institutional context in which identity groups make demands also matters. A group may deem it pointless to demand greater inclusion in formal political institutions if the context is one in which those institutions ultimately have little decision-making power. On the other hand, as examples from the former Communist countries suggest, numerical inclusion in formal decision-making institutions does not ensure equality or recognition of rights for women and other identity groups.

Institutions matter in another way as well. They create the avenues through which groups approach the state, and sometimes this also helps shape groups' demands. Whether to approach the state at the local or national level; through protests, votes, or lawsuits; and on which particular issues—all of these questions are deeply affected by the institutional context, as cases from gay rights in the United States to Muslim rights in the UK suggest.

Lastly, many aspects of the groups themselves play a key role in their success or failure in gaining their preferred policy outcomes. Most important, a critical mass of people must recognize themselves as part of a group with common interests vis-á-vis the state. These interests may be communal rights, as they often are for religious minorities, but they may also be individual rights of access and equal citizenship. Whatever their goals, a shared sense of identity allows members of these groups to form a social movement or interest group. At that point, their ability to mobilize resources, to frame a persuasive argument, and to exploit political opportunities can be crucial to their success. As several of our examples suggest, from Muslim traditionalists in Turkey to gays in the United States, their very mobilization may also encourage the countermobilization of groups with conflicting values. Struggles for recognition, whether they involve demands for equal citizenship or communal rights or both, are usually protracted and difficult.

Despite the obstacles to organizing and achieving political goals, more and more groups throughout the world appear to be demanding inclusion, recognition, and individual or communal rights. The rhetorical dominance of liberal democracy as well as the numerical dominance of formal electoral democracies explains some of this trend. As we've stressed throughout the book, the dominance of democratic discourse makes it important for virtually all states to justify their actions in terms of citizenship, and this provides an opening and a basis on which groups can demand inclusion and recognition. In addition, although many formally democratic states still only imperfectly respect civil liberties and freedoms, they do allow more space for civil society on the whole than do their authoritarian counterparts or predecessors. Thus the wave of democratization in the 1990s has opened political space for identity groups around the world. Indeed, women's movements and other identity-based movements were part of the social movement cohort that helped push the tide of democratization forward in the first place.

Globalization also has given more impetus to identity movements around the world, whether via globalized examples and inspiration or via assertions of local identity against the forces of global homogenization. As the European examples in the section on religion show, the movement of people across borders and especially postcolonial immigration has raised questions about inclusiveness and the definition of citizenship in long-established democracies. Media also certainly play a role, as news of identity group mobilizations in one place travels quickly and may provide a spark to similar organizing elsewhere. For this reason, people often speak of a wave of "global feminisms" of different types beginning in the 1970s. Although groups throughout the world developed feminist goals and tactics to suit their particular circumstances, news and ideas from other countries encouraged women everywhere to organize for their own agendas. Similarly, international institutions themselves have sometimes promoted policy goals, particularly with respect to women's education, health, and equality, that have interacted with local demands to help produce policy outcomes.

The trend toward greater mobilization around issues of identity is strong right now, but as always in comparative politics, we cannot assume that what is true today will be true tomorrow. We do believe that identity will continue to be a key challenge to the politics of nation-states, and particularly liberal democracies, for the foreseeable future, and these challenges are likely to arise in other places if more countries expand their openness to global markets and ideas, and increase the scope of their civil societies. In the future, however, new conflicts and new political trends will arise, and students of comparative politics will be challenged to document and explain the new patterns, sources, and outcomes of future political conflicts.

COUNTRY AND CONCEPT Policies and Politics of Inclusion and Clashing Values

Country	RELIGION Freedom of religion constitutionally guaranteed?*	% of respondents who say "I am a religious person"†	GENDER Gender Empowerment Measure (GEM) Value‡ (higher scores = less gender disparity)	Gender-related Development Index (GDI) Value§ (higher scores = less gender disparity)
Brazil	Yes.	85.4	0.490	0.789
China	Yes, but very little actual freedom of religion exists and the gov't tries to control religious institutions and practice.	14.7	0.534	0.776
Germany	Yes, but some small religious groups have lodged complaints about discrimination.	—§§	0.831	0.931
India	Yes, but minority Muslim and Christian populations complain of discrimination.	79.5	—	0.600
Iran	No. Islam declared official religion.	94.9	0.347	0.750
Japan	Yes. Religious corporations monitored by Ministry of Education in wake of Aum Shinrikyo attacks.	26.5	0.557	0.942
Nigeria	Yes, but in practice many parts of Nigeria under *sharia.*	96.6	—	0.456
Russia	Yes, but only certain religions afforded full legal status.	65.7	0.489	0.801
United Kingdom	No constitution, but customary legal protection against religious discrimination.	41.6	0.783	0.944
United States	Yes.	82.5	0.762	0.937

* Information is from the International Coalition for Religious Freedom.

† World Values Survey data.

‡ GEM, the UN's Gender Empowerment Measure, is a composite indicator that captures gender inequality in three key areas: political participation and decision-making power, as measured by women's and men's percentage shares of parliamentary seats; economic participation and decision-making power, as measured by two indicators—women's and men's percentage shares of positions as legislators, senior officials and managers and women's and men's percentage shares of professional and technical positions; and power over economic resources, as measured by women's and men's estimated earned income (PPP US$). See UN Data, http://data.un.org/DocumentData.aspx?id=88.

§ GDI, the UN's Gender Development Index, is a composite index that measures human development in the same dimensions as the HDI while adjusting for gender inequality in those basic dimensions. These dimensions are: a long and healthy life; access to knowledge; and a decent standard of living. These basic dimensions are measured separately for females and males in the GDI by life expectancy at birth; adult literacy and combined gross enrollment in primary, secondary and tertiary level education; and estimated earned income per capita in Purchasing Power Parity U.S. dollars (PPP US$), respectively.

		SEXUALITY		
Ratio of estimated female to male earned income**	Ratio of female to male adult literacy	Laws against homosexuality?; Extent of rights or extent of punishment††	% of respondents who say that "Homosexuality is never justifiable"‡‡	% of respondents who say that "Homosexuality is always justifiable"
0.58	1	No. Limited same sex unions. Some constitutional and de facto rights.	55.8	8.6
0.64	0.91	No. No same sex unions.	92.3	0.1
0.58	1	No. Registered partnership exists as well as some laws against discrimination. Some states have constitutional protections.	20.2***	21.25†††
0.31	0.65	Yes (for men), but government does not prosecute.	70.8	18.1
0.39	0.87	Yes, punishable by prison term or possibly death.	94.0	1.2
0.45	1	No. Some laws against discrimination exist.	29.8	9.4
0.41	0.77	Yes, in areas governed by *sharia*, punishable by death.	77.6	0.4
0.62	1	No. Some laws against discrimination exist.	31.6	—
0.66	1	No. Civil partnership and laws against discrimination exist. Adoption possible.	24.6	14.2
0.63	1	No. Some discrimination laws and some form of union or marriage permitted in some states.	31.6	14.1

** Data are from UN, see http://data.un.org/DocumentData.aspx?id=88.

†† Data are from Daniel Ottosson, LGBT World Legal Wrap Up Survey, November 2006. Available at www.ilga-europe.org/europe/issues/international/lgbt_world_legal_wrap_up_survey_november_2006. See also www.ilga.org/statehomophobia/LGBcriminallaws-Daniel_Ottoson.pdf.

‡‡ Response to World Values Survey Question: "Please tell me for each of the following statements whether you think it can always be justified, never be justified, or something in between?"

§§ Data available only for East and West Germany separately. In 1999, scores for each were 62.1 (West Germany) and 28.6 (East Germany).

*** Data shown for Germany is an average of West and East German scores for 1999, the last data available on this question from Germany. Scores for "never justifiable" were 17.9 (West Germany) and 22.5 (East Germany).

††† Data shown for Germany is an average of West and East German scores for 1999, the last data available on this question from Germany. Scores for "always justifiable" were 23.7 (West Germany) and 18.8 (East Germany).

Key Concepts

deliberative democracy (p. 490)   multicultural integration (p. 490)
liberationist approach (p. 519)   multiculturalism (p. 497)

Works Cited

Alaedini, Pooya, and Mohamad Reza Razavi. 2005. "Women's Participation and Employment in Iran: A Critical Examination." *Critique: Critical Middle Eastern Studies* 14, no. 1, 57–73.

Bahramitash, Roksana, and Shahla Kazemipour. 2006. "Myths and Realities of the Impact of Islam on Women: Changing Marital Status in Iran." *Critique: Critical Middle Eastern Studies* 15, no. 2, 111–128.

Bell, David, and Jon Binnie. 2000. *The Sexual Citizen: Queer Politics and Beyond.* Cambridge: Polity Press.

Equality and Human Rights Commission (UK). www.equalityhumanrights.com/en/aboutus/pages/aboutus.aspx.

Eskridge, William N., Jr. 1999. *Gaylaw: Challenging the Apartheid of the Closet.* Cambridge: Harvard University Press.

Fetzer, Joel S., and J. Christopher Soper. 2005. *Muslims and the State in Britain, France, and Germany.* Cambridge: Cambridge University Press.

Human Development Report 2005 Russian Federation Russia in 2015: Development Goals and Policy Priorities. 2005. Moscow: United Nations Development Programme–Russia.

Inter-Parliamentary Union. 2008. *Women in National Parliaments.* www.ipu.org/wmn-e/classif.htm.

Kirkpatrick, Jeane J. 1974. *Political Woman.* New York: Basic Books.

Kymlicka, Will. 1995. *Multicultural Citizenship: A Liberal Theory of Minority Rights.* Oxford: Oxford University Press.

Kymlicka, Will, and Wayne Norman, ed. 2000. *Citizenship in Diverse Societies.* Oxford: Oxford University Press.

Mansbridge, Jane. 2000. "What Does a Representative Do: Descriptive Representation in Communicative Settings of Distrust, Uncrystallized Interests, and Historically Denigrated Status." In *Citizenship in Diverse Societies,* ed. Will Kymlicka and Wayne Norman, 99–123. Oxford: Oxford University Press.

Marsiaj, Juan P. 2006. "Social Movements and Political Parties: Gays, Lesbians, and *Travestis* and the Struggle for Inclusion in Brazil." *Latin American and Caribbean Studies* 31, no. 62: 167–196.

Modood, Tariq. 2006. "British Muslims and the Politics of Multiculturalism." In *Multiculturalism, Muslims, and Citizenship: A European Approach,* ed. Tariq Modood, Ann Triandafyllidou, and Ricard Zapata-Barrero. New York: Routledge.

Paidar, Parvin. 1995. *Women and the Political Process in Twentieth-Century Iran.* Cambridge: Cambridge University Press.

Pateman, Carole. 1988. *The Sexual Contract.* Stanford: Stanford University Press.

Racioppi, Linda, and Katherine O'Sullivan See. 1995. "Organizing Women before and after the Fall: Women's Politics in the Soviet Union and Post-Soviet Russia." *Signs* 20, no. 4: 818–850.

Rao, Badrinath. 2006. "The Variant Meanings of Secularism in India: Notes toward Conceptual Clarification." *Journal of Church and State* (Winter): 47–81.

Roschin, S.Yu, and N.V. Zubarevich. 2005. "Gender Equality and Extension of Women's Rights in Russia in the Context of Millennium Development Goals." Moscow: United Nations Development Programme.

Servicemembers Legal Defense Ntwork. 2008. www.sldr.org/templates/index.html.

Teplova, Tatyana. 2007. Welfare State Transformation, Childcare, and Women's Work in Russia." *Social Politics* 14, no. 3: 284–322.

White, Anne. 2005. "Gender Roles in Contemporary Russia: Attitudes and Expectations among Women Students." *Europe-Asia Studies* 57, no. 3: 429–455.

Young, Iris Marion. 2000. *Inclusion and Democracy.* Oxford: Oxford University Press.

Resources for Further Study

Hunter, Shireen T., ed. 2002. *Islam: Europe's Second Religion.* Westport, Conn.: Praeger.

Lovenduski, Joni, et al. 2005. *State Feminism and Political Representation.* Cambridge: Cambridge University Press.

Mazur, Amy G. 2002. *Theorizing Feminist Policy.* Oxford: Oxford University Press.

Parekh, Bhikhu. 2000. *Rethinking Multiculturalism: Cultural Diversity and Political Theory.* Cambridge: Harvard University Press.

Rex, John. 2002. "Islam in the United Kingdom." In *Islam: Europe's Second Religion,* ed. S. Hunter, 51–76. Westport, Conn.: Praeger.

World Values Survey. www.worldvaluessurvey.org.

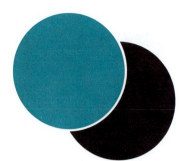

Country Bibliography

Aborisade, Oladimeji, and Robert J. Mundt. 1998. *Politics in Nigeria*. New York: Longman.

Alves, Maria Helena Moreira. 1985. *State and Opposition in Military Brazil*. 1st ed. Austin: University of Texas Press.

Clemens, Elisabeth Stephanie. 1997. *The People's Lobby: Organizational Innovation and the Rise of Interest Group Politics in the United States, 1890–1925*. Chicago: University of Chicago Press.

Edozie, Rita Kiki. 2002. *People Power and Democracy: The Popular Movement against Military Despotism in Nigeria, 1989–1999*. Trenton, N.J.: Africa World Press.

Hashim, S. Mohsin. 2005. "Putin's Etatization Project and Limits to Democratic Reforms in Russia." *Communist and Post-Communist Studies* 38, no. 1.

Herskovits, Jean. 2007. "Nigeria's Rigged Democracy." *Foreign Affairs* 86, no. 4.

Hrebenar, Ronald J. 2000. *Japan's New Party System*. Boulder, Colo: Westview Press.

Jaffrelot, Christophe. 2003. *India's Silent Revolution: The Rise of the Lower Castes in North India*. New York: Columbia University Press.

Kingstone, Peter R., and Jeffrey Cason. 2000. "Muddling through Gridlock: Democracy Looks South." In *Democratic Brazil: Actors, Institutions, and Processes*, ed. Peter R. Kingstone and Timothy J. Power, 185–217. Pittsburgh: University of Pittsburgh Press.

Kingstone, Peter R., and Timothy J. Power. 2000. *Democratic Brazil: Actors, Institutions, and Processes*. Pittsburgh: University of Pittsburgh Press.

Roberts, Geoffrey K. 1997. *Party Politics in the New Germany*. London: Pinter.

Roett, Riordan. 1978. *Brazil: Politics in a Patrimonial Society*. Rev. ed. New York: Praeger.

Rotberg, Robert I. 2004. *Crafting the New Nigeria: Confronting the Challenges*. Boulder, Colo.: Lynne Rienner Publishers.

Schrecker, J. E. 1991. *The Chinese Revolution in Historical Perspective*. New York: Greenwood Press.

Shah, Ghanshyam. 2002. *Caste and Democratic Politics in India*. Delhi: Permanent Black. Distributed by Orient Longman.

Shefter, Martin. 1994. *Political Parties and the State: The American Historical Experience*. Princeton: Princeton University Press.

Shi, Tianjian. 1997. *Political Participation in Beijing*. Cambridge: Harvard University Press.

Stoner-Weiss, Kathryn. 2006. "Russia: Authoritarianism without Authority." *Journal of Democracy* 17: 104–118.

Streeck, Wolfgang, and Anke Hassel. "The Crumbling Pillars of Social Partnership. In *Germany: Beyond the Stable State*, ed. Herbert Kitschelt and Wolfgang Streeck, 101–124. London: Routledge.

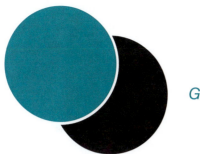

Glossary

absolutism   Rule by a single monarch who claims complete, exclusive power and sovereignty over a territory and its people (chapter 2)

acephalous society   Stateless; ruled by very local level government only (chapter 4)

amakudari   In Japan, the "descent from heaven," in which senior bureaucrats get positions in the industries they formerly regulated (chapter 6)

assimilationist   Someone who believes immigrants or other members of minority cultural communities ought to adopt the culture of the majority population (chapter 4)

assymetrical federal system   Division of constitutionally assigned power to national and subnational governments, with different subnational governments (states or provinces) having distinct relationships with and rights in relation to the national government (chapter 6)

authoritarian regime   A regime lacking democratic characteristics, ruled by a single leader or small group of leaders (chapter 1)

autonomy   Ability and right of a minority group to partially govern themselves within a larger state (chapter 4)

bicameral legislature   A legislature that has two houses (chapter 6)

Bolshevik   Vladimir Lenin's branch of the communist movement in Russia that led the Russian communist revolution (chapter 3)

bourgeoisie   The class that owns capital; Marxists argue they are the ruling elite in all capitalist societies (chapter 1)

bureaucracy   A large set of appointed officials whose function is to implement the laws of the state, as directed by the executive (chapter 2)

bureaucratic-authoritarian state   A state or regime characterized by institutionalized rule under a military government with a primary goal of economic development; coined by Guillermo O'Donnell to describe Latin American military regimes in the 1970s (chapter 3)

cadre parties   Parties that have a small membership of political elites who choose candidates and mobilize voters to support them; in contrast to mass parties (chapter 7)

cap and trade system   Market-based pollution control system in which the government sets an overall limit on how much of a pollutant is acceptable from an entire industry or country and issues vouchers to pollute to each company; individual companies are then free to trade these vouchers (chapter 11)

capitalism   The combination of a market economy with private property rights (chapter 5)

charismatic legitimacy   The right to rule based on personal virtue, heroism, sanctity, or other extraordinary characteristics; one of Max Weber's three versions of legitimacy (chapter 2)

Christian democratic welfare states   States whose social policies are based on the nuclear family with male breadwinner, designed primarily to achieve income stabilization to mitigate the effects of market-induced income insecurity; Germany is key example (chapter 11)

citizen   A member of a political community or state with certain rights and duties (chapter 3)

civic culture   Political culture in which citizens hold values and beliefs that support democracy, including active participation in politics but also enough deference to the leadership to let it govern effectively (chapter 1)

civic nationalism   A sense of national unity and purpose based on a set of commonly held political beliefs (chapter 4)

civil rights   The first of T. H. Marshall's rights of citizenship; those rights that guarantee individual freedom as well as equal, just, and fair treatment by the state (chapter 3)

civil society   The sphere of organized, nonviolent activity by groups smaller and less inclusive than the state or government, but larger than the family or individual firm (chapter 1)

clientelism   The exchange of material resources for political support (chapter 2)

closed-list proportional representation   Electoral system in which each party presents a ranked list of candidates for all the seats in the legislature; voters can see the list and know who the "top" candidates are, but they vote for the party, and each party is awarded legislative seats based on their percentage of the total vote and awards those seats to the candidates on its list, in the order in which they are listed (chapter 7)

coalition government   Government in a parliamentary system in which at least two parties negotiate an agreement to rule together (chapter 6)

code law   Legal system originating in ancient Roman law and modified by Napoleon Bonaparte in France, in which judges may only follow the law as written, interpreting it as little as necessary to fit the case; past decisions are irrelevant, as each judge must look only to the existing law; in contrast to common law (chapter 6)

codetermination   In Germany unions are represented on the supervisory boards of all German firms of more than two thousand employees (chapter 5)

cohabitation   Sharing of power between a president and prime minister from different parties in a semi-presidential system (chapter 6)

collective action problems   The unwillingness of individuals to undertake political action because of the rational belief that their individual action will have little or no effect; a problem democratic regimes must overcome via parties and interest groups (chapter 7)

collective responsibility   All cabinet members must publicly support all government decisions in a parliamentary system (chapter 6)

command and control policies   Pollution control system in which a government directly regulates the specific amount of pollution each polluting entity is allowed (chapter 11)

common law   Legal system originating in Britain in which judges base decisions not only on their understanding of the written law but also on their understanding of past court cases; in contrast to code law (chapter 6)

communist regime   System of government established on the principles of Marxist belief that strives to achieve a communist society and is led by a communist party that claims the exclusive and unquestioned right to rule (chapter 1)

comparative advantage   Theory of trade that argues that economic efficiency and well-being will be maximized if each country uses its resources to produce whatever it produces relatively well compared to other countries and then trades what it has produced with other countries for goods it does not produce (chapter 5)

comparative institutional advantage   Idea in the "varieties of capitalism" school of thought that argues that different kinds of capitalist systems have different institutional advantages that they usually will try to maintain, resulting in different responses to external economic pressures (chapter 10)

comparative politics   One of the major subfields of political science in which the primary focus is on comparing power and decision making across countries (chapter 1)

comparativists   Political scientists who study comparative politics (chapter 1)

competitive authoritarian regime   Type of hybrid regime in which formal opposition and some open political debate exist and elections are held to select the executive and legislative branches; these processes are so flawed, however, that the regime cannot be considered democratic in any real sense; also called semiauthoritarian and electoral authoritarian (chapter 9)

consociationalism   A democratic system designed to ease communal tensions via the principles of recognizing the existence of specific groups and granting some share of power in the central government to each, usually codified in specific legal or constitutional guarantees to each group (chapter 4)

constructivism   A theory of identity group formation that argues identities are created through a complex process usually referred to as social construction; societies collectively "construct" identities as a wide array of actors continually discusses the question of who "we" are, and identity groups are not frozen in time, though change relatively slowly, and each individual can be part of more than one group (chapter 4)

convergence   The argument that globalization will force similar economic and social policies across all countries (chapter 10)

coordinated market economies (CMEs)   Part of the varieties of capitalism approach; capitalist economies in which firms, financiers, unions, and government consciously coordinate their actions via interlocking ownership and participation; Germany and Japan are examples (chapter 10)

corporatism   Interest group system in which one organization represents each sector of society; originally from the Catholic belief in society as an organic whole; two subtypes are societal and state corporatism (chapter 3)

coups d'etat   Military takeovers of a government (chapter 3)

cultural nationalism   National unity based on a common cultural characteristic, and those people who don't share that particular cultural characteristic cannot be included in the nation (chapter 4)

deficit spending   Government spending that occurs when more is spent than is collected in revenue (chapter 5)

delegative democracies   Democracies in which free and fair elections take place but neither vertical nor horizontal accountability is strong enough to prevent the emergence of elected executives with nearly unlimited power (chapter 9)

deliberative democracy   Democracy that asks citizens not only to assume their rights and minimally participate through voting but also to engage actively in democratic discussion in the effort to build a better society (chapter 12)

democracy   A regime in which citizens have basic rights of open association and expression and the ability to change the government through some sort of electoral process (chapter 1)

democratic breakdowns The replacement of democratic regimes with authoritarian or semi-authoritarian regimes (chapter 1)

democratic centralism The organization of a ruling party, primarily in communist regimes, in which lower organs of a party and state vote on issues and individuals to represent them at higher levels, ultimately reaching the top level, which would make final, binding decisions that all must then obey without question; key organizational innovation of Vladimir Lenin, leader of the Russian Communist party (chapter 3)

democratic consolidation The idea that democracy has become widely accepted as the permanent form of political activity in a particular country, and all significant political elites and their followers accept democratic rules and are confident everyone else does as well (chapter 9)

democratic deepening Improvement in the quality of democracy, including the extent of participation, rule of law, and vertical and horizontal accountability (chapter 9)

democratic transition A type of regime change involving typically a negotiated process that removes an authoritarian regime and concludes with a founding election for a new, democratic regime; also called transition to democracy (chapter 1)

developmental state A state that consciously seeks to create national strength in particular economic areas; it takes an active and conscious role in the development of specific sectors of the economy; Japan is a key example (chapter 5)

dictatorship of the proletariat The first stage of communism in Marxist thought, characterized by absolute rule by workers as a class over all other classes (chapter 3)

dominant party system Party system in which multiple parties exist but one wins every election and governs continuously (chapter 7)

dual convergence Part of varieties of capitalism approach; convergence of economic policies occurring within LMEs and CMEs (chapter 10)

Duverger's Law French political scientist Maurice Duverger argued that FPTP electoral systems will produce two major parties, eliminating smaller parties (chapter 7)

electoral authoritarianism Type of hybrid regime in which formal opposition and some open political debate exist and elections are held to select the executive and legislative branches; these processes are so flawed, however, that the regime cannot be considered democratic in any real sense; also called competitive authoritarian and semi-authoritarian. (chapter 3)

electoral democracy Political system in which opposition parties are legal and elections take place, but full civil and political rights of liberal democracy are not secure (chapter 3)

electoral systems Formal, legal mechanisms that translate votes into control over political offices and shares of political power (chapter 7)

elite theory Theory that all societies are ruled by a small group that has effective control over virtually all power; contrast to pluralist theory (chapter 1)

empirical theory An argument explaining what actually occurs; empirical theorists first notice and describe a pattern, and then attempt to explain what causes it (chapter 1)

environmental justice movement A movement focused on exposing and fighting against racial and class inequalities in the presence of pollution, started in the United States in 1982 (chapter 11)

ethnic group A group of people who see themselves as united by one or more cultural attributes or a sense of common history but do not see themselves as a nation seeking their own state (chapter 4)

executive   The branch of government that must exist in all modern states, it is usually the chief political power in a state and implements all laws (chapter 6)

export-oriented growth (EOG)   Development policy based on encouraging economic growth via exports of goods and services, usually starting with light manufacturing such as textiles (chapter 10)

externality   A cost or benefit of the production process that is not fully included in the price of the final market transaction when the product is sold (chapter 5)

external sovereignty   Sovereignty relative to outside powers and legally recognized in international law (chapter 2)

failed state   A state that is so weak that it loses effective sovereignty over part or all of its territory (chapter 2)

fascist regime   System of government based on fascist doctrine that the state should be supreme over all, including over individual rights; includes corporatism and a belief in a supreme leader, and specifically rejects the individual rights of liberal democracy and the materialism of communist thought (chapter 1)

federalism   A system in which a state's power is legally and constitutionally divided among more than one level of government; in contrast to a unitary system (chapter 2)

feudal states   Premodern states in Europe in which power in a territory is divided among multiple and overlapping lords claiming sovereignty (chapter 2)

fief   A relationship between lord and vassal in which the lord gave a vassal the right to rule a piece of land, its products, and people in exchange for political and military loyalty; the central relationship in feudal states (chapter 2)

"first-past-the-post" (FPTP)   Electoral system in which individual candidates are elected in single-member districts; the candidate with the most votes, but not necessarily a majority, wins (chapter 7)

fiscal policy   Government budgetary policy (chapter 5)

foreign direct investment (FDI)   Investment from abroad in productive activity in another country (chapter 10)

founding election   The first democratic election in many years (or ever), marking the completion of a transition to democracy (chapter 9)

free wage labor   Labor that can move from place to place and is paid based on the time worked; required by capitalism (chapter 3)

glasnost   Political policy launched by Mikhail Gorbachev in the late 1980s in the Soviet Union; a partial political liberalization (chapter 3)

globalization   A rapid increase in the flow of cultural symbols, political ideas and movements, economic activity, technology, and communications around the globe (chapter 5)

guanxi   In China, networks of personal supporters, including but not exclusively family, that are important for economic and political survival and advancement (chapter 8)

hardliners   Leaders in an authoritarian regime who believe in repressing any opposition and preserving the status quo when faced with a demand for political liberalization or democratization (chapter 9)

head of government   The key executive power in a state; usually a president or prime minister (chapter 6)

head of state   The official, symbolic representative of a country, authorized to speak on its behalf and represent it, particularly in world affairs; usually a president or monarch (chapter 6)

hegemony   The ruling class's political dominance via its manipulation of cultural values and ideas (chapter 1)

Hindu nationalism   In India, a movement to define the country as primarily Hindu; the founding ideology of the BJP party (chapter 7)

historical institutionalists   Theorists who believe institutions explain political behavior and shape individuals' political preferences and what they see as their self-interests, and that institutions evolve historically in particular countries and change relatively slowly (chapter 1)

historical materialism   The assumption that material forces are the prime movers of history and politics; a key philosophical tenet of Marxism (chapter 3)

horizontal accountability   The ability of state institutions to hold one another accountable (chapter 6)

hybrid regime   Regime that mixes elements of democracy with authoritarian rule (chapter 9)

hyperglobalization   Thesis that globalization is so powerful it will overwhelm the power of nation-states, forcing convergence of economic policies (chapter 10)

illiberal democracies   Similar to electoral democracies, in which opposition and elections are present, but not the fully protected rights of liberal democracy (chapter 9)

import-substitution industrialization (ISI)   Development policy popular in the 1950s–1970s that uses trade policy, monetary policy, and currency rates to encourage the creation of new industries that will domestically produce goods that the country imported in the past (chapter 5)

institutionalization   The degree to which government processes and procedures are established, predictable, and routinized (chapter 8)

instrumentalism   An elite theory of identity politics: rational and self-interested elites manipulate symbols and feelings of identity to mobilize a political following (chapter 4)

interest aggregation   The bringing together of a number of discrete interests into a coalition of broadly shared interests, which enhances the power of individual votes by aggregating them and potentially overcomes the collective action dilemma; in democracies, typically performed by political parties (chapter 7)

interest group pluralism   An interest group system in which many groups exist to represent particular interests and the government remains officially neutral among them; the United States is a key example (chapter 7)

interest groups   Organizations that represent and champion particular concerns or social groups but do not seek to gain power themselves, instead seeking only influence over those in power; a key element of civil society (chapter 1)

internal sovereignty   The sole authority within a territory capable of making and enforcing laws and policies; an essential element of a modern state (chapter 2)

international capital flows   Movements of capital in the form of money across international borders (chapter 10)

international relations   The study of politics among national governments and beyond national boundaries (chapter 1)

iron triangles   Three-sided cooperative interaction among bureaucrats, legislators, and business leaders in a particular sector that serves the interest of all involved but keeps others out of the policy-making process (chapter 6)

Islamism   The belief that Islamic law, as revealed by God to the Prophet Mohammed, can and should provide the basis for government in Muslim communities, with little equivocation or compromise (chapter 3)

jihad   Derived from an Arabic word for "struggle"; an important concept in Islam; the Quran identifies three kinds of *jihad:* internal struggle to live faithfully, struggle to resist evil and right injustice, and struggle to protect the Muslim community (chapter 3)

judicial independence The belief and ability of judges to decide cases as they think appropriate, regardless of what other people, and especially politically powerful officials or institutions, desire (chapter 6)

judicial review The right of the judiciary to decide whether a specific law contradicts a country's constitution (chapter 6)

judiciary Branch of government that interprets the law and applies it to individual cases (chapter 6)

jus sanguinis Citizenship based on "blood" ties; Germany is a key example (chapter 4)

jus soli Literally, citizenship dependent on "soil," or residence within the national territory; France is a key example (chapter 4)

Keynesian theory Named for British economist John Maynard Keynes, who argued that governments can reduce the "boom and bust" cycles of capitalism via active fiscal policy, including deficit spending when necessary (chapter 5)

legislative oversight Members of the legislature, usually in key committees, oversee the working of the bureaucracy by interviewing key leaders, examining budgets, and assessing how successfully a particular agency has carried out its mandate (chapter 6)

legislature Branch of government that makes the law in a democracy (chapter 6)

legitimacy The recognized right to rule (chapter 2)

liberal democracy A system of government that provides eight key guarantees: freedom of association, freedom of expression, the right to vote, broad citizen eligibility for public office, the right of political leaders to compete for support, alternative sources of information, free and fair elections, and institutions that make government policies depend on votes and other forms of citizen preferences (chapter 3)

liberal market economies (LMEs) In the varieties of capitalism approach, countries that rely heavily on market relationships to govern economic activity,

meaning that firms interact with other firms and secure sources of finance through purely market-based transactions; the United States and UK are key examples (chapter 10)

liberal welfare states States whose social policies focus on ensuring that all who can, gain their income in the market; more concerned with preserving individual autonomy via market participation than with reducing poverty or inequality; the United States is a key example (chapter 11)

liberationist approach Branch of the LGBT movement that seeks to transform sexual and gender norms, not simply to gain equal rights with heterosexuals but also to liberate everyone to express whatever sexual orientation and gender identity they wish in order to gain social acceptance and respect for all regardless of their conformity to preexisting norms or institutions (chapter 12)

majoritarian systems Electoral systems in which, if no candidate wins an absolute majority (50 percent plus one), a second election takes place between the top two candidates to achieve a majority win (chapter 7)

market-based private insurance system Health care system that relies on private insurance for the bulk of the population; the United States is a key example (chapter 11)

market economy An economic system in which individuals and firms exchange goods and services in a largely unfettered manner (chapter 5)

market failure Occurs when markets do not perform their expected functions, which is usually because they fail to perform efficiently or they fail to perform according to other widely held social values; often caused by externalities, high risk, or imperfect information (chapter 11)

marketing boards Government entities with monopoly control over the domestic and international marketing of key crops; usually found in Africa (chapter 5)

Marxism   Structuralist argument that says that economic structures largely determine political behavior; philosophical underpinning of communism (chapter 1)

mass parties   Parties that recruit as many members as possible who expect to have some control, and from whom the parties gain financial support, labor, and votes; in contrast to cadre parties (chapter 7)

means-tested public assistance   Social programs that provide benefits to individuals who fall below a specific income level (chapter 11)

member of parliament (MP)   An elected member of the legislature in a parliamentary system (chapter 6)

military regimes   System of government in which military officers control power (chapter 3)

Millennium Development Goals (MDGs)   Targets established by the United Nations to reduce poverty and hunger, improve education and health, improve the status of women, and achieve environmental sustainability (chapter 10)

mixed representation system   Also called a semi-proportional representation system; an electoral system that combines single-member district representation with overall proportionality in allocation of legislative seats to parties; Germany is a key example (chapter 7)

mode of production   In Marxist theory, the economic system in any given historical era: feudalism and capitalism in the last millennium in Europe (chapter 3)

moderates   Leaders of democracy movements who are willing to compromise with the authoritarian regime to make some gains toward democracy, even if partial (chapter 9)

modernists   Theorists of political culture who believe that clear sets of attitudes, values, and beliefs can be identified in each country that change very rarely and explain much about politics (chapter 1)

modernization   The transformation from poor agrarian to wealthy industrial societies, usually seen as the process of postcolonial societies becoming more like the West (chapter 1)

modernization theory   Theory of development that argues that postcolonial societies need to go through the same process that the West underwent in order to develop (chapter 3)

modernizing authoritarian regime   System of government that arose in postcolonial states and based its legitimacy on the claim to be able to provide development, which requires national unity under the leadership of an educated elite (chapter 1)

modern state   The primary political unit of the last several centuries; a state characterized by territory, sovereignty, a claim to internal and external legitimacy, and bureaucracy (chapter 1)

monetarist theory   Economic theory that only monetary policy can affect economic well-being in capitalist economies; rejects Keynesian idea of using fiscal policy to regulate economy, arguing instead for reduced role for government (chapter 5)

monetary policy   The amount of money a government prints and puts into circulation and the basic interest rates the government sets (chapter 5)

monopoly   The control of the entire supply of a valued good or service by one economic actor (chapter 5)

moral hazard   Occurs when someone does not bear the full consequences of his actions in a transaction, which gives him an incentive to overuse a beneficial resource (chapter 11)

mulatto   In Brazil and elsewhere in Latin America, a member of a mixed race group (chapter 4)

multicultural integration   Accepts that ethnocultural identities matter to citizens, will endure over time, and must be recognized and accommodated within political institutions, in contrast to assimilation (chapter 12)

multiculturalism   In general, the belief that different cultures in a society ought to be respected; in the

UK, the policy governing how the state treats racial and religious minorities (chapter 12)

multiparty systems   Party systems in which more than two parties could potentially win a national election and govern (chapter 7)

multiple case studies   Research method that examines the same phenomena in several cases to try to mimic laboratory conditions by carefully selecting cases that are similar in many ways but differ in the area being studied (chapter 1)

national health insurance (NHI)   A healthcare system in which the government mandates that virtually all citizens must have insurance; Germany is a key example (chapter 11)

nationalism   The desire to be a nation and thus to control a national state (chapter 4)

national health system (NHS)   A government financed and managed healthcare system, often called a single-payer system; the government creates a system into which all citizens pay, either through a separate insurance payment or via general taxation, and through which they gain medical care; the UK is a key example (chapter 11)

nations   Groups that share an identity and also share or seek to share a territory and state (chapter 1)

natural monopolies   The control of the entire supply of valued goods or services by one economic actor in sectors of the economy in which competition would raise costs and reduce efficiency (chapter 5)

neocolonialism   Relationship between postcolonial societies and their former colonizers in which leaders benefit politically and economically by helping outside businesses and states maintain access to the former colonies' wealth and come to serve the interests of the former colonizers and corporations more than they serve their own people (chapter 1)

neocorporatism   Also called societal corporatism; corporatism that evolves historically and voluntarily rather than being mandated by the state; Germany is a key example (chapter 7)

neofascist   Description given to parties or political movements that espouse a virulent nationalism, often defined on a cultural or religious basis and opposed to immigrants as threats to national identity (chapter 3)

neofundamentalist   Term coined by French scholar Olivier Roy; Islamic movements that focus only on implementing an extremely rigid vision of *sharia* at the local level, focused on how people live their daily lives, while ignoring the state; key example is the Taliban in Afghanistan (chapter 3)

neoliberalism   Development theory supporting structural adjustment programs; argues that developing countries should reduce the role of government and open themselves to global trade to allow the market to allocate resources to maximize efficiency and thereby economic growth (chapter 5)

neopatrimonial regimes   Systems of government that combine the trappings of modern, bureaucratic states with underlying informal institutions of clientelism that work behind the scenes to determine real power; most common in Africa (chapter 3)

New Public Management (NPM)   Theory of reform of bureaucracies that argues for the privatizing of many government services so that they would be provided by the market, creating competition among agencies and subagencies within the bureaucracy to simulate a market, focusing on customer satisfaction (via client surveys, among other things), and flattening administrative hierarchies to encourage more team-based activity and creativity (chapter 6)

nongovernmental organizations (NGOs)   Volunteer organizations, most commonly working to make countries more democratic or to provide assistance with development (chapter 7)

normative theory   An argument explaining what ought to occur rather than what does occur; contrast with empirical theory (chapter 1)

one-party regimes A system of government in which a single party gains power, usually after independence in postcolonial states, and systematically eliminates all opposition in the name of development and national unity (chapter 3)

open-list proportional representation Electoral system with multiple candidates in each district; voters are presented with a list of all candidates and vote for the individual candidate of their choice; each party receives a number of legislative seats based on the total number of votes cast for all candidates from that party, and candidates with the most votes in the party get those seats; Brazil is a key example (chapter 7)

pact In a transition to democracy, a conscious agreement among the most important political actors in the authoritarian regime and in civil society to establish a new form of government (chapter 9)

parliamentarism A term for a parliamentary system of democracy (chapter 6)

parliamentary sovereignty Parliament is supreme in all matters; key example is the UK (chapter 3)

participation The involvement of citizens in a country's political process (chapter 1)

participatory democracy A form of democracy that encourages citizens to participate actively, in many ways beyond voting; usually focused at the local level (chapter 3)

party system The number of parties and each one's respective strength as an institution (chapter 7)

patriarchy Rule by men (chapter 1)

patron-client relationships Top leaders (patrons) mobilize political support by providing resources to their followers (clients) in exchange for political loyalty (chapter 1)

Peace of Westphalia Agreement among European powers in 1648 that codified the idea of states as legal equals that recognized each other's external and internal sovereignty within specified territories prepared to defend that sovereignty and their interests via diplomacy if possible or war if necessary (chapter 2)

peak associations Organizations that bring together all interest groups in a particular sector to influence and negotiate agreements with the state; in the United States, an example is the AFL-CIO (chapter 7)

perestroika Economic policy launched by Mikhail Gorbachev in the Soviet Union in the late 1980s that opened the economy to some elements of the market (chapter 3)

personalist regimes Systems of government in which a central leader comes to dominate a state, typically eliminating not only all opposition, but also weakening the state's institutions to centralize power in his hands (chapter 3)

personality cult Occurs in the most extreme cases of personalist rule; followers constantly glorify the ruler and attempt to turn his every utterance into not only government fiat but also divine wisdom; Mao Zedong in China was a key example (chapter 8)

pluralist theories Argue that society is divided into various political groups and power is dispersed among these groups so that no group has complete or permanent power; contrast to elite theory (chapter 1)

plurality The receipt of the most votes, but not a majority (chapter 7)

policymaking The process of creating policies carried out by public officials (chapter 1)

politburo The chief decision-making organ in a communist party; China is a key example (chapter 3)

political accountability The ability of the citizenry, directly or indirectly, to control political leaders and institutions (chapter 6)

political actor Any person or group engaged in political behavior (chapter 1)

political appointees   Officials who serve at the pleasure of the president or prime minister and, among other things, are assigned the task of overseeing their respective segments of the bureaucracy (chapter 6)

political culture   A set of widely held attitudes, values, beliefs, and symbols about politics (chapter 1)

political development   The process through which and study of how and why modern nations and states arose, and how political institutions and regimes evolve (chapter 1)

political discourse   The ways in which people speak and write about politics; post-modern theorists argue it influences political attitudes, identity, and actions (chapter 1)

political economy   The study of the interaction between political and economic phenomena (chapter 1)

political ideology   A systematic set of beliefs about how a political system ought to be structured (chapter 1)

political institution   A set of rules, norms, or standard operating procedures that is widely recognized and accepted by the society, and that structures and constrains political actions (chapter 1)

political liberalization   The opening of the political system to greater participation; typically before a transition to democracy (chapter 9)

political parties   Organizations that represent citizens' concerns in the formal political process and seek to gain political office (chapter 1)

political rights   The second of T. H. Marshall's rights of citizenship; those rights associated with active political participation: right to association, expression, voting, and running for office (chapter 3)

political saliency   The degree to which something is of political importance (chapter 4)

political science   The systematic study of politics and power (chapter 1)

political socialization   The process through which people, especially young people, learn about politics and are taught a society's common political values and beliefs (chapter 1)

political violence   The use of violence by nonstate actors for political ends (chapter 9)

politics   The process by which human communities make collective decisions (chapter 1)

politics of recognition   The demands for recognition and inclusion that have arisen since the 1960s in racial, religious, ethnic, gender and other minority or socially marginalized groups (chapter 4)

populism   A broad and charismatic appeal to poor people on the part of a leader to solve their problems directly via governmental largess; most common in Latin America in the early-mid twentieth century (chapter 7)

postmaterialist   Set of values in a society in which most citizens are economically secure enough to move beyond immediate economic (materialist) concerns to "quality of life" issues like human rights, civil rights, women's rights, environmentalism, and moral values (chapter 1)

postmodernist   An approach that sees cultures not as sets of fixed and clearly defined values, but rather as sets of symbols subject to interpretation (chapter 1)

power   The ability of one person or group to get another person or group to do something it otherwise would not do (chapter 1)

precautionary principle   Environmental and health policy that emphasizes risk avoidance even when the science predicting a risk is uncertain (chapter 11)

presidentialism   A term denoting a presidential system of democracy (chapter 6)

prime minister (PM)   The head of government in parliamentary and semipresidential systems (chapter 6)

primordialism   A theory of identity that sees identity groups as in some sense "natural" or God given, having existed since "time immemorial," and able to be defined unambiguously by such clear criteria as kinship, language, culture, or phenotype (chapter 4)

principal-agent problem   A problem common in any hierarchical situation in which a superior (principal) hires someone (agent) to perform a task, but the agent's self-interests do not necessarily align with the principal's, so the problem is how the principal makes sure the agent carries out the task as assigned; in politics, common when the elected or appointed political leadership in the executive or legislative branches assigns a bureaucrat a task to implement laws in a particular way (chapter 6)

privatize   Sell off public assets to the private sector (chapter 5)

proletariat   A term in Marxist theory for the class of free wage laborers who own no capital and must sell their labor to survive; communist parties claim to work on its behalf (chapter 1)

proportional representation (PR)   Electoral system in which seats in a legislature are apportioned on a purely proportional basis, giving each party the share of seats that matches its share of the total vote (chapter 7)

psychological theories   Explanations of political behavior based on psychological analysis of political actors' motives (chapter 1)

public goods   Those goods or services that cannot or will not be provided via the market because their costs are too high or their benefits too diffuse (chapter 5)

quantitative statistical techniques   Research method used for large-scale studies; involves the reduction of evidence to sets of numbers that statistical methods can analyze to systematically compare a huge number of cases (chapter 1)

quasi-states   States that have legal sovereignty and international recognition but lack almost all the domestic attributes of a functioning modern state (chapter 2)

race   A people who sees itself as a group based primarily on one or more perceived common physical characteristics and common history (chapter 4)

radicals   In democratic transitions, members of civil society who wish to achieve immediate and complete democracy and are unwilling to compromise with the existing regime (chapter 9)

rational-choice institutionalists   Institutionalist theoristswho follow the assumptions of rational choice theory and argue that institutions are the products of the interaction and bargaining of rational actors (chapter 1)

rational choice theory   Explanation of political behavior that assumes that individuals are self-interested and rational beings who bring a set of self-defined interests, adequate knowledge and ability to pursue those interests, and rationality to the political arena; these assumptions are then used to model political behavior in particular contexts (chapter 1)

rational-legal legitimacy   The right of leaders to rule based on their selection according to an accepted set of laws, standards, or procedures; one of Max Weber's three versions of legitimacy (chapter 2)

regime   A set of fundamental rules and institutions that govern political activity (chapter 1)

regime change   The process through which one regime is transformed into another (chapter 1)

regime types   Categories used by political scientists to classify regimes (chapter 1)

relative deprivation   A belief that a group or individual is not getting its share of something of value relative to others in the society or relative to members' own expectations (chapter 4)

rent-seeking   Gaining an advantage in a market without engaging in equally productive activity; usually involves using government regulations to one's own benefit (chapter 6)

representation The degree to which political officials accurately reflect the views and govern per the desires of the population (chapter 1)

research methods Systematic processes used to ensure that the study of a specific item or situation is as objective and unbiased as possible (chapter 1)

revolution A sudden and violent socioeconomic and political transformation that fundamentally changes the political, economic, and social order; constitutes the most dramatic form of regime change (chapter 1)

revolutions from above Revolutions in which the outcomes are often negotiated among political elites, each with the backing of a segment of the populace (chapter 9)

revolutions from below Revolutions that involve the mass uprising of the populace to overthrow the government as a central part of the process (chapter 9)

risk assessment Analysis of what the risks of damaging outcomes are in a particular situation (chapter 11)

risk management Policy used to keep risks to acceptable levels (chapter 11)

ruling class An elite who possess adequate resources to control a regime; in Marxist theory, the ruling class is the class that controls key sources of wealth in a given epoch (chapter 1)

semi-authoritarian regimes Type of hybrid regime in which formal opposition and some open political debate exist and elections are held to select the executive and legislative branches; these processes are so flawed, however, that the regime cannot be considered democratic in any real sense; also called competitive authoritarian and electoral authoritarian (chapter 3)

semipresidentialism A political system in which executive power is divided between a directly elected president and a prime minister elected by a parliament; Russia and France are key examples (chapter 6)

semiproportional representation system Also called a mixed representation system; an electoral system that combines single-member district representation with overall proportionality in allocation of legislative seats to parties; Germany is a key example (chapter 7)

separation of powers Constitutionally explicit division of power among the major branches of government (chapter 6)

sharia Muslim law (chapter 3)

single, nontransferable vote (SNTV) An electoral system in which multiple seats exist in each legislative district but each voter only votes for one candidate; Japan prior to 1993 was a key example (chapter 7)

single case study Research method that examines a particular political phenomenon in just one country or community and can generate ideas for theories or test theories developed from different cases (chapter 1)

single-member district Electoral system in which each geographic district elects a single representative to a legislature (chapter 7)

single-payer system A government financed and managed healthcare system, often called a national healthcare system (NHS); the government creates a system into which all citizens pay, either through a separate insurance payment or via general taxation, and through which they gain medical care; the UK is a key example (chapter 11)

social capital Social networks and norms of reciprocity important for a strong civil society (chapter 7)

social classes In Marxist theory, groups of people with the same relationship to the means of production; more generally, groups of people with similar occupations, wealth, or income (chapter 1)

social construction Part of constructivist approach to identity; process through which societies collectively "construct" identities as a wide array of actors continually discusses the question of who "we" are (chapter 4)

social contract theory Philosophical approach underlying liberalism that begins from the premise that legitimate governments are formed when free and independent individuals join in a contract to permit representatives to govern over them in their common interests (chapter 3)

social democracy   Combines liberal democracy with much greater provision of social rights of citizenship and typically greater public control of the economy (chapter 3)

social democratic welfare states   States whose social policies strongly emphasize universal entitlements to achieve greater social equality and promote equal citizenship; Sweden is prime example (chapter 11)

social insurance   Provides benefits to categories of people who have contributed to a (usually mandatory) public insurance fund; typically used to provide retirement pensions (chapter 11)

social market economy   In Germany, postwar economic system that combines a highly productive market economy with an extensive and generous welfare state and unusually active involvement of both business and labor associations in setting and implementing economic policy (chapter 5)

social movements   Part of civil society; have a loosely defined organizational structure and represent people who have been outside the bounds of formal institutions, seek major socioeconomic or political changes to the status quo, or employ noninstitutional forms of collective action (chapter 7)

social policy   Policy focused on reducing poverty and income inequality and stabilizing individual or family income (chapter 11)

social revolution   In Marxist theory, the transition from one mode of production to another; Marxist understanding of revolution (chapter 3)

social rights   The third of T. H. Marshall's rights of citizenship; those rights related to basic well-being and socioeconomic equality (chapter 3)

societal corporatism   Also called neocorporatism; corporatism that evolves historically and voluntarily

rather than being mandated by the state; Germany is a key example (chapter 7)

softliners   In democratic transitions, members of the authoritarian regime willing to consider compromising with opponents as a means to survive demands for democratization (chapter 9)

sovereign   Quality of a state in which it is legally recognized by the family of states as the sole legitimate governing authority within its territory, and as the legal equal of other states (chapter 2)

soviets   Legislative bodies in the communist regime of the Soviet Union (chapter 3)

stagflation   Simultaneous high inflation and high unemployment; term coined in the 1970s (chapter 5)

stare decisis   Literally, "let the the decision stand"; in common law, the practice of accepting the precedent of previous similar cases (chapter 6)

state corporatism   Corporatism mandated by the state; common in fascist regimes (chapter 7)

states   Ongoing administrative apparatuses that are internationally recognized as legally sovereign, control territory, and monopolize the use of force to govern (chapter 1)

structural adjustment programs (SAPs)   Development programs created by the World Bank and International Monetary Fund beginning in the 1980s; based on neoliberalism (chapter 5)

structuralism   Approach to explaining politics that argues that political behavior is at least influenced and limited, and perhaps even determined, by broader structures in a society such as class divisions or enduring institutions (chapter 1)

subcultures   Groups that hold partially different beliefs and values from the main political culture of a country (chapter 1)

supreme leader Individual who wields executive power with few formal limits in an authoritarian regime; in the Islamic Republic of Iran, the formal title of the top ruling cleric (chapter 8)

sustainable development Economic development that can continue over the long term (chapter 11)

symmetrical federal system Division of constitutionally assigned power to national and subnational governments; with all subnational governments (states or provinces) having the same relationship with and rights in relation to the national government (chapter 6)

technocratic legitimacy A claim to rule based on knowledge or expertise (chapter 3)

terms of trade The prices of a country's exports relative to its imports (chapter 5)

territory An area with clearly defined borders to which a state lays claim (chapter 2)

terrorism Political violence targeted at civilian noncombatants (chapter 9)

theocracy Rule by religious authorities (chapter 3)

theocratic regime A system of rule based on theocratic beliefs (chapter 1)

theory An abstract argument that provides a systematic explanation of some phenomena (chapter 1)

totalitarian regime A regime that controls virtually all aspects of society and eliminates all vestiges of civil society; Germany under Hitler and the Soviet Union under Stalin were key examples (chapter 3)

trade The flow of goods and services across national borders (chapter 10)

traditional legitimacy The right to rule based on a society's long-standing patterns and practices; one of Max Weber's three versions of legitimacy (chapter 2)

tragedy of the commons Without a collective effort to limit use and abuse, no individual has the in-

centive or ability to preserve a common, shared good that is free, so it's likely to be overused and perhaps ultimately depleted (chapter 11)

transnational corporations (TNCs) Large firms that operate in multiple countries simultaneously (chapter 10)

transition to democracy A type of regime change typically involving a negotiated process that removes an authoritarian regime and concludes with a founding election for a new, democratic regime (chapter 9)

two and a half party system Party system in which two large parties win the most votes but typically neither gains a majority, which requires a third (the "half" party) to join one of the major parties to form a legislative majority; Germany is key example (chapter 7)

two party system Party system in which only two parties are able to garner enough votes to win an election, though more may compete; the United Kingdom and United States are key examples (chapter 7)

typology A classification of some set of phenomena into distinct types for purposes of analysis (chapter 1)

umma The global Muslim community (chapter 3)

unitary systems Political system in which the central government has sole constitutional sovereignty and power, in contrast to a federal system (chapter 6)

universal entitlements Benefits that governments provide to all citizens more or less equally, usually funded through general taxation; in the United States, public education is an example (chapter 11)

vanguard party Vladimir Lenin's concept of a small party that claims legitimacy to rule based on its understanding of Marxist theory and its ability to represent the interests of the proletariat before they are a majority of the populace (chapter 3)

varieties of capitalism approach School of thought analyzing wealthy market economies that focuses primarily on business firms and how they are governed in terms of their interactions with government, each other, workers, and such sources of finance such banks and stock markets; divides such economies into LMEs and CMEs and argues that globalization will not produce convergence between them (chapter 10)

vertical accountability　The ability of individuals and groups in a society to hold state institutions accountable (chapter 6)

vote of no confidence　In parliamentary systems, parliament voting to remove a government (the prime minister and cabinet) from power (chapter 6)

weak state　State that cannot provide adequate political goods to its population (chapter 2)

welfare states　Distinct systems of social policies that arose after World War II in wealthy market economies, including liberal welfare states, social democratic welfare states, and Christian democratic welfare states (chapter 11)

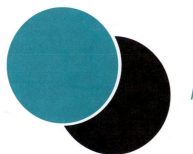

Index

NOTE: Page numbers with *b, f, m,* or *t* indicate boxes, figures, maps, and tables respectively. Italicized *page numbers* indicate photographs.